THE FUND AGREEMENT
IN THE COURTS:
VOLUME II

The Fund Agreement in the Courts: Volume II

*Further Jurisprudence Involving
the Articles of Agreement
of the
International Monetary Fund*

By
JOSEPH GOLD

INTERNATIONAL MONETARY FUND
Washington, D.C.   •   1982

International Standard Book Number: 0-939934-17-5

CONTENTS

PREFACE

This book consists of material published over a number of years as well as material hitherto unpublished. The published material has raised some editorial problems because there have been three versions of the Articles: the original Articles, the First Amendment, and the Second Amendment, which became effective, respectively, on December 27, 1945, July 28, 1969, and April 1, 1978.

One problem was whether references to provisions of the Articles should be modified if they have a place in the present version of the Articles that differs from the place they had in the former versions. Substitution of the present references would be anachronistic. The solution has been to record in the footnotes that the references are to the original Articles or to the First Amendment if there seemed to be the risk of confusion. No problem has arisen if a provision retains its former place in the Articles. Fortunately, a number of the provisions to which frequent references occur (for example, Section 2(a) and Section 2(b) of Article VIII and Section 3 of Article VI) have not been moved. It is worth mentioning that the provision on authoritative interpretation of the Articles was Article XVIII until the Second Amendment but is now Article XXIX.

Another problem was what to do about references to the various editions of the publication *Selected Decisions of the International Monetary Fund and Selected Documents*. Once again, references have not been changed but frequently references have been added in the footnotes to the latest editions, the Eighth Issue (1976) or the Ninth Issue (1981), in which a decision appears.

I have not been reluctant to make changes in the original text of material published in the past whenever changes seemed desirable for reasons of style or clarity. I have observed much greater restraint on matters of substance. Few changes of this kind have been made, so that the development and the modification of views as time went by will be apparent. Once again, less restraint has been practiced when it seemed that the presentation of a view could be improved, but only a few contexts have been revised for this purpose.

I owe much to some of my former colleagues in the Legal Department of the International Monetary Fund. They reacted to drafts of my articles, we had energetic exchanges, and then, for better or worse, I had to make up my mind. I thank these colleagues for the pleasure and usefulness of this good disputing, and I absolve them from any responsibility for my views. The same absolution must be granted to the Fund. The Introduction explains that the Fund has adopted few interpretations of the Articles on the problems that are the subject matter of this book. If the Fund has taken relevant decisions, I have made the fact clear. For the rest, all opinions are solely for my account. (I am aware of the *dictum* of an English judge that "every expert has a weakness—you just have to find it.")

I am indebted to the Editors of *Staff Papers* who have been hospitable in finding room in that extraordinary publication of the Fund for the many articles that have appeared so far on the *Fund Agreement in the Courts*. Members of the Editorial Division of what is now the External Relations Department of the Fund have worked their way through the text and footnotes of the published articles with a devotion and skill that have resulted in friendship.

I must express my gratitude to members of the staff of the Fund who have had a special connection with this volume. Mr. Norman K. Humphreys, Chief Editor of the Fund, suggested the project. Miss Mary Ellen Lucas of the Editorial Division has made an outstanding contribution by the scrupulous but speedy performance of numerous editorial and other tasks. Mr. Amokrane Touami of the Legal Department willingly prepared the List of Cases and helped in other ways. Mrs. Esther Parsons, also of the Legal Department, typed the new material and undertook many duties in assembling all material for transmission to the Editorial Division and in keeping track of the progress of the volume toward publication.

April 1982   Joseph Gold

THE FUND AGREEMENT
IN THE COURTS:
VOLUME II

Introduction

In 1962, eight articles that had appeared in the International Monetary Fund's journal *Staff Papers* were collected and published by the Fund under the title *The Fund Agreement in the Courts*.[1] The first of these articles appeared in 1951 and the eighth in 1962. The subject matter of the book was the first, but already substantial, body of cases decided by national and international tribunals in which the Articles of Agreement of the International Monetary Fund had affected issues raised in the proceedings. These earlier cases continue to be of interest because they go on affecting later cases.

Since 1962 the number of cases involving the Articles of Agreement and the range of issues raised in them have increased considerably. Ten further articles in the series have appeared, together with a pamphlet entitled *The Cuban Insurance Cases and the Articles of the Fund*, which was published outside the series because of its length. Reprints of these eleven contributions have been in demand because old and new problems of the effects of the Articles continue to arise in litigation in many countries.

It has become apparent that it would be convenient to litigants and scholars to republish in the form of a single volume the ten articles published in *Staff Papers* together with the pamphlet. Five hitherto unpublished additions have been made to these eleven contributions. Chapter 12 is a discussion of the reactions of courts, academic scholars, practitioners, and officials to the issues involving the Fund's

---

[1] Joseph Gold, *The Fund Agreement in the Courts* (Washington, 1962). (Hereinafter cited as Gold, *Fund Agreement in the Courts* (1962).) Full citations for the shortened references used in this volume are given in the Selected Bibliography, pp. 467–70.

1

Articles that were thought to arise as a result of the U.S. Government's freeze of Iran's assets in 1979–81. The reactions that are noted, though many, are probably only the first in what is likely to be a prolonged debate. The issues involving the Articles were not resolved because of the discontinuance of legal proceedings involving the freeze. In this respect, the cases resemble the Cuban insurance cases in which the issues raised by the Articles were not pursued, or were not pursued further, because of Cuba's withdrawal from the Fund.

Appendix A deals with the history of the drafting of Article VIII, Section 2(*b*), on the origin of which some new material has become available in Volume XXVI of the *Collected Writings of John Maynard Keynes.*[2] This provision declares, in effect, that certain contracts that are offensive to the exchange control regulations of a member country of the Fund other than the one in which the forum is situated shall be treated as unenforceable by the forum. Article VIII, Section 2(*b*) has been responsible for more litigation and more debate among legal scholars than any other provision of the Articles. It will be obvious from this book that the last word on the meaning of the provision has not been uttered by courts or authors.

Appendix B deals with many of the cases decided so far in which courts have been called on to apply a unit of account defined in terms of gold for the purposes of a treaty in which a new unit of account has not yet been substituted for gold by amendment. These cases involve the Articles of Agreement because the Second Amendment of the Articles abolishes the official price of gold and prohibits maintenance of the external value of currencies in terms of gold. The cases involve the Articles for the further, and equally important, reason that the special drawing right (SDR) is now the Fund's unit of account and is being adopted increasingly as the unit of account for the purposes of other international organizations and other conventions.

Appendix C discusses some aspects of exchange control regulations in relation to nonmembers of the Fund, including those that become contracting parties to the General Agreement on Tariffs and Trade (the GATT). Appendix D considers an arbitral award that raised the question of the relationship of Article VIII, Section 2(*b*) to governments and private parties. Appendix D also includes a discussion of

---

[2] *The Collected Writings of John Maynard Keynes, Vol. XXVI: Activities 1941–1946, Shaping the Post-War World, Bretton Woods, and Reparations,* ed. by Donald Moggridge (Macmillan and Cambridge University Press, for the Royal Economic Society, 1980). (Hereinafter cited as *Keynes, Vol. XXVI.*)

Article VIII, Section 2(*b*) in relation to the choice of law to govern an arbitration.

The topics relating to the Articles that have been examined by the courts have been numerous. If, for example, the impact of the Articles on private international law alone is considered, the topics include, among others, the unenforceability of certain contracts, unjust enrichment, the enforcement of foreign judgments, exchange control and tort, public policy, the act of state, revenue laws, and the application of units of account defined in terms of gold that are included in private international law conventions and domestic legislation giving effect to them.

At one time, there was little realization that the Articles might be relevant to private litigation. The Articles were a treaty, and it might have been assumed that private parties were not affected because the rights and obligations created by the treaty applied exclusively to states. The reader of Volume XXVI of Keynes' *Collected Writings* will see what weight he gave to the principle that the Articles created no rights for private parties in his interpretation of some provisions of the Articles.[3] The fact that the rights and obligations created by a treaty exist only on the official plane does not mean that the legal position of private parties cannot be affected. Another reason for the neglect of the legal impact of the Articles in earlier years may have been that the treaty is economic in character and that lawyers are not comfortable with economics.

The growing awareness of the relevance of the Articles to certain legal problems that affect private parties has not always led to legal solutions that are fully compatible with the economics of the Articles. It should be a cardinal rule of interpretation that the solution of a legal problem involving the Articles should make maximum economic sense. This rule can be difficult to apply in some cases. The purposes of the Fund as stated in Article I of the Agreement are complex and not necessarily in harmony with each other in some circumstances. The problem then will be to decide which purpose or purposes are to be given decisive weight in order to increase the likelihood that over time all the purposes of the Fund can be realized. There is some evidence of increased reliance by lawyers on the expert knowledge of

---

[3] *Ibid.*, pp. 119–21, 135. Joseph Gold, *The Multilateral System of Payments: Keynes, Convertibility, and the International Monetary Fund's Articles of Agreement*, IMF Occasional Paper No. 6 (Washington, 1981). (Hereinafter cited as Gold, Occasional Paper No. 6.)

economists in the preparation of legal arguments when issues relate to the Articles. It is possible, however, that monetary authorities are not always willing to provide assistance on matters within their competence when approached by lawyers on behalf of their clients. If monetary authorities stand aside, it is because they do not wish to appear partisan or because they wish to preserve as much freedom as possible for themselves in the affairs of the Fund.

In order to bring the Articles to the notice of the legal profession, the Fund adopted its authoritative decision of June 10, 1949 on some legal aspects of Article VIII, Section 2(b). This decision and a few early contributions to journals did succeed in creating an awareness of the fact that the Articles had legal effects on private parties in connection with exchange controls. Exchange restrictions have been radically reduced since the early years of the Fund, but exchange controls have been more persistent, although they too are much reduced. An increase in protectionism by measures applied to trade has been an unfortunate phenomenon in recent years,[4] and exchange controls are often applied as auxiliary measures. Notwithstanding the accumulation of cases in which the Articles have been cited, particularly in connection with exchange controls, and the mass of academic discussion of this jurisprudence, cases are still reported in which the Articles should have been cited but were overlooked.

In some of the early decisions the courts were disposed to fit the provisions of the Articles into traditional legal doctrines and in this way to negate or minimize the changes made by the Articles. Contracts were treated as unenforceable under Article VIII, Section 2(b) only if the court found that the exchange control regulations that had not been observed were part of the law governing the contract under the private international law of the forum. This form of conservatism has diminished, but it has been followed by other judicial action that counteracts the effect of the provision. Some courts, without narrowing the scope of the provision directly, have deprived it of practical effect by collateral action. One example of this approach has been the fragmentation into discrete contracts of a complex design to circumvent exchange control regulations. By enforcing the last of the severed contracts, the courts complete the design.

Although some courts have been conservative in their approach to particular provisions, other courts have discovered in the interstices of

---

[4] International Monetary Fund, Trade and Payments Division (Bahram Nowzad, Chief), *The Rise in Protectionism*, IMF Pamphlet Series, No. 24 (Washington, 1978).

the Articles a public policy of collaboration among members that moderates older doctrines or even inspires the rejection of them in the circumstances of the case. This tendency can be observed in the United States, but the conservative approach is evident when the interests of domestic financial markets could be affected adversely. In some countries, the courts have been conservative when the interests of residents of the country of the forum could be prejudiced.

Even when courts are made aware of the relevance of the Articles to issues that are being litigated, the courts are not given the benefit of the full store of jurisprudence and critical material. Often, lawyers have relied exclusively on material published in the country in which they are practicing. This limitation does not exclude foreign material altogether because sometimes a domestic author has discussed some of the cases decided in other countries. The republication of some of the articles that have appeared in *Staff Papers* in German or French in legal periodicals published in the Federal Republic of Germany, France, and Belgium has helped to draw attention to jurisprudence involving the Articles. In England, excerpts from decisions discussed in the articles published in *Staff Papers* have been included in *International Law Reports,* beginning with Volume 22 for 1955 (published in 1958). Nevertheless, it is apparent from the reports of some cases that not all the relevant material was discovered. There is evidence, however, of collaboration across national boundaries among some lawyers when the same issue is being litigated in more than one country.

The neglect of decisions and critical material that are not readily available in the country of the forum means that the prospects for uniform interpretation of the Articles are reduced. Whatever may be the explanation, courts, when interpreting the Articles, have been less emphatic about the desirability of uniformity in the decisions of the courts of contracting parties than they have been when interpreting other multilateral treaties.[5] This attitude leads courts to interpret the

---

[5] See, for example, Lord Diplock in *Fothergill v. Monarch Airlines Ltd.* [1980] 2 All E.R. 696, at 706.

"It is, however, otherwise with that growing body of written law in force in the United Kingdom which, although it owes its enforceability within the United Kingdom to its embodiment in or authorisation by an Act of Parliament, nevertheless owes its origin and its actual wording to some prior law-preparing process in which Parliament has not participated, such as the negotiation and preparation of a multilateral international convention designed to achieve uniformity of national laws in some particular field of private or public law, which Her Majesty's government wants to ratify on behalf of the United Kingdom but can only do so when the provisions of the convention have been

language of the Articles as if the treaty was a domestic legal instrument. In some countries, the result is more emphasis on verbal considerations than on purpose.

The decisions of foreign courts may be difficult to discover, but when discovered they may be difficult to evaluate. If the decision of a foreign court is cited, the forum has a delicate task in assessing the weight it should attribute to the court and therefore to the decision.[6]

---

incorporated in our domestic law. The product of this law-preparing process is generally contained in texts expressed in several different languages all of which are of equal authenticity and can be looked at to clarify the meaning of any one of them. The Warsaw Convention of 1929 and its later protocols are exceptions inasmuch as the only authentic text is that expressed in the French language which is set out in the Carriage by Air Act 1961, Sch 1, Part II.

"The language of that convention that has been adopted at the international conference to express the common intention of the majority of the states represented there is meant to be understood in the same sense by the courts of all those states which ratify or accede to the convention. Their national styles of legislative draftsmanship will vary considerably as between one another. So will the approach of their judiciaries to the interpretation of written laws and to the extent to which recourse may be had to 'les travaux préparatoires', 'la doctrine' and 'la jurisprudence' as extraneous aids to the interpretation of the legislative text.

"The language of an international convention has not been chosen by an English parliamentary draftsman. It is neither couched in the conventional English legislative idiom nor designed to be construed exclusively by English judges. It is addressed to a much wider and more varied judicial audience than is an Act of Parliament that deals with purely domestic law. It should be interpreted, as Lord Wilberforce put it in *James Buchanan & Co Ltd v Babco Forwarding and Shipping (UK) Ltd* [1977] 3 All ER 1048 at 1052, [1978] AC 141 at 152, 'unconstrained by technical rules of English law, or by English legal precedent, but on broad principles of general acceptation'."

See also *Director of Public Prosecutions v. Henn* [1980] 2 C.M.L.R. 229, and "The 'purposive' versus the 'literal' construction of statutes," *Australian Law Journal*, Vol. 55 (1981), pp. 175–76.

[6] "As respects decision of foreign courts, the persuasive value of a particular court's decision must depend on its reputation and its status, the extent to which its decisions are binding on courts of co-ordinate and inferior jurisdiction in its own country and the coverage of the national law reporting system. For instance your Lordships would not be fostering uniformity of interpretation of the convention if you were to depart from the prima facie view which you had yourselves formed as to its meaning in order to avoid conflict with a decision of a French court of appeal that would not be binding on other courts in France, that might be inconsistent with an unreported decision of some other French court of appeal and that would be liable to be superseded by a subsequent decision of the Court of Cassation that *would* have binding effect on lower courts in France. It is no criticism of the contents of the judgments in those foreign cases to which your Lordships have been referred if I say that the courts by which they were delivered do not appear to me to satisfy the criteria which would justify your Lordships in being influenced to follow their decisions in the interest of uniformity of interpretation." (*Fothergill v. Monarch Airlines Ltd.*, cited in fn. 5, at 708.)

The difficulty of this assessment may explain why it is rarely attempted.

The Fund is empowered to adopt authoritative interpretations of its Articles,[7] which members must make effective under their laws if the interpretations are not automatically effective.[8] The Fund has adopted few interpretations of this kind, and only one that relates to Article VIII, Section 2(b). Further interpretations would resolve some of the many controversies that still swirl around that provision or that are stimulated by other provisions. The absence of more numerous authoritative interpretations can be explained in a number of ways. The Fund is reluctant to act as if it were a court of appeal that contradicts or confirms the decisions of its members' courts. An interpretation would not overrule decisions in domestic cases already concluded, but the interpretation would affect later cases. The Fund could be requested, however, to give an interpretation before legal proceedings in a member's courts had been completed. In these circumstances the Fund's interpretation would affect the outcome of a pending case as well as future cases.

Members can raise questions of interpretation under the procedure established by the Articles for authoritative decision of such questions by the Fund, but members have shown no disposition to make the Fund a tribunal that, in effect, would oversee or guide their courts. Litigants have sometimes urged their monetary authorities to request the Fund for interpretations but have not succeeded in moving their authorities to take this step. The authorities may fear that the responses of the Fund will not be in accordance with the policies that they favor. The Articles do not enable the courts themselves to invoke the procedure for authoritative interpretation, but the Fund has responded to courts' inquiries of a factual character.

Another explanation of the modest number of authoritative interpretations is that they are made in the first instance by the Executive Board. Normally, there are few lawyers among Executive Directors, and although the Executive Board is called upon frequently to interpret the Articles, the issues are rarely of the kind that arise under private law. The Executive Board would be reluctant to assume the role of a tribunal deciding issues of this character. It would also be reluctant to treat them as matters fit for intergovernmental debate. The procedure for authoritative interpretation is considered more suitable for

---

[7] Article XXIX; Article XXI(d). See Joseph Gold, *Interpretation by the Fund*, IMF Pamphlet Series, No. 11 (Washington, 1968). (Hereinafter cited as Gold, Pamphlet No. 11.)

[8] Article XXXI, Section 2(a).

questions that have an intergovernmental impact with little or no direct impact on private parties.

The Executive Board has had a strong preference for informal decisions when dealing with problems of a legal character that it must face in its activities. These decisions are not taken under the procedure for authoritative interpretation. Informal decisions may have a persuasive effect on courts, but these decisions do not have the legal cogency of authoritative interpretations. This distinction does not imply any intrinsic legal difference between informal and authoritative interpretations or in the legal techniques the Fund applies in reaching them.

The Executive Board has preferred informal interpretative decisions because it wishes to avoid the finality of authoritative interpretations. Informal decisions can be adapted more readily if circumstances change or if error becomes manifest. Moreover, questions have been raised about the legality of rescinding or amending authoritative interpretations. Although there is no legal impediment to rescission or modification, neither course would be undertaken lightly, particularly if some members might conclude that either action was detrimental to their interests.

Finally, if the procedure for authoritative interpretation were pursued beyond the first stage of decision by the Executive Board, difficulties would complicate the second stage. A Committee of the Board of Governors on Interpretation is the body to which decisions of the Executive Board are referred on appeal at the request of any member. The First Amendment of the Articles made provision for the Committee as a compromise when the procedure for authoritative interpretation under the original Articles became controversial. Some members saw the problem as predominantly one of legal doctrine, while others saw it as predominantly one of the distribution of power. Most members did not believe that there was a problem, but they were anxious that agreement should be reached on the SDR as the main feature of the First Amendment. The provision expressing the compromise was drafted in broad terms, not only because of the inherent difficulties of reaching agreement on all aspects of the compromise but also because most members had no enthusiasm for engaging in further negotiation on procedures that had seemed to them satisfactory in the past. As a result, many features of the Committee were left for subsequent determination by the organs of the Fund, but the same forces that were responsible for leaving the issues open in the First Amendment of the Articles have been responsible for not resolving them later. The steps necessary to put the Committee into operation have not been taken.

The Fund Agreement in the Courts—VIII*

This article discusses six cases, in most of which basic questions of law under the Articles of Agreement of the International Monetary Fund were raised. Two cases decided by German courts dealt with the unenforceability of certain exchange contracts; a case in New York and another in the Philippines involved exchange surrender requirements; a fifth case, decided in Brazil, considered multiple rates of exchange; and the last case, decided by the courts of the District of Columbia, dealt with the privileges and immunities of the Fund.

Unenforceability of Certain Exchange Contracts

HAMBURG COURT OF APPEALS

On July 7, 1959, the Court of Appeals (*Oberlandesgericht*) of Hamburg delivered a judgment that involved a discussion of Article VIII, Section 2(*b*).[1] The plaintiff company, a resident of the Federal Republic of Germany, agreed in June and July 1957 to sell a number of pinball gambling machines to the defendant, a resident of the Saar Territory, under invoices expressed in deutsche mark, and brought this action for the unpaid price. The plaintiff claimed that the defendant had agreed to take delivery of the machines at a railroad depot in German territory, but had failed to do this. The defendant

---

* Originally published in November 1964.
[1] *Entscheidungen zum Interzonalen Privatrecht*, 1958–59, No. 135A.

replied that the contract was void because a regulation of June 4, 1958 of the Ministry of Commerce, Traffic and Agriculture of the Saar Territory prohibited the importation of the gambling machines into the Saar Territory. In addition, a license was required under foreign exchange legislation, but had not been obtained.

The court gave judgment for the plaintiff on the ground that the contract was for the delivery of the machines within German territory, and importation into the Saar Territory was solely at the risk of the defendant. For this reason, the regulations of the Saar Territory did not affect the validity of the contract. Although this reasoning was sufficient to dispose of the case, the court went on to give other reasons for its opinion. Even if the contract did provide for importation of the machines into the Saar Territory, the regulation of June 4, 1958 provided only that a license was necessary for the movement of goods across the border, and that an importation without license was a customs violation. The regulation did not apply to the underlying contract, and, therefore, the contract was not rendered invalid by the absence of a license.

Passing to the argument based on exchange control, the court held that the regulations in force in the Saar Territory were foreign law. Under the Agreement of October 27, 1956 between the Federal Republic and France, the economic reintegration of the Saar Territory into the former had been postponed. In the interval French foreign trade and exchange control was to continue to apply to the Saar Territory as French and not as German law. The court then continued as follows:

> Since foreign law is involved, it is irrelevant whether the defendant's payments obligation is contrary to a prohibition of French exchange control. For the latter is not to be taken into consideration by a German judge, since it involves foreign public law (cf. RGZ 156, 158 [160], also RGZ 108, 241 [243]). Nor can any other result be derived for this case from the Bretton Woods Agreement, to which the Federal Republic of Germany has acceded (Articles of Agreement of the International Monetary Fund of July 1944, BGBl 1952 II 728). Article VIII, Paragraph 2b of the Agreement contains the following provision:
>
> "Exchange contracts which involve the currency of any member and which are contrary to the exchange control regulations of that member maintained or imposed consistently with this Agreement shall be unenforceable in the territories of any member."
>
> The interpretation of this provision, especially of the concept "exchange contract" is very controversial. If it is held to mean that in the case of "exchange contracts" the German judge must abide by prohibitions of

foreign exchange control regulations, which is also controversial (cf. *Hjerner*, Främmande Valutalag och Internationell Privaträtt 42; *Bülck*, Jahrbuch für internat. Recht V, 119), there still does not exist any reason to abide by French payment prohibitions that may exist; for no "exchange contract" is involved in this case. If one gives this concept a narrow interpretation and limits it to transactions involving exclusively foreign exchange, i.e., international means of payment, (for the controversy regarding interpretation refer to *Mann*, JZ 1953, 444; *Nussbaum*, Money in the Law 542 f.; *Bülck*, idem 116; *Hjerner*, idem 43–46), then no reasoning is required. But even if one accepts a broader interpretation and includes under "exchange contracts" all transactions that in any manner affect the exchange holdings of a member country, this concept does not cover *per se* the sale of goods for money. If as in the case in question the contractual commitment of the nonresident is solely a money debt without the debtor being required to make payment in a particular manner that would affect the exchange holdings of the country, there can even under the broadest interpretation of the term be no question that an international purchase of goods is not an "exchange contract" pursuant to Article VIII.

Accordingly, in this case only German exchange control legislation is applicable, which, in accordance with the opinion under 2(a), does not obstruct the payment obligation of the defendant.[2]

There are three comments that must be made on this passage from the court's opinion. The first is that the "narrow interpretation" of "exchange contracts" as involving only means of payment rests on a reading of the provision that is neither exclusive nor necessary. After the learned international discussions of the last decade or more, this reading can be taken seriously only if the normal scope of exchange control and the purpose of Article VIII, Section 2(*b*) in the Fund's Articles are ignored. Second, the court qualified the assumption that the "broader interpretation" covered contracts for the sale of goods with the proviso that a contract of this kind must affect the exchange resources of the member whose exchange control regulations are involved. The further elaboration of this point, however, is not clear. Apparently, the court did not consider that a member's currency was involved if the contract between a resident and a nonresident merely called for payment without requiring payment in "a particular manner that would affect the exchange holdings" of the member. This remark is obscure because it is indicated in the report that the invoices for the machines were in deutsche mark. If this fact meant that payment

---

[2] The rest of the opinion dealt at some length with the question whether the plaintiff was a participant in a smuggling operation and concluded that it was not.

had to be made in that currency, the exchange resources of the Saar Territory were affected because discharge of the defendant's obligation would directly reduce those exchange resources. However, the exchange resources of the Saar Territory were affected by any obligation of the resident defendant to make payment to the nonresident plaintiff, whether or not a currency of payment was specified by the contract. If any foreign currency was specified, the effect was obvious, as already explained. If the domestic currency of the Saar Territory was specified, the exchange resources of the Saar Territory were affected because the nonresident's holding of the currency would represent a charge against the economy of the Saar Territory that could be realized either by the conversion of the currency or by its use to acquire goods or services there for which foreign exchange might have been earned. If payment were made in either foreign or domestic currency under a contract that did not specify the currency of payment, the effect would be exactly the same as payment pursuant to a term specifying payment in the currency in which it was in fact made. Obviously, payment would have to be made in some currency, and a conclusion that payment in one currency affected exchange resources but payment in another did not could be accepted only by ignoring the economics to which the Fund's Articles give a legal formulation. It will be seen that the views of the majority of the New York Court of Appeals in the *Banco do Brasil* case, discussed below, are open to the same criticism. It is a strange fact, however, that while the majority of the New York court doubted whether there was an exchange contract where a foreign currency was the currency of payment, the opinion of the Hamburg court is open to the interpretation that this same doubt was expressed because the contract did not unequivocally call for payment in a foreign currency.

It is also possible that the Hamburg court had another theory in mind in holding that there was no adequate demonstration of the fact that the exchange resources of the Saar Territory were affected. This possibility is suggested by the fact that, as noted, the invoices were in deutsche mark. Perhaps the court thought that if the defendant had deutsche mark balances in Germany, his disposition of them would not affect the exchange resources of the Saar Territory. This conclusion would not be correct. Whether or not there is exchange control, but clearly if there is control, the foreign exchange resources of residents must be deemed to be resources of the country in which they reside. These are resources that, at least in theory, can be mobilized, and their character as resources of the country is not changed if they are not centralized but allowed to remain in private hands for use in accordance with exchange control regulations.

The third comment is that the court concluded that the issue in connection with Article VIII, Section 2(*b*) was whether the contract between the parties was an "exchange contract." It is submitted that this was not the substantive issue because, as explained above, the contract was clearly an "exchange contract." The substantive issue was whether the regulation of June 4, 1958 of the Saar Territory was an "exchange control regulation" within the meaning of Article VIII, Section 2(*b*). This concept has not been defined with legal precision in the Fund's Articles or in any decision of the Executive Directors of the Fund. However, part of the reasoning that led to a decision of the Executive Directors on the meaning of "restrictions on the making of payments and transfers for current international transactions" in Article VIII, Section 2(*a*) can throw some light on "exchange control regulations."

It must be clearly understood that the two concepts are not the same. "Exchange control regulations" is a wider concept than the "restrictions" of Article VIII, Section 2(*a*), because there are controls that can require the observance of certain procedures before payments may be made but without hindering any payments or without hindering payments for current international transactions. A control will be a restriction on payments if certain payments are prohibited, limited, or unduly delayed. Another type of measure that is an exchange control but not a restriction is an exchange surrender requirement. This measure does not in itself restrict the "making" of payments and transfers, and may not even be part of a restrictive system if the monetary authorities provide all the exchange that is required for making payments and transfers. Again, the concept of "restrictions on the making of payments and transfers" in Article VIII, Section 2(*a*), on which the Executive Directors have taken a decision, relates to "current international transactions," while "exchange control regulations" in Article VIII, Section 2(*b*) embraces both current international transactions and capital movements.

In elucidating the meaning of "restrictions on the making of payments and transfers," etc., three views were considered. One view was that any governmental interference or impediment that reduced the freedom of private parties to make payments was a restriction. A second view was that a practice was a restriction if the purpose of the member in imposing it was to protect its balance of payments. Neither of these views was accepted, for reasons that need not be gone into here except to say that under either of these views the jurisdiction of the Fund to approve or disapprove certain practices would have covered, under the first view all, and under the second view many, of the practices that are normally regarded as trade controls. This result could not have been reconciled with the international negotiations that preceded and succeeded the Bretton Woods Conference on the establishment of an international trade organization or with Resolution VII of the Conference itself.[3] These negotiations have resulted in the GATT and not the international organization that was envisaged, but there is no evidence in the legislative history of the Articles that the drafters contemplated a wider interpretation of the jurisdiction of the Fund if the plans for a trade organization did not succeed.

It followed from the unacceptability of the two views that have been mentioned that a third view had to be adopted. This view was that the "restrictions" that were subject to the jurisdiction of the Fund must be on the financial aspect of transactions, and that the test for this purpose must be objective and technical. In short, does the restrictive measure address itself to the transaction that gives rise to a payment or to that payment? This principle has been expressed in a sentence in a decision of the Executive Directors on the convertibility of currencies under the Articles of Agreement, which reads: "The guiding principle in ascertaining whether a measure is a restriction on payments and transfers for current transactions under Article VIII, Section 2 is whether it involves a direct governmental limitation on the availability or use of exchange as such."[4]

---

[3] "The United Nations Monetary and Financial Conference
RECOMMENDS:

To the participating Governments that, in addition to implementing the specific monetary and financial measures which were the subject of this Conference, they seek, with a view to creating in the field of international economic relations conditions necessary for the attainment of the purposes of the Fund and of the broader primary objectives of economic policy, to reach agreement as soon as possible on ways and means whereby they may best:

(1) reduce obstacles to international trade and in other ways promote mutually advantageous international commercial relations, . . ."
See also Section 14 of the U.S. Bretton Woods Agreements Act (59 Stat. 512 (1945)).

[4] *Selected Decisions of the Executive Directors*, Second Issue (Washington, September 1963), pp. 76–77. (Hereinafter cited as *Selected Decisions*, Second Issue.) Also, *Selected Decisions of the International Monetary Fund and Selected Documents*, Ninth Issue (Washington, June 15, 1981), pp. 209–10. (Hereinafter cited as *Selected Decisions*, Ninth Issue.)

It must be repeated, in order to avoid any misunderstanding, that the concept of "exchange control regulations" is not the same as the concept of "restrictions on the making of payments and transfers," etc. and that there are many measures that would undoubtedly fall within the former category but not the latter. There has been no formal decision of the Executive Directors with respect to the meaning of "exchange control regulations," but the proposal of a trade organization that influenced the decision with respect to the meaning of restrictions could justify the conclusion that "exchange control regulations" do not include regulations that are formulated and applied solely as controls of trade transactions.

It must also be said that the question of the meaning of "exchange control regulations" in Article VIII, Section 2(b) depends on the proper construction of that provision and the Articles as a whole, and that the solution of this question is not much helped by judicial or other pronouncements not related to that provision.[5] For example, it is necessary to take into account the fact that the concept to be elucidated is "exchange control regulations . . . maintained or imposed consistently with this Agreement." In a certain sense it could be argued that pure trade controls are consistent with the Articles because, on the one hand, there is nothing in the Agreement that prohibits them. On the other hand, there is no express or implied authority to adopt them, and it is difficult, therefore, to hold that they are "maintained or imposed" consistently with the Agreement. In other respects, these words are taken to mean that there is express or implied authority in the Agreement for certain practices and not merely that there is a neutral silence on them.

There are certain indications in the court's opinion that the regulation of June 4, 1958 was a control of importation into the Saar Territory and not a control of payments for imports, but these *dicta* must be read with caution because the court did not concentrate on the classification of the regulation. If the license that was required did relate only to the ability of the defendant to make the import, and did not prescribe that he must get a license in order to obtain

---

[5] For example: ". . . this court is entitled to be satisfied that the foreign law is a genuine foreign exchange law, i.e., a law passed with the genuine intention of protecting its economy in times of national stress and for that purpose regulating (inter alia) the rights of foreign creditors, and is not a law passed ostensibly with that object, but in reality with some object not in accordance with the usage of nations." *Re Helbert Wagg & Co., Ltd.* [1956] 1 All E.R. 129, 142, *per* Upjohn, J.

or use foreign exchange or pay in domestic currency for the import, it was probably not an "exchange control regulation." It would be necessary to study the precise text and operation of the regulation before arriving at a firmer view. It must not be assumed, however, that exchange controls and trade controls are necessarily exclusive categories. Frequently, the same measure can fall into both categories,[6] and it is possible that this analysis was true of the present case.

To sum up, to the extent that the case before the Hamburg Court of Appeals turned on the application of Article VIII, Section 2(b), the substantive issue was not whether there was an "exchange contract" but whether the regulation of June 4, 1958 was an "exchange control regulation." The answer depended on the technical character of the regulation, and it will have become apparent that the effect of the regulation was not decisive. If the regulation was an exchange control regulation, it was a direct control of payment by the defendant. If it was a trade control regulation, it was an indirect control of payment, but this effect would not convert it into an exchange control regulation. Finally, the regulation could have been a direct control of both trade and exchange.

Two further aspects of the case are worth noting. The first is that the agreements between the parties seem to have been made in June and July 1957, while the regulation that was involved was adopted on June 4, 1958. The court made no reference to the retroactive application of the regulation. It may be assumed, therefore, that the court did not consider this fact to be relevant under Article VIII, Section 2(b). Nor did the court take into account the fact that on July 5, 1959, two days before the court delivered its opinion, the special economic regime

---

[6] This point was made in the Report of the Special Sub-Group working on the relations between the Fund and the GATT in the field of quantitative restrictions for balance of payments purposes in the course of the Review Session of 1954–55.

"2. Generally there is a fairly clear division of work between the International Monetary Fund on the one hand and the CONTRACTING PARTIES to the General Agreement on Tariffs and Trade on the other. The division, however, being based on the technical nature of government measures rather than on the effect of these measures on international trade and finance, is inevitably somewhat arbitrary in some respects. In many instances it is difficult or impossible to define clearly whether a government measure is financial or trade in character and frequently it is both. It follows that certain measures come under the jurisdiction of both the IMF and the CONTRACTING PARTIES and that decisions in relation to such measures have to be taken against a background of the objectives and rules both of the Fund and the General Agreement." (General Agreement on Tariffs and Trade, *Basic Instruments and Selected Documents*, Third Supplement (June 1955), p. 196.)

of the Saar Territory was terminated and integration with Germany became complete. These facts have a bearing on the question of the date as of which it must be determined whether an exchange contract is contrary to the relevant exchange control regulations and therefore enforceable or unenforceable. Other cases have raised the issue whether this date is necessarily the date at which the contract is made, if there are changes in the regulations or in such other facts as membership in the Fund before a court decides whether there should be a remedy for nonperformance of the contract.[7]

The other aspect of the case involves the special status of the Saar Territory. Article VIII, Section 2(b) imposes on one member the duty to treat as unenforceable certain exchange contracts that are contrary to the exchange control regulations of another member. For these purposes, a member must be taken to include, in both instances, "all their colonies, overseas territories, all territories under their protection, suzerainty, or authority and all territories in respect of which they exercise a mandate."[8] Under the Treaty for the Settlement of the Saar Question entered into by France and Germany on October 27, 1956, the Saar Territory was to be integrated politically into Germany by the application of German constitutional and other law as from January 1, 1957, except to the extent specified, but for a transitional period, to end not later than December 31, 1959, the Saar Territory was to remain part of the customs and currency area of France. The French franc was to remain legal tender, and French exchange control and other legal regulations relating to the franc were to continue to apply during the transition. The court had no difficulty in regarding the customs and exchange regulations of the Saar Territory as foreign law. By implication, therefore, the court treated the Saar Territory as under the authority of France for the purposes of Article VIII, Section 2(b).[9]

---

[7] Gold, *Fund Agreement in the Courts* (1962), pp. 62–66, 77–78.

[8] Article XX, Section 2(g): "By their signature of this Agreement, all governments accept it both on their own behalf and in respect of all their colonies, overseas territories, all territories under their protection, suzerainty, or authority and all territories in respect of which they exercise a mandate." (Article XXXI, Section 2(g) of the Second Amendment.)

[9] Note Article 6(4) of the Treaty: "France shall share with the Saar economy the international finance facilities which result from her sovereignty in the matter of currency"; and Article 13(2): "International agreements in the sphere of customs and currency, which have been or will be concluded by France with third countries, shall be applicable to the Saar Territory during the transitional period. . . ."

SUPREME COURT OF FEDERAL REPUBLIC OF GERMANY

On April 9, 1962, the Supreme Court of the Federal Republic of Germany delivered a judgment marked by a confident application of Article VIII, Section 2(*b*).[10] The contrasts between this case and the opinion of the Hamburg court are discussed below. The defendant was an Austrian resident that processed maize for foreign account to produce dextrose and waste dextrose sugar at its factory in Austria. In 1948, the defendant entered into agreements by which the plaintiff was to receive "commission or goods" in respect of all maize processed for all German firms except those named. The "commission quantity" was to be a defined number of kilograms of dextrose for defined amounts of maize. In 1948 and 1949 the defendant processed certain large amounts of maize for two German firms, and in these proceedings the plaintiff sought "monetary compensation" in deutsche mark in respect of the "commission quantity" which he claimed to be entitled to under the agency agreements.

The Supreme Court found that the parties had agreed to be governed by German law and noted that for this reason the lower court had found it unnecessary to consider the applicability of Austrian exchange control regulations. The Supreme Court disagreed. It said that normally the foreign exchange legislation of a country was regarded as effective only within the country's territory. As the defendant's main office was in Austria, the claim against it was situate there and consequently was subject to Austrian foreign exchange control regulations. The plaintiff alleged, however, that the defendant had assets in Germany. To this argument, the court reacted as follows:

> The assets of a defendant outside a country are not in themselves, according to the principle of territoriality, subject to the restrictions of the foreign exchange legislation of that country (cf. Drobnig, loc. cit., page 1091, BGHZ 7, 397).
>
> However, the plaintiff in this case cannot obtain any judgment against the defendant in German courts, even if the defendant possesses assets in the Federal Republic of Germany, if the Austrian exchange regulations are opposed to the satisfaction of his claim. For in the present case it must be borne in mind that both the Federal Republic of Germany and Austria have acceded to the Articles of Agreement of the International Monetary Fund (the so-called Bretton Woods Agreement) (cf. German BGBl 1952 II 637; Austrian BGBl No. 105/1949). Thereby, inter alia, Art. VIII, Section 2b, of these Articles of Agreement has been

---

[10] *Wertpapier-Mitteilungen*, No. 21 of May 26, 1962, pp. 601–602.

raised by both countries to the status of internal law. This provision states that exchange contracts which are contrary to the exchange control regulations maintained or imposed by a member consistently with that agreement are unenforceable in the territories of any member. It can be concluded from this that the member countries have contractually agreed, within the field covered by the agreement, mutually to observe each other's foreign exchange regulations (cf. BGHZ 31, 367, 373 WM 1960, 370; Staudinger BGB 11th edition, Art. 134, Note 20; OLG Schleswig, in *Jahrbuch fuer intern. ausl. oeff. Recht* 1955, 113, with note by Buelck; Mann JZ 1953, 442).

In these circumstances the judgment appealed against cannot stand. On the contrary, the Appeal Court will have to examine whether Austrian foreign exchange regulations which, under the aforementioned Articles of Agreement, are to be observed, are opposed to the legal action taken by the plaintiff, and whether an Austrian foreign exchange permit, if required, has been issued. This means both a permit for the agreements of March 1 and November 7, 1948 and a permit for the payment now claimed in this action.

It is not clear precisely what followed from the court's finding that the parties intended German law to govern their agreements. The court might have meant that German law, including its private international law, applied, because it seems to have been willing to recognize the application of Austrian exchange control regulations to the extent that the claim against an Austrian resident was to be satisfied from assets in Austria. This view was based not on Article VIII, Section 2(b) but apparently on a principle of the territoriality of exchange control regulations, although often this principle has been taken in private international law, apart from Article VIII, Section 2(b), to exclude recognition of the exchange control regulations of another country. This aspect of the case will not be pursued further except to say that to the extent that the court found that German law governed the contract but was nevertheless willing to recognize Austrian exchange control regulations—which was certainly the position insofar as assets in Germany were concerned—the case is one in which Article VIII, Section 2(b) led to a result that would not have followed from the traditional private international law of the forum. In a number of cases,[11] courts have reinforced the application of Article VIII, Section 2(b) by concluding that the result of applying the provision was the same as the result of applying their traditional private international law.

---

[11] See Gold, *Fund Agreement in the Courts* (1962), pp. 89, 152.

Perhaps the most notable feature of the case is that the Supreme Court, in deciding that Article VIII, Section 2(b) required the recognition of Austrian exchange control regulations, showed no hesitation on the question whether the agreements were "exchange contracts." In the Hamburg case, the court found that there was no "exchange contract" before it because, even if it was conceded that a contract for the sale of goods for money could be included in this category, it would be classified in this way only if it could be shown that the contract established something more than a bare pecuniary obligation. It was necessary to show that the payment would affect the exchange resources of the Saar Territory. The Hamburg court was not satisfied that this effect was demonstrated, perhaps because the defendant could have paid in the domestic currency of the Saar Territory or from assets outside the Saar Territory.

In the Supreme Court case, the whole of the discussion of Article VIII, Section 2(b) and the conclusion that it required the recognition of Austrian exchange control regulations were postulated on the assumption that there were assets in Germany. The fact that these assets were outside the territory of Austria did not lead the Supreme Court to doubt that the disposition of them by a resident of Austria would affect the exchange resources of Austria.

The contrast between the two cases is even more striking. To begin with, the agreements provided for "commission or goods." Therefore, if this provision was treated as a term entitling the plaintiff to call for money at his discretion, the currency of payment was not prescribed. There would have been no more than the "money debt" that the Hamburg court found an inadequate basis for classifying a contract as an "exchange contract." There is room for doubt, however, whether the contract called for a pecuniary consideration at all. On the one hand, the plaintiff was to receive "commission or goods," but on the other hand this reward was expressed solely in terms of weights of dextrose. It is possible, of course, that the parties expected that the plaintiff would be entitled to and would call for the pecuniary equivalent of the dextrose, and that the reference to the dextrose was a formula for determining the amount of a pecuniary reward that could fluctuate.

The nature of the plaintiff's rights is not clarified by the following passage in the judgment:

> The Appeal Court states that there is no offense against Art. II of Military Government Law No. 51 and against Art. 3 of the Currency Law. The appeal wrongly challenges this.
> (a) Both of these legal provisions relate to debts in *money*. In the

present case, on the other hand, the debt was originally a debt in *goods* (dextrose). The plaintiff in this case is demanding money only as compensation for the dextrose which he alleges was owed under the agreement (Art. 326 BGB).

(b) The fact that under the agreement of March 1, 1948 the plaintiff was to receive "commission or goods" in no way alters the fact that a debt of the defendant to the plaintiff in respect of the delivery of a commission quantity of dextrose was not a monetary debt. This is so even if this clause could be regarded as giving the plaintiff an option (cf. BGH WM 1961, 451; Senate Decision VII ZR 64/60 of April 24, 1961).

(c) It is immaterial whether at the most 200 kg of pure dextrose can be produced from 1,000 kg of maize. Even if that were so, so that the defendant could not have taken the commission quantity for the plaintiff from the returnable yield of the maize, this would not in any way have altered the nature of the dextrose debt as a debt in goods.

In this passage, the Supreme Court concluded that the debt was not a monetary debt, perhaps because it was *expressed* in goods. This finding was made for the purpose of Article II of Military Government Law No. 51[12] and Article 3 of the Currency Law of June 18, 1948.[13]

It is not intended to discuss the finding in relation to these two monetary laws of the occupation authorities in Germany. If, however, the finding that there was no monetary debt under these laws is taken to apply more generally to the issues in the case, the judgment of the Supreme Court would have to be understood to be that a contract for the payment of a commission in goods is an "exchange contract." Moreover, the statement that it would have to be ascertained whether there had been the grant of "both a permit for the agreements . . . and a permit for the payment now claimed in this action" could be interpreted to mean that a contract, even though not an exchange contract in its inception, could be converted into one by a claim for damages. Both of the propositions advanced in this paragraph as interpretations of the decision must be regarded as tentative, in view of the fact that the court seems to have been willing, in the second passage quoted above, to consider the possibility that the agreements gave the plaintiff an option to demand money in lieu of goods.

---

[12] "Except as authorized by Military Government, no person shall make or enter, or offer to enter, into any arrangement or transaction providing for payment in or delivery of a currency other than Marks."

[13] "Money debts may be contracted in a currency other than deutsche marks only with the permission of the competent foreign exchange control agency. The same rule applies to money debts, the deutsche mark amount of which is to be fixed in terms of the exchange rate for some other currency, or by the price or quantity of fine gold or other goods or performances."

Exchange Surrender Requirements

NEW YORK COURT OF APPEALS

On April 4, 1963, the New York Court of Appeals delivered its judgment in *Banco do Brasil, S.A. v. A.C. Israel Commodity Co., Inc., et al.*[14] The defendant, a Delaware corporation with its principal place of business in New York, was an importer of Brazilian coffee. The plaintiff was a Brazilian banking corporation and quasi-governmental agency with functions that included the supervision of all matters relating to foreign exchange and with powers to act for the enforcement of Brazilian foreign exchange laws and the recovery of moneys due to Brazil under them. The gist of the plaintiff's complaint was that the defendant conspired with a Brazilian exporter of coffee to pay the exporter dollars that the exporter could sell in the Brazilian free market for 220 cruzeiros per dollar instead of surrendering the dollars to the plaintiff, in accordance with Brazilian exchange control regulations, at the rate of 90 cruzeiros per dollar. The defendant profited by paying a lower price for the coffee than the minimum price established by Brazilian law. The plaintiff alleged that the evasion of Brazilian exchange control regulations had been accomplished by the exporter's forgery of documents evidencing receipt of the dollars by the plaintiff, without which the coffee could not have left Brazil. The plaintiff claimed damages of more than $1.3 million against the defendant. The arguments addressed to the Court of Appeals, in the course of which the plaintiff relied heavily on Article VIII, Section 2(*b*), were summarized in an earlier article.[15]

The Court of Appeals, by the narrow margin of four judges to three, denied the plaintiff's claim. Burke, J., delivering the opinion of the majority, first dealt with the question whether there was an exchange contract that involved Brazilian currency:

> It is far from clear whether this sale of coffee is covered by subdivision (b) of section 2. The section deals with "exchange contracts" which "involve" the "currency" of any member of the International Monetary Fund, "and *** are contrary to the exchange control regulations of that member maintained or imposed consistently with" the agreement. Subdivision (b) of section 2 has been construed as reaching only "transactions which have as their immediate object 'exchange,' that is, international media of payment" (Nussbaum, Exchange Control

---

14 12 N.Y. 2d 371, 190 N.E. 2d 235, 239 N.Y.S. 2d 872 (1963).
15 Gold, *Fund Agreement in the Courts* (1962), pp. 135–39.

and the International Monetary Fund, 59 Yale L.J. 421, 426), or a contract where the consideration is payable in the currency of the country whose exchange controls are violated (Mann, The Exchange Control Act, 1947, 10 Mod. L. Rev. 411, 418). More recently, however, it has been suggested that it applies to "contracts which in any way affect a country's exchange resources" (Mann, The Private International Law of Exchange Control Under the International Monetary Fund Agreement, 2 International and Comp. L.Q. 97, 102; Gold and Lachman, The Articles of Agreement of the International Monetary Fund and the Exchange Control Regulations of Member States, Journal du Droit International, Paris (July-Sept. 1962)). A similar view has been advanced to explain the further textual difficulty existing with respect to whether a sale of coffee in New York for American dollars "involves the currency" of Brazil, the member whose exchange controls were allegedly violated. Again it is suggested that adverse effect on the exchange resources of a member *ipso facto* "involves" the "currency" of that member (Gold and Lachman, op. cit.). We are inclined to view an interpretation of subdivision (b) of section 2 that sweeps in all contracts affecting any members' exchange resources as doing considerable violence to the text of the section. It says "involve the currency" of the country whose exchange controls are violated; not "involve the exchange resources." While noting these doubts, we nevertheless prefer to rest this decision on other and clearer grounds.

The first of the grounds on which the majority based its decision was that the sanction of unenforceability in Article VIII, Section 2(*b*) required New York courts in certain circumstances to withhold judicial remedies to enforce a contract but did not require them to grant damages for a tort if the contract was performed:

> The sanction provided in subdivision (b) of section 2 is that contracts covered thereby are to be "unenforceable" in the territory of any member. The clear import of this provision is to insure the avoidance of the affront inherent in any attempt by the courts of one member to render a judgment that would put the losing party in the position of either complying with the judgment and violating the exchange controls of another member or complying with such controls and refusing obedience to the judgment. A further reasonable inference to be drawn from the provision is that the courts of no member should award any recovery for breach of an agreement in violation of the exchange controls of another member. Indeed, the International Monetary Fund itself, in an official interpretation of subdivision (b) of section 2 issued by the Fund's Executive Directors, construes the section as meaning that "the obligations of such contracts will not be implemented by the judicial or administrative authorities of member countries, for example, by decreeing performance of the contracts or by awarding damages

for their non-performance." (International Monetary Fund Ann. Rep. 82–83 [1949], 14 Fed. Reg. 5208, 5209 [1949].) An obligation to withhold judicial assistance to secure the benefits of such contracts does not imply an obligation to impose tort penalties on those who have fully executed them.

From the viewpoint of the individuals involved, it must be remembered that the Bretton Woods Agreement relates to international law. It imposes obligations among and between states, not individuals. The fact that by virtue of the agreement New York must not "enforce" a contract between individuals which is contrary to the exchange controls of any member, imposes no obligation (under the law of the transaction—New York law*) on such individuals not to enter into such contracts. While it does mean that they so agree at their peril inasmuch as they may not look to our courts for enforcement, this again is far from implying that one who so agrees commits a tort in New York for which he must respond in damages. It is significant that a proposal to make such an agreement an "offense" was defeated at Bretton Woods. (1 Proceedings and Documents of the United Nations Monetary and Financial Conference 334, 341, 502, 543, 546—referred to in Nussbaum, Exchange Control and the International Monetary Fund, 59 Yale L.J. 421, 426, 429, supra.)

The second ground was the principle of law that the courts of one country will not enforce the revenue laws of another country:

> Lastly, and inseparable from the foregoing, there is a remedial consideration which bars recovery in this case. Plaintiff is an instrumentality of the Government of Brazil and is seeking, by use of an action for conspiracy to defraud, to enforce what is clearly a revenue law. Whatever may be the effect of the Bretton Woods Agreement in an action on "A contract made in a foreign country between citizens thereof and intended by them to be there performed" (See Perutz v. Bohemian Discount Bank in Liquidation, 304 N.Y. 533, 537, 110 N.E. 2d 6, 7), it is well established since the day of Lord Mansfield (Holman v. Johnson, 1 Cowp. 341, 98 E.R. 1120 [1775]) that one State does not enforce the revenue laws of another. (Government of India v. Taylor, 1 All E.R. 292 [1955]; City of Philadelphia v. Cohen, 11 N.Y. 2d 401, 230 N.Y.S. 2d 188, 184 N.E. 2d 167; 1 Oppenheim, International Law, §144b [Lauterpacht ed., 1947].) Nothing in the Bretton Woods Agreement is to the contrary. In fact its use of the unenforcibility device for effectuation of its purposes impliedly concedes the unavailability of the more direct method of enforcement at the suit of the

---

* "All of respondent's acts allegedly in furtherance of the conspiracy took place in New York where it regularly did business." (Footnote to the opinion of the majority.)

aggrieved government. By the second sentence of subdivision (b) of section 2, further measures to make exchange controls more effective may be agreed upon by the member States. This is a matter for the Federal Government which not only has not entered into such further accords but has not even enacted the enabling provision into law (U.S. Code, tit. 22, §286 h).

The minority, in an opinion delivered by Chief Judge Desmond, held that if this was a suit to enforce a foreign revenue law, the adherence of the United States to the Articles of Agreement made it impossible to object on the basis of New York public policy:

> If there had never been a Bretton Woods Agreement and if this were a suit to enforce in this State the revenue laws of Brazil it would have to be dismissed under the ancient rule most recently restated in City of Philadelphia v. Cohen, 11 N.Y. 2d 401, 230 N.Y.S. 2d 188, 184 N.E. 2d 167. But Cohen and its predecessor cases express a public policy which lacks applicability here because of the adherence of the United States to the Bretton Woods Agreement. As we noted in Perutz v. Bohemian Discount Bank in Liquidation, 304 N.Y. 533, 537, 110 N.E. 2d 6, 7, the membership of our Federal Government in the International Monetary Fund and other Bretton Woods enterprises makes it impossible to say that the currency control laws of other member States are offensive to our public policy.

The minority concluded, however, that this was not a suit to collect taxes levied by the Brazilian Government and therefore was not a suit to enforce a foreign revenue law. The action was not even an effort to enforce Brazil's currency regulations. It was an action to recover damages in tort for fraud and conspiracy to deprive the plaintiff of the dollar proceeds to which it was entitled. The defendant not only knew of and intended to benefit by the fraud but also participated in it in New York "by making its purchase agreements here and by here receiving the shipping documents and making payments." The minority concluded that "refusal to entertain this suit does violence to our national policy of co-operation with other Bretton Woods signatories and is not required by anything in our own State policy."

The opinions in the New York Court of Appeals have been quoted at some length because of the obvious importance of the case, but at this stage of the discussion of the case only one comment need be made. It is on the views expressed by the majority on the meaning of the words "involve the currency" in Article VIII, Section 2(b). The majority was inclined to hold that these words could not be understood to mean that the contract affected the exchange resources of the member whose exchange controls were violated. This *dictum* is unfortunate. Its seriousness is enhanced by the fact that it was delivered by the highest court of a U.S. state that has a leading role in international trade and finance.

The majority's *dictum* on this issue cannot be accepted once the objectives of the Agreement and the particular purposes of Article VIII, Section 2(*b*) are grasped.[16] The Agreement seeks the elimination of exchange restrictions but authorizes them in special circumstances, usually related to the economic difficulties of a member. In the Agreement, members have agreed to cooperate with the Fund and among themselves in various ways, one of which is that they will not enforce exchange contracts that violate the exchange control regulations of another member. In this way, they avoid intensifying any economic difficulties of that member. This cooperation would be reduced drastically in scope if an exchange contract were deemed to "involve" the currency of a member only if, as implied by the majority, it called for payment in the member's currency. Exchange control regulations make no distinction between payments in domestic and foreign currency for the reasons explained above in the discussion of the Hamburg case, and it would have been quixotic on the part of the drafters to make this distinction for the purposes of Article VIII, Section 2(*b*). Probably, many people who are unfamiliar with exchange control would more readily expect that if the protection given by such a provision was to be narrower than the normal scope of exchange control regulations, the contracts that it would apply to would be those requiring payment in foreign exchange rather than domestic currency. Indeed, it has already been noted that this is one possible interpretation of the opinion in the Hamburg case.

The majority based its *dictum* solely on the language of Article VIII, Section 2(*b*). Even then, the argument was oversimplified. The negotiators and drafters of the Articles were men highly expert in finance and economics, including exchange control, who had no difficulty with the concept that a currency was "involved" if the resources that supported it could be drained away. They understood that this consequence would involve a currency in the sense that its stability could be impaired and disorderly exchange arrangements or competitive exchange depreciation could be provoked.[17] What they would have

---

[16] See 63 *Columbia Law Review* (1963), p. 1336: ". . . the generally accepted view is that the provision applies to any transaction that *affects* the exchange resources of a member nation."

[17] See Article I (iii) and Article IV, Section 4(*a*) of the Articles of Agreement.

found difficult to understand was why a currency was involved only to the extent of a drain resulting from payments in domestic currency or, to take the other limited view, only to the extent that the drain resulted from payments in foreign exchange. Finally, even the commentator who is intent only on the language of the provision cannot really maintain that "involve the currency" can mean nothing but "expressed in the currency" or "requiring payment in the currency." There is some comfort in the reflection that the view of the majority was only an *obiter dictum*.

UNITED STATES SUPREME COURT

The Banco do Brasil petitioned the U.S. Supreme Court for a writ of certiorari to review the judgment of the New York Court of Appeals. It asserted that the question justifying review was whether the national policy of the United States, as evidenced by its adherence to the Articles of Agreement, prevented a state court from refusing on grounds of state policy to consider the civil claim of an instrumentality of the Government of Brazil for the dollars that would have accrued to it but for a fraudulent conspiracy to evade Brazil's exchange control law.

In their brief in support of the petition, counsel for the Banco do Brasil vigorously attacked the application to this case of the rule that the revenue laws of one country are not enforced by the courts of another country. In this argument, they relied on the general effect of the Agreement on U.S. public policy and moved away from the argument based on Article VIII, Section 2(*b*), to which so much emphasis had been given by the Banco do Brasil in the New York courts. The brief argued that, in concentrating on Article VIII, Section 2(*b*), the majority in the Court of Appeals had ignored the decision of the U.S. Supreme Court in the *Kolovrat* case,[18] in which the court held that, because of the United States' membership in the Fund, Oregon could not validly cut off the right of Yugoslav nationals to inherit American property because of Oregon's public policy objections to exchange controls maintained by Yugoslavia as a member of the Fund. Similarly, New York should not be able, by relying on its rule of public policy with respect to "revenue" laws, to cut off the right to sue for damages for conspiracy to violate exchange controls maintained by Brazil as a member of the Fund.

---

[18] 81 S. Ct. 922 (1961); Gold, *Fund Agreement in the Courts* (1962), pp. 128–35.

The brief pointed out that the Fund had helped Brazil with financial resources and technical advice, but Brazil still found it necessary to have broad exchange controls as permitted by the Articles. As a member of the Fund, the United States was bound to cooperate with the Fund and Brazil to make Brazil's controls effective. The action of the New York court ignored this national policy by encouraging frauds directed against Brazilian exchange controls. The resulting losses that might be suffered by Brazil and other members of the Fund that had exchange surrender requirements could fall ultimately on the U.S. taxpayer because of an increase in U.S. foreign economic aid that might become necessary. U.S. aid to Brazil since the war had been vast, and had continued, both under independent programs and through the Fund, since the alleged conspiracy.

The Supreme Court invited the Solicitor General to express the views of the United States, and, after consultation with the Department of State and the Department of the Treasury, he submitted a memorandum in which he stated the view of all three that the case did not present a problem requiring resolution by the Supreme Court. The memorandum regarded Article VIII, Section 2(b) as the relevant provision, and argued that it did not require state courts to go beyond its terms and give a remedy in tort based on alleged violations of exchange control regulations. As for the argument of petitioner "that notwithstanding the limited scope of Article VIII, Section 2(b), the United States' adherence to the Bretton Woods Agreement *per se* manifests an overriding national policy favoring the enforcement of foreign exchange control regulations, so that the New York courts were compelled to entertain petitioner's tort action," the two Departments consulted and the Solicitor General agreed that "the bare acceptance of the Bretton Woods Agreement did not establish a national policy requiring the courts of the State of New York to entertain this suit." He pointed out that the views of the two Departments particularly charged with the negotiation and performance of the Agreement must be given great weight.

The Solicitor General distinguished the *Kolovrat* case in a passage that is not easy to understand:

> All that was held in *Kolovrat* was that the Bretton Woods Agreement constituted an expression of national policy on the subject of foreign exchange, which the State of Oregon was not at liberty to disregard. The claim rejected in *Kolovrat* as inconsistent with this established national policy was based on the assumption that a Bretton Woods member might fail to meet obligations which were *expressly* set out in

28

the agreement. No question as to the scope of an obligation imposed by the agreement was involved. The present case, unlike *Kolovrat*, concerns the meaning to be given to a particular provision in light of the United States' adherence to the agreement.

Since the language and history of the provision is explicit, and since the governmental agencies primarily concerned are not of the opinion that adherence to the agreement *ipso facto* establishes the overriding policy urged by petitioner, we suggest that, from the standpoint of the United States, there is no impelling need for review by this Court.

The Banco do Brasil replied to the Solicitor General's memorandum by stating that it did not contend that Article VIII, Section 2(*b*) imposed an obligation to entertain the suit. Nor did it argue that this provision or the Agreement as a whole was the source of its cause of action. Its cause of action was in tort for damages for conspiracy. The contention was that the national policy resulting from the United States' acceptance of the Agreement prevented New York courts from refusing to entertain the claim because the alleged fraud involved Brazil's foreign exchange regulations. On the Solicitor General's treatment of the *Kolovrat* case, the reply contended that if the Solicitor General was arguing that the basis of the *Kolovrat* decision was that Oregon was not entitled to assume that Yugoslavia might fail to meet an express obligation in the Agreement to refrain from controlling the transfer of inheritances to residents in the United States, the argument failed because there was no such express obligation in the Agreement.

The Supreme Court denied the petition for a writ of certiorari.[19] No reasons were given, and it must not be assumed that they are necessarily those set out in the Solicitor General's brief, although they probably weighed heavily against the argument of an implied treaty obligation. The case is of considerable importance as one of three decided by U.S. courts in which the central issue seems to have been the impact of the Agreement as a whole, in contrast to the effect of Article VIII, Section 2(*b*) in isolation, on the public policy of the United States. The other two cases are the *Kolovrat* case and *Perutz v. Bohemian Discount Bank in Liquidation.*[20] Later cases will have to decide to what extent these cases establish a pattern and what that pattern is. In this connection, it seems impossible to argue that the *Kolovrat* case turned on some specific provision of the Agreement and not the Agreement as a whole. There is no provision in the Articles

---

[19] 84 S. Ct. 657 (1964).
[20] 110 N.Y.S. 2d 446 (1952); 304 N.Y. 533, 110 N.E. 2d 6 (1953); Gold, *Fund Agreement in the Courts* (1962), pp. 50–55.

that would require Yugoslavia to permit the transfer of inheritances.[21] The precise *ratio decidendi* of the *Kolovrat* case, however, is even more obscure than that of the *Perutz* case.

The issue that faced the courts in the *Banco do Brasil* case was a difficult one. On the one hand, it would not have been surprising if it had been held that the public policy of the United States now required that the suit for damages should be entertained. The arguments of counsel for the Banco do Brasil in which the financial and economic aid of the Government of the United States to Brazil is contrasted with the action of the New York court are powerful. On the other hand, the rule refusing the enforcement of revenue laws is an old one and it is not easy to shake its authority. Moreover, it might have been feared that if the Banco do Brasil had succeeded, the burdens on New York bankers and merchants doing business with countries having exchange control regulations could be considerably increased, and the New York courts could find themselves forced to deal with a mass of litigation involving the implementation of these regulations. It is interesting to note that it was not asserted that the Brazilian participants in the alleged conspiracy had been punished in Brazil, or that steps had been taken in Brazil to tighten procedures and avoid similar evasions in future. It might also have been thought that the Brazilian exchange system was an unduly complicated one, whether it was consistent with the Articles or not.[22]

Even after all of this is said, there remains an uncomfortable feeling in the minds of some commentators that perhaps the most desirable balance was not struck on the issue of public policy.[23]

---

[21] Gold, *Fund Agreement in the Courts* (1962), pp. 132–33. There was in the *Kolovrat* case a treaty between Yugoslavia and the United States, but it would be difficult to regard the treaty as implicitly bringing the case under the second sentence of Article VIII, Section 2(b): "In addition, members may, by mutual accord, co-operate in measures for the purpose of making the exchange control regulations of either member more effective, provided that such measures and regulations are consistent with this Agreement." The effect of the treaty was not that the controls of each party should be made effective but, if anything, that controls should not be applied. The New York Court of Appeals noted that the second sentence of Article VIII, Section 2(b) has not been enacted into law in the United States. If there were a "mutual accord," would U.S. courts refuse to apply it for this reason? See 62 *Michigan Law Review* (1964), p. 1234.

[22] On this aspect of the case, it should be noted that exchange surrender requirements in themselves are not restrictions, do not require the approval of the Fund, and are consistent with the Articles. Surrender at a rate of exchange that constituted a multiple rate of exchange, as in the Brazilian case, did require the approval of the Fund in order to be consistent with the Articles.

[23] F. David Trickey, "The Extraterritorial Effect of Foreign Exchange Control

SUPREME COURT OF THE PHILIPPINES

In *Bacolod Murcia Milling Co., Inc. v. Central Bank of the Philippines*,[24] the Supreme Court of the Philippines on October 25, 1963 denied an appeal from a decision of the Court of First Instance of Manila dismissing a petition praying that Circular No. 20 promulgated by the Central Bank on December 9, 1949, and in particular section 4(a) thereof, be declared null and void on the ground that it was *ultra vires* and also because it constituted a confiscation of private property without the justification of public use and fair compensation. Section 4(a) provided, inter alia, that all receipts of foreign exchange should be sold by the recipient to an authorized agent of the Central Bank within one business day following receipt, and authorized agents were required to sell the exchange to the Central Bank daily. The petitioner received U.S. currency for an export of sugar to the United States in December 1956, but objected to the sale of this exchange to the Central Bank at the rate of two pesos per dollar paid by the Central Bank. This ratio was the par value for the peso established by the Philippines under the Articles, and also the rate at which the Bank sold dollars to importers, but the petitioner objected to payment based on anything less than the prevailing rate for the peso in foreign markets, principally in the United States, which rate the petitioner alleged was at least three pesos per dollar. Of the issues that were raised, the Supreme Court considered the most important to be whether the exchange control provision in section 4(a) of the circular was authorized by Section 74 of the charter of the Central Bank (Republic Act No. 265), pursuant to which the circular purported to have been promulgated:

Laws," 62 *Michigan Law Review* (1964), pp. 1232–41: "The decision in the principal case, if followed by other state courts, will have the unfortunate effect of denying IMF members the right to seek compensation in American courts for acts which undermine their financial stability and economic development" (p. 1241). This author also questions the thesis that exchange control laws are "revenue laws" within the meaning of the traditional rule (p. 1238). "Bretton Woods Agreement Held Not to Provide Tort Action for Evasion of Foreign Exchange Control Laws," 63 *Columbia Law Review* (1963), pp. 1334–41. "In light of American efforts to fulfill the purposes of the Bretton Woods Agreement, the dissent's statement (in the Court of Appeals) that national policy requires New York to entertain the plaintiff's suit is probably correct" (p. 1340). See also G.W. Pohn, "Court Refuses to Put Export-Import Contract Within Bretton Woods Agreement," 15 *Syracuse Law Review* (1963), pp. 100–103. *Contra:* R.K. Baker, "Extraterritorial Enforcement of Exchange Regulations," 16 *Stanford Law Review* (1963), pp. 202–209.

[24] The decision, No. L-12610, is summarized in *Complete Monthly Digest of Supreme Court Decisions*, Quezon City, No. 10, October 1963, pp. 364–66.

Emergency restriction on exchange operations.–. . . . in order to protect the international reserve of the Central Bank during an exchange crisis and to give the Monetary Board and the Government time in which to take constructive measures to combat such a crisis, the Monetary Board [of the Central Bank], with the concurrence of at least five of its members, and with the approval of the President of the Philippines, may temporarily suspend or restrict sales of exchange by the Central Bank and may subject all transactions in gold and foreign exchange to license by the Central Bank. The adoption of the emergency measures authorized in this section shall be subject to any executive and international agreements to which the Republic of the Philippines is a party.

The court below had found that there was a monetary crisis, and the Central Bank argued that the express and implied provisions of the charter empowered the Bank to impose exchange control of the kind that had been imposed. The word "restrict" in Section 74 was synonymous with "control" and the compulsory surrender of foreign exchange to the monetary authorities and their sale of it to exporters constituted a recognized form of exchange control. Again, Section 2 charged the Bank with the duty "to administer the monetary and banking system of the Republic; to maintain monetary stability in the Philippines; to preserve the international value of the peso." Another provision on which the Bank relied was Section 70:

*Action when the international stability of the peso is threatened.–*Whenever the international reserve of the Central Bank falls to an amount which the Monetary Board considers inadequate to meet the prospective net demands on the Central Bank for foreign currencies, or whenever the international reserve appears to be in imminent danger of falling to such a level, or whenever the international reserve is falling as a result of payments or remittances abroad which, in the opinion of the Monetary Board, are contrary to the national welfare, the Monetary Board shall:

(a) Take such remedial measures as are appropriate and within the powers granted to the Monetary Board and the Central Bank under the provisions of this Act; . . .

The writer of the opinion, and perhaps certain other members of the court, concluded that the Central Bank had not made out a power to compel the surrender of foreign exchange to it. Under Section 70, the remedial measures that could be taken had to be within the statutory powers. Section 74 and other provisions merely authorized the Monetary Board of the Central Bank to restrict or regulate foreign exchange, but these provisions did not include the power to commandeer that had been exercised. Such a power was confiscatory. If justified by a monetary crisis, it could be adopted by the Legislature but not by the Bank. It was true that the measure had helped to ward off a monetary crisis, but it was not necessary for that purpose. The licensed recipients of foreign exchange could have been directed to sell it directly to licensed importers. The members of the court holding these views concluded, therefore, that the disputed section 4(a) of Circular No. 20 was not valid.

Although the writer and perhaps some other members of the court held this view, the majority nevertheless concluded that the petitioner could not succeed on any claim to compel payment by the Bank at the rate of three pesos per dollar for exchange surrendered to it. The petitioner had applied for and obtained a license to export under the provisions of Circular No. 20, and it was, therefore, estopped from challenging the Bank's power to enforce those provisions of the circular that required the surrender of the proceeds of licensed exports.

The defense of estoppel did not operate against that part of the petition that sought the prohibition of the enforcement of the circular prospectively, i.e., when licenses had not yet been applied for under the circular. The court found, however, that the petitioner could not succeed on this part of its case either:

> One last defense raised by the Bank against the action is that under present laws and because of international agreements which the country has entered into, the Bank may not unilaterally change the present rate of exchange of ₽ 2 to the dollar. The members of the Court agreed that this defense is valid and bars the present suit.
>
> Sections 3 and 4 of Article IV of the International Monetary Fund Agreement of which the Philippines is a signatory, provides as follows:
>
> "Sec. 3. *Foreign Exchange dealings based on parity.*—The maximum and the minimum rates for exchange transactions between the currencies of members taking place within their territories shall not differ from parity;
>
> (i) in the case of spot exchange transactions, by more than one per cent; and
>
> (ii) in the case of other exchange transactions, by a margin which exceeds the margin for spot exchange transactions by more than the Fund considers reasonable."
>
> "Sec. 4. *Obligations regarding exchange stability*—
>
> (a) Each member undertakes to collaborate with the Fund to promote exchange stability, to maintain orderly exchange arrangements with other members, and to avoid competitive exchange alterations.
>
> (b) Each member undertakes, through appropriate measures consistent with this Agreement, to permit within its territories exchange

transactions between its currency and the currencies of other members only within the limits prescribed under section 3 of this article."[25]

The main purpose of the agreement is to promote exchange stability, to maintain orderly exchange arrangements among members, and to avoid competitive exchange depreciation. (Art. 1, par. iii, International Monetary Fund Agreement.)

To comply with its obligations under the agreement, especially as regards exchange stability, the Bank may not change the par value of the peso in relation to the dollar without previous consultation or approval by the other signatories to the agreement. Circular No. 20 must have been communicated to the other members of the agreement—and it is assumed that no contemplated change therein had been communicated to the other signatories at the time of the filing of this case.

The Central Bank, therefore, may not be compelled to ignore Circular No. 20, which was adopted with the advice and acquiescence of the other members of the International Monetary Fund, and it may not be compelled by mandamus to prohibit its enforcement.

Furthermore, under Article 49 of Republic Act No. 265, the Central Bank does not have the power to change the par value of the peso, a change which the present suit would require. This can be done only by the President upon proposal of the Monetary Board and with the approval of Congress. Were the petition of the petitioner for the payment of his dollar earnings at the rate of ₱ 3 to the dollar granted, the Central Bank would be violating the above provision of Republic Act No. 265 because it would be consenting to an actual change in the par value of the peso in relation to the dollar without previous approval or authority of those empowered to make the change.

The petitioner moved for a rehearing on the ground, inter alia,[26] that the court had not properly understood the provisions of the Fund's Articles that it had cited. They dealt not with the establishment or change of par values but with the margins for exchange transactions. For spot exchange transactions the margins were 1 per cent from parity, but for other exchange transactions, "such as those involving bank notes, drafts or bills of exchange expressed in foreign currency, like the U.S. dollar currency involved in our case," the margin could be wider by an amount that the Fund considered reasonable. No evidence had been presented of what the Fund regarded as

---

[25] The provisions as quoted by the court have not been corrected to eliminate certain deviations in punctuation and the like from the authentic text.

[26] The arguments of the petitioner and the replies of the respondent on the motion for rehearing are not noted here except to the extent that they involve the Articles of Agreement.

reasonable, but it had been shown that a rate of at least three pesos per dollar prevailed in the United States and it could not be presumed that the United States was in violation of the Articles. Therefore, the case did not involve any inconsistency with the par value for the peso, but rested instead on the fact that the rate claimed as just compensation was within the permitted margins based on parity.

Moreover, the petitioner continued, the current practice of the Central Bank under the latest amendment of Circular No. 20 required the surrender of only 20 per cent of export receipts at the official rate and permitted the sale of the other 80 per cent by the authorized banks at the prevailing free market rate in the Philippines. It must be assumed that this practice was valid under the Articles of Agreement, and it supported the petitioner's contention that the Agreement did not prevent a higher rate than the official rate in 1956.

In opposing the petitioner's motion, the Central Bank replied that the petitioner's claim was really to the difference between the official rate of exchange that it had received, which was also the par value, and the market rate abroad. The claim was to recover damages for the depreciation of the Philippine currency. Such a claim was inconsistent with Philippine public policy and called on the court to recognize a change in the par value of the peso that had not been adopted in accordance with the law. The court has not yet passed upon these arguments and decided whether or not to permit a rehearing.

Multiple Rates of Exchange

FIRST TAXPAYERS COUNCIL OF BRAZIL

The case of *Cobrazil, Cia. de Mineraçao de Metalurgia Brazil* (Brazil Metallurgy Mining Co.), decided by the Second Chamber of the First Taxpayers Council of Brazil on March 29, 1963,[27] involved the question of the meaning of an exchange rate. The issue arose under a provision of the Brazilian income tax regulations which declared that certain calculations for tax purposes involving foreign currency should be made by converting the currency at the rate of exchange effective on the date of payment, credit, remittance, receipt, or use, or at the rate of exchange at which the pertinent operations were actually carried out. More particularly, the issue involved certain remittances made in Belgian francs. Cobrazil objected to the conversion of these

---

[27] *Contribuinte Fiscal*, Vol. 7, No. 82, Rio de Janeiro, Oct. 5, 1963, pp. 346–50.

amounts at a rate of exchange that included the surcharge imposed by the Superintendência da Moeda e do Crédito (SUMOC) on the purchase of the foreign exchange.

Cobrazil argued that there were only two exchange rates in Brazil at the relevant date, the par value (official rate) as declared to the Fund and the free rate. The surcharges imposed by SUMOC were not part of the amount of Brazilian currency that was converted into Belgian francs but were in the nature of expenditures required in order to obtain conversion. These expenditures should not be taken into account in determining the rate of exchange under the income tax regulations.

The Council rejected Cobrazil's contention. An exchange rate was the rate at which an exchange operation is carried out. It was the effective rate at which units of one currency are acquired in return for units of another currency. A surcharge paid on the acquisition of foreign currency or a bonus received on its disposition was part of the exchange operation and thus part of the exchange rate. There was no justification for adopting, as the basis for calculation, either the par value or the free market rate when the operation was performed at the par value and surcharge or bonus, because this calculation would depart from the rate at which the operation was actually carried out. The Council concluded that the various premiums, surcharges, and bonuses associated with exchange operations in Brazil were integral parts of the Brazilian system of multiple rates of exchange.

The views of the Council as summarized above are consistent with the conclusions reached by the Fund in applying various provisions of the Articles of Agreement that deal with rates of exchange. For example, Article IV, Section 3 prescribes the maximum and minimum rates, in terms of variations from parity, for exchange transactions in a member's territories involving its own and another member's currency. Under Article VIII, Section 3, members are required to avoid "multiple currency practices" (i.e., multiple rates of exchange), except as authorized by provisions of the Articles of Agreement or approved by the Fund. In determining whether a member is observing the obligations imposed by these provisions, the Fund has always applied the concept of the "effective" rate of exchange. This is the rate at which one currency is in fact exchanged for another. The cost of one currency in terms of another may be the result of a diversity of procedures or devices imposed by monetary authorities, but it is this cost that the Fund regards as relevant for arriving at the rate of exchange for the purposes of the Articles. A vast body of precedent has grown up around the concept of the effective rate. Sometimes it may take close inspection and fine reasoning to determine whether or not a particular expenditure or receipt relates to the purchase or sale of one currency in return for another. But in many cases the answer will be clear. For example, it has been held since the early days of the Fund that taxes on the purchase or sale of exchange are part of the exchange rate for that purchase or sale. "An effective buying or selling rate which, as the result of official action, e.g., the imposition of an exchange tax, differs from parity by more than one per cent, constitutes a multiple currency practice."[28]

Another feature of the Council's opinion that accords with the Fund's practice is the fact that the motive with which the surcharge was imposed did not affect the result. Cobrazil appears to have argued, without success, that the surcharge was not part of the rate because it was a fiscal measure. The Fund in its practice regards an exchange surcharge as part of the exchange rate whatever might be the motive of the monetary authorities in imposing it. Their motive might be to raise revenue, protect domestic industry, or something else, but the Fund's determinations are not based on these considerations but on such objective facts as the way in which the surcharge is levied.

Although there is a close correspondence between the conclusions of the Council and the practice of the Fund as described above, there are certain *dicta* involving the Articles of Agreement that do not command support:

> The official rate, as it is called, is simply the nominal value in accordance with the Bretton Woods Agreement of 1944, approved by Decree No. 21,177 of May 27, 1946, which was published in the *Diario Oficial* of June 27, 1946, page 9,559.
>
> That Agreement does not and could not control the exchange system of any of the Parties.
>
> And the par value there established is limited to the direct relations of Fund members with one another and with the institutions created at that time. If this were not the case there would be a restriction of national sovereignty which would be inadmissible under the Constitution.
>
> This is evident, in refutation of the appellant's reasoning, from the text of the Agreement, which was published in the *Diario Oficial*.

---

[28] *Selected Decisions*, Second Issue, p. 86. (*Selected Decisions*, Ninth Issue, pp. 223–25.) Cf. Hans Aufricht, "Exchange Taxes," XXII *Zeitschrift für Nationalökonomie* (1962), pp. 20–40, and especially p. 21.

"A member may change the par value of its currency without the concurrence of the Fund if the change does not affect the international transactions of members of the Fund" (Article 4, Section 5(e)).

A reading of the full text will never bear out the appellant's interpretation.

The Bretton Woods Agreement does not require the country to maintain an unalterable value of its currency for all purposes; much less does it institute an exchange system or system of foreign-trade control to be effective in Brazilian territory, preventing the country from issuing regulations and establishing the kind of system best consonant with national commercial interests.

There should be no doubt about the following legal propositions:

(1) A par value established under the Articles of Agreement may be regarded as the "nominal value" of a currency because the Articles do not require that exchange transactions shall take place at that value. It is the value on which exchange transactions are to be based, and Article IV, Sections 3 and 4(b) establish the rules for the margins from parity within which members may permit exchange transactions within their territories.

(2) The par value is not simply the basis for exchange transactions between the governmental or monetary authorities of member countries or between the Fund and those authorities. The provisions of the Articles of Agreement with respect to par values and exchange rates apply to all exchange transactions taking place within a member's territories, including all the exchange transactions to which private entities or persons are parties.

Article IV, Section 5(e) does not authorize a member to permit certain exchange transactions to take place within its territories beyond the permitted margins from the parity resulting from par values established in accordance with the Articles of Agreement. In other words, the provision does not give a member freedom to decide to what extent it will or will not make its par value effective in exchange operations. The function of Article IV, Section 5(e) is to enable a member not to ignore its existing par value but to change it consistently with the Articles of Agreement without getting the concurrence of the Fund that is normally necessary in order to ensure that a change of par value will be consistent with the Agreement.

There is reason to believe that Article IV, Section 5(e) was inserted in the Articles of Agreement as the result of the contention that if the central authorities of a member had a complete monopoly of the trade and payments of that country, and if the member's currency was not employed in international payments, the par value of the currency was irrelevant internationally because it would affect no international payments. It was argued, therefore, that a member in such a position should be able to change its par value after consulting the Fund as required by Article IV, Section 5(b), but without the necessity for getting the Fund's concurrence. There was some skepticism that a case of the kind postulated as the basis for the provision could ever be demonstrated, and none has in fact been proved to the satisfaction of the Fund. Nor is it clear that a case would come under the provision even in the unlikely event that no payments of any kind, whether for invisibles or trade, were made in the member's currency. The exchange rate might still be a factor affecting the allocation of resources in the country and hence the volume of external transactions, and it might therefore be held that "the international transactions of members of the Fund" were affected. In any event, what should be clear is that in referring to "the international transactions of members of the Fund" unaffected by the change of par value, the provision is not referring solely to the transactions of governmental or monetary authorities, as is assumed in the *dicta* quoted from the Council's opinion, but to all transactions within the member's territories, including the transactions of the member's residents.

(3) It is true that rates of exchange not based on a par value established under the Articles of Agreement may exist within a member's territories. The explanation is not that the Agreement is limited in its application to the exchange systems of members. Once a member joins the Fund, it will be subject thenceforth to a code of international obligations in relation to its exchange system. If there are nonparity rates, they either will be permitted by this code or will be violations of it. In certain circumstances, multiple currency practices may be permitted by the Articles of Agreement. They may be maintained, although not permanently, if they were engaged in when the member joined the Fund, but any adaptation of them or any introduction of new ones requires the prior approval of the Fund. Even though multiple currency practices may be consistent with the Articles, they are no more than temporary expedients because the objective of the Articles is a unitary rate system based on a par value established under the Articles. This objective means an exchange system in which all exchange transactions take place within the permitted margins from a parity that is itself consistent with the Articles.

Privileges and Immunities

U.S. Court of Appeals for the D.C. Circuit

On July 27, 1962 the United States Congress approved a Joint Resolution,[29] which, after reciting, inter alia, that it was in the interest of the United States to promote international monetary cooperation through the Fund, and that the principal office of the Fund in Washington, D.C. had become inadequate, went on to authorize the Administrator of General Services, on the basis of full reimbursement by the Fund, to acquire by purchase, condemnation, or otherwise, certain defined land adjacent to the Fund's principal office and to convey the property to the Fund for the expansion of its principal office. On December 28, 1962 the United States brought an action in the U.S. District Court for the District of Columbia for the taking of the property under power of eminent domain for conveyance to the Fund and for the ascertainment and award of just compensation to the owners. The defendant owners answered the complaint by alleging that the Joint Resolution was unconstitutional on the ground that the interest of the United States in the Fund, amounting to only 26 per cent of the total voting power, was not such that a taking by the United States could be considered as made for a public use of the United States. The owners also objected that the Fund, the real party in interest, had not been joined as a party to the action.[30] The owners argued that the condemnation of property by the United States for the benefit of another international organization, the Pan American Health Organization, which had been upheld by the court,[31] was not a precedent because the United States was not to be reimbursed in that case. The United States was making a contribution to the work of that organization and was not simply acting as its purchasing agent.

The United States deposited with the court an amount that it estimated as just compensation. On February 1 and 5, 1963, the court, treating the owners' answer as motions to dismiss the complaint and deny possession, dismissed the owners' motions and ordered that possession be surrendered on or before May 1, 1963. The owners appealed from these orders to the U.S. Court of Appeals for the District of Columbia Circuit, whereupon the United States moved that

---

[29] Public Law 87-552, 76 Stat. 222, Report No. 1941 of the House of Representatives, 87th Congress, 2nd Session, contains some information about the negotiations to purchase the property that preceded the Joint Resolution.

[30] The Fund was not a party to these proceedings at any time.

[31] *U.S.A. v. All of Square 59*, District Court Docket No. 4-61 (1961).

this appeal be dismissed on the ground that the court lacked the jurisdiction to review them. The United States argued, on the strength of *Catlin v. United States*,[32] that there was jurisdiction to review orders in a condemnation suit only when they finally disposed of the whole case and adjudicated all aspects of it. The District Court's dismissal of the owners' motions was not a final action in this sense. The District Court's dismissal was interlocutory, and judgment would not be final until just compensation was determined and judgment for it granted. In the determination of just compensation, the owners could present their contentions as to the invalidity of the transfer of title.

It was at this stage of the case that the legal argument began to revolve around the Articles of Agreement. The owners argued that if their appeal resisting the transfer of possession were denied, they might suffer irreparable harm. That would be the situation if their building was demolished or if the United States conveyed title to the Fund. In the latter event, the owners could not recover their property if the final decision was in their favor because the immunities of the Fund under Article IX, Section 3 would shield it from judicial process.

The United States argued that the Fund's immunities were not relevant. A condemnation suit was an *in rem* proceeding in which the court acquired jurisdiction over the property and retained that jurisdiction until final settlement. It was true that, under the declaration of taking procedure that had been followed, the United States could acquire title, but it would be set aside if final judgment were given for the owners. The United States could convey this defeasible title to another, but this consequence would not terminate the court's jurisdiction over the property itself. The United States could not convey a greater title than it had, so that, if title were conveyed but the court later found that the condemnation was unconstitutional, physical possession could be restored by the court to the former owners. The owners replied that the Articles of Agreement made no distinction between *in rem* and *in personam* proceedings in granting immunity to the Fund.

The Court of Appeals found for the owners on the question that involved the Fund's privileges and immunities. Senior Circuit Judge Prettyman, speaking for the court, said:

> The International Monetary Fund was established by Articles of Agreement between the United States and other powers, known as the

---

[32] 65 S. Ct. 631, 324 U.S. 229 (1945).

Bretton Woods Agreement, effective December 27, 1945, 60 Stat. 1401 *et seq.* The Agreement provides (Article IX, Section 3, *Id.* at 1413):

"The Fund, its property and its assets, wherever located and by whomsoever held, shall enjoy immunity from every form of judicial process except to the extent that it expressly waives its immunity for the purpose of any proceedings or by the terms of any contract."

The Fund has not waived its immunity for the purpose of the present proceeding, nor has its immunity been removed by the terms of any contract.

The Government says that upon the effective date of the judgments of the District Court it will transfer the title to the property and its possession to the Monetary Fund. The statute under which it would acquire the property would require it to do so. Therefore immediately after transfer of the title to the United States that title will be transferred to an entity which is immune from all judicial process of the United States. We think this circumstance takes this case out of the doctrine of the *Catlin* case and makes these judgments of the District Court final judgments.

The Government argues that the proceeding, being a condemnation action, is *in rem*, and that the court, having acquired jurisdiction over the property, never loses that jurisdiction. But the statute in this particular case (Pub. L. No. 87-552) authorizes the Administrator to acquire and to convey this property to an entity which is not only itself immune from process but whose property is also immune. Unless either that statute or that paragraph in the Bretton Woods Agreement is invalid, this property, as well as its prospective owner, would pass beyond the jurisdiction of this court the instant it passed to the Fund.

The court concluded that there should be a prompt resolution of the basic issue of the validity of the taking, and that until then the effect of the orders of the lower court should be stayed. The issue was never finally resolved, because shortly after this judgment of the Court of Appeals the parties agreed on a price for the property.

The detached observer may view the predicament of the Fund as a bystander in this litigation with a certain amusement. The Fund's building project would be accelerated by the success of the United States' argument but at the cost of the contraction of the Fund's privileges and immunities in the courts of the host member. If the United States' argument failed, the building program would not prosper but the Fund's privileges and immunities would remain intact. Time has disposed of the dilemma. Now that the extension of the headquarters building is well under way, the undetached observer can feel even greater satisfaction in the court's confirmation of the Fund's privileges and immunities.

2

The Cuban Insurance Cases and the Articles of the Fund*

I. Introduction

The change of regime in Cuba in 1959 led to a considerable migration of citizens from that country. Many of these émigrés held insurance policies issued by U.S. or Canadian companies that had been doing business in Cuba. A wave of litigation based on these policies flooded into courts in the United States against both groups of companies.[1] One company alone had more than 6,000 policies outstanding that had been issued through its Havana branch. "The pending suits involve all kinds of policy claims, including death claims, suits for cash surrender values of policies, annuity benefits and endowment proceeds, as well as actions to force insurers to accept premiums and maintain policies in force."[2]

The actions instituted by policyholders involved a wide range of legal problems including issues of the act of state doctrine, nationalization, and private international law. They also raised many questions relating to Article VIII, Section 2(b) of the Fund's Articles of Agreement:

---

* Originally published in 1966.

[1] There has been some litigation in Canada also. See *Colmenares v. Imperial Life Assurance Co. of Canada* (1965) 51 D.L.R.(2d) 122; (1966) 54 D.L.R.(2d) 386.

[2] Brief of petitioners on a petition to the U.S. Supreme Court for a writ of certiorari to the Supreme Court of Louisiana in *Pan American Life Insurance Co. v. Theye y Ajuria*, p. 11.

> Exchange contracts which involve the currency of any member and which are contrary to the exchange control regulations of that member maintained or imposed consistently with this Agreement shall be unenforceable in the territories of any member. In addition, members may, by mutual accord, co-operate in measures for the purpose of making the exchange control regulations of either member more effective, provided that such measures and regulations are consistent with this Agreement.[3]

Indeed, they raised almost all the questions that had already been discussed in the growing body of case law involving that provision, together with a number of questions that were considered for the first time. The cases were remarkable not only because of the issues that were involved but also because of the amount of money at stake. Estimates of the total maturity values of the policies range from US$100 million to US$250 million, but it is doubtful that any estimate can be regarded as reliable. "Never before in a series of cases has the potential effect, both legal and economic, of the Fund Agreement on the rights of individuals and private corporations been more clearly brought into focus than in the suits brought by Cuban refugees seeking to recover the cash surrender value of their policies of life insurance in this country." [4]

All aspects of the cases deserve close study, and one detailed examination of them in relation to the Fund's Articles has already appeared.[5] The present chapter also is confined to that aspect of the cases; the only cases considered are those in which the courts dealt expressly in some way with the Articles. In other cases the briefs of counsel discussed the Articles, but the courts did not react overtly to these arguments. The implications of this silence are, on the whole, too problematical to warrant speculation here. It must be said at the outset, although the point will be discussed later, that the issues involving the Articles of the Fund disappeared with the withdrawal of Cuba from the Fund and ceased to affect those cases that had not yet been finally decided. But the judicial treatment of these issues while

---

[3] The Fund's interpretation of this provision (Executive Board Decision No. 446-4, June 10, 1949) is reproduced in the Appendix to this chapter, p. 94. See also *Selected Decisions of the Executive Directors and Selected Documents*, Third Issue (Washington, January 1965), pp. 73–74, hereinafter cited as *Selected Decisions*, Third Issue. (*Selected Decisions*, Ninth Issue, pp. 201–202.)

[4] Richard R. Paradise, "Cuban Refugee Insureds and the Articles of Agreement of the International Monetary Fund," *University of Florida Law Review*, Vol. 18 (1965), pp. 29–77, particularly pp. 37–38.

[5] Paradise, *op. cit.*

they remained active deserves study because of the possible impact of these cases on future litigation, in the United States or elsewhere, in which Article VIII, Section 2(*b*) is relevant.

CUBA AND THE FUND

Cuba became a member of the Fund on March 14, 1946 and notified the Fund, in accordance with Article XIV, Section 3, that it intended to avail itself of the transitional arrangements of Article XIV, Section 2. On December 18, 1953, Cuba notified the Fund that it was prepared to accept the obligations of Article VIII, Sections 2, 3, and 4. As a result, Cuba was required, inter alia, to avoid the imposition, without the approval of the Fund, of restrictions on the making of payments and transfers for current international transactions (Article VIII, Section 2(*a*)). On April 2, 1964 the Fund received Cuba's notice of withdrawal from the Fund, and, in accordance with Article XV, Section 1, the withdrawal became effective at once.

From time to time in the course of the litigation discussed here, the Fund was asked by counsel about the consistency with the Fund's Articles of the exchange restrictions applied by Cuba. The Executive Directors of the Fund authorized the following reply:

> This is in response to your inquiry concerning the consistency with the Articles of Agreement of exchange restrictions maintained or imposed by Cuba.
>
> A member of the Fund, like Cuba, which has accepted the obligations of Article VIII is required to obtain Fund approval of exchange restrictions on payments and transfers for current international transactions, multiple currency practices and discriminatory currency arrangements pursuant to Article VIII, Sections 2 and 3 of the Fund's Articles of Agreement. The Fund has approved the maintenance by Cuba of a two per cent exchange tax on remittances abroad. Any other existing restrictions on current transactions, multiple currency practices or discriminatory currency arrangements do not have the Fund's approval.
>
> In accordance with the Articles of Agreement, Fund approval for controls of capital transfers is not required. Thus, to the extent any controls are confined to capital transfers, they are maintained or imposed consistently with the Fund's Articles of Agreement.

CUBAN LEGISLATION AND DECREES

The Cuban laws and decrees that have been regarded in the cases as relevant to the issues are a mixture of enactments dealing with legal tender, exchange control, and nationalization.[6] They begin with Law No. 13 of December 23, 1948, which established the National Bank of Cuba as the central bank and dealt with the national currency. Article 90 provided that the bank-notes of the National Bank would be legal tender and have unlimited power to discharge obligations. Under Article 95 the national currency would be the only legal tender currency in Cuban territory and would have to be accepted in payment of obligations contracted or payable in Cuba. Article 97 provided that U.S. currency would cease to be legal tender in Cuba one year after the National Bank began operating or for an additional period of not more than one year thereafter if that was decreed. Decree No. 1384 of April 9, 1951 established June 30, 1951 as the effective date under Article 97. From that date, U.S. currency would cease to be legal tender in Cuba, and "all obligations contracted or payable in the national territory shall be expressed and settled in national currency," the substitution of pesos for dollars to be at par.

Law No. 568 was enacted on October 2, 1959, after the Government of Dr. Castro had taken office, in order to establish a sweeping exchange control. Article 1 declared a list of actions to be "felonies of monetary contraband." Those treated as relevant in the cases were set forth in paragraphs 6 to 12:

6. To export currencies or securities, or to transfer funds to points abroad by means of checks, transfers, drafts, letter-orders, orders of payment, compensations, travellers checks, letters of credit, reimbursements of collections, purchases or sales of passage tickets or through any other similar means, regardless of the origin or source of the funds, except for those cases authorized by the Currency Stabilization Fund, through a member bank or a firm duly authorized by Banco Nacional de Cuba.

7. To export or import national currency in excess of the limit that [sic] set now or hereafter by the Currency Stabilization Fund.

8. To establish credits in national currency for persons residing abroad or for residents of Cuba for the account of residents abroad.

9. To assign or transfer credits in national currency to residents abroad, make payments for their account in national currency and set up credits in bank accounts the holders whereof reside abroad without first complying with the rules issued by the Currency Stabilization Fund in this respect.

10. To receive and credit to bank accounts kept abroad, or to transfer to third parties collections made abroad for business transacted or

---

[6] Not all the laws and decrees were relied on by the defendants in each of the cases.

46

services rendered in Cuba, regardless of the source of the respective funds.

11. To secure financing payable abroad in foreign currency without the prior authorization of the Currency Stabilization Fund, except for transactions of banks associated to the Banco Nacional de Cuba with their home offices or foreign correspondents, for the establishment of letters of credit, overdrafts and other normal activities of the banking business.

12. Any other violation or infringement of the rules of the Currency Stabilization Fund under which funds are transferred or remitted abroad in violation of the prohibitive rules of the same Fund or in a larger amount than is permitted thereby.[7]

Law No. 851 of July 6, 1960 was adopted in order to permit the nationalization of all businesses and properties of natural or juridical persons of the United States or in which they had a majority share or interest even though the enterprise was organized under Cuban law. The payment for nationalized properties was to be made in bonds of the Republic of Cuba, which would be amortized from a fund constituted by annual allocations of foreign exchange based on a formula related to purchases of sugar in each calendar year by the United States from Cuba in excess of a stated price. Interest also was to be payable from this fund. The bonds were to be amortized in a period not less than 30 years from the date of nationalization.[8]

Resolution No. 3 of October 24, 1960 was promulgated under Law No. 851 for the purpose of effecting the nationalization of all the properties and firms in Cuba of U.S. persons. Among them were the U.S. insurance companies that were the defendants in the cases. The Canadian insurance companies were not affected and continued to do business under policies issued in the past. The Resolution declared that the Cuban State was "subrogated in place and grade of the natural and juridical persons referred to . . . with respect to the properties, rights and rights of action mentioned, as well as the assets and liabilities constituting the capital of the concerns referred to." [9]

Finally, Law No. 930 of February 23, 1961 provided that operations involving foreign currencies were a monopoly of the State, which would carry them out exclusively through the National Bank. Only

---

[7] This translation has been quoted, notwithstanding some obvious infelicities, because it is the one used in most of the cases.

[8] *American Journal of International Law*, Vol. 55 (1961), pp. 822–24.

[9] Richard C. Allison, "Cuba's Seizures of American Business," *American Bar Association Journal*, Vol. 47 (1961), pp. 48–51.

the Bank was authorized to hold foreign currencies, and any foreign exchange received in Cuba had to be surrendered to the Bank. Only the Bank might authorize the acquisition and holding of foreign currencies within or outside Cuban territory by persons domiciled in Cuba (Article 23). "All receipts and payments in foreign currency and, similarly, all settlements with foreign countries and natural or juridical persons abroad shall be carried out only through and under the control of the National Bank of Cuba" (Article 24). "Holdings in local currency maintained at credit institutions or other agencies which belong to natural or juridical persons domiciled abroad may be utilized only by these persons with the express authorization of the President of the National Bank of Cuba or such officers as he may designate" (Article 26). "All exports and transfers to foreign countries of foreign exchange, checks, securities or other kinds of monetary instruments or instruments representing foreign means of payment are prohibited without authorization of the National Bank of Cuba" (Article 42). Coins and notes issued by the National Bank "shall be the only currency of legal tender status and shall be accepted in payment of all obligations payable" in Cuba (Article 14). "When other currency has been or is specified, the obligations shall be liquidated and paid necessarily in legal tender currency" (Article 14).

II. The Cases

THE PLAINTIFF SUCCEEDS

Pan American Life Insurance Co. v. Blanco

In 1945 the defendant company, a Louisiana corporation, issued to the plaintiff three single-premium annuity contracts under which his daughters were the annuitants and under which monthly payments were to begin as each of the plaintiff's three daughters reached the age of 21. The signatures of the defendant's officials executing the policies were authenticated before a notary in Havana, and the policies were delivered to the plaintiff there on payment of the premium in dollars by the plaintiff. The contracts provided that the annuities were to be paid in dollars, and that all liquidations were to be paid at the defendant's head office in New Orleans on delivery of the contract to the defendant. The plaintiff, who was vested with control of the contract, demanded its cash surrender value in Florida after he became a resident of that state. On the defendant's refusal to pay, the plaintiff sued and the defendant counterclaimed for a declaratory judgment of nonliability. One policy matured in May 1957 before suit was brought, and another in May 1961 in the course of the litigation.

The U.S. District Court for the Southern District of Florida struck out the defendant's answer and counterclaim, which argued that the defendant was relieved of liability because of Law No. 13 and Decree No. 1384 thereunder, Law No. 568, and Law No. 851 and Resolution No. 3 thereunder. An interlocutory appeal was taken to the U.S. Court of Appeals, Fifth Circuit, on a question certified by the District Court.[10] In support of its contention that

> ... the Blancos' rights to enforce payment in dollars in the United States were made unenforceable by Cuban Law No. 568 of September 29, 1959 requiring payments to Cuban nationals to be made in Cuba in pesos, Pan American argues that Cuban Law No. 568 is valid and binding under The Bretton Woods Monetary Agreement of 1945 to which Cuba and the United States are signatories, which was incorporated into the laws of the United States in 22 U.S.C. §286; that the annuity policies in controversy are "exchange contracts" within the meaning of such Agreement and subject to the exchange control regulations of Cuba. In this connection Pan American's Reply Brief states that "only one other question remains: Is Cuban Law 568 'maintained or imposed consistently with' The Bretton Woods Agreement?" It then quotes portions of a letter from the General Counsel of the Monetary Fund which Pan American contends establishes the fact "that Law No. 568 is a currency control regulation which is 'maintained or imposed consistently with' The Bretton Woods Agreement." No such letter appears in the record. Application of The Bretton Woods Agreement involves other questions of fact and law as to which there is no proof in the record.

These questions were stated in a footnote as follows:

> ... Has Cuba incorporated the Bretton Woods Agreement into its law as did the United States, in Title 22 U.S.C. §286? Has Cuba complied with its obligations under such agreement? Did Cuba's withdrawal from the International Bank for Reconstruction and Development, on November 14, 1960 ... constitute such a breach of the purposes of the fund as set forth in Art. I as to render such Agreement ineffective as to Cuba? Are the annuity policies in question "exchange contracts" within the meaning of Art. VIII, Sec. 2(b) of the Bretton Woods Agreement?[11]

---

[10] 311 F. 2d 424 (decided November 7, 1962).
[11] *Ibid.*, at 427, fn. 8.

The Court of Appeals noted that, with the exception of Resolution No. 3, none of the Cuban laws or resolutions had been placed in the record, and the court decided that it would not take judicial notice of them. It followed that the defendant must lose on the part of its case that rested on Article VIII, Section 2(b). The Court of Appeals held, however, that the action of the District Court was wrong in striking out the defendant's counterclaim based on Resolution No. 3 and the alleged substitution of the Cuban Government for the defendant. The Court of Appeals held, therefore, that the District Court should not have dismissed the counterclaim and should now decide the case on the merits.

The *Blanco* case was then consolidated for trial by the U.S. District Court for the Southern District of Florida with two other cases against *Pan American Life Insurance Co.*, by *Conill* and by *Aguirregaviria Zabaleta*, and with a fourth case, *Lorido y Diego v. American National Insurance Co.*[12] The three further cases involved actions by plaintiffs, on certain policies of life insurance, for a declaratory judgment that the policies were in full force and effect; that the cash surrender value where applicable was payable on demand; or that where there were annuity or endowment features, these would be payable on maturity. In the *Blanco* case there was, as already noted, a counterclaim by Pan American for a declaratory judgment.

American National was a corporation organized and existing under the laws of Texas, with a principal place of business in Galveston. Both defendants had conducted life insurance business in Cuba until some time in October 1960, Pan American through a branch office and American National through a general agent. Cuban law did not require the companies to maintain a certain volume of assets in Cuba, beyond an initial deposit of $25,000, as a condition of doing business there.

All the plaintiffs were Cuban nationals and refugees residing in Florida. None of the contracts provided that the policyholder would be paid solely from assets of the defendant located in Cuba, and the District Court found that all of the defendants' assets were available for payment under the policies issued by them. All applications for the policies had been made in Cuba in Spanish and had been sent to the defendants' home offices in the United States, where they were accepted and where the policies were issued. The Pan American policies were in Spanish and the American National policies in English.

---

[12] 221 F. Supp. 219 (decided July 15, 1963).

The policies were forwarded to the defendants' representatives in Cuba, who had them authenticated and who delivered them to the policyholders. Except as noted below in the *Zabaleta* case, all the Pan American policies provided that all payments, whether of premiums or benefits, were to be made in New Orleans. The Cuban peso was the designated currency in the American National policies, but all payments were to be made in Galveston.

In the *Conill* case, the defendant issued to the plaintiff in 1941 a life insurance policy under which, in consideration of annual payments, the defendant would pay a stipulated amount to the plaintiff's beneficiary on proof of the plaintiff's death. The plaintiff demanded, and was refused, the cash surrender value of the policy.

In the *Zabaleta* case, the defendant issued a life insurance policy to the plaintiff in 1938 that provided various life insurance and endowment benefits and other options at the plaintiff's election. The policy had a maturity value and various cash surrender values. In 1952 the plaintiff agreed with the defendant that payments to or by the plaintiff should be made in Cuban pesos in Havana. Before that date, the plaintiff had paid all premiums in U.S. dollars. In October 1958 the plaintiff exercised an option to cease paying premiums and to receive an endowment payment 15 years thereafter. In July 1962 the plaintiff demanded the cash surrender value of the policy. The defendant refused the demand and also refused to consider that the policy had full force and effect.

In the *Lorido y Diego* case, the plaintiff received two policies of life insurance in 1950, which provided that stipulated amounts be paid to the plaintiff, if living, or to his named beneficiary on the maturity dates. The plaintiff demanded, and was refused, the cash surrender value of the policies.

By pretrial stipulation it was agreed that the issues of law were the same as stated by the Circuit Court of Appeals in the *Blanco* case, i.e., whether or not

> . . . Pan American is relieved of liability and performance of its obligations under the contracts by reason of certain Cuban laws and decrees, referring to: (1) Cuban Law No. 13 of 1948 and Cuban Monetary Decree of 1951 under Law No. 13, which Pan American alleged "required all contracts theretofore payable in dollars to or by Cuban nationals in Cuba to be payable in Cuban pesos." (2) Cuban Law No. 568 of September 29, 1959, which Pan American alleges prohibited the defendant from paying any monies to Cuban nationals anywhere except in Cuba, (3) Cuban Law No. 851 of July 6, 1960 and Cuban

Resolution No. 3 of October 24, 1960 under Law No. 851 "which in substance and effect" expropriated the Cuban assets of Pan American "and substituted the Cuban government as the obligor" in "the annuity contracts herein sued on."

District Judge Choate observed that on December 18, 1953 Cuba had notified the Fund, in accordance with Article XIV, Section 3, that Cuba accepted the obligations of Article VIII, Sections 2, 3, and 4 of the Fund's Articles of Agreement. He also noted that Cuba had withdrawn from the International Bank for Reconstruction and Development while continuing to remain a member of the Fund, but that there was no requirement in the Articles of the Fund that a member must continue to be a member of the Bank. He quoted the statement that the Executive Directors of the Fund had authorized in connection with the exchange system of Cuba and that has been quoted earlier in this chapter.

The court went on to say:

> The pre-trial stipulation states the issue in terms of whether or not the court is required to recognize and give effect to these Cuban decrees and laws either under our municipal law or under the two Bretton Woods Agreements and 22 U.S.C. §286 et seq., Acceptance of Membership by United States in International Monetary Fund.[13]

The court held that it was not required to give extraterritorial effect to the Cuban laws and decrees. The defendants had assumed that because the plaintiffs were Cuban nationals by origin, they were subject to Cuban sovereignty and bound by Cuban law. That argument could not be accepted, because the plaintiffs were refugees and residents of the United States. Neither the parties nor the subject matter of the actions was subject to Cuban sovereignty. The defendants' assets in Havana bore no necessary relation to the causes of action.

Passing from the question whether the Cuban legislation had extraterritorial effect, the court then considered the question whether that legislation must nevertheless be applied under the private international law of the forum. It recognized that by applying traditional choice-of-law rules, a strong argument could be made for holding that the contracts were governed by Cuban law. The court preferred a choice-of-law rule based on the consideration of giving maximum protection to the insured, and on this basis the law of the domicile of the insurers governed. The court held, nevertheless, that the choice

---

[13] *Ibid.*, at 226.

of law was not necessary for the determination of these cases, and repeated its opinion that the legislation had no extraterritorial effect.

> . . . Even if the court is mistaken as to the National status of the plaintiffs as refugees, these laws do not apply to cover the situation of a Cuban national enforcing an executory contract in the forum of another jurisdiction according to the terms of an obligation existing prior to the passage of those laws. Further, we do not believe that such laws and decrees can have any force and effect over the persons of these litigants who are not only without Cuba, but, as refugees, are not subject to its in personam jurisdiction. . . . On the basis of the foregoing, The Bretton Woods Agreement and 22 U.S.C. §286 et seq. would not appear to have any applicability.[14]

Menendez Rodriguez v. Pan American Life Insurance Co. and Vento Jaime v. Pan American Life Insurance Co.

In January 1945, the defendant insured the lives of the plaintiffs in these suits, who were then resident in Havana, in the amount of $20,000 each. The applications were accepted by the defendant in New Orleans. The policies provided that annual premiums would be paid for 20 years, and that all payments by either party would be "verified in the City of New Orleans in the legal money of the United States." From 1945 to 1952 the plaintiffs had paid the premiums in dollars, and from 1952 to 1958 in pesos. In July 1960, the plaintiffs, after having become refugees and residents of Florida, demanded the cash surrender value of the policies in Tampa and were refused. The plaintiffs were advised by the defendant to make the premium payment in Havana and to apply for the cash surrender value there.

The defendant argued that the controversy was justiciable solely under the laws of Cuba and in its courts. It argued, inter alia, that Cuban law prevented it from paying in dollars. For a variety of reasons, including the finding that the policies were governed by Cuban law, the U.S. District Court dismissed the actions on the ground of *forum non conveniens*. The U.S. Court of Appeals, Fifth Circuit, reversed this decision on the ground that the defendant had not discharged the burden of showing that the plaintiffs could obtain justice in the Cuban courts and that those courts would be more convenient for the determination of the cases. The court also held that the act of state doctrine did not lead to a different result, but it did not deal specifically with Article VIII, Section 2(b).[15] This silence led to

---

[14] *Ibid.*, at 229.
[15] 311 F. 2d 429 (decided October 17, 1962).

a petition for rehearing, which the court denied as follows:

> Appellee further suggests here that the Bretton Woods Agreement and certain Cuban currency control statutes require dismissal of this complaint. Since the entry of our opinion in this case this Court has on November 7, 1962 rejected this contention in Pan American Life Insurance Company v. Inocencio Blanco, 311 F. 2d 424.[16]

It will be noted that the court relied on the decision of the Court of Appeals in the *Blanco* case, but that court merely held that it would not take judicial notice of the Cuban laws on which the argument involving Article VIII, Section 2(*b*) rested.

Theye y Ajuria v. Pan American Life Insurance Co.

As in the other cases against Pan American, the plaintiff, a Cuban national, applied, in May 1928, for a policy of life insurance through the defendant's representative in Havana; the application, in Spanish, was referred to the home office in New Orleans; the application was approved, returned to the local representative, authenticated, and delivered to the plaintiff. The policy stipulated that all premiums were payable in advance at the home office and that on presentation of the policy and proof of the death of the insured, the defendant would pay the proceeds to the beneficiary at its home office. All the annual premiums were paid in dollars until 1942, when the plaintiff exercised one of the options in the policy and had it converted into a paid-up policy. The defendant paid a bonus and made three loans to the plaintiff in 1948, 1950, and 1952; the plaintiff received and repaid all three loans in pesos in Havana. The plaintiff left Cuba in November 1960 and was residing as a refugee in Florida. On arrival in the United States, he demanded the cash surrender value of the policy at the New Orleans office. After the defendant refused the demand, the plaintiff brought suit in the District Court for the Parish of Orleans. In answer to the plaintiff's petition, the defendant argued that (1) the contract was governed by Cuban law; (2) if the contract had originally been governed by Louisiana law, its situs had been changed to Cuba by the subsequent acts of the parties in connection with the bonus and loans; and (3) under the act of state doctrine and certain provisions of the Fund's Articles, the laws of Cuba passed since the execution of the policy governed the contract.[17] The trial judge held that the policy when issued and converted was governed

---

[16] *Ibid.*, at 437 (rehearing denied December 20, 1962). See also 376 U.S. 779, 84 S. Ct. 1130 (1964).

[17] 161 So. 2d 70, 71.

by Louisiana law, and that subsequent Cuban laws could not affect obligations under the policy. He gave judgment for the plaintiff in the amount of $7,090.

The defendant appealed to the Court of Appeal of Louisiana, Fourth Circuit, which reversed the judgment of the lower court.[18] The court held that a sovereign government could enact legislation controlling insurance business within its bounds for the benefit of its citizens. Law No. 568 was adopted before the plaintiff left Cuba on November 4, 1960. Furthermore, the defendant's business and assets in Cuba were nationalized on October 24, 1960. A sovereign nation had the power to change the situs of its nationals' contracts and could impair the obligations of contracts.

> With these legal propositions before us, the Court must recognize and give effect to the Bretton Woods Agreement signed by the United States, Cuba, and some ninety-five sovereign Nations in 1945. Each signatory to the Compact, which included an International Monetary Fund, bound itself to take steps to implement the principles of the international accord, as part of its domestic law. Our own Congress honored its commitment by enacting a statute to that effect. (22 U.S.C.A. §286 et seq.).

After quoting Article VIII, Section 2(b), the court continued:

> By accepting and implementing the above, our Congress has undertaken to make the above principle, a part of our national law. On June 14, 1949, the International Monetary Fund, binding on all its members, including Cuba and the United States, issued the following interpretation of Article VIII, Section 2(b):

> "An obvious result of the foregoing undertaking is that if a party to an exchange contract referred to in Article VIII, Sec. 2(b) seeks to enforce such a contract, the tribunal of the member country before which the proceedings are brought, will not, on the ground that they are contrary to the public policy of the forum, refuse recognition of the exchange control regulations of the other member which are maintained or imposed consistently with the Fund Agreement. It also follows that such contracts will be treated as unenforceable notwithstanding that under [the] private international law of the forum [the law under which the foreign exchange control regulations are maintained or imposed] is not the law which governs the exchange contract or its performance * * * ."

> Cuban Law 568 of September 29, 1959, required payments between plaintiff and defendant be made in Cuba, regardless of the language

---

[18] 154 So. 2d 450 (rehearing denied July 1, 1963).

of the contract. Despite this, plaintiff attempts to defy the decrees and laws of Cuba, the sovereign to whom he owed allegiance to come into this country and collect his debt in the currency of another nation. This would nullify and frustrate his own sovereign's legislative will and powers.

Prior to the Bretton Woods Agreement, plaintiff's position might have been upheld. Our Courts have held it to be the public policy of the forum State to refuse to give effect to exchange control legislation of a foreign sovereign, where such was labelled by the forum as penal, punitive, confiscatory or violative of fundamental concepts of justice. In this connection, the Court calls attention to the cases and authorities cited therein of Menendez Rodriguez v. Pan American Life Insurance Co., 5 Cir., 311 F. 2d 429 and Menandez v. Aetna Insurance Co., 5 Cir., 311 F. 2d 437.

This Court believes, and so holds, that the Bretton Woods Agreement and our Acts of Congress (22 U.S.C.A. §286 et seq.) supersede the principles enunciated in the above authorities, as to parties or nations who signed the agreement or treaty. It is now our national policy to deny enforcement, in the Court of this land, of contracts which would frustrate the exchange control regulations of another member of the agreement. Our Congress gave recognition to the will of the signatories to the agreement, declaring that the public policy of its members would be better served by a measure of collaboration among them designed to give effect to each other's exchange control regulations. The U.S. Supreme Court, in Kolovrat v. Oregon, 366 U.S. 187, 81 S. Ct. 922, 928, 6 L.Ed. 218, decided May 1, 1961, interpreted the Bretton Woods Agreement as follows:

"These treaties and agreements show that this Nation has adopted programs deemed desirable in bringing about, so far as can be done, stability and uniformity in the difficult field of world monetary controls and exchange. * * * Doubtless these agreements may fall short of that goal. But our National Government's powers have been exercised so far as deemed desirable and feasible toward that end, and the power to make policy with regard to such matters is a national one from the compulsion of both necessity and our Constitution."

We find that the Court below disregarded the above treaty accord between the United States and Cuba and our own Congressional enactments to implement this agreement. Our Courts should not and cannot enforce a contract which transcends the sovereign will of Cuba touching on monetary contracts involving its own nationals. Plaintiff demands should have been rejected.[19]

---

[19] *Ibid.*, at 453–54.

Having disposed of the case on the basis of Article VIII, Section 2(b), the court went on to note that the defendant had maintained reserves in Cuba to meet its Cuban obligations, including the policy involved in this action. The Cuban Government had taken over those reserves and the defendant's obligations. If judgment went against the defendant in Louisiana, it would have to pay the obligation twice, because it could not satisfy the judgment from the Cuban assets that had been nationalized.

The plaintiff appealed to the Supreme Court of Louisiana, which held that there was no room for speculation as to the law that the parties intended as the governing law.[20] It was the law of Louisiana, and the trial judge was right in holding that Cuban legislation passed after the policy became a paid-up policy had no effect on the obligation in existence at that time.[21] Nothing that had happened later showed that the parties intended to change the situs of the contract to Cuba.

The court then passed on to the argument based on Article VIII, Section 2(b):

> Conceding that Cuba had adopted the Articles thereof as part of its national law as alleged by the defendant, an exhaustive study of the Bretton Woods Agreement, as well as all authorities relied on by the defendant, fails to show where the Agreement or any of the cases are controlling under the particular facts of the case at bar inasmuch as a contract payable in the state of Louisiana in United States currency is not a foreign exchange contract.
>
> In Blanco v. Pan American Life Insurance Company, 221 F. Supp. 219, see also 311 F. 2d 424, the same defenses to claims by policyholder Blanco and other Cuban refugees were urged therein as here, and in support thereof, the defendant cited the Court of Appeal opinion in the case at bar. That court concluded, however, that Federal courts are not bound by state decisions in interpreting a federal question and disposed of the matter by holding the Bretton Woods Agreement had no applicability in that case because the Cuban government lost whatever jurisdiction it possessed over not only the subject matter of the litigation but also over the persons of the plaintiffs when they fled from Cuba, became alien residents of the United States, political citizens of nowhere, but civil citizens of Florida as they were domiciled there. The court further remarked "* * these laws (relied on by defendant) do not apply to cover the situation of a Cuban national enforcing an

---

[20] 161 So. 2d 70 (decided February 24, 1964).

[21] In a footnote, the laws and decrees referred to are Laws Nos. 13, 568, and 851; Decree No. 1384; and Resolution No. 3 (ibid., at 71, fn. 2).

executory contract in the forum of another jurisdiction according to the terms of an obligation existing prior to the passage of those laws. Further, we do not believe that such laws and decrees can have any force and effect over the persons of these litigants who are not only without Cuba, but, as refugees, are not subject to its in personam jurisdiction. * * *"

Moreover, courts, including those of this country as well as those of foreign jurisdictions, in interpreting contracts involving matters affected by the Bretton Woods Agreement are uniform in their holding that the laws of the state or nation where the parties intended the contract to be performed govern.[22,23]

Judgment for the plaintiff was affirmed.

Pan American Life Insurance Co. v. Raij

The plaintiff applied for and received a 20-year endowment policy according to the practice of Pan American as described in the other cases. The policy provided that all payments by either party would be made in dollars in New Orleans. All premiums were paid until November 1960, when the premium was refused and returned by the defendant. Subsequent tenders of premium were refused, and the plaintiff sued for a declaration that he was entitled to pay the premiums and have them accepted and that the policy was in full force and effect. The defendant relied on Resolution No. 3 and Decree No. 1384. On June 6, 1962 the Circuit Court found for the plaintiff on the ground that these measures did not change the contract in the absence of agreement by the parties on a change.

The District Court of Appeal of Florida, Third District, affirmed this decision. On a petition for rehearing, the court said:

---

[22] 161 So. 2d 74. For the last proposition, the court's citations were: "Menendez Rodrigues v. Pan American Life Insurance Company, 5 Cir., 311 F. 2d 429, 432; Pan American Life Insurance Company v. Recio, Fla. App., 154 So. 2d 197 (Florida); Pan American Life Insurance Company v. Raij, Fla. App. 156 So. 2d 785 (Florida); Menendez v. Aetna Insurance Company, 5 Cir., 311 F. 2d 437; Ahmen Bey Naguib v. Heirs of Moise Abner, abstract appears in J.T.M., No. 4003, Nov. 24/25, 1948; Kraus v. Zivostenska Banka, 187 Misc. 681, 64 N.Y.S. 2d 208; Cermak, et al. v. Bata Akciova Spoiecnost, Sup., 30 N.Y.S. 2d 782; Frankman v. Ango-Prague Credit Bank (London office), 1 All E.R. 337; Frankman v. Ango-Prague Credit Bank, 2 All E.R. 1025; Zivnostenska Banka National Corporation v. Frankman, 2 All E.R. 671." (Note that some names are misspelled.)

[23] After the decision of the Supreme Court in *Banco Nacional de Cuba v. Sabbatino*, 376 U.S. 398 (1964), the defendant petitioned the Supreme Court for a writ of certiorari to review the decision of the Supreme Court of Louisiana. Certiorari was denied, 377 U.S. 997, 84 S. Ct. 1922 (1964).

The appellant has filed a petition for rehearing, pointing out that, in rendering the opinion in this cause, the court overlooked and failed to consider its contention that this transaction was governed by the Bretton Woods Agreement relating to the International Monetary Fund and the Federal legislation pertaining thereto. See: 22 U.S.C.A. §286 et seq. At the time of the original opinion in this cause, this Agreement was considered and deemed to be not applicable, for the reason that the contract involved was a contract with an American company, made in the United States, payable in United States Dollars; that premiums had been accepted in United States Dollars since 1942, and that the effect of the chancellor's decree was only to require the appellant to continue to accept premium payments in United States Dollars. Not only were we of the opinion that the Bretton Woods Agreement was not applicable to the contract in the instant case, we were further of the opinion that the Bretton Woods Agreement pertained only to contracts "involving the currency of any member" of the Fund and that an American contract, upon which payments were to be made to or by the appellant in United States currency, was not an unenforceable contract within the provisions of Article VIII, §2(b) of the Bretton Woods Agreement.[24]

On a further appeal, the Court of Appeal held that the decision of the District Court must be quashed on the ground that it was in conflict with the *Ugalde* case, which is summarized below, but on further consideration, the Court of Appeal held that it was not clear that there was a conflict and reversed itself.[25]

Varas v. Crown Life Insurance Co.

In 1944, the plaintiff's mother, as guardian of the plaintiff, applied to the defendant, a Canadian company with a place of business in Cuba, for insurance on the life of the plaintiff, who was then a resident of Cuba. The defendant executed and delivered a 20-year endowment policy in the face value of $5,000 to the plaintiff or her mother in Havana. The contract was in Spanish, but provided that all payments by either party were to be in U.S. dollars. All premiums were paid in Cuba, in dollars from 1944 to 1951, and in pesos thereafter. In August 1960 the plaintiff left Cuba as a refugee and became a resident of the United States. In April 1961 the plaintiff demanded the cash surrender value of the policy at an office of the defendant in Pennsylvania. On the defendant's refusal, the plaintiff sued for the cash surrender value, or, alternatively, the return of the premiums.

[24] 156 So. 2d 785, 786 (1963).
[25] 164 So. 2d 204 (rehearing denied June 10, 1964). Certiorari denied, 379 U.S. 920, 85 S. Ct. 275 (1964).

The court of first instance found for the plaintiff in the amount of the premiums. Both parties appealed, with the plaintiff claiming the cash surrender value. The defendant argued, inter alia, that its obligation was to pay in Havana, which it was prepared to do. It also argued that Decree No. 1384 modified its dollar obligation and Law No. 568 prohibited payment in dollars, and that, as a result of provisions in the Fund's Articles, it was prevented from paying in the United States. The appellate court, the Court of Common Pleas, Montgomery County, Pennsylvania, held that when a life insurance contract fixes no place of performance, the presumption is that the place is where the contract was made. Therefore, no demand for performance could be made in Pennsylvania. But the plaintiff could not return to Cuba to recover there, and any agent collecting for her in Cuba would not be able to forward the money to the United States. In these circumstances, the plaintiff was entitled to recover in quasi-contract the value of the premiums that had been paid.

> The plaintiff is obligated to go to Cuba in order to receive any benefits under the insurance contract. It is excusably impossible for her to do so. She had partly performed the contract before this impossibility arose. She is entitled to recover the value of that performance.
>
> Her right to recovery is not based on the contract but is under the theory of unjust enrichment. . . . Therefore, the law governing the performance of the insurance contract is not applicable, and any Cuban law which might bar such a recovery is of no effect. Since no contractual right is being enforced here, the International Monetary Fund Agreement is not involved.
>
> It is true that the defendant has partly performed the contract on its side in that it insured the life of the plaintiff for a period of 17 years. In return for this service the defendant had the use of the plaintiff's money during this period. The total premiums paid are less than the cash surrender value of the policy at the time the demand was made. The use of the plaintiff's money free of any charge for interest is fair compensation for the insurance coverage provided. The result reached is equitable as well as legally proper.[26]

The parties appealed to the Superior Court of Pennsylvania, which noted that:

> . . . Since oral argument, we have been asked by the defendant company to disregard the question raised as to the impact of the International Monetary Fund Agreement as on April 2, 1964, effective on that date, the Republic of Cuba had withdrawn from membership.[27]

---

[26] 83 Montg. Co. L.R. 71, 73 (decided December 2, 1963).
[27] 204 Pa. Super. 176, 203 A. 2d 505, 507 (decided September 17, 1964).

The Superior Court disagreed with the lower court's decision that the plaintiff could recover only the premiums, and held that the plaintiff was entitled to recover on the cash surrender option in Pennsylvania, and that the Cuban monetary laws were not applicable. The theory on which it proceeded was that the cash surrender option was an irrevocable offer that became a contract when and where the election was made to exercise the option, and the law of this place was the law governing performance. This contract was distinct from the principal contract and could be subject to a different governing law.

On the subject of Article VIII, Section 2(b), the Court said:

> We agree that the currency laws of Cuba must be honored by the government of the United States and by our courts if Cuban law is applicable. The power of a sovereign state over its currency is absolute. This was especially true when both countries were signatories to the Breton [sic] Woods Agreement, a treaty of the United States and therefore a part of the supreme law of the land. The Breton Woods agreement specifically requires the recognition and honoring of Cuba's currency laws. The Breton Woods agreement brought into being the "International Monetary Fund Agreement", 60 Stat. 1401–1411, 1945. However, Cuba has withdrawn from membership so that a new look must perchance be taken at the cases based on the fund agreement when membership was held by both countries. It is true, however, that even prior to the currency treaty foreign exchange regulations were held to be applicable in suits in the United States. This is in line with our public policy to prevent evasion of currency obligations in the nation where the obligation is payable.[28]

THE PLAINTIFF FAILS

Confederation Life Association v. Ugalde

In 1948, the plaintiff, then a resident of Havana, applied to the defendant, a Canadian company, for a life insurance policy. The policy was delivered to the plaintiff in Havana. Both the application and the policy were in Spanish. The policy provided that all payments under it were to be made in dollars, and the place of payment was to be Havana. After the adoption of Decree No. 1384, the defendant informed its policyholders in Cuba that pesos would be substituted for dollars under the contracts. The plaintiff made subsequent payments of premium in pesos. In October 1961, the plaintiff demanded the cash surrender value of the policy in the United States, but the

---

[28] 203 A. 2d 505, 510. Certiorari denied, 382 U.S. 827, 86 S. Ct. 62 (1965).

defendant offered to pay pesos in Havana and refused to pay dollars in the United States. The plaintiff sued in a Florida court of first instance, and summary judgment was entered for him for $13,825.52, the cash surrender value of the policy.

The defendant appealed to the District Court of Appeal of Florida, Third District, which reversed part of the decision of the lower court by a majority of two judges to one.[29] The defendant argued that the contract was governed by the law of Cuba, and that payments under it had to be made in pesos at par with the dollar. The plaintiff argued that the law of Florida applied, and that it would be against public policy under that law to enforce a Cuban law that enabled the defendant to discharge its obligation in pesos. The District Court of Appeal held that neither Florida nor any jurisdiction other than Cuba had any contacts with the contract, which was made and was to be performed in Cuba, and the law of which was therefore the governing law. The defendant had offered performance in accordance with that law. Cuba had the right to prescribe its legal tender and to provide that contracts payable in Cuba must be discharged in Cuban legal tender. There was nothing in this repugnant to the public policy of Florida. The majority opinion did not deal with Article VIII, Section 2(b).

Notwithstanding the line of argument that it had adopted, the majority did not dismiss the plaintiff's claim. It held that the courts of Florida were open to the plaintiff, and the error of the lower court was not in entertaining the action or giving judgment for the plaintiff, but in the amount of the judgment. The majority saw the issue, therefore, as one of the applicable rate of exchange. It remitted the case to the lower court with instructions to enter judgment for the plaintiff in dollars in such amount as represented 13,825.53 pesos at the rate of exchange on the date of the original judgment.

The minority judge held that two contracts were involved. The first of these was made in 1948 and insured the plaintiff's life. It contained a continuing irrevocable offer by the plaintiff to enter into a contract to pay a cash surrender value. This offer became a second contract when the plaintiff accepted the offer by demanding the cash surrender value in Florida on October 11, 1961. The defendant had broken this contract; Florida law governed it; and the plaintiff was entitled to the full cash surrender value in dollars. If, however, Cuban

---

[29] 151 So. 2d 315 (decided March 26, 1963).

law applied, the Cuban legislation and decrees prohibited the transfer of funds from Cuba but did not affect funds "which may have already been located abroad or possessed by nationals in other states." The defendant had resources in Florida to discharge its obligation to the plaintiff, and the defendant could use them for this purpose without violating Cuban law.

The defendant appealed to the Supreme Court of Florida, which confirmed the statement of law and conclusion of the District Court of Appeal that Cuban law governed the contract.[30] The court also dealt with the impact of the Fund's Articles:

> The Cuban laws relating to the establishment of currency control are similar to those which have been enacted in this country with respect to our own currency and are not violative of United States policy. The Florida Courts are obligated by the International Monetary Fund Agreement to apply the cited Cuban laws to the contract here involved.[31]

The conclusion that Cuban law governed, reinforced by the effect of the Articles, led the court to conclude not that the plaintiff could recover the dollar equivalent of the peso cash surrender value but that he could not recover at all. The defendant had offered performance in accordance with the contract, and therefore there was no breach of contract and no cause of action.[32]

After the withdrawal of Cuba from the Fund, the plaintiff presented a motion for the reconsideration and modification or reversal of the judgment. He argued that the Supreme Court of Florida had based its judgment on the membership of Cuba and the United States in the Fund and on Article VIII, Section 2(b). The provisions of the Articles, he continued, were for the benefit of member states, and Cuba was no longer a member. The date of proposed relief determined the applicability of Article VIII, Section 2(b), so that it would not now be a violation of the Articles if that provision were

---

[30] 164 So. 2d 1 (decided February 24, 1964; rehearing denied April 8, 1964); order modified accordingly by District Court of Appeal, 163 So. 2d 343 (1964); certiorari denied by U.S. Supreme Court, 379 U.S. 915, 85 S. Ct. 263 (1964).

[31] Ibid., at 2.

[32] On April 8, 1964 the Supreme Court of Florida denied a petition for rehearing that had been presented after the Supreme Court of Louisiana reversed the decision of the Louisiana Court of Appeal in the Theye y Ajuria case. The Florida court had referred to the Louisiana Court of Appeal decision in the latter case as a "similar case," but on the petition for rehearing the Florida court held that the decision of the Louisiana Court of Appeal was not vital to its own decision, so that the reversal did not affect its decision (164 So. 2d 1, 3).

not applied.[33] The defendant replied that the court's opinion that the contract was governed by Cuban law, under which there had been no breach, was not affected by the withdrawal of Cuba from the Fund. On July 1, 1964, the Supreme Court of Florida denied the plaintiff's motion, and a subsequent petition to the U.S. Supreme Court for certiorari was denied.[34]

III. Major Issues of Article VIII, Section 2(*b*)

RELATION BETWEEN THE PROVISION AND PRIVATE INTERNATIONAL LAW

A fundamental question raised by the cases is the relation of Article VIII, Section 2(*b*) to private international law. That branch of the law of each country includes a set of rules that determine the law by which contracts, including their performance, are governed. Article VIII, Section 2(*b*) also establishes a rule for the recognition of certain provisions of a particular system of law. It declares that if suit is brought in a member's court to enforce an exchange contract, the court must refuse enforcement if the contract is contrary to the exchange control regulations of another member whose currency is involved. In short, the law of the member whose currency is involved must be recognized in the circumstances and for the purpose prescribed by Article VIII, Section 2(*b*).

The rule established by Article VIII, Section 2(*b*) produces two questions in relation to the choice-of-law rules of private international law. The first of these is whether the rule of the provision is an independent one. There has been a tendency by some courts to hold that the law indicated by the provision will be recognized only if it is the law selected as the governing law under the choice-of-law rules of the private international law of the forum. This interpretation would not render Article VIII, Section 2(*b*) meaningless, because some courts might find that a particular system of foreign law was the governing law under their private international law and nevertheless reject recognition of the exchange control regulations of that foreign law as contrary to domestic public policy were it not for Article VIII, Section 2(*b*). On this assumption, the sole effect of the provision would be to change the public policy of the forum but not

---

[33] The plaintiff cited *Stephen v. Zivnostenska Banka National Corporation*, 31 Misc. 2d 45, 140 N.Y.S. 2d 323 (1955), as authority.

[34] 379 U.S. 915, 85 S. Ct. 263 (1964).

to affect its rules with respect to the determination of the applicable law.

In at least one of the cases there is evidence of the belief that Article VIII, Section 2(b) operates to compel the recognition of the exchange control regulations of a particular system of law if this is the law selected by the private international law of the forum as the law governing the contract. This case is *Theye y Ajuria*, in which the Supreme Court of Louisiana seems to have said that the provision requires recognition of the exchange control regulations of another legal system if the contracting parties intended that system to govern their contract. The court said that foreign and domestic courts had been uniform in observing this principle. The cases cited by the court do not support this proposition, even if one ignores the fact that, apart from Cuban insurance cases, they were decided in that primitive period in the history of Article VIII, Section 2(b) in which courts were usually unaware of the provision. The non-U.S. cases cited by the court seem all to have been drawn from the first installment of the series of articles "The Fund Agreement in the Courts."[35] There was no reference to later cases decided after years of international consideration had clarified aspects of the provision.[36]

---

[35] In *Ahmed Bey Naguib v. Heirs of Moise Abner*, the provision was not referred to. In *Kraus v. Zivnostenska Banka*, the Articles were mentioned by the court "in passing." In *Cermak et al. v. Bata Akciova Spolecnost*, the court said that before considering the effect of the Articles, it would await the decision of some trailblazing appellate court or at least a case in which counsel briefed the issue and decision was necessary. There are *dicta* in *Zivnostenska Banka National Corporation v. Frankman* that seem to support the proposition of the Louisiana court, but they merely note the parallel effect of the governing law and Article VIII, Section 2(b), and do not say that the latter operates only within the ambit of the former. See Gold, *Fund Agreement in the Courts* (1962), pp. 14–17.

[36] For example, *Moojen v. Von Reichert*, Gold, *Fund Agreement in the Courts* (1962), pp. 148–53, and the decision of April 9, 1962 of the Supreme Court of the Federal Republic of Germany; see also Joseph Gold, "Fund Agreement in the Courts—VIII," pages 18–21 in this volume, particularly p. 19.

On June 13, 1966 the U.S. Court of Appeals for the Fifth Circuit decided appeals from the U.S. District Court for the Southern District of Florida in the *Blanco, Conill, Lorido y Diego*, and *Zabaleta* cases (*Pan American Life Insurance Co. v. Blanco*, 362 F. 2d 167 (1966)). The Court of Appeals held that "although the determination of these cases may require consideration of the act of state doctrine and the Bretton Woods International Monetary Fund Agreement," the court had to apply the private international law of the forum. The court noted, however, that Cuba had withdrawn from the Fund, so that the Articles would not preclude payment under the policies, for which proposition it cited *Stephen v. Zivnostenska Banka, etc.* (The court added the following *obiter dictum*, citing the *Theye y Ajuria* case: "Even though this were not so, the Bretton Woods Agreement would not be applicable to contracts such as the insurance policies here involved.")

There should be no doubt that recognition of the exchange control regulations indicated by Article VIII, Section 2(b) does not depend on the determination that they are part of the governing law under the private international law of the forum. The purpose of Article VIII, Section 2(b) is to provide a certain measure of support for the exchange control regulations of a member if they are consistent with the Articles of Agreement. The criterion adopted by the provision is consistency of the regulations with that international agreement and not the uncertain and diverse rules of private international law applied by members. The issue was settled long ago in the Fund's authoritative interpretation addressed to members on June 14, 1949, in which the Fund said that the contracts covered by the provision "will be treated as unenforceable notwithstanding that under the private international law of the forum, the law under which the foreign exchange control regulations are maintained or imposed is not the law which governs the exchange contract or its performance."[37]

The principle, therefore, is that Article VIII, Section 2(b) establishes a rule that requires recognition of the exchange control regulations of the member whose currency is involved without any necessity to show that its system of law is the governing law under the private international law of the forum. With this settled, the second question must be faced. Does the principle mean that when the issue is whether the exchange control regulations of another member must be recognized, Article VIII, Section 2(b) has become the sole rule and has abrogated those rules of the private international law of the forum that deal with the determination and application of the governing law? Alternatively, does the principle mean that Article VIII, Section 2(b) has not abrogated those rules, which remain in reserve until it is seen how Article VIII, Section 2(b) operates? If the provision has had the former effect (abrogation), it would follow that if an exchange contract was contrary to the exchange control regulations of the member whose currency was involved, the contract would be unenforceable. But it would also follow that if the contract was not contrary to those regulations, it would be enforceable. This would necessarily be the result because the law of the forum would no longer refer to any other law as the law governing the contract. It is this latter result that would not necessarily follow from a different view of the relationship between Article VIII, Section 2(b) and private international law. If it were held that the provision does not abrogate the choice-of-law rules of the private international law of

---

[37] See Appendix to this chapter, p. 94 in this volume.

the forum, it would still be true that the inconsistency of a contract with the exchange control regulations of the member whose currency was involved would lead to the unenforceability of the contract. If, however, there was no such inconsistency, it would still be possible to apply the law, including the exchange control regulations, of some other country under the private international law of the forum, as a result of which the plaintiff might not succeed on his contract even though this result was not required by Article VIII, Section 2(*b*).

It should not be held that Article VIII, Section 2(*b*) is an exclusive rule that has abrogated private international law. The object of the provision is to ensure that a currency is not undermined by the non-recognition of the exchange control regulations of a member whose currency is involved when the conditions of the provision are satisfied. The policy of the provision does not extend to those cases in which Article VIII, Section 2(*b*) does not require the unenforceability of contracts. In those cases, it is no part of the purpose of the provision to interfere with the normal workings of private international law. If the provision does not result in unenforceability, the question whether exchange control regulations are to be recognized or not can be left to the vagaries of private international law.

This brief analysis of the relations between Article VIII, Section 2(*b*) and private international law is necessary for an understanding of the Cuban insurance cases. It will be seen that in some of them Article VIII, Section 2(*b*) did not require the recognition of the exchange control regulations of Cuba because Cuba's currency was not involved. This situation left the way open to the private international law of the forum. This approach justified the weight that was given to certain points of contact in determining the applicable law. They were relevant under private international law but not under Article VIII, Section 2(*b*).

Finally, the analysis that has been offered may explain why some courts continue to approach problems of the recognition of the exchange control regulations of other countries by the route of the traditional private international law of the forum. It may be possible to follow that approach and find on the facts of the case that the governing law is the law that includes certain exchange control regulations, and that the regulations are to be recognized for this reason. In these circumstances, it is unnecessary to plunge into the profundities of Article VIII, Section 2(*b*), because the result will not be affected. The foreign law may also be the law of the currency "involved" under Article VIII, Section 2(*b*). The law will then be applicable on this basis also; but it will only reinforce and not alter the result with respect to the enforcement of the contract.[38] Alternatively, the law that includes the exchange control regulations and that is selected as the governing law may not be the law of the currency that is "involved," but it will be applicable nonetheless under the private international law of the forum. Again, therefore, the result will not be altered by Article VIII, Section 2(b). It would only be on a finding that the law of which the exchange control regulations were part was not the governing law under the private international law of the forum, so that the regulations were not entitled to recognition on this basis, that it would then be necessary to see if Article VIII, Section 2(b) compelled a different result.

The analysis in the preceding paragraph might be clearer in terms of an actual example. Suppose that under the private international law of the forum, Cuban law, which includes certain exchange controls, is the governing law. If Cuban law is applied as the governing law, the Cuban controls will be recognized, and this will not be changed by a finding that Cuban currency is "involved." The Cuban controls will be entitled to recognition on both bases. Similarly, if Cuban currency is not "involved," the controls will not be entitled to recognition under Article VIII, Section 2(b), but they will still be recognized as part of the governing law. Only if Cuban law is not the governing law, so that the controls are not entitled to recognition on this basis, does the possibility exist that the provision may lead to a different result on the issue of recognition.

EXCHANGE CONTRACTS

Under Article VIII, Section 2(b), the contracts that may be unenforceable are "exchange contracts." In the *Blanco* case, the District Court, in a footnote to its opinion, raised the question whether the insurance policies in that case were "exchange contracts," but the court did not try to answer the question. In the *Raij* case, a *dictum* of the District Court of Appeal can be read to suggest that the court thought the contract was not an exchange contract because it was for the payment of dollars, although the court couples this fact with further facts showing the relationship of the contract to the United States. In the *Theye y Ajuria* case, the Supreme Court of Louisiana dismissed an argument based on Article VIII, Section 2(b) on the

---

[38] This analysis must not be taken to imply that the legal effect will necessarily be the same on both bases. For example, under the private international law of the forum, the effect may be invalidity in contrast to unenforceability under Article VIII, Section 2(b).

ground that "a contract payable in the state of Louisiana in United States currency is not a foreign exchange contract."

These are the only reasonably direct references to the question whether insurance contracts are "exchange contracts." It is interesting that although the courts in these cases were attempting to formulate some delimitation of the concept, they did not suggest that the concept could not include insurance contracts as such. They have therefore, avoided the too simple view, which had a little support at one time, that "exchange contracts" were confined to contracts for the exchange of international media of payment, usually the exchange of one currency for another. Exchange control regulations normally control other categories of transactions as well, and there is no reasonable explanation, based on the economic purposes of Article VIII, Section 2(b), or the Articles as a whole, for restricting the provision to only one of the categories of contracts that affect the exchange resources of a member.[39]

The *Raij* and *Theye y Ajuria* cases imply a limitation of another kind. Some of the language of the opinions can be read to suggest that the test of an exchange contract is whether it calls for payment in a currency foreign to the forum or perhaps foreign to the law governing the contract under private international law. The only virtue of these tests would be their mechanistic character. They would have no necessary relation to the objective of Article VIII, Section 2(b). For U.S. courts to hold that they will enforce contracts providing for payment in U.S. dollars because these are not exchange contracts ignores the fact that they are most obviously exchange contracts when viewed by the member in which an obligor-defendant is resident. That member's foreign exchange resources would be directly drained away by a judgment. Similar unfortunate consequences could follow from the test of the governing law under private international law. The tests of forum or governing law to determine whether an exchange contract is before the court makes the application of Article VIII, Section 2(b) depend largely on the will of contracting parties. These tests, therefore, are in opposition to the international monetary objective of Article VIII, Section 2(b), which is that international recognition should be given to regulations controlling the will of contracting parties when, because the tests of the provision are met, this recognition is necessary for the defense of members' currencies.

---

[39] For earlier discussions of "exchange contracts," see Gold, *Fund Agreement in the Courts* (1962), pp. 83–84, 91–93, 96, 116–17, 146. See also Gold, "Fund Agreement in the Courts—VIII," pp. 13, 20–21 in this volume.

The Currency "Involved"

Recognition of the exchange control regulations of a member in accordance with Article VIII, Section 2(b) depends on a determination that they are the regulations of a member whose currency is involved in the performance of the exchange contract that someone seeks to enforce. Although other views are still expressed from time to time, the more expert and more generally held opinion is that the currency of a member is involved if the contract affects that member's exchange resources. Where other views are expressed, they tend to be based on a purely linguistic approach to the provision that ignores the economic considerations that were responsible for its adoption.[40]

The criterion of effect on a member's exchange resources is not a traditional one for lawyers. It is tempting, therefore, to wonder whether the criterion is an economic formulation of the legal principle that the member had legislative jurisdiction under established norms of public international law to adopt the exchange control regulations in question. Another possibility is that Article VIII, Section 2(b) establishes a new norm in the concept of the currency involved that goes beyond earlier norms of legislative jurisdiction.

States sometimes write legislation with the intention that it shall regulate matters with which, in the eyes of some foreign observers, the legislation has an insubstantial contact, or they may use language that is loose enough to permit this application. Legislation of this kind is likely to be applied uncritically by the courts of the legislator, but other states may hold that the legislator has gone beyond the bounds of legislative jurisdiction. They are then likely to hold that the legislation does not produce legal results that they will recognize. Of course, it does not necessarily follow that they will recognize the effects of foreign legislation even when the existence of legislative jurisdiction is uncontested, but in that event, if they refuse recognition, it will be for different legal reasons. For example, in the field of exchange control, they may hold, apart from Article VIII, Section 2(b), that the exchange control regulations of another state cannot be recognized because they purport to be more than "territorial" and, therefore, to that extent, go beyond the bounds of legislative jurisdiction to adopt them. Where the objection of the absence of legislative jurisdiction is

---

[40] See, for example, the majority opinion of the New York Court of Appeals in *Banco do Brasil, S.A. v. A.C. Israel Commodity Co., Inc.*, 12 N.Y. 2d 371, 190 N.E. 2d 235, 239 N.Y.S. 2d 872 (1963), discussed in Gold, "Fund Agreement in the Courts—VIII," pp. 22–27 in this volume.

not available on the facts, they may hold that recognition would conflict with the public policy of the forum.

The difficulty of reaching a conclusion on the relationship between the criterion in Article VIII, Section 2(b) that a currency is involved (in the sense of effect on exchange resources) and the test of legislative jurisdiction is twofold. On the one hand, the norms of legislative jurisdiction in international law are still to some extent controversial.[41] On the other hand, the determination of when a country's exchange resources are affected has not been made with precision.

In the absence of the further analysis that needs to be made to answer the question that has been posed above as to the scope of the criterion, it is submitted that the currency of a member is undoubtedly involved when the member regulates the transactions of its residents or transactions dealing with assets within its territory. It must not be assumed that this is a simple rule that can be applied without difficulty. For example, in numerous cases the courts have struggled to establish where certain kinds of property are situated. One of these, debts, will be referred to in more detail later. Nevertheless, once it is decided that persons are resident or assets are present within the legislator's territory, it will be possible to say with confidence that there is legislative jurisdiction to adopt exchange control regulations affecting those residents or assets, and also that the exchange resources of the legislator are affected by the contracts thus controlled. If regulations seek to go beyond the control of residents or of assets within the territory, the burden should then be on anyone who argues that the regulations affect the exchange resources of the legislator to prove that fact. If the fact is proved, the case will have to be treated as one that is covered by Article VIII, Section 2(b). If the case is one that is not covered by traditional norms of public international law on legislative jurisdiction, it will follow that Article VIII, Section 2(b) has created a new norm in the field of exchange control.

An examination of the Cuban exchange control legislation and decrees does not lead to an incontrovertible conclusion that an effort had been made to go beyond the control of residents or local assets. No comment will be made here on Law No. 13 and Decree No. 1384 for reasons that will be explained later. Law No. 568 is written in general terms, but they could be read as relating only to residents or

---

[41] F.A. Mann, "The Doctrine of Jurisdiction in International Law," *Académie de Droit International, Recueil des Cours*, Tome 111 (The Hague, 1964, I), pp. 9–162.

to assets situated within Cuban territory. There is no language that unambiguously shows an intention to go beyond these jurisdictional bases. The exchange control features of Law No. 930 give even less evidence of an intention to exercise control on some basis other than residence or the situs of assets in Cuba. The minority judge in the Florida District Court of Appeal in the *Ugalde* case,[42] the U.S. District Court in the *Blanco* case,[43] and then the cases consolidated with that case[44] suggest that the Cuban enactments were intended to have this limited application.

It is more important to see what the U.S. courts actually decided than to speculate about the scope that the Cuban legislator intended for the legislation and decrees. There is little discussion of the question whether Cuban currency was "involved." In the *Blanco* case, the U.S. District Court held that the legislation could not affect litigants who were not only outside Cuban territory but were also refugees, and that for this reason the Articles of the Fund did not apply. In an earlier part of its opinion, the court noted that the contracts did not call for performance from the defendants' assets in Cuba, the implication of which is that the legislation could not affect the defendants' assets outside Cuba. The court seemed to be reaching for a thesis that Article VIII, Section 2(b) did not require the recognition of exchange control regulations if they purported to control nonresidents in transactions involving assets outside the jurisdiction. The *Blanco* case influenced the decision in a number of other cases. In the *Theye y Ajuria* case, the Louisiana Court of Appeal used language suggesting that Article VIII, Section 2(b) required the recognition of exchange control regulations based on the control of nationals, but it is not impossible that the court intended residents by this expression. The Louisiana Supreme Court, however, followed the *Blanco* decision in holding that Cuba had no jurisdiction over the refugee plaintiffs. In the *Raij* case, there is a suggestion in the opinion of the Florida District Court of Appeal that Cuban currency was not involved because the contract called for payments in dollars. It must be added, however, that the court referred to the contract as an "American contract," by which it undoubtedly meant that there were many other contacts with the United States.

If a contract between two nonresidents of Cuba provides, expressly or implicitly, that it can be performed outside Cuba without affecting

---

[42] 151 So. 2d 315 (1963).
[43] 311 F. 2d 427, 428, fn. 9.
[44] 221 F. Supp. 219, 229.

assets situated in Cuba, and such performance is in fact sought outside Cuba, any Cuban exchange control regulations that purport to prevent or control that performance are not entitled to recognition under Article VIII, Section 2(*b*) on the ground that Cuban currency is involved. This was the situation and result in the *Blanco* and similar cases. The contracts were made with nonresident American companies through resident Cuban agents or branches, but the suits were against the companies and not against the agents or branches. Cuban exchange control regulations could have regulated payments and transfers by the agents or branches, and these regulations would have fallen within the ambit of Article VIII, Section 2(*b*). The courts found, however, in the *Blanco* and similar cases that the contracts did not require payments from assets held by the agents or branches in Cuba, and that the assets of the companies, wherever they were situated and could be reached, were available for the performance of the contracts.

If the contract calls for performance in Cuba, the problem is more difficult.[45] The issue can be stated in this form: if nonresident parties to a contract agree that performance shall be made in Cuba, does this enable Cuba to adopt regulations requiring performance in Cuba that would be entitled to recognition under Article VIII, Section 2(*b*)?

A traditional way of looking at this question in private international law would be to consider whether the debt is property situated in Cuba because it is payable there. This is an issue relating to the debt as intangible property and is not necessarily the same as the issue whether the law of the place of performance regulates the mode of performance of the contract giving rise to the property right. For example, if a resident of France agrees to pay a resident of England in Germany, the fact that German law may determine how the debt shall be discharged does not necessarily lead to the conclusion that the debt is situated in Germany instead of France, where the debtor can be reached. Even if it could be demonstrated that it is established in private international law that a debt as property is situated where it is payable, it still would not follow that this was the rule that had to be adopted for Article VIII, Section 2(*b*). The situs of a debt is a legal fiction, and the situs can be held to be in different places for different rules if the purposes of the rules are not the same.

Although there is some authority for holding for some purposes of private international law that a debt is situated where it is payable,

---

[45] This is not the same as saying that the contract calls for payment with assets situated in Cuba. The discharge of a contract in Cuba can be made with assets that are not situated in Cuba but are transferred there.

73

it has been questioned whether this is or should be the rule, at least when the debts of insurance companies doing business in several jurisdictions are involved. It has been argued that

> . . . the selection of the place where the principal or home-office of a corporation is situated is the natural and obvious solution of the problem which arises where a corporation maintains branches in different countries. The corporation may be present, in the sense of being amenable to jurisdiction, in many countries but its principal presence which must determine the situs of the debts owed by it should be at the place where the home-office is established.[46]

If traditional private international law provided any valid analogy for the special purposes of Article VIII, Section 2(b), it would follow from the conclusion quoted above that the debts payable in Cuba by the foreign insurance companies were not situated in Cuba, and therefore were not subject to Cuban exchange control regulations that would have to be recognized under Article VIII, Section 2(b). This result would follow to the extent that the involvement of a currency is deemed to depend on the presence of assets within Cuban territory.

It is interesting to note one consequence of the view that a debt payable in Cuba by one nonresident to another nonresident is an asset situated in Cuba and therefore subject to control by regulations entitled to recognition under Article VIII, Section 2(b). It would follow that Cuba could prevent the two nonresidents from amending their contract so as to provide for payment elsewhere than in Cuba, because that would amount to the withdrawal of an asset from Cuba. Other members would be required to respect regulations of this kind.

If a solution is sought without the dubious assistance of private international law in attributing a situs to debts, it is not easy to accept the idea that, because nonresidents have agreed to pay a debt in Cuba, Cuban currency is involved and Cuba's exchange control regulations may preclude payment elsewhere. Even if payment is made in Cuba, it may be argued that Cuban currency is not involved. If the debtor pays with pesos newly acquired for foreign exchange, Cuba's foreign exchange assets are increased, but the increase is

---

[46] J. Unger, "Life Insurance and the Conflict of Laws," *The International and Comparative Law Quarterly*, Vol. 13 (1964), pp. 482–501, especially p. 497. Professor Unger points out that the author of the leading U.S. monograph on the subject (C.W. Carnahan, *Conflict of Laws and Life Insurance Contracts*, Second Edition (Buffalo, New York, Dennis, 1958), pp. 438–47) comes to the same conclusion.

matched by Cuba's currency liability represented by the peso balance in the payee's hands. If payment is made with an existing peso balance, Cuba's currency liability is transferred from one nonresident holder to another. It may be replied that what counts is Cuba's gross foreign exchange position, or Cuba's ability to improve its net position by restricting the use of peso balances, and therefore that Cuba's currency would be involved if payment were made in Cuba. These hypotheses show the ambiguity of the test that a member's exchange resources must be affected and the need for the further refinement of that test. It is not necessary to resolve these ambiguities because the real issue is not whether Cuba's currency would be involved in payment in Cuba, but whether it would be involved in payment by one nonresident to another nonresident outside Cuba with assets outside Cuba. That, it is submitted, is the real issue because the exchange control regulation that was relied on in the cases was said to be one that forbade payment outside Cuba. In more general terms, this submission can be restated as follows. A member's currency will be involved in an exchange contract if the member's exchange resources will be affected by the performance of the contract that is sought. There appears to be no way in which it could be demonstrated that payments between nonresidents outside Cuba with assets outside Cuba would affect Cuba's exchange resources by adding to or subtracting from those resources.

To the extent that the insurance companies were relying on Article VIII, Section 2(*b*) when they argued that they were bound to pay in Cuba and were prevented by Cuban regulations from paying elsewhere, they were implicitly arguing that Cuban currency was involved because they had agreed on payment in Cuba. The issue arose in its sharpest form in the *Ugalde* case, in which the courts held that the place of payment was indeed Cuba, in contrast to the finding in the cases against U.S. insurance companies in which the Supreme Court of Florida held that the place of payment was in the United States. The *Ugalde* case is of some importance because of its influence on a number of other decisions.[47]

One basis for the decision in the *Ugalde* case was that Article VIII, Section 2(*b*) required the recognition of Cuban exchange control

---

[47] *Crown Life Insurance Co. v. Calvo*, 151 So. 2d 687 (1963), quashed in part per *Ugalde* decision, 164 So. 2d 813 (1964); *Sun Life Assurance Co. of Canada v. Klawans*, 162 So. 2d 704 (1963), quashed in part per *Ugalde* decision, 165 So. 2d 166 (1964); *Trujillo v. Sun Life Assurance Co. of Canada*, 166 So. 2d 473 (1964); *Confederation Life Association v. Brandao*, 173 So. 2d 515 (1964).

regulations.[48] If it were concluded that Cuba's currency was not "involved," it would follow that the case was decided on the wrong principle to the extent that the *ratio decidendi* was Article VIII, Section 2(*b*). There is, however, one version of the facts that would show that Cuba's currency was "involved." It is possible that in this case the plaintiff was not a refugee but continued to be a resident of Cuba even though he brought suit in Florida. This fact has been alleged in a discussion of the cases that appeared in a periodical.[49] It is interesting that in the report of the *Ugalde* case there is no mention of the residence or émigré status of the plaintiff. Although the court did not rely on the fact that the plaintiff was a resident of Cuba, Article VIII, Section 2(*b*) was clearly applicable if he was. Resources accruing to a resident of Cuba are resources that could be conscribed for the support of Cuba's currency. Cuba could therefore control the place and form in which a resident should receive payment, and regulations that were intended to do this would be entitled to recognition under Article VIII, Section 2(*b*), on the assumption, of course, that the provision was satisfied in all other respects.

The basic test for determining whether the currency of a member is involved in an exchange contract, it has been submitted, is whether the contract is entered into by a resident of that member or deals with assets situated within the member's territory. This test is not affected by the currency in which payment is called for, although the District Court of Appeal in the *Raij* case may have taken the view that Cuba's currency could not be involved in a contract requiring payment to be made in dollars. Moreover, observers might be tempted to explain the different results in the *Ugalde* and *Blanco* lines of cases in terms of the currency of payment. Cuba's resources may be affected if a contract calls for payment in dollars and not affected

---

[48] Cf. the *Zabaleta* case, in which the parties had agreed on payment in Cuba but in which the plaintiff nevertheless succeeded in the Florida courts.

[49] According to the article, "Insurance Claims—Cubans Raise a Storm," *Business Week*, No. 1728, October 13, 1962, p. 120, the plaintiff returned to Cuba after filing his suit in the United States and went on paying premiums in pesos in Cuba. In the brief for the appellee on appeal to the Superior Court of Pennsylvania in the *Varas* case, this article is referred to (pp. 14–15) as explaining the passage in the opinion of the court in the *Ugalde* case (151 So. 2d 315, 323) that reads as follows: "The courts of Florida were open to the *Cuban citizen, while here*, to seek redress . . ." (italics in the brief). Note that the plaintiff filed suit in Florida on November 6, 1961 and made a premium payment in pesos in Cuba on March 7, 1962. (See brief of appellant on appeal to District Court of Appeal of Florida, Third District, in the *Ugalde* case, p. 3; reply brief of appellant, p. 2, fn.; and brief of petitioner, Supreme Court of Florida, p. 24.)

if a contract calls for payment in pesos. If a resident pays a non-resident in dollars, Cuba's foreign exchange assets are reduced; and if a resident receives payment in dollars from a nonresident, Cuba's assets are increased.[50] (If the same payments are made in pesos, the economic effects are comparable in that Cuba's liabilities are increased or decreased, respectively.) If a nonresident pays another nonresident in pesos, prima facie Cuba's exchange resources are not affected, because there is simply the transfer of a liability from one nonresident to another. Cuba's resources may be affected, however, if the transfer is of an asset within Cuban territory, such as a peso bank balance, because of the possible greater propensity of the transferee to withdraw the balance and obtain another currency for it, which would reduce Cuba's assets.

The circumstance that a contract calls for payment in Cuba or in pesos does not in itself justify the conclusion that Cuban currency is involved under Article VIII, Section 2(*b*). Of course, it does not follow from this conclusion that the place or currency of payment is irrelevant for all purposes. It has been explained that private international law can still apply when a contract is not unenforceable under Article VIII, Section 2(*b*). If it is assumed that the contract in the *Ugalde* case was not unenforceable under Article VIII, Section 2(*b*), it would still be possible to conclude that under the private international law of the forum Cuban law was the governing law, for example, because it was the law intended by the parties or the *lex loci solutionis*. It would also be possible for the forum to decide whether it would recognize exchange control regulations that were part of this law or whether it would refuse recognition because of the public policy of the forum. If the court found that the regulations were offensive to the public policy of the *lex fori*, Article VIII, Section 2(*b*) could not be relied on to compel recognition in circumstances in which the court had decided that the contract was not unenforceable under that provision. This conclusion must not be taken to suggest that a court would be unable to find that the effect of the Articles as a whole had changed public policy and abrogated the former principle of the non-recognition of the exchange control regulations of other countries even though the case was not covered by Article VIII, Section 2(*b*).

---

[50] Cf. the opinion of the Court of Appeals of Paris in *Moojen v. Von Reichert:* "There is no doubt that, although the transfer was expressed in French francs, it could have an effect on the Dutch economy, for the Treasury of that country has an interest in the resident's repatriation of the foreign currency obtained after selling the shares for a just price. . . ." See also Gold, *Fund Agreement in the Courts* (1962), p. 146.

EXCHANGE CONTROL REGULATIONS

Article VIII, Section 2(*b*) refers to exchange contracts that are contrary to "exchange control regulations." It has been shown in an earlier chapter that these words must not be taken to include all forms of economic regulation, and, in particular, must not be understood to embrace controls on trade in contrast to exchange.[51] The Cuban insurance cases involved a limitation of a different kind.

The cases tend to deal with all the laws and decrees that have been mentioned earlier in this chapter as if they were of the same character. For example, the pretrial stipulation in the *Blanco* case stated that the issue was whether all of them were entitled to recognition under the Articles of the Fund. There is a similar implication in the *dictum* of the Supreme Court of Florida in the *Ugalde* case in which a parallel is drawn between "the Cuban laws relating to the establishment of currency control" and laws enacted in the United States with respect to the U.S. currency.[52]

Law No. 13 and Decree No. 1384 are legal tender laws in contrast to exchange control legislation.[53] The purpose of legal tender legislation (*cours légal*) is to prescribe the currency that payees must accept in discharge of obligations. In these days, this legislation frequently declares also that the notes and coins issued by the monetary authorities of the legislator have the quality of legal tender.[54] This aspect of the law is sometimes referred to as dealing with the *cours forcé*. Laws dealing with the *cours légal* and the *cours forcé* may be coupled in practice with exchange control legislation, but they are not in themselves exchange control legislation. Although usually it

---

[51] Gold, "Fund Agreement in the Courts—VIII," pp. 13–16 in this volume.

[52] However, the U.S. District Court in the *Blanco* case may have been reaching for a distinction in quoting the following passage from the appellee's brief: "The 1948 law, for example, does not require that payment of obligations due Cuban nationals be made only in pesos. The law does require that, if an obligation is paid within the Republic of Cuba, then, and in that event only, the national currency of Cuba, pesos, must be accepted in payment of obligations" (311 F. 2d 427, 428, fn. 9). Cf. petitioner's brief to the Supreme Court of Florida in the *Ugalde* case: "The legal tender statute and decrees of 1948–1951 . . . are similar to those that have been adopted by this country with respect to our own currency. The exchange control measures imposed after 1959 . . . , although not having any present counterpart in United States law. . . ." (p. 18).

[53] Law No. 851 and Resolution No. 3 deal with nationalization and fall into a third category.

[54] See F.A. Mann, *The Legal Aspect of Money*, Second Edition (London, Clarendon Press, 1953), pp. 33–39; Arthur Nussbaum, *Money in the Law, National and International* (Brooklyn, Foundation Press, 1950), pp. 45–59.

is not difficult to distinguish between them in practice, formulation of the difference is more difficult because of the absence of precise definitions. Normally, legal tender legislation deals with the establishment and characteristics of a currency, and exchange control legislation deals with the defense of a currency by husbanding national resources.[55] It must be repeated that this is not a precise formula by which to distinguish between them. For example, the experience of the Fund itself shows that exchange control regulations are sometimes adopted for such nonbalance of payments reasons as the preservation of national or international security.[56]

If, however, the rough distinction that has been made is accepted as adequate for normal working purposes, Law No. 13 and Decree No. 1384 should be regarded as no more than legal tender legislation. They provided for the establishment of a national currency as the sole legal tender within Cuba, but they did not deal with the control of Cuba's exchange resources. For example, a Cuban resident obligor was given the right to settle his obligation in pesos, but there appears to be nothing that prevented a Cuban resident from undertaking a dollar obligation abroad. Moreover, Cuban residents were expressly permitted to make foreign exchange deposits in Cuban banks and to draw against them in the form of foreign exchange. That Law No. 13 and Decree No. 1384 were not exchange control regulations is demonstrated by the fact that Cuba was not required to get approval of them under Article VIII, Section 2(*a*) when Cuba gave notice that it was prepared to perform the obligations of Article VIII, Sections 2, 3, and 4.[57] Of course, Law No. 568 and Law No. 930 were obviously "exchange control regulations," so that before Cuba withdrew from the Fund the question of the application of Article VIII, Section 2(*b*) to these laws could not have been avoided on the ground that they were not exchange control regulations.

Capital and Current Transactions

One of the more troublesome issues raised by the cases before Cuba withdrew from the Fund was whether the Cuban exchange control

---

[55] See *de Sayve v. de la Valdene*, 124 N.Y.S. 2d 143 (1953); Gold, *Fund Agreement in the Courts* (1962), p. 74.

[56] *Selected Decisions*, Third Issue, pp. 75–76; see also p. 82. (*Selected Decisions*, Ninth Issue, pp. 203–204 and 209–11.)

[57] Restrictions on payments and transfers for current international transactions introduced by a member before it gives notice that it is prepared to perform the obligations of Article VIII, Sections 2, 3, and 4 require the approval of the Fund for the maintenance of the restrictions after the notice becomes effective.

regulations that the defendants relied upon were "maintained or imposed consistently with this Agreement." Cuba had notified the Fund that it was prepared to accept the obligations of Article VIII, Sections 2, 3, and 4. Therefore, it was bound by Article VIII, Section 2(*a*) to obtain the approval of the Fund for the imposition of any "restrictions on the making of payments and transfers for current international transactions." It remained free, however, to control capital transfers under the authority of Article VI, Section 3:

> Members may exercise such controls as are necessary to regulate international capital movements, but no member may exercise these controls in a manner which will restrict payments for current transactions or which will unduly delay transfers of funds in settlement of commitments. . . .

Payments for current transactions are defined as follows by Article XIX(*i*):

> Payments for current transactions means payments which are not for the purpose of transferring capital, and includes, without limitation:
> (1) All payments due in connection with foreign trade, other current business, including services, and normal short-term banking and credit facilities;
> (2) Payments due as interest on loans and as net income from other investments;
> (3) Payments of moderate amount for amortization of loans or for depreciation of direct investments;
> (4) Moderate remittances for family living expenses.
> The Fund may, after consultation with the members concerned, determine whether certain specific transactions are to be considered current transactions or capital transactions.

The Fund authorized the issuance to counsel for a number of litigants, who applied for it, of the statement that was quoted by the U.S. District Court in the *Blanco* case. That statement referred to the legal position of a member like Cuba under Article VIII, Sections 2, 3, and 4 and Article VI, Section 3. It declared that, apart from a 2 per cent exchange tax on remittances abroad, the Fund had not approved any restrictions under Article VIII, Section 2 or any of the other exchange practices that require approval under Section 3.

The upshot, therefore, was that any Cuban exchange control regulations that restricted payments and transfers for current international transactions, apart from the exchange tax, were not maintained or imposed consistently with the Articles. By contrast, any regulations that merely controlled capital movements were maintained or imposed consistently with the Articles.

It will be apparent from what has been said that, while Cuba was still a member of the Fund, it was necessary for the courts, if all other elements of Article VIII, Section 2(*b*) were present, to determine whether the Cuban exchange control regulations dealing with insurance on which the defendants relied affected payments and transfers for current transactions or capital transfers. This question is a difficult one on which the Fund has not adopted any interpretations. The following comments do not purport to arrive at a final conclusion.

One difficulty in reaching a view on the classification under the Articles of the exchange controls adopted by Cuba results from the facts. It has been seen that the problem of classification calls for a determination on whether Cuba was controlling capital transfers or payments for current transactions. It can be assumed that the determination is whether the controls were on capital transfers or payments for current transactions from the viewpoint of Cuba. For example, it is understandable that the drafters of the Articles should accept the idea that a member could control payments that were capital movements, whether inward or outward, of its own economy. It would not be easy to understand why the right to control capital transfers should depend on some abstract definition of capital transfers unrelated to any particular member. If it is accepted, therefore, that the classification implies a member in relation to which the classification must be made, payments under a contract between two nonresidents of Cuba not affecting assets situated in Cuba do not appear to be either capital transfers or payments for current transactions of Cuba. This statement is perhaps another way of saying that Cuba had no legislative jurisdiction to adopt exchange regulations controlling these payments.

The analysis cannot stop at this point because the facts may not have been as stated above in all the cases, and they seem to have been different in the *Ugalde* case. It is necessary, therefore, to consider the case in which Cuba attempts to control payments between a resident insured and a nonresident insurance company.

A first approach to the question of classification might be that it is settled by Article XIX(*i*). This approach might be that any of the payments listed in categories (1) to (4) in that provision are decisively for current transactions and are not affected by the words "which are not for the purpose of transferring capital." The argument would then proceed that "all payments due in connection with . . . other current business" are included in category (1) and that insurance is

81

"other current business." [58] If this view were accepted, all payments to or by insurance companies, whether of premiums or benefits, and whatever the form of insurance, would be considered to be payments for current transactions. But it does not follow that this is the final answer, and that one should conclude forthwith that, as Cuba would be controlling payments for current transactions, it was not entitled to apply these controls because they had not been approved by the Fund. The doubt that this is the final answer is induced by the reflection that it would provide an easy and obvious technique for the wholesale transfer of capital abroad. The single-premium endowment or annuity policy is a good example of what could be done to transfer resources abroad as payments for alleged current transactions notwithstanding a member's policy of controlling capital transfers.

The suggestion that the problem may not be wholly resolved by classification from the viewpoint of the nonresident insurance company means, once again, that the payments should be examined from the viewpoint of Cuba. How does Cuba view the payments made by its residents to nonresident insurance companies or by nonresident insurance companies to its residents? The answer to this question might turn on the particular form of life insurance policy that is involved. For example, it might be held that term insurance differs from whole-life and endowment contracts in that the last two involve a savings and investment element as well as protection against risk while the first provides only protection against risk. Under term insurance, nothing is payable at the end of the term, and no cash surrender value accrues during the term. It might be argued, therefore, that when the insured pays premiums for term insurance, he is making payments for a return in the form of a current service and therefore for current transactions. In contrast to term insurance, some forms at least of annuity contracts are considered to include no insurance benefit. If the annuitant dies and a cash value is paid to a named beneficiary, the payment is treated as a death benefit and not insurance against risk. [59] It might be concluded that premiums paid under this form of insurance are not paid in respect of current transactions. [60] Between term insurance at one extreme and these annuity

---

[58] See Bernard S. Meyer, "Recognition of Exchange Controls After the International Monetary Fund Agreement," *Yale Law Journal*, Vol. 62 (1953), pp. 867–910, particularly p. 903.

[59] *Principles of Life Insurance*, published for Life Office Management Association, Vol. 1 by J.E. Greider and W.T. Beadles (Homewood, Illinois, Irwin, 1964), pp. 247–48.

[60] Subject to what is said below about covering the administrative cost of the

contracts at the other are whole-life and endowment contracts under which it might be held that premiums are paid partly for the insurance service and partly for savings and investment. If this view were accepted, it would lead to the conclusion that the premiums are paid for both current transactions and as capital transfers.

The Fund has made no official determinations on the classification of insurance, but its *Balance of Payments Manual* contains the following passage:

> 294. Three aspects of life insurance transactions may be distinguished. First, life insurance premiums represent additions to, and life insurance claims payments represent withdrawals from, the funds which the insurance companies have set aside as cover for future claims on the basis of an actuarial calculation (hereinafter referred to as their life funds). Life funds, including the interest accrued on them, constitute savings of the policy holders; therefore, changes in residents' share of the life funds of foreign insurance companies are appropriate to the capital account of the balance of payments. Second, the interest accruing on the policy holders' accumulated shares of the life funds of the insurance companies represents investment income and should be recorded in Table VI. Third, part of insurance premiums and interest accruals, net of claim payments, is used to cover the administrative cost of the insurance companies, including their profits. This part, which represents payment for a pure insurance service, is the only element of life insurance transactions that is appropriate to Table VIII, item 1.[61]

It will be observed that this passage makes no distinction among the various types of life insurance. Second, the point is made that some part of the premiums can be treated as paid in respect of the administrative cost of the insurance companies, and, therefore, in respect of current transactions. Probably, this analysis would be true of premiums paid under all forms of insurance contract. If this view were adopted, the contrast between term and other forms of insurance would not be absolute. It must be borne in mind that the *Balance of Payments Manual* does not seek to present legal interpretations of the Articles. It might still be held, therefore, that the

---

insurance companies. It should be noted that the courts have had to decide for various reasons whether particular forms of insurance are predominantly for protection or for savings. See, for example, *Penn Mutual Life Insurance Co. v. Lederer*, 252 U.S. 523, 531, 40 S. Ct. 397, 400 (1920).

[61] International Monetary Fund, *Balance of Payments Manual*, Third Edition (Washington, 1961), p. 97. (Hereinafter cited as *Balance of Payments Manual*, Third Edition.)

element of payment for the administrative cost of the insurance company in premiums paid under term insurance was secondary or consequential and did not prevent a country from controlling the payments of premium as capital transfers. This element would not affect the view that has been advanced of payments of premium under other forms of life insurance, because these payments may be regarded as payments for current transactions on other grounds.

The cases summarized earlier in this article did not involve term insurance. They involved the other forms of life insurance and a variety of claims under them, including claims to recover the cash surrender or maturity value of policies, to compel the defendants to accept premiums, and to get the return of premiums. Whatever the analysis that may be applied to the payment of premiums, there might be greater agreement that the payment of the cash surrender or maturity value of a policy to a resident represents the receipt by him of a capital transfer.[62] Therefore, the member would be able to prescribe for its residents how and where they should receive such transfers, and the member would not need the approval of the Fund for these prescriptions. It may be objected, however, that the proceeds are not exclusively of a capital nature, because they include some element of interest and, therefore, recent interest. Here again the interest might be of too subsidiary a character to obstruct the conclusion that the payment must be treated as a capital transfer.

Before the discussion of the "current" and "capital" dichotomy is

---

[62] In *Catz and Lips v. S.A. Union Versicherung*, a Belgian court held that the transfer of insurance moneys was a capital transfer under Article VI, Section 3 (see Gold, *Fund Agreement in the Courts* (1962), pp. 30–31), but it is doubtful that life insurance was involved. In the *Ugalde* case, the appellant argued as follows in its brief to the Florida District Court of Appeals: "It may be that the purely insurance feature of an insurance contract is a service and that the premium payment is a payment for a current service within the definition of Article XIX(i)(1). The cash surrender value of a policy represents, however, not a payment for a service but a repayment on an investment much like an ordinary savings account. The establishment of a savings deposit is the most obvious kind of capital transaction. The transfer of such a deposit from one country to another is thus an international capital movement. The transfer from one country to another of the savings portion of an insurance policy—in this case the cash surrender value—is likewise an international capital movement" (p. 29). Paradise, *op. cit.*, pp. 70–72, disagrees on the ground that there is no debtor-creditor relationship under an unmatured policy until the insured exercises the option to get the cash surrender value. His theory of a current transaction involves the idea of a current liability, but it is unusual to classify transactions according to the contingent or accrued character of the liability of a party to the transaction instead of according to the subject matter of the transaction. See *Balance of Payments Manual*, Third Edition, pp. 23–24.

terminated, it is legitimate to wonder whether it was necessary to make a final classification of the payments in the Cuban insurance cases. It will be recalled that, under Article VI, Section 3, a member is authorized to regulate international capital movements but not in a manner "which will restrict payments for current transactions or which will unduly delay transfers of funds in settlement of commitments. . . ." It might be argued that even if a member was authorized to control payments connected with insurance policies as capital transfers, it could not do this consistently with the Articles if commitments to make these payments had been entered into. This argument would rely more particularly on the words "which will unduly delay transfers in settlement of commitments," although it would be necessary to imply that the commitments referred to were entered into before the capital controls were adopted in order to avoid the absurdity of the total negation of authority to control capital transfers. This line of argument would rely on the fact that Article VI, Section 3 does not expressly confine the commitments to those connected with current transactions. Indeed, the separate mention of current transactions would imply the rejection of any such limitation. The conclusion of this reasoning would be that the Cuban controls were inconsistent either with Article VIII, Section 2(a), if they affected current transactions, or with Article VI, Section 3, if they affected capital transfers, and that in either event they were not entitled to recognition under Article VIII, Section 2(b).

The clause dealing with commitments in Article VI, Section 3 is undoubtedly obscure, but it is most unlikely that it applies to capital transfers. For example, it would be difficult to understand why there was so much discussion at the Bretton Woods Conference of the drafting of "payments of moderate amount for amortization of loans, etc.," in Article XIX(i)(3) if a member would be unable under Article VI, Section 3 to restrict transfers in settlement of commitments to pay more than moderate amounts. Furthermore, if "commitments" applies to capital transfers, a member that was availing itself of the transitional arrangements of Article XIV, Section 2 would have less authority to control capital transfers than payments and transfers for current transactions. Under Article XIV, Section 2 the member would be able to control payments and transfers for current transactions whether or not commitments had been entered into, but its ability to control capital transfers would not extend to transfers covered by commitments. This result could not be reconciled with the purpose of the Fund "to assist in the establishment of a multilateral system of payments in respect of current transactions between members" and the absence of any comparable purpose with respect to capital transfers. In order to help members availing themselves of the transitional arrangements of Article XIV, Section 2, special authority was given by that provision to restrict payments and transfers for current transactions notwithstanding the purpose of the Fund to work toward the elimination of these restrictions. The absence of a similar provision with respect to capital transfers is to be explained by the fact that there was full freedom to control them whether or not a member was availing itself of the transitional arrangements and not by reference to any decision of the drafters to prevent interference with capital transfers when there were commitments to make them.

The pre-Bretton Woods history of Article VI, Section 3 gives some assistance in clarifying the obscure phrase relating to commitments. Among the unpublished drafts that were discussed at the preparatory conference held at Atlantic City were the following proposals:

> . . . a member country may not use its control of capital movements to restrict payments arising out of current transactions in goods and services *or to delay unduly transfers of earnings, interest and amortization.*
>
> Not to impose restrictions on payments arising out of current transactions in goods and services *or to delay unduly transfers of earnings, interest and amortization.* . . .

One reaction to the italicized words was that they should be transferred to the definition of payments for current transactions in what became Article XIX(*i*). Indeed, the words seem quite obviously to be the ancestors of categories (2) and (3) in Article XIX(*i*), which would have been regarded as capital transfers but for that provision. It is possible, therefore, that the original words were intended to single out certain types of payments of a capital nature in order to ensure that they would be treated as payments for current transactions.

A later draft at the Atlantic City conference read as follows:

> No member country may control international capital movements in a manner which will restrict payments for current transactions or which will unduly delay transfers of funds in settlement of commitments arising from such transactions. . . .

This language confirms the impression of the purpose of the earlier drafts, and would have made it quite clear that the commitments related to payments for current transactions. Unfortunately, there is no explanation for the omission of the words "arising from such transactions" in the final text of Article VI, Section 3. Nevertheless, the provision should be understood as if they were still there. The object of the clause would then be the perfectly sensible one of making it clear that the concept of restrictions on current payments and transfers included not only the prohibition of such payments but also undue delay in allowing transfers to be carried out when payments were permitted. With this analysis, it must be concluded that, if Article VIII, Section 2(*b*) was applicable, it was not possible to avoid the classification of the Cuban insurance payments as capital or current.

IV. Other Issues of Article VIII, Section 2(*b*)

WITHDRAWAL FROM THE FUND

The Cuban insurance cases support the thesis that if a country withdraws from the Fund it loses the benefit of Article VIII, Section 2(*b*), even in respect of contracts that were entered into when it was a member. This conclusion had already been reached by the New York Supreme Court in *Stephen v. Zivnostenska Banka National Corporation*.[63] In the *Ugalde* case, the plaintiff's motion for reconsideration of the case because Cuba had withdrawn from the Fund was dismissed, but no reason was given by the court. The defendant had opposed the motion on the ground that there was an alternative basis for the verdict, the determination that Cuban law governed the contract under private international law. In the *Varas* case, after the withdrawal of Cuba the defendant company asked the Superior Court of Pennsylvania to disregard the defendant's argument based on the Articles, and the court said that, as a result of the withdrawal, a new look had to be taken at the cases that had been based on the Articles when both Cuba and the United States were members.

As a result of the Cuban insurance cases, there is also available now the opinion of the law officers of the United States. In *Pan American Life Insurance Co. v. Lorido*,[64] the petitioner sought writs of certiorari from the U.S. Supreme Court to the courts of Florida, and the Solicitor General was invited to express the views of the United States. The Florida courts had given judgment for the plaintiff on the ground that the place of performance under the contract was the United States. One of the grounds on which the petitioner relied

---

[63] See fn. 33 *supra*; Gold, *Fund Agreement in the Courts* (1962), pp. 77–78.
[64] 19 Fla. Supp. 167; 154 So. 2d 200 (1963).

was Article VIII, Section 2(*b*). On this point, the Solicitor General's Memorandum for the United States states:

> Further review is not warranted with respect to the petitioner's other contention—that granting recovery to the respondent is contrary to Article VIII (2)(b) of the International Monetary Fund Articles of Agreement. In April of this year, Cuba withdrew from the International Monetary Fund. The provisions of Article VIII (2)(b) are for the benefit of member states and not for the benefit of private parties. Since Cuba is no longer a member of the Fund and since the date of proposed relief determines the applicability of Article VIII (2)(b), a decree granting recovery to the petitioner will not violate the provisions of the Agreement. See *Stephen v. Zivnostenska Banka, National Corporation*, 140 N.Y.S. 2d 323, 326.
>
> In the view of the United States, therefore, this case does not present any substantial question of federal law or policy.[65]

The implications of this view go beyond the immediate question that was raised. For example, it supports the thesis that the sanction of unenforceability under Article VIII, Section 2(*b*) is not invalidity. A contract that was invalid *ab initio* could not be resuscitated by a subsequent event like the withdrawal from the Fund of the member under whose regulations the contract had been invalidated. The view that the sanction is not invalidity permits the conclusion that a contract originally unenforceable may become enforceable because of a change in or the repeal of exchange control regulations, and the reverse will also be true.[66] A contract may also become enforceable or unenforceable as the result of a change in circumstances. A resident party may become nonresident before the performance of the contract, and exchange control regulations may cease to apply. This was the position in most of the Cuban insurance contracts. The reverse may also occur. A nonresident may become a resident and find that the exchange control regulations of the country of his residence apply to a contract he made before he changed his residence.

Withdrawal from IBRD

The withdrawal of Cuba from the Fund on April 2, 1964 was preceded by withdrawal from the International Bank for Reconstruc-

---

[65] Certiorari was denied, 379 U.S. 871, 85 S. Ct. 15 (1964).

[66] Gold, *Fund Agreement in the Courts* (1962), pp. 62–66. See also Gold, "Fund Agreement in the Courts—VIII," pp. 16–17 in this volume. In the *Blanco* and consolidated cases, the remark of the District Court that Cuban laws could not affect an obligation entered into before the laws were passed must be regarded as an *obiter dictum*. The laws were not entitled to recognition under Article VIII, Section 2(*b*) because the plaintiffs had become nonresidents.

tion and Development on November 14, 1960. In the *Blanco* case, the District Court, in a footnote to its opinion, thought that one of the questions raised by the case was whether Cuba's withdrawal from the Bank constituted such a breach of the purposes of Article I of the Fund's Articles as to render the Articles "ineffective as to Cuba."[67] Later in the history of the case, the District Court noted that there was nothing in the Fund's Articles that required a member to remain a member of the Bank. This finding is correct. The Articles of the Bank make membership available to countries that are members of the Fund,[68] and any member that ceases to belong to the Fund automatically ceases to be a member of the Bank unless the Bank by three fourths of the total voting power agrees to allow it to remain a member.[69] There is nothing corresponding to these provisions in the Articles of the Fund.

RECIPROCITY

In the *Blanco* case, among the questions posed by the District Court in the footnote to its opinion that has been mentioned already[70] were the questions whether Cuba had incorporated the Bretton Woods Agreement into its law as had the United States and whether Cuba was performing its obligations under the Agreement. These questions were not confined to Article VIII, Section 2(*b*), but whatever the scope of the questions, the implication of them cannot be accepted as sound law.

It is true that the Articles envisage benefits for all members of the Fund as a result of the obligations of the Articles. This principle does not mean that there is a legal principle of reciprocity in accordance with which the failure by one member to perform an obligation releases other members from a similar obligation or other obligations that are beneficial to the defaulter. On the contrary, the purpose of the Articles is to preserve an objective legal order notwithstanding departures from the obligations of the Articles by individual members from time to time. It is not for each member to judge whether and to what extent there have been violations of the Articles by other members and the legal effect on itself. It is the function of the Fund to decide whether there have been violations and what are the legal consequences of them. It should not be assumed, however, that even

---

[67] 311 F. 2d 427, fn. 8.
[68] Article II, Section 1.
[69] Article VI, Section 3.
[70] See fn. 67 *supra*.

if the Fund is satisfied that there has been the breach of an obligation by one member, the legal consequence will be that other members are absolved from that same obligation or other obligations in relation to the defaulter or other members.

It is appropriate to recall the words of a Netherlands court in a case involving the recognition of exchange control regulations under Article VIII, Section 2(b):

> The Dutch forum must refrain from evaluating the Indonesian foreign exchange provisions and must also refrain from judging the question whether in view of its behavior Indonesia can be considered as a treaty partner. Apart from the fact that a partner to a treaty which has had to protest against violations of international agreements must itself fulfill its obligations, the paramount interest is that the international order to which the Netherlands and Indonesia have both adhered be respected.[71]

QUASI-CONTRACT

In the *Varas* case, one of the lower courts held that the plaintiff's contractual right was to payment in Cuba, and because she could not return to Cuba to collect the benefits under her policy, she should be allowed to recover the value of the premiums that she had paid. This quasi-contractual remedy was available in order to prevent an unjustified enrichment of the defendant insurance company. The court held that Article VIII, Section 2(b) did not prevent this recovery because the remedy was in quasi-contract and did not call for enforcement of the contract. The Pennsylvania Superior Court did not adopt this theory and allowed the plaintiff to recover on the contract.

The relationship of quasi-contractual claims to Article VIII, Section 2(b) is an interesting one. The Schleswig-Holstein Oberlandesgericht [72] and the Supreme Court of Hong Kong [73] have both held that if a contract is unenforceable under Article VIII, Section 2(b), a party that has performed its part cannot recover what he has paid. This conclusion is sound. If it were not adopted, parties would be encouraged to run the risk of flouting exchange control regulations because at worst the courts would restore them to their precontract positions to the extent that this could be done by restitu-

---

[71] *Frantzmann v. Ponijen*, Nederlandse Jurisprudentie (1960), No. 290; Gold, *Fund Agreement in the Courts* (1962), pp. 113–18.

[72] *Lessinger v. Mirau*, Gold, *Fund Agreement in the Courts* (1962), pp. 90–91.

[73] *White v. Roberts*, 33 Hong Kong Law Reports (1949) 231–82; Annual Digest (1962) and Reports of Public International Law Cases, Year 1949, pp. 27–36; Gold, *Fund Agreement in the Courts* (1962), pp. 87–90.

tion. Moreover, a remedy in quasi-contract in a forum foreign to the exchange control regulations that have been violated could produce the very result that was sought by the unenforceable contract.[74] It must be repeated that this caveat with respect to quasi-contractual remedies applies to contracts that are unenforceable under Article VIII, Section 2(*b*). In the *Varas* case, the contract was not unenforceable under the provision after the plaintiff became a nonresident of Cuba.

FRAGMENTATION OF AGREEMENTS

After Cuba withdrew from the Fund, the Superior Court of Pennsylvania delivered its decision in favor of the plaintiff on the theory that the exercise of the cash surrender option completed a contract that was independent of the original contract of insurance. Because of the withdrawal, this theory did not determine whether or not Article VIII, Section 2(*b*) required the recognition of Cuban exchange control regulations. The technique by which a single agreement is fragmented into two or more contracts is questionable, and on occasion it could result in the circumvention of Article VIII, Section 2(*b*). *Southwestern Shipping Corporation v. National City Bank of New York*[75] is an example of a case in which the willingness of the courts to hold that there were separate contracts made it possible to complete the evasion of exchange control regulations that private parties had planned.[76]

V. Summary

The litigation in U.S. courts in which claims have been made under life insurance policies issued by U.S. or Canadian companies to applicants then resident in Cuba is the most extensive body of cases involving Article VIII, Section 2(*b*) that has come into the courts so far. The cases suggest the following reactions.

1. The benefits of Article VIII, Section 2(*b*) cease to be available to a country once it withdraws from the Fund, even in respect of contracts entered into when the country was a member. This conclusion seems to have been accepted by both courts and counsel in the cases. The conclusion has a wider significance in that it supports the view that Article VIII, Section 2(*b*) does not provide for the invalidity of

---

[74] Gold, *Fund Agreement in the Courts* (1962), pp. 93–94.

[75] 173 N.Y.S. 2d 509 (1958); 178 N.Y.S. 2d 1019 (1958); 190 N.Y.S. 2d 352 (1959); certiorari denied, 361 U.S. 895, 80 S. Ct. 198 (1959).

[76] Gold, *Fund Agreement in the Courts* (1962), pp. 97–100, 102–108.

contracts, but only their unenforceability. Whether a contract is unenforceable is determined by the facts at the time when enforcement is sought.

2. Notwithstanding the view that seems to have been held in one of the cases, the application of exchange control regulations under Article VIII, Section 2(b) does not depend on a finding that they are part of the governing law under the private international law of the forum.

3. Article VIII, Section 2(b) does not abrogate the choice-of-law rules of private international law. Therefore, if a contract is not unenforceable under Article VIII, Section 2(b), the forum may still apply the law that its private international law determines to be the governing law. This principle may result in the recognition of exchange control regulations that are part of the governing law, even though this result is not required by Article VIII, Section 2(b).

4. The cases did not exclude life insurance contracts from the category of "exchange contracts." Suggestions that the test of an exchange contract is whether it calls for payment in a currency foreign to the forum or to the governing law under private international law should not be accepted.

5. The test for determining whether a member's currency is involved in an exchange contract is that its exchange resources would be affected by the performance that is sought. This test may be equivalent to the principle that the member whose exchange control regulations are in issue has legislative jurisdiction under public international law to adopt the regulations. This conclusion would seem to mean that the regulations control the transactions of residents or transactions dealing with assets situated within the member's territory. In order to conclude that Article VIII, Section 2(b) has created a further norm of legislative jurisdiction, it would be necessary to show that a member's exchange resources are affected by transactions that do not involve residents or local assets.

6. The *Blanco* case and cases like it are consistent with the view that a member's currency is not involved in contracts between nonresidents that do not require the transfer of an asset situated in the member's territory. The *Ugalde* case cannot be reconciled with this view except on the assumption that the plaintiff was a resident of Cuba. The fact that nonresident parties have agreed that payment should be made in pesos in Cuba should not lead to the conclusion that Cuba's currency would be involved in performance of the contract elsewhere with assets outside Cuba. It should not be concluded therefore that Cuba was entitled to adopt exchange control regulations

forbidding performance elsewhere that would be entitled to recognition under Article VIII, Section 2(b). This conclusion does not prevent a finding by the forum that the regulations must nevertheless be recognized as part of Cuban law because it is the governing law under the private international law of the forum.

7. The currency of payment, whether foreign or domestic, is not a test by which to determine whether a currency is "involved" in a contract. Whether a member's resources are affected will be determined by other facts relating to the contract.

8. "Exchange control regulations" should not be understood to include legal tender laws (*cours légal* or *cours forcé*). Some of the legislative provisions treated as relevant in the cases were of this other character.

9. The cases raise the question whether exchange control regulations affecting life insurance control payments for current transactions or capital transfers. If the payments for current transactions or capital transfers of Cuba were involved in any of the cases, the classification of Cuba's regulations as controlling the one or the other would have determined whether the regulations were maintained or imposed consistently with the Articles. The classification of the payment of premiums may depend on the type of life insurance that is in issue. If there is an element of insurance against risk, and not solely an element of savings and investment, one view might be that the premium is paid in part for a current service. It has also been suggested that all premiums involve payment for a current service to the extent that they recompense the insurer for administrative cost. The payment of the cash surrender or maturity value of a life insurance policy may be regarded as a capital transfer, although there may again be present a minor element of a current nature, i.e., to the extent that recent interest is included.

10. The words "transfers of funds in settlement of commitments" in Article VI, Section 3 should be understood to refer to transfers within a reasonable period of the proceeds of unrestricted payments for current transactions.

11. Withdrawal from membership in the IBRD does not affect the benefits that a member of the Fund is entitled to under Article VIII, Section 2(b).

12. A member's enjoyment of the benefits of Article VIII, Section 2(b) does not depend on a demonstration to the forum that the member is giving reciprocal treatment under that or other provisions of the Articles.

13. Remedies in quasi-contract or the fragmentation of an agreement into two or more contracts should not be resorted to as techniques for frustrating the purpose of Article VIII, Section 2(*b*).

APPENDIX

Unenforceability of Exchange Contracts: Fund's Interpretation
of Article VIII, Section 2(*b*)

The following letter shall be sent to all members:

The Board of Executive Directors of the International Monetary Fund has interpreted, under Article XVIII of the Articles of Agreement, the first sentence of Article VIII, Section 2(b), which provision reads as follows:

Exchange contracts which involve the currency of any member and which are contrary to the exchange control regulations of that member maintained or imposed consistently with this Agreement shall be unenforceable in the territories of any member.

The meaning and effect of this provision are as follows:

1. Parties entering into exchange contracts involving the currency of any member of the Fund and contrary to exchange control regulations of that member which are maintained or imposed consistently with the Fund Agreement will not receive the assistance of the judicial or administrative authorities of other members in obtaining the performance of such contracts. That is to say, the obligations of such contracts will not be implemented by the judicial or administrative authorities of member countries, for example by decreeing performance of the contracts or by awarding damages for their non-performance.

2. By accepting the Fund Agreement members have undertaken to make the principle mentioned above effectively part of their national law. This applied to all members, whether or not they have availed themselves of the transitional arrangements of Article XIV, Section 2.

An obvious result of the foregoing undertaking is that if a party to an exchange contract of the kind referred to in Article VIII, Section 2(b) seeks to enforce such a contract, the tribunal of the member country before which the proceedings are brought will not, on the ground that they are contrary to the public policy (*ordre public*) of the forum, refuse recognition of the exchange control regulations of the other member which are maintained or imposed consistently with the Fund Agreement. It also follows that such contracts will be treated as unenforceable notwithstanding that under the private international law of the forum, the law under which the foreign exchange control regulations are maintained or imposed is not the law which governs the exchange contract or its performance.

The Fund will be pleased to lend its assistance in connection with any problem which may arise in relation to the foregoing interpretation or any other aspect of Article VIII, Section 2(b). In addition, the Fund is prepared to advise whether particular exchange control regulations are maintained or imposed consistently with the Fund Agreement.

Decision No. 446-4
June 10, 1949

3

The Fund Agreement
in the Courts—IX*

The ninth article in this series discusses six cases in which certain aspects of the Articles of Agreement of the International Monetary Fund have been considered by the courts in six member countries. A Venezuelan case dealt with the effect of the Articles on the choice of an exchange rate by the court in awarding judgment on a claim expressed in a foreign currency. A case decided in the United States dealt with the question whether countervailing duties could be imposed because of multiple rates of exchange when they had been approved by the Fund with the concurrence of the United States. In a third case, an English court, for the first time, interpreted certain features of the English legislation giving the force of law to Article VIII, Section 2(b). A German case also dealt with that provision and is particularly interesting because of a novel development in procedure. A Netherlands court considered the relationship of Article VIII, Section 2(b) to nationalization. Finally, Philippine litigation involving the legality of certain exchange surrender requirements, in which aspects of the Fund's Articles had been vigorously argued, has come to an end.

Judicial Application of Exchange Rates

An opinion delivered on May 15, 1961 by a Venezuelan court (the Commercial Court of First Instance of the Judicial Federal District and

---

* Originally published in July 1967.

of the State of Miranda) in *Adriática Venezolana de Seguros S.A. v. The First National City Bank of New York*[1] includes a lengthy discussion of a number of legal aspects of monetary theory. The views of the court were heavily influenced by the Spanish translation of the late Professor Nussbaum's book, *Money in the Law, National and International*.[2] The opinion is of special interest, however, on the question of the effect of the Articles of Agreement on the determination that courts must often make of the appropriate rate of exchange on which to base their judgments when there are multiple rates. This problem is one on which there is little judicial authority.

Adriática, a Venezuelan commercial company, came into court to make a formal offer to the Caracas branch of City Bank, also domiciled in Venezuela, of the equivalent in Venezuelan bolívares of US$118,722.78 at the rate of Bs 3.35 per U.S. dollar in payment of certain bills of exchange and interest from the date of maturity to the date of formal offer. City Bank was willing to accept the offer in full discharge of one of the bills, but, in respect of the others, was willing to accept bolívares in discharge only if and to the extent that foreign exchange could be obtained with the bolívares from the Venezuelan Central Bank. Adriática rejected this counteroffer; the court ordered Adriática to deposit the amount of its offer in court, and summoned City Bank to appear and state its arguments against the offer and deposit.

The court confirmed that the U.S. dollar in which the bills were expressed was the money of account and not the money of payment, and that the defendant was entitled to tender bolívares. It also decided that under Venezuelan law the exchange rate between the bolívar and the dollar at the date of the demand, and not at the date when the obligation was incurred or matured, must be applied. This decision led the court to examine Venezuela's exchange system at the date of the demand. The court found that before November 1960 there were two markets, "controlled" and "free." For the controlled market before November 1960, the Central Bank fixed the rate at which foreign exchange could be obtained at Bs 3.35 per U.S. dollar, but the rate was the same in the free market because all persons needing foreign exchange could get it in the controlled market without limitation. There was thus no reason for any divergence in rate to develop.

---

[1] *Revista de la Facultad de Derecho* (Caracas), Vol. 21 (1961), pp. 287–337, hereinafter cited as *Revista*.

[2] Arthur Nussbaum, *Money in the Law, National and International* (Brooklyn, 1950); *Derecho monetario nacional e internacional*, translation and notes by Alberto D. Schoo (Buenos Aires, 1954).

The situation changed, however, with the exchange regime that was initiated by Presidential Decree No. 390 on November 8, 1960 and adapted thereafter, because this regime no longer ensured that even those parties who were eligible to get their foreign exchange in the controlled market would actually get it. These parties were now required to get a foreign exchange license. The issue of licenses was discretionary on the part of the authorities, who would be governed by such factors as the availability of foreign exchange in the market, the monetary reserves of the country, the general payments needs of the economy, and the particular payments needs of the applicant. The selling rate in this market remained Bs 3.35 per U.S. dollar. Other specified purchases and sales of foreign exchange, not eligible for the controlled market, could be made in the free market, to which, in addition, those who had been refused an exchange license for the controlled market could have recourse. The Central Bank was authorized to intervene in the free market and to determine the selling rate on the basis of the state of the country's reserves and the exchange rate fluctuations in the free market. The rate was established at Bs 4.70 per U.S. dollar, and was later changed to Bs 4.67 and again to Bs 4.63. Even access to the free market was possible only if the purchaser came within certain defined categories. For this reason, yet a third market emerged for other transactions. This market also was legal. The rate in it was a little higher than in the free market.[3]

The court held that the burden was on Adriática to prove that the rate of Bs 3.35 per U.S. dollar was the appropriate one unless this fact was established by some legal text of which the court should take judicial notice. Adriática argued that two decisions of the highest Venezuelan tribunal in 1950 and 1951 constituted a text of that character. The court found, however, that these decisions, which took judicial notice of the official rate established by the Central Bank, were distinguishable, because they were delivered when the Central Bank was regulating the rate in both the controlled and the free markets at Bs 3.35 per U.S. dollar by supplying unlimited amounts of foreign exchange at that rate. The situation was now different: exchange could be obtained in the controlled market for certain specific purposes only, and even for these purposes a license had to be sought and might be refused. As a result, the rates in the two

---

[3] On April 18, 1961 the selling rate in this market was approximately Bs 4.81 per U.S. dollar. See International Monetary Fund, *Twelfth Annual Report on Exchange Restrictions* (Washington, 1961), p. 367; see also *Eleventh Annual Report* (1960), pp. 339–42, and *Thirteenth Annual Report* (1962), pp. 359–62.

markets had diverged. Therefore, the courts could continue to take judicial notice of the rate in the controlled market, but it did not follow that this was the rate at which to value foreign currencies in terms of the bolívar.

The court held that the appropriate valuation could be made only in the free market:

> The general norm in matters of assessment of a foreign currency in terms of a local currency is the one which places reliance on the exchange rate operating in the "spontaneous" market, namely, the one which results from the free play of supply and demand—with the possible softening action of the official authorities—provided that this "spontaneous," parallel, or free market is permitted under the law as is our situation and does not therefore constitute a black or illegal market.
>
> In support of this statement, it should be pointed out that the above principle wholly satisfies the demands of equity. Equity requires that the creditor can, in the same place and on the same day as he is paid, obtain with the Venezuelan bolívares that he receives, the amount of foreign currency which constitutes the object of the debt. This result can only be achieved when the conversion is affected at the exchange rate prevailing in the "spontaneous," parallel, or free market.[4]

The importance of this conclusion is enhanced by the fact that the debt that was the source of Adriática's offer was included within the categories of payments for which foreign exchange could be obtained in the controlled market. The court held that this fact did not affect its conclusion because the debtor was not able to get foreign exchange automatically on proof that his payment was eligible for the controlled market. It was still necessary for him to apply for a license, and the authorities might refuse his application. There is no evidence in the report of the case that he had applied for a license.

The court gave a further reason for its view. Exchange control and the official rate that it implies are established to regulate international transactions involving the movement of foreign exchange from one country to another. When, however, the debtor pays in foreign exchange the amount of a debt incurred in foreign exchange and the creditor receives the amount within the same country, this transaction does not necessarily imply a transfer of foreign exchange from one country to another. The payment is an internal operation that is outside the orbit of exchange control and of the official rate established by it. This second reason is much less persuasive than the first. It is

---

[4] *Revista*, pp. 334–35.

difficult to believe that payments in foreign exchange or payments in domestic currency when made to a nonresident are not of legitimate concern to exchange control authorities until withdrawal of the balance across the boundary is contemplated.

The court concluded that Adriática had not discharged the burden of proof that rested on it, for which reason its offer and deposit were null. In reaching its conclusion, the court dealt with the impact of the Articles of Agreement in two passages of its lengthy opinion. Before these passages are examined, it must be recalled that the par value for the bolívar agreed by Venezuela with the Fund on April 15, 1947, with effect from April 18, 1947, was Bs 3.35 per U.S. dollar, and that this has remained the par value at all times since then.

In the more theoretical part of its opinion, the court spoke as follows, after dealing with the difficulties of ascertaining the value of one currency in terms of another when there are multiple rates or black markets:

> . . . all these problems of valuation of foreign exchange under the exchange control system have apparently been very much simplified through the establishment of "par values" by the International Monetary Fund. These values will largely replace the "official values" of the past but they have not yet entirely eliminated the basic problem. Although it seems probable that courts will have recourse to the "par values", this is not binding upon them, says Professor Nussbaum. . . . And tax authorities will be even less bound by this. There exist, on the other hand, numerous currencies which lack "par values". Besides, the regulations of the International Monetary Fund have nothing to do with valuation when there are multiple rates for a foreign currency. Moreover, this is so even with respect to transactions in foreign exchange because the enforcement of par values will necessarily encounter resistance in the ever-changing conditions of our shaky present. Early in 1948 tension generated by the pressure of financial conditions against the rigid "par value" system led to an explosion. France introduced a dual market system for certain foreign currencies over the Fund's disapproval, a measure which actually destroyed the proclaimed par value of the French franc, and through the years Canada has been allowed to maintain divergent "official" and "free" rates for her dollar at odds with the par value. Generally, whenever "free" or "parallel" markets exist, deviations from the par value are bound to appear. . . .

> These considerations show that in the concrete realities of international life, the "par values" fixed by convention in the Agreement that created the International Monetary Fund cannot be taken as the only criteria for the purpose of the evaluation of one currency in terms of

another, because of the necessity to prove beforehand that the monetary legislation under which the currencies are issued conform in effect to the provisions of the Articles.[5]

In the final part of its opinion, in which the court reached its conclusion, it returned to the subject of the Fund as follows:

> The reference to the Agreement of the International Monetary Fund signed at Bretton Woods in 1944 and ratified by Venezuela is not relevant in this matter. It is true that in such Articles "par values" have been established for the currency of all the signatory states. But it is also evident that this "fixing", even if it had been complied with by all the countries (which in fact has not occurred), does not by any means bind the courts of a specific country to matters which are not included within the object of the Agreement. The payment of debts stipulated in foreign currency and the method of conversion of a currency for these purposes is not taken into account within the Articles. "The regulations of the International Monetary Fund, besides, have nothing to do with valuation when there are multiple currency rates for a foreign currency" . . .[6] as is our situation. Equally, it should be remembered that the imposition of this "par value" did not by any means disturb the existence of "dual" markets in France, Italy and Canada, despite the opposition of the International Monetary Fund.[7]

Much of these two passages is irrelevant to the legal issue. There is not much logic in arguing that, in principle, currencies should not be valued on the basis of par values because from time to time one or another member may fail in its duty to make its par value effective in accordance with the Articles.[8] What is really involved in this argument, and the further argument that there may be multiple rates for a currency, is that the par value, or rates based on it, may fail to do justice between the parties. There can be no dispute about that propo-

---

[5] *Ibid.*, pp. 311–12.

[6] The court cited Nussbaum, *op. cit.*, p. 669.

[7] *Revista*, p. 335.

[8] Article IV, Section 3: "*Foreign exchange dealings based on parity.*—The maximum and the minimum rates for exchange transactions between the currencies of members taking place within their territories shall not differ from parity
  (i) in the case of spot exchange transactions, by more than one percent; and
  (ii) in the case of other exchange transactions, by a margin which exceeds the margin for spot exchange transactions by more than the Fund considers reasonable."
Article IV, Section 4(b): "Each member undertakes, through appropriate measures consistent with this Agreement, to permit within its territories exchange transactions between its currency and the currencies of other members only within the limits prescribed under Section 3 of this Article. A member whose monetary authorities, for the settlement of international transactions, in fact freely buy and sell gold within the limits prescribed by the Fund under Section 2 of this Article shall be deemed to be fulfilling this undertaking."

sition, and there will be no difficulty in accepting what it implies unless some provision in the Articles compels members to make sure that their courts apply par values when faced with the need to determine the value of one currency in terms of another. The only relevant point made in the two passages is that the Articles contain no provision dictating the use of par values as conversion factors when courts must calculate the value of one currency in terms of another. This proposition is correct. It is correct even if both of the currencies involved have effective par values, and it would remain true even if the currencies of all members of the Fund had effective par values.

What the Articles seek to do, substantially, is to have members establish viable par values, which would mean that members would have little or no economic difficulty in observing their obligations to adopt appropriate measures to make those par values effective as the basis for exchange transactions in their territories. If this result is achieved, the courts will apply the effective rates of exchange, not because there is an obligation to do so under the Articles, but because it is the logical and equitable consequence of the obligations that are laid on members. What the courts must do, as is indicated by the Venezuelan case, is render justice between the parties, and this obligation will mean the application of the prevailing rate of exchange on the appropriate date. If the rates are not unified or if they fluctuate, the choice of the appropriate rate may be difficult; and the rate that is chosen may have no connection with any par value that has been agreed under the Articles.

A less important point, but nevertheless one worth making, is that it is misleading to speak of the par value as the appropriate rate of exchange for a court to select. The Articles intend that a par value shall be the basis for exchange rates, in the sense that members have obligations to permit exchange transactions in their territories only within the prescribed margins of parity as the ratio between the par values of the currencies involved. Therefore, even when par values are effective in this sense, the courts should apply the actual rates that are quoted for transactions, and not the parities that are the basis for these quotations, at which transactions will occur only by chance.

In connection with its own jurisdiction over exchange rates, the Fund has always been meticulous in distinguishing between rates of exchange and conversion factors. The Fund's jurisdiction over rates of exchange applies not only to par values as the bases for exchange rates but also to multiple rates of exchange. Initial par values must be agreed with the Fund, and later changes must be the subject of consultation with the Fund and, normally, may be made only if the Fund concurs. In addition, the introduction or change of multiple rates of exchange, which by definition will depart from the prescribed margins around parity, must receive the Fund's approval in order to be valid under the Articles. In applying these principles of jurisdiction, the Fund satisfies itself that it is really dealing with exchange rates. The Fund has to decide that it is dealing with rates at which one member's currency is to be exchanged for another member's currency.

Sometimes, however, a conversion factor is needed for translating one currency into another without the exchange of the one currency for the other. The factor applied by courts in translating the foreign currency of a claim into the domestic currency of the forum if the latter is the only currency that the courts can award is a good example of circumstances in which no exchange transaction is involved. The Fund has never held that the rate that courts adopt for this purpose must be approved by the Fund. Of course, as shown above, for certain purposes courts tend to recognize rates already in existence, and therefore, their legal status under the Articles may have arisen in other contexts.[9] It remains true, nevertheless, that the Fund would not assert jurisdiction over the practices of the courts in evaluating currencies in terms of each other, whatever rates the courts might think fit to apply. This principle would be equally true in other circumstances, e.g., where customs authorities adopted factors for levying duties without the actual exchange of currencies.[10] The

---

[9] The court was aware of the indirect effect of par values under the Articles on questions of the judicial determination of rates of exchange. For example: "As is well known, the creation of the International Monetary Fund may have influence over these questions when they are of an international nature by virtue of having instituted for the monetary units of member states—among which Venezuela is numbered—'par values' on a gold base which a member must not alter without the Fund's consent. Hence the organization has created 'international gold management standards'" (*Revista*, p. 307). The Fund's approval, however, may be required of rates of exchange even though they are not related to a par value, and these rates may be multiple rates as they were in the Venezuelan case (see *Selected Decisions*, Third Issue, pp. 84–91; *Selected Decisions*, Ninth Issue, pp. 223–25), or unitary rates (see, for example, Article XX, Section 4(d)(iii), *original* and *first*). The passage in the judgment taken from Nussbaum to the effect that "the regulations ... of the Fund have nothing to do with valuation when there are multiple rates for a foreign currency" must not be taken to imply an absence of jurisdiction on the part of the Fund over multiple rates.

[10] See Gold, *The International Monetary Fund and Private Business Transactions*, IMF Pamphlet Series, No. 3 (Washington, 1965), p. 6. (Hereinafter cited as Gold, Pamphlet No. 3.)

Fund's practice shows that the rates adopted for these computations are not subject to the Fund's exchange rate jurisdiction.[11] It follows, therefore, that the courts should conclude that the Agreement does not bind them to apply any particular rates when they make their computations.[12]

This last conclusion raises a further issue. It will be recalled that the Venezuelan court noted that the exchange rates in effect were legal and had not developed in an illegal black market. It is not at all clear that the court was announcing a doctrine that only legal rates should ever be applied. If it is accepted that the essential task of a court is to apply a rate of exchange that does justice between the parties, this may conflict with the undeviating selection of a legal rate. For example, if there is an exchange system in which most exchange transactions are carried out at legal rates but in which there is also a peripheral black market, the rates in the latter market may reflect the risks of evading the law and not the economic value of the currency. The implications of such an exchange system may differ greatly from those of a system in which most or all exchange transactions are conducted at illegal rates. In any event, what is meant by

---

[11] In theory at least, the Fund's jurisdiction might become involved. If it is possible to imagine such widespread practices of adopting conversion factors that the value of the currency as approved by the Fund was called into question, the Fund might request the member to take appropriate action pursuant to the member's undertaking under Article IV, Section 4(a) to collaborate with the Fund to promote exchange stability, maintain orderly exchange arrangements with other members, and avoid competitive exchange alterations. There is a precedent for such action in the Fund's statement of policy concerning subsidies for gold production. The Fund has stated that even if a subsidy was not in violation of Article IV, Section 2, which deals with the price at which gold may be bought and sold by monetary authorities, the subsidy might be inconsistent with Article IV, Section 4(a), because it cast widespread doubt on the uniformity of the monetary value of gold or contributed to monetary instability (*Selected Decisions,* Third Issue, p. 15. See also *Selected Decisions of the International Monetary Fund and Selected Documents,* Eighth Issue (Washington, 1976), pp. 8–10; hereinafter cited as *Selected Decisions,* Eighth Issue). See also the Fund's policy statements on external transactions in gold at premium prices (*Annual Report of the Executive Directors for the Fiscal Year Ending June 30, 1947* (Washington, 1947), pp. 78–79 (hereinafter cited as *Annual Report*); and *Selected Decisions,* Third Issue, pp. 13–14 (*Selected Decisions,* Eighth Issue, pp. 10–11)).

[12] The discussion is not meant to preclude the possibility that the parties may agree, or be taken to have agreed, that for the purposes of their contract, conversion factors shall be determined by parities or rates of exchange consistent with the Fund's Articles, and that the forum would apply such clauses where permitted by the *lex fori.* An example of such a technique, although on the intergovernmental level and for purposes of customs valuation and not contract, can be found in Article VII of the GATT, and, in particular, paragraphs 4(a), (b), and (c) of that Article. Note that these provisions use the term "conversion rate of exchange" for what has sometimes been called "conversion factor" in the present chapter.

legality in this context is ambiguous. It may mean rates that are consistent with the *lex fori*, or it may mean rates that are consistent with the Articles of the Fund; although in the Venezuelan case the rates in issue were consistent with both. A rate can be consistent with the former criterion but not with the latter. It is possible, however, that in some legal systems rates are not consistent with the *lex fori* unless they are also consistent with the Articles. The principle of selecting the rate that does justice between the parties will probably induce courts, whenever possible, to select realistic rates even if those rates are inconsistent with the Articles. It is likely that courts will not want to penalize private litigants because governments have failed to observe their international obligations.

What has been said in the preceding paragraph about the legality of rates may have a different aspect when rates of exchange are established by other members and not by the member in whose territories the forum is situated. A forum may hold that it will apply a rate of exchange established by its own monetary authorities even though that rate is inconsistent with the Agreement; but if rates of exchange are established by another member, Article VIII, Section 2(*b*) may come into play. If particular rates of exchange are prescribed by the exchange control regulations of another member but have not been approved by the Fund, a court may be disposed to refuse recognition of them on the ground that the exchange control regulations are not maintained or imposed consistently with the Articles. It is also conceivable that a court may hold that it is not being asked to apply the exchange control regulations of the other member, but rather to apply the rates of exchange between that member's currency and the domestic currency that have developed in the domestic market of the forum. Even though these rates may reflect the other member's unapproved exchange control regulations, the court may still hold that it is recognizing market facts and not foreign regulations.

Multiple Rates of Exchange and Countervailing Duties

It has been seen that the Venezuelan court referred to the domestic validity of exchange rates in determining the rate to which the plaintiff was entitled, and this reference led, in the discussion of that case, to some reflections on the relevance of the international validity of exchange rates to the issue before the court. In *Energetic Worsted Corporation v. The United States* [13] one aspect of the case was the

---

[13] Customs Appeal No. 5160 (April 7, 1966).

international validity of Uruguay's multiple rates of exchange under the Fund's Articles in relation to the imposition of countervailing duty under section 303 of the U.S. Tariff Act of 1930.[14] The importer in this case appealed against the judgment of the Third Division of the U.S. Customs Court overruling the importer's protest against the assessment of countervailing duty on five entries of wool tops exported from Uruguay and entered at Philadelphia during 1953. The assessment had been based on a notice, promulgated by the Secretary of the Treasury on May 6, 1953, determining under section 303 that Uruguay was paying a net bounty or grant of 18 per cent of the invoice value and dutiable charges on wool tops. A majority of the trial court agreed that this was the effect of Uruguay's multiple rates of exchange, and a third judge dissented.[15]

In supporting the position of the Treasury Department, the majority of the trial court stated:

> It is clear from the record in this case that the Treasury Department imposed the countervailing duty on wool tops only after careful consideration of the entire situation and after circumstances had changed sufficiently to show that the preferential exchange rate had given such an advantage to Uruguayan exporters as to constitute a bounty or grant within the meaning of section 303. Although the United States and other countries may have recognized or approved multiple exchange rate systems in general and although there may have been various causes for Uruguay's action, nevertheless, section 303 of our tariff act imposing countervailing duties in certain circumstances has

---

[14] Section 303, U.S. Tariff Act of 1930: "Whenever any country, dependency, colony, province, or other political subdivision of government, person, partnership, association, cartel, or corporation shall pay or bestow, directly or indirectly, any bounty or grant upon the manufacture or production or export of any article or merchandise manufactured or produced in such country, dependency, colony, province, or other political subdivision of government, and such article or merchandise is dutiable under the provisions of this Act, then upon the importation of any such article or merchandise into the United States, whether the same shall be imported directly from the country of production or otherwise, and whether such article or merchandise is imported in the same condition as when exported from the country of production or has been changed in condition by remanufacture or otherwise, there shall be levied and paid, in all such cases, in addition to the duties otherwise imposed by this Act, an additional duty equal to the net amount of such bounty or grant, however the same be paid or bestowed. The Secretary of the Treasury shall from time to time ascertain and determine, or estimate, the net amount of each such bounty or grant, and shall declare the net amount so determined or estimated. The Secretary of the Treasury shall make all regulations he may deem necessary for the identification of such articles and merchandise and for the assessment and collection of such additional duties."
[15] 224 F. Supp. 606 (decided October 21, 1963).

not been repealed. It must be applied whenever it is shown that a bounty or grant has been bestowed. The fact that United States representatives on the International Monetary Fund and the National Advisory Council did not object to Uruguay's multiple exchange rate system in general is not relevant. Whether or not such a system is objected to, whenever the result is a bounty as to any particular article, the statute requires that countervailing duties be imposed. The facts here show that the preferential exchange rate did result in a bounty to the Uruguayan exporter.[16]

One feature of the opinion of the majority on which the dissenting judge disagreed was the relevance of the Fund, and on this feature he said:

The exchange rate governing the involved exportations was preceded by a number of fiscal events of international significance, the importance of which cannot be overlooked in the total appraisal of currency controls as a basis of subsidization of exports. . . . One such event was the emergence, in 1945, of the International Monetary Fund, of which organization the United States and Uruguay were charter members. One of the principal purposes of the Fund is "To promote exchange stability, to maintain orderly exchange arrangements among members, and to avoid competitive exchange depreciation." Thus, through participation in the Fund, Uruguay gained multilateral recognition and support for its currency system and practices from the Fund members which, of course, included the United States. It is said that in the matter of foreign exchange controls "the Bretton Woods agreements have somewhat enlarged the field of recognition."[17]

In the light of this development, it is difficult to understand how the majority could brush aside the United States participation in the Bretton Woods agreements as being irrelevant to this matter of subsidization through currency manipulation. . . . The International Monetary Fund and the United States, acting through the Secretary of the Treasury and others constituting the National Advisory Council on International Monetary and Financial Problems, gave approval to Uruguay in no uncertain terms for the use of the multiple exchange rates governing its imports and exports. This attitude was not formulated in a vacuum. It was formulated with a conscious awareness of the impact of such currency reforms on all phases of American activities of an economic and fiscal nature involving intercourse with Uruguay in such matters. Indeed, the Treasury Department's earlier

---

[16] *Ibid.*, at 614.

[17] *Ibid.*, at 618. A footnote cites Nussbaum, *op. cit.*, p. 475, for this latter quotation. In the passage quoted, Nussbaum seems to be referring to the recognition of the exchange control law of one country under the private international law of other countries.

defense of Uruguay's currency system against the claim here made was based upon knowledge and information derived from United States participation in Fund activities and investigations of monetary activities of Fund members.[18]

The dissenting judge distinguished certain earlier cases relied on by the majority as based on unilateral action by the German Government before the existence of the Fund and decided therefore at a time when rates carried no international endorsement.[19]

To recapitulate, the trial court held, notwithstanding the dissent of one of its three members, that the approval of multiple rates by the Fund, with the concurrence of the U.S. Executive Director, did not prevent a finding that the rates constituted a bounty in respect of which countervailing duty could be imposed. The U.S. Court of Customs and Patent Appeals reversed the decision of the trial court but did so on the ground that it did not agree with the method used by the Treasury Department to calculate the bounty that Uruguay was alleged to have granted. The court quoted the passage from the majority opinion set forth above, but did not comment on it. Once the court determined that there was no satisfactory proof that the multiple rates actually resulted in a bounty, it became unnecessary to decide whether multiple rates approved by the Fund, with the concurrence of the U.S. Executive Director, could be treated in law as involving a bounty under section 303 of the Tariff Act.

Unenforceability of Certain Exchange Contracts

ENGLAND

Sharif v. Azad, decided by the Court of Appeal on October 5, 1966,[20] is an important case not only because it is the first close

---

[18] *Ibid.,* at 618.

[19] *Ibid.* Other considerations involving the Fund that are mentioned in the dissenting judgment are that: (i) The Uruguayan devaluations of October 1949 were preceded by widespread multiple currency changes by Argentina, which was at that time not a member of the Fund and therefore "was subject to no external surveillance or control in its currency practices as was Uruguay" (*ibid.,* at 621). See also references to Spain (*ibid.,* at 625). (ii) "Under the International Monetary Fund operations currency controls, such as those employed in Uruguay, are regarded as being only 'transitory expediencies'" (*ibid.,* at 621).

These considerations related to the calculation of a bounty and not to the prior question of principle, i.e., whether in view of the relevance of the Fund the question of bounty could arise at all.

[20] [1966] 3 W.L.R. 1285; [1966] 3 All E.R. 785.

scrutiny of Article VIII, Section 2(b) by an English court but also because an eminent English court has now confirmed a number of interpretations of that provision that give effect to its purpose within the framework of the Articles. Latif, a resident of Pakistan, had an account with the Habib Bank in Karachi, on which he could draw rupees. Under Pakistan's exchange control regulations, he could not take those rupees out of Pakistan or exchange them for sterling without the permission of the exchange control authorities. Early in 1964, Latif came on a short visit to England and in Manchester met a Pakistani named Sharif, the plaintiff, who was living in England. Latif, needing sterling, obtained £300 in sterling from Sharif; in return, Latif gave Sharif a check for 6,000 rupees drawn on the Habib Bank. At prevailing rates of exchange between sterling and the rupee, 6,000 rupees were the equivalent of about £450.[21] The check given to Sharif was signed by Latif, but the payee's name was left in blank. Sharif took the check to another Pakistani in Manchester, Azad, the defendant, a travel agent who lived in England and arranged passages for Pakistanis. The name of Azad's brother, who was living in Pakistan, was inserted in the check as payee, and Azad sent the check to him for collection. In return for the check, Azad gave Sharif a sterling check for £300, signed by Azad in favor of Sharif, and drawn on a Manchester bank. This check was postdated because Azad wanted to make sure that his brother succeeded in collecting the rupees from the Habib Bank. The Pakistani authorities became suspicious about the rupee check and did not allow payment to be made freely to Azad's brother. The Habib Bank placed the rupees in a blocked account on which the brother could not draw without the permission of the authorities. The reaction of Azad to this development was to stop payment of the sterling check. Sharif sued for the amount of the check, and the Manchester County Court entered judgment for him. The Articles of Agreement were not referred to in those proceedings, but were relied on for the first time in support of the defendant's argument on appeal that the transaction on which the suit was based was illegal.

The three members of the Court of Appeal (Lord Denning, Master of the Rolls, and Lords Justices Diplock and Russell) were unanimous

---

[21] This amount is stated in the opinion of Lord Justice Diplock (ibid., at 1294), but there were multiple rates of exchange, and it is possible, by using certain rates as the appropriate rates, to show that Latif received more than the sterling equivalent of 6,000 rupees and that Azad's brother received more than the rupee equivalent of £300. See Fifteenth Annual Report on Exchange Restrictions (1964), pp. 368–74.

in distinguishing two transactions, the first between Sharif and Latif, and the second between Sharif and Azad. The court held that the first of these transactions would have been unenforceable as a result of the United Kingdom's Bretton Woods legislation that gave the force of law to Article VIII, Section 2(*b*) in the United Kingdom.[22] The court also held, however, that the second transaction was not illegal or unenforceable and that the plaintiff succeeded in his claim based on it. The court dealt with the following topics:

(1) On the fundamental issue of the effect of Article VIII, Section 2(*b*) on English private international law, the most elaborate statement was made by Lord Justice Diplock.

> Latif in drawing the rupee cheque as consideration for his receipt from the plaintiff of £300 in England was in my view acting in contravention of section 5(1)(f); and any payment of the cheque by him, unless authorised by the State Bank, would have been in contravention of section 5(1)(e).[23] On the other hand, it is to be observed that the section applies only to acts done by persons who are in or resident in Pakistan.

> The drawing of the rupee cheque by Latif was an act done in England. The payment of the rupee cheque when it took place would be an act done in Pakistan. Sovereignty being territorial, the English courts do not in general recognise the right of a foreign state to legislate as to the legality or legal effect of acts done in England unless some United Kingdom statute so provides. But where the law of the foreign state purports to affect contractual rights between parties, the English court may give effect to it, even in respect of an act done in England, if the proper law of the contract is that of the foreign state. Even where the proper law of the contract itself is not that of the foreign state, the English court may also give effect to the law of the foreign state so far as it relates to acts required to be done in the foreign state in performance of the contract. Both these general rules of English conflict of laws are subject to the qualification that the English courts will not enforce legislation of a foreign state which is penal or fiscal, and nice questions may arise as to the scope of this qualification.

> But they do not arise in the present case, for where the foreign law which is relied upon as affecting the contractual rights of parties is the exchange control regulations of a state which is a party to the Bretton Woods Agreements, the matter is not regulated by the general rules of English conflict of laws but by an English statute, the Bretton Woods

---

[22] 9 and 10 Geo. 6, c. 19; and S.R. & O. 1946 No. 36.
[23] Of the Foreign Exchange Regulation Act, 1947 of Pakistan. The text of this provision is quoted later in the discussion.

Agreements Act, 1945, and an English statutory order made under that statute, the Bretton Woods Agreements Order, 1946, the relevant provision of which is to be found in Part I, art. 8 s. 2(b), of the Schedule to the Order and reads as follows:

"Exchange contracts which involve the currency of any member and which are contrary to the exchange control regulations of that member maintained or imposed consistently with that Agreement shall be unenforceable in the territories of any member."

The effect of this is that an "exchange contract," whatever may be its proper law and wherever acts may be required to be done in performance of the "exchange contract," is unenforceable by an English court if it is contrary to the exchange control regulations of the foreign state.[24]

The opinion of Lord Denning on this part of the case was briefer:

Let me say at once that England and Pakistan are both members of the International Monetary Fund and, as such, each country will respect the currency regulations of the other. This derives from the Bretton Woods Agreement which has been incorporated into our law by the Bretton Woods Agreements Act, 1945, and the Bretton Woods Agreements Order in Council [S.R. & O. 1946 No. 36] made under the Act.[25]

No mention was made in any of the opinions of the interpretation under Article XVIII of Article VIII, Section 2(b), adopted by the Fund on June 10, 1949.[26] One of the main purposes of that interpretation was to clarify the relation of Article VIII, Section 2(b) to private international law. The reason for the absence of any reference to the interpretation may have been the question that would be raised of the effect of Article XVIII interpretations under English law.[27] There was no need for the court to face this question in circumstances in which there was no conflict between its views and the interpretation.

(2) The court held that the effect of the Bretton Woods legislation was to declare the contracts covered by Article VIII, Section 2(b) "unenforceable," and the court refused to treat this expression as equiv-

---

[24] [1966] 3 W.L.R. 1285, 1292–93.

[25] Ibid., at 1289.

[26] Selected Decisions, Third Issue, pp. 73–74. (Selected Decisions, Ninth Issue, pp. 201–202.)

[27] Gold, "The Interpretation by the International Monetary Fund of its Articles of Agreement," International and Comparative Law Quarterly, Vol. 3 (1954), pp. 271–72. It should not be overlooked that the court showed none of the reluctance expressed by Lord Justice Evershed in Kahler v. Midland Bank Ltd. [1948] 1 All E.R. 811, 819, when it adopted interpretations on questions on which the Fund had not spoken (see p. 272 of the article cited here).

alent to "illegal." In the words of Lord Justice Diplock: "It is to be noted that such contract is not made 'illegal' in English law, merely unenforceable." [28]

(3) The court did not permit itself to be deflected by verbal pedantries from arriving at a sensible economic interpretation of "exchange contracts." According to Lord Justice Diplock:

> The expression "exchange contract" is nowhere defined in the Act or the Order or even in the Bretton Woods Agreement itself. I think that it should be liberally construed having regard to the objects of the Bretton Woods Agreement to protect the currencies of the states who are parties thereto; and I should be prepared to hold that the following were "exchange contracts," viz. (1) the agreement between the plaintiff and Latif whereby the plaintiff agreed to pay Latif £300 for the rupee cheque; (2) the agreement between the defendant and the plaintiff whereby the defendant agreed to issue to the plaintiff his cheque for £300 in exchange for the rupee cheque drawn by Latif; and (3) the contracts between Latif and the successive holders of the rupee cheque created by the rupee cheque itself, at any rate in so far as they were not in or resident in Pakistan.
>
> But not all these "exchange contracts" were contrary to the provisions of the Foreign Exchange Regulations Act, 1947, of Pakistan.[29]

According to Lord Denning:

> The words "exchange contracts" are not defined, but I think that they mean any contracts which in any way affect the country's exchange resources. The contracts with which we are concerned here are all clearly exchange contracts. They affect the exchange resources of Pakistan and England. If they offend against the currency regulations of Pakistan or England, they are unenforceable. It is not suggested now that they offend against the currency regulations of England; but it is said that these contracts offend against the currency regulations of Pakistan and are therefore unenforceable.[30]

An interesting feature of this last passage should not be overlooked. In referring to the unenforceability of exchange contracts that offend against the currency regulations of the United Kingdom, Lord Denning suggests that Article VIII, Section 2(b) applies to the exchange control regulations of the forum. The provision should be understood, however, to deal only with the recognition of the exchange control regulations of other members of the Fund and not

---

[28] [1966] 3 W.L.R. 1285, 1293.

[29] *Ibid.*, at 1293.

[30] *Ibid.*, at 1289–90. [The Court of Appeal has since repudiated this view in *Wilson, Smithett & Cope Ltd. v. Terruzzi* [1976] 1 All E.R. 817.]

of the member in which the forum is established. For that court, Article VIII, Section 2(b) does not override the will of its own legislator. For example, it should not be held as a result of that provision that the court has the task of determining whether the exchange control regulations promulgated by its authorities are maintained or imposed consistently with the Articles of Agreement. Yet it would be required to make this finding if it were held that domestic exchange control regulations were embraced by Article VIII, Section 2(b). Furthermore, those regulations might impose some sanction other than unenforceability, and it should not be open to the court to substitute unenforceability on the thesis that Article VIII, Section 2(b) applied.[31]

Even if a forum should hold that it would not apply the regulations of the *lex fori* that were maintained or imposed inconsistently with the Articles because this result was thought to follow from the way in which the Articles had been given the force of law or because of some other principle of domestic law, the refusal to apply the regulations would follow from the principle of domestic law and not from Article VIII, Section 2(b). That provision requires each member to collaborate with all other members, but to conclude that it applies to domestic regulations as well would mean that the drafters had held the strange idea that each member could collaborate with itself.

(4) The crucial issue in the case was the severability of the transaction between Sharif and Latif, on the one hand, and between Sharif and Azad, on the other. The main line of reasoning by which the court permitted Sharif to recover was as follows. The exchange control regulations of Pakistan purported to apply to a contract only if one of the parties was in or resident in Pakistan. The check issued by Azad to Sharif was a sterling check issued in England by one resident of that country to another. It was not contrary to the exchange control regulations of Pakistan and therefore was not unenforceable under the United Kingdom's Bretton Woods legislation. Azad had argued that the sterling check was "affected with illegality" within the meaning of section 30 of the English Bills of Exchange Act, 1882. The conclusion of Lord Justice Diplock on this argument was that:

> Even assuming that the defendant's cheque was issued pursuant to a tripartite contract to which Latif was a party as well as the plaintiff and the defendant themselves—a matter which it was for the defendant to prove but which was never investigated at the trial—such tripartite

---

[31] Gold, *Fund Agreement in the Courts* (1962), p. 66.

contract would not have been "illegal" in English law, although it would have been unenforceable under the Bretton Woods Agreements Act, 1945, and the Bretton Woods Agreements Order, 1946, notwithstanding that the proper law of the contract was English law.

But the plaintiff is not suing on this contract, whether it was bipartite or tripartite. He is suing on the cheque which was issued by the defendant in performance of this contract. A cheque issued in performance of an agreement which is merely unenforceable is not "affected by illegality". . . .[32]

Lord Justice Diplock also pointed out that another defense open to the drawer of a check in an action by an immediate party to it is that the latter did not give value for it. Azad did not plead this defense; therefore, the subsequent history of the rupee check delivered by Sharif to Azad as consideration for the sterling check was not investigated in detail at the trial. Under the Pakistani law, the legal effect of the payment of the rupees into the blocked account was therefore unclear, but in any event it was not relevant because the defense of an absence of consideration had not been pleaded.

Even though the interpretation of various features of Article VIII, Section 2(b) gives powerful support to the realistic application of that provision, there is room for some disquiet when the result in this case is examined. It is true, as Lord Denning pointed out, that Azad would be damnified:

I see no reason why the plaintiff should not enforce the sterling cheques for £300 against Abdulla Azad. This enforcement will teach Azad a sharp lesson not to engage in transactions of this kind. He will have to pay £300 to Sharif and may get nothing back: for I do not suppose the authorities in Pakistan will allow the brother to use the 6,000 rupees. At all events, the matter is in their control. It is for them to say whether they will permit those rupees to be used by the brother in Pakistan or not.[33]

There is cold comfort in this reaction because Sharif would not be taught any lesson. He had been a party to all the arrangements that were designed to circumvent the exchange control regulations of Pakistan, but the court was enabling him to be made whole.

The decision that there were two distinct transactions and that the second of them was a wholly domestic English transaction is based on somewhat ambivalent reasoning. Sometimes, the result appears to follow from the interpretation of Pakistan's exchange control regula-

---

[32] [1966] 3 W.L.R. 1285, 1294.
[33] Ibid., at 1290.

tions, but sometimes it appears to be drawn from the English Bills of Exchange Act. If the issue was really the interpretation of the regulations—and it is submitted that this was the correct issue—perhaps the court might have held that Sharif's action on the check was an action to enforce a contract that offended the regulations. It was obvious to Sharif and Latif, if only because the name of the payee was left blank in the rupee check, that Sharif might sell that check to another for sterling. The absence of the name of the payee meant that Latif was giving Sharif implied authority to fill in the name of the payee in any way that Sharif thought fit. It might have been possible, therefore, to hold that, for the purposes of the regulations, Latif's transfer of the rupees was not complete until the name of Azad's brother was inserted as payee, and that Azad gave the sterling check to Sharif in return for Latif's transfer of the rupees to Azad's brother.

Alternatively, it might have been possible to hold that Latif made two transfers of the rupee balance, one to Sharif and another to Azad's brother. If either of these analyses had been accepted, it might have been concluded that the sterling check was given in return for an action by Latif, a resident of Pakistan, and that the transaction viewed in this way was caught by the exchange control regulations of Pakistan. In support of either of these suggested approaches, it might be argued that one purpose of the regulations was to avoid the transfer of the rupees without the accrual of the sterling counterpart to the exchange control authorities. The authorities had been deprived of sterling paid on two occasions as counterpart for the transfer, first by Sharif and then by Azad. They were as interested in the latter payment as in the former, for which the blocking when Azad's brother sought to draw was evidence.

The provisions of Pakistan's Foreign Exchange Regulation Act, 1947 that were considered relevant read as follows:

> Save as may be provided in and in accordance with any general or special exemption from the provisions of this sub-section which may be granted conditionally or unconditionally by the State Bank, no person in or resident in the provinces and the capital of the Federation shall—(e) make any payment to or for the credit of any person as consideration for or in association with (i) the receipt by any person of a payment . . . outside Pakistan; (ii) the creation or transfer in favour of any person of a right whether actual or contingent to receive a payment . . . outside Pakistan; (f) draw, issue or negotiate any bill of exchange . . . or acknowledge any debt, so that a right (whether actual

114

or contingent) to receive a payment is created or transferred in favour of any person as consideration for or in association with any matter referred to in cl.(e).

This language is broad, and the words "in association with" are particularly interesting. In addition, Section 21(1) of the Act, which was not mentioned, provides that:

No person shall enter into any contract or agreement which would directly or indirectly evade or avoid in any way the operation of any provision of this Act or any rule, direction or order made thereunder.

Could it have been held that all the steps in the arrangements were indirect evasions of the prohibited transfer of rupees from Latif to Azad's brother and contrary to the exchange control regulations under this provision also?

In the final analysis, of course, there would be no alternative to the decision adopted by the Court of Appeal if the exchange control regulations of Pakistan did not apply to the sterling check given by Azad to Sharif. This view was taken by the court, although it was the court's own construction of the regulations. This construction was not based on any statement by the exchange control authorities of Pakistan and was in opposition to such expert evidence as had been adduced.

It will be apparent that one of the most difficult issues raised by the case is the extent to which courts should be willing to dissect contractual arrangements put together with the design of evading exchange control regulations if the result of this dissection is to require the courts to carry out the design in some important respect. It has been noted that this was the result in *Sharif v. Azad.* It was also the result of the majority decision of the New York Court of Appeals in *Southwestern Shipping Corporation v. National City Bank of New York.*[34] The same tendency toward dissection is apparent in the decision of the Superior Court of Pennsylvania in *Varas v. Crown Life Insurance Company,*[35] although before this stage of the litigation had been reached, Article VIII, Section 2(b) had ceased to be applicable because Cuban exchange control regulations were involved and Cuba had withdrawn from the Fund. In cases of the kind referred to here, the result may be affected by judicial motivations that are given

---

[34] 173 N.Y.S. 2d 509 (1958); 178 N.Y.S. 2d 1019 (1958); 190 N.Y.S. 2d 352 (1959); certiorari denied 361 U.S. 895, 80 S. Ct. 198 (1959). Discussed by Gold, *Fund Agreement in the Courts* (1962), pp. 97–100, 102–108.

[35] 203 A. 2d 505; certiorari denied 382 U.S. 827, 86 S. Ct. 62 (1965).

greater weight than the consideration that the evader is being helped to succeed in his scheme of evasion. For example, in the *Southwestern* case the court may have wanted to hold the bank accountable as "repository" notwithstanding the machinations of the evaders. In *Sharif v. Azad* the court may have been concerned with the impact of Article VIII, Section 2(*b*) on negotiable instruments. These motivations are obviously not improper in view of the necessities of commercial and financial life, but the question to be faced is whether they should be given precedence over the public policy of Article VIII, Section 2(*b*).

FEDERAL REPUBLIC OF GERMANY

In *Loeffler-Behrens v. Beermann*, the parties, both German nationals, met in Brazil, and the plaintiff agreed to lend the defendant a sum of money for business purposes. The amount handed over by the plaintiff to the defendant in April 1959 was in dispute, but according to the plaintiff it was US$5,500. On April 14, 1959 the defendant gave the plaintiff a written promise, which read as follows:

> I confirm and declare that I undertake to deliver to [the plaintiff], residing here, the value of Cr$777,000, covered by a promissory note of the same value and with a due date of May 15, 1959, equivalent to exactly US$5,550. Sao Paulo, April 14, 1959.

On May 15, 1959 the defendant gave the plaintiff the promissory note that was mentioned, but the plaintiff failed to get payment of the debt or interest beyond US$66. On October 1, 1959, he obtained a new written promise to pay from the defendant, but this promise also was dishonored. The acknowledgment read as follows:

> I [the defendant] undertake to fulfill the following:
> 1. To do all I can to remit within the next two weeks US$100–200 towards repayment of the principal debt.
> 2. In any case, to pay the amount of US$5,550 by October 15, 1959.
> 3. The interest of 3 per cent monthly on US$5,550 for the period from May 15–October 15, 1959, that is to say, US$832.50 less the amount entered under (1) and the sum of US$66 that was paid to [the plaintiff] on August 13, 1959, will be paid by me by November 15, 1959.

The defendant returned to Europe and lived in Germany after 1961. The plaintiff remained resident in Brazil.

The plaintiff sued in the Mannheim Regional Court (*Landgericht*) on the basis of the documents of April 14 and October 1, 1959. The plaintiff argued that the defendant had received U.S. dollars and must repay dollars and that, in a loan between Germans, Brazilian exchange legislation was irrelevant. The defendant relied on a number of arguments, among them the argument that the acknowledgment of October 1, 1959 was void because it was in breach of Brazilian law to contract an obligation in foreign currency. The Regional Court gave judgment for the plaintiff, in substance, for the deutsche mark equivalent of US$5,500 (perhaps an erroneous reference to $5,550) plus interest, minus US$66 to be offset against interest, at the rate of exchange prevalent at the place and time of payment. Both parties appealed from the judgment of that court to the Karlsruhe Regional Court of Appeals (*Oberlandesgericht*).

On appeal, the defendant requested that the judgment of the lower court be rescinded or, alternatively, that if judgment was given for the plaintiff, it should not exceed the deutsche mark equivalent of 777,000 cruzeiros at the commercial bank free market rate less the equivalent of US$66 at the same rate. The defendant's main argument rested on the nullity of the two acknowledgments of debt under Brazilian law.

In its judgment of December 15, 1965 the Court of Appeals concurred in the finding of the lower court that the contract was governed by Brazilian law. At the time of the contract, both parties were domiciled and had their business interests in South America. The loan was to finance business to be carried on in Brazil, and repayment was to be made there. The reference to cruzeiros in the document of April 14, 1959 and the use of Portuguese in both documents confirmed that neither party contemplated the application of German law because of German nationality.

Brazilian law included Decree No. 23501 of November 27, 1933, in which Article 2 provided that it was "prohibited on pain of nullity, in contracts to be fulfilled in Brazil, to stipulate payment in a currency that is not the national currency according to its legal value." Expert opinion on Brazilian law advised that if there was the stipulation of payment in a foreign currency, Brazilian currency was payable.

The Court of Appeals held that it did not follow that this rule of Brazilian law had to be applied. Public law regulations, which included foreign exchange regulations, were not effective beyond the legislator's borders. Decree No. 23501 was obviously adopted for purposes of monetary and economic policy because of the instability of the cruzeiro, and according to prevailing opinion it would have to be regarded as territorial only.

The Court of Appeals continued:

To be sure, recognition of foreign monetary intervention beyond the sphere of power of the foreign country is possible on the basis of treaties under international law. In regard to international foreign exchange regulations, the necessity to recognize Brazilian foreign exchange regulations could arise from the International Monetary Fund Agreement, to which the Federal Republic acceded under the Law of July 28, 1952 . . . as did Brazil, according to information provided by the Deutsche Bundesbank on August 12, 1965. However, the Brazilian foreign exchange regulations relevant to the case before the court are not opposed to a judgment ordering the defendant to pay U.S. dollars or deutsche mark, because they are not "exchange control regulations" within the meaning of Article VIII(2)(b) of the Articles of Agreement of the International Monetary Fund. This is to be inferred from the information provided by the Deutsche Bundesbank and by the Legal Department of the International Monetary Fund. Therefore, the Court has to proceed on the assumption that the importation of foreign exchange into Brazil is not subject to control, in any case is not prohibited. Thus the matter rests with the above arguments that the Brazilian foreign exchange regulations are not applicable.

The Court of Appeals concluded that although Brazilian law governed the contractual liability, German law would have to be applied as the law governing the monetary liability. On this basis, the defendant owed the plaintiff US$5,550 plus interest, minus US$66 to be deducted from interest, and therefore, under German law, judgment had to be given for the deutsche mark equivalent.

This case is notable for a number of reasons. To begin with, it is the first case in which a court in a member country has approached the Fund with a formal request for a finding on whether certain exchange control regulations of another member were "exchange control regulations . . . maintained or imposed consistently with this Agreement" for the purposes of Article VIII, Section 2(*b*). In its interpretation of that provision, the Fund has said that it

> will be pleased to lend its assistance in connection with any problem which may arise in relation to the foregoing interpretation or any other aspect of Article VIII, Section 2(b). In addition, the Fund is prepared to advise whether particular exchange control regulations are maintained or imposed consistently with the Fund Agreement.[36]

In practice, the Fund has not gone beyond assistance under the second of these sentences, and on all other occasions on which it has given advice on the consistency of exchange control regulations it has done

---

[36] *Selected Decisions*, Third Issue, p. 74. (*Selected Decisions*, Ninth Issue, pp. 201–202.)

so at the request of a litigant. In the Karlsruhe case, the request was made by the court itself in a letter transmitted to the Fund by the Executive Director appointed by the Federal Republic of Germany. The court's letter was addressed to the Managing Director of the Fund, and the Executive Directors authorized the General Counsel of the Fund to reply in accordance with a draft that was laid before them.

A second interesting feature of the case is that in order to reply to the question whether Brazilian Decree No. 23501 was an exchange control regulation that was maintained or imposed consistently with the Articles, the reply had necessarily to express a view on the meaning of this concept in relation to *cours forcé* legislation. Article 1 of the Brazilian decree declared that any agreement was void if it called for payment in gold or foreign currency or aimed at nonrecognition of the enforced rate of exchange for the Brazilian paper currency. Article 2 has been noted already.

The General Counsel's reply stated that the Articles of Agreement contain no definition of "exchange control regulations" and that the Fund has not interpreted these words. In the opinion of the General Counsel, however, they did not include laws that had been designed to ensure the acceptance of paper currency as legal tender in the country of issue. The decree applied even between residents and even though no payment in foreign exchange or gold was stipulated, which suggested that it had not been adopted for the purpose of husbanding Brazil's foreign exchange resources. The court's attention was drawn to *de Sayve v. de la Valdene*,[37] in which a New York court noted, without any expression of dissent, that it had been conceded that the category of foreign exchange control laws did not include French legislation prohibiting clauses in French domestic contracts calling for payment in gold or foreign currency. In view of these considerations, it was suggested that the question of the consistency of the decree with the Articles did not arise.

The Karlsruhe Court of Appeals accepted the view expressed in the Fund's reply. But it is not clear why, although the letter to the Fund set forth only Article 1 of the Brazilian decree, the court referred solely to Article 2 in its opinion. It must be said, however, that the language of these Articles in the Portuguese original and in German or English translation is not clear. Article 1 seems, on the whole, to constitute the prohibition of gold and foreign currency

---

[37] 124 N.Y.S. 2d 143 (1953). Gold, *Fund Agreement in the Courts* (1962), p. 74.

clauses, and Article 2 to prohibit payment at some rate of exchange for Brazilian currency other than the official rate. If this reading of them is correct, Article 1 would have greater relevance to the case than Article 2.

In purporting to accept the view expressed in the Fund's letter, the court distinguished between "foreign exchange regulations" and "foreign exchange control regulations," a distinction that could produce confusion. The concept in Article VIII, Section 2(b) is "exchange control regulations." In addition, the court concluded that because exchange control regulations were not involved, there was no bar to a judgment ordering the defendant to pay U.S. dollars or deutsche mark, and no control or prohibition of the importation of foreign exchange into Brazil. Whether or not the court was justified in assuming that exchange control regulations would not prevent payments in foreign exchange by nonresidents to residents, it seems clear enough that the Brazilian decree, as *cours forcé* legislation, was drafted in terms that applied even between a resident and a nonresident.

Finally, the case sharply illustrates the change that Article VIII, Section 2(b) has brought about in connection with the recognition of the exchange control regulations of other countries. Had the Brazilian decree fallen within the scope of Article VIII, Section 2(b), the Karlsruhe Court of Appeals would have been willing to recognize it. But the decree did not, and therefore the court felt free to ignore it even though it was part of the law that governed the contractual obligation. The court held that the decree was part of Brazilian public law and therefore not entitled to recognition.

Exchange Control and Nationalization

Indonesian Corporation P.T. Escomptobank v. N.V. Assurantie Maatschappij de Nederlanden van 1845 [38] poses questions of the relationship of Article VIII, Section 2(b) to nationalization. A Netherlands insurance company (the N. Corporation) owned all the shares in five Indonesian insurance companies. One of these companies (the M. Company) had a number of accounts, in which the other subsidiaries also had rights, in U.S. dollars, sterling, Hong Kong dollars, Malayan dollars, and Netherlands guilders with an Indonesian bank (Escomptobank). On November 26, 1959 the M. Company,

---

[38] *Nederlands Tijdschrift voor Internationaal Recht (Netherlands International Law Review)*, Vol. XIII, No. 1 (1966), pp. 58–70.

acting on behalf of itself and the other subsidiaries, assigned its claims against Escomptobank to the N. Corporation. The assignment was executed in the Netherlands by the Managing Director of the M. Company. The N. Corporation attached the assets of Escomptobank in the Netherlands and brought an action for payment of the balances and validation of the attachment.

The subsidiaries had been brought under state control by Indonesian decrees of 1957 and 1958 and subsequently nationalized with retroactive effect by a decree of 1960. According to all the courts that heard the case, this nationalization was confined to Netherlands-owned enterprises, was without compensation, and was intended to exercise pressure on the Netherlands in connection with the dispute over the western part of New Guinea. Escomptobank argued that these decrees deprived the Managing Director of the M. Company of any power to make the assignment to the N. Corporation; that the assignment was in violation of Indonesian exchange control law because a license had not been granted by the Indonesian authorities; and that the balances could not be collected without a license. The Foreign Exchange Control Ordinance of 1940 adopted by the Netherlands East Indies prohibited residents of what was later Indonesia from disposing of foreign currency and foreign claims to nonresidents, but the M. Company had received a general license to dispose of the foreign currencies in question. This license was canceled under measures adopted by Indonesia in 1958 in connection with the imposition of state control.

The District Court of The Hague gave judgment for the N. Corporation. It dismissed Escomptobank's argument that a Netherlands court could not review the legality of Indonesia's acts of state, on the ground that this doctrine did not apply to violations of international law, and the nationalization was a violation because it was without compensation, discriminatory, and political in motivation. The termination of the general license and the control of the balances were also affected by this violation of international law. The court continued:

> Apart from this, legislation of a public law character such as laws dealing with foreign exchange control, has, as a matter of principle, only territorial effect. Since the assignment was contracted in the Netherlands and concerned claims which, for Indonesia, were foreign claims, i.e., balances in foreign currencies to be collected abroad, there is no reason at all to consider them as being governed by Indonesian foreign exchange control law.

Escomptobank further invoked the Agreement concluded at Bretton Woods in July 1944 relative to the International Monetary Fund to which both the Netherlands and Indonesia were parties. This Agreement establishes an obligation on the part of the contracting States to recognise each other's foreign exchange control legislation. This provision was superseded by the Financial and Economic Agreement entered into by the Netherlands and Indonesia at the Round Table Conference. This Agreement regulated foreign exchange control matters, but it has been unilaterally broken by Indonesia. Consequently, a Netherlands court has no obligation to take into account agreements previously made with Indonesia concerning foreign exchange control.[39]

Whatever may be the validity of the principle in the first paragraph of this quotation as a principle of private international law, it cannot operate against Article VIII, Section 2(b). Under that provision the law governing an assignment is not relevant. As for the argument that the claims were "foreign claims" from Indonesia's standpoint, this classification does not mean that they were beyond the scope of Indonesian exchange control for the purpose of the provision. The court disposed of the argument that Article VIII, Section 2(b) now required recognition of Indonesian exchange control legislation with the reply that the provision had been superseded by the Financial and Economic Agreement. This statement cannot be taken literally. It is impossible to see on what basis the bilateral treaty between the Netherlands and Indonesia could affect the obligation imposed by Article VIII, Section 2(b), which binds all members under the multilateral Articles of Agreement of the Fund.

Perhaps what the court meant was that Indonesia had undertaken under the bilateral agreement not to impose exchange control of the kind that it imposed in 1958, and therefore that under this agreement Indonesia had committed itself to the Netherlands not to exercise the power to impose exchange controls that it had under the Articles of the Fund. This version of the court's opinion would not mean that Article VIII, Section 2(b) as such had been superseded, but that the provision did not require the recognition of exchange control legislation that had been imposed in violation of some other international agreement under which a country undertook not to have such legislation. This argument could not be considered seriously if the other agreement were deemed to be inconsistent with the provisions of the Articles. But even if there were no such inconsistency, there would still be a problem because Article VIII, Section 2(b) speaks of ex-

---

[39] *Ibid.*, at 61.

change control regulations that are maintained or imposed "consistently with this Agreement" and not consistently with other agreements.[40]

Escomptobank appealed to the Court of Appeal of The Hague, which upheld the decision of the lower court. Escomptobank had argued that the act of state doctrine did not depend on any demonstration that the act for which recognition was demanded was in accordance with international law. The Court of Appeal refused to accept this argument as valid and held that it would disregard acts of state that were inconsistent with international law when the contest was between private parties. The Court of Appeal also refused to upset the decision on the basis of Indonesian exchange control. It gave a number of reasons for this conclusion but did not refer to the Fund's Articles.

Escomptobank appealed to the Supreme Court and advanced a series of grievances, many of which alleged the erroneous application of the Articles of Agreement and among which the one relating to exchange control was argued as follows:

> The Court of Appeal did not evaluate Escomptobank's argument that the claims of the subsidiaries, which were transferred to *de Nederlanden van 1845* were governed by Indonesian law, the foreign exchange control legislation included, and irrespective of the circumstances under which the assignment took place. That legislation should in each case be represented in so far as it declares contracts entered into under violation of its provisions null and void under civil law. As Escomptobank argues, this is the case here. In pursuance of rules of Netherlands private international law, these provisions preclude *de Nederlanden van 1845* from collecting the equivalent in Netherlands currency of balances in foreign currencies due to her subsidiaries. The Financial and Economic Agreement and its annexes as well as the membership of both countries of the International Monetary Fund both create an obligation for the Netherlands and Indonesia to collaborate in the field of foreign exchange control and to recognise reciprocally

---

[40] The implications of Article VIII, Section 6 would have to be considered in connection with this issue: *"Consultation between members regarding existing international agreements.*—Where under this Agreement a member is authorized in the special or temporary circumstances specified in the Agreement to maintain or establish restrictions on exchange transactions, and there are other engagements between members entered into prior to this Agreement which conflict with the application of such restrictions, the parties to such engagements will consult with one another with a view to making such mutually acceptable adjustments as may be necessary. The provisions of this Article shall be without prejudice to the operation of Article VII, Section 5."

each other's law in this matter. This obligation further entails that no contracts shall be recognised [if] entered into under violation of the foreign exchange control legislation of the country the law of which governs the contract. The courts shall not refuse to enforce this legislation on the ground that it would be irreconcilable with principles of public policy [of] the State of the *forum*. This conclusion is not changed by the fact that the assignment also has certain factors connecting it with the Netherlands legal order.[41]

The Supreme Court dismissed the appeal. It found that Indonesia had established the control and nationalization without compensation of the five subsidiaries. The court held that the Indonesian measures of nationalization could not be relied on in the Netherlands to challenge the disposition of rights in Indonesia by a company that had its seat in Indonesia if the shares in it were owned in the Netherlands. It was repugnant to Netherlands public policy that legal effect be given to foreign measures enacted to prejudice Netherlands interests in the manner and for the purpose involved in this case. The Supreme Court held that to reach this result it was not necessary for the Court of Appeal to decide whether the Indonesian measures violated international law.[42]

On the argument based on exchange control, the Supreme Court was willing to hold that claims arising from the balances and the assignment were governed by Indonesian law, but even if, in normal circumstances, the assignment and collection required a license under Indonesian exchange control provisions, those provisions could not be invoked in this case. The N. Corporation would not be granted a license, and therefore application of the exchange control provisions would have exactly the same effect as recognizing those measures of nationalization that had been held repugnant to Netherlands public policy.

The court continued as follows:

This conclusion is not changed by the provisions of the Financial and Economic Agreement and its annexes, mentioned in the grievance —in so far as they may still be operative—, since they relate to regular financial intercourse between the Netherlands and Indonesia and cannot be deemed to be applicable to the very exceptional circumstances created by the Indonesian measures against Netherlands interests.

---

[41] Fn. 38 *supra*, at 67.

[42] April 17, 1964, N.J. 1965, No. 22, pp. 81–98. On this point, the decision has been followed in *Kjellberg Elektroden und Maschinen G.m.b.H. v. N.V. Nederlandse Kjellberg Elektroden Fabrick NEKEF, Nederlands Tijdschrift voor Internationaal Recht,* Vol. XIII, No. 2 (1966), pp. 203–206.

Nor do the articles of the Agreement of Bretton Woods which have been cited, constitute a bar, since they may likewise be held to concern exclusively regular financial intercourse between the States.[43]

Whatever the merits of the Supreme Court's judgment, it is doubtful that its gloss on Article VIII, Section 2(b) can be accepted. The court held that the provisions of the Articles that had been cited are confined to "regular financial intercourse" between states.[44] It is not clear what this means but it may be that exchange control for economic reasons was what the court had in mind. The Fund has made it clear, however, that "restrictions on payments and transfers for current international transactions" in Article VIII, Section 2(a) include "all restrictions on current payments and transfers, irrespective of their motivation and the circumstances in which they are imposed."[45] The decision of the Executive Directors from which these words are taken established a special procedure for the approval of one category of restrictions, namely, those imposed by members solely for the preservation of national or international security. This reference is not meant to suggest that the Indonesian restrictions in the present case were of this character, but the Fund's decision shows that restrictions that fall within the words of Article VIII, Section 2(a) because of their form are not excluded from the scope of that provision because of the motives with which they are imposed. It should follow that the words "such controls as are necessary to regulate international capital movements" in Article VI, Section 3 are also comprehensive and not limited by motive. With this understanding of restrictions and controls, it becomes impossible to hold that the words "exchange control regulations . . . maintained or imposed consistently with this Agreement" in Article VIII, Section 2(b) are narrower in scope than the provisions of the Articles authorizing the maintenance or imposition of the controls.

It does not follow that the decision of the Supreme Court was wrong and that Article VIII, Section 2(b) did require recognition of the Indonesian measures that were in issue. A much closer look at them would be necessary before any such conclusion could be ac-

---

[43] Fn. 38 *supra*, at 69.

[44] The English interpretation in *Netherlands International Law Review* of the judgment uses the words "may . . . be held," which are ambiguous and may suggest a somewhat tentative view. The report in *Nederlandse Jurisprudentie*, however (see fn. 42), has been translated as follows: "because these, too, were intended to apply only to regular financial intercourse between states."

[45] *Selected Decisions*, Third Issue, pp. 75–76. (Also, *Selected Decisions*, Ninth Issue, pp. 203–204.)

cepted. For example, were the measures imposed consistently with the Articles? If they were not adopted for balance of payments reasons, then, to the extent that they restricted payments and transfers for current international transactions, they required the approval of the Fund under Article VIII, Section 2(*a*), even though Indonesia had the benefit of the transitional arrangements of Article XIV, Section 2. To the extent that the measures were capital controls, and therefore in themselves did not require the approval of the Fund, were they exercised in "a manner which will restrict payments for current transactions or which will unduly delay transfers of funds in settlement of commitments"? And again, if the measures were confiscatory because they did not provide for compensation, were they "exchange control regulations" within the meaning of Article VIII, Section 2(*b*)?

One important aspect of the case is that the Supreme Court, unlike the two lower courts, found it unnecessary to deal with the act of state doctrine and its relationship to international law. It decided that it would not recognize the effects of the Indonesian decree on the independent ground of repugnancy to Netherlands public policy. If, however, the case was one that fell within Article VIII, Section 2(*b*), the court would not have been able to rely on domestic public policy to refuse recognition of Indonesian exchange control regulations. This conclusion has been made clear in the Fund's interpretation of Article VIII, Section 2(*b*).[46]

The decision of the Netherlands Supreme Court on public policy made it possible for the court to avoid the issue faced by the U.S. Supreme Court in the famous *Sabbatino* case.[47] In that case, the Supreme Court held that courts in the United States "will not examine the validity of a taking of property within its own territory by a foreign sovereign government, extant and recognized by this country at the time of suit, in the absence of a treaty or other unambiguous agreement regarding controlling legal principles, even if the complaint alleges that the taking violates customary international law."[48] One author has raised the question whether the *Sabbatino* decision means that courts in the United States will no longer be concerned with the question whether the exchange control regulations of another member are consistent with provisions of the Articles.[49]

---

[46] *Ibid.*, pp. 73–74. (*Selected Decisions*, Ninth Issue, pp. 201–202.)

[47] *Banco Nacional de Cuba v. Sabbatino*, 376 U.S. 398, 84 S. Ct. 923 (1964).

[48] 376 U.S. 398, 428.

[49] Richard R. Paradise, "Cuban Refugee Insureds and the Articles of Agreement of the International Monetary Fund," *University of Florida Law Review*, Vol. 18 (1965), pp. 29–77, particularly pp. 66–67, 74–75.

In other words, will the courts recognize exchange control regulations even though they are inconsistent with the Articles? The *Sabbatino* case, however, dealt with the taking of property, and it is not at all clear that cases of this kind, or that all cases of this kind, would be considered exchange control regulations. For example, an outright confiscation, i.e., a taking without compensation of any kind, would clearly be beyond the scope of exchange control regulations as these are normally understood. The centralization of foreign exchange, which is a normal feature of exchange control, is not the same as the expropriation of foreign exchange. Moreover, the *Sabbatino* case itself makes a reservation for a treaty or other unambiguous agreement, and the Fund's Articles would be within that reservation. Whatever ambiguities may be found in Article VIII, Section 2(*b*), there is no ambiguity about the principle that the recognition of exchange control regulations under that provision is confined to those that are consistent with the Articles. There seems to be little reason, therefore, to fear that the *Sabbatino* case will lead to results contrary to Article VIII, Section 2(*b*), and there is no more reason to expect such results under the Netherlands doctrine of public policy.

Exchange Surrender Requirements

In *Bacolod Murcia Milling Co., Inc. v. Central Bank of the Philippines*,[50] the Supreme Court of the Philippines refused to hold that Circular No. 20, promulgated by the Central Bank on December 9, 1949, was null and void. The circular required recipients of foreign exchange to sell it to an authorized agent of the Central Bank within one business day following receipt. A leading issue in the case was whether the circular was authorized by Section 74 of the charter of the Central Bank (Republic Act No. 265), and various aspects of the Fund's Articles were relied upon in argument and also in the petition for rehearing.[51] That petition was denied,[52] partly on the ground that the issue as to the enforcement of Circular No. 20 had become moot because the circular had been replaced by Circular No. 133, promulgated by the Central Bank on January 21, 1962 to implement the later Republic Act No. 2609. After the expiration of that Act, Circular No. 133 was extended by Circular No. 171. The effect of these two

---

[50] *Official Gazette, Republic of the Philippines*, Vol. 60 (September 7, 1964), p. 5533. (Hereinafter cited as *Official Gazette*.)

[51] See pp. 31–35 in this volume.

[52] *Official Gazette*, p. 5546.

circulars has now been considered by the Supreme Court in later litigation.

The later case is *Chamber of Agriculture and Natural Resources of the Philippines, et al. v. Central Bank of the Philippines*, in which the validity was contested of circulars requiring exporters to surrender 20 per cent of their receipts to the Central Bank at the par value of 2 pesos per U.S. dollar and authorizing the sale of the rest in the free market. The petitioners, seven exporters, insisted that the continuation of the surrender requirement was illegal, relying, inter alia, on the decision in the *Bacolod Murcia* case and on the fact that the four-year period prescribed for decontrol by the later statute had expired four years after April 25, 1960. The circular establishing the 20 per cent surrender requirement had been passed in accordance with the provisions of that Act, but the circular had been extended by a circular taking effect on April 25, 1964, under Section 74 of the Central Bank's charter. Therefore, the issue was raised again whether Section 74 empowered the Central Bank to impose exchange surrender requirements at the rate fixed by the Central Bank in authorizing it to subject foreign exchange transactions to suspension, restriction, and licensing. The opinion in the *Bacolod Murcia* case had concluded that Section 74 could not be given this meaning but found for the Central Bank on other grounds. It was not clear in the earlier case whether this interpretation was accepted only by the judge who wrote the opinion or whether it was shared by other judges. In the later case, this ambiguity has been resolved. Mr. Justice Reyes, with whom eight of the other nine judges concurred, held that the interpretation must be taken to have been that of the author of the opinion only and not of the majority of the court. The court then held by the same majority of nine to one that Section 74 did give the Central Bank authority to compel the surrender of exchange at the legal parity and that the circular was a valid exercise of this power.

There is no need to go into the complexities discussed in the judicial opinions because, in contrast to the *Bacolod Murcia* case, few of them concerned the Fund. An interesting aspect of the Articles, however, was involved in the court's treatment of petitioners' argument that the surrender of 20 per cent of export receipts was confiscatory. The court found this an "exaggeration" in view of the payment for it at the legal parity. The court conceded that the surrendered exchange was resold by the Central Bank at a higher rate in terms of pesos for dollars, so that the Bank realized a profit. The court pointed out, however, that this profit was credited to a "Revaluation of International Reserve" account, under Section 44 of the Bank's charter, and it could not be included in the Bank's computation of its annual profit or loss. Under Section 44, any profit on a revaluation must be offset against any amounts payable to the Fund or the International Bank for Reconstruction and Development as a consequence of the revaluation, and any balance carried to a special segregated account. In the case of the Fund, the reference is to Article IV, Section 8, under which a member is required to maintain the gold value of the Fund's holdings of the member's currency, and under which a member must pay further currency to the Fund on a devaluation or depreciation of the member's currency.[53]

In connection with the objection that the surrender requirement was an invalid exercise of police power, the court quoted with approval the following passage in an earlier judgment:

> . . . this Court held that Circular No. 20, which subjects to licensing by the Central Bank all transactions in gold and foreign exchange, was in fact approved by the President of the Philippines. As regards the necessity of approval by the International Monetary Fund, this Court said in People vs. Koh, *supra*, that "it is not incumbent upon the prosecution to prove that the provisions of Circular No. 20 complied with all pertinent international agreements binding on our Government. The Central Bank and the President certify that it accords therewith, and it is presumed that said officials knew whereof they spoke, and that they performed their duties properly. It is rather for the defense to show conflict, if any, between the Circular and our international commitments."[54]

The issue raised in this passage involves that part of Section 74 of the Central Bank's charter under which the measures adopted pursuant to the provision "shall be subject to any executive and international agreements to which the Republic of the Philippines is a party." The introduction of an exchange surrender requirement is not a restriction on payments and transfers for current international transactions and therefore does not require the approval of the Fund under Article VIII, Section 2(a).[55] Nevertheless, if the measure involves a new effective rate of exchange, the Fund's approval would be required under the Fund's jurisdiction with respect to multiple

---

[53] Gold, *Maintenance of the Gold Value of the Fund's Assets*, IMF Pamphlet Series, No. 6 (Washington, 1965), hereinafter cited as Gold, Pamphlet No. 6. Revaluation in the charter must be taken to mean any change in valuation and not simply an increase in the value of the currency.

[54] *People v. Tan*, L.–9275, June 30, 1960.

[55] Gold, Pamphlet No. 3, p. 8.

currency practices.[56] If the proportion of export proceeds to be surrendered is varied, with part paid for at the parity and the rest sold in
the free market, there is a new effective rate of exchange formed by
the combination of the two.

In a concurring opinion, Mr. Justice Bengzon dealt at somewhat
greater length with the argument petitioners had based on the following language in Section 1 of Act No. 2609:

> In implementing the provisions of this Act, along with other monetary,
> credit and fiscal measures to stabilize the economy, the monetary
> authorities shall take steps for the adoption of a four-year program of
> gradual decontrol.

The court held that this provision did not necessarily mean complete
decontrol by the end of the four years for which the Act ran. The
concurring opinion reads:

> . . . Congress must have been aware, as it is presumed to be aware, of
> the Articles of Agreement of the International Monetary Fund, to
> which the Philippines is a signatory, providing, in effect, that before
> exchange restrictions may be withdrawn a stable economic position
> must first be in existence. . . .

For this proposition, Mr. Justice Bengzon quoted Article XIV, Section 2 of the Articles and gave special emphasis to the last sentence:

> In particular, members shall withdraw restrictions maintained or im-
> posed under this Section as soon as they are satisfied that they will
> be able, in the absence of such restrictions, to settle their balance of
> payments in a manner which will not unduly encumber their access to
> the resources of the Fund.[57]

---

[56] *Selected Decisions*, Third Issue, pp. 84–91 (*Selected Decisions*, Ninth Issue,
pp. 223–25). The Central Bank relied on this decision in its brief (pp. 34–55) and
argued that the Fund had given its approval (pp. 106–107).

[57] Cf. *Selected Decisions*, Third Issue, p. 82 (*Selected Decisions*, Ninth Issue,
pp. 209–11): "Before members give notice that they are accepting the obligations
of Article VIII, Sections 2, 3, and 4, it would be desirable that, as far as possible,
they eliminate measures which would require the approval of the Fund, and that
they satisfy themselves that they are not likely to need recourse to such measures
in the foreseeable future."

4

The Fund Agreement
in the Courts—X*

All the cases discussed in this latest contribution to the jurisprudence involving the Articles of Agreement of the International Monetary Fund deal with Article VIII, Section 2(b):

> Exchange contracts which involve the currency of any member and which are contrary to the exchange control regulations of that member maintained or imposed consistently with this Agreement shall be unenforceable in the territories of any member. In addition, members may, by mutual accord, cooperate in measures for the purpose of making the exchange control regulations of either member more effective, provided that such measures and regulations are consistent with this Agreement.

All the cases were decided by the highest tribunal within the jurisdiction in which the proceedings were conducted.

In the first of the cases to be discussed, the Court of Appeals of the State of New York examined the relationship of the act of state doctrine to exchange control. The other five cases dealt with the unenforceability of certain exchange contracts. Three were decided by the Federal Supreme Court of Germany, and the other two by the Court of Cassation of France.

Exchange Control and Act of State

In *French v. Banco Nacional de Cuba* [1] the Court of Appeals of New York considered the relationship of exchange control to the act of

---

* Originally published in July 1972.
[1] 295 N.Y.S. 2d 433, 23 N.Y. 2d 46 (1968).

state doctrine, and held by a decision of four judges to three that an act of state of Cuba prevented the plaintiff from succeeding on her claim. The Currency Stabilization Fund of Cuba had issued certificates to Ritter, an investor in Cuba, in respect of the proceeds of his investment in that country. The certificates stated that the owner of them, on tendering a certain number of Cuban pesos, would receive a check drawn on the defendant's New York account for an equal number of U.S. dollars. The certificates had been signed by both the Currency Stabilization Fund and the defendant. Ritter presented certificates but was refused dollars under Decision No. 346 of the Currency Stabilization Fund. The Decision suspended the processing of certificates "for the time being." It had been adopted pursuant to decrees of the Cuban Government that prevented U.S. and other investors from receiving currency other than Cuban pesos in respect of their Cuban investments.[2] Ritter assigned the certificates to the plaintiff, who obtained a judgment on them in an action in the Supreme Court of New York. In an appeal from this judgment to the Appellate Division, which failed, one of the defenses was that Decision No. 346 was an act of state of the sovereign Government of Cuba, which U.S. courts could not question. This defense was reargued before the Court of Appeals of New York.

It has been affirmed by the *Sabbatino* case[3] that courts in the United States will not inquire into the validity under the law of a foreign country of acts performed by the government of that country within its own territory. The Supreme Court said in the *Sabbatino* case that:

> . . . [R]ather than laying down or reaffirming an inflexible and all-encompassing rule in this case, we decide only that the Judicial Branch will not examine the validity of a taking of property within its own territory by a foreign sovereign government, extant and recognized by this country at the time of suit, in the absence of a treaty or other unambiguous agreement regarding controlling legal principles, even if the complaint alleges that the taking violates customary international law.[4]

---

[2] Joseph Gold, "The Cuban Insurance Cases and the Articles of the Fund," pp. 43–94 in this volume (hereinafter cited as Gold, "Cuban Insurance Cases"); Joseph Gold, "The International Monetary Fund and the International Recognition of Exchange Control Regulations: The Cuban Insurance Cases," *Revue de la Banque* (1967), pp. 523–38.

[3] *Banco Nacional de Cuba v. Sabbatino*, 376 U.S. 398, 84 S. Ct. 923 (1964). See pp. 126–27 and also pp. 120–25 in this volume.

[4] 376 U.S., at 428; 84 S. Ct., at 940.

The Court of Appeals noted that although the Cuban action had imposed losses on Ritter, they resulted from an exchange control regulation that did not amount to a "taking" or "expropriation" as in the *Sabbatino* case.[5] The court held that the *Sabbatino* principle must surely apply to the lesser action of the imposition of exchange control.

If Cuba had been a member of the Fund at the time of the suit, would the Fund's Articles have been considered "a treaty or other unambiguous agreement regarding controlling legal principles" on the ground that the Articles apply to exchange control and Decision No. 346 was an exchange control regulation? The question did not arise, but the court noted that it might have arisen. A footnote to the opinion of Chief Judge Fuld, who delivered the opinion of the majority of the Court of Appeals, states that no treaty had been cited:

> In point of fact, Cuba withdrew, in 1964, from the International Monetary Fund Agreement, the only arguably applicable international instrument, and the defendant does not claim its benefits.[6]

Article VIII, Section 2(*b*) requires courts to deny the enforcement of exchange contracts when they are contrary to exchange control regulations that are consistent with the Articles. The provision is intended to ensure that a forum will recognize exchange control regulations for this purpose even though, before the country in which the forum is situated became a member of the Fund, recognition would have been refused on the principle that the exchange control regulations of other countries offended the public policy of the forum. The decision of the New York Court of Appeals recognized the effect of the exchange control regulations of Cuba even though they might offend the public policy of New York and even though the Articles were inapplicable.

The act of state doctrine as applied by the Court of Appeals produces a liberal attitude to the exchange control regulations of other countries. The attitude might be less liberal if it implied some limitation by analogy to the concept of the "taking" or "expropriation" of property within Cuba. A limitation of this kind, however, is not consistent with the court's treatment of the Hickenlooper Amendment to the U.S. Federal Foreign Assistance Act of 1961,[7] which the U.S.

---

[5] "The Government of Cuba, by its Decision No. 346, has actually done nothing more than enact an exchange control regulation similar to regulations enacted or promulgated by many other countries, including our own. . . . A currency regulation which alters either the value or character of the money to be paid in satisfaction of contracts is not a 'confiscation' or 'taking' " (295 N.Y.S. 2d, at 442).

[6] 295 N.Y.S. at 442.

[7] U.S. Code, tit. 22, §2370, subd. (e), par. (2); 78 U.S. Stat. 1009 (1964), as amended 79 U.S. Stat. 653 (1965).

Congress passed as a result of the *Sabbatino* decision. The amendment declares that no court in the United States shall decline on the ground of the act of state doctrine to make a determination on the merits giving effect to the principles of international law in a case in which "a claim of title or other right to property" is asserted by any party, including a foreign state, "based upon (or traced through) a confiscation or other taking" by an act of that state in violation of the principles of international law. The court pointed out that before Decision No. 346, Ritter had pesos and a contract made in Cuba, governed at all times by the law of Cuba and to be performed there by the delivery of a check for U.S. dollars in return for the pesos. He had not held any specific fund of dollars that had been taken from him. Neither had his pesos or his contract right been taken from him and vested in the Cuban Government or anyone else. Therefore, in the opinion of the majority, there was no confiscation or other taking of property within the meaning of the Hickenlooper Amendment. Those concepts in the amendment were not intended to include breaches of contract.

With this conclusion, it was not necessary for the majority to consider whether the action of the Cuban Government violated principles of international law, but Chief Judge Fuld decided to examine this question because the minority took the view that there was a taking within the meaning of the Hickenlooper Amendment. He concluded that exchange control was an essential function of government and that the exercise of it had become common practice. An exchange control measure was not contrary to international law if it was "reasonably necessary" to "protect the foreign exchange resources of the state,"[8] and this was the nature of Decision No. 346.

Judge Hopkins, who concurred in the opinion of Chief Judge Fuld, held that the act of state in this case was the refusal of the defendant, an instrumentality of the Cuban Government, to perform its obligations under a contract to be performed within Cuba, and it was not necessary to regard the exchange control regulations as the act of state. They were merely the basis on which the defendant justified its refusal to perform. On the view taken by Judge Hopkins, it could not be said that the case established that exchange control in itself was an act of state. It does not necessarily follow from this view of the case, however, that Judge Hopkins would have held that the act of state doctrine could apply to a refusal to perform by the instru-

---

[8] 295 N.Y.S. 2d, at 449, citing *Restatement of the Law, Second, Foreign Relations Law of the United States*, §198.

mentality of a government but not to a refusal by a private party.[9] The impression that Judge Hopkins was not narrowing the doctrine in this way is strengthened by the concurrence of Chief Judge Fuld in this separate opinion. If in the opinion of Judge Hopkins there is a bias in favor of the defense of an act of state when asserted by governmental instrumentalities, it is in contrast to the dissenting opinion of Judge Keating. In that opinion, there are *dicta* that suggest a greater readiness to allow private parties to rely on the defense.[10]

Judge Keating and two other judges dissented on the ground that the evidence did not establish that Decision No. 346 applied to the certificates held by the plaintiff. But even if the Decision did apply to them, the defense of act of state would not be available because the facts showed not merely a breach of contract but "a confiscation clothed in the disguise of a valid currency regulation."[11] In their view, the word "property" in the Hickenlooper Amendment included contractual rights.

In the main dissenting opinion, Judge Keating said that New York law had "always recognized the validity of regulations by foreign countries to protect their economies," but Decision No. 346 was not "a legitimate exercise of a sovereign nation's right to protect its international economic position."[12]

> There is sufficient authority in international law for the proposition that a taking of property can occur without first depriving the owner of legal title if the foreigner is effectively deprived of all benefit of the property. . . . Moreover, simply because Decision No. 346 was initially necessitated by Cuba's need to protect its foreign exchange, it does not follow that it remains valid under international law permanently. . . . I see no reason to determine the validity of Decision No. 346 by a simple reference to the date it was enacted, July 15, 1959. Though this might be justified when the currency regulations of a country are in accord with the principles of the International Monetary Fund, even though the enacting country is not a member or has subsequently withdrawn, this view is not justified when these monetary policies are inconsistent with the purpose of the Fund. (International Monetary Fund . . . art. VI, §3. This section contains the limitation that "no member may exercise these controls in a manner which will restrict payments for current transactions or which will unduly delay transfers of funds in settlement of commitments.")[13]

---

[9] There is an ambiguous footnote on this question on p. 452 of 295 N.Y.S. 2d.
[10] For example, 295 N.Y.S. 2d, at 470.
[11] 295 N.Y.S. 2d, at 460.
[12] *Ibid.*, at 469.
[13] *Ibid.*, at 470.

Judge Keating seems to be asserting a number of propositions in this passage. First, exchange control regulations are valid under international law if they are imposed by a member of the Fund and are consistent with its Articles. Second, the exchange control regulations of a nonmember or former member of the Fund may be valid under international law. In this connection, it should be recalled that Cuba withdrew from the Fund on April 2, 1964. Third, exchange control regulations may be valid when adopted but may become invalid later. It is certainly true that exchange control regulations may cease to be consistent with the Articles, for example, by the withdrawal or expiration of the Fund's approval of them. Fourth, in no circumstances will exchange control regulations be valid under international law if they are inconsistent with the principle of Article VI, Section 3 of the Articles.

The last proposition appears to treat Article VI, Section 3 as declaratory of nontreaty international law and therefore applicable to the exchange control regulations of all countries, whether they are members or ex-members of the Fund or have never been members. The provision reads as follows:

Controls of capital transfers

Members may exercise such controls as are necessary to regulate international capital movements, but no member may exercise these controls in a manner which will restrict payments for current transactions or which will unduly delay transfers of funds in settlement of commitments, except as provided in Article VII, Section 3(*b*), and in Article XIV, Section 2.

Article VI, Section 3 authorizes members to regulate international capital movements, provided that this authority is exercised without restricting payments for current transactions or unduly delaying transfers of funds in settlement of commitments. These qualifications do not require a member to permit transfers in settlement of all commitments without regard to the restrictions that it is applying consistently with the Articles. If it applies restrictions on capital movements or applies restrictions on payments and transfers for current international transactions under the authority of some provision of the Articles, it may rely on those restrictions in order to refuse to permit settlements whether the commitments are entered into before or after the adoption of the restrictions. In particular, the member is not bound to relax restrictions on balances of its currency that it has controlled as capital because the holders wish to use them for settlements. The function of the clause referring to undue delay is to make it clear that if payments for current transactions are permitted, there will be a restriction nevertheless if there is undue delay in permitting transfers by payees to their own country of what they receive in the settlement of commitments connected with these transactions.[14] It was useful to clarify this point in the Articles because the application of capital controls necessitates administrative procedures that segregate movements of capital from payments and transfers for current transactions, and these procedures could produce delays in the transfers of funds received in the settlement of commitments to make the latter payments. Moreover, if payees wish to transfer these receipts within a reasonable period, the balances must not be treated as capital and controlled as such.

If this analysis were being applied to Cuba at a date on which it was a member of the Fund, the results would be as follows. Cuba had accepted the obligations of Article VIII, Sections 2, 3, and 4. To the extent that Decision No. 346 involved restrictions on payments and transfers for current international transactions, the restrictions would be consistent with the Articles only if the Fund had approved them under Article VIII, Section 2(a). To the extent that controls on the movement of capital were involved, the controls would be consistent with the Articles without the necessity for approval by the Fund, provided that they were exercised in a manner that did not restrict payments for current international transactions and did not delay unduly transfers of funds received in unrestricted payments. The case before the court related to the proceeds of the liquidation of an investment in Cuba, the purchase of a farm, and therefore what was in issue was a control on the transfer of capital.[15]

In concluding that Decision No. 346 was not valid under international law, Judge Keating held that it must be examined together with all the related economic regulations applied by Cuba, because they were elements in a single consistent pattern. The design was not to protect Cuba's balance of payments by preventing the flight of capital or devaluation of the currency but to eradicate foreign private capital. The effect of the regulations had been the complete and prolonged blocking of the peso balances of Americans.[16]

---

[14] For a full discussion of the provision, see Gold, "Cuban Insurance Cases," pp. 84–87 in this volume.

[15] See Article XIX(i) for a definition of payments for current transactions for the purposes of the Articles. (References to particular Articles are to provisions of the Articles of Agreement of the International Monetary Fund.)

[16] Even the use of pesos by nonresidents within Cuba was subject to authorization by the National Bank. 295 N.Y.S. 2d, at 473, fn. 5, par. (5).

Four cases involving Czechoslovak exchange control regulations had been cited by the appellant,[17] including *Perutz v. Bohemian Discount Bank in Liquidation*, from which Judge Keating quoted the following statement by the New York Court of Appeals:

> A contract made in a foreign country by citizens thereof and intended by them to be there performed is governed by the law of that country. . . . *Our courts may, however, refuse to give effect to a foreign law that is contrary to our public policy. . . .*[18] But the Czechoslovakian currency control laws in question cannot here be deemed to be offensive on that score, since our Federal Government and the Czechoslovakian Government are members of the International Monetary Fund. . . .[19]

Judge Keating distinguished these cases from the one before the Court of Appeals on the ground that the earlier cases had been argued solely on the basis of exchange controls and not in relation to Czechoslovak nationalization decrees.

The decision of the Court of Appeals applying the act of state doctrine raises the question of the relationship of that doctrine to Article VIII, Section 2(*b*) in New York courts. In a case in which the exchange control regulations of a member are consistent with the Articles, a plaintiff seeking performance of a contract that is contrary to the regulations would be denied a remedy under the doctrine and under the provision. If the regulations are inconsistent with the Articles, the plaintiff again would be denied a remedy under the doctrine. Two questions then arise. First, is the court bound in such a case to ignore the effect of the Articles? Second, if the court does not ignore the Articles, what is the result under them? The answer to the first question appears to be that the court is not required to ignore the Articles, because the *Sabbatino* decision makes a reservation in favor of "a treaty or other unambiguous agreement regarding controlling legal principles." The Articles of Agreement could come within that reservation. If the Articles are considered, it would seem that Arti-

---

[17] *Kahler v. Midland Bank Ltd.* [1949] 2 All E.R. 621; *Zivnostenska Banka National Corporation v. Frankman* [1949] 2 All E.R. 671; *Kraus v. Zivnostenska Banka*, 187 Misc. 681, 64 N.Y.S. 2d 208 (1946); *Perutz v. Bohemian Discount Bank in Liquidation*, 304 N.Y. 533, 110 N.E. 2d 6 (1953). See Gold, *Fund Agreement in the Courts* (1962), pp. 14–19, 28–30, 50–55, 75–76, 78–79, 124, 134–35, 137–39, 155.

[18] 295 N.Y.S. 2d, at 471.

[19] 304 N.Y., at 537; 110 N.E. 2d, at 7, quoted by Judge Keating, 295 N.Y.S. 2d, at 471–72. See also the reference to *In the Matter of Heddy Brecher-Wolff*, Title Claim No. 41668, Docket No. 1698; Gold, *Fund Agreement in the Courts* (1962), pp. 78–79; 295 N.Y.S. 2d, at 472, fn. 4.

cle VIII, Section 2(b) does no more than declare that a contract is unenforceable if it is contrary to regulations that are consistent with the Articles. It does not provide for enforceability if the regulations are inconsistent with the Articles, and it can be assumed that the question of enforceability is determined by the law of the forum. On this view, there would be no conflict between the refusal of a remedy under the doctrine and the effect of the provision, because the provision does not require that the contract be treated as enforceable. With this analysis, it is not apparent that there would be any conflict in New York between its application of the doctrine of the act of state to exchange control regulations and Article VIII, Section 2(b).

Discussion of the case can be concluded with a final comment on the opinion of Judge Keating. In explaining why he thought that the Cuban regulations were invalid, he said: "The Cuban Government, by rescinding the tax certificates, has simply added to its currency reserves by this ploy."[20] The conscription of foreign exchange is as much a purpose of exchange control as the prohibition or limitation of payments and transfers. The conscription is not in itself a confiscation, and it is necessary to examine other facts to see whether it has this effect. The statement of Judge Keating need not be understood to imply a general principle but can be taken to relate to the facts of the case, in which, it has been seen, he concluded that the plaintiff had been deprived for a prolonged period of any use of her holdings of pesos.

Unenforceability of Certain Exchange Contracts

FEDERAL REPUBLIC OF GERMANY

Federal Supreme Court Judgment of April 27, 1970 [21]

The plaintiff bank sought to recover the amounts of two bills of exchange from the drawee, a Dutch company. The bills had been made by K, a nonresident of the Netherlands, accepted by B, a member of the defendant's board of directors, and endorsed by K to the plaintiff. The bills had been dishonored and protested. One of the defenses was that the acceptance was invalid because the license required by Dutch law had not been obtained. The Oldenburg State

---

[20] 295 N.Y.S. 2d, at 471.
[21] BGH Urt. v. 27.4.1970—II ZR 12/69 (Oldenburg), *Neue Juristische Wochenschrift*, Vol. 23 (August 20, 1970), pp. 1507–1508.

Court gave judgment for the plaintiff, but it was reversed by the Oldenburg State Court of Appeal. An appeal was taken to the Federal Supreme Court, which delivered a judgment on April 27, 1970 in the course of which it made an important statement of its understanding of various aspects of Article VIII, Section 2(b).

(i) The Supreme Court agreed with the Court of Appeal that Article VIII, Section 2(b) affects only the enforceability of claims under a contract to which the provision applies. It dismissed the view, for which there had been minor support in the past, that the provision prescribes invalidity for exchange contracts that are contrary to the exchange control regulations of members of the Fund if those regulations are consistent with the Articles. The court noted that its view was in keeping with the authoritative English text ("shall be unenforceable") and the German translation of it. The purpose of the provision, the court continued, was to reverse former judicial rulings and to ensure that members of the Fund would recognize each other's exchange control regulations when they were consistent with the Articles, whatever might be the law governing the contract under the law of the forum (lex fori) and notwithstanding the principle of the, nonrecognition of foreign public law. For this purpose, it was sufficient for the courts and administrative authorities of members of the Fund to refrain from giving help to contracting parties to get the performance of contracts that are forbidden by exchange control regulations, and it was not necessary to declare contracts invalid. On this and other aspects of its opinion, the court cited with approval certain published views, including some expressed in articles on the "Fund Agreement in the Courts" that had first appeared in *Staff Papers* and later in *Rabels Zeitschrift für ausländisches und internationales Privatrecht*.[22]

The principle that Article VIII, Section 2(b) does not declare contracts invalid because they are entered into in defiance of exchange control regulations means that the circumstances at the time when a contract is made are not necessarily decisive for the purposes of suit on the contract. Article VIII, Section 2(b), in declaring contracts

---

[22] Joseph Gold, "Das Währungsabkommen von Bretton Woods vom 22.7.1944 in der Rechtsprechung—II," *Zeitschrift für ausländisches und internationales Privatrecht (RabelsZ.)*, Vol. 22 (1957), pp. 601–36, at p. 629. See also Joseph Gold, "Das Währungsabkommen von Bretton Woods vom 22.7.1944 in der Rechtsprechung," *Zeitschrift für ausländisches und internationales Privatrecht (RabelsZ.)*, Vol. 19 (1954), pp. 601–42; "Das Währungsabkommen von Bretton Woods vom 22.7.1944 in der Rechtsprechung—III," *Rabels Zeitschrift für ausländisches und internationales Privatrecht*, Vol. 27 (1962), pp. 605–65.

unenforceable but not invalid because they are entered into in defiance of exchange control regulations, makes it possible to examine the facts at the date when enforcement is sought. Moreover, it will be seen from the discussion in (iv) below that the effect on the balance of payments or exchange resources of a member is a criterion in the understanding and application of certain aspects of the provision. It is not contracts but the performance of obligations under them that affects the balance of payments or exchange resources. The purpose of Article VIII, Section 2(b) will be promoted, therefore, if the effect on the balance of payments or on exchange resources at the time when the performance of obligations is sought is taken into account in applying the provision.

If a contract was contrary to exchange control regulations when made but by the time of suit the regulations are abrogated or amended so that the contract is no longer contrary to them, the contract becomes enforceable even though it was originally unenforceable. If the contract had been invalid when made, it could not become valid simply by the revocation or modification of exchange control regulations. Unenforceability produces the obviously sensible result that when a member no longer seeks protection for its balance of payments, other members are no longer required to give protection.

It is possible that the law of the foreign exchange control regulations prescribes that contracts contrary to them are invalid. This prescription does not alter the meaning of unenforceability in Article VIII, Section 2(b). That provision still binds the forum to do no more than treat the contract as unenforceable. If, however, the foreign law is the law governing the contract under the private international law of the *lex fori*, the forum may treat the contract as invalid, but that result will follow from the private international law of the forum and not from the Articles. There is nothing in the Articles to suggest that Article VIII, Section 2(b) is substituted for private international law beyond ensuring that contracts will not be treated as enforceable in circumstances in which the provision requires that they be unenforceable.

It has been seen that a contract that was unenforceable when made may cease to be unenforceable under Article VIII, Section 2(b). The reverse may happen. A contract that was not contrary to exchange control regulations when made may become unenforceable as a result of the subsequent modification or introduction of exchange control regulations.

Similarly, changes in the consistency of exchange control regulations with the Articles may affect the enforceability of a contract. Article VIII, Section 2(b) provides that a contract shall be unenforceable if it is contrary to exchange control regulations "maintained or imposed consistently with this Agreement." Regulations may have been approved by the Fund as restrictions under Article VIII, Section 2(a) [23] before a contract was made but approval may expire or be withdrawn before the contract is performed. Regulations may have lacked approval when a contract was entered into but may receive approval later. Changes in the consistency of regulations with the Articles may also occur under other provisions of the Articles.

A distinction similar to the one involving changes in exchange control regulations or in their consistency with the Articles can be based on changes in the circumstances of the contracting parties. Exchange control regulations may be unchanged but they may cease to apply to a party because he has become a nonresident of the member country maintaining the regulations, although he was a resident when he entered into the contract.[24] The contract is no longer unenforceable under Article VIII, Section 2(b), even though it was unenforceable when made. Once again, the reverse may happen. A contract originally enforceable may become unenforceable because a party has changed his status from a nonresident to a resident of the member maintaining exchange control regulations in accordance with the Articles.

Finally, a contract may cease to be unenforceable under Article VIII, Section 2(b) because the exchange control regulations that have not been observed are those of a country that is no longer a member of the Fund. Cuba, Czechoslovakia, and Poland have all withdrawn from the Fund. Indonesia withdrew for a time but rejoined the organization. Cases have occurred in the courts of members of the Fund involving the exchange control regulations of Cuba [25] and Czechoslovakia [26] after the withdrawal of those countries. The decisions have

---

[23] "Subject to the provisions of Article VII, Section 3(b), and Article XIV, Section 2, no member shall, without the approval of the Fund, impose restrictions on the making of payments and transfers for current international transactions" (Article VIII, Section 2(a)).

[24] Gold, "Cuban Insurance Cases," p. 72 in this volume.

[25] Ibid., pp. 43–94 in this volume. See also fn. 45 infra.

[26] Cermak et al. v. Bata Akciova Spolecnost, 80 N.Y.S. 2d 782 (1948) (Gold, Fund Agreement in the Courts (1962), pp. 15–17); Stephen v. Zivnostenska Banka National Corporation, 140 N.Y.S. 2d 323 (1955) (Gold, Fund Agreement in the Courts (1962), pp. 77–78; see also fn. 17 at p. 31); Basso v. Janda, Recueil Dalloz Sirey, July 3, 1968, Jurisprudence, p. 445 (infra, pp. 153–55).

been consistent with the principle that unenforceability under Article VIII, Section 2(*b*) is determined by the facts at the time of suit, that the provision is for the benefit of members, and that if a country withdraws from the Fund it loses the protection of the provision.[27]

(ii) In arriving at its conclusion on the meaning of unenforceability under Article VIII, Section 2(*b*), the Supreme Court noted that its view was in accord with the Fund's "official interpretation" of June 10, 1949. The court did not examine the question whether it was bound by the interpretation, perhaps because its opinion was consistent with the interpretation. The judgment adds little, therefore, to the body of jurisprudence on the question whether interpretations adopted by the Fund under Article XVIII are binding on tribunals in member countries under their domestic law as it stands at the time of decision.[28]

When a country joins the Fund it deposits an instrument, which states that the country accepts all the obligations of the Articles and has taken all the steps necessary to give effect to those obligations under its law. A member that becomes a participant in the Special Drawing Account deposits a similar instrument with respect to the obligations of that Account.[29] The Fund decides with finality any question of the interpretation of the Articles that arises between members or between a member and the Fund.[30] The obligation of Article VIII, Section 2(*b*) means the obligation as interpreted by the Fund under Article XVIII. The obligation under Article VIII, Section 2(*b*) to treat certain contracts as unenforceable can be performed only through a member's courts and administrative agencies. If the courts and agencies of a member do not consider themselves bound under their domestic law by the Fund's interpretation of the provision, and if they take actions that are inconsistent with the interpretation, the member will not be performing an obligation in accordance with the instrument that it deposited on joining the Fund or participating in the SDR arrangements. If domestic law does compel the courts and agencies to act inconsistently with the obligation as interpreted under Article XVIII, the member must take action to make good its declaration that it has taken all necessary steps under its law to enable it to perform its obligations. In short, it must take whatever steps are

---

[27] *Stephen v. Zivnostenska Banka National Corporation,* 140 N.Y.S. 2d 323 (1955) (Gold, *Fund Agreement in the Courts* (1962), p. 142; Gold, "Cuban Insurance Cases," pp. 87–88 in this volume).

[28] Gold, Pamphlet No. 11, pp. 31–42.

[29] Article XX, Section 2(*a*), *original* and *first,* and Article XXIII, Section 1, *first.*

[30] Article XVIII, *original* and *first.*

necessary to ensure that its courts and agencies will act in accordance with the interpretation.

(iii) An argument that has been made for the minority view that unenforceability must mean invalidity has been the principle of Anglo-American domestic law that allows the defendant to decide whether or not to raise the defense of unenforceability, while Article VIII, Section 2(b) requires respect for foreign exchange regulations in the public interest and not in the private interest as seen by the defendant. The fallacy in this argument is obvious: there is no reason why the concept of unenforceability under the Articles must carry with it the idiosyncrasies of the concept in a particular system of private law. The Supreme Court rejected the argument and held that, in order to give effect to the public law purposes of the Articles, a court must raise the objection based on Article VIII, Section 2(b) even though neither party to the litigation has relied on the provision. If the contract on which an action is brought is contrary to exchange control regulations that are consistent with the Articles, an essential "precondition" of the suit is lacking and the court must reject the claim. By its decision on this aspect of the case, the court held that the public interest that induces it in certain cases to raise the defense of invalidity on its own initiative justified a similar procedure even though it was dealing with an unenforceable and not an illegal contract.

The Supreme Court held that the duty of a court to raise the issue of the enforceability of a claim does not affect the rules relating to the burden of proof. The Court of Appeal had decided correctly, on the basis of information provided by the Nederlandsche Bank, the central bank of the Netherlands, that under Dutch exchange control regulations a resident must obtain a license to accept a bill of exchange drawn by a nonresident if the purpose of the transactions was to give or to secure credit given to the nonresident. A license was not required if bills were accepted for certain other purposes. The Court of Appeal had acted on the defendant's statement that the bill of exchange had been accepted by the defendant to secure credit given to the nonresident K by the plaintiff. For the plaintiff to succeed, it was necessary, therefore, that it should prove, if it could, that the bills had been given for some purpose that did not require a license under the Dutch exchange control regulations. The plaintiff had not inquired into the underlying transaction between the defendant and K, but the court held that

> [a]s long as account must be taken domestically of foreign exchange restrictions, the complication of discounting acceptances by persons

whose domicile or place of business is abroad, feared by the appellant, cannot be avoided, and is to be remedied by means of appropriate investigation and verification.

(iv) The Supreme Court also expressed a view on the meaning of "exchange contracts" in Article VIII, Section 2(b). It held that obligations deriving from bills of exchange were within the meaning of that concept "since it is just such obligations that can especially affect the balance of payments, and therefore if they were not included in this concept, it would hardly be feasible to restrict foreign exchange transactions effectively." This passage deserves closer analysis.

The two elements of "exchange contracts" and the currency "involved" in the provision have been regarded sometimes as the duplication of a single element but, although they are associated, they are distinct. The first element identifies the contracts to which the provision applies, and the second identifies the member that is entitled to have its exchange control regulations recognized for the purposes of the provision when exchange contracts are contrary to these regulations. The alleged duplication arises from the fact that sometimes "exchange contracts" have been defined in such a way that the definition also determines the currency "involved."

A number of definitions of "exchange contracts" have been attempted. For example, it has been said that they are contracts that affect,[31] or in any way affect,[32] the exchange resources of a country. In the case discussed here, the Supreme Court defined them as contracts that affect the balance of payments. These formulations recognize quite properly that the concept must be given an economic meaning. It is possible that any contract that is not purely domestic in all its aspects can be shown to have some effect of an economic character on two or more countries, although the effect may be remote. The purpose of the qualifying word "exchange" must serve to eliminate contracts that have no obvious economic content, although the contracts that remain will still be diverse. Five basic types of economic transaction have been distinguished:

(a) purchases and sales of goods or services against financial items (the exchange of goods or services for means of payment);
(b) barter (the exchange of goods or services for goods or services);
(c) the exchange of means of payment for other means of payment;

---

[31] *Lessinger v. Mirau, Jahrbuch für Internationales Recht,* Vol. 5, Part 1 (1955), pp. 113–23 (Gold, *Fund Agreement in the Courts* (1962), p. 91).

[32] E.g., *Sharif v. Azad* [1966], 3 W.L.R., at 1289–90, [1966] 3 All E.R., at 787, see p. 111 in this volume.

(d) the provision or acquisition of goods or services without requital (e.g., grants-in-kind);

(e) the provision or acquisition of means of payment without requital (e.g., gifts).[33]

Transactions in any of these categories may enter into the balance of payments or affect the exchange resources of a country. They can affect exchange resources because they represent an addition to or diminution of the assets or liabilities of a country in the sense that ultimately they could increase, reduce, or forgo an increase in the reserves of the monetary authorities of a country. Therefore, "exchange contracts" are not restricted to category (c) above. Moreover, they are not confined to transactions that give rise to transfers of money. For example, they may provide for barter. If a transfer of money is involved, it need not be made through the banking system in which the contracting party resides. For example, an importer may pay for his import with a credit from the exporter's country. If a transfer is made, it may be in the domestic currency of the payor or payee or in a currency that is foreign to the importer. An understanding of "exchange contracts" on these lines has been described as "liberal," [34] although with approbation, but this understanding does no more than reflect the economic character of the Articles in which the concept of "exchange contracts" is embedded and the function it is meant to serve.

When the discussion is directed to the currency "involved," the connection with "exchange contracts" is obvious. The currency "involved" is the currency of the member in which there is an effect on the balance of payments or on exchange resources. It has been the practice to speak of "the" currency that is involved, but a balance of payments is a statement of the transactions of a country with other countries. Therefore, any exchange contract will involve two currencies, i.e., the currencies of the two members in which the parties to the exchange contract are resident. It does not follow that both members have exchange control regulations. Either or both of them may maintain exchange control regulations, or neither of them. If both have exchange control regulations, the courts will apply their own country's regulations. If the domestic regulations do not deny a remedy, the forum will still have to treat a contract as unenforceable if it is

---

[33] *Balance of Payments Manual,* Third Edition, pp. 1–2; *Balance of Payments Concepts and Definitions,* IMF Pamphlet Series, No. 10, Second Edition (Washington, 1969), pp. 2–3.

[34] *Sharif v. Azad* [1966] 3 W.L.R., at 1293; [1966] 3 All E.R., at 789.

contrary to the regulations of the other member,[35] and the courts of a third member will have to treat a contract as unenforceable if it is contrary to the regulations of either of the two countries issuing the currencies involved.

It is sometimes said that the test for determining whether or not the currency of a member is involved turns on whether exchange control regulations are for the protection of the balance of payments of that member.[36] A definition of exchange control that is often referred to, even though it does not involve the application of Article VIII, Section 2(b), stresses the test of the defense of the balance of payments:

> In my judgment, these courts must recognize the right of every foreign state to protect its economy by measures of foreign exchange control. . . . [T]his court is entitled to be satisfied that the foreign law is a genuine foreign exchange law, i.e., a law passed with the genuine intention of protecting its economy in times of national stress and for that purpose regulating (inter alia) the rights of foreign creditors, and is not a law passed ostensibly with that object, but in reality with some object not in accordance with the usage of nations. . . .[37]

The test of "protection" of the balance of payments is adequate in most cases but it can be misleading. It is not the test of the Supreme Court, which preferred to speak of exchange control regulations as regulations that control transactions that "affect" the balance of payments. The test as expressed by the Supreme Court is more precise because Article VIII, Section 2(b) requires recognition, for the purposes of that provision, of exchange control regulations that are "maintained or imposed consistently" with the Articles if they are authorized by any one of a number provisions.[38] The authority conferred by these provisions is related most frequently, but not invariably, to the protection of the balance of payments. For example, a member may impose exchange control regulations for reasons of national or international security, and the Fund has made it clear that a member must obtain the Fund's approval of them, which means, of course, that they can be authorized under the Articles.[39] In some circumstances, a mem-

---

[35] The discussion deals with the exchange control regulations of other members. Article VIII, Section 2(b) does not deal with the exchange control regulations of the *lex fori*.

[36]*Sharif v. Azad* [1966] 3 W.L.R., at 1293; [1966] 3 All E.R., at 789.

[37] *Re Helbert Wagg & Co. Ltd.* [1956] 1 All E.R., at 142.

[38] Article VI, Section 1; Article VII, Section 3(b); Article VIII, Section 2(a); Article XI, Sections 1 and 2; Article XIV, Section 2.

[39] *Selected Decisions of the Executive Directors and Selected Documents*, Fifth Issue (Washington, 1971), pp. 94–95. (*Selected Decisions*, Ninth Issue, pp. 203–204.)

ber may impose exchange control regulations as a sanction against another country or territory in accordance with a resolution of the United Nations. A number of members imposed exchange control restrictions against Rhodesia, and these restrictions were approved by the Fund under Article VIII, Section 2(*a*). In cases such as these, the purpose of the exchange control regulations is not to protect the balance of payments of the member adopting them but to produce an adverse effect on the balance of payments of the country or territory against which they are directed.

Language that refers to protection of the balance of payments may be misleading in another way. It may suggest that exchange control regulations are imposed only by members in deficit in their balances of payments, and that a member in surplus will not impose exchange controls or will not be entitled to have them recognized under Article VIII, Section 2(*b*) if it does impose them. None of these propositions is correct. A member may impose exchange control regulations because it has a troublesome surplus, for example, as the result of an inflow of capital, and these regulations will be recognized no less than the regulations of a member in deficit.

Although the test that the performance of a contract would affect a member's balance of payments normally will serve to determine whether its currency is involved, the question may be raised whether the test produces the same results in all cases as two other tests. One of these is jurisdiction to adopt regulations and the other is effect on exchange resources. It has been suggested that the concept of the currency "involved" is simply another way of stating that a member has legislative jurisdiction in accordance with familiar legal principles to apply regulations on the basis of residence within the member's territory or the location of assets within its control.[40] There are circumstances in which the equivalence of jurisdiction of this kind and effect on the balance of payments may not be obvious. For example, a member has jurisdiction to control contracts for the transfer between nonresidents of an asset within its territory. If the nonresidents are residents of different countries, the transfer might not affect the member's global balance of payments, but the transfer might affect the member's regional balances of payments, and for this reason the transfer might have economic importance for the member. If the transfer is between two nonresidents, whether of the same country or of different countries, a change in the class of obligee might have

---

[40] Gold, "Cuban Insurance Cases," pp. 70–77 in this volume.

economic relevance. The transfer of a bank deposit in a member's territory between a foreign central bank and a private resident of the country of the central bank is an example of a change of this character. Other transfers between nonresidents might not affect the balance of payments even though the member would have jurisdiction to control the transfers.[41] Finally, transfers between a member's residents must not be overlooked. It can control transfers among them of assets situated abroad, but the transfers may not affect its balance of payments.

In those cases in which an effect on the balance of payments is not obvious, there is a sense in which its exchange resources can be said to be affected. They are affected in the sense that the contracts relate to resources within the member's control, unually by providing for the transfer of them.

Federal Supreme Court Judgment of February 17, 1971 [42]

In a judgment of February 17, 1971 the Federal Supreme Court followed the judgment of April 27, 1970 but applied it to new facts. The exchange control regulations that had applied to a contract when made were repealed before suit and, as noted above, this kind of case is one of those that illustrate the difference between the unenforceability of a contract under Article VIII, Section 2(b) and invalidity.

The plaintiff, a firm operating in the Federal Republic of Germany, in July and August 1963 supplied the defendant, a French firm, with hog sides from the German Democratic Republic under a contract entered into in East Berlin. The price was in excess of a quarter of a million U.S. dollars. Under French exchange control regulations in force at that time, payment for goods from Eastern Germany could not be made to the seller in the Federal Republic but had to be credited to a "bilateral franc account" held with an East German bank. The holder of an account of this type could operate it only in a specified manner and only for specified purposes. The plaintiff received bilateral francs for an amount outstanding under the contract, and in September 1963 the parties agreed in Switzerland with a third party on a switch transaction that involved a discount of 7 per cent. The court found that the defendant undertook to bear this disagio. The plaintiff claimed the balance, after deduction of a counterclaim, in

---

[41] Ibid., p. 75.

[42] BGH Urt. v. 17.2.1971—VIII ZR 84/69 (Frankfurt), Neue Juristische Wochenschrift, Vol. 24 (June 1, 1971), pp. 983–85; Wertpapier-Mitteilungen, No. 14 of April 3, 1971, pp. 411–12.

proceedings instituted in the Federal Republic. The defendant argued that the agreement was void under French exchange control regulations.

The agreement of September 1963 was contrary to French exchange control regulations then in effect. After January 30, 1964 such a transaction ceased to be unlawful under French regulations, but a license was necessary for transfers to the Federal Republic. On January 31, 1967 these transfers ceased to be subject to any kind of control.

In its opinion, the Supreme Court noted that both France and the Federal Republic of Germany were members of the Fund and referred to Article VIII, Section 2(b). The court accepted the conclusions that the contract by which the defendant undertook to absorb the disagio was contrary to French exchange control regulations when made and that the currency of France was involved. The court held that the purpose of Article VIII, Section 2(b) was to protect the foreign exchange reserves of the member of the Fund that had issued the exchange control regulations, by ensuring that the courts of other members would not ignore them on the basis of the public law character of the regulations or conflict with the public policy of the forum. The Supreme Court's decision of April 27, 1970 had decided that the provision prevented the enforcement of contractual claims but did not require that they be regarded as void. If a member repeals exchange control regulations, it declares thereby that it no longer needs the protection of the regulations. The court held, therefore, that other members should be bound no longer to give protection, and that contractual claims could be enforced. The court, in support of its conclusions, referred once again to the views expressed in the articles that had appeared in *Rabels Zeitschrift für ausländisches und internationales Privatrecht*, as well as to the work of other authors.

The Supreme Court went on to decide other issues connected with the claim. First, the conclusion that Article VIII, Section 2(b) was no longer a bar to the enforcement of the claim would stand even if it could be shown that under French domestic law the contract remained void after the repeal of the exchange control regulations. It was the purpose of Article VIII, Section 2(b) to ensure that all other members would not enforce exchange contracts that were contrary to any member's exchange control regulations, but it was not the purpose of the provision to ensure that other members would give these contracts the same treatment that they received under the law of the member that had adopted the regulations.

Second, because the claim was not unenforceable under Article VIII, Section 2(b), it was admissible, but whether it was well founded depended on the domestic law that governed the contract. The facts showed that the parties intended German law to apply, and there was no provision of that law prohibiting the agreement. It was not relevant under German law that the contract violated French exchange control regulations when it was made. The legal consequences of a violation did not go beyond those prescribed by Article VIII, Section 2(b).

Third, under German law a contract having as its object an impossible act is void, but the payment of the disagio was to be made in Germany, and it was possible there.

Federal Supreme Court Judgment of March 11, 1970 [43]

The plaintiff, a credit institution in Germany, financed the purchase in early 1965 of equipment for a coin-operated laundry by a Dutch firm, which on January 22, 1965 agreed to be a surety for the loan. The agreement declared: "The surety recognizes the provisions of German law under which the suretyship may be invoked against him." The plaintiff brought this action against the defendant to recover the outstanding balance of the loan.

The State Court of Appeal of Düsseldorf treated the defendant's contract of suretyship as an "exchange contract" and the Dutch foreign exchange law as "exchange control regulations" for the purpose of Article VIII, Section 2(b), and the Supreme Court accepted these findings.

The parties agreed that under the Dutch foreign exchange control regulations, the defendant's contract of suretyship was subject to approval by the Nederlandsche Bank. Approval was not requested or given when the contract was entered into, but, on the request of the plaintiff, approval was given on February 2, 1968.

The parties disagreed on the question whether under Dutch law the subsequent approval validated the contract, which originally was invalid under that law. Under German law, a contract would be validated in these circumstances. The Supreme Court confirmed the view of the Court of Appeal that the question of validation must be decided according to German law because the defendant had recog-

---

[43] BGH Urt. v. 11.3.1970—VIII ZR 147/68 (Düsseldorf), *Neue Juristische Wochenschrift*, Vol. 23 (May 27, 1970), p. 1002.

nized that the provisions of German law were applicable. It was unnecessary, therefore, to decide what was the effect of the subsequent approval under Dutch law.

At first sight, it might seem that the question whether the suretyship contract was contrary to Dutch exchange control regulations was decided according to German law. On closer analysis, this is not what the Supreme Court decided, and its decision is consistent with the other two decisions by it that have been discussed in this chapter. The basic thesis of all three decisions is that Article VIII, Section 2(b) deals with the unenforceability of contracts and not with their invalidity. This principle is stated most forcefully in the decision of April 27, 1970. If a contract is invalid when made, it cannot become valid later, but unenforceability under the provision can be determined in relation to the facts at the time of suit. Therefore, the decision of February 17, 1971 established the proposition that if exchange control regulations are repealed before suit, a contract that was contrary to them when made ceases to be unenforceable. In the earlier decision of March 11, 1970, the grant of approval by the Nederlandsche Bank after the contract was made but before suit meant that at the time of suit the contract ceased to be contrary to the exchange control regulations of the Netherlands and, therefore, ceased to be unenforceable in Germany. As a result, Article VIII, Section 2(b) had no further function, the claim was admissible, and the question whether it was sound had to be determined by German law as the law governing the contract under the *lex fori*. Under German law, a contract that depended for its validity upon the grant of a license was validated by the grant of a license after the contract was entered into. This aspect of the case resembled the treatment of the repeal of French exchange regulations in the decision of February 17, 1971. That decision held that after the repeal the contract ceased to be unenforceable under Article VIII, Section 2(b), and because the contract was governed by German law the question whether it remained invalid under French law after the repeal was irrelevant.

In both cases, it must be assumed that the contract ceased to be contrary to exchange control regulations, in the one case because a license was granted in the Netherlands and in the other because the regulations were abrogated in France. The contracts then became enforceable in Germany even though they may have continued to be invalid in the Netherlands or in France because the contract had been contrary to the regulations of those members when made. It is necessary, however, to clarify what is meant by invalidity. If the contract is invalid in the Netherlands or France because of the general law, there is no reason why continuing invalidity there should require other members to treat the contract as unenforceable under Article VIII, Section 2(b). Their only obligation is to decree unenforceability if a contract is contrary to exchange control regulations. If, however, the contract remained invalid in the Netherlands or in France because exchange control regulations remained in existence, even if their only remaining purpose was to perpetuate the invalidity of past contracts, there would still be an obligation on Germany to treat the contract as unenforceable.

The cases clarify the extent to which Article VIII, Section 2(b) has modified the pre-existing law, including private international law, of members of the Fund. If the provision results in the unenforceability of a contract, the pre-existing domestic law under which it was enforceable has been changed. If, however, for whatever reason, the provision does not require that a contract be treated as unenforceable, the provision does not establish a new principle of law which requires that the contract be regarded as enforceable. The *lex fori*, including its private international law, continues to apply, with the result that in some cases a contract may be treated as valid and in others as invalid. In the two cases in which the Federal Supreme Court held that the contract was not unenforceable under Article VIII, Section 2(b), it then held that under the private international law of the forum German law applied and the contract was valid under that law.

France

Basso v. Janda[44]

The First Civil Chamber of the Court of Cassation of France adopted a decision on October 16, 1967 affirming the proposition that Article VIII, Section 2(b) does not prescribe unenforceability for an exchange contract contrary to the exchange control regulations of a country that has never been a member of the Fund. The proposition is not surprising, but it is surprising that the country involved was Czechoslovakia, which was a member of the Fund from December 27, 1945, the date on which the Articles of Agreement took effect, until December 31, 1954, when Czechoslovakia withdrew.

In March 1948, Janda, a resident of Czechoslovakia, entrusted US$30,000 to Kosek, a citizen of the United States who was about to

---

[44] *Recueil Dalloz Sirey*, July 3, 1968, Jurisprudence, p. 445.

leave Prague, with the agreement that Kosek would retransfer the money to Janda abroad. Later, both Janda and Kosek became domiciled in Nice, and on July 1, 1951 Kosek signed a document acknowledging that he held the amount in question on behalf of Janda. Kosek died in New York in 1960, and Janda brought suit against Basso as Kosek's executor in Nice, where Janda was able to attach some assets belonging to Kosek. The Court of Appeal of Aix-en-Provence gave judgment for Janda on May 10, 1965, and Basso appealed to the Court of Cassation on the ground that the Court of Appeal had neglected Article VIII, Section 2(b) and the Fund's interpretation of it. Basso argued that the decision of the Court of Appeal was based on the finding that Czechoslovakia had not adhered to the Articles of the Fund, although Czechoslovakia had been an original member and did not withdraw until after the date of the contract. The claim should be treated as unenforceable, Basso went on, because Czechoslovakia's currency was involved within the meaning of the provision. The transfer affected Czechoslovakia's reserves by depriving it of foreign currency at a time when foreign currency was vital for its economy. Janda argued that the acknowledgment of 1951 was distinct from the original verbal contract made in Prague and was governed by French law. Basso replied that the acknowledgment could not be dissociated from the original contract, which had violated Czechoslovak exchange control regulations. Basso contended, therefore, that the Court of Appeal was wrong in deciding that Janda could recover because the acknowledgment was valid under French law.

The finding of fact by the Court of Appeal that Czechoslovakia had participated in the Bretton Woods Conference but had not adhered to the Articles was binding on the Court of Cassation, and the court concluded, as a consequence, that the finding of law that the effects of the exchange control regulations of Czechoslovakia could not be recognized in France was correct.[45] The judgment was based on a patent

---

[45] In *Confederation Life Association v. Vega y Arminan,* 207 So. 2d 33 (1968), 211 So. 2d 169 (1968), 393 U.S. 980 (1968), a Cuban refugee, resident in Florida, claimed the cash surrender value of a life insurance policy issued in Cuba by the defendant, a Canadian insurance company, when the plaintiff was resident there. All payments under the policy were to be made in Havana. Cuban exchange control laws required the payment in pesos of all obligations payable in Cuba, and the defendant refused to make any payment of the cash surrender value except in pesos in Havana. The court held that the cash surrender value clause was a continuing offer, which matured when accepted by the insured, in Florida, and that the law of Florida governed as the *lex loci contractus.* The defendant had relied on Article VIII, Section 2(b) and had cited *Confederation Life Association v. Ugalde,* 151 So. 2d 315 (1963); 163 So. 2d 343 (1964); 164 So. 2d 1 (1964); 379 U.S. 915

error of fact, but the result should have been the same even if the error had been avoided or corrected, because Czechoslovakia had left the Fund before the action was instituted. Janda had not failed to advance this argument before the Court of Cassation.

The terse refusal of the court to consider the effect of Czechoslovak exchange control regulations once it was determined that Article VIII, Section 2(b) did not apply is in sharp contrast to the more amiable attitude of the New York Court of Appeals in *French v. Banco Nacional de Cuba* to the exchange controls of other countries. The contrast is even sharper because Basso argued that it was against French public policy to enforce a contract that had been invalidated by the legislation of another sovereign state. The Court of Cassation announced its view without even asking what law governed the contract under French private international law. The case differs therefore from the two cases decided by the Federal Supreme Court of Germany in which the court determined that German law governed the contract under the private international law of Germany and refused to give effect to the foreign exchange control regulations of another country for that reason.

Constant v. Lanata[46]

The facts in *Constant v. Lanata* are similar to those in *Basso v. Janda*, except that the exchange control regulations in issue were those of a member and not a former member of the Fund. In the course of 1964, Constant, a French citizen, who appears to have been resident in Algeria, handed 420,000 Algerian dinars to Lanata, another French citizen, who seems to have been a nonresident of Algeria. The transfer was made in Algeria, apparently in currency notes, with the intention that they would be transferred to intermediaries in return for French francs to be delivered in France. As a result of these arrangements, Lanata gave Constant a postdated check drawn on a French bank, in the amount of 300,000 French francs. The official rate for the dinar was equal to the par value for the franc. Unless there was some other obligation of Lanata to Constant, the amount of the check may reflect the purpose of the transaction, which was to evade Algerian exchange

---

(1964); 85 S. Ct. 263 (1964). The court held that Article VIII, Section 2(b) did not apply because Cuba had withdrawn from the Fund, and relied on *Pan American Life Insurance Company v. Blanco*, 362 F. 2d 167 (1966): "It is settled that the laws of a nonmember nation are not given extraterritorial effect by the terms and conditions of the Bretton Woods Agreement" (207 So. 2d, p. 38).

[46] *Revue critique de droit international privé*, Vol. 59 (No. 3, 1970), pp. 464–74.

control regulations, or a commission Constant agreed to pay Lanata, or both of these circumstances. Constant smuggled the check out of Algeria and presented it for encashment in France, but Lanata's account was overdrawn and the check was dishonored. It is possible that Constant had become a nonresident of Algeria by the time he presented the check, but the residence of the parties from time to time is not clear.

Constant brought an action to recover the amount of the check, and on October 21, 1965, the Marseille court (*tribunal de grande instance*) gave judgment for him. An appeal was taken to the Court of Appeal of Aix-en-Provence, which set aside the judgment on December 15, 1966. Lanata had contended that the claim must be rejected because it was based on an illegal transaction. Constant had replied that, because exchange control regulations were territorial, the Algerian prohibition of the export of capital could not be taken into account by a French court in a suit between French citizens. The Court of Appeal decided that, in principle, the exchange control regulations of another country were inapplicable in France, but the principle could be displaced by a treaty. The court noted that both France and Algeria were members of the Fund, and it referred, therefore, to Article VIII, Section 2(*b*). It referred also to the Evian Agreement between France and Algeria, which authorized Algeria to regulate transfers of funds from Algeria to France.[47] The court concluded that Algerian exchange control regulations were applicable to legal relationships involving payments and transfers from Algeria to France. The court held that as Constant's claim was based on a check that was the counterpart of an illegal transfer of funds from Algeria, the contract had an illegal purpose (*cause*), and the claim must fail. Constant's only remedy was to claim restitution of the 420,000 dinars from Lanata in Algeria.

Constant appealed to the Court of Cassation (First Civil Chamber), which reversed the decision of the Court of Appeal on June 18, 1969. In a brief opinion, the court began with the proposition that under Article 1376 of the Civil Code an action for money not due may be brought by a claimant who requests the return of payments made in performance of a contract that is void because of the illegality of its purpose. The court noted that Constant's claim had been dismissed on the ground that, pursuant to Article VIII, Section 2(*b*), Algerian exchange control regulations, which were consistent with the Evian

---

[47] There is no evidence that, in its treatment of the Evian Agreement, the court relied on the second sentence of Article VIII, Section 2(*b*).

Agreement, applied to transfers from Algeria to France; that therefore the check had an illegal purpose; and that Constant's sole remedy, if he wished to resort to it, was to claim restitution in Algeria. The next step in the opinion was the Delphic statement that by adjudicating as it did the Court of Appeal implied that it had not been impossible for Lanata to perform the contract because of the exchange control regulations of Algeria, supervening circumstances, or *force majeure,* but that instead of performing Lanata had misappropriated the funds he should have delivered.

The Court of Cassation did not challenge the determination by the Court of Appeal that the purpose of the contract was illegal under French law because the parties had intended to violate applicable Algerian exchange control regulations. The Court of Cassation drew from this determination the conclusion that the Court of Appeal had treated the contract as illegal because of the rule of French law that a contract is void if it has an illegal purpose (Articles 1108, 1131, and 1133 of the Civil Code). The Court of Cassation also concluded that the Court of Appeal had failed to grant Constant the remedy to which he was entitled as a result of this determination, because under French law a party to an illegal contract may obtain the restitution of any payment that he has made under the contract (Article 1376). The Court of Cassation pointed out that because the proceedings were between French nationals, the Court of Appeal should not have refused to exercise jurisdiction by withholding the remedy of restitution from Constant.

The decision was based on the thesis that, because of Article VIII, Section 2(b), the Algerian exchange control regulations governed the transfer of funds from Algeria to France. French law was then applied, and it was held that because the purpose of the contract was to contravene Algerian regulations the contract was illegal and Constant was entitled to restitution. If this analysis of the decision is correct, however, Article VIII, Section 2(b) did not simply require the French courts to recognize the relevance of Algerian exchange control regulations to the transfer. It also required the courts to hold that the contract that provided for the transfer was unenforceable. The provision does not prescribe illegality. If it had been held that the contract was unenforceable, Constant would not have been entitled to restitution under the rules that govern the restitution of payments made under illegal contracts.

The cause of action appears to have been on the check and, therefore, was an attempt to get enforcement of the contract. It is possible,

157

however, that Constant relied on another cause of action in which the contract was a necessary circumstance but in which enforcement of the contract was not requested. The other cause of action that Constant might have been pursuing was a claim to the restitution of money paid under a contract void for illegality. Whether or not Constant did advance this claim, the Court of Cassation proceeded as if he had. The court's willingness to consider Constant's claim as one for restitution led to the paradoxical result that he might receive treatment that would be even more favorable to him than a judgment on the contract. If he were given judgment on the contract, he would recover 300,000 francs, but if he were entitled to restitution he might be able to recover the value in francs of 420,000 Algerian dinars. The equivalent in French francs at something like the official rate of exchange would be highly profitable to Constant when compared with the contract he had made. As a result, the French courts, having found that the contract was void for the illegality of its purpose, would be giving Constant a remedy that, in its effect, more than carried out the illegal purpose of the contract. If, by restitution, the court meant not the restoration of the 420,000 dinars handed over to Lanata or the equivalent in French francs of that amount but the 300,000 French francs that he probably realized as a result of his dealings with intermediaries and after deducting the amount of his commission, the court would be executing the purpose not only of Constant but also of Lanata.

The case is another in a small group of cases in which the courts have held that a claim could be sustained by distinguishing the basis for it from a contract affected by Article VIII, Section 2(b). Sometimes, the courts have held that the plaintiff's claim was *ex contractu* but based on a contract that could be severed from the contract that violated exchange control regulations even though the contract treated as severable was part of a single design of evasion.[48] Sometimes, the

---

[48] *Southwestern Shipping Corporation v. National City Bank of New York,* 173 N.Y.S. 2d 509 (1958), 178 N.Y.S. 2d 1019 (1958), 190 N.Y.S. 2d 352 (1959), certiorari denied 361 U.S. 895, 80 S. Ct. 198 (1959) (Gold, "Cuban Insurance Cases," p. 91 in this volume; Gold, *Fund Agreement in the Courts* (1962), pp. 97–100, 102–108); *Varas v. Crown Life Insurance Co.,* 83 Montg. Co. L.R. 71 (1963), 204 Pa. Super. 176, 203 A. 2d 505 (1964), 382 U.S. 827, 86 S. Ct. 62 (1965) (Gold, "Cuban Insurances Cases," pp. 59–61 in this volume); *Sharif v. Azad* [1966] 3 W.L.R. 1285, [1966] 3 All E.R. 785, see pp. 115–16 in this volume.

A decision of the German Federal Supreme Court of May 21, 1964 (VII ZR 23/64) resisted the tendency noted in the text. The plaintiff, a corporation organized under the law of Liechtenstein, entered into an agreement with the defendant, a resident of Germany, under which the plaintiff was to transfer an amount of deutsche mark to the defendant in Hamburg and receive in return an

courts have held that the plaintiff could recover on a noncontractual basis, usually the unjust enrichment of the defendant.[49] The effect of both techniques has been to give remedies that were equivalent to, or better than, the enforcement of a contract that was unenforceable under Article VIII, Section 2(b). Often, in these cases, the courts appear to be favoring some other legal purpose or to be expressing their disapproval of one party. In the case discussed here, Lanata would have to account for his misappropriation but Constant would be helped to carry out his evasion of Algerian exchange control regulations.

The difficulty with denying a claim to the restitution of a payment made under a contract that is unenforceable under Article VIII, Section 2(b), on the ground that restitution would be equivalent to or better than enforcement, is that the provision appears to deal only with the contract. It could be argued, therefore, that it does not deal with remedies outside the contract. Nevertheless, the effect of granting restitution may be to encourage the violation of exchange control regulations because a party making a payment incurs no financial risk. It would seem that courts should refuse such a privileged position to parties either by holding that their domestic doctrines of restitution do not permit recoveries in these cases or by holding that the concept of unenforceability in Article VIII, Section 2(b) is broad enough to deny restitution. The latter attitude would be consistent with the deci-

---

amount in French francs from firms in France. The defendant guaranteed that the payment in French francs would be made within a fixed period. The plaintiff alleged that the payment had not been made and brought this action under the guarantee. Most of the facts were contested, but both parties admitted that the contract was intended to evade French exchange control regulations.

Although the contract was governed by German law, the court held that Article VIII, Section 2(b) must be taken into account. It declared that normally an obligation such as the obligation of the defendant to the plaintiff in this case to pay in deutsche mark outside France would not be affected by French exchange control regulations, but the obligation was to arise only if the French firm failed to make the payment.

The guarantee agreement, therefore, was so "closely and inseparably" linked with the principal and prohibited obligation that it must share the fate of that obligation (*Aussenwirtschaftsdienst des Betriebs-Beraters: Recht der Internationalen Wirtschaft*, No. 7 (July 1964), p. 228).

[49] *Varas v. Crown Life Insurance Co.*, 83 Montg. Co. L.R. 71 (1963), 204 Pa. Super. 176, 203 A. 2d 505 (1964), 382 U.S. 827, 86 S. Ct. 62 (1965) (Gold, "Cuban Insurance Cases," pp. 60, 90–91 in this volume). Cf. *Lessinger v. Mirau*, *Jahrbuch für Internationales Recht*, Vol. 5, Part 1 (1955), pp. 113–23 (Gold, *Fund Agreement in the Courts* (1962), pp. 90–94, 118, and "Cuban Insurance Cases," p. 90 in this volume); *White v. Roberts*, 33 Hong Kong Law Reports (1949), pp. 231–82 (Gold, *Fund Agreement in the Courts* (1962), pp. 87–94, 118, and "Cuban Insurance Cases," p. 90 in this volume).

sion of the Federal Supreme Court of Germany that the court should raise the objection of Article VIII, Section 2(b) because of the public interest served by that provision.

It is likely that when the suit was brought both Constant and Lanata had become residents of France, and the question arises whether, on the test of impact on the balance of payments, the currency of Algeria was still involved under Article VIII, Section 2(b). It has been said that changes in exchange control regulations, the consistency of regulations with the Articles, and membership in the Fund that occur by the time of suit must be taken into account in applying the provision. These facts are not related to the question whether a currency is "involved," but changes in the residence of parties are related to that question. Does it follow that all other changes in the facts related to this question must be taken into account? In particular, would it be proper to hold that Algeria's currency was no longer involved because the only obligation that remained unperformed could not affect its balance of payments, even though the obligations that had affected, or could have affected, its balance of payments—such as the transfer of the dinars (to unreported intermediaries) and removal of the check from Algeria— had been performed? An approach of this kind would mean that whenever the parties succeeded in carrying out that part of the contract that was peculiarly within the mischief against which Article VIII, Section 2(b) was directed, the courts would be available to assist in completing their design. To avoid this result, it would be necessary to consider the contract on which a suit was brought as consisting of all the obligations for which it had provided and not simply as consisting of those that remained unperformed.

5

The Fund Agreement
in the Courts—XI*

This latest installment in the series of articles dealing with jurisprudence in which the Fund's charter has been involved discusses
cases decided by the Federal Maritime Commission of the United
States and the U.S. District Court for the Southern District of New
York, the European Court of Justice, and the Supreme Court of the
Netherlands. The issues raise or suggest some of the problems that
the decline of the par value system has created or may create for the
parties to transnational transactions and the drafters of international
or private agreements.

What Is a "Devaluation"?

In *Australia/U.S. Atlantic & Gulf Conference, Proposed Imposition
of Currency Adjustment Surcharge*,[1] a proceeding before the Federal
Maritime Commission of the United States, the issue involved a surcharge on freight rates of 6.32 per cent imposed by the Conference as
from January 8, 1972. The surcharge had been agreed by the Conference with shippers in Australia and was designed to prevent them
from enjoying a profit by paying freight in U.S. dollars, compared
with the increase in effective costs for lines that had to pay expenses
in Australian currency in Australia. The surcharge had been calcu-

---

* Originally published in March 1975.
[1] Federal Maritime Commission, Docket No. 72-5, January 28, 1972.

lated on the basis of a so-called devaluation of 8.57[2] per cent of the U.S. dollar and a decision of the Australian Government to revalue the Australian dollar and to tie it to the U.S. dollar at an appreciation of 6.32 per cent. The Conference filed notice of the surcharge with the Federal Maritime Commission of the United States, to take effect within 15 days in accordance with Article 23(b) of the Shippers Rate Agreement the Conference had entered into with shippers. The Commission challenged the action under the Shipping Act, 1916[3] on the ground that a surcharge could be imposed on 15 days' notice under Article 23(b) of the agreement only in the conditions described in Article 23(a) and those conditions had not occurred. Article 23(a) reads as follows:

> In the event of . . . currency devaluation by governmental action, regulations of any governmental authority pertaining thereto, or any other official interferences with commercial intercourse arising from the above conditions, which prejudicially affect the operations of any of the Carriers in the trade covered by this Agreement so as to render it reasonably impracticable or partially impracticable to continue such operations. . . .[4]

The Commission ordered the Conference to show cause why the surcharge should not be subject to a provision of the Act under which 90 days' notice was required. The Conference persisted in its position that its tariff was properly filed, and the Commission resorted to the courts for a temporary restraining order. On February 4, 1972, in *Federal Maritime Commission v. Australia/U.S. Atlantic & Gulf Conference et al.*, the U.S. District Court for the Southern District of New York granted the temporary injunction. In order to be able to grant an injunction the court had to find that the party requesting the injunction was likely to succeed on the merits and that irreparable injury was likely unless the injunction was granted. On the issue of the probable outcome on the merits, the court held that the Shippers Rate Agreement was written in terms of U.S. currency, and it was unlikely therefore that the agreement was meant to refer to a devaluation by some government other than the Government of the United States. The court was motivated by the consideration that "in

---

[2] The U.S. Administration had agreed as part of the Smithsonian agreement to propose to Congress an increase of 8.57 per cent in the price of gold in terms of U.S. dollars, which corresponded to a devaluation of the U.S. dollar by 7.89 per cent.

[3] 46 U.S.C.A. §817(b).

[4] Shippers Rate Agreement, Article 23 (printed in Federal Maritime Commission, Docket 72-5, cited in fn. 1), p. 13.

view of the ease and frequency with which other governments throughout the world"[5] had taken action to affect the value of their currencies, it was questionable whether the parties to the agreement would have agreed, or the Commission would have approved an agreement, that "could have been so easily and often changed on short notice."[6] The court then held that it was a "simple and undeniable fact"[7] that the U.S. dollar had not been devalued officially, and that only Congress could take that action.

On the issue of irreparable damage, the court accepted the argument that the increased tariff would cause damage to the U.S. wool industry, which had made firm commitments based on rates of exchange prevailing at the time the commitments were entered into, so that increases in cost could not be passed on to consumers.

On January 18, 1972 the Commission issued an Order to Show Cause why the Commission should not find the imposition of the surcharge to be in violation of various provisions of the Shipping Act. Counsel for the Commission argued that the language of Article 23(a) of the Shippers Rate Agreement meant an official devaluation of the U.S. dollar by Congress because the tariffs of the Conference quoted freight rates in U.S. dollars. The Conference argued that the words "governmental action" were not confined to action by the Congress of the United States to change the par value of the dollar, and that those words as well as the phrases "governmental authority" and "any other official interferences" referred to actions by other governments in addition to the Government of the United States. Moreover, the Conference tariff had been amended in certain respects to refer to the conversion of the U.S. dollar into Australian currency. The Australian Government had taken action on December 22, 1971 to recognize the devaluation of the U.S. dollar by revaluing the Australian dollar, an action that fell within the scope of Article 23(a) of the agreement.

In any event, the Conference argued, the U.S. dollar had been devalued by governmental action within the meaning of Article 23(a) by the participation of the United States in the Smithsonian agreement of December 18, 1971, under which the Government agreed to an immediate effective devaluation of 8.57 per cent and the removal of the surcharge on imports in return for the revaluation of certain other currencies. These actions, the Conference argued, were within the powers of the President of the United States.

---

[5] 337 F. Supp. 1032, at 1036 (1972).
[6] *Ibid.*
[7] *Ibid.*

The Conference advanced a further argument, which it based on certain actions of the Fund. On December 18, 1971 the Fund had adopted a decision to give effect to certain aspects of the Smithsonian agreement by establishing a temporary regime of wider margins for exchange rates based on the par values resulting from the realignment of currencies under the Smithsonian agreement. The U.S. Government, the Conference argued, had joined in a decision of the Fund under which the Fund had revalued SDRs against the U.S. dollar in advance of any formal action by the United States. Therefore, in practice, the dollar had been devalued against SDRs, because a country wishing to obtain U.S. dollars could obtain them at the rate of $1.08 instead of the former rate of $1 for each SDR. The international value of the U.S. dollar had already been adjusted in practice, and the change in the par value of the dollar in terms of gold would not have any further effect on exchange rates in the market.

The Maritime Commission, in an opinion of four Comissioners delivered on September 12, 1972,[8] preferred the narrower meaning of "currency devaluation" on the ground that the clause in which it appeared had been inserted in Article 23(a) by amendment after an official devaluation of sterling. It followed that interpretation of the clause had to take that event into account. The Commission agreed with the District Court that the formulation of the agreement and the tariff in terms of U.S. dollars was relevant. The Commission further agreed with the court that the purpose of Article 23(a) would not be assured if shippers could "be buffeted by an unforeseeable number of short-notice increases" resulting from the actions taken by other governments to change the value of their currencies. The Commission concluded that if the Conference had intended the meaning for which it had argued, it would have been easy to employ such language as "action of any government" instead of "governmental action" and "*de facto* devaluation" instead of "devaluation."

A fifth Commissioner dissented from the view of the majority that the filing of the revised tariff was an obvious nullity, and that it could be rejected for that reason without a hearing. He thought that the intention of the parties to the Shippers Rate Agreement, and of the Commission when it approved the amendment of the agreement that dealt with devaluation, had to be investigated. It was not obvious that they had been thinking only of devaluation by Congress. *De facto* devaluation by or flowing from governmental action might have been

---

[8] Pikes and Fischer, 13 SRR 289–99.

within the intent of the agreement. The declaration by the President of the United States on August 15, 1971 or the Smithsonian agreement may have amounted to a *de facto* devaluation of the U.S. dollar. He pointed out that the converse of the assumption that shippers were not to be buffeted by changes in rates made easily and frequently on short notice was that carriers could be buffeted by devaluations made easily and frequently on short notice. He concluded, however, that the Conference had not submitted evidence of intent, and therefore he would construe the language strictly and adversely to the Conference, so that in the event he concurred in the result reached by the other Commissioners.

The Conference petitioned the U.S. Court of Appeals for the District of Columbia Circuit for a review of the Commission's Order. The appeal was dismissed as moot because a subsequent tariff had become effective that was the same as the one that the Commission had ruled invalid. The Court noted that the issues that had been raised might recur in other circumstances, and if these issues should arise again, judicial review of them would not be precluded.

The practical result of the proceeding was that the Conference was unable to levy the surcharge for any period before the change in par value of the U.S. dollar took effect on May 8, 1972.

The main feature of the case is the conclusion that "devaluation" of the U.S. dollar meant devaluation as the result of action by Congress.[9] The words "devaluation," "depreciation," "revaluation," and "appreciation" are useful because they can describe different phenomena, but they are often employed loosely.[10] It would contribute to clarity if "devaluation" were confined to a reduction in par value in terms of gold as a common denominator, and "depreciation" to a reduction in terms of other currencies, usually in the market. It cannot be asserted, however, that this usage is always observed[11] or that a precise legal

---

[9] Section 5 of the Bretton Woods Agreements Act (59 Stat. 514 (1945)): "Unless Congress by law authorizes such action, neither the President nor any person or agency shall on behalf of the United States . . . (b) propose or agree to any change in the par value of the United States dollar under Article IV, Section 5, or Article XX, Section 4, of the Articles of Agreement of the Fund, or approve any general change in par values under Article IV, Section 7. . . ."

[10] Cf. the frequent confusion between "par value" and "parity."

[11] Note, for example, the words "normally" and "generally" in the following passage: "The terms devaluation and revaluation normally are reserved for changes in the par value which make the currency concerned cheaper or more expensive in terms of other currencies. Where similar changes occur in an exchange rate that is not a par value, the terms depreciation and appreciation are

terminology has become established. The etymological difference between them is not likely to promote precision. "Devaluation" means a reduction in worth, and "depreciation" a reduction in price. As the dissenting commissioner suggested, it is not impossible that the parties had used the word "devaluation" to include "depreciation" in the sense of a decline in terms of other currencies or in the sense of what the four commissioners called "*de facto* devaluation."

It may be pertinent that Article 23(a) refers to devaluation by governmental action. If "devaluation" was intended to mean only a change in par value, the phrase "by governmental action" was redundant. It is at least conceivable that the drafters of the agreement were emphasizing governmental action, in order to encompass all changes in exchange rates that resulted from deliberate governmental action.

The Fund's Articles do not employ the term "devaluation," but refer in one context to a reduction in par value.[12] "Depreciation" does appear in the clause "the foreign exchange value of a member's currency has, in the opinion of the Fund, depreciated to a significant extent within that member's territories." In this clause, "depreciation" is used in contrast to "devaluation," but another provision declares that the avoidance of "competitive exchange depreciation" is a purpose of the Fund. In that context, "depreciation" must include both phenomena.[13]

If the parties had intended the word "devaluation" in Article 23 of the Shippers Rate Agreement to have a broad meaning, the Commission would have had to decide whether the U.S. dollar had depreciated within the territories of the United States and whether it had depreciated "by governmental action." The announcement of August 15, 1971 declaring that foreign official holdings of U.S. dollars would not normally be converted into gold or other reserve assets by the U.S. authorities was certainly "governmental action." Another govern-

---

generally used. Depreciation or appreciation may involve either discrete or gradual changes in value," in "Glossary of Exchange Concepts," *IMF Survey*, Vol. 1 (August 28, 1972), p. 32.

See also *The International Monetary Fund, 1945–1965: Twenty Years of International Monetary Cooperation*, ed. by J. Keith Horsefield (Washington, 1969), Vol. II, pp. 111 *et seq.*; Vol. III, pp. 24 and 111 (hereinafter cited as *History, 1945–65*); Gottfried Haberler, "U.S. Balance of Payments Policy and the International Monetary System," in *Convertibility, Multilateralism and Freedom: World Economic Policy in the Seventies—Essays in Honour of Reinhard Kamitz*, ed. by Wolfgang Schmitz (Vienna, 1972), pp. 187–91; "SDRs: New Look," *The Economist*, Vol. 252 (July 6, 1974), p. 96.

[12] Article IV, Section 8(*b*), *original* and *first*.

[13] Article I(iii).

mental action was taken by the Secretary of the U.S. Treasury in notifying the Managing Director of the Fund, in a letter dated August 15, 1971, that "effective August 15, 1971, the United States no longer, for the settlement of international transactions, in fact, freely buys and sells gold" under the second sentence of Article IV, Section 4(b).[14] On August 20, 1971 the Fund adopted a decision in which it noted that

> exchange transactions in the territories of the United States have been occurring outside the limits prescribed by Article IV, Section 3, and the actions taken by the United States authorities do not at the present time ensure that transactions between their currency and the currencies of other members take place within their territories only within the limits prescribed by Article IV, Section 3.[15]

The participation of the United States in the Smithsonian agreement could have been regarded as a further "governmental action." Paragraph 5 of the Communiqué of the Ministerial Meeting of the Group of Ten on December 17 and 18, 1971 announcing the Smithsonian agreement included the following statement:

> The United States agreed to propose to Congress a suitable means for devaluing the dollar in terms of gold to $38.00 per ounce as soon as the related set of short-term measures is available for Congressional scrutiny. Upon passage of required legislative authority in this framework, the United States will propose the corresponding new par value of the dollar to the International Monetary Fund.[16]

The announcement by the issuer of a major currency of its intention to make a future change in the par value of its currency was an extraordinary action,[17] and one may wonder what was the appropriate word to describe the immediate effect of the announcement on exchange rates. A bill to modify the par value of the U.S. dollar was introduced

---

[14] IMF Press Release No. 853, August 20, 1971, reproduced in *International Financial News Survey*, Vol. 23 (August 25, 1971), p. 261. (Hereinafter cited as *IFNS*.)

[15] Executive Board Decision No. 3399-(71/90), August 20, 1971. (This decision is paraphrased in IMF Press Release No. 853, cited in fn. 14.)

[16] *IFNS*, Vol. 23 (December 22–30, 1971), p. 418; *Annual Report of the Secretary of the Treasury on the State of the Finances for the Fiscal Year Ended June 30, 1972* (Washington, 1972), p. 370.

[17] It occurred again with respect to the subsequent change in the par value of the U.S. dollar. The Secretary of the U.S. Treasury announced on February 12, 1973—IMF Press Release No. 957, February 13, 1973, reproduced in *IMF Survey*, Vol. 2 (February 26, 1973), p. 53—that the President was requesting Congress to authorize the change, which took effect with the concurrence of the Fund on October 18, 1973. Once again the proposed change became effective in the exchange markets immediately after the announcement.

167

in Congress on February 9, 1972. The change in par value was made on May 8, 1972, but it did not affect the relationships among currencies in the markets that had resulted from the Smithsonian agreement. In the words of the Secretary of the Treasury, "devaluation of the dollar will formalize the pattern of exchange rates negotiated last December and which since then, de facto, has prevailed in the exchange markets."[18]

In its arguments before the Maritime Commission, the Conference argued that certain decisions of the Fund supported the case presented by the Conference. The change in the par value of the U.S. dollar from $35 to $38 per fine ounce of gold was not established under the Articles until May 8, 1972. The actions of the Fund after the Smithsonian agreement and before May 8, 1972 were complex. If the par value of a member's currency is changed, the member must adjust the Fund's holdings of the currency so that the gold value of the holdings corresponds to the new par value. The Fund is authorized, however, to find that although there has been no change in the par value of a member's currency, its foreign exchange value has depreciated to a significant extent within the member's territories, and the member must then pay to the Fund an amount of its own currency equal to the reduction in the gold value of the Fund's holdings of the currency.[19] At no time after August 15, 1971 or after the Smithsonian agreement did the Fund find that there had been a depreciation in the foreign exchange value of the U.S. dollar for the purpose of requiring the United States to maintain the gold value of the Fund's holdings of U.S. dollars.

After the Smithsonian agreement the Fund took other decisions, however, based on a change in the value of the U.S. dollar to the equivalent of $38 per fine ounce of gold. In order to help to minimize disorder in the exchanges, the Fund adopted a decision on December 18, 1971 by which it defined arrangements that members could observe and be deemed thereby to be fulfilling their obligation "to collaborate with the Fund to promote exchange stability, to maintain orderly exchange arrangements with other members, and to avoid competitive exchange alterations."[20] These arrangements involved "central rates," as a substitute for new par values, and margins wider

---

[18] U.S. Congress, House, Committee on Banking and Currency, *To Provide For a Modification in the Par Value of the Dollar*, Hearings on H.R. 13120 (92nd Congress, 2nd Session, Washington, March 1–3 and 6, 1972), p. 4.

[19] Article IV, Section 8(b), *original* and *first*.

[20] Article IV, Section 4(a), *original* and *first*.

than those permitted by the Articles for exchange rates in exchange transactions.[21] The margins permitted by the Articles are around the parity between the two currencies involved in any exchange transaction, that is, around the ratio between the two currencies based on their par values. The decision permitted the calculation of wider margins to be made on the basis of the central rates of the currencies involved in an exchange transaction. Neither central rates nor wider margins are compatible with the provisions of the Articles on par values and exchange rates. The Fund's decision could not validate the practices it was recognizing, even though the Fund was willing to accept them as a mitigation of the harm that could follow from totally unregulated exchange rates.

One issue that had to be faced in formulating the decision was whether the ratio between the U.S. dollar and another currency would be based on the par value of the dollar, which remained unchanged at $35 per fine ounce of gold. The Fund was unwilling to assume for all its purposes that there had been no change in the value of the dollar, because it was expected that the promised change in par value would be reflected in exchange rates without delay. It was decided, therefore, that margins would be calculated for the purposes of the decision as if the change in par value had taken effect already. This working assumption was expressed in the novel phrase "effective parity relationships."[22] In a sense, however, the assumption affected the conduct of other members and not the United States. Other members continued to intervene in the exchange markets to maintain exchange rates within margins, and the effect of the decision was to enable them to enjoy the greater flexibility of central rates and wider margins. The United States continued to refrain from intervention, and therefore it was not faced with the practical necessity of calculating margins for the guidance of its conduct in the exchange market on the assumption that the change in par value had become effective. Indeed, the decision was written in such a way that the United States would not have been able to declare a central rate and to employ wider margins unless it had adopted a practice of intervening in the exchange market.

On January 4, 1972 the Fund adopted a decision that established the principles according to which members would be required to

---

[21] See Joseph Gold, "The Legal Structure of the Par Value System," *Law and Policy in International Business*, Vol. 5 (No. 1, 1973), pp. 194–98.

[22] *Selected Decisions of the International Monetary Fund and Selected Documents*, Sixth Issue (Washington, 1972), p. 12; hereinafter cited as *Selected Decisions*, Sixth Issue. (*Selected Decisions*, Eighth Issue, pp. 14–17.)

adjust the Fund's holdings of their currencies pursuant to the obligation of members to maintain the gold value of those holdings. Once again the decision was formulated so as not to require the United States to adjust the Fund's holdings of U.S. dollars even though other members were required to adjust the Fund's holdings of their currencies on the basis of their effective parity relationships with the U.S. dollar as explained above.

By the same decision the Fund made a temporary change in Rule O-3, which determines the rates of exchange at which participants provide currency, or convert it, when SDRs are transferred between participants. Under Rule O-3, the exchange rate for the U.S. dollar was taken to be its par value and the rates for other currencies were certain representative rates in the markets for the spot delivery of U.S. dollars. After the Smithsonian agreement, the par value for the U.S. dollar was unacceptable as the basis for determining the amount of dollars to be provided in return for SDRs, and the Fund therefore suspended the operation of that part of Rule O-3 under which the par value was prescribed in transfers of SDRs for U.S. dollars. A formula was adopted by which sterling or French francs would be provided on the basis of the par values of those currencies adjusted by reference to their effective parity relationships to the U.S. dollar and their representative rates. The formula ensured that if the amount of sterling or French francs provided for SDRs were converted into U.S. dollars for the benefit of the transferor of SDRs, it would receive the same amount of U.S. dollars as if dollars had been provided directly and on the basis that the par value had in fact been changed. In short, the transferor would receive dollars as if one SDR were equal to $1.08571 instead of $1.00.

The effect of the Fund's decisions can be summarized by saying that the Fund did not decide that, as a result of the Smithsonian agreement, the par value of the U.S. dollar had been reduced or that its foreign exchange value had declined, but for the purposes of transactions and operations involving other currencies conducted through the General Account and the Special Drawing Account, the Fund acted as if the prospective change in the par value of the dollar, announced in the Smithsonian agreement, had already taken place.

The Conference contended that something similar to the Fund's decisions should be recognized for the purposes of the revised tariff. The Commission refused, basically because of the way in which it understood the word "devaluation" in the Shippers Rate Agreement. If the drafters of that agreement had indeed intended to confine the meaning of the word to a change in par value, they probably had done so in the belief that an effective par value system with narrow margins would be maintained. Since August 15, 1971 the drafters of agreements have been forced to abandon that belief, and they are faced with even greater difficulties of concept and terminology than in the past.

Narrow Margins

A case before the European Court of Justice illustrates reliance on a system of par values and narrow margins for another purpose, that is, the rates of exchange to be used in calculations involving the conversion of currencies in connection with the common agricultural policy of the European Economic Community.[23] In *Gesellschaft für Getreidehandel AG v. Einfuhr- und Vorratsstelle für Getreide und Futtermittel,*[24] the plaintiff received a license on January 28, 1966 from the competent German authority, under which the plaintiff imported a quantity of maize from France in February 1966. The import was made at a free-at-frontier price of 508.86 French francs per *tonne,* in accordance with a decision of the Commission of the Common Market, with a levy of 11.59 deutsche mark per *tonne* fixed by the German authority on the basis of that price. The plaintiff instituted proceedings before the Finanzgericht Hessen in which it claimed that the levy was too high, and the Finanzgericht concluded that the issue depended on the validity of the decision of the Commission. Thereupon, the Finanzgericht, acting under Article 177 of the Treaty of

---

[23] Regulation No. 129 adopted by the Council of the European Economic Community. ". . . WHEREAS it is necessary to fix the exchange rates to be used for transactions within the framework of the common agricultural policy which involve expressing in one currency sums shown in another currency; whereas all Member States and a large number of third countries have declared a parity for their currency to the International Monetary Fund, which has recognised the same; whereas under this body's rules the exchange rates applying to current transactions and quoted on foreign exchange markets, which, subject to supervision by the monetary authorities of countries the parity of whose currency has been recognised by the Fund, are allowed to fluctuate only within narrow limits about that parity figure; whereas in consequence the use of the exchange rate corresponding to the said parity normally makes it possible to avoid the monetary difficulties which might prevent the common agricultural policy being carried out . . ." Alan Campbell, *Common Market Law* (London, 1969), Vol. II, p. 502; hereinafter referred to as Campbell, *Common Market Law.*

[24] *Common Market Law Reports,* Vol. 13 (February 1974), pp. 186–202; *Recueil de la Jurisprudence de la Cour,* Vol. 18 (No. 7, 1972), pp. 1071–90.

Rome,[25] requested the European Court of Justice for a preliminary decision on the question of the validity of the Commission's decision. This aspect of the case need not be pursued further in this discussion, but in July 1972 the Finanzgericht transmitted an additional question to the European Court of Justice as the result of a further argument by the plaintiff. The new argument was that the levy was invalid because the Commission had erred in failing to authorize the Federal Republic under Article 2(2) of the Council's Regulation No. 129 of October 23, 1962 to convert French francs into deutsche mark at the rate of exchange in the German foreign exchange market instead of the parity relationship between the two currencies established under the Articles of Agreement of the Fund. The plaintiff argued that there was a considerable difference between the two at the relevant date, and that if the exchange rate had been applied, the free-at-frontier price would have been approximately 1 per cent higher and the levy correspondingly lower.

Article 1 of Regulation No. 129 provides that whenever accounting units are referred to in formal measures adopted by the Council concerning the common agricultural policy, or in provisions pursuant to those measures, the value of the unit is to be 0.88867088 gram of fine gold. Under Article 2(1) when transactions pursuant to the measures or provisions require the expression of a currency in terms of another currency, the exchange rate to be applied shall be "the parity declared to the International Monetary Fund recognised by the latter." Article 2(2), however, provides for departures from this rule:

> There may be cases, in one or more countries, where, on the foreign exchange market which is subject to supervision by the country's monetary authorities, there are fluctuations in the exchange rate from the rate corresponding to the parity declared to the International Monetary Fund and recognised by the latter which though within the

---

[25] Article 177 of the Treaty Establishing the European Economic Community: "The Court of Justice shall be competent to make a preliminary decision concerning: (a) the interpretation of this Treaty; (b) the validity and interpretation of acts of the institutions of the Community; and (c) the interpretation of the statutes of any bodies set up by an act of the Council, where such statutes so provide.

"Where any such question is raised before a court or tribunal of one of the Member States, such court or tribunal may, if it considers that its judgment depends on a preliminary decision on this question, request the Court of Justice to give a ruling thereon.

"Where any such question is raised in a case pending before a domestic court or tribunal from whose decisions no appeal lies under municipal law, such court or tribunal shall refer the matter to the Court of Justice."

limits prescribed under this body's rules, are in exceptional cases such as to endanger effect being given to the measures or provisions referred to in Article I. In such cases the Council of the Commission, acting in accordance with the powers conferred by such measures or provisions and the procedures laid down in such measures or provisions in each instance, may decide that, for the currencies in question, the exchange rates quoted on the most representative market or markets, as provided in paragraph 4, should temporarily be applied in transactions to be effected for the purposes of those measures or provisions.[26]

The Commission argued that Article 2(2) applied only exceptionally, namely, when there were severe market disturbances that threatened the common agricultural policy, and that there had been no circumstances of this kind in February 1962. The plaintiff relied on the Commission's Regulation No. 67 of July 11, 1962 with respect to the criteria for the modification of levies on grains, flours, cereal groats, and semolinas. According to this regulation, no modification is to be made in a levy on these products if a calculation based on the elements that determine the levy show a variation of not more than 0.75 or less than 0.45 unit of account from the existing levy. The plaintiff argued that a deviation in excess of 0.75 unit could be taken to indicate the existence of a market disturbance within the meaning of Article 2(2) of Regulation No. 129. The Court held that the plaintiff had not established that there had been exceptional circumstances in which fluctuations in exchange rates had endangered the common marketing arrangements or policy. The Commission had adopted Regulation No. 67 in the interest of administrative simplification. The purpose was to avoid adjustments in the levy within a certain range

---

[26] Campbell, *Common Market Law*, Vol. II, p. 503.

See also Article 3(1) of Regulation No. 129:

"*Exceptional measures*

"1. Where monetary practices of an exceptional nature are such as to endanger effect being given to the measures or provisions referred to in Article I, the Council or the Commission, acting in accordance with the powers conferred by such measures or provisions and the procedures laid down in such measures or provisions in each instance, may, after consulting the Monetary Committee, take measures which are exceptional to the present regulation, in particular in the following cases:

"(a) when a member country of the International Monetary Fund, having declared to that institution a parity for its currency and that parity being recognised by the same, permits fluctuations in the value of its currency in excess of the limits laid down under this body's rules;

"(b) when a country resorts to abnormal exchange techniques such as variable or multiple exchange rates or applied a barter agreement;

"(c) in the case of countries whose currency is not quoted on official foreign exchange markets." Campbell, *Common Market Law*, Vol. II, pp. 503–504.

as the result of variations in exchange rates. The Regulation did not imply that variations outside the range were in themselves an indication of serious disturbance.[27]

The practice of the Fund in valuing currencies in the changing circumstances of the last few years illustrates the problems that must be faced by the draftsmen of legal provisions now that they can rely no longer on the observance of par values and narrow margins. In February 1966, the relevant date in the case before the European Court, the Fund's system of valuation was based on par values. Calculations involving a member's currency for the purposes of the Fund's operations and transactions and for all other purposes were made on the basis of the par value of the currency established by the member under the Articles even though exchange transactions in the market between the member's currency and the currency of any other member were permitted to take place within certain margins around the parity between the two currencies. Under the Articles, the margin that a member is required to observe for spot exchange transactions taking place within its territories is 1 per cent on either side of the parity between its currency and the other currency involved in each transaction.[28] The Fund continued to base its calculations on par values even after it exercised its authority to approve multiple currency practices in order to permit what was in effect a broadening of the margins for exchange transactions.[29] In December 1958, a number of European members, including those in the Common Market, decided to adopt margins for exchange transactions involving the issuer's currency and the U.S. dollar of approximately or exactly 0.75 per cent of the parity between the two currencies. The result of this practice when adopted by two members that used the U.S. dollar for intervention was a cumulation of margins, up to 1.5 per cent of parity, for transactions involving their two currencies. Moreover, the margins might be even wider in transactions involving a currency pegged on a currency that was itself pegged on the U.S. dollar. The European members decided to employ these margins in order to make it easier for them to establish free exchange markets and the *de facto* (or "external") convertibility of their currencies for the benefit of nonresidents, and at the same time to economize somewhat in the use of

---

[27] For subsequent action on the unit of account, see Campbell, *Common Market Law*, Vol. II, pp. 535–37; and Council Regulation No. 2543/73 of September 19, 1973, in *Official Journal of the European Communities*, Vol. 16, No. L 263 (September 19, 1973).

[28] Article IV, Sections 3 and 4(b), *original* and *first*.

[29] Article VIII, Section 3, *original* and *first*.

reserves. The Fund held that these objectives justified approval of the practice. It decided therefore on July 24, 1959 to approve, as multiple currency practices, margins of 2 per cent of parity when they resulted from the maintenance of margins of 1 per cent for transactions between a member's currency and the convertible or *de facto* convertible currency of another member.[30]

In 1966, the only circumstances in which the Fund made its calculations on some basis other than the par value of a currency for which a par value had been established were circumstances in which the issuer of the currency was failing to observe margins consistent with the Articles for transactions involving its currency. Under the Articles, this failure does not result in the legal abrogation of the par value, but the Fund nevertheless has the authority, under a provision that compels members to maintain the gold value of the Fund's holdings of their currencies,[31] to apply rates of exchange that reflect the foreign exchange value of currencies that have depreciated or appreciated in the issuer's market. Because the issuer of what was called a fluctuating currency was bound to maintain the gold value of the Fund's holdings of the currency, the Fund applied the exchange rate for spot exchange transactions involving the member's currency and the U.S. dollar in the member's main exchange market. The principle on which the U.S. dollar was chosen for this purpose was that the United States had announced to the Fund that it observed a policy of maintaining the value of its currency by means of gold transactions with the monetary authorities of other members.[32] The Fund applied these rates of exchange in calculations involving a fluctuating currency even if from time to time rates were within the margins prescribed by the Articles or approved by the Fund.

In 1968, when the amendment of the Articles was drafted in order to establish the Special Drawing Account, it was decided that SDRs would be defined in terms of gold.[33] It became necessary, therefore, to determine how the equivalent in currency of the defined amount of gold would be calculated when SDRs were transferred between participants in the Special Drawing Account. It was agreed that if a participant transferred SDRs to another participant designated by the

---

[30] Executive Board Decision No. 904-(59/32), July 24, 1959, *Selected Decisions*, Third Issue, p. 11. (*Selected Decisions*, Eighth Issue, p. 13.)

[31] Article IV, Section 8, *original* and *first*. See also Gold, Pamphlet No. 6, Second Edition, 1971.

[32] Article IV, Section 4(*b*), *original* and *first*.

[33] Article XXI, Section 2, *first*.

Fund to receive them, the transferor should be allowed to choose the currency convertible in fact that it wished to receive but the transferee should be allowed to choose the currency convertible in fact that it wished to provide. If it had been agreed that par values should be applied in calculating the amount of currency to be provided for a transfer of SDRs, the transferor would have been likely to call for the currency that was most appreciated in the market, while the transferee would have been likely to provide the currency that was most depreciated. It was necessary, therefore, to reconcile the choices that were to be allowed to both transferor and transferee, and to do this in a way that did not favor the one or the other. This requirement meant that the solution could not be based on par values, even though in 1968 most members were maintaining par values and narrow margins, because if par values were applied either the transferor or the transferee might gain an advantage in relation to the exchange rate for the currency provided compared with the rate for some other currency that might have been provided.

The problems were solved by means of the so-called principle of equal value, according to which the value of the amount of currency received by the transferor does not vary materially with the choice of transferee or currency. If the currency provided by the transferee of SDRs is not the currency requested by the transferor, the issuer of the currency provided must convert it into the currency requested by the transferor. The transferee must provide an amount of currency which, when converted, will yield to the transferor the same value that would have been received had the transferee provided directly the currency requested by the transferor. The principle of equal value was achieved by a rule that based the necessary calculations on the par value for the U.S. dollar and, for any other currency, on a representative rate for exchange transactions between that currency and the U.S. dollar in the market of the currency.[34] The representative rate for a currency is determined according to a standing procedure agreed between the Fund and the issuer of the currency.

Calculations for the purpose of carrying out operations and transactions conducted through what became the General Account of the Fund once the amendment took effect on July 28, 1969, including operations and transactions in SDRs conducted with the Fund itself through that Account, continued to be made in the manner already

---

[34] Rules and Regulations, Rule O-3, *By-Laws, Rules and Regulations,* Thirty-Second Issue (Washington, July 10, 1974), pp. 54–56.

described, that is, on the basis of the par value of the currency involved, except when it was fluctuating. After December 18, 1971 a fundamental change occurred because the exception became widespread in practice and ceased to be exceptional. With the Fund's recognition of central rates and margins wider than those approved by the Fund, on July 24, 1959, and with few, if any, members observing the narrow margins of the past, the Fund decided on January 4, 1972 that calculations based on par values had become almost wholly inappropriate. With few exceptions, therefore, calculations were to be made thereafter on the basis of the representative rates that were being applied for the purposes of the Special Drawing Account.[35]

Gold Value

On October 27, 1967, a collision occurred on a waterway in the Netherlands between the motor ship Hornland, which belonged to Hornlinie, a corporation subject to the law of the Federal Republic of Germany, and the motor ship Président Pierre Angot, which belonged to Société Nationale des Pétroles, a corporation subject to the law of France. Both vessels sank, and large expenses were incurred in raising the Hornland and its cargo. It was found that both vessel and cargo had suffered great damage. The collision led to litigation that was decided finally by the Supreme Court of the Netherlands on April 14, 1972 in *Hornlinie v. Société Nationale des Pétroles Aquitaine*.[36] In the appeal to the Supreme Court, the German corporation was the plaintiff and the French corporation the defendant.

The parties agreed that the collision was attributable to the negligence of the defendant's vessel to such an extent that the defendant was liable in damages for not less than the amount to which it had limited its liability. This amount was governed by Article 740(d), paragraph 4 of the Commercial Code of the Netherlands, which had been adopted to give effect to Article 3, paragraph 6 of the Treaty Concerning the Limitation of Liability of Owners of Seagoing Vessels, signed at Brussels on October 10, 1957. The two provisions permit the limitation of liability by reference to a franc with a content of 65.5 milligrams of gold nine-tenths fine. This franc is often called the Poincaré franc. It is, of course, no longer in circulation, but it has

---

[35] Executive Board Decision No. 3537-(72/3) G/S, January 4, 1972, reproduced in *Annual Report, 1972*, pp. 87–88.
[36] *Nederlandse Jurisprudentie*, 1972, No. 269, pp. 728–38.

been employed in a number of international treaties as a unit of value.[37] Article 740(d) of the Commercial Code provides that "this franc is to be converted into Netherlands currency at the rate of the day." According to the treaty, the amounts mentioned in the treaty "shall be converted into the national currency of the State in which limitation is sought on the basis of the value of that currency by reference to the unit defined above at the date on which the ship-owner shall have" taken certain actions to limit his liability. The parties agreed that May 2, 1969 was the day for which a rate should be chosen for the conversion of 2,313,360 Poincaré francs into Netherlands guilders.

The defendant computed the value of the francs at 555,515 guilders on the basis that one franc was equal to 0.240133 Netherlands guilder. This computation was based on a gold price of US$35.00 per troy ounce of fine gold under the Fund's Articles and the par value of the guilder of 3.62 guilders per U.S. dollar established by the Netherlands with the Fund on May 2, 1969. The plaintiff argued that the computation should be based on the "real value" of gold, which was higher than $35 per ounce. The defendant agreed to pay any excess over 555,515 guilders that might be found to be payable in these proceedings.

The plaintiff contended that until March 1968 the price of gold in the free market had been based on $35 per ounce, but that the central banks of the countries that formed the gold pool had then decided to stop supplying gold to the market at that price, with the result that the market price had diverged from the former price. The central banks of members of the Fund continued to maintain the former price among themselves, but their practice was irrelevant for "third parties," because the central banks no longer provided gold to them at that price. On May 2, 1969, transactions in gold in the market were freely permitted, and were taking place in the Netherlands. The plaintiff

---

[37] See, for example, Article 22 of Convention for the Unification of Certain Rules Relating to International Carriage by Air, signed at Warsaw, October 12, 1929 (137 L.N.T.S. 11–33 (1933)); Article 6(1) of International Convention for the Unification of Certain Rules Relating to the Carriage of Passengers by Sea, done at Brussels, April 29, 1961 (Nagendra Singh, *International Conventions of Merchant Shipping*, Second Edition (London, 1973), p. 1359); Article 6(4) of International Convention for the Unification of Certain Rules Relating to Carriage of Passenger Luggage by Sea, done at Brussels, May 27, 1967 (*ibid.*, p. 1364); Article III (4) of Convention on the Liability of Operators of Nuclear Ships done at Brussels, May 25, 1962 (*ibid.*, p. 1370). The gold value of the Poincaré franc was fixed by the law of June 25, 1928 under the Poincaré Government.

claimed 705,788.67 guilders on the basis of the price in the market on that day.

The lower court examined the *travaux préparatoires* of the Treaty of Brussels in order to discover the intention of the parties because neither the provision in the Commercial Code nor the provision in the treaty answered the question of valuation clearly. Various delegations participating in the negotiation of the treaty had referred to the difficulties of converting gold francs into currency, particularly because of the difference between the official price and the market price for gold. For this reason some delegations had proposed that conversion should be made at the "official rate of exchange," but it was pointed out that some countries had two official rates, and the proposal was rejected. Another proposal had favored the current market rate of exchange for the currency involved, but this solution was opposed by those who supported the official rate of exchange, and the proposal was not pursued.

The lower court drew from the *travaux préparatoires* the conclusion that the drafters intended that conversion should be at the official rate but that they did not want to provide expressly for this practice because it might not solve all problems, particularly when there were two official rates. The failure to give expression to this mode of valuation, however, did not mean that it had been rejected as the preferred practice.

The court thought nevertheless that because of the changed circumstances since 1968 the question whether computations should be based on the price in the free market should be considered. The clause in the treaty originated with the Warsaw Convention[38] and was adopted in that treaty in order to deal with the possible devaluation of currencies. It was incorporated in the Treaty of Brussels in order to achieve certainty for international maritime creditors as to the maximum amount for which they would be able to have recourse against a vessel owner whatever might be the exchange rate of the currency of payment. Certainty for the vessel owner with respect to the limit of his liability was also an objective, although this certainty

---

[38] For some cases decided by courts in the United States on the Warsaw Convention, see *Koninklijke Luchtvaart Maatschappij N.V. KLM v. Tuller*, 292 F. 2d 775, at 776 (D.C., Cir. June 23, 1961); *Kelley v. Société Anonyme Belge d'Exploitation de la Navigation Aérienne*, 242 F. Supp. 129, at 138 (U.S.D.C., N.Y., April 12, 1965); *Pierre v. Eastern Air Lines*, 152 F. Supp. 486, at 487–88, (U.S.D.C., N.J., June 27, 1957).

was not designed to protect him against the devaluation of his domestic currency.

The lower court pointed out that an accessory but not unimportant consideration in the minds of the drafters was that gold had a stable value. This consideration did not mean, however, that they had sought to give protection against the progressive reduction in the purchasing power of currencies. If the drafters had had this objective they would have drafted the provision in another form. The price of gold had fluctuated and at the date relevant for the proceedings was below the level it had attained earlier, but the purchasing power of money continued to decrease annually. Moreover, the price of gold varied with place as well as time. In some countries the free fixing of price was not tolerated. The choice of a free market price, therefore, would involve much uncertainty for the vessel owner.

Finally, the lower court noted that although the official price of $35 per troy ounce under the Articles of the Fund could be altered, considerable stability in the official price could be expected as a consequence of the operation of the Fund. The court concluded, therefore, that the official price must be applied, and that a German plaintiff pursuing a claim against a French defendant in a Netherlands court could not complain if the amount of the recovery was computed on the basis of a price established by international regulation to which all three countries had adhered.

The plaintiff appealed to the Supreme Court, which confirmed the decision of the lower court. The Supreme Court noted that the provisions of the treaty and of the code refer to conversion (i.e., calculation of one currency in terms of another) on the basis of the value of the national currency, and this suggested that conversion should be based on the official par value of the guilder expressed in gold and not on the price of gold. Most of the states that cooperated in bringing the treaty into existence had accepted the Articles of the Fund, under which understandings existed with respect to the relationships among their currencies expressed, directly or indirectly, in specific amounts of gold. The franc referred to in the treaty was no longer a national currency, but the fact that the drafters adopted as an accounting unit not a weight of gold but a currency with a specific gold content implied that they had in mind the monetary significance of gold and not its commercial value.

The Supreme Court then examined the question whether either of the two theses advanced by the parties would be more effective in realizing the objectives of the provisions in the treaty and in the code, even though the history of the provisions showed that neither the drafters nor the legislature had adopted any particular solution. The Supreme Court noted two objectives. The drafters of the treaty had chosen a fictitious currency in order to avoid tying the destiny of the amount to which liability could be limited to the devaluations and revaluations of a particular currency. Similarly, the prescription in the treaty with respect to the date of conversion was intended to prevent legislatures from destroying the uniformity that was intended by fixing the amount in the national currency in advance. The objectives of avoiding a tie to an existing currency and of not freezing amounts in a currency could be served equally well by either of the two theses that were in contest. Moreover, neither would ensure constancy in terms of purchasing power. Computations based on the price of gold in the market would arrive at larger amounts than computations based on official parities. These larger amounts would not necessarily be related to the purchasing power of the currency involved but would be determined by such factors as speculation.

In these circumstances, the Supreme Court concluded that the objective of uniformity of the Brussels Treaty would be served more effectively by observing the relationships among currencies on the basis of the common valuation of gold according to the Articles of the Fund, to which the great majority of parties to the Brussels Treaty had adhered.[39] This approach would give better results than the diverse and changeable prices for gold in the free markets. The case for applying the official gold value of the guilder was not affected by the disparity between the official price of gold and the price that had developed in the market as a result of the action taken in March 1968 by the countries that had formed the gold pool. The Supreme Court considered that this conclusion was confirmed by the fact that in 1969 the diplomatic conference that had drafted the treaty regarding legal liability for damage by oil pollution [40] had discussed the question at issue in this case, had adopted the same franc for calculating the limitation of liability as was used in the Brussels Treaty, and had accepted the official value of national currency in relation to the franc as the basis for conversion.

---

[39] Article IV, Section 1, *original* and *first*.

[40] International Convention on Civil Liability for Oil Pollution Damage, signed at Brussels, November 29, 1969, *American Journal of International Law*, Vol. 64 (April 1970), pp. 481–90.

The problem in the *Hornlinie* case has been the subject of increasing discussion not only because of the international monetary developments of the last few years but also because at least two conventions that have been opened for signature raise the issue. The Guatemala Protocol to the Warsaw Convention, which was opened for signature on March 8, 1971 but has not yet come into force, does not abandon the use that the Warsaw Convention makes of the Poincaré franc. The proposed International Convention on the Establishment of an International Fund for Compensation for Oil Pollution Damage is intended to supplement the International Convention on Civil Liability for Oil Pollution Damage, 1969, which was mentioned by the Supreme Court of the Netherlands in support of its conclusion. It is a coincidence worth noting that the text of the supplementary convention was agreed at Brussels on December 18, 1971, the day on which the Smithsonian agreement was reached and on which the Fund adopted its decision on central rates and wider margins.

The purposes of the Compensation Fund are to provide compensation for damage resulting from pollution when the protection afforded by the Liability Convention is inadequate, and to give relief to shipowners in respect of certain financial burdens imposed on them by the Liability Convention. The financial terms that give effect to these purposes employ the Poincaré franc.

One view advanced in recent discussions is in opposition to the decision in the *Hornlinie* case and holds that the conversion required by the Guatemala Protocol should be made on the basis of the market price of gold. This argument has been based in part on the legal principle that a market for gold was not invalid under the Articles of the Fund.[41] It has also been argued that the par value of the U.S. dollar is artificial, that the market price has more meaning for private persons, and that the provisions of the conventions in which the Poincaré franc appears are intended to "protect potential victims from the effects of inflation." [42]

Recently, a different view, consistent with the conclusions in the *Hornlinie* case, has been expressed. On April 17 and 18, 1973, hear-

---

[41] Paul P. Heller, "The Warsaw Convention and the 'Two-Tier' Gold Market," *Journal of World Trade Law*, Vol. 7 (January 1973), pp. 126–29. Mr. Heller has elaborated his views in "The Value of the Gold Franc—A Different Point of View," *Journal of Maritime Law and Commerce*, Vol. 6 (October 1974), pp. 73–103.

[42] Allan I. Mendelsohn, "The Value of the Poincaré Gold Franc in Limitation of Liability Conventions," *Journal of Maritime Law and Commerce*, Vol. 5 (October 1973), p. 127.

ings were held before the Subcommittee on Oceans and International Environment of the Committee on Foreign Relations of the U.S. Senate on a bill to implement the proposed convention to create a compensation fund for damage by oil pollution. Senator Pell asked Mr. Herter, Special Assistant to the Secretary of State for Environmental Affairs, to explain the Poincaré franc and what effect the change in the par value of the U.S. dollar and the impending further change would have on the value of the Poincaré franc under the provisions of the convention.

> Is the value of the Poincare Franc to be valued in terms of the relatively artificial price of gold (i.e. $42 per ounce) pegged by the U.S. for purposes of stabilizing international exchange rates or is it to be valued by the more meaningful price established in the free world monetary market? . . .[43]

In a written reply, Mr. Herter explained that the Poincaré franc represents a particular quantity of gold, which must be translated into "the local currency equivalent" to implement the provisions of the proposed convention. The franc is used as a measure of relative value or a standard in a number of multilateral conventions "because it has a specified gold content which will not change, since it is not in use as a national currency. It is thus a stable measure of value." He went on as follows:

> The gold content of the Poincare franc should be valued in the national currencies of the parties to the conventions on the basis of the official price of gold, not on the basis of the price in the free commercial market. Under the two-tier gold system adopted in March 1968 and still in operation, governments and their entities use only the official gold price for transactions and value computations. Under the devaluation legislation now pending in the Congress the dollar official price will be $42.2222 per fine ounce. Since the conventions are agreements between governments, only the official gold price would be used in translating Poincare francs into the domestic currencies of the nations party to the conventions. The negotiators at the 1969 and 1971 Conference clearly had these official gold prices in mind, as is reflected in the dollar estimates of the Convention figures in their reports.
>
> The purpose of such a stable unit is to ensure that the obligations of the shipowners of each country participating in the conventions have the same value as those of all other participants, regardless of fluctuations between currencies. The management of the International

---

[43] U.S. Congress, Senate, Committee on Foreign Relations, Subcommittee on Oceans and International Environment, *International Compensation Fund for Oil Pollution Damage*, Hearings on Executive K, 92nd Congress, 2nd Session, and S. 841, 93rd Congress, 1st Session (Washington, April 17–18, 1973), pp. 120–21.

[Compensation] Fund, the assessment of contributions from oil receivers, the obtaining of insurance or guarantees by shipowners to satisfy liability limits, and the certifications of financial responsibility by national authorities all depend on use of such a stable unit, and they could not function effectively without it. The [Compensation] Fund Convention itself provides in Article 4(6), that the Fund Assembly may increase the compensation limits up to twice the original figure to take into account, among other things, "changes in . . . monetary values"; this was obviously intended to be the mechanism for adjustment for general inflationary trends.[44]

One author, discussing the *Hornlinie* case, has argued that when the equivalent of gold value in a currency must be determined for the purposes of a treaty such as the Brussels Convention as of some date after the establishment of a central rate for the currency, the central rate and not the par value should be applied.[45] Although the *Hornlinie* case was decided by the Supreme Court of the Netherlands on April 14, 1972, the conversion had to be made as of a date that preceded the establishment of a central rate for the guilder.

If the thesis is accepted that the official gold value of a currency and therefore its par value must be applied, it is natural to think of the central rate, when there is one, as a solution. If a domestic court were disposed to adopt this solution, it would probably have to face the question whether there was a sufficient basis under its law to apply the central rate for the currency of the forum.

The Telegraph Regulations and the Telephone Regulations adopted on April 11, 1973 at Geneva as the Final Acts of the World Administrative Telegraph and Telephone Conference of the International Telecommunication Union adopted the solution of central rates in certain circumstances. The Regulations, which entered into force on September 1, 1974, provide for the settlement of accounts by administrations and private operating agencies. In the absence of special arrangements, the accounts, which are to be kept in Germinal francs, another international unit with a gold value,[46] can be settled in the currency

---

[44] *Ibid.*, p. 121. According to the current draft of one international convention in the field of transportation that is being negotiated, the Poincaré franc would be used, and conversion would be made into the currency of the forum on the basis of the official value of the currency. If there were no official value, the competent authority of the state of the forum would determine what should be considered the official value for the purposes of the convention.

[45] S. Royer, "De omrekeningskoers van goudfranken in guldens: pariwaarde of spilkoers?" *Nederlands Juristenblad*, Jaargang 48, 73/20 (May 19, 1973), pp. 601–606.

[46] The Germinal franc was established after the French Revolution by the law of March 28, 1803 (7 Germinal of year XI of the revolutionary calendar) with a gold content of 10/31 gram, nine-tenths fine. In 1865 it was adopted as the

chosen by the creditor. The gold value of the selected currency is to be determined by the par value approved by the Fund or the central rate if established under the Fund's decision after approval of the par value. If the par value or central rate has been adopted unilaterally by the issuer, the use of the selected currency must be acceptable to the debtor.[47]

Two problems arise in connection with the application of central rates. The proposal in favor of the judicial choice of central rates was made, and the Telegraph and Telephone Regulations were adopted, when the Fund's original decision on central rates was still in effect.[48] That decision was drafted on the assumption of fixed and stable relationships among currencies based on par values or on central rates for those currencies for which the issuers preferred the informal concept of a central rate. Whether a central rate for a currency was communicated to the Fund in terms of gold, SDRs, or another currency, it was possible to convert the central rate as communicated into terms of gold, because a communication in terms of another currency was accepted only if a par value or central rate was being observed for that currency. If par values were acceptable as a solution of the problem of uniform value under the conventions that apply a concept of gold value, central rates could have been defended just as readily under the original decision on central rates.

The Fund has amended the original decision on central rates [49] in a way that weakens the justification for the application of them as a

---

gold franc of the Latin Union. Among the conventions in which it appears are International Convention Concerning the Carriage of Goods by Rail (CIM), done at Berne, February 25, 1961 (U.K. Cmnd. 2187) and International Convention Concerning the Carriage of Passengers and Luggage by Rail (CIV), done at Berne, February 25, 1961 (U.K. Cmnd. 2186).

[47] Appendix 1 to each of the two Regulations deals with other situations, and prescribes the rate of exchange between currencies "on the official or generally accepted foreign exchange market" if there is no par value or central rate or if margins recognized by the Articles or the Fund's decisions or previously established by an issuer are not being observed. The Regulations also provide that "[i]f there should be a radical change in the international monetary system (e.g. a substantial general change in the official price of gold, or if gold ceased to be used generally as a basic reference for currencies)" that invalidates or makes it inappropriate to apply the provisions of the Appendix, the administrations and agencies would be free to agree on different provisions pending revision of the Appendix.

[48] Executive Board Decision No. 3463-(71/126), December 18, 1971, *Selected Decisions*, Sixth Issue, pp. 12–15. (*Selected Decisions*, Eighth Issue, pp. 14–17.)

[49] Executive Board Decision No. 4083-(73/104), November 7, 1973, reproduced in *Annual Report, 1974*, Appendix II (Washington, 1974), pp. 103–105. (*Selected Decisions of the International Monetary Fund and Selected Documents*, Seventh Issue (Washington, 1975), pp. 18–21, and *Selected Decisions*, Eighth Issue, pp. 18–21.)

solution of the problem. Certain members of the European Economic Community that purported to maintain central rates under the original decision confine transactions among their own currencies within announced margins around central rates but not transactions involving their currencies and the U.S. dollar. It became difficult, therefore, to resist the argument that a member should be entitled to regard a rate for its currency as a central rate, if it wished, when it was maintaining a rate for its currency within margins of a relationship to a currency, such as sterling, for which the issuer itself was not maintaining a stable rate based on a par value or central rate. If a central rate for a currency was defined in terms of a currency that was not itself stable in the way that has been described, the central rate could not be turned into a gold value. Furthermore, it could no longer be held that a fixed and stable pattern of exchange changes would prevail among currencies on the basis of par values or central rates that would satisfy the objective of uniform value in the discharge of obligations under conventions providing for compensation or the limitation of liability. The amendment of the decision on central rates recognized that currencies are fluctuating in different degrees against each other in the markets.

A second and equally telling criticism of the use of central rates, or indeed of par values, to solve the problem of valuation, whether under the original or the amended decision, is that they can be associated with wide margins. As the Fund's practice in connection with transactions conducted through the General Account shows, it was justifiable to use par values in measuring the equivalent of gold value in terms of a currency only when narrow margins were observed for exchange transactions. Even in such circumstances, the drafters of the amendment to the Articles preferred not to use par values as a basis for determining the equivalent in terms of a currency of the gold value of SDRs. Once a member availed itself of wider margins, whether in association with a par value or a central rate, the Fund employed market rates of exchange in determining the gold value of the member's currency.[50] Exchange rates could vary too much from the relationship based on the par values or central rates of the currencies involved in a transaction to justify the use of the par value or central rate as an equitable measurement of gold value. Under the original decision it was possible that exchange rates might differ by as much as $4\frac{1}{2}$ per cent, and in some circumstances even $6\frac{1}{2}$ per cent, from the relationship based on par values or central rates. The mar-

---

[50] Executive Board Decision No. 3637-(72/41) G/S, May 8, 1972, *Selected Decisions*, Sixth Issue, pp. 17–19. (*Selected Decisions*, Eighth Issue, pp. 32–33.)

gins are defined in a different way under the amended decision, but they continue to be wider than those that are valid under the Articles.[51] If the objective of a treaty is to ensure the payment of uniform amounts of currency as the equivalent of gold value, whatever currency may be used for the purpose of payment, the use of central rates, or for that matter par values, is unlikely to achieve the result of uniformity if they are associated with wide margins.

The Supreme Court of the Netherlands emphasized the importance of a solution based on the practice of the Fund because the Fund is the central international institution in monetary matters and because the countries involved in the litigation were members of the Fund. The unsatisfactory results that would be achieved by applying par values or central rates in present conditions does not mean that a solution can no longer be based on the practice of the Fund. It has been seen that operations and transactions under the Articles are based on two gold clauses. One of them requires members to maintain the gold value of the Fund's holdings of their currencies in the General Account, and the other requires that designated transferees of SDRs must provide equal value in terms of currency, on the basis of the gold value of SDRs, whatever the currency they provide. For both these purposes, the Fund prescribes the appropriate rates of exchange for any currency that is involved in an operation or transaction. Until the end of June 1974, the exchange rate for the U.S. dollar for this purpose was taken to be its par value, and for other currencies the representative market rate for spot delivery of the U.S. dollar was applied. The Fund made a temporary exception, however, for certain transactions in SDRs, at the instance of the European members that were maintaining margins for exchange transactions between their currencies but not for transactions involving U.S. dollars. They objected to the assumption that the exchange rate for the U.S. dollar was equivalent to par for a number of reasons, including the fact that the United States was not intervening in the markets, converting official holdings of dollars into gold or other reserve assets, or taking other appropriate measures to maintain margins for exchange transactions. Participants in the Special Drawing Account transferring SDRs within the scope of the temporary exception were allowed to conduct the transactions on the basis of the par value or central rate of the currency provided in return for the transfer.

---

[51] For the margins under the amended decision, see paragraphs 1, 3, and 7 of the decision.

The exchange rates employed by the Fund under the practice as described above may seem to have been fictitious as determinations of gold value, but they were no more fictitious than any other so-called official gold value in circumstances in which no member maintains the value of its currency by means of transactions in gold. If the hypothesis of a fixed value for the dollar equal to its par value is accepted, the solution of the rates of exchange employed by the Fund for its own purposes would have been superior to the use of par values or central rates for the purposes of the conventions. The Fund's practice was based on market rates, and therefore achieved equal value among currencies and did so in a realistic way.

The Fund's move on July 1, 1974 to a new mode of valuation in its two Accounts was based on the principle that the gold content of the SDR is equivalent to a prescribed combination of 16 currencies. This technique also can be regarded as determining gold value [52] because it is being applied under the two gold clauses in the present Articles. The new mode of valuation is available, therefore, for determining the equivalence of gold value in any currency that must be calculated under international conventions of the kind that was involved in the *Hornlinie* case. The technique is being applied by the Fund to give effect to the express requirement in the Articles of equal value in transactions involving SDRs, and it might be applied therefore under conventions in which a concept similar to equal value is implicit. This conclusion rests on the assumption that courts will prefer the reasoning of the Supreme Court of the Netherlands in choosing an official mode of valuation and one that is consistent with the practice of the Fund. The solution has been recommended already by the author of a recent study of the problem.[53]

---

[52] See IMF Press Release No. 74/29, June 13, 1974, reproduced in *IMF Survey*, Vol. 3 (June 17, 1974), pp. 177 and 185.

[53] See T.M.C. Asser, "Golden Limitations of Liability in International Transport Conventions and the Currency Crisis," *Journal of Maritime Law and Commerce*, Vol. 5 (July 1974), pp. 645–69. Mr. Asser quotes extensively from the judgment in the *Hornlinie* case.

6

The Fund Agreement in the Courts—XII*

This installment in the series dealing with jurisprudence in which the Fund's Articles of Agreement have been involved discusses some important cases dealing with exchange control. The cases that are examined have been decided by the Court of Cassation and other courts of France, the Court of Appeals of the State of New York, the Queen's Bench Division and the Court of Appeal of England, and the Commercial Court of Brussels. The broad topics with which the cases deal are the relation of the unenforceability of certain contracts under the first sentence of Article VIII, Section 2(*b*) of the Fund's Articles of Agreement to delictual claims involving these contracts, certain restrictive interpretations of that provision by some courts, and the effect of the doctrine of public policy (*ordre public*) on a litigant's reliance on the exchange control laws of members of the Fund other than the country of the forum. In the discussion of this last topic, it is proposed that the interdependence among countries that they have recognized by becoming members of the Fund should lead their courts to apply the doctrine of public policy in a manner favorable to the exchange control regulations of other members if the regulations are consistent with the Articles. This approach would be particularly appropriate when followed by courts that have taken a narrow view of Article VIII, Section 2(*b*).

---

* Originally published in March 1977.

189

Foreign Exchange Control and Delict

THE ZAVICHA CASE

On July 18, 1966 Daiei Motion Picture Company, a Japanese corporation, entered into a contract dated September 1, 1966 with Zavicha, a resident of France, under which for a period of ten years from the date of the contract he was to be the sole representative of the company for all European countries and the manager of its European business. He undertook that, at his own expense, he would make premises available, open an office, and hire employees for conducting business under the contract. Zavicha was to receive a monthly salary of F 10,000 and bonuses based on the commercial value of films selected by him for distribution by the company in Japan. The parties would agree on the bonus for each film. He was also to select for distribution in Europe films produced by the company. The contract stated that in case of dispute the courts of the Seine would have competence and French law would apply. Zavicha began work under the contract in October 1966, and incurred expenses in opening an office and in arranging publicity. On February 21, 1967 the company informed Zavicha that it was having difficulty in getting approval of the contract by the Japanese exchange control authorities. It offered to renegotiate the contract so that there would be a better chance of getting it approved. On June 5, 1967 the company informed him that it considered itself released from the contract because it was null and void under Japanese law, and on August 24 reaffirmed the nullity of the contract and gave him formal notice to stop purporting to act as its representative. Zavicha sued for F 1 million as the expenses that he had incurred in performing the contract and for F 2.25 million as damages for loss of profit resulting from breach of contract. The company advanced various defenses and counterclaims.

The company's main defense was that the contract was contrary to Japanese exchange control regulations and therefore unenforceable under the first sentence of Article VIII, Section 2(*b*) and the interpretation of that provision adopted by the Fund on June 10, 1949.[1] The first sentence of the provision reads as follows: "Exchange contracts which involve the currency of any member and which are contrary to the exchange control regulations of that member maintained

---

[1] *Selected Decisions*, Eighth Issue, pp. 131–32. (*Selected Decisions*, Ninth Issue, pp. 201–202.)

or imposed consistently with this Agreement shall be unenforceable in the territories of any member." Under Japan's Foreign Exchange and Foreign Trade Control Law (Law No. 228 of December 1, 1949) and Cabinet Order No. 203 of June 27, 1950, no resident was allowed to enter into a service contract involving payments to a nonresident without the approval of the Exchange Office. Zavicha replied that the exchange control regulations were not consistent with Article VII of the Fund's Articles,[2] and were not justified by Japan's monetary and economic conditions. The Court of Commerce held that this was not the only provision that authorized exchange control regulations and cited Article XIV.[3] To support the consistency of the regulations with the Articles, the company relied upon a letter from the General Counsel of the Fund stating that the exchange control regulations of Japan did not contain any provision inconsistent with the Articles.[4] Zavicha argued that Article VIII, Section 2(b) did not apply to payments for current international transactions, which were governed by Article VIII, Section 2(a). On this last argument, the court held that

> this way of seeing things is not consistent with the wording of paragraph (b), which makes no distinction between the exchange contracts to which it applies; that it therefore suffices that contracts are in issue that involve the currency of a member State, that is to say, contracts the implementation of which affects the exchange resources of that State, according to the most general definition that has been given and the one that has already been accepted in judicial decisions. . . .[5]
> (Translation)

In *Daiei Motion Picture Co. Ltd. v. Zavicha*, the Fourth Division of the Court of Appeal of Paris on May 14, 1970 affirmed the decision

---

[2] The argument seemed to be that exchange restrictions are consistent with the Articles only when a member's currency has been declared scarce under Article VII, Section 3, because the declaration is designed to safeguard the position of that member. The provision is designed, however, to safeguard the interests of other members.

[3] Japan accepted the obligations of Article VIII, Sections 2, 3, and 4 on April 1, 1964, and therefore was no longer able to take advantage of the transitional arrangements of Article XIV in 1966 or at any later date.

[4] The second paragraph of the letter reads as follows:

"I have been authorized to inform you that Japan does not maintain any restrictions on the making of payments or transfers for current international transactions that would require approval under Article VIII, Section 2(a), and in this connection I refer you to Executive Board Decision No. 1034-(60/27), adopted June 1, 1960, which states in part: 'The guiding principle in ascertaining whether a measure is a restriction on payments and transfers for current transactions under Article VIII, Section 2, is whether it involves a direct governmental limitation on the availability or use of exchange as such.' "

[5] *La Semaine Juridique*, No. 21 (May 26, 1971), II. Jurisprudence, 16751.

of the Court of Commerce of May 31, 1968 in favor of the company. The Court of Appeal refused Zavicha a remedy on the contract because of Article VIII, Section 2(*b*). The Court held,[6] however, that the company owed him a duty to do all that it could to obtain the necessary authorization from the Japanese exchange control authorities. The company had failed to perform this duty, and it had allowed him to incur expenses under the contract before informing him that the authorization had not been obtained. The court held that this claim was delictual (*une faute quasi-délictuelle*) and not contractual, so that Article VIII, Section 2(*b*) did not apply to it. The court relied on the fact that the company had made only an informal application for a license, that there had been a postponement for minor reasons and not a refusal, and that the difficulties could easily have been overcome. The company had deliberately refrained from taking further steps in order to renegotiate the contract. In addition, the company knew of the difficulties in October 1966 but did not inform Zavicha of them until February 1967, by which time he had incurred expenses. On June 3, 1971, following an appraisal by experts, the court ordered the company to pay Zavicha F 1 million in reimbursement of expenses and F 2,430,000 as damages.[7] The company was adjudged bankrupt on December 23, 1971.

The decision is notable not only because the court accepted the broad interpretation of "exchange contracts" and the currency "involved" but also because it recognized that, in view of the Japanese regulations, the contract was unenforceable even though French law governed the contract and was the *lex fori*. According to certain judicial decisions,[8] if a party's claim under a contract is unenforceable under Article VIII, Section 2(*b*), he cannot succeed by reformulating the claim as one for damages for tort, or as a claim for the performance of a natural obligation, or for the restitution of an unjustified enrichment. These claims can, but need not, have the same effect as enforcing the contract.[9] Damages were awarded to Zavicha because of the company's failure to take all possible steps to comply with

---

[6] It has been argued that the cause of action in the Court of Commerce was based on contract but was transformed into one based on delict by the Court of Appeal. Article VIII, Section 2(*b*) was not relied on in the lower court. (Georges Durry, "Responsabilité civile," *Revue trimestrielle de droit civil*, Vol. 69 (1971), pp. 844–46.)

[7] See the judgment of March 16, 1974 of the Paris Court of Appeal, Fourth Chamber/B.

[8] Gold, *Fund Agreement in the Courts* (1962), pp. 89–90, 97–100, 118.

[9] Jean-Pierre Eck, Note, *Revue critique de droit international privé* (July/September 1974), pp. 497–98. (Hereinafter cited as Eck, Note.)

exchange control regulations and to make the contract enforceable. The decision has been defended on the ground that it was not based on the nonfulfillment of the contract, and could not have been because the court held that the contract did not have to be performed.[10] The decision has also been attacked on the ground that it negated the effect of Article VIII, Section 2(*b*) by adding a condition that the defendant should not be at fault.[11] A question that the case raises is how far courts should go in refusing remedies that are not legally equivalent to, but approximate in effect, the enforcement of an unenforceable contract in order to discourage parties from entering into such contracts.

The court assumed, without examining Japanese law on this point, that in the circumstances of the case it was reasonable to hold that the company had the duty to apply for a license. The court noted that the company operated in Japan and was familiar with Japanese exchange control regulations. It is not clear whether the court held that a duty arose between the parties as the result of an implied agreement between them or as the result of some general doctrine of law that all parties have a duty to make their contracts effective. Even on the latter hypothesis, the doctrine would seem to be one that establishes an implied term. If the duty to apply for a license was an implied term of the agency contract, the failure would have been contractual and not delictual, and if contractual it would have been caught by Article VIII, Section 2(*b*).

The court declared that the contract was no more enforceable in France than it was in Japan. It did not accept the company's argument that the contract was null and void, because the company had not proved that this was the position under Japanese law. The court found that Japanese law did not provide that an unauthorized contract was absolutely void, but that it could not be performed without a license. Had the court declared the contract null and void, it would have gone beyond Japanese law, which, according to the majority opinion adopted by the Supreme Court of Japan in 1965 in *Tomita v.*

---

[10] *Ibid.*, pp. 493–94; Durry, "Responsabilité civile" (cited in fn. 6), pp. 844–46; François Gianviti, "Réflexions sur l'article VIII, section 2 *b*) des Status du Fonds Monétaire International," *Revue critique de droit international privé* (1973), pp. 657–59. (Hereinafter cited as Gianviti, "Réflexions sur l'article VIII, section 2*b*)".)

[11] See Patrick Juillard, "La nullité d'un contrat de change conclu en violation de l'article VIII-2-b des statuts du Fonds Monétaire International : à propos de l'arrêt de la Cour de Paris du 14 mai 1970," *La Semaine Juridique*, No. 21 (May 26, 1971), I. Doctrine, 2399.

Inoue, provides only that a contract entered into without the necessary license was not invalid under private law even though it subjected a party to criminal penalties.[12]

The validity of the contract raised another issue, which, however, the court did not investigate. The regulation requiring a license was not a restriction on payments and transfers for current international transactions within the meaning of the Articles because the restriction was on entry into contracts, that is, on the transaction of business, and not on payments even though the restriction was supported by an exchange control regulation. Insofar as the restriction on entry into the contract was concerned, the approval of the Fund under Article VIII, Section 2(a) was not necessary. The Fund does not have jurisdiction to approve or disapprove restrictions on the import and export of goods, the business of insurance, arrangements for the distribution of films, or the transaction of any other forms of business, of which these examples are but a few chosen at random. The Fund's jurisdiction is to approve or disapprove restrictions applied directly on payments and transfers for current international transactions that are permissible under the applicable law. Restrictions on the transaction of business may be within the jurisdiction of other international organizations. Whether particular restrictions on the transaction of business are or are not within the jurisdiction of another international organization, the normal consequence of these restrictions will be that payments may not be made in respect of the transactions that are subject to the restriction. To have given the Fund authority to disapprove this consequential prohibition of payments would have had the effect of giving it jurisdiction over the import and export of goods, the business of insurance, arrangements for the distribution of films, and the

---

[12] *Saiko Saibansho Hanrei-Shu* (Supreme Court Reporter), Vol. 19, Pt. 2 (1965), pp. 2306–30. See also Teruo Doi, "The Validity of Contracts Made in Violation of the Forum's Exchange Controls," *Law in Japan: An Annual,* Vol. 2 (1968), pp. 180–93; Tomohei Taniguchi, "Comment on *Tomita v. Inoue,*" *ibid.,* pp. 194–97. According to the minority opinion, the validity or invalidity of a contract could not be determined until a license was applied for and either granted or refused. Until then, it was "inconclusively invalid." The position under French law with respect to the absence of authorization when required by French exchange control regulations differs from the result reached in *Tomita v. Inoue.* A contract for which authorization is not obtained is null, whereas formerly this was the result only if fraud was present. If, however, authorization is being sought, an obligation arises that cannot be repudiated even though it cannot be performed unless and until authorization is granted. Nullity gives rise to claims to restitution by both parties of what they have transferred pursuant to the purported contract. See Philippe Malaurie, Note, *Recueil Dalloz Sirey* (February 18, 1976), pp. 83 *et seq.*

transaction of all other forms of business requiring payments for their performance.

The restriction in the case was on entry into the contract,[13] and if this had been the only relevant provision of Japanese law, Article VIII, Section 2(b) would have had no role.[14] The proscription of payments under an unapproved contract is not, in the absence of special circumstances, a restriction on payments and transfers under Article VIII, Section 2(a), but the proscription is nevertheless an exchange control regulation under Article VIII, Section 2(b). A regulation that is not restrictive within the meaning of Article VIII, Section 2(a) does not require the approval of the Fund, and therefore can be "maintained or imposed consistently" with the Articles within the meaning of Article VIII, Section 2(b) without the approval of the Fund. This

---

[13] Articles 27 and 42 of the Foreign Exchange and Foreign Trade Control Law (Law No. 228, December 1, 1949, as amended by Law No. 99, June 15, 1968):

Art. 27. "Unless authorized as provided for in this Law or in Cabinet Order, no person shall in Japan:

    (1) Make any payment to a foreign country;

    (2) Make any payment to an exchange non-resident, or receive any payment from an exchange non-resident; . . ."

Art. 42. "Unless authorized as provided for by Cabinet Order, no person shall contract for services involving payment, settlement or any other transaction governed by provisions of this Law." (*Japan: Laws, Ordinances and Other Regulations concerning Foreign Exchange and Foreign Trade* (Osaka, 1976), pp. A-9–A-12.)

See also Article 17 of the Cabinet Order Concerning Control of Foreign Exchange (Cabinet Order No. 203, June 27, 1950, as amended by Cabinet Order No. 324, August 28, 1972):

Art. 17. "Except for the following cases, any person may make contracts concerning services restricted or prohibited under the provisions of Article 42 of the Law:

    (1) Where contract is made between an exchange resident and an exchange non-resident whereby the exchange resident receives offer of services, for which settlement of payment is to ensure . . .

    (3) In addition to cases the exception coming under the prescription of item (1) above, where contract is made between an exchange resident and an exchange non-resident giving rise to settlement by the non-standard method of settlement . . .

2. Any person who obtained license of the competent Minister for making contracts concerning services prescribed under any of the items of the preceding paragraph may do so in accordance with the terms of such license, provided, however, that the competent Minister shall not grant such license in case license, validation, approval or certification under the provisions of laws and orders listed under Article 11 paragraph 1 items (1) through (5) is required for making contracts concerning such services." (*Japan: Laws, Ordinances and Other Regulations concerning Foreign Exchange and Trade* (1976), pp. A-41–A-42.)

[14] See Gianviti, "Réflexions sur l'article VIII, section 2 b)" (cited in fn. 10), p. 641.

aspect of Article VIII, Section 2(*b*) was referred to in the letter of March 17, 1970 from the General Counsel of the Fund.[15] The court held that exchange control regulations were involved, although it did not distinguish between the contract and payments under it.

A problem arises, however, because the contract was classified in Japanese law as valid. The regulations proscribed payments under an unapproved contract, which raises the question whether a restriction on payments and transfers for current international transactions was involved as a result of the legal effect of an unapproved contract. If there were such a restriction, the regulation imposing it would not have been "maintained or imposed consistently" with the Articles within the meaning of Article VIII, Section 2(*b*) if the restriction had not been approved by the Fund. According to the Japanese authorities, however, the purpose of the licensing procedure was to prevent the disguised transfer of capital. All contracts were approved for invisible transactions that were genuine current international transactions, so that there was no restriction on payments and transfers for these transactions.

The company appealed to the Commercial Division of the Court of Cassation to have the decision of the Court of Appeal set aside and a new trial ordered. It argued, inter alia, that Zavicha had undertaken to obtain the necessary license; that it was impossible to obtain a license; that the alleged tort was inseparable from the contract; that a party cannot sue on a contract that it knows to be null and void; and that a tort cannot be based on a contract that is contrary to *ordre public* in the monetary field, particularly in view of the membership of France in the Fund. The Court of Cassation rejected these arguments and confirmed the judgment of the Court of Appeal.[16]

Zavicha sued the Bank of Japan, the central bank of Japan, in Paris for F 20.5 million as damages for the loss imposed on him by its *fautes délictuelles ou quasi-délictuelles*. This claim was based, inter alia, on the alleged wrongful acts of the Bank of Japan in refusing to approve the contract of September 1, 1966. The refusal was alleged to be in violation of the Articles of the Fund because the contract related to a current international transaction, for which a license could

---

[15] Excerpt from the third paragraph of the letter:
"Article VIII, Section 2(*b*), refers to 'exchange control regulations' but the Fund has not defined the scope of this term. To the extent that the Law and Cabinet Order cited above were deemed to involve 'exchange control regulations', such regulations would have been maintained consistently with the Articles. . . ."
[16] Eck, Note (cited in fn. 9), pp. 491–92.

not be withheld. The claim was based also on alleged false statements by the Bank about its exchange control procedures and the application of them to the contract in issue. On March 16, 1974, the Paris Court of Appeal, Fourth Chamber, decided on appeal from a judgment of the Paris Tribunal of Commerce delivered on September 19, 1972, that the Bank of Japan was immune from suit. It applied the principle that

> immunity from jurisdiction may be invoked by foreign governments and organizations acting on their instructions or on their behalf with regard to acts of public authority or carried out in the interest of a public service.

The court held that the Bank of Japan, when acting as the authority in charge of exchange control, does so by order and on behalf of the Japanese Government. If it were assumed, although it had not been demonstrated, that Japanese legislation or the Bank of Japan had misinterpreted the Articles of the Fund, or even that the Bank had misinterpreted national legislation, these errors would be covered by the Bank's immunity from jurisdiction, because they would constitute either a violation by the Japanese Government of its international obligations or the commission of actions in the course of public service. The court applied the same analysis to the alleged false statements. On May 19, 1976, the Court of Cassation confirmed the judgment of the Court of Appeal.[17]

THE BANCO FRANCES CASE

The relationship between a claim for damages for tort and the unenforceability of exchange contracts under Article VIII, Section 2(b) is a complex one. In the *Zavicha* case, the court held that a contract was unenforceable under the provision because a license had not been obtained but that damages could be awarded because of the defendant's failure to apply for a license. *Banco do Brasil, S.A. v. A.C. Israel Commodity Co., Inc.*[18] has achieved some prominence as a case in which the New York Court of Appeals refused to award damages for conspiracy to evade Brazilian exchange control regulations. It held

---

[17] See the judgment of March 16, 1974 of the Paris Court of Appeal, Fourth Chamber/B. See also the judgment of May 19, 1976 of the Court of Cassation, First Civil Chamber, and Ph. Kahn, Note, *Journal du Droit International*, No. 3 (July 1976), pp. 687–91. Cf. *Trendtex Trading Corporation v. Central Bank of Nigeria* [1976] 3 All E.R. 437, *The Times* (London), January 18, 1977, p. 11; *Statni Banka and Banque d'Etat Tchécoslovaque v. Englander*, discussed later in this chapter.

[18] 216 N.Y.S. 2d 669 (1961); 12 N.Y. 2d 371, 190 N.E. 2d 235, 239 N.Y.S. 2d 872 (1963); 376 U.S. 906, 84 S. Ct. 264 (1964).

that New York courts were required in certain circumstances to withhold judicial remedies to enforce a contract but not to grant remedies for a tort if the contract was performed. Neither Article VIII, Section 2(*b*) nor any other provision of the Articles had changed the principle that the courts of one country do not enforce the revenue laws of another country.

The effect of *Banco do Brasil* was cut down to slim proportions by the New York Court of Appeals in its decision of May 8, 1975 in *Banco Frances e Brasileiro S.A. v. Doe.*[19] The principal question before the court was whether a foreign private bank might avail itself of the New York courts in an action for damages for tortious fraud and deceit and for rescission of contracts arising from alleged violations of foreign exchange control regulations.

The plaintiff was a private Brazilian bank that brought an action for fraud and deceit, and for conspiracy to defraud and deceive, against 20 "John Doe" defendants whose identities were unknown to it. The gravamen of the plaintiff's complaint was that these defendants had participated, in violation of Brazilian exchange control regulations, in the submission of false applications to the plaintiff, which had relied upon them and made improper exchanges of Brazilian cruzeiros into travelers checks in U.S. dollars. The plaintiff claimed that as a result it had been exposed to penalties under Brazilian law and to injury to its business and reputation. The regulations allowed a Brazilian resident to obtain no more than $1,000 in return for cruzeiros when making a trip abroad. A large amount of the checks that had been obtained in violation of these regulations was deposited by two of the unknown John Does in accounts bearing code names with two banking institutions in New York. An order of attachment was granted against the property of John Doe Nos. 1 and 2 held with the two institutions. Motions were made by the plaintiff for disclosure by the institutions of the true names and addresses of the two John Does and to direct the attorney for John Doe No. 1 to disclose the true names and addresses of the defendants and the basis for his authority to act, or, in the alternative, to vacate his appearance in the action. John Doe No. 1 moved to vacate the order of attachment, to dismiss the plaintiff's complaint, and to intervene in the motion for disclosure so as to resist it. After various steps in the proceedings, the Appellate Division, relying on the *Banco do Brasil* case, granted the defendant's motion to dismiss the complaint and dismissed all ancillary applica-

---

[19] 36 N.Y. 2d 592, 331 N.E. 2d 502, 370 N.Y.S. 2d 534 (1975).

tions by the plaintiff on the ground that the New York courts were not open to an action arising from a tortious violation of foreign currency regulations. The plaintiff appealed, and the Court of Appeals, in a decision of six judges to one, modified the decision of the Appellate Division and granted various forms of relief.

The majority opinion referred to the "old chestnut"[20] of the conflict of laws that one state does not enforce the revenue laws of another state, but rejected the modern extension of the category of revenue laws to include foreign exchange regulations. According to the majority, that extension was unjustifiable on the basis of both precedent and analysis. Analysis led the court to make the following pronouncement:

> . . . [M]uch doubt has been expressed that the reasons advanced for the rule, if ever valid, remain so. . . . Some do consider that, in light of the economic interdependence of all nations, the courts should be receptive even to extranational tax and revenue-claims as well, especially where there is a treaty involved, but also without such constraint. . . . Indeed, there may be strong policy reasons for specially favoring a foreign revenue regulation, using that term in its broadest sense, especially one involving currency exchange or control.
>
> In the international sphere, cases involving foreign currency exchange regulations represent perhaps the most important aspect of the revenue law rule. This assumes, of course, that a currency exchange regulation, normally not designed for revenue purposes as such, but rather to prevent the loss of foreign currency which in turn increases the country's foreign exchange reserves, is properly characterizable as a revenue law. . . . At any rate, it is for the forum to characterize such a regulation and in this State the question would appear to have been resolved for the present at least by *Banco do Brasil v. Israel Commodity Co.* . . .
>
> But even assuming the continuing validity of the revenue law rule and the correctness of the characterization of a currency exchange regulation thereunder, United States membership in the International Monetary Fund (IMF) makes inappropriate the refusal to entertain the instant claim. The view that nothing in [A]rticle VIII, [Section 2(b)] . . . requires an American court to provide a forum for a private tort remedy, while correct in a literal sense (see *Banco do Brasil v. Israel Commodity Co.* . . .) does not represent the only perspective. Nothing in the agreement prevents an IMF member from aiding, directly or indirectly, a fellow member in making its exchange regulations effective. And United States membership in the IMF makes

---

[20] 36 N.Y. 2d 592, at 596.

it impossible to conclude that the currency control laws of other member States are offensive to this State's public policy so as to preclude suit in tort by a private party. Indeed, conduct reasonably necessary to protect the foreign exchange resources of a country does not offend against international law. . . . Moreover, where a true governmental interest of a friendly nation is involved—and foreign currency reserves are of vital importance to a country plagued by balance of payments difficulties—the national policy of co-operation with Bretton Woods signatories is furthered by providing a State forum for suit.[21]

The majority distinguished the *Banco do Brasil* case on the ground that the Government of Brazil itself, through the Banco do Brasil, sought redress for fraudulent violations of the Government's exchange control regulations. In the case now before the court, a private bank was seeking damages and rescission of fraudulent exchange transactions.[22] The court was aware of no case in which a remedy in tort arising from exchange control regulations had been denied in proceedings between private parties under the rule relating to foreign revenue laws, and the court declined to extend the *Banco do Brasil* case so as to deny a remedy in these circumstances.

The court referred to *Perutz v. Bohemian Discount Bank in Liquidation*.[23] This case has been the subject of much discussion not only because of the conclusion reached but also because the *ratio decidendi* implicit in it is not clear. The majority had this interesting comment on the effect of Czechoslovakia's exchange control regulations in that case:

> *Perutz v. Bohemian Discount Bank in Liquidation* . . . is consistent with an expansive application of the IMF agreement to which we here ascribe (cf. *Kolovrat v. Oregon* . . .), although there it is true defensive use of foreign currency exchange regulation was made and upheld by this court. But interestingly, in *Perutz*, in contrast to the instant case, political relations at the time were not conducive to comity which nevertheless was extended.[24]

The dissenting judge held the view that although relief was sought by a private bank, what was involved was "an aspect of the Brazilian Government's sovereign management of the economy of its own coun-

---

[21] *Ibid.*, at 597–98.

[22] For a similar distinction, see Viscount Simonds in *Regazzoni v. K.C. Sethia Ltd.* [1957] 3 All E.R. 286, at 289, and *Re Lord Cable (deceased)* [1976] 3 All E.R. 417.

[23] 110 N.Y.S. 2d 446 (1952); 304 N.Y. 533, 110 N.E. 2d 6 (1953). See Gold, *Fund Agreement in the Courts* (1962), pp. 28–30, 50–55.

[24] 36 N.Y. 2d at 599.

try" and not solely the resolution of private rights as defined under the law of another state. The issue for him was whether a claim for which enforcement is sought is a manifestation of sovereign authority in the pursuit of "fiscal regulation and management." The plaintiff had not suffered a loss in the private sense by providing travelers checks for value received. The heart of the claim was exposure to penalties applied by the Brazilian Government for breach of its regulations. The *Banco do Brasil* case had decided that foreign exchange control regulations may present an aspect of sovereign power by a foreign state, and it was for this reason that a remedy was refused even though the court invoked the rule relating to foreign revenue laws. This principle can be modified by treaty, but no modification had been made that applied in the circumstances of this case.

> Nothing in the Bretton Woods Agreement Act or in any other agreement between the United States and Brazil of which we are aware, however, mandates a complete abrogation of the normal conflicts rule or requires our courts *affirmatively* to enforce foreign currency regulation, as we are invited to do in the present case . . .
>
> The majority, however, argues that the time may have come for a change in what historically has been the applicable rule. I recognize that strong arguments can be mounted for a change in view of the increased frequency and importance of international commerce and the significantly different perspective in today's world in which one nation views another nation and its interests. In my opinion, however, the responsibility for any change lies with our Federal Government rather than with the highest court of any single State. Change, if at all, in my view, would better come at the hands of the State Department and the Congress, through the negotiation of international agreement or otherwise in the discharge of the constitutional responsibility of the Federal Government "to regulate commerce with foreign nations" (cf. Bretton Woods Agreement Act). A fitting sense of judicial restraint would dictate that the courts of no single State should enunciate a change, however large that State's relative proportion of foreign commerce may be, particularly since the authoritative effect thereof would necessarily be confined to the borders of that State.[25]

The effect of the decision in New York is that the rule relating to foreign revenue laws will not prevent claims in tort between private parties because a violation is involved of the exchange control regulations of a foreign state that is a member of the Fund. The court did not inquire whether the exchange control regulations were consistent with the Articles of the Fund, but probably assumed that they were.

---

[25] 36 N.Y. 2d at 602, 604.

The *ratio decidendi* may be applied to claims other than those in tort. The court did not decide that the same principle would apply to an action brought by the instrumentality of a foreign government and was content simply to refer to the *Banco do Brasil* case, but the court did cast doubt on that decision even within its newly defined narrow compass by doubting that exchange control regulations are revenue laws.

Restrictive Interpretations of Article VIII, Section 2(*b*)

Terruzzi Case in Queen's Bench Division

Wilson, Smithett & Cope Ltd. v. Terruzzi,[26] decided in England by the Queen's Bench Division on January 31, 1975 and by the Court of Appeal on January 20, 1976, seriously limits the scope of Article VIII, Section 2(*b*) in English courts. The plaintiffs were members of the London Metal Exchange and carried on business as dealers and brokers in metals. The defendant, a resident of Italy, dealt in metals in Milan. The plaintiffs alleged that between January 11, 1973 and November 7, 1973 they concluded with the defendant, on the standard terms of contract of the London Metal Exchange and subject to its rules and regulations, a series of contracts for the purchase or sale of copper wirebars, lead, and zinc futures. On November 14, 1973 the plaintiffs, having failed to receive any payment from the defendant, either as margin or in any other way, in respect of the debit balance of his account, "closed out" the defendant on his open contracts by transactions that left the defendant liable, after certain credits that were due to him, in an amount equal to almost £200,000. The losses resulted largely from an increase in the price of zinc sold forward for three months' delivery on behalf of the defendant in circumstances in which he was "short." In an action by the plaintiff for this amount, the defendant pleaded that the contracts were unenforceable because they were unlawful under Italian law and were exchange contracts within the meaning of Article VIII, Section 2(*b*), which had been incorporated into English law.[27]

The defendant relied on Decree-Law No. 476 of June 6, 1956, by means of which the Italian authorities introduced regulations that included the following articles:

---

[26] [1976] 1 Q.B. 683; [1976] 1 Q.B. 703 (C.A.).
[27] Bretton Woods Agreements Order in Council 1946 (S.R. & O. 1946 No. 36).

2. Residents are forbidden from performing any act whatsoever which produces obligations between them and nonresidents, except contracts for the sale of goods for export and contracts for the purchase of goods for import, save with ministerial authorization. Residents are forbidden from effecting the export or import of goods save upon ministerial authorization. Debts due to residents by nonresidents must be declared in the manner and within the terms laid down by the Ministry for Foreign Trade.

Residents who are creditors or debtors by virtue of any right toward nonresidents must recover their credits or pay their debits in the manner and within the provisions laid down by the Ministry for Foreign Trade. . . .

4. Residents cannot receive payments from nonresidents or effect payments to nonresidents directly or on behalf of the same, save in conformity with the provisions of Articles 2 and 3. (*Translation*)

Article 3 was not relevant to the proceedings. Article 13 of the Decree prescribes the authorizations that must be obtained from the Treasury, the Ministry for Foreign Trade, or both, as the case might be, for the actions by residents that are otherwise prohibited. The two government departments were empowered to delegate the task of issuing authorizations to the Italian Exchange Office and the Bank of Italy. The defendant did not obtain the authorization required by the Decree.

The court of first instance, the Queen's Bench Division, held, on the basis of the concessions made by the parties with respect to various aspects of the case, that the meaning and effect of Article VIII, Section 2(*b*) had to be decided purely as a question of English law. The court also decided that nothing turned on the point that the contracts were made for the purpose of speculating in "futures" without either party contemplating actual deliveries of metal. It was not contested that in English law contracts such as these are treated as ordinary contracts for the sale and purchase of goods, because the delivery and acceptance of the goods may be required.

The court noted Article XVIII of the Articles and the Fund's interpretation under that provision of some aspects of Article VIII, Section 2(*b*),[28] but found that the interpretation cast no light on the issues in this case.[29]

---

[28] See fn. 1.

[29] "Article XVIII of the fund agreement deals generally with its interpretation but is unfortunately of no assistance for present purposes. It only applies if any question arises between a member and the fund or between member states, in which cases any question of interpretation is to be submitted to the executive directors for their decision with a right of appeal to the board of

The plaintiffs argued that the lira was not "involved" within the meaning of Article VIII, Section 2(b) because the contracts provided for payment in sterling. The court was clearly unsympathetic to this view but at the same time was reluctant to endorse the view that the word referred to the economic effects of the contract. The court preferred the view that the phrase "which involve the currency of any member" must be taken as a whole and understood to mean that the purpose of the provision is to protect states that are members of the Fund and not nonmembers. "In such cases, if an 'exchange contract' infringes the exchange control regulations of a member, then I think that it follows that it also involves the currency of that member."[30] This view would mean that a member's currency could be "involved" even though an exchange contract had no economic effect on the member. Had the intention of the drafters been the one attributed to them, they could simply have omitted the phrase "which involve the currency of any member" and changed "that member" to "a member" later in the provision.

It is doubtful whether the court was endorsing the proposition that Article VIII, Section 2(b) refers to the exchange control regulations of any member that has adopted regulations affecting the contract. In rejecting the view that a currency is "involved" only if an obligation under the contract is denominated in that currency, the court referred to *Theye y Ajuria v. Pan American Life Insurance Co.*, a decision of the Supreme Court of Louisiana,[31] as a case that at first sight appeared to support the proposition. The real ratio of that decision in favor of the defendant was not, the court thought, that the insurance contracts

---

governors. However, if any such decision had been given throwing light on the questions which I have to decide, then I would clearly have given great weight to it." ([1976] 1 Q.B. 683, at 693.)

If a decision of the kind referred to had been adopted under Article XVIII, the duty of members of the Fund would be to take any steps that might be necessary under their law to make it binding and not merely persuasive. This conclusion follows from the assurance that a country gives on joining the Fund that "it has accepted this Agreement in accordance with its law and has taken all steps necessary to enable it to carry out all of its obligations under this Agreement." (Article XX, Section 2(a).) The obligations are the obligations as interpreted authoritatively by the Fund under Article XVIII. A member is bound to take whatever steps are necessary to ensure that its governmental authorities, acting within the sphere of their competence, will act in accordance with the member's obligations as authoritatively interpreted. A member is also bound to take the necessary steps to ensure that its courts will act in the same way in relation to obligations of the member that are to be performed through the courts.

[30] [1976] 1 Q.B. 683, at 694.

[31] 154 So. 2d 450 (1963); 161 So. 2d 70 (1964); 377 U.S. 997, 84 S. Ct. 1922 (1964); Gold, "Cuban Insurance Cases," pp. 54–58, 68–69 in this volume.

were expressed in U.S. dollars. "The ratio was that both parties were at the material time residents of the United States, so that a contract payable in dollars could not be affected by Cuban exchange control legislation which no longer applied to the plaintiff after he had ceased to be a resident of Cuba."[32] The regulations provided, inter alia, that payments should be made in Cuba in respect of business that had been transacted there. The reason why Article VIII, Section 2(b) no longer applied to this regulation was that the parties had ceased to have any economic connection with Cuba.

The court dealt with the plaintiff's argument that there should be no presumption that the exchange control regulations in the Italian decree were "maintained or imposed consistently with" the Articles. The plaintiff argued that the decree imposed restrictions on the making of payments and transfers for current international transactions within the meaning of Article VIII, Section 2(a) and Article XIX(i), a view with which the court sympathized, but that there was no evidence that the approval of the Fund was ever sought or obtained. The court concluded, however, that it should assume that the decree was maintained or imposed consistently with the Articles. The reasoning was as follows:

> The effect of the Italian decree is no different from the effect of the legislation of many countries which one has encountered in practice. In my judgment, the real test concerning legislation of this kind is not merely its wording but also the manner in which it is administered. The words are "maintained or imposed," and I think that "maintained" may well have been intended to include the manner in which the legislation is administered. The Italian decree contains no absolute prohibition but provides in each case for the possibility of obtaining ministerial authorisation. An English court should not assume without evidence, of which there is none in the present case, that the Italian authorities administer their exchange control regulations in a sense contrary to the obligations of Italy as a member of the I.M.F. In the absence of such evidence, and in relation to legislation of a kind which is internationally fairly commonplace in this field, it seems to me that a court of a member state should not assume without evidence that such legislation is not "maintained or imposed consistently with the I.M.F. agreement."[33]

This passage can be understood to mean that the English courts will decide for themselves where the burden of proof rests in relation to

---

[32] [1976] 1 Q.B. 683, at 693–94.
[33] Ibid., at 696.

the consistency or inconsistency of exchange control regulations with the Articles. The danger of such an approach is that it may produce a result that is in conflict with the decision of the Fund on the consistency of particular exchange control regulations with the Articles. The determination of consistency depends not only on interpretation of the Articles but also on the exercise by the Fund of its discretion to approve or not to approve certain restrictions. If a court were to deal with the issue solely as one of interpretation or of the burden of proof in circumstances in which consistency depended on approval by the Fund, the court would substitute itself for the Fund as the administrator of the Articles.

The court's suggested interpretation of the words "maintained or imposed" is not in accordance with the Fund's understanding of those words or the way that it operates in the application of them. The word "maintained" is taken to refer to the privilege that a member has to continue to apply those restrictions on payments and transfers for current international transactions that it applied when it entered the Fund, without the necessity for approval by the Fund, if the member decides to avail itself of the transitional arrangements of Article XIV. For this reason, "maintained" precedes "imposed" in the text, whereas logically, on the court's reasoning, "imposed" should precede "maintained." The word "maintained" does not refer to the day-to-day operation of exchange control regulations. It is true, however, that a member must administer its exchange control regulations in accordance with the Articles at all times. If regulations have been approved by the Fund as restrictions under Article VIII, Section 2(a), but are being operated otherwise than in accordance with the terms of the approval, they will cease to be approved and therefore will cease to be consistent with the Articles. Sometimes approval is not sought because the authorities intend to grant licenses for all genuine payments and transfers for current international transactions and to impede only capital transfers. The purpose of the regulations will then be to isolate capital transfers, including those that are disguised. If the member observes its intention, the regulations will not be restrictions under Article VIII, Section 2(a). Once the regulations are operated so as to produce restrictions under that provision, the regulations will cease to be consistent with the Articles. In short, the necessity for operation at all times in accordance with the Articles follows from the word "restrictions" and not from the word "maintained."

Italy became a member of the Fund on March 27, 1947 under a

Resolution of the Board of Governors that prescribed the terms for membership.[34] Various provisions of the Articles give special privileges to members whose territories were occupied by an enemy of the United and Associated Nations.[35] Italy was not one of the United and Associated Nations, but after Italy became a cobelligerent of the United and Associated Nations it was occupied by an enemy of them. The Fund wanted to give Italy the benefits that the Articles accorded to countries occupied by the enemy. The Resolution declared, therefore, that the provisions under which these benefits were enjoyed should apply to Italy.[36] One of the provisions that was made to apply was "the parenthetical statement of Article XIV, Section 2."[37] That statement, in the context of the first sentence of Article XIV, Section 2, reads as follows:

> In the post-war transitional period members may, notwithstanding the provisions of any other articles of this Agreement, maintain and adapt to changing circumstances (and, in the case of members whose territories have been occupied by the enemy, introduce where necessary) restrictions on payments and transfers for current international transactions.

Italy's restrictions were maintained under Article XIV. Decree-Law No. 476 codified pre-existing exchange control laws and regulations apart from one measure in the decree that is not relevant for the present purpose.[38] If the decree had contained new restrictions on payments and transfers for current international transactions, Italy might have asserted in 1956 that it was authorized to introduce them without the necessity for approval by the Fund under the parenthetical statement in Article XIV, Section 2.[39] The Fund did not find that the decree introduced new restrictions for which approval was necessary.

A later occasion on which it became necessary to consider the decree was when Italy ceased, on February 15, 1961, to avail itself of the transitional arrangements of Article XIV and undertook to perform the obligations of Article VIII, Sections 2, 3, and 4 without qualifica-

---

[34] Resolution No. 1-6, adopted effective October 2, 1946.

[35] Article III, Section 3(*d*); Article XIV, Section 2; Article XX, Sections 2(*h*), and 4(*a*), (*d*), (*e*), and (*g*); Schedule B, par. 4, *original* and *first*.

[36] See Joseph Gold, *Membership and Nonmembership in the International Monetary Fund: A Study in International Law and Organization* (Washington, 1974), pp. 71–76. (Hereinafter cited as Gold, *Membership and Nonmembership*).

[37] Resolution No. 1-6, par. 4.

[38] *Eighth Annual Report on Exchange Restrictions* (1957), p. 202.

[39] Unless the restrictions were multiple currency practices as well. See *Selected Decisions*, Eighth Issue, p. 151. (*Selected Decisions*, Ninth Issue, pp. 223–25.)

tion. At that time, any restrictions on payments and transfers for current international transactions that Italy would continue to apply would cease to be "maintained" under Article XIV, Section 2, but would be "imposed" under Article VIII, Section 2(a). What, then, was the Fund's analysis on that occasion? As noted in the discussion of the *Zavicha* case, there is a restriction on payments and transfers for current international transactions only if the restriction is applied directly to the payment or transfer and not to some other aspect of the transaction that gives rise to an obligation to make a payment or transfer. In the words of the Fund's decision on the subject, "The guiding principle in ascertaining whether a measure is a restriction on payments and transfers for current transactions under Article VIII, Section 2 is whether it involves a direct governmental limitation on the availability or use of exchange as such."[40] Applying this criterion to the 1956 decree, the Fund concluded that any restrictive effect that there might be in the administration of it applied to the export or import of goods under Section 2 of the decree. Section 4 of the decree was an exchange control regulation but not a restriction on payments or transfers for current international transactions under the Articles, because an independent discretion was not exercised with respect to these payments or transfers. An importer's ability to make payments was determined exclusively and automatically by the granting or withholding of authority to make the import.

The term "exchange control regulations" appears in Article VIII, Section 2(b). The issues in this part of the case, therefore, were, first, whether the provisions of Decree-Law No. 476 included exchange control regulations and, second, if there were such regulations whether they were "maintained or imposed consistently" with the Articles in the sense in which those words are used in Article VIII, Section 2(b). Article VIII, Section 5(a)(xi) refers to "exchange controls" and continues:

> *i.e.*, a comprehensive statement of exchange controls in effect at the time of assuming membership in the Fund and details of subsequent changes as they occur.

The word "controls" is used in Article VI, Sections 1 and 3 in relation to international capital movements. There is no textual evidence that the "exchange control regulations" of Article VIII, Section 2(b), or the "exchange controls" of Article VIII, Section 5(a)(xi), exclude any

---

[40] *Selected Decisions*, Eighth Issue, p. 139. (*Selected Decisions*, Ninth Issue, pp. 209–11.)

controls of payments and transfers for current international transactions or capital transfers. The Fund would not be able to discharge its duties effectively[41] if it did not receive national data on all exchange controls so that it could determine, for example, whether they were restrictions on payments and transfers for current international transactions or controls on capital transfers or controls on capital transfers that "restrict payments for current transactions or . . . unduly delay transfers of funds in settlement of commitments. . . ."[42] Various aspects of Article VI, Section 3 show that the word "controls" applies to restrictions on payments and transfers for current international transactions as well as to capital transfers:

> Members may exercise such controls as are necessary to regulate international capital movements, but no member may exercise these controls in a manner which will restrict payments for current transactions or which will unduly delay transfers of funds in settlement of commitments, except as provided in Article VII, Section 3(*b*), and in Article XIV, Section 2.

This provision shows that "controls" may be applied to payments for current international transactions if they are not restrictive or if they do not unduly delay transfers, or even when they are restrictive if they are authorized by Article VII, Section 3(*b*) or Article XIV, Section 2.

The conclusion to be derived from these textual elements is that "exchange control regulations" include regulations that restrict payments and transfers for current international transactions, nonrestrictive regulations applied to such payments and transfers, and regulations that control capital transfers. This conclusion is in accord with the normal understanding of the expression. Exchange control regulations can deal with all international payments and transfers of foreign or domestic currency.

Once this conclusion is reached on the content of "exchange control regulations" in Article VIII, Section 2(*b*), it becomes possible to answer the second question, that is, whether exchange control regulations that deal with payments and transfers for current international transactions but do not restrict them, and therefore do not require the approval of the Fund, are "maintained or imposed consistently" with the Articles. Exchange control regulations applied to capital transfers are maintained or imposed consistently with the Articles because Article VI, Section 3 authorizes members to control capital transfers

---

[41] Article VIII, Section 5(*a*), *original* and *first.*
[42] Article VI, Section 3, *original* and *first.*

without the necessity for the Fund's approval. Other exchange controls that do not restrict payments and transfers for current international transactions do not require the approval of the Fund, although it is true that there is no provision that states this proposition with the same forthrightness as Article VI, Section 3.

It is not difficult to see why exchange control regulations that do not require the approval of the Fund should nevertheless be considered to be "maintained or imposed consistently" with the Articles for the purpose of Article VIII, Section 2(b). If a member decides to apply exchange control regulations in order to determine whether payments and transfers are disguised capital transfers, so as to be able to exercise its right to control capital movements, or if a member wants to determine that authorization has been granted for trade transactions before permitting payments in respect of them, other members should not enforce contracts that deprive a member of these opportunities to protect itself. The conclusion on this part of the judgment is that the court was correct in holding that the Italian regulations relating to payments were consistent with the Articles, but based this holding on incorrect reasoning.

According to the court, the crucial and most difficult question in the case was whether or not the contracts were "exchange contracts" within the meaning of Article VIII, Section 2(b). One view, as expressed by Lord Radcliffe in *In re United Railways of Havana and Regla Warehouses Ltd.*,[43] a case not involving the Articles, was that a "true exchange contract" is one "which is a contract to exchange the currency of one country for the currency of another."[44] This definition, the court said, represents what one would normally understand by the expression as a matter of ordinary English in any context dealing with foreign currencies. The other and broader view was represented by the definition offered by Lord Denning, Master of the Rolls, in *Sharif v. Azad*,[45] a case involving Article VIII, Section 2(b). According to that definition, "exchange contracts" are "any contracts which in any way affect the country's exchange resources." The court considered the language of various provisions of the Articles, the views of authors, certain cases involving Article VIII, Section 2(b)

---

[43] [1961] A.C. 1007, at 1059.

[44] *Ibid.* The *dictum* was *obiter* in the case in which it was delivered, and the decision itself has since been overruled. See *Miliangos v. George Frank (Textiles) Ltd.* [1975] 3 All E.R. 801.

[45] [1966] 3 All E.R. 785. See Joseph Gold, "Fund Agreement in the Courts—IX," p. 111 in this volume.

decided by the courts of other countries, and *Sharif v. Azad.* The result of this survey was a conclusion in favor of Lord Radcliffe's view. Some of the reasons were that, as pointed out in the *Banco do Brasil* case, the broad interpretation would give no independent effect to the word "exchange" in the expression "exchange contracts," that the broad interpretation would interfere with international trade, that contracting parties would find it too burdensome to seek to satisfy themselves before entering into international contracts that all necessary permissions had been obtained, and that the broad interpretation would embrace all contracts except those for barter.

Terruzzi Case in Court of Appeal

The opinion of the lower court deserves detailed examination because of its scope and vigor, but the decision of the Court of Appeal, which affirmed the decision of the lower court, will be authoritative as a precedent in English courts unless it is overruled on some future occasion. The opinions of the three members of the Court of Appeal were confined largely to the meaning of the words "exchange contracts." The court included Lord Denning, M.R., whose view of the meaning of "exchange contracts" in *Sharif v. Azad* has been referred to as the broad interpretation. In the *Terruzzi* case, he noted that he had adopted his earlier view without question, and he now resiled from it in favor of the other view. Lord Denning referred to a "notorious case," decided by an English court in 1928,[46] that involved speculation in foreign exchange at a time when exchange rates were fluctuating. The judge in that case castigated the speculators in language of unusual forcefulness, which Lord Denning quoted.[47] The mischief perpetrated by speculators in foreign exchange and castigated in the 1928 case was, in the opinion of Lord Denning, the one that the participants at Bretton Woods intended to stop by means of Article VIII, Section 2(*b*). He went on:

> I do not know of any similar mischief in regard to other contracts, that is, contracts for the sale or purchase of merchandise or commodities. Businessmen have to encounter fluctuations in the price of goods, but this is altogether different from the fluctuations in exchange rates. So far from there being any mischief, it seems to me that it is in the interest of international trade that there should be no restriction on contracts for the sale and purchase of merchandise and commodities; and that they should be enforceable in the territories of the members.[48]

---

[46] *Ironmonger and Co. v. Dyne,* 44 T.L.R. 497 (1928).
[47] *Ibid.,* at 498.
[48] [1976] 1 Q.B., at 713 (C.A.).

The contracts in this case were intended by the defendant to be speculations in the prices of metals, but the plaintiff had a contractual right to insist on the completion of purchases and sales of the metals, for which reason it has been seen that the contracts are treated by English law as contracts for the purchase and sale of metals and not gaming contracts. The plaintiffs, by "closing" out the contracts, did sell the defendant sufficient quantities of zinc to enable him to meet his forward commitments as and when they fell due.

There is no good reason for assuming that while contracts for the sale of currency can be harmful to a country, contracts requiring payments for trade transactions cannot. Nor can there be more of a presumption of possible harm in connection with one category compared with the other. If payments for trade were never harmful there would have been no reason to grant authority to restrict these payments under Article VIII, Section 2(a) or to restrict trade transactions under the GATT, which expressly recognizes the need for restrictions in certain circumstances to safeguard the balance of payments.[49] In policy after policy the Fund has emphasized that restrictions on payments for trade transactions are detrimental to currencies.[50] If both categories of contract can undermine the strength of currencies, there is no reason to assume that authorized derogations from a multilateral system of payments for current international transactions are less deserving of respect if the derogation relates to payments for trade.

Lord Denning cited Article I(ii), Article VI, Section 3, Article VIII, Section 2(a), and Article XIX(i) as fortifying his view that "the Bretton Woods Agreement should not do anything to hinder legitimate contracts for the sale or purchase of merchandise or commodities."[51] This objective would be achieved by interpreting "exchange contracts" as contracts for the exchange of one currency for another. He found it difficult to give sensible meaning to the words "which involve the currency of any member" on any other reading, whereas in his view they were intended to distinguish between the currencies of members and nonmembers. He added this thought, however:

> It is no doubt possible for men of business to seek to avoid article VIII, section 2(b), by various artifices. But I hope that the courts will be

---

[49] Article XII of the GATT.

[50] See, for example, the Fund's decisions on bilateralism and convertibility, retention quotas, discrimination for balance of payments reasons, and payments arrears (*Selected Decisions*, Eighth Issue, pp. 134–43). (*Selected Decisions*, Ninth Issue, pp. 204–13.)

[51] [1976] 1 Q.B. 683, at 713–14 (C.A.).

able to look at the substance of the contracts and not at the form. If the contracts are not legitimate contracts for the sale or purchase of merchandise or commodities, but are instead what Professor Nussbaum calls "monetary transactions in disguise," . . . as a means of manipulating currencies, they would be caught by section 2(*b*).[52]

Lord Justice Ormrod also found sufficient evidence in various provisions in which "exchange" appears, perhaps most clearly in the reference to "exchange transactions" in Article IV, Section 3, to support the conclusion that the phrase "exchange contracts" was used in its "primary sense."[53] For him also the interpretation should be favored that interfered as little as possible with international trade.

Lord Justice Ormrod seemed to believe that a distinction could be drawn between current international transactions, such as contracts for the sale of goods, and exchange contracts, which explained for him why "such a restrictive provision"[54] as Article VIII, Section 2(*b*) appears as the second of two subsections under the common heading "Avoidance of restrictions on current payments." The thought seems to be that restrictions on payments for trade will be less effective, and to this extent "avoided," if other members can enforce contracts notwithstanding the restrictions. On this view, the purpose of Article VIII, Section 2(*b*) is to exhort or require members not to take cognizance of restrictions adopted by fellow members.

Payments under contracts for the purchase and sale of currency are payments for current international transactions if they are not for the purpose of transferring capital. For example, the Fund has frequently decided that limitations on the amount of foreign currency that residents may purchase for visits abroad as tourists or businessmen are restrictions on payments for current international transactions. Furthermore, the "transfers" for current international transactions referred to in Article VIII, Section 2(*a*) involve purchases and sales of currency. The transfers relate to the proceeds of recent current international transactions. Under Section 2(*a*), parties to these transactions must be allowed to dispose of the currency of receipt and get their own currency with it unless the Fund approves restrictions on these dealings. If the Fund authorized restrictions on these dealings, the authorization would be given under Article VIII, Section 2(*a*), and the exchange control regulations by which the restrictions were imposed would relate to "exchange contracts" under Section 2(*b*).

---

[52] *Ibid.*, at 714.
[53] *Ibid.*, at 715.
[54] *Ibid.*, at 716.

Lord Justice Ormrod advanced a new theory of the meaning of the word "involve" in Article VIII, Section 2(b), which, however, he thought had no special significance. He thought that its function was to bring within the scope of "exchange contracts" monetary transactions in disguise. The contract in the case before him was not a transaction of this kind. If it involved any currency, it was sterling and not lire. It had not been shown that the defendant would have to acquire sterling for lire, but even if he did, lire would not be "involved" in the contract.

Those who support the interpretation of exchange contracts adopted in this case are led to regard the phrase in which the word "involve" appears as unimportant or to explain it unconvincingly as referring to monetary transactions in disguise or as excluding the exchange control regulations of nonmembers. Some such analysis is necessary in order to avoid the criticism that is made of the broad interpretation that it gives no independent meaning to the word "exchange" in the phrase "exchange contracts." A reasonable meaning can be given to all elements in the provision if "exchange contracts" are understood to be all contracts that provide for international payments or transfers and if "involve" is taken to refer to the exchange control regulations of the member whose balance of payments or exchange resources would be affected by enforcement of the contract, provided that the regulations are maintained or imposed consistently with the Articles.

Lord Justice Ormrod was aware of the difficulty of deciding whether the regulations were maintained or imposed consistently with the Articles. He thought that this question could be resolved only by evidence that the Fund had approved the regulations, or by applying a presumption of validity, or by expert evidence as to the effect of the regulations.

Lord Justice Shaw reasoned that if some special meaning not to be found in a dictionary had been intended for "exchange contracts" they would have been defined in Article XIX. The words used for all concepts in the Articles are defined by dictionaries, but the meaning of many of the concepts not defined in Article XIX has proved to be controversial in the context of the Articles. The Fund has had to adopt decisions defining many of these concepts. In any event, there is more than one dictionary meaning of "exchange." One meaning is foreign or domestic currency when involved in international payments. This is the meaning of the word "exchange" in the phrase "exchange control."

Lord Justice Shaw expressed the opinion that the broad view of exchange contracts would embrace transfers of capital, but that such an extension of meaning would be unnecessary in order to serve the objects of the Articles. In his opinion, members are free to restrict capital transfers because they are outside the protection of Article VIII, Section 2(*a*) and therefore do not need the protection of Section 2(*b*). Current international transactions are within the protection of Section 2(*a*), but it would frustrate the purposes of the Articles to apply Section 2(*b*) to them. According to this analysis, there are three categories of international transaction: current transactions, capital transactions, and exchange contracts. Economists would not accept this classification. The courts made much of the presence of lawyers at Bretton Woods, but economists also were there. The Articles were drafted on the assumption that transactions would be classified either as current or capital. On the thesis of Lord Justice Shaw, Article XIX(*i*), which begins "Payments for current transactions means payments which are not for the purpose of transferring capital . . ." should have gone on to say "or which are not made under exchange contracts."

The language of Article VIII, Section 2(*b*) does not exclude from exchange control regulations the control of capital transfers or of payments and transfers for current international transactions. Moreover, even if the courts' definition of "exchange contracts" were accepted, it would include contracts to make capital transfers. The transferor moves from one currency into another. The harm that outflows of capital might do to a currency was one of the dominating concerns of the drafters of the Articles. The drafting history of Article VIII, Section 2(*b*) shows that it was regarded as a contribution to the deterrence of undesirable capital movements.[55] The suggestion of Lord Justice Shaw that they can be effectively controlled "at source"[56] without any need to make contracts for them unenforceable could equally be made with respect to contracts requiring payments and transfers for current international transactions. These payments also can be controlled at the source, and neither more nor less effectively than capital transfers. Exchange controls are normally applied through the legislator's authorized dealers, to whom parties must go whether they wish to make payments and transfers for current international transactions or capital transfers. Furthermore, the fact that

---

[55] See Gold, *Fund Agreement in the Courts* (1962), pp. 114–15.
[56] [1976] 1 Q.B. 683, at 724.

payments are impeded at the source may be the reason why a contracting party sues in a foreign court and seeks damages for nonperformance or other relief notwithstanding the exchange control regulations. Finally, it has been seen that "exchange contracts" as defined by the courts in the *Terruzzi* case can provide for payments and transfers for current international transactions within the meaning of Article VIII, Section 2(*a*). A barrier has not been erected between the two subsections of Article VIII, Section 2.

SOME FURTHER REFLECTIONS ON THE TERRUZZI CASE

In both the lower and the appellate court the judges found support for their view of the meaning of "exchange contracts" in various provisions of the Articles, particularly Article IV, Sections 3 and 4, in which the word "exchange" appears in such formulations as "foreign exchange dealings," "exchange transactions," and "exchange operations." The judges thought that these phrases clearly bore the meaning given to "exchange contract" by Lord Radcliffe. It has been noted that no reference was made in this connection to any of the provisions of the Articles in which the words "exchange control" appear.

A related textual point to be considered is that a purpose of the Articles is to establish a multilateral system of payments and transfers for current international transactions by prohibiting restrictions inconsistent with that system. The Articles are concerned, therefore, with all payments and transfers of this kind and not merely with those that take the form of contracts for the purchase and sale of currency. When derogations from the system are permitted in the form of restrictions, and members other than the legislating member are required to take the action required by Article VIII, Section 2(*b*), it is not obvious why the drafters should narrow their concern from all payments and transfers for current international transactions to any one class of them.

The courts were unwilling to give paramount effect to the Fund's purpose of promoting international monetary cooperation because the Fund has the important purpose of promoting international trade as well. It is true that the attempt to establish a hierarchy of purposes is a dangerous and probably erroneous undertaking. Nevertheless, the jurisdiction of the Fund is confined to payments and transfers and does not extend to imports and exports. Even at the Bretton Woods Conference it was agreed that another international organization would be created with jurisdiction over trade.[57] Moreover, the issue in the case

---

[57] Resolution VII of the United Nations Monetary and Financial Conference,

was not the effect to be given to the purposes of the Fund, but, on the assumption made by the courts that the Italian regulations were restrictions under Article VIII, Section 2(*a*), the effect to be given to an authorized derogation from the obligation to avoid these restrictions. Under Article I, the Fund must be guided in all its decisions by the purposes of the Fund. Therefore, if the Fund had decided to approve the restrictions, that decision would have been taken because in the particular circumstances of Italy the approval would promote the purposes of the Fund, taken as a whole, over the longer run. The assumption that the regulations amounted to restrictions under Article VIII, Section 2(*a*) was unfounded, but the regulations were exchange control regulations within the meaning of the Articles, and they must be regarded as consistent with the Articles even though approval of them was unnecessary under the Articles.

A more reasonable reading of Article VIII, Section 2(*b*), it has been suggested, is that exchange contracts mean contracts requiring international payments or transfers in foreign or domestic currency. This interpretation would explain various aspects of the provision that puzzled the courts. It would explain why the expression "exchange transactions" is not used. It would also explain why Article VIII, Section 2(*b*) is not part of the provisions dealing with exchange rates, in which the expression "exchange transactions" occurs, although at one time during the drafting of the Articles the substance of Article VIII, Section 2(*b*) was included in the other provisions. Furthermore, the words "involve the currency of any member" take on a more likely meaning than the exclusion of nonmembers. This exclusion, it was explained, was not necessary but was made out of an abundance of caution.[58] There was no need to exclude nonmembers in this provision because it follows of necessity from other provisions, such as Article XI, that nonmembers are not the beneficiaries of any obligations of members under the Articles.[59] On the reading that has been suggested, the words would point to the member whose balance of payments or exchange resources were affected and whose exchange control regulations were designed to protect them. The Cuban insurance cases[60]

Proceedings and Documents of the United Nations Monetary and Financial Conference, Bretton Woods, New Hampshire, July 1–22, 1944, Department of State Publication 2866, International Organization and Conference Series I, 3 (Washington, 1948), p. 941. (Hereinafter cited as *Proceedings and Documents*.)

[58] [1976] 1 Q.B. 683, at 717.

[59] *Menendez v. Saks and Company*, 485 F. 2d 1355, at 1367 (1973).

[60] Pp. 43–94 in this volume.

show that parties may attempt to rely on the exchange control regulations of a member in circumstances in which the regulations do not affect the member's economic position.

The approach that has been suggested is different from the interpretation that was rejected in the *Terruzzi* case. The condition that a member's balance of payments or exchange resources must be affected is derived from the words "involve the currency of any member" and not from "exchange contracts." The language of Article VIII, Section 2(*b*), examined in the tranquillity that was not a feature of the three weeks of the Bretton Woods Conference, is not as good as it might be for conveying the meaning that has been suggested, but no reading is free from difficulty. It is submitted that the reading suggested here is far more reasonable than the one adopted in the *Terruzzi* case, and is indeed the correct reading.

The courts in the *Terruzzi* case were bothered by the breadth of any interpretation other than the one that they chose, but a more liberal interpretation would not be broader than the exchange control regulations that are regarded by a member as necessary and are authorized by or under the Articles.

The courts examined the decisions of a number of courts in member countries other than the United Kingdom, particularly because of the argument that it was important to achieve conformity in the interpretation of a provision that was now part of the domestic law of all members. Lord Justice Ormrod felt that this submission was weakened by the divergence that had developed between the courts in France and in the Federal Republic of Germany, on the one hand, and a court in Belgium, on the other hand. The survey of cases neglected decisions delivered in the last few years and, therefore, failed to note that the Supreme Court of the Federal Republic of Germany[61] and the Court of Cassation in France,[62] the highest tribunals in these countries, have now adopted the view that exchange contracts are contracts that affect a member's exchange resources. Much emphasis was placed on the *obiter dictum* in the *Banco do Brasil* case, but there was no mention of the treatment of that case in the *Banco Frances* case, although it must be noted that the judgments in the later case do not discuss the meaning of "exchange contracts."

---

[61] Gold, "Fund Agreement in the Courts—X," p. 145 in this volume.
[62] See Eck, Note (cited in fn. 9), pp. 491–98.

ZEEVI CASE

The New York Court of Appeals in its decision of June 16, 1975 in *J. Zeevi and Sons, Ltd., et al. v. Grindlays Bank (Uganda) Limited*[63] gave a restrictive application to Article VIII, Section 2(*b*), but the basis of the decision is not clear. On March 24, 1972 an Israeli corporation deposited with the defendant, Grindlays Bank, Ugandan currency valued at US$406,846.80 for the purpose of establishing a fund on which the plaintiff, an Israeli partnership, could draw money. On the same date, the defendant opened its irrevocable credit for US$406,846.80 in favor of the plaintiff and issued a letter of credit acknowledging that it had opened an irrevocable credit for the amount referred to and providing that the credit would be available against clean drafts drawn on the depositor in ten equal monthly installments beginning April 15, 1972. The defendant guaranteed the payment of drafts. The negotiating bank was authorized to claim reimbursement for its payments from First National City Bank (Citibank) by debits against the defendant's account with Citibank. By directives of March and April 1972, the Bank of Uganda, acting with the authority of the Minister of Finance under the Exchange Control Act of Uganda, notified the defendant that foreign exchange allocations in favor of Israeli companies and nationals should be canceled and ordered the defendant to make no payments pursuant to the letter of credit. On April 14, 1972 the defendant informed Citibank of the action of the Ugandan authorities and directed it to make no payments. On December 28, 1972 Chemical Bank presented to Citibank for reimbursement ten drafts totaling the amount of the credit. Citibank returned the drafts and refused payment. The plaintiff as beneficiary of the letter of credit and the assignee of the plaintiff commenced this action by order of attachment on the defendant's funds on deposit with Citibank. The defendant relied on various defenses, one of which was that refusal to dismiss the complaint was contrary to Article VIII, Section 2(*b*) of the Fund's Articles.

The Court of Appeals emphasized the value to those in commerce of having a place at a financial center where they could be certain of the prompt availability of funds under an irrevocable letter of credit. A vast amount of this business was transacted in New York.

> The parties, by listing United States dollars as the form of payment, impliedly . . . set up procedures to implement their trust in our policies.

---

[63] 37 N.Y. 2d 220, 333 N.E. 2d 168, 371 N.Y.S. 2d 892 (1975).

In order to maintain its preeminent financial position, it is important that the justified expectations of the parties to the contract be protected. . . .[64]

The court held that no effect could be given to the confiscatory and discriminatory act of the Ugandan Government. The act of state doctrine did not apply. Under that doctrine, the courts of the United States cannot question an act of a recognized foreign nation committed within its own territory.[65] In this case, however, the debt was not located in Uganda because it had no power to enforce or collect it.

With respect to the defense based on Article VIII, Section 2(b), the court held:

Contrary to defendants' position, the agreement [i.e., the Articles], even when read in its broadest sense, fails to bring the letter of credit within its scope, since said letter of credit is not an exchange contract. In *Banco do Brasil, S.A. v. Israel Commodity Co.,* . . . this court frowned on an interpretation of said provision of the Bretton Woods Agreement which "sweeps in all contracts affecting any members' exchange resources as doing considerable violence to the text of the section."[66]

Even if the broad interpretation of exchange contracts is rejected in accordance with the *dictum* in the *Banco do Brasil* case, the letter of credit might fall within some narrower interpretation. It would certainly seem to fall within the interpretation adopted in the *Terruzzi* case. The court may have proceeded on the principle, however, that suit by the beneficiary on the letter of credit could be severed from the contract between the defendant and the depositor to issue the letter of credit, which incontestably would fall within the *Terruzzi* definition.[67]

---

[64] 37 N.Y. 2d at 227, 371 N.Y.S. 2d at 898.

[65] See *French v. Banco Nacional de Cuba*, 295 N.Y.S. 2d 433, 23 N.Y. 2d 46 (1968). (Gold, "Fund Agreement in the Courts—X," pp. 131–39 in this volume.)

[66] 37 N.Y. 2d at 229, 371 N.Y.S. 2d at 900.

[67] John S. Williams, "Foreign Exchange Control Regulation and the New York Court of Appeals: *J. Zeevi & Sons, Ltd. v. Grindlays Bank (Uganda), Ltd.,*" *Cornell International Law Journal*, Vol. 9 (May 1976), pp. 243–44. Cf. the severance of the check from the underlying transaction that gave rise to it in *Sharif v. Azad* [1967] 1 Q.B. 605. (Gold, "Fund Agreement in the Courts—IX," pp. 107–16 in this volume.)
"To a Continental lawyer this might appear as a somewhat surprising result, because the giving of these cheques was clearly part of an overall exchange transaction which might well be considered as falling within the object of article VIII, section 2(b). But to an English lawyer the decision would appear correct and logical because we tend to favour a more precise analytical approach to construction and interpretation." (*Wilson, Smithett & Cope Ltd. v. Terruzzi* [1976] 1 Q.B. 683, at 699, *per* Kerr J.)

The court did not inquire whether the discriminatory restriction had been imposed consistently with the Articles. Restrictions on payments and transfers for current international transactions cannot be introduced consistently with the Articles unless they are approved by the Fund.

Exchange Control and Public Policy of Other Members

It is an accepted idea that there is great and growing interdependence among countries.[68] The word is used in many ways, but most uses involve the idea that increasingly the policies and activities of one country affect the policies and activities of other countries. In such a world, countries have at the same time less effective autonomy and more impact on other countries than in the past. Interaction would be more descriptive than interdependence. Whatever may be the precise word to describe it, the reality stimulates cooperation among countries. The communiqué dated June 22, 1976 of the Council of the Organization for Economic Cooperation and Development meeting at ministerial level is a recent example of the many affirmations of the idea and the moral drawn from it:

> 3. Member Governments agreed that the high degree of interdependence among their countries, their recognition, in a spirit of solidarity, of each other's problems and their dedication to the same basic principles demand close consultation and co-operation among themselves in formulating and implementing their economic policies. Where appropriate, this co-operation may extend to the adoption of rules or guidelines for their behavior as had been the case in specific areas such as trade environment, energy and international investment and multinational enterprises. . . .

> 11. Ministers reaffirmed that co-operation among industrialised countries within the OECD in pursuit of improved relations with the developing countries is essential to achieve a coherent approach to the evolving economic relations between the industrialised and developing countries and to lead to agreements on practical measures. . . .

It is submitted that the courts in adopting restrictive interpretations of Article VIII, Section 2(b) and in neglecting public policy as an independent basis for relief are not merely failing to give effect to the consequences of interdependence but are acting in opposition to the

---

[68] Miriam Camps, *The Management of Interdependence: A Preliminary View* (New York, 1974), pp. 42–59. See also *Cebora S.N.C. v. S.I.P. (Industrial Products) Ltd.* [1976] 1 Lloyd's Rep. 271 (C.A.), at 274–75 and 279.

actions of their governments. In negotiating treaties, governments consider the general welfare. Courts must consider problems from the standpoint of the litigants before them. It is not surprising that the result in a number of cases involving Article VIII, Section 2(*b*) corresponds to the view taken by the court of the morality or immorality of the litigants. The courts have delivered their opinions on the moral behavior of the parties, sometimes in stern language, although sometimes the courts disavow any intention of giving legal weight to these judgments. *Sharif v. Azad* and the *Terruzzi, Zeevi, Zavicha,* and *Banco Frances* cases are examples of this tendency to moralize.

At the same time courts do not neglect interests that go beyond those of the parties. *Miliangos v. George Frank (Textiles) Ltd.*[69] shows the concern of English courts for London as a financial center, and the *Zeevi* case shows a similar concern of New York courts for their city. These cases are not isolated examples of this preoccupation.[70] The interests that are taken into account in cases such as these are domestic. What is now proposed is that courts should weigh the interests of other members of the Fund when issues related to international monetary relations arise in litigation. There are circumstances in which the public policy of the *lex fori* should dictate concern for the interests of other contracting parties even though there is no specific provision of the Articles that compels this concern.

The Supreme Court of the United States in *Kolovrat v. Oregon*[71] has shown sympathy for the application of the doctrine of public policy in an issue involving inheritance by taking into account the fact that Yugoslavia and the United States were both members of the Fund and that Yugoslavia's exchange controls met the standards of the Articles. The Supreme Court seems to have held that the United States, by adhering to the Articles, had established a public policy in the field of inheritance that the individual states had to respect and against which they could not assert their own public policy.

The opinion of the New York Court of Appeals in the *Banco Frances* case is the clearest recent expression in favor of public policy as a

---

[69] [1975] 3 All E.R. 801.

[70] "Any erosion of the certainties of the application by our Courts of the law merchant relating to bills of exchange is likely to work to the detriment of this country, which depends on international trade to a degree that needs no emphasis." (*Cebora S.N.C. v. S.I.P. (Industrial Products) Ltd.* [1976] 1 Lloyd's Rep. 271 (C.A.), at 278, *per* Sir Eric Sachs.)

[71] 81 S. Ct. 922, 366 U.S. 187 (1961). See Gold, *Fund Agreement in the Courts* (1962), pp. 128–35; Gold, Pamphlet No. 3, pp. 28–29.

reason for taking cognizance of the exchange control regulations of other members of the Fund if the regulations are consistent with the Articles. In various cases, the New York Court of Appeals has established a pattern of restrictive interpretation of Article VIII, Section 2(b) but a liberal application of the doctrine of public policy. The court has based this approach on considerations of economic interdependence. It has given affirmative relief in tort for the fraudulent evasion of the exchange control regulations of another member of the Fund. The considerations that induced the court to act in this way would justify recognition of these regulations, if consistent with the Articles, as a defense in an action to enforce a contract even though Article VIII, Section 2(b), in the view of the court, did not provide a defense. The Court of Appeals was disposed as early as the *Perutz* case to accept exchange control regulations as a defense in these circumstances.

Two other cases have a bearing on the doctrine of public policy in relation to exchange control. A decision of a French court can be understood to support the principle that a result of the Articles of Agreement is to sweep aside the objection that recognition of the effect of the foreign exchange control legislation of another country is contrary to the *ordre public* of the forum even though Article VIII, Section 2(b) is not involved. In *Statni Banka and Banque d'Etat Tchécoslovaque v. Englander*,[72] decided by the Court of Appeal of Aix-en-Provence on February 14, 1966, Rodan, a resident of Czechoslovakia, sought in 1948 to transfer an amount of Czechoslovak currency to Englander, a resident of France, via Tatra Banka. The bank deposited the money in an account opened in the name of Englander, but returned the money to Rodan when it failed to get authority from the Czechoslovak exchange control authorities to make the transfer to Englander. By action of the Minister of Finance taken under a Czechoslovak law of 1950, Statni Banka succeeded to the rights and obligations of Tatra Banka. On January 14, 1964, the Court of Appeal of Aix-en-Provence awarded judgment in favor of Englander against Statni Banka in a suit he had instituted to collect the equivalent in French francs of the debt owed to him. Englander then succeeded in obtaining an order for the attachment of funds held to the credit of Statni Banka by a Paris bank.

Statni Banka appealed successfully on the ground that its funds were immune from seizure. The Court of Appeals noted that the bank

---

[72] *International Law Reports*, ed. by E. Lauterpacht, Vol. 47 (London, 1974), pp. 157–63.

was charged with the duty of making payments on behalf of the Czechoslovak State in foreign countries, and that the funds it held abroad belonged to the state. The court held that it was impossible to distinguish between the public and private funds held by the bank and therefore all the funds were immune from execution.

The Court of Appeal considered a further argument in opposition to the attachment, which was based on Czechoslovak exchange control legislation. The court declared that the exchange control legislation of other countries could not be given effect in France because it was contrary to French *ordre public,* but an exception was admitted if an international agreement required a different result. The court noted that at the time of the original request to Tatra Bank to make the transfer both Czechoslovakia and France were members of the Fund, and that members were authorized by Article XIV, Section 2 to maintain exchange restrictions.[73]

> As Czechoslovakia believed it necessary, on account of economic conditions, to incorporate in its exchange control legislation the prohibition of the export of capital without authorization, this foreign regulation was binding on France in application of the Articles of Agreement of the I.M.F. Validation of the attachment effected in Paris on the capital belonging to the Statni Banka would result in annulling the refusal to transfer funds made by the Czechoslovak authorities in application of the exchange control regulations in force in that country, and would constitute an intervention in that regulation.[74]

The court was aware that Czechoslovakia was no longer a member of the Fund, but cited a payments agreement concluded on January 16, 1964 between the two countries, under Article I of which payments between the franc area and Czechoslovakia were to be effected in conformity with the exchange control regulations in force in the two countries. Article VI of the bilateral agreement applied Article I to payments under contracts concluded before the date of entry into force of the payments agreement. The court concluded that:

> By the effect of two successive Agreements to which France and Czechoslovakia were parties, Czechoslovak exchange control legislation is binding on France from the date of the deposit in issue, as it is now binding as regards the attachment.[75]

Various aspects of this decision should be noted:

---

[73] If the case involved a capital transfer, authority to control it would have been granted by Article VI, Section 3, and not by Article XIV, Section 2.

[74] *International Law Reports* (cited in fn. 72), p. 162.

[75] *Ibid.,* p. 163.

(i) Immunity was sufficient to justify cancellation of the attachment, so that the further basis for the decision involving exchange control was *obiter.*

(ii) The further basis for the decision could have been limited in turn to the bilateral payments agreement, but the reference in the judgment to successive agreements after the court noted the withdrawal of Czechoslovakia from the Fund suggests that in this part of the judgment the court relied on both agreements.

(iii) Nowhere in the judgment is there a reference to Article VIII, Section 2(*b*), even though Article XIV, Section 2 is cited as authority for the maintenance of exchange restrictions. The judgment can be read to mean that the effect of Article XIV, Section 2 of the Articles was that the restriction in question was "binding on France in application" of the Articles. As a consequence, perhaps on the basis of the Articles or under some principle not derived from the Articles, French courts could not render the restriction nugatory by permitting the attachment. As noted already, the court did not rely on Article VIII, Section 2(*b*), or on some other specific provision of the Articles, in order to decide that the attachment must be canceled, although it did preface its discussion of the Articles by stating that *ordre public* would not be an impediment to the effectiveness of the foreign exchange control regulations of another country "in performance of an international agreement."[76]

---

[76] *Ibid.,* p. 162. The "Bretton Woods Agreements of July 1944" were cited by the Court of Cassation in its judgment of January 25, 1966 in *Cassan v. Koninklijke Nederlandsche Petroleum Maatschappij (International Law Reports* (cited in fn. 72), pp. 58–60) and by the *tribunal de grande instance* of the Seine in its judgment of June 29, 1966 in *Plichon v. Société Koninklijke Nederlandsche Petroleum Maatschappij (International Law Reports* (cited in fn. 72), pp. 67–72) to support rejection of the argument that recognition of the effect of a Dutch Decree on French nationals holding in France share certificates issued by Dutch corporations was contrary to French *ordre public.* The Decree required the holders to declare the certificates in order to enable them to be validated. If certificates were not declared, they would be canceled and substitutes issued to the rightful possessors or, if there were none, to the Dutch authorities. To protect French shareholders, with the agreement of the Dutch authorities, a law was passed in France to establish a special validation procedure in France. Cassan and Plichon had not declared their share certificates in Royal Dutch. Cassan requested the French court to order Royal Dutch to issue to him the certificates that had been issued in substitution for those he held. Plichon requested similar relief, or, as a subsidiary remedy, the value of the certificates. Both argued that forfeiture under the Dutch Decree was contrary to French *ordre public.* The courts held that the purpose of the Decree was not confiscation but the restoration of plundered property. In holding the Decree to be in conformity with the Bretton Woods Agreements, as well as with the London Declaration of January 5, 1943 (U.S.

(iv) It is not clear why a similar result should not have been reached, on the basis of the reasoning with respect to exchange control, in the proceedings that led to the decision of January 14, 1964 in favor of Englander.

(v) *Dicta* in the judgment are not consistent with the principle recognized by a number of courts that Article VIII, Section 2(*b*) confers no benefit on nonmembers or ex-members of the Fund.[77]

(vi) The court rejected the argument that the performance in France from funds located there of an obligation recognized by a French court was not a transfer subject to Czechoslovak foreign exchange control.

The second case is *Ceulemans v. Jahn and Barbier*, decided by the Commercial Court of Brussels on April 19, 1968.[78] In 1965, three Belgian citizens entered into a partnership arrangement in Belgium for the purpose of carrying out operations by which Congolese currency would be converted into U.S. dollars in contravention of the exchange control law of the Democratic Republic of Congo (now Zaïre). The role of the defendants was to sell in Congo the Congolese francs purchased in Brussels and to remit the proceeds to Brussels. The operations were not contrary to Belgian law. The plaintiff sued his two associates for US$124,600, which they admitted was owing to him, but they contended that they had handed this amount to a crew member of SABENA. This person handed over to the plaintiff in Waterloo an envelope containing wastepaper. The courier claimed that this was the envelope handed to him by the defendants. It was not determined who had perpetrated the fraud, but the plaintiff argued that it was not he who should bear the loss.

The court made no reference to Article VIII, Section 2(*b*). It decided that it would not provide a remedy to a plaintiff who entered into a contract entailing the performance of acts in another country that were

---

Department of State, *Bulletin*, January 9, 1943, pp. 21–22), the courts were referring not to the Articles of Agreement but to Resolution VI of the Bretton Woods Conference (on Enemy Assets and Looted Property). (*Proceedings and Documents*, pp. 939–40.)

[77] See *Basso v. Janda, Recueil Dalloz Sirey*, July 3, 1968, Jurisprudence, p. 445 (Gold, "Fund Agreement in the Courts—X," pp. 153–55 in this volume); *French v. Banco Nacional de Cuba*, 23 N.Y. 2d 46, 295 N.Y.S. 2d 433 (1968) (Gold, "Fund Agreement in the Courts—X," pp. 131–39 in this volume); *Stephen v. Zivnostenska Banka National Corporation*, 140 N.Y.S. 2d 323 (1955) (Gold, *Fund Agreement in the Courts* (1962), pp. 77–78). See also Gold, "Cuban Insurance Cases," pp. 63–64 in this volume.

[78] *Jurisprudence commerciale de Belgique*, 1968, No. 11–12, Pt. IV, pp. 765–85; *Pasicrisie Belge*, 1969, Pt. III, pp. 22–28.

contrary to the law of that country. There is nothing surprising about this principle, but the court's emphasis on "the good relations that should exist between nations, . . . the notions of solidarity that each day enlist greater support" is worth noting.[79] If a contract calls for the performance of acts outside the territory of a country that will produce the effect within the territory of weakening the economic and financial position of the country, should not the same notions of solidarity apply in order to justify the denial of remedies based on the contract?

Professor François Rigaux, in a discussion of the case,[80] comments that the objective of the foreign law should be considered in determining whether the violation of it is contrary to the concept of morality (bonnes mœurs) in Belgian law and whether the violation should be discouraged by the refusal of a remedy. In this connection he notes that

> on occasion, foreign regulations are the implementation of a concerted action of international policy, i.e. in order that their violation offend the contractual morality of another state, the judge in this state must determine whether or not his government's position is aligned with that of the other state.[81] (Translation)

In his view, the common membership of Belgium and Congo in the Fund made it unnecessary to examine the objective of the exchange control law of Congo, if consistent with the Articles, in order to decide that violation of the law was contrary to the concept of morality in Belgian law.

> . . . the Bretton Woods Agreements set forth, as between the member countries, this common policy and spirit of solidarity the existence of which, with regard to a matter not governed by a similar agreement, the national courts are entitled to verify if the foreign regulation has an international policy objective.[82] (Translation)

Two problems must be considered in connection with public policy. The first is the principle subscribed to by the courts of some countries that they will not enforce the penal, revenue, confiscatory, or fiscal laws of another country. The principle is sometimes extended to justify the disregard of these laws even though enforcement in a narrow sense is not involved. In England, the House of Lords has now

---

[79] Jurisprudence commerciale de Belgique (cited in fn. 78), p. 772.
[80] Ibid., pp. 777–85.
[81] Ibid., p. 783.
[82] Ibid., p. 785.

made it clear that normal exchange control laws do not fall into any of these categories.[83] It is interesting to note the following statement in a case decided by the House of Lords in which a parallel was drawn between the prohibition by India of certain exports, which was directly involved in the case, and the exchange control laws of other countries:

> . . . [F]urther, it must, I think, be borne in mind that . . . [the older cases that had been cited] date from a time when international relationships were somewhat different and when theories of political economy now outmoded were generally accepted. Many dealt with revenue laws or penal laws which have always been regarded as being in a special position, and I do not wish on this occasion to say more than that probably some re-examination of some of these cases may in future be necessary.[84]

The New York Court of Appeals, it has been seen, was willing to reject the "old chestnut" about revenue laws but in any event found it inappropriate in relation to exchange control regulations among members of the Fund. This attitude is consonant with the decisions of courts in other countries that have been responding to changes in international monetary relations and have been finding legal solutions more suitable to new conditions.[85]

The other problem relating to public policy is suggested by the second sentence of Article VIII, Section 2(b):

> In addition, members may, by mutual accord, cooperate in measures for the purpose of making the exchange control regulations of either member more effective, provided that such measures and regulations are consistent with this Agreement.[86]

---

[83] *Kahler v. Midland Bank Ltd.* [1949] 2 All E.R. 621, at 623–24, 629, and 642.

[84] *Regazzoni v. K.C. Sethia Ltd.* [1957] 3 All E.R. 286, at 293.

[85] See *Hornlinie v. Société Nationale des Pétroles Aquitaine, Nederlandse Jurisprudentie*, 1972, No. 269, pp. 728–38 (Gold, "Fund Agreement in the Courts—XI," pp. 177–88 in this volume; *Transarctic Shipping Corporation, Inc. Monrovia, Liberia v. Krögerwerft (Kröger Shipyard) Company, European Transport Law*, Vol. 9 (1974), pp. 701–10 (Gold, *Floating Currencies, Gold, and SDRs: Some Recent Legal Developments*, IMF Pamphlet Series, No. 19 (Washington, 1976), pp. 17–33), hereinafter cited as Gold, Pamphlet No. 19; *Miliangos v. George Frank (Textiles) Ltd.* [1975] 3 All E.R. 801 (Gold, Pamphlet No. 19, pp. 35–38).

[86] One kind of cooperation that was contemplated is suggested by the following passage in the *Questions and Answers on the International Monetary Fund* issued by the U.S. Treasury on June 10, 1944: "Even though it never becomes necessary for a country to prevent a flight of capital, a country may find it helpful to cooperate with other member countries in controlling capital movements. Such cooperative measures might appropriately include a refusal to accept or permit acquisition of deposits, securities, or investments by nationals of any member country imposing restrictions on the export of capital except with the permission of the

This sentence might be taken to proscribe any resort to public policy on the ground that application of the concept would be cooperation for which the mutual accord of governments was required. This version of the second sentence is not the only possible version. The power of governments to enter into agreements can be reconciled without difficulty with the authority of the courts to apply legal principles. The New York Court of Appeals favored the first version in the *Banco do Brasil* case but decided in favor of the second in the *Banco Frances* case.

The objection might be raised that "mutual accord" between governments will ensure reciprocity while the application of public policy may not achieve that result. To this objection, an enlightened member of the House of Lords in one of the cases referred to above replied:

> It [i.e., the principle that was being applied] is a principle of our municipal law. Its aim is no doubt to preserve comity with other friendly states, but it is in no sense dependent on proof of universality or reciprocity.[87]

Indeed, the application of public policy by the courts of members that take a narrow view of Article VIII, Section 2(*b*) may extend a measure of reciprocity to those members whose courts take a broad view.

Finally, if public policy is relevant to ensure that courts take cognizance of the exchange control regulations of another member when they are consistent with the Articles, cognizance might be refused when the regulations are inconsistent with the Articles. There are circumstances in which courts that start with the proposition that they will not recognize the exchange control regulations of other countries nevertheless admit exceptions. They may recognize the effect of regulations if the doctrine of the act of state applies.[88] They may refuse to compel performance of a contract if it requires that an act be done within the territory of a foreign country that is invalid under the exchange control law of that country.[89] They may refuse to compel performance of a contract or trust in violation of the exchange control

---

government of that country and the Fund. Member countries might also undertake to make available to the Fund or to the government of any member country information on property, deposits, securities, and investments of the nationals of that member country." (*History, 1945–65*, Vol. III, p. 179)

[87] Lord Somervell of Harrow in *Regazzoni v. K.C. Sethia Ltd.* [1957] 3 All E.R. 286, at 297.

[88] See *French v. Banco Nacional de Cuba*, 295 N.Y.S. 2d 433, 23 N.Y. 2d 46 (1968) (Gold, "Fund Agreement in the Courts—X," pp. 131–39 in this volume.)

[89] See *Ceulemans v. Jahn and Barbier, Jurisprudence commerciale de Belgique*, 1968, No. 11–12, Pt. IV, pp. 765 *et suiv.; Pasicrisie Belge*, 1969, Pt. III, pp. 22–28. See also *Foster v. Driscoll* [1929] 1 K.B. 470 (C.A.).

law that is part of the proper law of the contract or the trust.[90] Should the courts refuse, on the basis of public policy, to act in accordance with these exceptions if the exchange control law is inconsistent with the Articles?

---

[90] See *Re Lord Cable (deceased)* [1976] 3 All E.R. 417.

7

The Fund Agreement in the Courts—XIII*

Par Values and Exchange Rates

This installment in the series of articles dealing with jurisprudence in which the Fund's Articles of Agreement have been involved discusses some cases that deal with par values and exchange rates. Problems arise under legal instruments that refer to par values and parities established under the Articles. If these instruments are not modified, problems will continue to arise even after the Second Amendment of the Articles. Courts have shown a tendency to be flexible when dealing with references to par values, but they have also recognized certain limits. It is a paradox that solutions may be easier after the Second Amendment because present par values have been abrogated by that event. It is clear that the par value system for which the Second Amendment makes provision will not be initiated forthwith after the Second Amendment, and it may never be initiated. Unless courts consider themselves compelled by the facts to look back to some date when a par value was in existence, they will have no alternative but to find a realistic solution.

The cases discussed in this article are prefaced by a summary of some aspects of the law on par values before the Second Amendment, and are followed by a summary of similar aspects of the law governing the par value system that could be called into existence under the Second Amendment.

---

* Originally published in June 1978.

Par Values Before Second Amendment

Under the Articles before the Second Amendment, a member that, within the meaning of the second sentence of Article IV, Section 4(b), was freely buying and selling gold for its currency in transactions with the monetary authorities of other members on the basis of the par value for its currency was deemed to be fulfilling its obligations with respect to rates for exchange transactions within its territories.[1] A member that was not freely buying and selling gold and was not taking appropriate measures that succeeded in keeping exchange transactions in its territories between its own currency and the currency of another member within the margins around the parity between the two currencies, i.e., the ratio between them based on the par values for them under the Articles, was failing to fulfill its obligations under the Articles.[2] The Fund was then able, but not required, to declare the member ineligible to use the resources of the Fund,[3] and to compel it to withdraw from the organization.[4] Moreover, the Fund had no authority to approve a unitary floating rate or a unitary fixed rate that was not proposed as a par value.

The par value last established under the Articles remained the par value as a legal concept under the Articles until a new one was established. The principle was settled by the Executive Board in its *Annual Report* of 1951:

> A member of the Fund cannot, within the terms of the Articles of Agreement, abandon a par value that has been agreed with the Fund except by concurrently proposing to the Fund the establishment of a new par value.[5]

This aspect of the provisions on par values and exchange rates led in many instances to a huge discrepancy between the last par value and the actual rate of exchange for a currency. The explanation of what seemed to some observers the absurdity of insisting on the continued legal existence of a par value that was clearly unrelated to a current rate of exchange is twofold. The purpose of the legal principle was,

---

[1] Joseph Gold, *The Fund's Concepts of Convertibility*, IMF Pamphlet Series, No. 14 (Washington, 1971), pp. 33–37. (Hereinafter cited as Gold, Pamphlet No. 14.)

[2] Joseph Gold, "The Legal Structure of the Par Value System," *Law and Policy in International Business*, Vol. 5 (No. 1, 1973), pp. 177–84. (Hereinafter cited as Gold, "Legal Structure of Par Value System.")

[3] Article XV, Section 2(a), *original* and *first*.

[4] Article XV, Section 2(b), *original* and *first*.

[5] *Annual Report, 1951* (Washington, 1951), p. 40.

first, to deny the Fund authority to give tacit recognition to a floating rate that might seem to result from acquiescence in the abandonment of a par value, and, second, to deny the Fund authority to give tacit recognition to a fixed rate that had not been concurred in by the Fund in accordance with the procedures prescribed for the establishment of par values. The legal position can be explained in other terms: the intent of the Articles was the establishment and maintenance of fixed rates of exchange based on par values arrived at by procedures providing for international scrutiny and concurrence. If a member failed to maintain the effectiveness of a par value established in accordance with these procedures, it was to be regarded as violating its obligations to maintain rates for exchange transactions within the prescribed margins around the parity that continued to exist in the contemplation of the Articles.

Treatment of a member as a violator of its obligations, in order to promote the objective of international approval or concurrence in the exchange rate for a member's currency and the rejection of unilateral determination of it by the member,[6] was subject to a limited qualification in the case of an "unauthorized change" of par value. The Articles provided that if a member, after consultation with the Fund, changed the par value of its currency despite the objection of the Fund in circumstances in which the Fund was entitled to object, the member was not failing to fulfill its obligations within the meaning of the Articles because of its unilateral action.[7] The consequence, however, was that the member became automatically ineligible to use the resources of the Fund unless the Fund decided to prevent this consequence. This treatment of the unauthorized change of par value was the reverse of the treatment of those actions that were violations of the Articles. Violations by a member did not give rise to ineligibility unless the Fund took a decision declaring the member ineligible. If, after a reasonable period following the adoption of an unauthorized change of par value, the difference between the member and the Fund on an appropriate par value continued to exist, the member could be compelled to withdraw from the Fund. The effect, therefore, was that although a member was able to change the par value of its currency despite the objection of the Fund without the stigma of acting in

---

[6] Article IV, Section 5, *original* and *first*; Article XX, Section 4(a) and (d)(iii), *original* and *first*.

[7] See Joseph Gold, "Unauthorized Changes of Par Value and Fluctuating Exchange Rates in the Bretton Woods System," *American Journal of International Law*, Vol. 65 (1971), pp. 117–20; Gold, "Legal Structure of Par Value System," pp. 174–75.

violation of the Articles, the consequences of that action were designed to deter a member from undertaking it.

The concept of an action that was not a violation, even though it was subject to consequences that resembled, and with respect to ineligibility were even more rigorous than, the consequences attendant on a violation, was a compromise between those negotiators of the Articles who wanted the Fund to have extensive authority over exchange rates and those negotiators who wanted members to have final authority over the external value of their currencies. The latter negotiators were willing, however, that the cost of supporting an unauthorized par value should not be borne by the Fund's resources unless the Fund permitted the use of them. Notwithstanding the unusual compromise that was reached, the emphasis was still on a fixed rate of exchange. The compromise did not extend to the adoption of a floating rate. Moreover, it did not apply unless the contemplated change of par value had been submitted to the Fund for its concurrence. The withdrawal of support from a par value established under the Articles and the substitution of a fixed rate that was not submitted to the Fund for its concurrence as a new par value was inevitably a violation of the Articles. The reason for the distinction between this case and the unauthorized change in par value was the policy of the Articles in favor of scrutiny by the Fund of changes in exchange rates.

The legal principle that the par value last established under the Articles continued to be the par value under the Articles in all circumstances in which a member was failing to maintain it, whether or not the member was in violation of its obligations, did not, in principle, impede the conduct of operations and transactions under the Articles. Whether a member was allowing its currency to float, or had adopted a fixed official rate that it had not submitted to the Fund as a change in par value, or had made an unauthorized change in par value, the Fund was able to conduct operations and transactions in the member's currency. The Fund could do this by applying the exchange rate in the member's market between its currency and the U.S. dollar.[8] Because the United States was freely buying and selling gold within the meaning of the Articles, it was regarded as maintaining the value of its currency in terms of gold in accordance with its par value, and therefore the exchange rate between a member's currency and the

---

[8] Article IV, Section 8, *original* and *first*. See also Gold, Pamphlet No. 6, Second Edition, 1971, pp. 20–21.

U.S. dollar enabled the Fund to ascertain the actual gold value of the member's currency. The Articles authorized the Fund to apply that gold value, instead of the gold value represented by the par value most recently established under the Articles, as the basis for its operations and transactions involving the currency. The negotiators of the original Articles, however, did not think the unthinkable. The procedure as described became inappropriate once the central currency of the international monetary system, the U.S. dollar, became a floating currency. The assumption that the par value of the U.S. dollar was being maintained by means of the willingness of the U.S. authorities to support the par value with gold transactions was no longer tenable. It then became difficult for the Fund to continue to conduct its operations and transactions, and because it did not decide to suspend them,[9] the Fund had to find new and sometimes complicated procedures to continue them.[10]

After the announcement of August 15, 1971 that foreign official holdings of U.S. dollars would no longer be converted into gold or other reserve assets by the U.S. monetary authorities, the Fund adopted two successive decisions under which it sought to preserve as much order as possible in circumstances in which no members were observing their obligations with respect to exchange arrangements under the Articles.[11] The decisions invented the concept of the "central rate," and, in order to permit greater flexibility in exchange arrangements, defined wider margins for exchange transactions. The effort was intended to establish a simulacrum of the par value system, although without some of the constraints to which it had been subject. The decisions did not, and could not, absolve members from the nonobservance of their obligations with respect to par values and exchange rates.[12] The decisions attempted to minimize disorder by

---

[9] Article XVI, Section 1, *original* and *first*. For the partial suspension of one provision, see Executive Board Decisions No. 4078-(73/102) S, November 5, 1973 and No. 4145-(74/6) S, February 1, 1974, *Annual Report, 1974* (Washington, 1974), pp. 103, 108–109.

[10] See, for example, Executive Board Decisions No. 3865-(73/12) G/S, February 16, 1973, *Annual Report, 1973* (Washington, 1973), p. 98, No. 3537-(72/3) G/S, January 4, 1972 and No. 3637-(72/41) G/S, May 8, 1972, *Annual Report, 1972*, (Washington, 1972), pp. 87–89. (*Selected Decisions*, Eighth Issue, pp. 32–33.) The process culminated in the "basket" valuation of the SDR (Executive Board Decision No. 4233-(74/67) S, June 13, 1974, as amended by Executive Board Decisions No. 4261-(74/78) S, July 1, 1974 and No. 4234-(74/67) S, June 13, 1974, *Annual Report, 1974* (Washington, 1974), pp. 116–18.

[11] Executive Board Decisions No. 3463-(71/126), December 18, 1971 and No. 4083-(73/104), November 7, 1973, *Selected Decisions*, Eighth Issue, pp. 14–21.

[12] See Gold, Pamphlet No. 19, pp. 15–33, Appendices A and B.

invoking the obligation of members to collaborate with the Fund to promote exchange stability, to maintain orderly exchange arrangements with other members, and to avoid competitive exchange alterations.[13]

LIVELY LTD. AND ANOTHER V. CITY OF MUNICH

In this English case, decided by the Queen's Bench Division in June 1976,[14] there was much discussion of the question whether par values as referred to in the Articles continued to be in force for sterling and the U.S. dollar when both currencies were floating. In 1928, the City of Munich raised a loan of £1,625,000 six per cent sterling bonds under an agreement with Lazard Brothers & Co., Ltd. of London acting on behalf of the bondholders. The principal and interest were expressed in sterling, but the bondholders were given the option of requiring payment and repayment either in sterling or in "United States Gold Dollars . . . at the fixed rate of exchange of $4.86 to the pound sterling," which was the value of the dollar of the weight and fineness in effect on November 24, 1928 in terms of sterling. The latest date for redemption was December 1, 1953, but the loan had gone into default on the outbreak of war. On June 14, 1955 an agreement was entered into between Lazard Brothers and the City of Munich that modified the terms of the bonds in a number of respects, the most important of which was the elimination of the dollar option. The removal of this option was the result of a number of postwar developments. The Fund had come into existence, and both the United States and the United Kingdom were members. In September 1953 the intergovernmental agreement on German external debt had come into effect. It will be referred to below as the LDA (London Debt Agreement). The par value of the pound had been devalued in March 1949 to $2.80 per pound, or 2.48828 grams of fine gold per pound.

The modified terms of the reissued bonds provided for payments in sterling only, in amounts calculated "on the basis that the equivalent in U.S. Dollars of the nominal amounts due at the rate of $4.86 to the £ will be re-converted into sterling at the appropriate rate of exchange (determined in accordance with Article 13 of the said Agreement of 27th February 1953) applicable to the date when the respective amount is payable." Article 13 of the LDA read as follows:

---

[13] Article IV, Section 4(a), *original* and *first*.
[14] [1976] 3 All E.R. 851.

Rates of Exchange Wherever it is provided in the present Agreement and the Annexes thereto that an amount shall be calculated on the basis of a rate of exchange, such rate shall . . . be—(a) determined by the par values of the currencies concerned in force on the appropriate date as agreed with the International Monetary Fund under Article IV, Section 1, of the Articles of Agreement of the International Monetary Fund, or (b) if no such par values are or were in force on the appropriate date, the rate of exchange agreed for current payments in a bilateral payments agreement between the Governments concerned or their monetary authorities; or (c) if neither par values nor rates in bilateral payments agreements are or were in force on the appropriate date, the middle rate of exchange generally applicable for transactions ruling for cable transfers in the currency of the country in which payment is to be made in the principal exchange market of the other country on that date, or on the last date before that date on which such rate was ruling; or (d) if there is or was no rate of exchange as specified under (a), (b) or (c) at the appropriate date, the cross-rate of exchange resulting from the middle rates of exchange ruling for the currencies in question in the principal exchange market of a third country dealing in those currencies on that date or the last date before the said date upon which such rates were ruling.[15]

The court held that the issue was whether the applicable rate of exchange was the one prescribed by (a) or (c) of Article 13.

The court set out most of Article IV of the Fund's Articles,[16] and explained these provisions, but not always correctly. Par value and parity were confused in describing the margins for exchange transactions, which were regarded as being of fundamental importance for the resolution of the problem posed in the case. The second sentence of Article IV, Section 4(*b*) on the free purchase and sale of gold was

---

[15] *Ibid.*, at 854. Article IV, Section 1 of the original Articles read as follows:

"(*a*) The par value of the currency of each member shall be expressed in terms of gold as a common denominator or in terms of the United States dollar of the weight and fineness in effect on July 1, 1944.

"(*b*) All computations relating to currencies of members for the purpose of applying the provisions of this Agreement shall be on the basis of their par values."

It will be apparent that par values were not agreed with the Fund under this provision as stated in Article 13 of the LDA. The initial par value of the currency of an original member was established under Article XX, Section 4 of the original Articles as the result of a communication by the member to the Fund, or by agreement with the Fund if the Fund objected to the communicated par value. A subsequent par value was established under Article IV, Section 5. In some instances, the concurrence of the Fund was necessary, but not in others.

[16] The reference to all provisions of the Articles in the discussion of this case are to provisions of the Articles before the Second Amendment.

237

thought to refer to "a free market" in gold, but it referred only to transactions between monetary authorities.[17] The court noted that if a currency floated,[18] the issuer could be required to adjust the Fund's holdings of the currency. "The ultimate issue in this case," the court said, "is whether, when this happens, the member's par value is nevertheless still 'in force'" for the purposes of Article 13(a) of the LDA.

The court traced the history of international monetary arrangements, with particular reference to sterling and the U.S. dollar, for several years preceding December 1, 1973. It concluded that on that date, exchange rates for the two currencies were not maintained by the two countries, and were not being maintained for the currencies by other countries, in relation to parities, central rates, the "snake," or any other arrangements, and were floating against each other and all other major currencies. The only difference was a formal one, in that the United Kingdom had informed the Fund that it was allowing the pound to float, while the United States had made no such statement to the Fund.

The plaintiffs, the registered holders of some of the bonds, claimed that Article 13(a) of the LDA did not apply, and that Article 13(c) did, under which the market rate of exchange between the U.S. dollar and the pound on December 1, 1973 was $2.34 to the pound. The defendants, the City of Munich, relied on Article 13(a). The court noted the paradox that because the appropriate rate had to be divided into the rate of $4.86 to the pound, the higher the appropriate rate the less sterling the plaintiffs would receive. The reason was clear: the modified bonds were designed to compensate bondholders by giving them a correspondingly greater number of pounds if sterling depreciated against the fixed rate of $4.86 to the pound.

The defendants claimed that under Article 13(a) of the LDA the rate to be applied was $2.89 per pound. This rate was arrived at on the basis of the last par value of the pound, established under the Fund's Articles in November 1967 at 2.13281 grams of fine gold, or $2.40 per pound, and the last par value of the U.S. dollar, established under the Articles on October 18, 1973 at 0.7366 gram of fine gold.

---

17 [1976] 3 All E.R. at 856.

18 The court defined floating as a situation in which neither currency "was maintained in relation to gold within fixed margins on either side of their par values." (Ibid., at 855.) The situation should not be defined in relation to margins around the par values of the currencies, but in relation to margins around the parity between the currencies based on par values. Rates of exchange could be maintained within the same margins for the two currencies only in relation to the ratio between par values.

The court remarked that the resulting exchange rate of $2.89 per pound was one that had no relation to any market or commercial rate of exchange. Under another provision of the LDA, which need not be examined here, the defendants felt constrained to reduce the rate of $2.89 to $2.80 per pound, so that the difference of opinion between the parties can be stated as $2.34 versus $2.80 per pound.

The defendants advanced two contentions. The first was that the words "in force" in Article 13(a) added nothing, because the concept was "par values . . . in force . . . as agreed," and not par values that were (i) in force and (ii) agreed with the Fund. Under this contention, a par value once agreed with the Fund remained in force until a new par value was agreed with the Fund. The second contention, if the first contention was wrong, was that the par values of the two currencies were in fact still in force for various purposes.

The court could not agree with the first contention. The words "in force" were intended to have some effect additional to "as agreed." Even under the scheme of the Fund's Articles, there was one case in which the words "in force" would have an additional effect. This case was the one in which a member made an unauthorized change in the par value of its currency within the meaning of Article IV, Section 6. The unauthorized change would result in a par value that was "in force" but not "agreed."

Under the second contention, the following purposes were advanced as those for which par values remained in force even when currencies were floating:

(1) Under Article III, the amount of a member's currency subscription, both originally and when a quota is changed, continues to be determined by the par value of a member's currency. (The argument is incorrect because a subscription already paid is, in effect, adjusted if an adjustment in the value of the Fund's holdings of the currency is made under Article IV, Section 8 when the currency is floating. Any additional subscription as the result of a change of the member's quota is paid on the basis of the adjusted value. To avoid any misunderstanding, it should be clear that the contentions and the comments on them are based on the Articles before the Second Amendment.)

(2) The amount that a member may have to pay to the Fund under Article IV, Section 8 when its currency depreciates is measured by reference to the last agreed par value. (The measurement of any adjustment is in fact made in relation to the value at which the Fund is holding a currency and this value need not correspond to the par

239

value if there has been an earlier adjustment, but the argument can be accepted that the cumulative effect of all adjustments measures the net departure of the market value of the currency from the par value).

(3) On the withdrawal of a member from the Fund, settlement with it under Schedule D, and, on the liquidation of the Fund, the administration of liquidation under Schedule E, would be carried out on the basis of par values. (This argument is incorrect because both settlement and administration would be made on the basis of the values at which the Fund was holding currencies. Article IV, Section 1(b), which declares that all computations relating to the currencies of members for the purpose of applying the provisions of the Articles shall be on the basis of par values, is subject to an implied qualification in favor of the value at which the Fund is holding a currency. The qualification applies in calculations related to the normal operations and transactions and would apply in any settlement on withdrawal or in liquidation of the Fund. The fact that Article IV, Section 1(b) cannot be considered exhaustive is illustrated further by the necessity to make computations involving the currency of a member held by the Fund before an initial par value is established for the currency.)

(4) The par value determines the amount of the contribution of the United Kingdom to the budget of the European Economic Community.

(5) The par value is used as a statistical measure by the United Kingdom for computing its monetary reserves.

The court held that it was unable to accept these considerations as evidence that the par value for the pound was still "in force" within the meaning of Article 13(a) of the LDA when these words were construed in accordance with the commercial object of the bonds, in their original and modified form, and of the LDA. The object was to protect bondholders against a possible depreciation of sterling against the U.S. dollar. If margins for a currency were not being maintained in accordance with the Fund's Articles, commercially the par value was not "in force." The par value was as meaningless commercially in such circumstances as the rate of $2.89 per pound, on which the defendants relied (subject to reduction to $2.80 per pound), compared with the real rate of exchange of $2.34 per pound.

> In an issue concerning the applicable rate of exchange between a debtor and creditor under a bond which incorporates art 13 it is in my judgment essential to construe this article in a commercially realistic sense. The present issue is concerned with a rate of exchange applicable to a commercial transaction; it is not concerned with treaty obligations by governments to the IMF or inter se. It does not follow from

the fact that par values continued to be used for certain purposes in the latter field that they were "in force" for the purpose of construing these words when art 13(a) is incorporated into a bond. In that context, par values are in my view no longer in force when margins are no longer being maintained in relation to the currencies in question. The fact that par values continue to exist does not necessarily mean that they remain in force.[19]

The court supported this conclusion by referring to the words "in force" in relation to a bilateral payments agreement under Article 13(b) of the LDA. Suppose that on the date as of which a rate of exchange had to be applied there was a bilateral payments agreement that prescribed a fixed rate of exchange, but that the agreement was not being observed by the parties on the relevant date, although they had not formally abrogated the agreement. If the actual rates of exchange differed from the agreed rate, the latter rate could no longer be said to be "in force" under Article 13(b) of the LDA.

The fact that, from the point of view of the treaty creating the bilateral payments agreement, both governments would still be bound by its terms does not appear to me to affect the true construction of para (b) when incorporated into a commercial contract.[20]

The court held that Article 13(c) of the LDA was the relevant provision and that, in accordance with it, the middle market rate on December 1, 1973 had to be applied.

COURT OF JUSTICE OF THE EUROPEAN COMMUNITIES

The Fund's conclusion that under the Articles the par value of a currency continued to exist notwithstanding the floating of the currency was not arrived at on the basis of any demonstration that the par value continued to have any operational effects under the Articles. There was no need to go through the strenuous efforts employed by the defendants in the *Lively* case to show that the par value still produced practical consequences. For the Fund, the conclusion that the par value continued to exist under the law of the Fund was an integral part of the conclusion that the member was not observing its obligations under Article IV, Sections 3 and 4(*b*). The obligations were to observe certain margins around parities based on par values, and therefore these par values must continue to have a legal life, or else there would be no basis for holding that the obligations were not being observed. The proposition can be stated in another form: a member

---

[19] [1976] 3 All E.R. at 862.
[20] *Ibid.*

241

adopting a floating rate was failing to observe its obligations because it was not enforcing the margins around parity and not because it was failing to have a par value. It had a par value even during the period of floating. It should be noted that although a member had an obligation to establish an initial par value, the member had no obligation to establish a new par value at some other date. It had only the privilege of changing the existing par value.

The decision in the *Lively* case is admirable in its realism. It is consistent with the jurisprudence of courts in other countries that have sought ways in which to give effect to the actual values of currencies instead of relying on formalistic solutions.[21] In these cases, the courts have been called on to determine the equivalent in the domestic currency of a unit of account expressed in terms of gold. The courts have resisted a solution based on a par value or central rate that existed under domestic law or practice. Although they have not been embarrassed by a direct reference to a par value or central rate under the domestic legal provision they had to apply, the difficulties of arriving at a realistic decision were considerable. In the *Lively* case the problem might have been even more difficult, because of the reference to par values,[22] had it not been for the opportunity offered by the modest phrase "in force."

In *Fabrizio Gillet v. Commission of the European Communities*, decided by the Court of Justice of the European Communities on March 19, 1975, the Commission applied literally the Staff Regulation that required calculation of the remuneration payable to an official "on the basis of the parities accepted by the International Monetary

---

[21] See *Transarctic Shipping Corporation, Inc. Monrovia, Liberia v. Krögerwerft (Kröger Shipyard) Company* in Gold, Pamphlet No. 19, pp. 17–33, and Joseph Gold, *Floating Currencies, SDRs, and Gold: Further Legal Developments*, IMF Pamphlet Series, No. 22 (Washington, 1977), pp. 33, 56–57; hereinafter cited as Gold, Pamphlet No. 22; *Hornlinie v. Société Nationale des Pétroles Aquitaine* in Gold, "Fund Agreement in the Courts—XI," pp. 177–88 in this volume; *Matter of the Khendrik Kuivas* in Gold, Pamphlet No. 22, pp. 56–58.

[22] For a discussion of the reform of Article II: 6(a) of the General Agreement on Tariffs and Trade in present circumstances, see Frieder Roessler, *Specific Duties, Inflation and Floating Currencies*, GATT, Studies in International Trade, No. 4 (Geneva, 1977).

Article II: 6(a) reads as follows:

"The specific duties . . . included in the Schedules . . . are expressed in the appropriate currency at the par value accepted or provisionally recognized by the Fund at the date of this Agreement. Accordingly, in case this par value is reduced consistently with the Articles of Agreement of the International Monetary Fund by more than twenty per centum, such specific duties . . . may be adjusted to take account of such reduction. . . ."

Fund which were in force on 1 January 1965."[23] Both of the currencies involved, the Belgian franc and the Italian lira, had effective par values on the appropriate date. The court applied these par values even though it recognized that "in a period of monetary instability it is possible that the objective sought by these provisions may not be entirely achieved."[24] It should be noted that adjustments were made in the amounts calculated in this way to take account of living conditions in the place of residence or employment.

The judgment of the Court of Justice of the European Communities of March 9, 1977 in *Société anonyme générale Sucrière v. Commission of the European Communities*[25] again illustrates the tendency of courts to find realistic solutions in current conditions when the opportunity exists, notwithstanding a reference to par values in this case. In a decision of January 2, 1973, the Commission of the European Communities imposed fines on certain commercial undertakings that were found to have infringed Articles 85 and 86 of the Treaty of Rome, which proscribe agreements that may affect trade among member states and have as their object or effect the prevention, restriction, or distortion of competition within the Common Market or any abuse of a dominant trading position within the Common Market. The fines were expressed as a certain number of units of account[26] (u.a.), followed by the clause "that is" and then a certain amount in the currency of the country in which the undertaking had its principal place of business. The unit of account was equivalent to 0.88867088 gram of fine gold; the equivalent in currency was based on the par value for it established in accordance with the Fund's Articles. For example, for the French franc the last par value was established on August 10, 1969 as 0.160000 gram of fine gold per franc, which was equivalent to 5.554 francs for the unit of account on the basis of the definitions of them in terms of gold. Some of the undertakings succeeded in

---

[23] Case 28/74 [1975] E.C.R. 473.

[24] *Ibid.*, at 474.

[25] Joined Cases 41, 43, and 44/73 [1977] E.C.R. 445. See also Rebecca M.M. Wallace, "Currency Fluctuation and the Payment of Fines," *European Law Review*, Vol. 2 (August 1977), pp. 301–303.

[26] The European Communities employ a number of units of account, of which the one defined in terms of gold was relevant in the case. The European unit of account (EUA), based on a basket of currencies, was created in 1975. So far, it is being used for the purposes of the European Development Fund, the operational budget of the European Coal and Steel Community, and the balance sheet of the European Investment Bank. The European Commission proposed in 1976, and the Council of Ministers agreed, that the EUA should be used eventually in all activities of the European Communities. (See Gold, Pamphlet No. 19, pp. 40–45.)

getting the fines reduced by a judgment of December 16, 1975 in which the fines were expressed as a certain number of units of account followed by an amount in currency in parentheses calculated on the basis of the par value.[27]

Some of the undertakings paid the Commission, in purported discharge of fines expressed in units of account and French francs, an amount of Italian lire calculated on the basis of the par value for the lira established in accordance with the Fund's Articles on March 30, 1960 (0.00142 gram of fine gold per lira, which was equivalent to 625 lire for the unit of account on the basis of the definitions of them in terms of gold). The Commission did not object to payment in lire, but did not accept the amounts paid as a discharge, on the ground that the debt under the judgment was the amount expressed in national currency in the judgment, and if the undertakings wished to pay in the currency of another member state, the amount had to be calculated on the basis of the rate of exchange on the date of payment.

Payment on the basis of the par value of the lira instead of the rate claimed by the Commission represented savings of 33 per cent for the French, 35 per cent for the Belgian, 40 per cent for the Dutch, and 43 per cent for the German undertakings. The undertakings challenged the view of the Commission and sought an interpretative decision of the Court.

Articles 15 and 17 of Regulation No. 17 of the Council of Ministers of February 6, 1962[28] authorizes the Commission to impose fines of one thousand to one million u.a., or a higher amount determined by a formula, for infractions of Article 85 or 86 of the Treaty. Article 18 of the Regulation, which is headed "Unit of Account," provides that for the purposes of Articles 15 and 17, the unit of account shall be the one used in drawing up the budget of the Community. Article 10 of the Financial Regulation of April 25, 1973,[29] which derives from a Regulation of 1962, provides that the value of the unit of account in which the budget shall be established shall be 0.88867088 gram of fine gold. Article 27 provides as follows:

> The financial contributions from Member States fixed by the budget shall be expressed in units of account as defined in Article 10. They

---

[27] *Coöperatieve vereniging "Suiker Unie" UA and Others v. Commission of the European Communities*, Joined Cases 40 to 48, 50, 54 to 56, 111, 113, and 114/73 [1975] E.C.R. 2026.

[28] *Official Journal of the European Communities*, Vol. 5, No. 13 (February 21, 1962), p. 204.

[29] *Ibid.*, Vol. 16, No. L 116 (May 1, 1973).

shall be converted into the respective national currencies on the basis of the relationship existing on the day of their payment between the weight of fine gold contained in a unit of account as referred to above and the weight of fine gold corresponding to parity in respect of each of those currencies as declared to the International Monetary Fund. Should the currency of one or more of the Member States cease to have any declared parity with the International Monetary Fund, the Commission shall propose appropriate measures to the Council.

The undertakings argued that their debts were fixed by the Court solely in units of account, that this was the only power of the Court, that the figures in French francs were "merely intended to be an indication of the amount,"[30] and that under the Financial Regulations the debts could be discharged by amounts of Italian lire equivalent to the units of account on the basis of the par value for the lira. The reference to French francs was only for the purpose of facilitating execution in another currency if it should become necessary, but it had not been necessary in this case. The undertakings also argued, inter alia, that the Commission's view placed undertakings established in a country with a hard currency at a disadvantage and therefore contravened natural justice, and that the Commission's view abandoned the unit of account as a common denominator and required payment "on the basis of the actual value of the currencies."[31] The fact that the unit of account did not reflect the value of currencies in the market could not be taken into account, because the Commission's proposal to adopt a unit of account based on a basket of currencies and daily exchange rates had not yet gone into effect.[32]

The Commission explained that originally it had fixed fines only in units of account, but a case had occurred in which it had been impossible to enforce the fine in one jurisdiction because execution of a judgment expressed in units of account was not possible under the domestic law. Since 1972, therefore, the Commission has referred in addition to the amount of the fine expressed in the currency of the principal place of business of the undertaking on the basis of the par value of the currency, or, in certain circumstances, in a currency determined by other criteria. The Commission argued that a unit of account was meaningless unless it was accompanied by a technique for calculating the equivalent in a currency, so that the Court had authority to express the equivalent of the amount of units in a cur-

---

[30] Joined Cases 41, 43, and 44/73 [1977] E.C.R. 449.
[31] *Ibid.*, at 451.
[32] See fn. 26 *supra*.

rency. Its practice in selecting a currency was uniform and nondiscriminatory among undertakings. The debt was determined by this technique. An undertaking was not entitled to redefine the debt by expressing it in units of account and a different currency. The privilege of discharging the debt in a different currency did not give a right to redefine it. According to the Commission, this practice had been endorsed by the Court and its judgment was to be interpreted in accordance with the practice.

The Advocate-General, in his opinion, advised that there was no jurisdiction in the Community in which a judgment expressed only in units of account could be enforced, which led him to believe that the authority of the Commission and the Court was not confined to expressing fines in units of account. Statement of the fine in a currency was essential for enforcement, and it was not logical that the effective amount of the fine should depend on whether it was paid voluntarily or as the result of a levy of execution. If the fine is paid in some currency other than the one in which it is expressed, the Court is not thrown back into a position in which it must think only in terms of units of account, but can find the true value of the currency in which it expressed the fine together with the expression of it in units of account.

The Court held that nothing in the Regulations required the Commission or a court to express fines either in units of account or in a currency. Under Articles 187 and 192 of the Treaty of Rome, the decisions of the Commission and the Court imposing a pecuniary obligation on persons other than states shall be enforceable, and any necessary enforcement shall be governed by the rules of civil procedure in force in the state in which it is effected. Therefore, because the unit of account is not a currency in which payment can be made, it is necessary to establish the amount of a fine in a currency. Any difficulties in selecting the currency because undertakings may conduct business in several states or outside the Community do not invalidate this conclusion. In such circumstances, the amount of the debt is the amount expressed in the selected currency, and the sums expressed in units of account serve only to determine whether the prescribed limits on the amounts of fines have been observed. Nevertheless, no legal provision prevents the Commission from accepting payments, if it wishes, in the currency of another member state.

> As far as concerns the rate to be applied in this case for the purpose of converting one of these currencies into another the applicants cannot

rely on the fact that Article 18 of Regulation No. 17 refers to the provisions applicable to the budget of the Community.

Since it is a fact that the parities of the various national currencies adopted by these provisions no longer in most cases reflect the actual position in the market, it cannot be assumed that they apply by analogy to circumstances which, as in this case, are not explicitly covered by any legal provision.

Although the Commission is entitled to accept payments in a national currency of the Community other than that in which the debt has been determined, the fact remains that it must see to it that the actual value of the payments made in another currency corresponds to that of the sum fixed in national currency in the Court's judgment.

Therefore the conversion of the two national currencies in question must be effected at the exchange rate on the free foreign exchange market applicable on the day of payment.[33]

The judgment relies on a rigidly textual application of the Regulations. The fine is expressed in the selected currency on the basis of the par value (constantly referred to as the "parity") of the currency as established under the Articles, notwithstanding the realization that the Regulations were written during the life of the par value system and that exchange rates were no longer consistent with par values. The Regulations did not deal with the way to calculate the equivalent of the selected currency in a currency of payment, and the Court refused to extend the Regulations to this operation. The result was realistic in its treatment of conversion but not in its treatment of the selected currency.

The Court did not deal with the second sentence of Article 27 of the Financial Regulation of April 25, 1973:

Should the currency of one or more of the Member States cease to have any declared parity with the International Monetary Fund, the Commission shall propose appropriate measures to the Council.

On the principle of the original Articles "once a par value, always a par value until changed," this sentence would have no meaning under the law of the Fund. Yet the drafters of the Regulation must have attributed some meaning to the sentence. Was it a meaning equivalent to the words "in force" in the *Lively* case? Three provisions of the Regulation do indeed use the expression "in force."[34] Did the drafters

---

[33] Joined Cases 41, 43, and 44/73 [1977] E.C.R. at 463.
[34] Financial Regulation of April 25, 1973:
"Article 29
The amounts shown to the credit of the accounts referred to in Article 28 shall

have in mind circumstances in which a member declared to the Fund that it would not maintain the par value of its currency? The words "declared parity" appear in the sentence. If the drafters had some such intention in mind, what would be the effect of the declaration of central rates to the Fund? The issuers of some of the selected currencies had declared central rates under the Fund's decisions.

The questions raised here are relevant to the problem whether the use of par values for selected currencies was inescapable. If this problem were to be considered, it would probably be examined in relation to the more fundamental topic of contributions to the Community's budget. Problems such as these arise at the intergovernmental level, and in the *Lively* case a distinction was drawn between intergovernmental relations and the expectations of commercial entities. In both the *Lively* case and the *Sucrière* case, however, the legal provisions that were interpreted were adopted at the intergovernmental and not the private level, but the provisions affected private entities.

Although the sentence in Article 27 quoted above was probably not drafted in contemplation of the abandonment of a par value system, because in April 1973 the Committee of Twenty was still negotiating on the basis of stable but adjustable par values with floating in particular situations,[35] the sentence could provide a solution because the Second Amendment has taken effect before the Community has moved to a "basket" unit of account for the purposes that were relevant in the case. Par values have been abrogated for the purposes of the Articles by the Second Amendment, and therefore the Commission could propose "appropriate measures" to the Council.

---

retain the value corresponding to the parity in force on the day of deposit in relation to the unit of account as defined in Article 10.

Should the parity of the currency of a Member State in relation to the unit of account be modified, there shall immediately be an adjustment of the balance of those accounts, by means of a further payment made by the Member State or Member States concerned or a repayment made by the Commission."

"*Article 36*

Payments provided for in Articles 26 and 34 shall be made in national currencies; they shall be calculated on the basis of the parity declared to the International Monetary Fund in force on the day of payment."

"*Article 71*

Entries in the accounts of any amount in units of account shall comply with the parity in force on the date of payment or actual payment."

[35] Communiqué of the Committee of the Board of Governors on International Monetary Reform and Related Issues, March 27, 1973, par. 4(a), *IMF Survey*, Vol. 2 (April 9, 1973), p. 100; IMF Press Release No. 964, March 27, 1973.

EXISTENCE AND NONEXISTENCE OF PAR VALUES UNDER
SECOND AMENDMENT

Par values in existence under the Articles at the time when the
Second Amendment became effective were abrogated for the purposes
of the Articles because the provisions of the Articles under which the
par values were established have ceased to exist.[36] At one stage during
the drafting of the Second Amendment, before the final compromise
was reached on the provisions relating to exchange arrangements, the
Executive Board discussed the proposal that the par values of currencies should be abrogated for the purposes of the Articles because, even
if a par value system were restored at some date, there would be an
interim period in which all currencies would be floating. An associated
proposal was that it should be possible to abrogate the par value of a
currency, for the purposes of the Articles, if the currency floated after
the restoration of a par value system. The thesis in favor of abrogation was that parties to treaties or contracts could be misled if the
Fund were to tell them that a currency had a par value even though
it was not being maintained when they had probably entered into
their commitments on the assumption that a par value was being
maintained, or, in the language of the subsequent *Lively* case, that a
par value had been agreed with the Fund and was in force. Parties
to legal arrangements might assume from a statement by the Fund
that there was a par value under the Articles that it was effective,
and that a member's actual exchange arrangements had the endorsement of the Fund. In past practice, to guard against these possible
mistaken impressions, the Fund, when asked whether a par value
existed for a floating currency, or what the par value was, usually
coupled its reply with the statement that the par value was not
effective.

There was some opposition to the proposals on the ground that if
par values were abrogated, the position of members under other legal
instruments that involved par values as a basis for commitments
would be undermined. Some of the opposition was probably based on
the commitments of member states under the law of the European
Community. It will be seen that the objections did not prevail, but
some of the safeguards finally incorporated in Schedule C of the

---

[36] *Proposed Second Amendment to the Articles of Agreement of the International Monetary Fund: A Report by the Executive Directors to the Board of Governors* (Washington, March 1976), Part II, Chapter C, Section 6. (Hereinafter
cited as *Proposed Second Amendment.*)

Second Amendment can be traced back to the discussion of these proposals.

The abrogation of par values when the Second Amendment took effect was accompanied by the abrogation of the Fund's decision on central rates and wider margins.[37] The decision was based on Article IV, Section 4(a) of the Articles before the Second Amendment, which does not appear in the Second Amendment, and on Resolution No. 26-9 of the Board of Governors,[38] which called on all members to collaborate with the Fund and with each other in order to maintain a satisfactory structure of exchange rates within appropriate margins. The abrogation of par values for the purposes of the Articles does not prevent a member from adopting a value for its currency, even in terms of gold, for some domestic purposes under its domestic law. For example, Public Law 94-564 of October 19, 1976 passed by the United States Congress to provide for amendment of the Bretton Woods Agreements Act and for other purposes repeals Section 2 of the Par Value Modification Act[39] as of the date of the Second Amendment. Section 2 defined the last par value of the U.S. dollar. The provision repealing Section 2 preserves the gold value, although not as a par value, for the following purpose:

> Section 14(c) of the Gold Reserve Act of 1934 (31 U.S.C. 405b) is amended to read as follows: "The Secretary of the Treasury is authorized to issue gold certificates in such form and in such denominations as he may determine, against any gold held by the United States Treasury. The amount of gold certificates issued and outstanding shall at no time exceed the value, at the legal standard provided in section 2 of the Par Value Modification Act (31 U.S.C. 449) on the date of enactment of this amendment, of the gold so held against gold certificates." [40]

---

[37] Executive Board Decision No. 3463-(71/126), December 18, 1971 and Decision No. 4083-(73/104), November 7, 1973, *Selected Decisions*, Eighth Issue, pp. 14–21.

[38] *Summary Proceedings of the Twenty-Sixth Annual Meeting of the Board of Governors*, September 27–October 1, 1971 (Washington, 1972), pp. 331–32. (Hereinafter cited as *Summary Proceedings*.)

[39] 31 U.S.C. 449.

[40] Bretton Woods Agreements Act, Amendments, Public Law 94-564, October 19, 1976, Section 8.
"The legal standards for the dollar of $42.22 per fine troy ounce of gold would be retained solely with respect to gold certificates held by the Federal Reserve System—the only domestic purpose for which a value of the dollar in terms of gold is needed. Approximately $11½ billion of these certificates are now outstanding, and are being retired by the Treasury as its gold holdings are sold." (U.S. Congress, House, Committee on Banking, Currency and Housing, Subcom-

The value that is maintained under this provision for the specified purpose of SDR 0.828948, or 0.736662 gram of fine gold, per U.S. dollar.

The abrogation of par values does not prevent members from establishing values for their currencies in terms of a denominator they select as part of their exchange arrangements. These values will not be par values in the sense of the original Articles, because there is no prescription of a common denominator and no fixed relationships among all currencies on the basis of a common denominator. Moreover, in accordance with the objective of a gradual reduction in the role of gold under the Second Amendment, any denominator may be chosen except gold. The preservation of a value for the U.S. dollar in terms of gold by the provision quoted above is not for the purpose of applying the exchange arrangements of the United States.

The Second Amendment permits a member to establish a value for its currency in various ways notwithstanding the abrogation of par values. The first is the one already mentioned: "the maintenance by a member of a value for its currency in terms of the special drawing right or another denominator, other than gold, selected by the member."[41] Second, exchange arrangements may include "cooperative arrangements by which members maintain the value of their currencies in relation to the value of the currency or currencies of other members."[42] Third, to accord with a changing international monetary system, the Fund may decide by a majority of 85 per cent of the total voting power to recommend general exchange arrangements to members, without limiting their right to apply these or other exchange arrangements of their choice. The general arrangements could include denominators or a common denominator, other than gold, and could approach a par value system without being the par value system of Schedule C.

The provisions of the Second Amendment governing exchange arrangements, including those that have been mentioned already, are not designed explicitly for an interim period that will terminate with an inevitable introduction of the par value system set forth in Schedule C. The provisions could apply permanently, and Schedule C might

---

mittee on International Trade, Investment and Monetary Policy, *To Provide for Amendment of the Bretton Woods Agreements Act, Hearings on H.R. 13955*, 94th Congress, 2nd Session, June 1 and 3, 1976 (Washington, 1976), p. 12.)

[41] Article IV, Section 2(*b*), *second*.

[42] *Ibid.* See also William H.L. Day, "A Reform of the European Currency Snake," *Staff Papers*, Vol. 23 (November 1976), pp. 582–84.

never come into operation. If, however, the Fund determines, by an 85 per cent majority of the total voting power, that certain conditions exist permitting "the introduction of a widespread system of exchange arrangements based on stable but adjustable par values," it must inform members that the provisions of Schedule C are in operation.[43] The Articles prescribe in detail the circumstances that the Fund must take into account in arriving at a determination.

The provisions of Schedule C have a strong resemblance to the provisions that governed the original par value system, but there are some striking differences, most of which are regarded as improvements that were shown to be desirable by experience under the reign of the original system. The common denominator of the system is not determined by the Articles, although gold and currencies are excluded.[44] The implication is that the SDR will probably be the common denominator, but one reason why the choice is not made is the uncertainty about the method of valuing the SDR that may be in force in the future. No member will be required to establish a par value, so that there will be freedom to choose exchange arrangements even after the par value system of Schedule C is in operation.[45]

The provisions dealing with changes in par value are similar to those of the original Articles, although a change may be proposed not only to correct a fundamental disequilibrium but also to prevent its emergence.[46] A proposed change in par value is not to take effect for the purposes of the Articles if the Fund objects to it. The words "for the purposes of this Agreement" make explicit the distinction between these and other purposes that a member may have in mind in adopting a change in par value.[47] If a member changes the par value of its currency notwithstanding the objection of the Fund, the member may be declared ineligible to use the resources of the Fund and may be compelled to withdraw from the Fund in accordance with Article XXVI, Section 2.

The special concept of the unauthorized change of par value under the original Articles has been eliminated. Under the original Articles a member that adopted an unauthorized change of par value was not in violation of any obligation, although it was treated as severely as, and in one respect even more severely than, a violator. This result was

---

[43] Article IV, Section 4, *second.*
[44] Schedule C, par. 1, *second.*
[45] Schedule C, par. 3, *second.*
[46] Schedule C, par. 6, *second.*
[47] Schedule C, par. 7, *second.*

achieved by such subtle means that the casual reader of the Articles may not have been aware of it. Article IV, Section 6, which dealt with the unauthorized change, provided separately for ineligibility and did not bring ineligibility about by reference to the more general provision of Article XV, Section 2(a) of the original Articles. The latter provision dealt with ineligibility "if a member fails to fulfill any of its obligations under this Agreement." In contrast to the absence of a reference to Article XV, Section 2(a), Article IV, Section 6 provided for compulsory withdrawal by a reference to Article XV, Section 2(b). This latter provision made it clear that notwithstanding the reference to the provision in Article IV, Section 6, the consequence was not that withdrawal was based on a violation. Article XV, Section 2(b) covered two distinct situations: "the member persists in its failure to fulfill any of its obligations under this Agreement, or a difference between a member and the Fund under Article IV, Section 6, continues."

The distinction between these two situations has been abandoned by Schedule C, paragraph 7 because the consequence of an unauthorized change of par value is that "the member shall be subject to Article XXVI, Section 2" of the Second Amendment. That provision incorporates both subsections (a) and (b) of Article XV, Section 2 of the former Articles. The effect is that the member making an unauthorized change of par value may be declared ineligible and compelled to withdraw for the only reason that can justify these actions, namely, a failure to fulfill obligations. Article XXVI, Section 2(b) has been modified to refer only to these failures, and it does not mention the unauthorized change of par value as a separate category.

The abandonment of the special concept of the unauthorized change came about because the prospect of a return to a par value system was at best remote, but also because there was less reason to insist on the principle for which the United Kingdom fought before and at Bretton Woods. The principle was that ultimate authority over the par value of a member's currency must rest with the member itself. Furthermore, the new provisions of the Second Amendment were part of a complex that recognizes the freedom of members to choose their exchange arrangements. If a member contemplated a change of par value to which the Fund objected, the member might be willing to terminate the par value as such and adopt the new value under its freedom to apply exchange arrangements of its choice. It is true that, as will be seen, the Fund could take a decision to prevent the termination of a par value, but a high majority is necessary for this decision. It is also true that if the decision were not taken and the par value was terminated, the member would not receive the international endorsement of the exchange rate for its currency that it would enjoy by having a par value.

A member has the right to inform the Fund at any time that it is terminating the par value of its currency for the purposes of the Articles. The termination will be effective unless the Fund objects to termination by a decision taken by an 85 per cent majority of the total voting power.[48] This high majority was adopted not so much in order to assure members that they had ultimate authority over their exchange arrangements as to enable the United States to assure the public that it would have a veto over any decision to prevent the United States from terminating a par value for the dollar. The same majority is required for certain other decisions and gives the United States a controlling voice in the introduction of a par value system and in the recommendation of general exchange arrangements by the Fund.[49]

Notice of the termination of a par value is not the only way in which a par value can cease to exist for the purposes of the Articles after Schedule C is in operation. If a member terminates the par value of its currency even though the Fund has objected to termination, Schedule C is realistic in providing that the par value no longer exists.[50] The par value of a member's currency ceases to exist if the Fund finds that the member does not maintain rates for a substantial volume of exchange transactions in accordance with the provision on

---

[48] Schedule C, par. 8, *second.*

[49] See Joseph Gold, *Voting Majorities in the Fund: Effects of Second Amendment of the Articles,* IMF Pamphlet Series, No. 20 (Washington, 1977), pp. 11–12. "These new exchange rate provisions are of critical importance both for the system as a whole and for the United States. They focus on the essential need to achieve underlying stability in economic affairs if exchange stability is to be achieved. They provide a flexible framework for the evolution of exchange arrangements consistent with this broad focus. And they help to ensure that the United States is not again forced into the position of maintaining a value for its currency that is out of line with underlying competitive realities and that costs the United States jobs and growth due to loss of exports, increased imports and a shift of production facilities overseas. Under the new provisions, the United States will have a controlling voice in the future adoption of general exchange arrangements for the system as a whole; and will have full freedom in the selection of exchange arrangements to be applied by the United States, regardless of the general arrangements adopted, so long as it meets its general IMF obligations." (U.S. National Advisory Council on International Monetary and Financial Policies, *Special Report to the President and to the Congress on Amendment of the Articles of Agreement of the International Monetary Fund and on an Increase in Quotas in the International Monetary Fund* (Washington, April 1976), p. 23.)

[50] Schedule C, par. 8, *second.*

the margins around parities.[51] This language covers two situations. In one situation the member allows its currency to float but does not inform the Fund that it is terminating the par value for the currency. In the other situation, the member adopts multiple currency arrangements, with or without the necessary approval of the Fund,[52] under which a substantial proportion of exchange transactions within its territories take place at rates outside the prescribed margins. Under the original Articles, a par value would not cease to exist even if all exchange transactions took place outside the legal margins.

As a result of the discussion by the Executive Board of the abrogation of par values that has been referred to already, certain safeguards are adopted for members. The Fund cannot decide that a par value has ceased to exist for the purposes of the Articles unless it has consulted the member and given it 60-day notice of the Fund's intention to consider whether to make a finding that a substantial volume of exchange transactions are taking place outside the legal margins. These safeguards give the member an opportunity to express its wishes, and the Fund cannot rush to judgment when a currency begins to float. There is opportunity, therefore, to see whether the floating is temporary because of transitory influences. There is no definition, however, of "a substantial volume of exchange transactions," and the finding can be made by a decision taken with a majority of the votes cast.[53] At any time after a par value has ceased to exist, the member may propose a new par value for its currency. "New" for this purpose would include a former par value.

The Fund's power to find that a par value has ceased to exist is new. So too is its power to discourage maintenance of an unrealistic par value.[54] In fact, it is the duty of the Fund to take this action. It is not made clear what forms discouragement may take. The power does not include authority for the Fund to terminate or change a par value because it is unrealistic. The principle of the original Articles that only a member can propose a change in the par value of its currency is preserved by Schedule C.[55] The provision reflects opinion that one of the shortcomings of the former par value system was the retention of unsuitable par values for too long and that the limited powers of the Fund to press for a change because the member's exclusive right

---

[51] Schedule C, pars. 5 and 8, *second.*
[52] Article VIII, Section 3, *second.*
[53] Schedule C, par. 8, *second.*
[54] Schedule C, par. 7, *second.*
[55] Schedule C, par. 6, *second.*

to propose a change was often understood to preclude the Fund from suggesting that a proposal should be made. Schedule C makes it clear that there is no logical contradiction in affirming the member's exclusive right and giving the Fund authority to suggest that the right should be exercised.

One of the most radical differences between the provisions on par values in the original Articles and the Second Amendment is that a par value, once established, will not necessarily persist until it is replaced by a new par value. A par value can be terminated by a member, cease to exist automatically, or cease to exist as the result of a finding by the Fund without the concurrent adoption of a new par value. The balance of opinion was strongly in favor of abandoning the legal fiction that a par value was in existence when it was ineffective and there was no reasonable likelihood that it would ever be made effective.

In addition, it became unnecessary to retain the principle that a par value continued to exist under the Articles when it was ineffective because it served the purpose of ensuring that the member failing to make it effective would be treated as failing to perform its obligations. It is no longer necessary to insist on the existence of a par value for this purpose. A member that is not applying a par value may not be in violation of its obligations, for example, because it has terminated a par value in accordance with the Articles. If the member ceases to make its par value effective inconsistently with the Articles, it will be in violation of obligations without any necessity to rely on the par value in order to reach this conclusion. For example, the member may be in violation because it has terminated its par value notwithstanding the objection of the Fund. The termination is then the violation, and not the neglect of the margins around parity.

One conclusion to be drawn from Schedule C is that even if a par value system is restored, the drafters of legal instruments are likely to be wary about references to par values such as those that were in issue in the cases discussed in this chapter. The current tendency to employ a unit of account, such as the SDR, may persist even when Schedule C is in operation.

8

The Fund Agreement in the Courts—XIV*

This fourteenth installment in the series dealing with the impact of the Articles of Agreement of the International Monetary Fund on litigation discusses cases decided in England, France, the Federal Republic of Germany, and the State of New York. All four cases are considered in relation to the effect of the Articles on issues involving the exchange control regulations of a member of the Fund that was not the country of the forum. The New York case has an additional interest because of its bearing on the enforcement of contractual obligations arising from Eurodollar loans.

The main provision of the Articles in relation to which the cases are examined is Article VIII, Section 2(b), which reads as follows:

> Exchange contracts which involve the currency of any member and which are contrary to the exchange control regulations of that member maintained or imposed consistently with this Agreement shall be unenforceable in the territories of any member. In addition, members may, by mutual accord, cooperate in measures for the purpose of making the exchange control regulations of either member more effective, provided that such measures and regulations are consistent with this Agreement.

This provision was not modified by the sweeping Second Amendment of the Articles notwithstanding the differing interpretations of it that have been adopted by courts in various countries. There has

---

* Originally published in September 1979.

257

already been some speculation[1] about the fact that the provision has not been modified. Nothing that bears on the interpretation of the provision should be read into this fact. The provision was not examined during the negotiation and drafting of the Second Amendment, and no proposal was made to modify it. An enormous range of issues of more obvious and more pressing economic and financial interest to members had to be resolved. The hope that agreement on the text of the Second Amendment could be reached promptly was not realized because of the number and complexity of these issues. Even the Jamaica Accord of the Interim Committee of the Board of Governors on the International Monetary System did not settle all essential issues, although it was the popular impression that nothing controversial remained after that meeting of the Committee. It is impossible to say whether Article VIII, Section 2(b) would have been amended, or how it would have been amended, if amendment had been proposed in order to change its purpose or to encourage a greater uniformity of interpretation by tribunals. That members are content to go on leaving the task of interpretation to the courts is demonstrated by the absence of any request by a member for an authoritative interpretation by the Fund of some aspect of Article VIII, Section 2(b) that would complement the original interpretation of June 10, 1949.[2]

I. Sing Batra v. Ebrahim [3] (England)

A question that arises in connection with Article VIII, Section 2(b) is whether the court in which an action is brought on an exchange contract that is unenforceable under the provision must apply the provision even though it is not cited and relied upon by a party to the proceedings. The question has practical as well as intrinsic importance because Article VIII, Section 2(b) and the provision of domestic law that gives domestic effect to it where that has been necessary are not always well known.

---

[1] See Andreas F. Lowenfeld, *The International Monetary System* (New York, 1977), §9.26, p. 275; Brian D. Beglin, "United States Enforcement of Foreign Exchange Control Laws—A Rule in Transition?" *New York University Journal of International Law and Politics*, Vol. 10 (Winter 1978), p. 560.

[2] Executive Board Decision No. 446-4, June 10, 1949, *Selected Decisions*, Eighth Issue, pp. 131–32. (*Selected Decisions*, Ninth Issue, pp. 201–202.)

[3] *The Times* (London) (May 3, 1977), p. 11; *Halsbury's Laws of England: Annual Abridgment*, 1977 (London, 1978), p. 453, par. 1906.

In *Sing Batra v. Ebrahim*, the lower court had given judgment for Sing Batra, the plaintiff, on a claim arising from two transactions in which, in consideration of payments by check in London, Ebrahim, the defendant, undertook to arrange for the payment of Indian rupees to the plaintiff by banker's draft in India and to the account of the plaintiff's daughter at an Indian bank. The official exchange rate was 18 rupees to the pound sterling. The exchange rate contracted for was 30–31 rupees to the pound. The plaintiff claimed damages for breach of contract on the basis of the difference between the two exchange rates. The transactions were illegal under India's Foreign Exchange Regulations Act, 1947. The lower court had not been referred to the Indian law, the Fund's Articles, the Bretton Woods Agreements Act, 1945 of the United Kingdom, or the Bretton Woods Agreements Order in Council, 1946[4] that gives the force of law to Article VIII, Section 2(*b*) in the United Kingdom.

The Court of Appeal on May 2, 1977 reversed the judgment of the lower court and gave judgment for Ebrahim. The opinion of the Master of the Rolls, with whom the other two members of the Court of Appeal agreed, includes the following passage:

> If the transactions were illegal it was the duty of the court to take the point. An appellate court should take the point of illegality of its own initiative, if not taken by the judge at trial. . . .
>
> . . . .
>
> An unauthorized contract to exchange sterling for Indian rupees was contrary to the exchange control regulations of both England and India. The courts must not enforce the contract if it was contrary to Indian exchange control. The object of the Indian regulations dealing with authorization by the reserve bank was to prevent Indian currency being depreciated by speculators. Black market deals were prohibited by law.
>
> The present transactions were plainly contrary to the Indian exchange control regulations and so were unenforceable by English law under the Bretton Woods Agreement [*sic*] Act and the order in council. Dr. Batra was claiming damages for breach of contract to obtain Indian currency at black market rates. The appeal should be allowed.[5]

It should be noted that the Court of Appeal held that it is the duty of the lower court to take the point, and that if the lower court does not, the appellate court must do so.

---

[4] U.K., S.R. & O. 1946 No. 36.
[5] *The Times* (London) (May 3, 1977), p. 11.

The Master of the Rolls treated the contracts as contrary to the exchange control regulations of both India and England. The reference to England in this context probably was based on the provisions of English law that give effect to Article VIII, Section 2(*b*). No provisions of English exchange control law were cited. If English exchange control law is relevant to litigation in an English court, no one would doubt that the law must be applied by virtue of its own force. Article VIII, Section 2(*b*), however, deals with the exchange control regulations of a member of the Fund other than the country of the forum. Special measures must be taken in some jurisdictions to give effect to a provision such as Article VIII, Section 2(*b*).

The most interesting feature of the case is the willingness of the court to entertain the defense based on Article VIII, Section 2(*b*) and the provisions of English law giving effect to it even though the contracts are declared to be unenforceable. What makes this aspect of the case interesting is that normally under Anglo-American law it is left to the defendant to plead the defense of unenforceability.[6] If he does not rely on this defense, whether by deliberation or oversight, the court will not consider unenforceability. Indeed, it has been argued that the reference to unenforceability in Article VIII, Section 2(*b*) must be interpreted to mean invalidity because the cooperation among members of the Fund that the provision calls for by requiring respect for the exchange control regulations of other members should not depend on the pleadings of litigants.[7]

The reply has been made to this argument that not all the incidents of the concept of unenforceability in domestic law have to be imported into the concept in Article VIII, Section 2(*b*).[8] Therefore, courts should recognize the public interest and hold that the provision requires them to treat as unenforceable those exchange contracts declared by it to be unenforceable even though unenforceability has not been pleaded. Courts can act in this way without concluding that unenforceability means invalidity. The distinction between the two concepts should be observed, not only because there is no necessity to merge them to make the provision effective but also because invalidity would produce consequences that cannot be reconciled with the policy of Article VIII, Section 2(*b*). Some of these consequences are discussed below.

---

[6] *Halsbury's Laws of England*, Vol. 9, Fourth Edition (London, 1974), pp. 85, 261; Arthur Linton Corbin, *Corbin on Contracts: A Comprehensive Treatise on the Rules of Contract Law*, Vol. 2 (St. Paul, 1950), pp. 152–54.

[7] See Gold, *Fund Agreement in the Courts* (1962), pp. 61–62.

[8] See Gold, "Fund Agreement in the Courts—X," p. 144 in this volume.

The Master of the Rolls refers to the illegality of the contracts but this reference is to illegality under Indian law. Nevertheless, this mention of illegality introduces a slight note of ambiguity into the court's willingness to take the initiative in referring to the provisions of law overlooked by the defendant. The ambiguity is slight because the Master of the Rolls is clear in characterizing the contracts as unenforceable under English law. This point of law was the subject of an explicit ruling by the Court of Appeal in the earlier case of *Sharif v. Azad*,[9] in which the Court refused to treat "unenforceable" as equivalent to "illegal." *Sharif v. Azad* has been overruled by *Wilson, Smithett & Cope Ltd. v. Terruzzi*,[10] but not on this point. The Federal Supreme Court of Germany also has concluded that unenforceability is not the same as illegality for the purpose of Article VIII, Section 2(b).[11]

Other courts have examined the effect of Article VIII, Section 2(b) on the contracts they were considering, even though a litigant had not relied on the provision and the domestic law relating to it. The Karlsruhe Regional Court of Appeal seems to have done this in *Loeffler-Behrens v. Beermann*.[12] Certainly, the court took the initiative in addressing an inquiry to the Fund on whether the exchange control regulations in the case were within the scope of Article VIII, Section 2(b).[13] The Federal Supreme Court of Germany has left no doubt that a court must take the initiative in declaring a contract unenforceable as a result of Article VIII, Section 2(b), even though the provision has not been raised as a defense. The court held that the public interest must be vindicated for the same reasons that induce the courts to treat illegal contracts as such even though no party has pleaded illegality.[14]

The concept of unenforceability makes it possible for the courts to base their decisions on the facts when enforcement of a contract is sought. Invalidity would require the courts to make their determination on the basis of the facts when a contract is entered into. The purpose of Article VIII, Section 2(b) is to ensure that members of the Fund will not ignore the interests of another member by refus-

---

[9] [1966] 3 W.L.R. 1285, at 1289–90, 1293–94; [1966] 3 All E.R. 785, at 789–90. See also Gold, "Fund Agreement in the Courts—IX," pp. 110–13 in this volume.

[10] [1976] 1 Q.B. 683; [1976] 1 Q.B. 703 (C.A.). See also Gold, "Fund Agreement in the Courts—XII," pp. 202–18 in this volume.

[11] See Gold, "Fund Agreement in the Courts—X," p. 140 in this volume.

[12] Gold, "Fund Agreement in the Courts—IX," pp. 116–20 in this volume.

[13] *Ibid.*, p. 119.

[14] Gold, "Fund Agreement in the Courts—X," pp. 144–45 in this volume.

ing to take account of its exchange control regulations if they are consistent with the Articles and meet the other criteria of Article VIII, Section 2(*b*). The determination that the interests of a member are affected should be made in relation to current circumstances and not to past circumstances that may have changed. To base the determination on past circumstances might result in recognizing public interests that no longer exist or in ignoring public interests that do exist.

Circumstances may change in a number of ways after a contract is entered into. Exchange control regulations may be imposed, modified, or abrogated. The Fund may approve exchange restrictions or cease to approve them. A party to a contract may change his residence so that exchange control regulations begin, or cease, to apply to him. These changes in circumstances are not the only ones that can create or terminate interests on the part of members that Article VIII, Section 2(*b*) is intended to protect.[15]

The decision of the Court of Appeal in *Sing Batra v. Ebrahim* implies no departure from *Wilson, Smithett & Cope Ltd. v. Terruzzi*, in which the Court of Appeal interpreted "exchange contracts" as restrictively as possible by considering them to be contracts for the purchase and sale of currencies. The contracts in *Sing Batra v. Ebrahim* fell within the scope of that narrow interpretation. The court followed two lines of argument to reach its conclusion in the *Terruzzi* case. One was a *dictum* in an earlier English case on the meaning of "exchange contracts" for another purpose,[16] and the other was what the court considered to be the normal understanding of these words. The *dictum* in the earlier case was *obiter,* and the decision itself has been overruled.[17] Furthermore, Lord Wilberforce, in a more recent case, has expressed the following view on the resort to English legal precedent in the interpretation of a treaty:

> I think that the correct approach is to interpret the English text which after all is likely to be used by many others than British businessmen, in a normal manner, appropriate for the interpretation of an international convention, unconstrained by technical rules of English law, or

---

[15] See the section entitled *"Making v. performance of exchange contracts"* in Gold, *Fund Agreement in the Courts* (1962), pp. 62–64; see also the section entitled *"The Federal Supreme Court Judgment of April 27, 1970"* (Federal Republic of Germany) in Gold, "Fund Agreement in the Courts—X," pp. 139–49 inthis volume; Gold, "Cuban Insurance Cases," pp. 70–77 in this volume.

[16] *In re United Railways of Havana and Regla Warehouses Ltd.* [1961] A.C. 1007, at 1059.

[17] *Miliangos v. George Frank (Textiles) Ltd.* [1975] 3 All E.R. 801. The correctness of the *dictum* was not considered in this case.

by English legal precedent but on broad principles of general acceptation. . . .[18]

The argument of the normal understanding of language in the *Terruzzi* case was supported with an analysis of various purposes and provisions of the Articles of Agreement. It has been submitted that most of this analysis was erroneous.[19] The interpretation of Article VIII, Section 2(*b*) that is most compatible with the purposes and provisions of the Articles is that "exchange contracts" are contracts requiring international payments or transfers in foreign or domestic currency. The word "exchange" in "exchange contracts" should be understood in the same way as in "exchange control," which also is a normal understanding of language. This understanding is reinforced by the mission of the Fund, which is to concern itself not with a limited class of payments but with all payments and transfers for international transactions. Moreover, experience confirms that the contracts covered by the *Terruzzi* interpretation are likely to be the subject of litigation only rarely. It is scarcely credible that the Bretton Woods conferees, in the three weeks available to them for reaching agreement on a master plan for payments and transfers on a world scale, would have allowed their concentration to be diverted to the fashioning of a sledgehammer to crack so small a nut.

In the interpretation of the phrase that is recommended here, the words "international" and "foreign or domestic" are to be understood from the standpoint of the legislator whose exchange control regulations have not been observed. "International" in this formulation means "transnational" and not simply "intergovernmental." The words "involve the currency of any member" in Article VIII, Section 2(*b*) should be understood to refer to the member whose balance of payments is affected by an exchange contract. The Fund is an international organization whose primary interest is the balances of payments of its members, for which reason its concern relates to all international payments and transfers.

The criterion of the impact of payments or transfers under a contract on the balance of payments must be distinguished from certain other criteria that have been proposed and that have been discussed in earlier contributions to this series of articles.[20] In particular,

---

[18] *James Buchanan & Co. Ltd. v. Babco Forwarding and Shipping (U.K.) Ltd.* [1977] 3 All E.R. 1048, at 1052.

[19] See Gold, "Fund Agreement in the Courts—XII," pp. 202–18 in this volume.

[20] Gold, "Fund Agreement in the Courts—X," pp. 145–49 in this volume. See also Eloy Ruiloba Santana, "Aspectos Teoricos del Control de Cambios en Derecho Internacional Privado," *Anuario de Derecho Internacional* (Pamplona), 1975-II, pp. 112–14.

although most often the criterion of protection of a member's currency, or less often the protection of a member's monetary reserves, may be adequate in the circumstances of a case, these criteria should be subsumed under the general criterion of effect on the balance of payments.

In *Sing Batra v. Ebrahim* the court mentioned that the objective of the Indian exchange law was to avoid depreciation of the Indian currency by speculators. A troublesome consequence of the *Terruzzi* case is that it ignores the effects of all contracts other than contracts for the purchase and sale of currencies, even though other contracts fail to observe exchange control regulations that are consistent with the Articles of Agreement of the Fund. Moreover, the effect of not holding contracts to be unenforceable in these circumstances is that courts enforce contracts that can undermine the currencies and damage the economies of states with which the state of the forum has undertaken to collaborate to avoid such consequences.[21] It is even possible to foresee a situation in which the resources contributed to the Fund by the state of the forum may be made available by the Fund as balance of payments assistance to the member whose exchange control regulations have been flouted by the contract that the forum enforces. The exchange control regulations are likely to have the same objective as the balance of payments assistance provided by the Fund with the currency of the forum.

One other element in the case merits attention. The Court of Appeal held that the contracts were illegal under Indian law and unenforceable under English law. A finding of illegality under the law of which the exchange control regulations are part is not necessary to bring about the sanction of unenforceability under the law of the forum. The language of Article VIII, Section 2(*b*) is broad and avoids technicality: "contrary to the exchange control regulations." For the purpose of Article VIII, Section 2(*b*), therefore, it would suffice if the foreign law attached some consequence other

---

[21] Cf. the following answer by Dr. Fritz Leutwiler, President of the Swiss National Bank, in discussing a new code of conduct for Swiss Banks:

"Q. Does the agreement ask banks to avoid handling money that came from tax evasion or other illegal activities?

A. No, sir! Our banks cannot take over the tasks of foreign-exchange controls in other countries. They are here, they are open, and they can accept all funds except those that the bank knows came from criminal acts. I refuse to put countries on a black list, to tell banks you can take funds from some countries but not from others. . . . These are judgments that are not within the competence of Swiss banks. What we want is that Swiss banks not send their managers to countries where there are restrictions and organize illegal capital outflows." (*Time* (European edition), Vol. 110 (July 11, 1977), p. 13.)

than illegality to the neglect of its exchange control regulations, such as voidness or even unenforceability. In short, whether the contract is illegal, void, or unenforceable under the foreign law, it will be unenforceable under the law of the forum.

II. Achour v. Perrot and Bouderghouma [22] (France)

In this case, decided by the Court of Appeals of Reims on October 25, 1976, the court refrained from raising the possible effect of Article VIII, Section 2(b) in circumstances in which it had not been relied on by a party to the litigation. The attitude of the court is surprising because it declared that

> While the operation envisaged is manifestly illegal under Algerian law, it is not within the competence of the French courts to punish the evasion of foreign law, particularly in the domain of public economic order; *it could be otherwise only insofar as such actions violate commitments undertaken by France. . . .*[23] (Emphasis added)

In August 1964, Achour, a French national resident in Algeria, commissioned another French national, Bouderghouma, to transfer, by clandestine means, from Algeria to France, the sum of 310,000 French francs delivered by Achour to Bouderghouma and Perrot. Only two sums of F 60,000 each were transferred to Achour, who brought this action to recover the balance. The defendants pleaded, inter alia, that as the agreement violated Algerian exchange control law, the French customs code, and the Evian Agreements between Algeria and France, the suit was inadmissible. It appears that the defendants entered this procedural objection, rather than the substantive objection of illegality, because of the possibility that if the court held the contract ineffective on the ground of illegality, it might decree the restitution of funds to which the defendants were not entitled.[24] In those circumstances, the effect of restitution could be the indirect enforcement of a contract that was illegal under Algerian law. The Court of Cassation did indeed reach this result in *Constant v. Lanata*, which has been discussed in an earlier chapter.[25] A similar result was achieved in *Achour v. Perrot and Bouderghouma* by a determination of a different kind. The court held that as the agreement was made between French nationals and was to be performed in France, they had implicitly

---

[22] *Journal du Droit International*, Vol. 105 (1978), pp. 99–106.

[23] *Ibid.*, p. 100 (translation from the French original).

[24] *Ibid.*, p. 101 (Note by Pierre Mayer).

[25] *Revue critique de droit international privé*, Vol. 59, No. 3 (1970), pp. 464–74. See, for the discussion of this case, Gold, "Fund Agreement in the Courts—X," pp. 155–60 in this volume.

intended to exclude the application of Algerian law and to subject the agreement solely to French law. The court found that the agreement did not violate French law or the Evian Agreements. It therefore accepted the appeal of Achour against the decision of the lower court in favor of the defendants and rejected their objection of the inadmissibility of the action.

The case suggests questions of the application of Article VIII, Section 2(b), even though the provision was not relied on by either party or mentioned by the court. First, the parties to the suit were no longer resident in Algeria at the time of the proceedings, and it may be assumed that the French francs delivered to the defendants had been transferred in some way from Algeria to France. Would an action on the agreement in France seeking damages for nonperformance fall within the scope of Article VIII, Section 2(b)? Could it be argued that, as a result of the transfer, Algeria's currency was no longer "involved" within the meaning of Article VIII, Section 2(b) and that its exchange control regulations were no longer relevant? In the discussion of *Constant v. Lanata* already referred to, it was argued that Article VIII, Section 2(b) should not be frustrated by an interpretation that Article VIII, Section 2(b) no longer applied in such circumstances:

> An approach of this kind would mean that whenever the parties succeeded in carrying out that part of the contract that was peculiarly within the mischief against which Article VIII, Section 2(b) was directed, the courts would be available to assist in completing their design. To avoid this result, it would be necessary to consider the contract on which a suit was brought as consisting of all the obligations for which it had provided and not simply as consisting of those that remained unperformed.[26]

Some courts,[27] though not all,[28] have been willing to dissect a single arrangement into severable transactions and to enforce one of

---

[26] *Ibid.*, p. 160 in this volume.

[27] See *Southwestern Shipping Corporation v. National City Bank of New York*, 173 N.Y.S. 2d 509 (1958), 178 N.Y.S. 2d 1019 (1958), 190 N.Y.S. 2d 352 (1959), 361 U.S. 895 (1959); Gold, *Fund Agreement in the Courts* (1962), pp. 97–100, 102–108; Gold, "Fund Agreement in the Courts—IX," pp. 115–16 and "—X," pp. 158–59 in this volume. See also *Varas v. Crown Life Insurance Co.*, 83 Montg. Co. L.R. 71 (1963), 204 Pa. Super. 176, 203 A. 2d 505 (1964), 382 U.S. (1965); Gold, "Cuban Insurance Cases," pp. 59–61, 91 in this volume; *J. Zeevi and Sons, Ltd. et al. v. Grindlays Bank (Uganda) Limited*, 37 N.Y. 2d 220, 333 N.E. 2d 168, 371 N.Y.S. 2d 892 (1975); Gold, "Fund Agreement in the Courts—XII," pp. 219–21 in this volume.

[28] See a decision of the German Federal Supreme Court of May 21, 1964 (VII ZR 23/64) in Gold, "Fund Agreement in the Courts—X," p. 158 in this volume, fn. 48.

them even though it was an essential element in a design to evade the exchange control regulations of another country. This technique is different, however, from a finding that there is an unseverable transaction but that an obligation constituting part of it can be enforced because another component obligation has been performed.

Second, the case is a minor illustration of the difficulties created by the definition of "exchange contracts" in the *Terruzzi* case. In the desire to exempt payments for commercial transactions from Article VIII, Section 2(b), the court held in that case that the words must be understood to mean contracts for the purchase and sale of currency. According to this definition, if Achour had given the defendants Algerian currency in return for a promise to deliver French francs in France, the agreement would be an "exchange contract." If, however, Achour had not paid Algerian currency but had promised some reward in French francs, the agreement would not be an "exchange contract." The distinction is not a realistic one in relation to Article VIII, Section 2(b) or to any other provision of the Articles.

Third, the defendants based part of their defense on the Evian Agreements, apparently because the Agreements envisaged the possibility of exchange control regulations imposed by a joint commission if required to protect Algeria's exchange resources. The defendants may have assumed that Algeria's exchange control regulations were imposed in accordance with this element of the Agreements. It seems, however, that the regulations were imposed by Algeria unilaterally and not by the joint commission. The Evian Agreements provided that, in the absence of exchange control authorized by the joint commission, there was to be freedom for transfers between Algeria and France.[29]

The facts as set forth in the preceding paragraph suggest questions involving the relationship of discriminatory practices to Article VIII, Section 2(b). Suppose that Patria discriminates in favor of Terra by permitting payments and transfers for current international transactions or capital transfers to Terra and impeding them to other members. The first question that arises is whether Patria and Terra are entitled under the Articles to engage in this practice, because Article VIII, Section 3 proscribes "discriminatory currency arrangements." A discriminatory currency arrangement may be a measure adopted by a member as a unilateral policy or as the result of a bilateral or multilateral agreement.

Although Article VIII, Section 3 binds members to avoid dis-

---

[29] *Journal du Droit International,* Vol. 105 (1978), p. 102.

criminatory currency arrangements, the prohibition is not absolute. The Fund has interpreted this provision and Article VI, Section 3 to mean that the prohibition does not apply to capital transfers, although a reservation has been made with respect to exchange rates. Article VI, Section 3 provides that

> Members may exercise such controls as are necessary to regulate international capital movements, but no member may exercise these controls in a manner which will restrict payments for current transactions or which will unduly delay transfers of funds in settlement of commitments, except as provided in Article VII, Section 3(b) and in Article XIV, Section 2.

Subject to the reservation dealing with exchange rates, the interpretation declares that: "Members are free to adopt a policy of regulating capital movements for any reason, due regard being paid to the general purposes of the Fund and without prejudice to the provisions of Article VI, Section 1."[30]

The caveat with respect to the general purposes of the Fund was intended to be a reminder that the Fund is an organization devoted to collaboration in monetary matters, so that members should try to avoid discriminatory controls on capital movements. The caveat with respect to Article VI, Section 1 refers to a provision under which, in certain circumstances, the Fund can request a member to impose capital controls. The implication is that the controls should not be discriminatory if the Fund requests nondiscriminatory controls. The Fund has never made a request under Article VI, Section 1. The first caveat has been reinforced by Article IV, Section 1 of the Second Amendment, in which the exchange rate obligations of members are introduced by these words: "Recognizing that the essential purpose of the international monetary system is to provide a framework that facilitates the exchange of goods, services, and capital among countries, ..." Notwithstanding the caveats and the new language in the Second Amendment, the basic principle remains that members are able to discriminate in the imposition and administration of capital controls.

It follows from what has been said so far that the proscription of discrimination in Article VIII, Section 3 applies to payments and transfers for current international transactions. Even with respect to them, however, the right to discriminate is recognized in certain circumstances. The Fund may approve a departure from the obligation,

---

[30] Executive Board Decision No. 541-(56/39), July 25, 1956, *Selected Decisions,* Eighth Issue, p. 97. (*Selected Decisions,* Ninth Issue, pp. 201–202.)

but it is not likely to do so because its policy is to eliminate discrimination. The outstanding example of the right of a member to discriminate without the necessity for approval by the Fund is the right it has to discriminate if it is availing itself of the transitional arrangements of Article XIV. It may then maintain or adapt, but not introduce, restrictions on payments and transfers for current international transactions in effect when it entered the Fund, even if the restrictions are discriminatory. The Fund discourages discrimination of this kind even if a member is availing itself of the transitional arrangements,[31] but this policy is not a legal limitation on the member's privilege. The real limitation, however, derives from the fact that a member is not entitled to "introduce" restrictions under Article XIV, Section 2. As a result, the scope for discrimination in these days is not extensive. For completeness, it may be added that members are authorized to discriminate against a member whose currency has been declared scarce by the Fund under Article VII, Section 3 by limiting exchange operations in the scarce currency, including those necessary for payments and transfers for current international transactions. The Fund has never made a declaration of the scarcity of a currency.

After this brief survey of discrimination, the second question that arises on the facts in *Achour v. Perrot and Bouderghouma* can be posed. Patria and Terra have entered into an agreement that discriminates in favor of Terra and against other members. An action is brought on an exchange contract that is consistent with the agreement, and the defendant pleads that the agreement is inconsistent with the Articles because it is a discriminatory currency arrangement that is not approved under or authorized by the Articles. If the action is brought in Patria or Terra, the defense is not likely to prosper, if only because the courts may regard the agreement as binding on them. Even if the action is brought in the court of a third member, Article VIII, Section 2(b) may not be an impediment to the plaintiff. The provision declares that exchange contracts shall be unenforceable if they are contrary to exchange control regulations that are consistent with the Articles. The provision does not require exchange contracts to be treated as unenforceable if they are compatible with exchange control regulations, whether or not they are consistent with the Articles. It would seem that, in addition, the provision does not impose unenforceability on exchange contracts if

---

[31] Executive Board Decision No. 1034-(60/27), June 1, 1960, *Selected Decisions,* Eighth Issue, pp. 139–40. (*Selected Decisions,* Ninth Issue, pp. 209–11.)

exchange control regulations are not observed but are inconsistent with the Articles.

The second question suggested by the facts of *Achour v. Perrot and Bouderghouma* would arise if an agreement were entered into by Patria and Terra that discriminated in favor of Terra, but Patria then imposed exchange controls under the apparent authority of the Articles that were in breach of the agreement. A plaintiff brings an action on an exchange contract, and the defendant contends that the contract is unenforceable under Article VIII, Section 2(*b*) because it is contrary to the exchange control regulations that Patria has imposed. The Articles contain nothing explicit on the effect of exchange control regulations that are authorized by the Articles but are inconsistent with an agreement between two members.

The problem can be even more complicated because the agreement itself can be either consistent or inconsistent with the Articles. Once again, special considerations may enter into the response of the court if the action was brought in Patria or Terra. If the action was brought in a third member country, and the agreement was inconsistent with the Articles, the court might treat the contract as unenforceable under Article VIII, Section 2(*b*). That is to say, the court might give no weight to the agreement and deal with the case as a straightforward one involving exchange control regulations that were consistent with the Articles and an exchange contract that was contrary to the regulations. The court might hesitate, however, if the agreement was consistent with the Articles, because this circumstance might neutralize Patria's apparent authority under the Articles to impose the exchange control regulations.

The Fund has not had to face questions such as these. Nor were they considered by the French courts in *Constant v. Lanata* or *Achour v. Perrot and Bouderghouma*, even though in the latter case, the court, noting that the joint commission had not imposed the regulations, concluded that "regulations adopted solely within the context of Algerian legislation cannot be binding upon a French court."[32] This *dictum* is valuable, but not as illuminating as it would have been had the action been brought in the court of a country other than France, which corresponds to Terra in the example that has been discussed, and had Article VIII, Section 2(*b*) been considered.

Fourth, the subject of discrimination in relation to Article VIII, Section 2(*b*) has been examined so far from the point of view of dis-

---

[32] *Journal du Droit International*, Vol. 105 (1978), p. 100 (translation from the French original).

crimination in favor of a particular member. The subject can be examined from the standpoint of discrimination against a particular member or even a particular category of persons. The problem is that, as seen already, there is some authority in the Articles for discrimination, particularly in connection with capital transfers.

Whatever may be the relevance of Article VIII, Section 2(b), there is evidence that courts in the country that is discriminated against, or whose citizens or residents are discriminated against, are not going to be disposed to refuse remedies on contracts because they are contrary to the discriminatory exchange control regulations of another member.

A learned commentator has pointed out that, even apart from Article VIII, Section 2(b), the principle that the exchange control regulations of another country are part of its public law and therefore not entitled to recognition in the courts of another country is out of date.

> It is to be hoped that the courts will rarely raise this objection, for such a position means not only a refusal to cooperate in the implementation of a foreign policy, but actual opposition to that policy. To uphold a contract whose purpose is the transfer abroad of foreign exchange, prohibited by the State in whose territory the currency is located, is to encourage that transfer. From the moment when the court recognizes its jurisdiction, it can choose only between an attitude of cooperation and an attitude of hostility. The first seems preferable in all but exceptional cases; it is not sufficient to oppose the foreign law with a principle of free movement of exchange which French law itself does not uphold.[33] (*Translation*)

He goes on, however, to make a reservation in connection with discrimination:

> On the other hand, when the prohibition on exports of capital means the dispossession of persons having legitimate and pressing reasons to leave the country, the objection should be raised. Moreover, in the case at hand, it is highly probable that the Court of Reims was aware that the Algerian legislation was intended to dispossess French nationals wishing to move to France after independence. . . .[34] (*Translation*)

Both *Constant v. Lanata* and *Achour v. Perrot and Bouderghouma* can be regarded as illustrations of the tendency not to withhold remedies if the exchange control regulations of another country are thought to be discriminatory against citizens or residents of the country of the forum. The principle in the passage quoted immediately above, how-

---

[33] Pierre Mayer, *ibid.*, pp. 105–106.
[34] *Ibid.*, p. 106.

271

ever, is expressed broadly in terms of "persons having legitimate and pressing reasons to leave the country," and not citizens or residents of the country of the forum.

The two French cases illustrate different techniques for giving a remedy. In *Constant v. Lanata*, the court seems to have held that, as a result of Article VIII, Section 2(*b*), Algerian exchange control regulations governed the transfer of funds from Algeria to France, the contract was illegal because it was contrary to the regulations, and the plaintiff was entitled to restitution. In *Achour v. Perrot and Bouderghouma*, the court did not mention Article VIII, Section 2(*b*) and held that the parties had intended to exclude Algerian law and subject their contract to French law, so that the Algerian exchange control regulations were irrelevant.

J. Zeevi and Sons, Ltd., et al. v. Grindlays Bank (Uganda) Limited is an illustration of the distaste that the courts of a third country may have for discriminatory exchange controls that one country may impose against another. The material interests of the country of the forum, however, were involved because of the effect that withholding a remedy might have had on New York as a financial center. Article VIII, Section 2(*b*) was pleaded as a defense, but the provision was dismissed with the brief finding that an "exchange contract" was not involved.

Fifth, perhaps the tacit policy of the court in *Achour v. Perrot and Bouderghouma*, as suggested by the commentator quoted above, took precedence over the principle of some systems of law that contracts are illegal if they call for the performance of an act in foreign territory that is illegal under the law of that territory. In *Ceulemans v. Jahn and Barbier*, in which no consideration of discrimination was involved, a Belgian court applied the latter principle in an action on a contract that required dealing in currency in what is now Zaïre in contravention of the law of that country.[35]

III. Federal Supreme Court Decision of December 21, 1976, III ZR 83/74 [36] (Federal Republic of Germany)

By a document drawn up in Paris on April 24, 1970 and by another drawn up in Madrid on May 11, 1970, the defendant, a

---

[35] *Jurisprudence commerciale de Belgique*, 1968, Pt. IV, fns. 11–12, pp. 765–85; *Pasicrisie Belge*, 1969, Pt. III, pp. 22–28; Gold, "Fund Agreement in the Courts—XII," pp. 226–27 in this volume.

[36] *WM: Zeitschrift für Wirtschafts- und Bankrecht*, Jahrg. 31, No. 12 (March 19, 1977), pp. 332–34.

Swedish citizen, acknowledged that he had received two loans totaling US$25,000 from the plaintiff, a U.S. citizen living in Paris. The defendant had lived only occasionally and for short periods in Sweden, but he had been registered as a resident and owned an apartment there. Since January 1973, he had been living in the Federal Republic of Germany. He repaid part of the loans in deutsche mark, and the plaintiff brought an action for the balance. The defendant argued that the contracts were invalid because they were contrary to Swedish exchange control regulations. The Regional Court found for the plaintiff, but the Appeals Court overruled the decision because of the violation of Sweden's exchange control regulations. The plaintiff appealed to the Supreme Court, but before the case was decided on the merits a settlement was entered into.

The issue that remained was how the costs of the litigation were to be borne. Under German law, this issue was to be decided according to equity on the basis of the facts and the course of the litigation. The primary consideration is which party would have succeeded if there had been no settlement, because the party who is compelled to pay the costs is the one who would have been required to do so in the absence of a settlement. The determination for the purpose of costs only is made, however, without a complete analysis of all the issues that would have been undertaken had the case been decided on the merits. (It would seem, therefore, that views expressed in the court's opinion should have less weight as a contribution to the elucidation of Article VIII, Section 2(b) than if the opinion had been delivered on the merits.)

(i) The Supreme Court agreed with the Appeals Court that the suit would have been inadmissible, and the plaintiff would have lost, if the loan agreements were exchange contracts within the meaning of Article VIII, Section 2(b), because the agreements would have been unenforceable. The court explained that if the debtor discharges an indebtedness that is unenforceable, he cannot claim return of the money under the provisions governing unjustified enrichment, because an unenforceable obligation is nevertheless an obligation.

(ii) The Supreme Court stated that the debtor's acknowledgment of his obligation does not make an unenforceable obligation enforceable if it is unsatisfied. The attitudes of litigants cannot change the unenforceability of obligations that is established for the protection of currencies. It would follow from this view that the court must raise an objection based on Article VIII, Section 2(b) if the parties have not done so.

(iii) According to the court, because Article VIII, Section 2(*b*) is designed to protect currencies, only those obligations that can affect the balance of payments of the member or members involved are subject to the provision. The court held that it was unable to come to a definitive opinion on whether the balance of payments of Sweden was involved, because of the funds that were involved in the case. The plaintiff made the first loan from funds in the United States and the second from funds in Switzerland. The court also pointed out that the defendant invested the proceeds in Spain, with the knowledge of the plaintiff.

The court doubted that these capital movements fell under Article VIII, Section 2(*b*). The question whether Article VIII, Section 2(*b*) applied would depend on the facts at the time of repayment and whether the defendant's assets in Sweden would be affected. When a resident borrows abroad, the resulting indebtedness affects the borrower's currency (i.e., the balance of payments, it would seem) if a claim against the borrower's assets in the country of his residence is not ruled out. The documents showed that the loans were to be repaid in U.S. dollars, but it was not clear whether or not suit could be brought against the defendant in Sweden and judgment satisfied from assets there. The court was of the opinion that no international transfer from the standpoint of Sweden would occur if the claim could be satisfied only from assets outside Sweden, even if the defendant was resident in Sweden.

The court's view is not consistent with its premise of effect on the balance of payments. If the defendant was a resident of Sweden at the time of the action, whether it was brought in Sweden or elsewhere, the location of his assets should not determine whether Swedish currency was involved according to the criterion of effect on the balance of payments. The currency of Sweden would be "involved" according to Article VIII, Section 2(*b*) because of the defendant's residence. "The balance of payments of a given economy will record either an entity's transactions with the rest of the world, if the entity is considered a resident of the economy, or an entity's transactions with the economy, if the entity is considered a nonresident."[37] A change in the ownership of an asset as between a resident and a nonresident enters into the balance of payments of the resident's country (and the nonresident's) wherever the asset is situated.[38]

---

[37] International Monetary Fund, *Balance of Payments Manual*, Fourth Edition (Washington, 1977), p. 10.

[38] *Ibid.*, p. 12.

The court noted that all the cases dealing with Article VIII, Section 2(*b*) decided by the Supreme Court up to the date of its opinion had related, as the objects of the plaintiff's claims, to assets located in the state whose exchange control regulations required that a license be obtained for entry into the contracts that gave rise to the claims. Furthermore, the cases had dealt with claims involving payment or security for payment for goods or services or obligations under bills of exchange. If the court was implying that Article VIII, Section 2(*b*) is limited to these categories, it must be noted that nothing in the provision or in its rationale suggests that it is restricted in this way. Even these limited categories of contracts, however, are in sharp contrast to the view of exchange contracts that prevailed in the *Terruzzi* case.

(iv) In addition to raising the question whether the use of a resident's assets abroad had an effect on the balance of payments of the resident's country, the court hinted at the possibility that the use of these assets might not be covered by the words "[payments] for the purpose of transferring capital" in the former Article XIX(*i*) (the present Article XXX(*d*)). The implication was that the payments in the case might not have been capital transfers even if "exchange contracts" in Article VIII, Section 2(*b*) applied to contracts calling for payments of a capital character. The court seemed to suggest that an actual movement of an asset across boundaries might be a necessary element of "transfer." This kind of movement is not necessary to constitute a "transfer." The word connotes a change of ownership of an asset between resident and nonresident and covers assets situated outside the territory of the resident's country, as explained in (iii) above. In *Statni Banka and Banque d'Etat Tchécoslovaque v. Englander,* a French court held that the performance in France by an obligor subject to Czechoslovak exchange control regulations from funds located in France would be a transfer subject to the Czechoslovak regulations.[39] This conclusion is of the utmost importance in connection with Article VIII, Section 2(*b*). Often, suit is brought in a forum other than that of the legislator of the exchange control because the defendant has assets within the jurisdiction of the forum with which his obligation could be satisfied if Article VIII, Section 2(*b*) did not apply.

---

[39] *International Law Reports,* ed. by E. Lauterpacht, Vol. 47 (London, 1974), pp. 157–63; Gold, "Fund Agreement in the Courts—XII," pp. 223–26 in this volume.

(v) The Supreme Court recognized that Article VIII, Section 2(*a*) is intended to prevent restrictions on payments and transfers for current international transactions, and it wondered therefore whether restrictions on any capital transfers were covered by Article VIII, Section 2(*b*), but the court expressed no opinion on this question.

The language of Article VIII, Section 2(*b*) is not limited to the restrictions covered by Article VIII, Section 2(*a*). The latter provision is designed to promote a multilateral system of payments and transfers for current international transactions, but certain derogations are permitted, and it is to these derogations that the obligation of members under Article VIII, Section 2(*b*) applies. The obligation, however, is not confined to these derogations. The drafters of the original Articles were as concerned to ensure that members would be free to control capital movements as they were to ensure that members would not restrict payments and transfers for current international transactions, except when restrictions were authorized by or under the Articles. The concern with freedom to control capital transfers was inspired by the chaos that flows of "hot money" had produced in the period between the two World Wars. Therefore, the controls imposed on capital movements, which were authorized by the Articles, were to be the subject of the same cooperation among members that is the objective of Article VIII, Section 2(*b*) when derogations from the multilateral system of payments and transfers for current international transactions are authorized. This reason of policy explains why Article VIII, Section 2(*b*) is formulated without qualification.

(vi) The Supreme Court cited its decision of February 17, 1971, in which it held that a contract unenforceable when made because it was contrary to exchange control regulations at that time ceases to be unenforceable if the exchange control regulations are repealed before performance is sought.[40] This conclusion should apply with equal force if exchange control regulations are not repealed but no longer apply to the debtor because he has ceased to be a resident of the country that has imposed the regulations. The Sveriges Riksbank had stated that the Swedish regulations would not apply to the defendant in this case if he had become a resident of the Federal Republic of Germany. The Appeals Court had held that the defendant remained a resident of Sweden but had not pursued the inquiry that

---

[40] BGH Urt. v. 17.2.1971—VIII ZR 84/69 (Frankfurt), *Neue Juristische Wochenschrift*, Vol. 24 (June 1, 1971), pp. 983–85; *Wertpapier-Mitteilungen*, No. 14 of April 3, 1971, pp. 411–12; Gold, "Fund Agreement in the Courts—X," pp. 149–51 in this volume.

could have been made as a result of the statement by the Sveriges Riksbank.

The Supreme Court concluded that, in the circumstances of this case, there were doubts whether the contract would have been considered enforceable or unenforceable had the action proceeded without settlement. These doubts justified the conclusion that, on the basis of equity, each party should bear its own costs.

IV. Irving Trust Company v. Mamidakis [41] (New York)

The decision adopted by the New York Court of Appeals in *J. Zeevi and Sons, Ltd., et al. v. Grindlays Bank (Uganda) Limited* [42] has been criticized because it offered no definition of the expression "exchange contracts" in Article VIII, Section 2(*b*) but held that an exchange contract was not involved in circumstances in which the narrow interpretation of the *Terruzzi* case, the narrowest so far, would have led to a different conclusion. [43] On October 19, 1978 the United States District Court for the Southern District of New York delivered a judgment in which there is not even an express mention of Article VIII, Section 2(*b*), although there are quotations from the opinion in the *Zeevi* case on other aspects of that case.

The plaintiff bank, chartered in New York State, sued the defendant, a citizen of Greece, who had his office in Athens. He had the controlling interest in a Cypriot and two Panamanian shipping corporations. One corporation had received a Eurodollar loan from the plaintiff in 1975, and all three had received Eurodollar loans from the plaintiff in 1977. The defendant had guaranteed the performance of all obligations under the loan agreements and the payment of attorneys' fees if the plaintiff placed collection with an attorney. One agreement of guaranty was executed in London, and the other in Greece. One loan was disbursed through the plaintiff's branch in London, the other was a refinancing of accrued obligations. The corporations defaulted, and the plaintiff sued the defendant for approximately $2.5 million. The court gave judgment for the plaintiff.

---

[41] 78 Civ. 0265-CLB, October 18, 1978, U.S. District Court, Southern District of New York (unreported as of April 1, 1979).

[42] 37 N.Y. 2d 220, 333 N.E. 2d 168, 371 N.Y.S. 2d 892 (1975); Gold, "Fund Agreement in the Courts—XII," pp. 219–21 in this volume.

[43] See Keith L. Baker, "Enforcement of Contracts Violating Foreign Exchange Control Laws," *International Trade Law Journal*, Vol. 3 (Fall 1977), pp. 281–83.

The guaranty agreements provided that they "shall be governed by and construed and interpreted in accordance with the laws of the State of New York." The customary legal language of similar transactions entered into in the State of New York was employed. The underlying loan agreements and promissory notes also provided that they were "deemed to have been made under and governed by the laws of the State of New York as to all matters of construction, validity, effect and performance." Each note contained a covenant that payments to be made at New York should be "free and clear of and without deduction for any . . . restrictions or conditions of any nature hereafter imposed by the Republic of Panama, the Republic of Greece, the Republic of Cyprus or the United States of America." Repayment of the loans was to be made by requiring the charterers of certain vessels to pay hire to an account at the plaintiff bank in New York. Under the loan agreements, all notices, requests, and other communications were to be addressed to the plaintiff in New York. The plaintiff retained the power to transfer the loan, from time to time at its sole discretion, from any one of its branches to another branch. Any legal action was to be brought in the courts of the State of New York or of the United States for the Southern District of New York, as the plaintiff might elect. The defendant consented to all these provisions.

The defendant pleaded that the foreign exchange control regulations of Greece prevented the payment of U.S. dollars in New York to satisfy the guaranties without a license from the Bank of Greece, and that the guaranties were null and void under Greek law because they had not been licensed. The court held that Greek law had not been proved to its satisfaction, but the court would assume, although it did not decide, that in the absence of a license, the defendant would be subject to criminal penalties under Greek law.

The court held that it would apply the New York rule on the choice of law. That rule, with respect to commercial transactions, is that the selection by the parties of the domestic law to govern their agreement is binding when, as in this case, the law bears a reasonable relationship to the agreement. The guaranty of an agreement to be performed in New York in itself would be a sufficient contact with New York for this purpose. The court would have concluded that the law of New York was the governing law even in the absence of a choice-of-law clause. A passage from the opinion in the *Zeevi* case was quoted in which it was pointed out that New York could maintain its pre-eminent financial position only if the justified expectations of the parties to a contract were protected. A further passage was quoted for the proposition that foreign legislation will not be given effect if it conflicts with the public policy of New York. The Fund's interpretation of Article VIII, Section 2(b), however, emphasizes that the objection of the public policy of the forum cannot be raised against foreign exchange control regulations in circumstances in which Article VIII, Section 2(b) applies.[44]

The court disposed of an argument, based on §40 of the *Restatement of the Law (Second): Foreign Relations Law of the United States*, that a court when exercising its enforcement jurisdiction should compare the vital national interests of each state whose laws are involved in litigation.[45] The court held that it was doubtful whether this principle was applied by New York courts, but in any event the interests of New York were paramount in this case.

> ... it is doubtful that the New York courts would permit a borrower-guarantor from a New York bank in an international transaction having sufficient contacts with New York to justify exercise of its jurisdiction, [to] avoid his commercial obligations so easily. To do so would impede international financial transactions of precisely the sort present here. Traditionally, in the absence of treaty provisions to the contrary, our courts have not enforced the foreign exchange controls of other nations, because these controls are contrary to our professed faith in the free enterprise system. See *Zeevi, supra.*

Although the qualification of "treaty provisions to the contrary" was mentioned, there was no discussion, as noted already, of Article VIII, Section 2(b) as a possible provision of this kind. There is a

---

[44] Executive Board Decision No. 446-4, June 10, 1949, *Selected Decisions*, Eighth Issue, pp. 131–32. (*Selected Decisions*, Ninth Issue, pp. 201–202.)

[45] "Limitations on Exercise of Enforcement Jurisdiction:
Where two states have jurisdiction to prescribe and enforce rules of law and the rules they may prescribe require inconsistent conduct upon the part of a person, each state is required by international law to consider, in good faith, moderating the exercise of its enforcement jurisdiction, in the light of such factors as

(a) vital national interests of each of the states,
(b) the extent and the nature of the hardship that inconsistent enforcement actions would impose upon the person,
(c) the extent to which the required conduct is to take place in the territory of the other state,
(d) the nationality of the person, and
(e) the extent to which enforcement by action of either state can reasonably be expected to achieve compliance with the rule prescribed by that state."
(§40, adopted and promulgated by the American Law Institute at Washington, D.C., May 26, 1962; revisions adopted and promulgated on May 20, 1964, and May 20, 1965.)

reference to the opinion in the *Zeevi* case,[46] but there the provision was dismissed in two sentences on the basis of the tentative and *obiter* view of "exchange contracts" advanced in an earlier case.[47]

In another line of thought in the opinion, the court held that the defendant had undertaken to obtain the licenses required by Greek law, and he had to accept the consequences if he had failed to obtain them. A similar thought was based on the defendant's express warranty that payments were valid, and that he would compensate the plaintiff for any increased costs occasioned by the imposition of any regulation that conditioned the plaintiff's rights under the notes.

On the first of these conclusions, the court said:

> Assuming that Greek law would be violated by making payment as required by these agreements, Mr. Mamidakis would be obligated under his agreement with the Bank to seek and obtain the currency control licenses which he claims are necessary. Both plaintiff's and defendant's experts on Greek law agree in their affidavits, that payment of the debt could be made if a license were obtained from the Bank of Greece. Under those conditions, the risk of future inability to obtain such a license, and its refusal by a government is ordinarily not a defense in a suit for breach of contractual agreements. *Corbin on Contracts* §1347 (1962).

The effect of this reasoning is to place in the hands of any party who is subject to the exchange control regulations of a country the power to decide that they shall not apply to him. All that he has to do is to undertake to obtain a license to make him liable under an exchange contract even if he applies for the license and it is refused. This result would negate the intent of Article VIII, Section 2(b), which is to place national welfare above private interest.

A distinction can be made between the refusal of a license by exchange control authorities and a party's failure to apply for one or to take all reasonable steps to obtain one if the conclusion can be reached that he had a duty to apply. In the latter event, a party may be liable in tort in some legal systems even though he cannot be made liable on the contract because of Article VIII, Section 2(b). Liability in tort may have an effect equivalent or comparable to a recovery on the contract, and so produce a financial result that Arti-

---

[46] See Gold, "Fund Agreement in the Courts—XII," pp. 219–21 in this volume.

[47] *Banco do Brasil, S.A. v. A.C. Israel Commodity Co., Inc., et al.,* 12 N.Y. 2d 371, 190 N.E. 2d 235, 239 N.Y.S. 2d 872 (1963); Gold, "Fund Agreement in the Courts—VIII," pp. 22–30 in this volume.

cle VIII, Section 2(*b*) seeks to prevent. Nevertheless, the provision is confined to the field of contract.[48]

V. A Questionnaire

The four cases discussed in this chapter raise problems of the understanding and application of Article VIII, Section 2(*b*), many but not all of which have arisen in earlier cases. Some of the problems suggested by these cases, and the answers that they should receive, are set forth below.

(1) If the parties fail to plead Article VIII, Section 2(*b*) when it is applicable, should the court exercise an initiative and take the provision into account?

Courts in a member country should give effect to Article VIII, Section 2(*b*) whenever it applies. Promotion of the public policy expressed in the provision should not depend on the will of litigants.

(2) Are "exchange contracts" confined to contracts for the purchase and sale of currencies?

The word "exchange" in the expression "exchange contracts" should be understood in the same way as in the expression "exchange control." Exchange contracts are contracts between a resident and a nonresident calling for a payment or transfer in currency, whether domestic or foreign from the standpoint of the member referred to in (3) below, that can affect its balance of payments.[49]

(3) The balance of payments of which member must be affected as a basis for treating an exchange contract as unenforceable?

The balance of payments must be that of the member whose exchange control regulations have not been observed by the parties entering into an exchange contract. The currency of that member is "involved" in the sense of Article VIII, Section 2(*b*).

(4) Is a country's balance of payments affected only if assets situated within its territorial jurisdiction can be resorted to in satisfaction of obligations under an exchange contract?

---

[48] See *Daiei Motion Picture Co. Ltd. v. Zavicha* discussed in Gold, "Fund Agreement in the Courts—XII," pp. 191–95 in this volume. For a discussion of the liability of exchange control authorities for refusal of a license and sovereign immunity, see *Zavicha Blagojevic v. Banque du Japon* and Note by Henri Batiffol in *Review critique de droit international privé*, Vol. 66 (April/June 1977), pp. 359–62.

[49] For the question whether the balance of payments is affected by transactions between residents in foreign assets or transactions between nonresidents in domestic liabilities, and the bearing of this question, however it is answered, under the provision, see pp. 401–403.

An exchange contract affects a country's balance of payments even if a resident enters into an exchange contract under which the resident's obligations are to be performed exclusively with assets he owns that are situated abroad.

(5) Must the exchange control regulations be designed for the purpose of protecting the currency involved or increasing the monetary reserves of the member that imposed them?

Normally, the exchange control regulations referred to in Article VIII, Section 2(b) will be imposed for the purposes mentioned in the question, but they need not be. For example, they may be imposed in order to bring pressure to bear on the balance of payments of a country as a sanction under a resolution of the United Nations. As for increasing monetary reserves, exchange control regulations may be designed to limit the inflow of capital.

(6) Does Article VIII, Section 2(b), in referring to an exchange contract as "contrary" to exchange control regulations, mean that the law of which the regulations are part must treat the contract as illegal or void?

The exchange contract need not be treated as illegal or void by the law of which the exchange control regulations are part in order to require the foreign forum to hold the contract to be unenforceable. The forum should reach this result even if the contract is only unenforceable under the law of which the exchange control regulations are part.

(7) As of what date should the facts be considered in order to determine whether an exchange contract is unenforceable?

The policy of Article VIII, Section 2(b) and the concept of unenforceability lead to the conclusion that the facts at the time when enforcement of an exchange contract is sought should be decisive. In particular, the facts at the time when the contract was entered into should not be decisive if they have changed in any one of a number of ways that would remove the contract from, or bring it within, the scope of Article VIII, Section 2(b).

(8) Should the performance of the obligation of one party under an exchange contract be regarded as a change for the purposes of (7) above?

If one party has performed its obligation and performance was contrary to the exchange control regulations of the member whose currency was involved, a court should not enforce the obligation of the other party on the ground that this performance would not, in itself, affect the balance of payments of the member whose balance of payments has already been affected. If courts did not treat the contract as unenforceable, on the ground that it had been partially performed, they would be helping to carry out arrangements in opposition to the policy of the member whose exchange control regulations had been breached.

(9) Are capital controls included among the exchange control regulations referred to in Article VIII, Section 2(b)?

Article VIII, Section 2(b) requires members to collaborate by not enforcing exchange contracts that are contrary to other members' exchange control regulations when they are consistent with the Articles, whether the regulations control payments and transfers for current international transactions or capital transfers. Article VIII, Section 2(b) promotes the policy of the Articles, on the one hand, of authorizing certain derogations from the multilateral system of payments and transfers for current international transactions, and, on the other hand, of authorizing members to control capital transfers.

(10) If a party guarantees that it will perform its obligations under an exchange contract notwithstanding any exchange control regulations that may apply, can the contract be enforced notwithstanding Article VIII, Section 2(b)?

The contract should be treated as unenforceable, because if it were not, any obligor could immunize his contract from the effect of the provision.

(11) If a member agrees with another member not to impose exchange control regulations on payments and transfers for current international transactions or on capital transfers to the other member, but then imposes them under some authority in the Articles notwithstanding the agreement between the parties, does Article VIII, Section 2(b) apply to the regulations?

The answer might be affected in practice by such considerations as the validity of the agreement between the members under the Articles and the court in which an action on an exchange contract contrary to the exchange control regulations is brought, but the problem has not been examined by the Fund or by any tribunal.

(12) If exchange control regulations are discriminatory, are they within the reach of Article VIII, Section 2(b)?

The Articles authorize discriminatory exchange control regulations under certain provisions, so that, prima facie, Article VIII, Section 2(b) applies. In practice, however, courts might be reluctant to apply the provision if the discrimination is against the citizens or residents of the country of the forum, or even if it is directed against another member.

9

The Fund Agreement in the Courts—XV*

This fifteenth installment in the series dealing with the effect of the Articles of Agreement of the International Monetary Fund on litigation discusses three cases decided by courts in France, the Federal Republic of Germany, and the United Kingdom, respectively, and a fourth case decided by the High Court of Justice of the European Communities. The first case examines a constitutional issue that was raised in France in connection with an increase in the quota of France in the Fund and acceptance of the Second Amendment of the Articles. In addition, the case has prompted discussion of the question whether national courts are authorized to interpret the Articles. The second and third cases involved the unenforceability of certain exchange contracts under Article VIII, Section 2(b) of the Articles. The decision in the fourth case depended on the legal effect under the law of the European Community of the establishment of a central rate by a member of the Fund and the Community under the Fund's decision of 1971 on central rates and wider margins.

I. Quotas and Amendment

DECISION OF FRENCH CONSTITUTIONAL COUNCIL, APRIL 29, 1978 [1]

The Facts

Under the amended Article 61 of the French Constitution, the Constitutional Council can be seized of constitutional problems. A

---

* Originally published in September 1980.
[1] *Journal Officiel*, April 30, 1978, pp. 1942–43.

commentator has detected three stages in the practice of the Council so far.[2] In the first years of its existence, it was concerned mainly with ruling on the distribution of authority between the Legislature and the Executive. In a second stage, the Council was called upon to resolve conflicts between governmental prerogatives and individual rights. A possible third, and current, stage may be one in which the decisions of the Council, or at least those having the greatest potential impact, deal with the distribution of power between national sovereignty and new or newly strengthened international organizations. In two recent cases of this kind, the Council has been called upon to rule on monetary matters involving the International Monetary Fund and both the European Monetary System and the European Monetary Cooperation Fund. The case involving the International Monetary Fund was decided on April 29, 1978.

On April 26, 1978, a law was adopted, consisting of a single article, that authorized the Government to proceed with an increase in the quota of France from SDR 1,500 million to a maximum of SDR 1,919 million in accordance with Resolution No. 31-2 of the Board of Governors, dated March 22, 1976, on the Fund's Sixth General Review of Quotas.[3] Under the resolution, a member's proposed increase in quota in accordance with the resolution was not to become effective unless the member notified the Fund of its consent to the increase not later than one month after the Second Amendment became effective or such later date as the Executive Board might prescribe, and unless the member had paid the increase in its subscription in full. According to two provisos, however, no increase in quota was to become effective before the later of two dates: the effective date of the Second Amendment and the date of the Fund's determination that members having not less than three fourths of the total of quotas on February 19, 1976 had consented to increases in their quotas. These provisos were adopted as a matter of policy. The first was designed to ensure that members would have the benefit of increased quotas only when the Second Amendment became effective. The intention was to induce members to take the necessary steps to accept the Second Amendment. The other proviso was designed as a safeguard to ensure that quotas would be increased for both members likely to use the Fund's resources and members whose increased subscriptions were likely to be called upon by the Fund to finance these uses.

---

[2] See Léo Hamon, *Recueil Dalloz Sirey*, November 7, 1979, p. 543.

[3] *Selected Decisions*, Eighth Issue, pp. 222–24. (*Selected Decisions*, Ninth Issue, pp. 324–26.)

The Second Amendment became effective on April 1, 1978, so that members had to notify the Fund of their consents to increases in their quotas before May 1, 1978, unless before that date the Executive Board prolonged the period for notices. A member would have to take whatever steps were necessary under its domestic law, including the adoption of any parliamentary measures, before it would be in a position to give the notice and to pay the additional subscription. On April 24, 1978, the Executive Board extended the period to June 12, 1978 because a number of members had not yet consented to increases in their quotas. Some members had initiated the procedures leading to adoption of the necessary domestic legal measures but had not completed them. France was in that position. The National Assembly had acted on April 18, 1978, and the Senate was to act on April 25, 1978.

The Second Amendment became effective in accordance with the provisions of the Articles as they stood before that Amendment. Under those provisions, proposed modifications of all but three provisions became effective on a date prescribed by the Fund after three fourths of the members, having four fifths of the total voting power, had accepted the proposed modifications.[4] France had not passed the legislation necessary to enable it to accept the proposed Second Amendment, but it was bound by the Articles as modified. On October 30, 1976 the Prime Minister had submitted to Parliament, on behalf of the Government, a bill providing both for acceptance of the Second Amendment and consent to the increase in quota. The bill was never placed on the agenda of a session because a majority did not exist in favor of the bill as a result of objections to some features of the Second Amendment. The Government explained in 1978 that the Second Amendment had become effective and that it was unnecessary to proceed with the bill insofar as it related to the Second Amendment in order to help bring it into effect or to make it binding on France. Parliamentary approval of consent to the increase in quota, however, continued to be necessary because under Article 53 of the Constitution a treaty imposing a financial commitment on the State must be submitted for parliamentary ratification. A similar situation had arisen with respect to authorization for France to participate in what was then the Special Drawing Account after the First Amendment had become effective without acceptance of that amendment by France. The constitutionality of the bill confined to the authorization

---

[4] Article XVII(b), original and first.

of participation was not challenged on that occasion. The bill was enacted into law on December 26, 1969, in time for the first allocation of SDRs on January 1, 1970.

On the later occasion, members of the Opposition argued that the Second Amendment and the increases in the quotas of members were an inseparable whole, and that measures to approve both should have been submitted for parliamentary approval. A failure to follow this procedure would be improper (*détournement de procédure*) because it would be in contravention of Article 53 of the Constitution. A further argument, among others, was that the Second Amendment brought about a basic change in the initial equilibrium between the rights and obligations of members, which amounted to an impairment of national sovereignty. The responsibility for such a change rested with Parliament and could be accepted only with its express approval.

It was also argued that the procedure for amendment of the Articles by the acceptance of certain majorities of members and voting power applied only to amendments on secondary matters and not to the replacement of one international monetary system by another. The Second Amendment had this effect by eliminating the par value system.

On April 27, 1978 one of the Opposition parties in the National Assembly raised the constitutional question before the Constitutional Council, which delivered its decision on April 29, 1978.

The Decision

The Constitutional Council noted that the increases in quotas were proposed in accordance with Article III, Section 2, while the Second Amendment was proposed in accordance with Article XVII. The independence of the two actions suggested by the separate legal bases was reinforced by the fact that the actions were the subject of separate resolutions of the Board of Governors. This analysis was not affected by the proviso that made the effectiveness of the Second Amendment a condition precedent for the increases in quotas. This condition did not mean that the Second Amendment was made contingent on the increases in quotas. Nor was the analysis affected by the presentation to the National Assembly on October 30, 1976 of a single bill dealing with both matters. That step had been taken for the convenience of Parliament because the two matters involved the same international organization and not because there was a legal nexus between them. Therefore, the acceptance by France of an increase in its quota could be approved without the need for a simultaneous pronouncement on the Second Amendment.

The Constitutional Council then went on to discuss the requirements for amendment under Article XVII of the original Articles, which had not been affected by the First Amendment. These requirements called for special majorities of the total voting power of the membership, and unanimity for the amendment of three provisions. One of these three provisions was the original Article IV, Section 5(b), under which no change could be made in the par value of a member's currency except on the proposal of that member. The Constitutional Council pointed out that a provision corresponding to Article IV, Section 5(b) was to be found in Schedule C, paragraph 6 of the Second Amendment. It was true that this provision of the Second Amendment would come into play only if a widespread system of exchange arrangements based on stable but adjustable par values was to be introduced in accordance with Article IV, Section 4, but the purpose of the provision in the Schedule was to safeguard the sovereignty of members. This same purpose was served by the provisions on exchange arrangements as a whole, and in particular by the provision assuring each member of the right to apply the exchange arrangements of its choice even before a par value system was introduced.

The Constitutional Council decided that because the Second Amendment had become effective in accordance with the Articles, to which France had subscribed as authorized by the law of December 26, 1945, the Second Amendment was binding on France without the necessity for further legislative authorization. It followed that the law on the increase in quota that had been submitted to the Constitutional Council for adjudication on its constitutionality was contrary to neither the Constitution nor to the principle of national sovereignty.

The Commentators

Learned opinion supports the conclusion reached by the Constitutional Council, but one commentator has argued that part of the judgment was *obiter*.[5] In his opinion, the Council did not need to rely, and should not have relied, as it did in part of its judgment, on

---

[5] See Dominique Carreau, "L'augmentation de la quote-part de la France au Fonds Monétaire International: La décision du Conseil Constitutionnel du 29 avril 1978," *Revue générale de droit international public*, Vol. 83 (Paris, 1979), pp. 209–19.

its analysis of the exchange rate provisions. In dealing with what amounted to the argument that unanimous acceptance of the Second Amendment was necessary because the change in the exchange rate provisions affected the sovereignty of members, the Constitutional Council was passing on the legality of an amendment that, according to the Fund's finding, had become effective under the provisions of the Articles on amendment. The claim of a national court to adjudge the Fund's finding was a usurpation of authority. Moreover, there was an internal procedure in the Fund for the settlement of any question of interpretation that arises between the Fund and a member or between members,[6] but the French Government had not raised a question as to the legality of the Second Amendment.

This same commentator criticizes what he regards as an *obiter dictum* of the Constitutional Council on the ground that the *dictum* could be understood to mean that the Constitutional Council might have come to a different conclusion if it had thought that the new provisions on exchange arrangements were more onerous than the provisions governing the original par value system. Indeed, it was possible to argue that the Fund was able, at least in principle, to exercise more discipline over members under the "firm surveillance" that it must now exercise over the exchange rate policies of members,[7] but the Constitutional Council was not entitled to deliver an adverse judgment on any such restraint on the monetary sovereignty of members. Another commentator who agreed with this conclusion has written that the Constitutional Council would have lacked competence to determine the legality under the Articles of an amendment even if there had been a misuse of the Fund's procedure for amendment.[8]

It is incontestable that some provisions governing the par value system that can be called into existence under the Second Amendment are, in some respects, more rigorous for members than the

---

[6] Article XVIII, *first.*

[7] Article IV, Section 3(*b*), *second.*

[8] David Ruzié, *Journal du Droit International*, Vol. 105 (1978), p. 584. Professor Ruzié contends that the only available procedure in such circumstances would be a request by the Fund for an advisory opinion of the International Court of Justice. It is true that, under Article VIII of the Agreement between the Fund and the United Nations, the Fund can request advisory opinions, except on certain issues not relevant here (*Selected Decisions*, Eighth Issue (1976), pp. 230–31; *Selected Decisions*, Ninth Issue, pp. 351–58). Professor Carreau's view that the issue would be one of interpretation that the Fund itself could settle with finality under Article XXIX of the present Articles is to be preferred (see Gold, Pamphlet No. 11), although the Fund could decide to request an advisory opinion. It has never made a request.

provisions of the original system. For example, under the original provisions of the Articles, a par value continued to exist for the purposes of the Articles in all circumstances until a new par value was substituted. The Fund had no authority to terminate a par value. Under the provisions on par values in the Second Amendment, the Fund may find that a member does not maintain rates for a substantial volume of exchange transactions within margins from parity that are consistent with the Articles, and the par value for the currency will then cease to exist for the purposes of the Articles.[9] Again, the Fund must discourage maintenance of a par value that it considers unrealistic under a provision[10] for which there was no counterpart in the original Articles.

At the same time, it is not difficult to show that in many respects the new provisions on par values create fewer constraints for members than the original provisions. There are no objective criteria, however, for deciding whether on balance the new par value provisions as a whole would bear more heavily on members than the old.[11] But the validity of an amendment that has become effective in accordance with the provisions of the Articles cannot be challenged even if objective criteria did exist, and it was concluded that the new provisions on exchange arrangements, including the provisions on par values, were more onerous for members than the provisions of the original Articles. There is no special sanctity that attaches to the original provisions of a treaty that contains provisions on amendment. There is no principle that the amendment of a treaty must always be for the purpose of relaxing obligations under it unless all contracting parties agree, even though they have agreed on procedures for amendment that do not require unanimity.

In contrast to the views already mentioned, a third commentator has contended that it is not beyond the jurisdiction of French courts to inquire into the question whether a treaty that is alleged to bind France has been legally ratified or approved in accordance with French law, because, if it has not been, the effect of Article 55 of the Constitution is that it will not prevail over French domestic law.[12]

---

[9] Schedule C, par. 8, *second.*
[10] Schedule C, par. 7, *second.*
[11] For a more detailed comparison, see Gold, "Fund Agreement in the Courts—XIII," pp. 249–56 in this volume.
[12] Hamon (cited in fn. 2), p. 544.

Competence of National Courts on Interpretation

It is submitted that the following principles apply to the question whether national courts are entitled to resolve problems of interpretation of the Articles:

(i) If the Fund has adopted an authoritative interpretation of the Articles under Article XXIX of the present Articles or its predecessor, and the interpretation is binding under the law of the forum either because it is automatically binding or because it has been made binding, the court must apply the interpretation.

(ii) If the authoritative interpretation is not binding under the law of the forum of a member, the member is obliged by the Articles to take the necessary steps to make the interpretation binding. Meanwhile, the forum should regard the interpretation as persuasive.

(iii) If a question of the interpretation of the Articles has arisen between a member and the Fund or another member, neither member is bound to request an authoritative interpretation. Similarly, the Fund is not bound to initiate the procedure leading to an authoritative interpretation.

(iv) If a question of interpretation of the Articles has arisen between the parties described in (iii) above, a member may not seek the interpretation from any forum, body, or organization other than the Fund.

(v) If the Fund has not adopted an authoritative interpretation on a question that arises in litigation, the forum is entitled, subject to (vii) and (viii) below, to arrive at its own interpretation. A forum must be able to act in this way because its function is to decide the case before it.

(vi) A judicial interpretation under (v) above will cease to be a precedent for the decision of cases if it is inconsistent with a later authoritative interpretation of the Fund.

(vii) A court is not entitled to challenge a finding of fact that the Fund is authorized by the Articles to make with finality and has made. For example, the Fund is authorized to make with finality a finding that decisions have been supported by the necessary majorities.

(viii) If the issue that has arisen in litigation involves the exercise of discretionary authority by the Fund, the court cannot substitute itself and decide the issue as if it was one of interpretation. For example, in the English case *Wilson, Smithett & Cope Ltd. v. Terruzzi*,[13] the Court of Appeal treated the question whether certain

---

[13] [1976] 1 Q.B. 683; [1976] 1 Q.B. 703 (C.A.).

Italian exchange control regulations were "maintained or imposed consistently" with the Articles as if the court could resolve this question by interpretation. Various provisions authorize the Fund to approve or refuse to approve exchange control regulations or to find that they are consistent or not consistent with the Articles. The actions of the Fund to approve or disapprove restrictions or to find that they are consistent or inconsistent with the Articles are regulatory in character. Questions involving approval or consistency can be answered only by reference to the Fund's actions, and not as if they were abstract questions of interpretation.

If it had been relevant to decide the question of the requirements for amendment under the Articles, the principles set forth above would have entitled the Constitutional Council to decide this question as one of interpretation of the Articles. The answer would have been obvious: unanimity was not required. The problem would not be one of competence but of the correctness of an interpretation. The court would not be correct if it decided that the requirements for a particular amendment were not those set out in the Articles. If the court added or substituted a requirement, it would be acting inconsistently with a treaty that France had accepted in accordance with its law. It is pertinent to cite the hypothetical analogy of a reservation that a member sought to attach to its acceptance of the Articles requiring unanimity for a particular kind of amendment for which unanimity would not be required by the Articles. Such a reservation would be inconsistent with the Articles and would be rejected by the Fund.

Another distinction that must be made is between the binding effect of an amendment on a member and the domestic steps the member must take to enable it to perform its obligations under the amendment, including the obligation, when necessary, to make the amendment binding on its courts.

Suppose, for example, that Article VIII, Section 2(b), which is discussed in connection with the next two cases, had been incorporated in the Articles by an amendment. Under the laws of some members, such a provision must be given the force of law by a particular procedure in order to make it binding on its courts. It would be within the competence of a court called upon to apply the provision to determine whether the procedure had been followed. If the court found that the procedure had not been followed, it would be unable to apply the provision, but this conclusion would not imply that the amendment was not binding on the member whose court was seized of the litigation. Nor would the conclusion mean that the court was going beyond its competence. The situation would be one in which the member was failing to honor its commitment to the Fund that it had "accepted this Agreement in accordance with its law" and had "taken all steps necessary to enable it to carry out all of its obligations under this Agreement."[14]

Amendment, Unanimity, and Sovereignty

One commentator has raised the question whether a distinction should be drawn between restrictions on national sovereignty that states may accept and transfers of it that they may not accept.[15] In applying this possible distinction to amendment of the Articles, he appears to consider that, because France and all other members were invited by the Board of Governors to accept the proposed Second Amendment, an original requirement of unanimity may have been transformed by delay into a requirement of majorities. He questions whether delay can have this effect because it leads to a surrender of sovereignty. The argument appears to be that there was an original requirement of unanimous acceptance, that this requirement preserved national sovereignty, and that the Second Amendment had become effective without the acceptance of France and therefore without observance of the rule of unanimity. The reply to this argument is that there never was a requirement of anything other than the prescribed majorities in order to make the Second Amendment effective.

In the law relating to international organizations, the tendency has been to reject a rule of unanimity for the modification of a constitutive treaty but to permit members to withdraw from the organization. They can exercise this privilege if, for example, an amendment is adopted that is not to their liking and that they have not accepted.[16] A member of the Fund that does not take steps to accept an amendment of the Articles is bound by the amendment, and cannot be compelled to withdraw from membership for this reason, although this action can be taken in some organizations.

The privilege of withdrawal from an international organization is regarded as a safeguard. In the case of the Fund, a member may withdraw at any time by transmitting a notice in writing to the Fund at its principal office, and the member need not give any reason for

---

[14] Article XXXI, Section 2(a), *second.*

[15] Hamon (cited in fn. 2), p. 544.

[16] Joseph Gold, *Legal and Institutional Aspects of the International Monetary System: Selected Essays* (Washington, 1979), pp. 301–302. (Hereinafter cited as Gold, *Selected Essays.*)

its notice. Withdrawal becomes effective on the date when the Fund receives the notice.[17] The privilege of withdrawal is safeguarded by requiring unanimous acceptance of a proposal to modify the privilege.[18] Acceptance by "all" members is made explicit. There is no room, therefore, for holding that unanimity refers only to those members that respond. If members abstain, there is no unanimity.[19]

II. Unenforceability of Certain Exchange Contracts

FEDERAL SUPREME COURT OF GERMANY, DECISION OF MARCH 8, 1979 [20]

In this case, decided on March 8, 1979, the Supreme Court of the Federal Republic of Germany ruled once again[21] on the meaning and application of the first sentence of Article VIII, Section 2(b) of the Fund's Articles:

> Exchange contracts which involve the currency of any member and which are contrary to the exchange control regulations of that member maintained or imposed consistently with this Agreement shall be unenforceable in the territories of any member.

The defendant, a business agent residing in Spain, acted in 1972 to 1974 as the collection agent of the plaintiff, who was, apparently, a resident of the Federal Republic of Germany but clearly a nonresident of Spain. From the money he collected, the defendant retained a

---

[17] Article XXVI, Section 1, *second.*

[18] Article XXVIII(b), *second.*

[19] Gold, *Selected Essays,* p. 296.

[20] VII ZR 48/78, Cologne.

[21] For earlier cases decided by the Supreme Court, see

(i) *Neue Juristische Wochenschrift,* June 10, 1960, pp. 1101–1103; Gold, *Fund Agreement in the Courts* (1962), pp. 139–42.

(ii) *Wertpapier-Mitteilungen,* No. 21 of May 26, 1962, pp. 601–602; Gold, "Fund Agreement in the Courts—VIII," pp. 18–21 in this volume.

(iii) BGH Urt. v. 27.4.1970—II ZR 12/69 (Oldenburg), *Neue Juristische Wochenschrift,* Vol. 23 (August 20, 1970), pp. 1507–1508; Gold, "Fund Agreement in the Courts—X," pp. 139–49 in this volume.

(iv) BGH Urt. v. 17.2.1971—VIII ZR 84/69 (Frankfurt), *Neue Juristische Wochenschrift,* Vol. 24 (June 1, 1971), pp. 983–85; *Wertpapier-Mitteilungen,* No. 14 of April 3, 1971, pp. 411–12; Gold (cited in (iii) above), pp. 149–51 in this volume.

(v) BGH Urt. v. 11.3.1970—VIII ZR 147/68 (Düsseldorf), *Neue Juristische Wochenschrift,* Vol. 23 (May 27, 1970, p. 1002; Gold (cited in (iii) above), pp. 151–53 in this volume.

(vi) 21.12.1976—III ZR 83/74, *WM: Zeitschrift für Wirtschafts- und Bankrecht,* Jahrg. 31, No. 12 (March 19, 1977), pp. 332–34; Gold, "Fund Agreement in the Courts—XIV," pp. 272–77 in this volume.

certain amount in Spanish pesetas. The plaintiff sued in the Federal Republic of Germany to recover that amount from the defendant. The claim was for payment in pesetas, or alternatively in deutsche mark, and the plaintiff was also willing to have payment made to an account opened for him in Spain. The defendant argued that the plaintiff's claim was unenforceable as the result of Article VIII, Section 2(b). Both Spain and the Federal Republic of Germany were members of the Fund at all the times that could be relevant. The Regional Court dismissed the claim because it was in violation of Spanish exchange control regulations. The plaintiff then assigned his claim to a Spanish lawyer residing in Spain and petitioned the court to order payment to the assignee. The plaintiff succeeded in the Higher Regional Court and in the Court of Appeals. The defendant appealed to the Supreme Court, which endorsed the decision of the lower appellate tribunals.

The main aspects of the judgment of the Supreme Court are noted in the following paragraphs.

1. The court seems to have thought in one context, although it may have reserved the point elsewhere, that the agreement between the parties, under which the defendant (the appellant) acted as collection agent for the plaintiff (the respondent), was of a character that would have justified the conclusion that it was an exchange contract within the meaning of Article VIII, Section 2(b) had the provision been applicable. It would follow from this view that "exchange contracts" are not confined to contracts for the sale of one currency against another. That this has been the court's view is abundantly demonstrated by earlier cases.[22]

2. The court declared that the object of Article VIII, Section 2(b) is to protect the currencies of members, and for this reason the provision makes exchange contracts unenforceable if they are contrary to another member's exchange control regulations and have an effect on that member's balance of payments. Only the test of effect on the balance of payments should have normative influence in determining whether the currency of a member is involved within the meaning of the provision. The averment that the object of the provision is the protection of the currencies of other members is a broad but not comprehensive rationalization and should not be given normative effect. It implies that the purpose with which a member maintains or

---

[22] Gold, "Fund Agreement in the Courts—X," pp. 145–46 in this volume.

imposes exchange control regulations determines whether they are exchange control regulations within the meaning of Article VIII, Section 2(b), and that the provision applies only to those regulations that a member imposes to protect its currency.

Nothing in the provision supports that conclusion. The provision refers to exchange control regulations without any limitation relating to their purpose. It is true that frequently exchange control regulations are maintained or imposed in order to protect the currency of the legislator, that is, are applied for balance of payments reasons, but not invariably. They may be applied, for example, for the preservation of national or international security. The Fund has decided that restrictions imposed by exchange control regulations on the making of payments and transfers for current international transactions for these reasons are subject to its jurisdiction under Article VIII, Section 2(a).[23] Restrictions applied for these reasons are often intended to bring pressure to bear, through the medium of the balance of payments of the restricting member, on the balance of payments of a member that is responsible for a threat to national or international security.

The motives for exchange control regulations are diverse and not confined to those that have been mentioned. The motive may be, for example, the desire to protect an industry or agriculture, to levy taxation by an administrative procedure that is convenient, or to support the ties of a currency area. It should not be overlooked that there may be a mixture of motives, even when one of them is to protect the balance of payments.

The expression "exchange control regulations" cannot be restricted by reference to the motive or motives that have led to their adoption. The only qualification that exchange control regulations must satisfy in order to bring them within the scope of Article VIII, Section 2(b) is that they are "maintained or imposed consistently with this Agreement." This analysis is reinforced by the second sentence of Article VIII, Section 2(b), which authorizes members to cooperate by going beyond the refusal to enforce certain contracts:

> In addition, members may, by mutual accord, cooperate in measures for the purpose of making the exchange control regulations of either

---

[23] Executive Board Decision No. 144-(52/51), dated August 14, 1952, *Selected Decisions*, Eighth Issue, pp. 133–34. (*Selected Decisions*, Ninth Issue, pp. 203–204.)

member more effective, provided that such measures and regulations are consistent with this Agreement.[24]

Nothing in this sentence suggests that cooperation for making exchange control regulations more effective is authorized only if they are for the protection of the balance of payments of the member that is applying the regulations. The only condition once again is that the measures and regulations are consistent with the Articles.

There is a practical reason for skepticism about an interpretation that the motive of protecting the balance of payments determines whether exchange control regulations are within the scope of Article VIII, Section 2(b). Courts would have to find whether or not that motive is responsible for the exchange control regulations that are in issue in the litigation before them. This inquiry is a difficult one. The Fund is called upon to conduct it for various purposes in the course of its activities. Its findings are based on both subjective and objective elements. A member may announce its motive, but it may refrain. If it does declare that its intention in applying exchange control regulations is, or is not, to manage its balance of payments, the Fund will give the declaration the benefit of any reasonable doubt, but the Fund reserves the right to satisfy itself about the member's actual motive by taking account of objective facts. In this inquiry, the Fund may give weight to the effect of the regulations on the member's balance of payments and the exchange rate of its currency and on the balances of payments and currencies of other members as well, the member's domestic and external conditions or policies that help to explain its choice of the regulations, expectations as to the duration of the regulations, and the prevailing practice among members in applying regulations of the kind in issue for balance of payments or for other reasons.

3. The court pointed out that the plaintiff's claim was to the payment of Spanish pesetas by the defendant, a resident of Spain, to another resident of Spain. The payment, the court held, would be a domestic transaction with no impact on the balance of payments of Spain. There was no reason, therefore, why Article VIII, Section 2(b), which was designed to protect the balance of payments, should be applied.

---

[24] For a recent discussion of English law on extradition for the evasion of the exchange control regulations of a Commonwealth country, see *Regina v. Governor of Pentonville Prison, Ex Parte Khubchandani*, *The Times* (London), February 15, 1980, p. 25.

Furthermore, it was not clear to the court, and it had not been asserted by the defendant, that the payment demanded by the plaintiff would violate the exchange control regulations of Spain. This aspect of the case raises the question of the extent to which courts should take the initiative in addressing inquiries to the Fund for the purpose of applying Article VIII, Section 2(b). Judicial authority exists for the proposition that, as Article VIII, Section 2(b) is designed to promote public policy, the court should take the initiative in raising the question of the possible effect of the provision on the case before it, even if the parties have not relied on the provision. Moreover, an appellate court should take this step even if the lower court has not.[25] It can be assumed that a court willing to act in this way would make a prima facie finding that the provision might be relevant. Courts have also taken the initiative in asking the Fund whether the exchange control regulations in issue in proceedings brought before them are maintained or imposed consistently with the Articles.

The question raised by the case under discussion is whether the court should have taken the initiative to discover whether Spain applied exchange control regulations that affected the payment the plaintiff sought to have the defendant make. Whatever answer this question might receive in other circumstances, there would have been no point to an inquiry by the court in this case, because it found that Article VIII, Section 2(b) was not relevant. The court held that, in the absence of any effect on the balance of payments of Spain, the provision could not apply.

4. The defendant had argued that, in order to decide whether Article VIII, Section 2(b) was applicable, it was necessary to consider the facts at the time when the contract was entered into and not at the time when performance was sought. According to this test, Article VIII, Section 2(b) did render the contract unenforceable. The court, citing its established case law and the opinions of various authors, including the present author, held that, as the provision dealt with unenforceability and not validity, the facts at the date when enforcement is sought are decisive. This approach gives effect to the objective of protecting the balance of payments, which the court favored and which it understood to mean the present and not the past balance of payments. According to the practice of the court, the precise date at which the facts are relevant is when oral arguments have been concluded. At that date, the contract between the parties did not affect the balance of payments of Spain.

---

[25] Gold, "Fund Agreement in the Courts—XIV," p. 259 in this volume.

5. The defendant made the further argument that the plaintiff had interposed the assignee only as a "straw man" to evade the exchange control regulations. It is interesting to compare this aspect of the case with the English case that is discussed next. In the German case, the court refused to be swayed by the argument of the "straw man" for two reasons, neither of which faced the issue in substance. The first reason was purely procedural, the second partly procedural.

The first reason was that the argument had been made too late in the appellate proceedings to be entertained by the court. The second reason was that there had been no determination in the lower court of the question whether there had been an outright assignment or an assignment only for the purpose of collection. Even if the assignment was for collection only, it did not follow that the intention was to evade Spain's exchange regulations. The intention might have been to transfer the money to the Federal Republic of Germany only if transfer was permitted under the regulations, or the intention might have been to use the money to make valid payments for the plaintiff in Spain.

Subject to the caveat in (2) above, the judgment is in accord with the conclusions summarized in Section V of "The Fund Agreement in the Courts—XIV."[26]

UNITED CITY MERCHANTS (INVESTMENTS) LTD. AND GLASS FIBRES AND EQUIPMENTS LTD. V. ROYAL BANK OF CANADA, VITROREFUERZOS S.A., AND BANCO CONTINENTAL S.A. ("THE AMERICAN ACCORD"), 1979 [27]

A director (O) of a Peruvian company (Vitro), which operated in the glass fiber industry of Peru, negotiated a contract between his company and a British company (Glass Fibres) under which Glass Fibres would supply a plant to produce glass fiber against a confirmed and irrevocable letter of credit. O requested Glass Fibres to quote a price to Vitro that was double the price of the plant, because Vitro would need to make further purchases of equipment for its operations and because it would be more convenient and easier if a single letter of credit could be opened for all the purchases, including the purchase of the plant from Glass Fibres. The other purchases were to be made from suppliers in the United States, although it was not impossible to make some from Glass Fibres.

---

[26] Pp. 281–83 in this volume.
[27] Queen's Bench Division (United Kingdom), March 12, 1979, *Lloyd's Law Reports* 267.

Later, an agreement was entered into between Glass Fibres and a company (N Company) on the nomination of O, who was closely associated with it. N Company had an office in Miami, and the agreement was signed there. Under this agreement, Glass Fibres would remit to N Company 50 per cent of any amount duly drawn by Glass Fibres under the letter of credit in respect of the value of the goods it supplied, excluding freight.

Vitro then complied with the exchange control procedures of Peru, and Vitro's Peruvian bank (Banco Continental S.A.) opened an irrevocable letter of credit that was confirmed by the Royal Bank of Canada. The latter bank undertook to honor drafts drawn in accordance with the letter of credit by paying U.S. dollars in London. The credit provided for an immediate payment to Glass Fibres of 20 per cent of the f.o.b. value, and this amount was drawn. After complying with British exchange control regulations, Glass Fibres remitted 50 per cent of this payment to N Company in Miami. Subsequently, the payee to which Glass Fibres was to make remittances was changed from N Company to the Bankers Trust Company in Miami as payee, without the specification of any particular account at this bank. The Miami bank was informed by the London bank of Glass Fibres that it held irrevocable instructions from Glass Fibres to make the agreed remittances to the Miami bank. The total amount to be remitted was later reduced by agreement because of additional costs incurred by Glass Fibres for which Vitro was responsible.

Glass Fibres supplied the goods that it had contracted to provide, and presented its documents for payment under the letter of credit in December 1976. A dispute had developed between Vitro and Glass Fibres. The Peruvian issuing bank and Vitro took the position that payment should not be made, and the confirming bank, the Royal Bank of Canada, refused payment when the documents were presented. Glass Fibres and its London bank, United City Merchants (Investments) Ltd., to which Glass Fibres had assigned its rights under the letter of credit, sued the Royal Bank of Canada, which arranged for the Peruvian bank and Vitro to be joined as defendants. In the course of the proceedings, the Peruvian bank raised the defense of the violation of Peruvian exchange control regulations and unenforceability under Article VIII, Section 2(b). Subject to the later resolution of this issue, judgment was given in favor of the plaintiffs against the Royal Bank of Canada.

The exchange control regulations of Peru that were relied on in this case were Articles 1 and 2 of Decree Law No. 18275 and Article 7 of Decree Law No. 18891. Under Article 1 of the first of these laws, residents of Peru, with the exception of the Central Reserve Bank and the Banco de la Nación, were prohibited from maintaining and making deposits in foreign currency with Peruvian or foreign banks and other institutions. Under Article 2, residents were prohibited from maintaining or contracting credits or entering into contracts in foreign currency if the credits or contracts were to be executed in Peru. These provisions were intended to prohibit payments and transfers for international capital transactions but not to interfere with the making of payments and transfers for current international transactions. The provisions were consistent with the Articles of Agreement of the Fund under Article VI, Section 3 without the need for approval by the Fund.

Article 7 of Decree Law No. 18891 reads as follows:

> *Article 7.* The overvaluation of imports and obligations payable in foreign exchange, as well as the undervaluation of exports, in violation of the Regime of Foreign Exchange Certificates, shall constitute an offense of fraud against the State. Any person that commits the offense described in the preceding paragraph shall be penalized in accordance with Article 19 of Decree Law No. 18275. The Minister of Economy and Finance shall be competent to bring any such violations to the attention of the judicial authorities, through the assistance of the Attorney General of the Republic in charge of matters pertaining to that Ministry.
>
> All other violations of the provisions that regulate the Regime of Foreign Exchange Certificates shall be penalized as provided for in Articles 23 and 24 of Decree Law No. 17710.

This provision made misrepresentation of the value of the transactions referred to a violation of Peru's exchange control regulations and a criminal offense. This provision also was consistent with the Articles of the Fund without the necessity for approval by the Fund.

In response to an inquiry from the lawyers for one of the defendants, the Secretary of the Fund was authorized by the Executive Board to make the following statement:

> Articles One and Two of Decree Law No. 18275 and Article Seven of Decree Law No. 18891 did not, in themselves, involve any measures that were subject to approval by the Fund under Article VIII, during the period referred to. These Articles of the Decree Laws were consistent with the Fund's Articles and would not be rendered inconsistent by any necessity for the Fund's approval of other provisions of the Decree Laws.

The court held that the contract between Glass Fibres and Vitro was an exchange contract because it was a monetary transaction in disguise contrary to the exchange control regulations of Peru. It was unenforceable, therefore, under the Bretton Woods Agreements Order in Council that had given the force of law to Article VIII, Section 2(*b*) of the Fund's Articles of Agreement in the United Kingdom. If the plaintiffs could recover, remittances would be made in disregard of Peru's exchange control regulations and in circumvention of the Order in Council. The confirmed credit was unenforceable, therefore, and the Royal Bank of Canada was entitled to refuse to make payment.[28]

In *Wilson, Smithett & Cope Ltd. v. Terruzzi*,[29] the Court of Appeal in England held, incorrectly it has been submitted and in conflict with decisions of the highest courts in the Federal Republic of Germany and France,[30] that the concept of exchange contract in Article VIII, Section 2(*b*) is confined to contracts for the exchange of one currency against another. Lord Denning, Master of the Rolls, made the following reservation, however:

> It is no doubt possible for men of business to seek to avoid Article VIII, section 2(*b*), by various artifices. But I hope that the courts will be able to look at the substance of the contracts and not at the form. If the contracts are not legitimate contracts for the sale or purchase of merchandise or commodities, but are instead what Professor Nussbaum calls "monetary transactions in disguise," . . . as a means of manipulating currencies, they would be caught by section 2(*b*).[31]

The court did not sever the arrangements under which the Royal Bank of Canada was committed to make payments to the plaintiffs from the contract that had been entered into between Vitro and Glass Fibres. In *Sharif v. Azad*,[32] L (a resident of Pakistan) gave a check for Pakistani rupees to S (a resident of the United Kingdom) in return for pounds sterling. S gave the rupee check to B (also a resident of the United Kingdom) in return for a check for sterling. B filled in his brother's name as payee in the rupee check. The Pakistani authorities blocked the rupee proceeds of that check because they suspected that there had been a violation of Pakistan's exchange

---

[28] "Bank's Commercial Credit: Illegality," *New Law Journal* (London, March 29, 1979), p. 317; "Enforcing a Contract Which Violates Exchange Controls," *International Practitioner's Notebook*, No. 8 (New York, November 1979).

[29] [1976] 1 Q.B. 683; [1976] 1 Q.B. 703 (C.A.).

[30] See pp. 20, 145, 150, 151, and 191 in this volume.

[31] [1976] 1 Q.B., at 714.

[32] [1966] 3 All E.R. 785, at 789–90.

control regulations. B stopped payment of the sterling check and S sued him. The Court of Appeal held that, although a claim under the rupee check would have been unenforceable, the claim under the sterling check by one resident of the United Kingdom against another resident was severable and enforceable.[33] Possibly, *Sharif v. Azad* was distinguished on the ground that the first transaction—the exchange of the rupee check for pounds sterling—was in violation of Pakistan's exchange control regulations, but recovery in the second transaction —the exchange of that rupee check for a sterling check—would not be a violation in itself and would not lead to a further violation of Pakistan's regulations. In the case involving Peru's exchange control regulations, it may have been assumed that recovery against the Royal Bank of Canada would lead to a violation in the form of a remittance of part of the recovery to the Miami bank.

The judgment has not been reported at this time, and it is not possible, therefore, to describe how the court dealt with the principle that normally a letter of credit is independent of the underlying contract that gives rise to it.

III. Exchange Rates

FRATELLI ZERBONE S.N.C. v. AMMINISTRAZIONE DELLE FINANZE DELLO STATO (JUDGMENT OF COURT OF JUSTICE OF EUROPEAN COMMUNITIES, JANUARY 31, 1978) [34]

The European Court of Justice in this case had to consider a number of legal issues involving the application of monetary compensatory amounts in a total exceeding 140 million Italian lire to imports of frozen meat from various Latin American countries by an Italian importer. The contracts prescribed payments in U.S. dollars. One of the issues in the case turned on whether the Italian lira had been revalued as a result of the Smithsonian agreement and the Fund's Executive Board Decision No. 3463-(71/126) of December 18, 1971 on central rates and wider margins.[35] The court was aware of the correct legal character of exchange rates under that decision, but misunderstood the effect of Italy's central rate as communicated to the Fund under it.

---

[33] Gold, "Fund Agreement in the Courts—IX," pp. 107–16 in this volume.
[34] Case 94/77 [1978] E.C.R. 99.
[35] *Selected Decisions*, Eighth Issue, pp. 14–17.

The issue depended on the meaning and application of Article 1(1) of Regulation (EEC) No. 974/71:

> If, for the purposes of commercial transactions, a Member State allows the exchange rate of its currency to fluctuate by a margin wider than the one permitted by international rules, it shall be authorised to:
> (a) charge on imports from Member States and third countries,
> (b) grant on exports to Member States and third countries,
> compensatory amounts for the products referred to below under the conditions determined hereinafter.

The regulation was understood to authorize the imposition of monetary compensatory amounts only if a currency fluctuated upward, that is, was revalued or appreciated, but the question was revaluation or appreciation in relation to what standard?

To answer this question, it was necessary to determine what was meant by the words "international rules" in the regulation. The court interpreted these words to refer to the provisions on par values under the Articles. The words did not cover Executive Board Decision No. 3463-(71/126) because, as the decision itself recognized, the decision did not, and could not, validate the practices it recommended in order to minimize disorder in conditions that were inconsistent with the Articles. It followed that the standard by which to determine whether the lira had appreciated was the par value of the currency that had been established under the Articles. That par value was Lit 625 per U.S. dollar of July 1, 1944, with a possibility of fluctuation up to 1 per cent on either side of parity. The par value had not been changed, but Italy declared a central rate of Lit 581.50 per U.S. dollar with margins of 2.25 per cent on either side of this relationship with the U.S. dollar. The court concluded, therefore, that there had been an appreciation of the lira that, on this part of the case, would justify the imposition of monetary compensatory amounts.

This conclusion was incorrect. The central rate of Lit 581.50 per U.S. dollar as adopted by Italy was in relation to the current U.S. dollar and not the U.S. dollar of the weight and fineness of gold in effect on July 1, 1944. Under the "international rules" of the Articles, the par value for the lira was established in terms of gold and the U.S. dollar of 1944. Under the court's finding, the standard for determining whether there had been an appreciation was the relationship between the Italian lira and the U.S. dollar of 1944. The current U.S. dollar in terms of which the central rate was communicated was not the dollar of 1944, because the United States undertook in the Smithsonian agreement to propose a devaluation of the dollar from US$35 to

US$38 per fine ounce of gold, but it was understood that this change would take effect immediately in the exchange markets. The central rate was expressed in relation to this depreciated dollar. Executive Board Decision No. 3463-(71/126) recognized that central rates could be communicated in terms of this decision by referring not to the "parity" between a currency and the U.S. dollar but to "the effective parity relationship."[36]

The situation of the Italian lira, therefore, was as follows. As part of the Smithsonian agreement, the lira was to be devalued by 1 per cent in relation to the par value of Lit 625 per U.S. dollar of 1944. The current U.S. dollar depreciated immediately by 7.89 per cent against the dollar of 1944. The effect was an appreciation of the lira in the market of 7.48 per cent against the current U.S. dollar. This datum, however, was irrelevant under the court's ruling on what was meant by international rules. The only relevant datum was the devaluation of 1 per cent against the par value of the lira. The rates of exchange for the lira at the critical dates were maintained within the wider margins around the central rate in accordance with the decision. If these rates of exchange had been in accordance with "international rules," there would have been neither an appreciation nor a depreciation for the purposes of Regulation (EEC) No. 974/71. Once it was concluded, correctly, that the only standard compatible with "international rules" was the par value, it followed inexorably that the lira had been devalued and not revalued, or had not appreciated to use the language of the court. The relationship of the lira to the dollar of 1944 was the same as it was to the SDR, which was defined at the relevant date in terms of gold (i.e., 0.888671 gram of fine gold).[37] The relationship was Lit 631.343 per U.S. dollar, compared with the parity derived from par values of Lit 625 per U.S. dollar.

---

[36] *Ibid.*, p. 14.
[37] Article XXI, Section 2, *first.*

10

The Fund Agreement in the Courts—XVI*

This sixteenth installment in the series dealing with the effect of the Articles of Agreement of the International Monetary Fund on litigation examines a proceeding before an arbitral tribunal established under the Agreement on German External Debts in which the main issue was the meaning of the expression "the least depreciated currency" in relation to two revaluations of the deutsche mark. An important facet of this issue was whether the expression had to be understood within the context of the international monetary order established by the Articles.

"The Least Depreciated Currency"

On May 16, 1980, the Arbitral Tribunal for the Agreement on German External Debts, consisting of seven members, delivered a decision in the case of *The Government of the Kingdom of Belgium, the Government of the French Republic, the Swiss Federal Council, the Government of the United Kingdom of Great Britain and Northern Ireland, the Government of the United States of America, Applicants v. the Government of the Federal Republic of Germany, Respondent.*[1] The decision, which was concurred in by a majority of four

---

* Originally published in June 1981.

[1] *International Legal Materials*, Vol. 19 (November 1980), pp. 1357–1408; *Revue générale de droit international public*, Vol. 84 (1980), pp. 1157–1245; François Gianviti, "Garantie de Change et Réévaluation Monétaire : L'Affaire de l'Emprunt Young (Sentence du 16 Mai 1980 du Tribunal d'Arbitrage des Dettes Extérieures Allemandes)," *Annuaire Français de Droit International*, Vol. XXVI (1980), pp. 250–73. See also *German Yearbook of International Law*, Vol. 23 (1980),

members with three members dissenting, dealt with the interpretation of Article 13 of the Agreement on German External Debts, London, 27 February 1953.[2] The Agreement will be referred to as the LDA (London Debt Agreement) in this discussion of the majority and minority opinions of the arbitrators. The opinions and submissions of the parties take account of various aspects of the Fund's Articles.

BACKGROUND OF THE CASE

Under the Versailles Peace Treaty of July 28, 1919, Germany agreed to pay compensation for losses sustained as a result of the First World War. In April 1921, the amount of reparations was fixed at 132 billion gold marks, and a plan for payments was imposed in May 1921. Germany was unable to perform its obligations under this plan. A scheme—the Dawes Plan—was worked out to reduce the war debt. To help to stabilize the German currency and pay the debt, a foreign loan of 800 million gold marks was negotiated in various currencies. Reparation and interest payments on U.S. dollar bonds, which were issued in the United States, were to be made in gold. In September 1928, a new effort was made to solve the problem of reparations. The result was the Young Plan, under which the reparations debt was to be paid in annual installments. A proportion amounting to US$600 million was to be payable in foreign currency, but payments under the Dawes loan were to be set off against this sum. A further agreement to carry out the purpose of the Young Plan took effect in 1930. It provided for the issue in international markets of loan bonds in nine currencies, for a total value of $300 million. The Bank for International Settlements (BIS) was formed to ensure observance of commitments under the Young Plan. It acted as Trustee for creditors under the loan, and it drafted the General Bond, which was signed on June 10, 1930. The General Bond, which set forth the conditions for the loan bonds, including a gold clause, took the form of an agreement between the German Government and the BIS as Trustee for the holders of issued and outstanding bonds. Only part of the obligations was met in accordance with the terms of the General Bond before the Second World War.

In order to integrate the Federal Republic, which was founded in 1949, into the world economy, it was considered necessary to settle

---

pp. 414–87, and Ignaz Seidl-Hohenveldern, "Zum Urteil des Schiedsgerichtshofes für das Abkommen über deutsche Auslandsschulden zur Young-Anleihe," *German Yearbook of International Law*, Vol. 23 (1980), pp. 401–13.

[2] *United Nations Treaty Series*, Vol. 333 (1959), pp. 4–449.

the problem of outstanding foreign debts. The Government of the Federal Republic accepted liability for outstanding prewar debt and expressed its willingness to join in a plan for settlement of the debts of the Government and of public authorities, including debts in respect of the economic aid received after 1945, and all arrears of interest. In April 1951, the three Western occupying powers (hereinafter referred to as the Three Powers) set up the Tripartite Commission on German Debts to act on their behalf in the negotiation of a settlement. The Commission was to prepare a plan for settlement, which would be incorporated in an agreement among participating governments. The Three Powers made it clear that the settlement would not provide unfair or privileged treatment for any group of creditors and that the terms of settlement would include no variation based on the currencies in which obligations were expressed.

The meetings of the Tripartite Commission with representatives of the Federal Republic were attended on occasion by observers from the Belgian, Dutch, Swedish, and Swiss Governments and representatives of German debtor interests. The Tripartite Commission announced the willingness of the Three Powers to forgo substantial proportions of their claims in respect of economic aid given after the Second World War.

The Conference on German External Debts opened in London on February 28, 1952 and continued until August of that year. The Tripartite Commission represented the Three Powers; the private creditors of these countries were represented by separate delegations; 22 creditor countries sent national delegations composed of governmental representatives and, in many cases, representatives of private creditors; 3 countries sent observers; the BIS was represented as a creditor in its own right; and the delegation of the Federal Republic included representatives of the Government and of private debtors.

The German representatives pointed out that a gold clause would be invalid under both U.S. and German law and deduced that creditors would have to be satisfied with payments in currencies in their depreciated state. The Tripartite Commission also objected to a gold clause as a term of the settlement, but did not object to a protective clause in some other form. Other delegations insisted on a gold clause, because they considered it to be the most important feature of their existing rights. Various protective clauses were proposed as compromises, but, until a solution was found, they were resisted as favoring one group of creditors over another.

The LDA gave effect to the understandings reached in the London Conference. It was signed by the Federal Republic of Germany, the states represented by the Tripartite Commission, and 15 other creditor countries. Subsequently, other countries acceded to the agreement. The three texts—English, French, and German—in which the LDA was written were equally authentic.

CLAUSE IN DISPUTE

Article 2 of Annex I, Section A of the LDA dealt with outstanding obligations resulting from the Young Plan. Article 2(e) provided that the amounts due in respect of the various issues of the 1930 loan were to be payable only in the currency of the country in which the issue was made. The basis for calculating the amount of currency payable was to be the amount in U.S. dollars to which the payment due in a currency would have been equivalent at the rates of exchange ruling when the loan was issued. The nominal amount of U.S. dollars arrived at in this way was to be reconverted into a currency of payment at the rate of exchange on August 1, 1952. Conversion Bonds were issued for an amount in the original currency arrived at in this way. The nominal value of the American issue was the same in Extension Bonds as the nominal value of the bonds issued in 1930. Bonds issued originally with a nominal value of DM 1,000 became Conversion Bonds with a nominal value of DM 1,000.50.

The second part of Article 2(e) is the protective clause on which agreement was reached for the benefit of Young Loan bondholders, and which became the subject of controversy. The text in the three languages is as follows:

> Should the rates of exchange ruling any of the currencies of issue on 1st August, 1952, alter thereafter by 5 per cent. or more, the instalments due after that date, while still being made in the currency of the country of issue, shall be calculated on the basis of the least depreciated currency (in relation to the rate of exchange current on 1st August, 1952) reconverted into the currency of issue at the rate of exchange current when the payment in question becomes due.

> Au cas où les taux de change en vigueur le 1er août 1952 entre deux ou plusieurs monnaies d'émission subiraient par la suite une modification égale ou supérieure à 5%, les versements exigibles après cette date, tout en continuant à être effectués dans la monnaie du pays d'émission, seront calculés sur la base de la devise la moins dépréciée par rapport au taux de change en vigueur au 1er août 1952, puis reconvertis dans la

309

monnaie d'émission sur la base du taux de change en vigueur lors de l'échéance du paiement.

Sollte sich der am 1. August 1952 für eine der Emissionswährungen massgebende Wechselkurs später um 5 v.H. oder mehr ändern, so sind die nach diesem Zeitpunkt fälligen Raten zwar nach wie vor in der Währung des Emissionslandes zu leisten; sie sind jedoch auf der Grundlage der Währung mit der geringsten Abwertung (im Verhältnis zu dem Wechselkurs vom 1. August 1952) zu berechnen und zu dem im Zeitpunkt der Fälligkeit der betreffenden Zahlung massgebenden Wechselkurs wieder in die Emissionswährung umzurechnen.

Changes in External Value of Currencies

The majority of the tribunal noted that there was no "agreed rate" for the French franc from January 26, 1948 to December 29, 1958. This reference was to the period that began with the adoption of an "unauthorized change" of par value, to use the language of Article IV, Section 6 of the Fund's original Articles,[3] and terminated with the establishment of a par value in which the Fund concurred. The initial par value of the French franc established under the Articles was 0.00746113 gram of fine gold per franc, or 0.839583 U.S. cent per franc; the corresponding figures for the new par value were 0.00180000 and 0.202550. In 1957, France adopted a system under which a 20 per cent surcharge was imposed on all outgoing payments and a 20 per cent premium was paid on all incoming payments. The Fund regarded this system as equivalent in economic terms to a devaluation.[4]

The protective clause was applied to the changes in external value of the French franc in both 1957 and 1958. The U.S. dollar was treated on both occasions as "the least depreciated currency," and the new external value of the French franc on each occasion was taken to exceed the test of 5 per cent in Article 2(e) of Annex I, Section A of the LDA. The BIS, as Trustee for the bondholders, pointed out that the implication of applying the clause was that the expression "the least depreciated currency" covered a currency that had not depreciated. It appeared to the BIS that the expression was not quite adequate.[5]

---

[3] Gold, *Selected Essays*, pp. 540–41, 554–56; Joseph Gold, "Unauthorized Changes of Par Value and Fluctuating Exchange Rates in the Bretton Woods System," *American Journal of International Law*, Vol. 65 (1971), pp. 113–28.

[4] *Annual Report, 1958*, p. 94.

[5] Article 13(c) of the LDA was applied on both occasions because there did not exist at the relevant dates "a par value agreed" with the Fund or a rate of exchange under a bilateral payments agreement between the United States and France.

The first revaluation of the deutsche mark took place in 1961. The majority cited the following exchange rates and percentage changes between that currency and the U.S. dollar:

August 1, 1952   DM 4.20 = US$1
                  DM 1   = US$0.238095
March 6, 1961   DM 4   = US$1
                  DM 1   = US$0.25

The exchange value of one deutsche mark had increased by 1.1905 U.S. cents, or 5.000105 per cent of the exchange rate on August 1, 1952; the price of one U.S. dollar had been reduced by DM 0.20, or 4.761905 per cent of the exchange rate on that date. The majority referred to the "exchange rates" on the two dates, but the numbers represent the parity between the two currencies that resulted from the par values that were established for them under the Fund's Articles. Parities as a concept did not correspond to exchange rates, because rates were free to fluctuate provided that they did not move outside margins around parity that were consistent with the Articles.[6] The references by the majority to "exchange rates" were dictated no doubt by the terminology of Article 2(e) of Annex I, Section A of the LDA, but under Article 13(a) of the LDA an exchange rate for the purposes of the LDA meant, with some exceptions not relevant here, par values "in force . . . as agreed" with the Fund on the relevant date.

It followed from the values mentioned above that a change of 5 per cent or more from the "exchange rates" ruling on August 1, 1952 had occurred if the change in the parity between the two currencies was expressed as an "appreciation" of the deutsche mark against the U.S. dollar but not as a "depreciation" of the U.S. dollar against the deutsche mark. The majority did not discriminate between this terminology and the terminology of "revaluation" and "devaluation."

The BIS, on May 27, 1961, notified the Federal Debt Administration (FDA), the appropriate agency of the Federal Republic, that payments subsequent to the revaluation of the deutsche mark had to be adjusted because all currencies of issue had depreciated against the deutsche mark and because the test of the minimum of 5 per cent had been met in 1957 and had become irrelevant thereafter. The FDA rejected this claim on the basis of its understanding of the protective clause. The BIS informed the five governments that were the applicants in this proceeding of the FDA's reaction and recom-

---

[6] Article IV, Sections 3 and 4, *original*.

mended recourse to the arbitral tribunal that, under the LDA, had exclusive jurisdiction in all disputes regarding the interpretation or application of the LDA.

The deutsche mark was revalued again in 1969. The majority described this action as a change of 12.587 per cent in the 1952 rate of exchange for the U.S. dollar.[7] The German Government again refused to adjust payments. Negotiation did not dispose of the difference of opinion, and the five applicant governments instituted proceedings against the German Government in May 1971.

PRINCIPAL CONTENTIONS OF THE PARTIES

The main arguments of the applicants were, first, that Article 2(e) of Annex I, Section A of the LDA applied not only to the depreciation but also to the appreciation of a currency of issue. The English and French texts referred to "depreciation" and "*dépréciation*," which, unlike "devaluation" and "*dévaluation*," comprised the loss of a currency's value even if it was not the result of a governmental act. An appreciation of a currency automatically meant the depreciation of all other currencies in this broader sense.

Second, the object, purpose, and history of the LDA supported this analysis because the LDA was intended to achieve a fair settlement of German indebtedness in circumstances in which settlement had been made possible only because private creditors and their governments had waived a substantial part of their claims. The respondent's obligation to permit all creditors to have the benefit of an appreciation of the deutsche mark followed from the prohibition of discrimination among classes of creditors that was imposed by Article 8 of the LDA and was a fundamental principle of the LDA. If this interpretation was not adopted, bondholders entitled to receive payment in deutsche mark would receive more favorable treatment on a revaluation of that currency because they would not receive less than the principal amount as calculated on the basis of exchange rates ruling on August 1, 1952.

The applicants asked the tribunal to adjudge that the revaluations of the deutsche mark gave rise to the application of the protective

---

[7] The two changes in the par value of the deutsche mark and the effective dates of the changes were as follows:

Date	Gram of Fine Gold per Deutsche Mark	U.S. Cents per Deutsche Mark
March 6, 1961	0.222168	25.0000
October 26, 1969	0.242806	27.3224

clause and entitled the holders of each issue made in a non-German currency to have payments falling due after a revaluation made on the basis of the rate of exchange between the deutsche mark and the currency of issue on the due date.

The respondent moved to have the tribunal reject the applicants' submissions on the ground that the LDA should be interpreted according to the circumstances at the time when the LDA was negotiated. At that time, no participant thought of an appreciation of the deutsche mark. The clause was intended only as protection against devaluation of a currency of payment (i.e., a reduction in value by governmental action) as was demonstrated by the language of the German text. The revaluation of the deutsche mark had not led to a change under the Articles in the par values of the currencies of the creditor countries, and therefore an increase in the amounts due in those currencies was not justified according to Article 13 of the LDA. The respondent, in arguing that the protective clause did not apply on the occasion of the appreciation of a currency, conceded that the expression "the least depreciated currency" applied to a currency that had neither appreciated nor depreciated as well as to a currency that had depreciated.

The respondent also argued that the condition of a change of 5 per cent or more in the disputed clause was not satisfied for all time by the depreciation of a single currency on a single occasion. The clause was applicable each time that a currency of issue depreciated by 5 per cent or more, compared with its position on August 1, 1952, or when, as a result of several depreciations of less than 5 per cent each, a cumulative depreciation of 5 per cent or more was reached, compared with the position on August 1, 1952. The tribunal did not rule on this question because its conclusion on the meaning of "the least depreciated currency" made a ruling unnecessary.

MAJORITY DECISION

The majority [8] approached the problems of interpretation by invoking provisions of the Vienna Convention on the Law of Treaties of May 23, 1969. The Convention did not apply in the proceedings, but the view was widespread that the Convention, at least in regard to interpretation, was a codification of existing customary law. The majority relied mainly on Article 31 (1) of the Convention: "A treaty

---

[8] Issues involving the jurisdiction of the tribunal are not examined in this chapter.

313

shall be interpreted in good faith in accordance with the ordinary meaning to be given to the terms of the treaty in their context and in the light of its object and purpose." The decisive words to be interpreted were *"Abwertung,"* "depreciation," and *"dépréciation."*

The majority declared that it had to give equal effect to all three texts. The ordinary and everyday sense of the crucial terms might lead to one interpretation of *"Abwertung"* and a different interpretation of "depreciation" and *"dépréciation."* Although *"Abwertung"* in proper technical language meant a reduction by governmental action in the external value of a currency in relation to a yardstick such as gold, some uncertainty was introduced by the tendency to describe this phenomenon as *"formelle Abwertung"* in everyday usage. The English and French words, however, were used normally to describe a loss of value however it came about, while the result of governmental action was usually termed "devaluation" or *"dévaluation."* Even if "depreciation" and *"dépréciation"* could be distinguished from "devaluation" and *"dévaluation"* in this way in the two languages, they were also used interchangeably in both everyday and technical language. The *International Monetary Fund, 1945–1965: Twenty Years of International Monetary Cooperation,* which was published by the Fund, was among the sources cited for this indiscriminate practice. The majority concluded that the possibility of different meanings for the three texts could not be ruled out, which meant that the wording of the disputed clause offered no clear guidance in the attempt to arrive at the intended meaning and to give concordance to the interpretation of the texts.

No clearer guidance could be obtained by concentrating on the normal meaning of the terms at the time that the LDA was concluded. The words "depreciation" and *"dépréciation"* were often used interchangeably with "devaluation" and *"dévaluation"* even when the par value system was still in operation in accordance with the Fund's Articles. The fungibility of these terms could be demonstrated by reference to Article I(iii) of the original Articles, which referred to "competitive exchange depreciation." In the system of par values agreed with the Fund, this concept could refer only to devaluation.

Textual interpretation could not resolve the vagueness of the terms in the English and French texts and the possible discrepancy between them and the German version, and it was necessary, therefore, to examine them "in their context" as required by Article 31 (1) of the Vienna Convention. "Context" meant the language of the disputed clause as a whole and the LDA as a whole. The applicants argued that the word "alter" ("*ändern,*" "*subir une modification*") in relation to exchange rates in the first part of the disputed clause was appropriate for both a rise and a fall in an exchange rate, with the consequence that the clause would apply if a currency were revalued. The applicants argued from this premise that the word "depreciated" (and its equivalents) in the latter part of the clause must be given the larger meaning. The majority did not accept the logic of this argument: the word "alter" did not necessarily control the meaning of "depreciated."

The applicants contested the respondent's argument that the word "depreciation" and its equivalents meant only devaluation on the ground that this construction could lead to inequitable results. If a single currency were revalued and all others were equally devalued, or if only one currency were devalued and all others remained unchanged or were revalued, no upward adjustment could be made because there would be no "least depreciated currency" to serve as a standard for payment in a devalued currency. The majority rejected this argument on the ground that the basis for adjustment in these cases would be the nondevalued currency before its revaluation. A nondevalued currency could be considered as "least depreciated" even though a revalued currency could not. The position would be unreasonable if payment in a devalued currency could not be adjusted because another currency had not been devalued but instead had been revalued.[9]

The majority, in considering the LDA as a whole, gave special weight to Article 13 because that provision would have to apply if an adjustment had to be made under the disputed clause. There was a direct link, therefore, between the two provisions. The text of Article 13 is as follows:

> Wherever it is provided in the present Agreement and the Annexes thereto that an amount shall be calculated on the basis of a rate of exchange, such rate shall, except in the cases provided for in Annex III and in Article 8 of Annex IV of the present Agreement, be—
>
> (a) determined by the par values of the currencies concerned in force on the appropriate date as agreed with the International Monetary Fund under Article IV, Section 1, of the Articles of Agreement of the International Monetary Fund; or

---

[9] The minority did not subscribe to the view that the respondent's argument permitted the solution offered by the majority. The consequential unreasonableness demonstrated that the respondent's argument was wrong.

(b) if no such par values are or were in force on the appropriate date, the rate of exchange agreed for current payments in a bilateral payments agreement between the Governments concerned or their monetary authorities; or

(c) if neither par values nor rates in bilateral payments agreements are or were in force on the appropriate date, the middle rate of exchange generally applicable for transactions ruling for cable transfers in the currency of the country in which payment is to be made in the principal exchange market of the other country on that date, or on the last date before that date on which such rate was ruling; or

(d) if there is or was no rate of exchange as specified under (a), (b) or (c) at the appropriate date, the cross-rate of exchange resulting from the middle rates of exchange ruling for the currencies in question in the principal exchange market of a third country dealing in those currencies on that date or the last date before the said date upon which such rates were ruling.

Under this provision, the majority declared, par values "in force . . . as agreed" with the Fund had precedence in the determination of exchange rates. In 1952, all the parties concerned, except Switzerland, were members of the Fund, and all these members, except France, had par values in force as agreed with the Fund. The importance of Article 13, the majority held, was that by means of it the LDA in matters of monetary law was expressly fitted into the structure of the Bretton Woods system. The essential framework of this system was the par value agreed between a member and the Fund and the bonding of exchange rates to the par value.

A consequence of the system was the unacceptability of the applicants' argument that the revaluation of one currency automatically meant a depreciation of all currencies not simultaneously revalued. If the deutsche mark was revalued, the purchaser of this currency for Belgian francs had to spend more Belgian francs than would have been necessary before the revaluation, but this result was not the consequence of a devaluation of the Belgian franc in terms of gold or the U.S. dollar of fixed gold content under the Articles. The relationship of the Belgian franc to currencies other than the deutsche mark remained unchanged. The value of the Belgian franc in terms of them would be reduced only if it were devalued. There was no depreciation of the Belgian franc in the sense in which the disputed clause used this term within the framework of monetary law as it stood when the LDA was negotiated.

The majority attached importance also to the fact that in 1961 and 1969, when the revaluations of the deutsche mark occurred, all the applicants, except Switzerland, had par values that came within the terms of Article 13(*a*) of the LDA. The par values of members other than the Federal Republic of Germany had not been changed by the revaluations and would have to be applied under Article 13(*a*) in any necessary determinations under that provision.

The applicants had questioned recourse to Article 13 as an aid to interpretation, arguing that it was a purely technical provision and that there were different German expressions in the texts of Article 13 and the disputed clause. Article 13 referred to *"Umrechnungskurs"* (*"*conversion rate*"*) while the disputed clause referred to *"Wechselkurs"* (*"*exchange rate*"*). The latter expression, they argued, usually described the relation between or among currencies. The exchange rate for a currency could change without action by the government of the issuer. The majority rejected this argument, in part because there was no similar discrepancy in the English and French texts, which used *"*rate of exchange*"* and *"taux de change"* in both provisions, and in part because a study of the German text of Article 13 as a whole showed that *"Umrechnungskurs"* was used in that context to mean exchange rate.

To support the view that the disputed clause had nothing to do with gold or the U.S. dollar of fixed gold content as the common denominator of par values under the Articles, the applicants relied on the English case *Lively Ltd. and Another v. City of Munich.*[10] That case has been discussed in the thirteenth installment in this series of *The Fund Agreement in the Courts.*[11] A loan to the City of Munich in 1928 fell within the ambit of the LDA, under which the maturity date became December 1, 1973 instead of December 1, 1953. The issue in the case was whether the amount payable at the later date was to be calculated according to Article 13(*a*) or Article 13(*c*) of the LDA. Par values were still in existence under the law of the Fund, but the par value system had collapsed. The court preferred Article 13(*c*) because of the collapse. The majority held that the case did not support the applicants because the situation in 1973 was different from the situations in 1961 and 1969 with which the tribunal was concerned. The case did support the respondent's view, however, that the word *"*depreciated*"* in the disputed clause could be interpreted by reference to Article 13(*a*) in circumstances in which the relevant facts antedated the time at which it became appropriate to apply Article 13(*c*).

---

[10] [1976] 3 All E.R. 851.
[11] Pp. 236–41 in this volume.

The applicants argued that the prohibition of discrimination among classes of creditors under Article 8 of the LDA was part of the context that had to be considered in the interpretative process. The principle of equal treatment would be violated if other classes of creditors under the Young Loan did not receive as much value as the holders of the German issue after the revaluations of the deutsche mark. The tribunal agreed there was inequality, but it was countenanced by Article 8, which provided that differential treatment was not proscribed if it was the result of a "settlement in accordance with the provisions of the present Agreement and the Annexes thereto." The inequality in this case followed from Article 13 and the disputed clause. Moreover, the prohibition of Article 8 ensured only *pari passu* treatment of bondholders and other creditors in the servicing of loans, as provided for by the General Bond, and not equality in the value of redemption payments.[12] The prohibition meant that other creditors were not to rank ahead of bondholders in the receipt of repayment if the debtor was unable to repay both classes fully and uniformly at the same time.

The majority, pursuing its approach under Article 31(1) of the Vienna Convention, turned to the "object and purpose" of the LDA. The object was the settlement of German external debts, and the purpose a fair compromise, in order that the German economy could recover and the plan of settlement could be honored. This end could be achieved only if foreign creditors were prepared to waive a substantial part of their claims and refrain from placing an intolerable burden on the German economy. Problems of interpretation had to be resolved in this spirit and from the standpoint of the circumstances that existed in 1952. Neither the spirit nor the circumstances could be ignored because of the strength and speed of the economic recovery of the Federal Republic. The majority did not accept the applicants' argument that a broad interpretation was appropriate because of the applicants' concessions and the continuing strength of the German recovery.

The majority concluded, finally, that the approach it had taken in accordance with Article 31(1) of the Vienna Convention resolved the problem of reconciling the three texts of the LDA. Even if the view were accepted that there was an irreconcilable discrepancy between the German text and the other two texts, the German text and the

---

[12] The majority found further support in Article V(2)(b) of Annex II and Section B, Article 7 of Annex IV of the LDA for the conclusions it drew from the context.

strict meaning of *"Abwertung"* would prevail because of the principle of Article 33(4) of the Vienna Convention. According to that principle, when several authentic texts cannot be reconciled and a discrepancy remains, the meaning to be preferred is the one that "best reconciles the texts, having regard to the object and purpose of the treaty." The German text most closely approached the object and purpose of the LDA.

The majority, who began by referring to the word *"Abwertung"* as "relatively clear" and as affected by "at least, some uncertainty," ended by describing the word as having "quite unequivocal meaning."

DISSENTING OPINION

The minority also relied for guidance on Articles 31 and 33 of the Vienna Convention. The opinion begins by emphasizing that the object and purpose of the LDA was a fair and equitable settlement for debtors and creditors. This intention was expressed in Article 8 of the LDA, which prohibited "any discrimination or preferential treatment among the different categories of debts or as regards the currencies in which debts are to be paid or in any other respect." Any provision of the LDA that required interpretation and did not come within the exception to the general principle of Article 8 had to be interpreted to give effect to this principle. It would not accord with the object and purpose of the LDA to give the disputed clause an interpretation under which the tranche issued in German currency and tranches issued in other currencies would not receive equality of treatment.

The minority's understanding of the text of the disputed clause, confirmed by its reading of the *travaux préparatoires,* was that a fixed pattern of relationships was established among all the currencies of issue on the basis of exchange rates as of August 1, 1952, with the intention that each bondholder when paid would receive equality of treatment in terms of U.S. dollar value as of August 1, 1952. The disputed clause referred to exchange rates, which meant the relationships among currencies, and not relationships to some external and fixed standard. The clause applied therefore to both rises and falls in a rate of exchange. If the exchange rate for one currency rose, the exchange rates for other currencies fell. The drafters had intended to replace a gold clause with a general or multiple currency exchange guarantee against changes in the exchange rates of all currencies of issue and not simply protection against the devaluation (*"Abwertung"*) of a currency of issue in which payment was to be made.

The guarantee came into play whenever an alteration of 5 per cent or more occurred in the exchange rate, whether that alteration was the result of devaluation or revaluation or some other cause of depreciation or appreciation. The term "the least depreciated currency" should not be understood as a technical expression that restricted the ordinary and broad meaning of the opening part of the disputed clause ("alter," "ändern," "subiraient . . . une modification"). The search for the least depreciated currency arose as a basis for calculation only after it had been determined that an alteration had brought the guarantee into play.

The fallacy in the respondent's argument, the minority held, was its concentration on gold as the standard and on each currency separately in relation to it. The argument was based on the assumption that the guarantee under the LDA gave no more protection than was given by the original gold clause, namely, protection against the formal devaluation of the currency of issue and payment. This assumption was incorrect because the guarantee was intended to give bondholders the benefit of the most favorable currency among all the currencies of issue. A multiple currency exchange guarantee of this kind was normal, and it was not surprising that the way it operated on the revaluation of one of the currencies was not spelled out when the guarantee was adopted.

The majority, recalling that the Vienna Convention permitted recourse to *travaux préparatoires* to confirm an interpretation arrived at with the aid of the rules of Article 31, examined the preparatory work of the LDA. The majority and the minority took different views on the positive support they found for their conclusions in the *travaux préparatoires*.

A similar difference of opinion appears in the reaction to the practice that had been followed after the entry into force of the LDA. Under the Vienna Convention, interpretation must take account of subsequent agreements among contracting parties on interpreting the treaty and of subsequent practice in applying it, from which a consensus on interpretation might be inferred. The majority examined statements by the parties to the LDA in the period between the signing of it in 1952 and the first revaluation of the deutsche mark in 1961 but found them too contradictory to provide any assistance. The minority attached importance to what happened after the *de facto* alteration of the exchange rate for the French franc in 1957. The alteration was taken into account when subsequent payments were made in French francs, even though France had made no change in the official rate of the franc in relation to other currencies or in the par value of its currency under the Fund's Articles. This action was an unequivocal acceptance of the view that *"Abwertung"* did not have the strict meaning of devaluation as contended by the respondent. Moreover, the adjustment was calculated by reference to the U.S. dollar, which was accepted as "the least depreciated currency" although it had not depreciated and on the contrary had appreciated against the franc in the exchange markets. The depreciation of all currencies against the deutsche mark in 1961 and 1969 corresponded to the depreciation of the French franc against the U.S. dollar and all other currencies of issue in 1957. The deutsche mark in 1961 and 1969 corresponded to the U.S. dollar in 1957 as a nondepreciated currency that, just as cogently as the dollar, qualified as "the least depreciated currency."

The minority rejected the respondent's assertion that bondholders entitled to payment in other currencies had not been deprived of any value by revaluation of the deutsche mark. The Bundesbank itself had reassessed its reserves in foreign currency and shown a loss after the two revaluations. What was true for the Bundesbank was true for the bondholders of the non-German tranches, and even more obviously for those who resided inside the Federal Republic.

The minority held that, if reconciliation of the texts of treaties written in more than one language was not possible except by preferring one of them, then equal authenticity was not a bar to an order of precedence among them on specific points of interpretation. Nor was equal authenticity a bar in these circumstances to recognition of the superiority of the language in which negotiations were conducted or an original version from which the other versions were translated. Only the English version was employed during the negotiation of the LDA, while the other two versions were translations from the English. The negotiators did not participate in the process of translation. It should be possible to show that a translation does not correctly reflect the meaning of an original text. The affairs of sovereign states cannot be influenced by the fortuitous choice of words selected by a nameless translator. The minority, by means of this reasoning, was led to favor the word "depreciated" in the English text and its broad meaning in that language.

The contrast in technique followed by the majority and the minority is as strong here as elsewhere. The majority refused to apply a number of interpretative approaches that were advanced as valid and appropriate. Among them were various approaches that would favor

321

the German text: the lowest common denominator of obligation, the clearest text, the interpretation least favorable to the parties that had primary responsibility for offering the text in the negotiations preceding adoption of it. Similarly, the majority rejected the approach, followed by the minority, of establishing an order of precedence among texts. This approach would have given primary weight to the English and French texts. To all these approaches, the majority said nay because they would not necessarily have been compatible with the intention of the negotiators and would not have been directed toward fulfillment of the object and purpose of the treaty.

The minority did not agree that the alteration of a rate of exchange in Article 13(*a*) meant an alteration of par value under the Fund's Articles. "Rate of exchange" was not defined in the LDA, and therefore it could not be assumed that the expression was used in an abnormal sense. Each of the paragraphs of Article 13 was based on the same ordinary meaning of "exchange rate." They dealt with different situations of fact. Paragraph (*a*) did not give the concept a special meaning in the light of which all paragraphs had to be interpreted. Nor did the minority accept the argument that, because of the reference in Article 13(*a*) of the LDA to Article IV, Section 1 of the Fund's Articles, or for some other reason, the provisions of the LDA were subordinated to the provisions of the Fund's Articles. These reactions of the minority led it to reject the conclusion that "depreciated" meant "devalued" and to hold that a revalued currency could be "the least depreciated currency."

LANGUAGE OF THE LDA

A major problem in the case was created by the word "depreciated" in the LDA. The confusion with which the words "depreciation," "appreciation," "devaluation," and "revaluation" have been and are being used is widespread in both official and nonofficial publications. The first pair of words are regarded sometimes as equivalent to the second pair, sometimes as wholly different from them, and sometimes as covering them but as more extensive. These three versions appear in the opinions of the tribunal and the written arguments, but in them a preferred version is not always maintained with consistency. Discrete meanings for the four words would be desirable, but it should not be assumed that the definition of them is a simple matter. There would be complications, for example, in the treatment to be accorded to governmental action. A case discussed in an earlier installment in this series illustrates the problems that can arise with a definition of "devaluation" in terms of "governmental action."[13]

The majority concluded that Article I(iii) of the Fund's Articles, in referring to "competitive exchange depreciation," was referring only to devaluation (i.e., a change in par value by a member). This argument cannot be sustained. Article IV, Section 6 of the original Articles dealt with unauthorized changes of par values—which by hypothesis were not agreed with the Fund—and Article IV, Section 8 dealt with those cases in which a member's currency depreciated in the exchange markets in breach of the member's obligations. Furthermore, a member might adopt a new fixed rate of exchange for its currency without calling it a par value or attempting to establish it as such under the Articles. This action also would be in breach of the member's obligations if it had already established a par value under the Articles. The purpose of the Fund expressed in Article I(iii) would have been frustrated by competitive changes in these circumstances as effectively as it would have been by competitive changes of par value. It should be noted that Article I(iii) remains unchanged by the Second Amendment even though a par value system is not now in operation. Competitive depreciation is possible, therefore, even in the absence of a par value system.

The majority may have assumed that Article I(iii) would not refer to actions inconsistent with the Articles, from which the majority may have inferred that the provision must be taken to refer to governmental actions to change par values. But a currency might have been "floating" in the days of the par value system without being inconsistent with the Articles. This was the legal position before the Fund called on a member to establish a par value under a Membership Resolution of the Board of Governors. The Fund would have regarded a competitive depreciation in these circumstances as inconsistent with the Articles. To prevent such a situation from arising, the Fund included a term in Membership Resolutions under which, in the period between the acceptance of membership and the establishment of an initial par value, a member was required not to change the exchange

---

[13] *Federal Maritime Commission v. Australia/U.S. Atlantic & Gulf Conference et al.*, 337 F. Supp. 1032 (1972); Gold, "Fund Agreement in the Courts—XI," pp. 161–71 in this volume. Note also that the Fund could decide to make uniform proportionate changes in the par values of the currencies of all members under Article IV, Section 7, *original* although a member could prevent the decision from applying to its currency. See also Schedule C, paragraph 11 of the present Articles.

rate for its currency without consulting the Fund in advance of a change and without obtaining its agreement.[14]

Perhaps, because of the provisions referred to above, Article IV, Section 4(a) of the original Articles, in giving effect to Article I(iii) in the form of an obligation of members, required them to avoid "competitive exchange alterations." The language of the Articles does not confirm the proposition that in 1952 "depreciation" in the Articles meant "devaluation." The only proposition that can be derived from the Articles is either that the applicants' understanding was correct or that precision was lacking.

Neither the majority nor the minority discussed Article IV, Section 8(b) of the original Articles, in which the reduction in a par value is expressly distinguished from a depreciation. That provision would have cast doubt on the majority's conclusion that "depreciation" in Article I(iii) had to mean "devaluation." Similarly, the provision would not have supported the conclusion of the minority that "depreciation" covered any reduction in the value of a currency, whether or not it resulted from a change in par value.

A discussion of Article IV, Section 8 was relevant to another aspect of the case. The respondent argued that the French action of 1957 was a "formal devaluation" and that it confirmed the view that Article I(iii) meant devaluation in referring to depreciation. On October 2, 1957, however, the Fund decided that France was required to adjust the Fund's holdings of French francs under Article IV, Section 8(b)(ii) as a result of the action France had taken. The decision meant that the adjustment was necessary not because of a reduction in par value under Section 8(b)(i) but because, as described in Article IV, Section 8(b)(ii), the currency had "depreciated to a significant extent within that member's territories."

The expression "the least depreciated currency" was interpreted by the majority to include within its reach a currency that had neither depreciated nor appreciated. An appreciated currency is even further removed from depreciation than an undepreciated currency. It is not surprising, however, that there should be such a strong division of opinion about the resonance of the expression. A more surprising conclusion of the majority was the view that in certain circumstances, adduced by the applicants to illustrate the unreasonableness of the respondent's argument, the least depreciated currency could be taken

---

[14] Gold, *Membership and Nonmembership*, pp. 195–97.

to be a revalued currency at its value before revaluation. The relationship between two currencies on this basis would correspond to nothing in the real world when payments were made after the revaluation. In the *Lively* case,[15] a rate of exchange that the defendants argued should be applied under Article 13(*a*) of the LDA was rejected by the court on the ground that it had no relation to any market or commercial rate of exchange.

The minority could have made more of the drafting of Article 13 of the LDA. The majority and the minority differed on what was to be drawn from the reference to par values in Article 13(*a*). The majority gave predominant importance to this paragraph and held that the reference to par values showed an intention to fit the LDA into the Bretton Woods system and its basic relationship to gold. The minority rejected this analysis and gave predominant importance to paragraphs (*b*), (*c*), and (*d*) because they did not refer to par values. These paragraphs could not have referred to par values, because they dealt with situations in which par values were not agreed with the Fund or were not in force. Nothing was made of the argument, however, that gold was the substratum of the par value system and that even in these situations it would have been possible to determine the foreign exchange value of currencies in terms of gold. It is true that the minority pointed out that paragraphs (*b*), (*c*), and (*d*) had no link to "gold or the gold dollar." It attributed the absence of that link to the unacceptability of a gold clause in the negotiations leading to the LDA, but the explanation is not persuasive in view of paragraph (*a*). The argument could have been reinforced by demonstrating that even paragraphs (*b*), (*c*), and (*d*) could have been fitted into the Articles, and that the negotiators, in refraining from following this course, had shown that they were not adapting their solution to the monetary law of the Articles.

The drafters of the LDA could have taken cognizance of Article IV, Section 8 of the original Articles of Agreement if such a solution had been acceptable to them. Under that provision, the "gold value" of the Fund's assets had to be maintained by adjusting the Fund's holdings of a member's currency in accordance with changes in the par value or the foreign exchange value of the currency. If the Fund found that the foreign exchange value of a member's currency had depreciated to a significant extent within the member's territories, which meant that the gold value of the currency had been reduced, the

---

[15] [1976] 3 All E.R. 851.

member had to pay more currency to the Fund in an amount "equal to the reduction in the gold value" of its currency held by the Fund. The provision did not mention appreciation, but the Fund interpreted the provision to require it to return to the member an amount of currency equivalent to the appreciation. As noted already, "depreciation" and "appreciation" under Article IV, Section 8 were phenomena distinguishable from changes in par values.

Article IV, Section 8 was both appropriate and necessary for the Fund. It was appropriate because the Fund's functions included its jurisdiction over par values and exchange rates, from which the conclusion was drawn that the Fund should not make profits or suffer losses as the result of changes in par values or exchange rates. The provision was necessary because, if the Fund's holdings of currencies were not adjusted in accordance with changes in gold value, the Fund could avoid profits and losses by standing ready to conduct its operations and transactions on the basis of unreal (i.e., unadjusted) exchange rates. In those circumstances, however, the Fund would face a run on an appreciated currency, and it would be unable to dispose of a depreciated currency. If, alternatively, the Fund chose to conduct its activities on the basis of current (i.e., adjusted) exchange rates without the adjustment of its holdings, it could not avoid profits or losses. In short, Article IV, Section 8 was necessary for the effectiveness of the Fund's financial activities. In this respect, it could be regarded as analogous to Article 13 of the LDA because that provision also was intended to ensure effectiveness, in this case the protection of bondholders. It should be noted, furthermore, that the adjustment of the Fund's holdings of a currency under Article IV, Section 8 did not depend on the legality of the conditions that made adjustment necessary.

Not until 1954, when the possible floating of sterling was in the air, did the Fund decide how it would apply Article IV, Section 8 to what were then called "fluctuating currencies." The expression meant that exchange transactions in a currency were not conducted within the legal limits around parities (i.e., around the ratios resulting from the par value of that currency and the par values of other currencies). It was obvious how the gold value of a fluctuating currency would have to be determined in a system based on gold in which the United States was the only member of the Fund that had undertaken to maintain the value of its currency in relation to gold by means of purchases and sales of gold for U.S. dollars with the monetary authorities of other members of the Fund. The foreign exchange (gold) value of a member's fluctuating currency would be determined by the exchange rates between that currency and the U.S. dollar in the member's main financial center. What was meant by the exchange rates for the purpose of the decision was spelled out in detail by the decision.[16]

The Fund's solution for the application of Article IV, Section 8 could have been anticipated by the negotiators of the LDA had they intended to base all paragraphs of Article 13 of the LDA on gold value as the substratum of the Bretton Woods system, but they did not. If in 1952 the negotiators had wanted such a solution, nothing would have been simpler than a provision under which the protection of bondholders would be based on the relationship of the currencies of issue and payment to the U.S. dollar, with some caveat for the situation in which there would be a change in the par value of the U.S. dollar. Such a solution could have covered all cases, whether or not a par value agreed with the Fund was in force. This solution was proposed, with the understanding that there would be new negotiations if the par value of the U.S. dollar were changed, but the proposal was not acceptable to the United States because it conflicted with U.S. policy on the gold clause. It is unnecessary to dwell on the discrepancies between paragraphs (c) and (d) of Article 13 of the LDA, which were based on exchange rates in the market, and the Fund's 1954 decision on fluctuating currencies. Paragraph (b) alone is sufficient to show how far Article 13 as a whole was from the solution of gold value. The exchange rate for a currency specified by a bilateral payments agreement might have been inconsistent with the exchange rate between the currency and the U.S. dollar. The specified exchange rate would have been a multiple currency practice and discriminatory currency arrangement and, even worse, might not have received the approval of the Fund.[17] The implication of Paragraph 13 is that the negotiators of the LDA had not intended to fit that agreement into international monetary law as established by the Articles of the Fund.

The majority and minority had different reactions to the circumstances that, when the LDA was negotiated, France did not enforce a par value agreed with the Fund and Switzerland was not (and still is not) a member of the Fund. The majority regarded these circumstances as exceptional and not as proof that the LDA had not been,

---

[16] For a full discussion of Article IV, Section 8, *original* and the Fund's decision on computations involving fluctuating currencies, see Gold, Pamphlet No. 6, Second Edition (1971).

[17] Article VIII, Section 3, *original*.

or could not be, fitted into the monetary law of the Bretton Woods system. The minority held that the circumstances of these two countries disposed of any argument that the negotiators of the LDA had intended to fit it into the framework of the Bretton Woods system. On this point also the minority could have strengthened its opinion by showing that the currencies of even these two countries would not have been beyond the reach of a protective clause based on the gold value of the currencies. In the case of the French franc, the Fund was required to determine the gold value of that currency under Article IV, Section 8. In the case of the Swiss franc, the exchange rate between it and the U.S. dollar in the Swiss exchange market could have been considered the gold value of the Swiss franc by analogy to Article IV, Section 8.

Some Further Reflections on the Two Opinions

The narrow margin of difference in the size of the majority and the minority is evidence of the difficulty of the basic issues. The reader of the two opinions must be impressed by the quality of each analysis and the wealth of cited authority. Is it possible to venture a statement of some underlying attitudes that guided the two groups to their different conclusions? The different responses to the cases of France and Switzerland have been mentioned already, but some broader differences can be discerned.

First among these differences is the influence attributed to a system of international monetary law. The majority regarded the Articles of the Fund as such a system and was disposed to hold that the negotiators of the LDA intended to work within that system.[18] The minority did not share this disposition.

Second, the two groups probably held different views on what was the main objective of the LDA. The majority seems to have given predominant weight to the recovery of the German economy as the main objective. Therefore, they assumed that the negotiators of the LDA had wanted to avoid obligations that would overburden the economy. The minority gave greater weight to the protection of bondholders as the main objective of the LDA.

---

[18] Compare the discussion of the implications drawn from the conviction that there is or is not an international monetary system in Joseph Gold, *The Rule of Law in the International Monetary Fund*, IMF Pamphlet Series, No. 32 (Washington, 1980), pp. 13–17. (Hereinafter cited as Gold, Pamphlet No. 32.)

Third, the two groups might have had different attitudes to the terms of the settlement compared with the original gold clause. The majority seems to have assumed an intention to provide comparable protection for bondholders, and it found that there was comparability between the gold clause and the par value system of the Articles. The minority attributed less importance to comparability between the old and the new terms and was willing to assume that agreement had been reached on a better form of protection than had been represented by the gold clause.

A final word is necessary. The case dealt only with the effect of the revaluations of the deutsche mark in 1961 and 1969 on the application of the protective clause. The case did not deal with the effects of the breakdown of the par value system after August 15, 1971 or with the consequences of the Second Amendment of the Articles, as will be apparent from the Attachment to this chapter.

ATTACHMENT

The BIS in its capacity as Trustee under the Young Loan issued an announcement dated May 30, 1980 (*New York Times,* Vol. 129 (May 30, 1980), p. D6) that included the following passage:

"It should be emphasized that this arbitral award only concerns the formal revaluations of the Deutsche mark in 1961 and 1969. The Arbitral Tribunal was not asked to rule on the more recent question, which has existed since 1971, of whether or not the exchange guarantee is applicable when currencies of issue of the Young Loan undergo important de facto alterations in their rates of exchange which does [*sic*] not result from formal changes in par values agreed with the International Monetary Fund.

"As a consequence of the floating of the exchange rates for the currencies of issue of the Young Loan, which commenced in May 1971 with the floating of the exchange rate for the Deutsche mark and has been the case for all the remaining currencies of issue for many years now, the Trustee notified the German Federal Debt Administration and the various paying agents that the reservations which the Trustee had already made regarding the rights of bondholders, and the precautionary steps to protect these rights being taken by the paying agents, extended to the new question of interpretation of the exchange guarantee to which floating exchange rates had given rise.

"If it is considered, in the light of the recent Arbitral Award, that the exchange guarantee does not apply in the event of the de facto appreciation in the exchange rate of a given currency of issue, it remains to be established whether the same is true when a given currency of issue suffers a de facto depreciation in exchange value.

"It should be recalled in this connection that the German Federal Debt Administration has applied the exchange guarantee, and made adjustments in the amounts payable to bondholders of the American, British, French and Swedish issues of the Young Loan, as from the due date for bonds and coupons of 1st June 1978. These adjustments resulted from the abolition of formal par values—which in fact had long since ceased to be respected in commercial transactions—to which the amendment of the articles of agreement of the International Monetary Fund on 1st April 1978 gave rise. The adjustments so made in the amounts payable to the bondholders in question were calculated on the basis of the Belgian franc, the currency of issue which, in the opinion of the German Federal Debt Administration, was, on each occasion, the "least depreciated currency" for the purposes of the exchange guarantee.

"No adjustments have, however, been made in respect of the preceding period of de facto floating exchange rates, which had commenced in 1971. In the view of the German Federal Debt Administration, a view not shared by the Trustee, par values remained in force for the purposes of the exchange guarantee until the above-mentioned amendment of the IMF articles of agreement.

"The Trustee has already drawn to the attention of the governments concerned the consequences for bondholders which result from floating exchange rates, and the further question of interpretation of the exchange guarantee to which this situation has given rise.

"In these circumstances, the Trustee has informed the German Federal Debt Administration that until the outstanding questions are settled, the Trustee's earlier reservations of the possible rights of bondholders to additional payments remain in force irrespective of whether or not the final coupon and the bonds due for redemption are presented for payment on or after 1st June 1980. All the paying agents have been notified accordingly, and have been requested by the Trustee to maintain the protective measures which are necessary in the interests of bondholders. In addition, the Trustee may make a further approach to the governments concerned requesting them to take appropriate steps to reach the earliest possible solution of the outstanding questions to which floating exchange rates have given rise pursuant to the exchange guarantee."

11

The Fund Agreement
in the Courts—XVII*

This seventeenth installment in the series dealing with the impact of the Articles of Agreement of the International Monetary Fund on litigation discusses two cases involving Article VIII, Section 2(b) of the Articles. The first case, decided by an English court, dealt with the issue whether that provision of the Articles applied to a claim against a bank under a confirmed irrevocable letter of credit. Little authority has existed hitherto on the question whether the provision qualifies the important legal principle that an irrevocable letter of credit is independent of the underlying commercial contract that gives rise to the letter of credit. The second case, decided by the Supreme Court of the Netherlands, raised the question of the application of the provision by courts in a region of the Kingdom of the Netherlands to a contract contrary to the exchange control regulations of another region of the Kingdom that had become independent after the contract was made but before the action was instituted.

I. Unenforceability of Certain Exchange Contracts and Letters of Credit

THE GLASS FIBRES CASE (ENGLAND)

In the fifteenth installment[1] in this series there was a discussion of *United City Merchants (Investments) Ltd. and Glass Fibres and Equip-*

---

* Originally published in December 1981.
[1] Joseph Gold, "Fund Agreement in the Courts—XV," pp. 299–303 in this volume.

ment Ltd. v. Royal Bank of Canada, Vitrorefuerzos S.A., and Banco Continental S.A. ("The American Accord")[2] and subsequent proceedings in which an English court applied Article VIII, Section 2(*b*) of the Fund's Articles. The first sentence of that provision is as follows:

> Exchange contracts which involve the currency of any member and which are contrary to the exchange control regulations of that member maintained or imposed consistently with this Agreement shall be unenforceable in the territories of any member.

The earlier discussion was concluded with the remark that the case, insofar as it dealt with the application of this provision, had not been reported and that it was not possible, therefore, to describe how the court, the Queen's Bench Division (Commercial Court), had treated the principle that normally a letter of credit is independent of the underlying contract that gives rise to it. This part of the proceedings in the Queen's Bench Division has since been reported under the name *United City Merchants (Investments) Ltd. and Glass Fibres and Equipment Ltd. v. Royal Bank of Canada and Others (No. 2)*,[3] and has now been the subject of a decision by the Court of Appeal under the name *United City Merchants (Investments) Ltd. and Others v. Royal Bank of Canada and Others*.[4]

The first plaintiff in these proceedings, United City Merchants, had received from the second plaintiff, Glass Fibres, an assignment of Glass Fibres' rights under a letter of credit against the first defendant, Royal Bank of Canada. For the purpose of this litigation, it was accepted that the first plaintiff was in no better position than the second plaintiff. The action resulted from Royal Bank's refusal to make payment under a letter of credit that Vitro had instructed Banco Continental in Peru to open in favor of Glass Fibres. Banco Continental arranged for the opening of a credit by the Royal Bank of Canada, Montreal, payable in U.S. dollars in London. The credit was irrevocable and available by sight drafts drawn on the Royal Bank of Canada, Montreal, against clean bills of lading on or before a date extended to December 31, 1976. Banco Continental was to repay Royal Bank over a period of five years for any advances made by Royal Bank. The letter of credit had been issued in respect of a contract for the sale by Glass Fibres to Vitro and import into Peru of equipment for the manufacture of glass fiber that was to be exported on or before December 15, 1976.

---

[2] [1979] 1 Lloyd's Rep. 267.
[3] [1979] 2 Lloyd's Rep. 498.
[4] [1981] 3 W.L.R. 242.

Royal Bank contended, inter alia, that the letter of credit was unenforceable under the Bretton Woods Order in Council of 1946, which was promulgated under the British Bretton Woods Agreements Act to give the force of law to Article VIII, Section 2(b). This contention was based on the allegation that the letter of credit was obtained to engineer the transfer of funds from Peru by overinvoicing contrary to the exchange control regulations of that country. The arrangements were made on the initiative of Olguin, a director, general manager, and majority shareholder of Vitro. The excess U.S. dollar funds were to be retransferred by Glass Fibres and held in Florida for the benefit of Vitro. The arrangements for this purpose and the exchange control regulations are described in Chapter 9 in this volume. Vitro, Olguin, and Banco Continental were residents of Peru. Neither Banco Continental nor Royal Bank knew of the overinvoicing when the letter of credit was negotiated.

Queen's Bench Division (Commercial Court)

The court considered the issue of Article VIII, Section 2(b) to be "the most difficult and novel part of this case."[5] The court referred to the proposition accepted by the English Court of Appeal in *Wilson, Smithett & Cope Ltd. v. Terruzzi*[6] that an "exchange contract" under the provision means a contract for the purchase and sale of one currency against another and that contracts involving securities or merchandise are not exchange contracts except when they are monetary transactions in disguise. This proposition, declared the court in the *Glass Fibres* case, was not greatly helpful in defining monetary transactions in disguise.

The court analyzed the agreement as one that, if carried out, would lead to the receipt by Vitro, through an intermediary, of U.S. dollars and the obligation of Vitro, through Banco Continental, to make repayment over a period of five years by selling Peruvian soles for U.S. dollars. On this analysis, the contract of sale between Glass Fibres and Vitro could be described "as constituting an exchange contract by being a monetary transaction in disguise"[7] contrary to Peru's exchange control regulations and therefore unenforceable under the 1946 Order in Council.

---

[5] [1979] 2 Lloyd's Rep. at 503.
[6] [1976] 1 Q.B. 683; [1976] 1 Q.B. 703 (C.A.). See Gold, "Fund Agreement in the Courts—XII," pp. 202–18 in this volume.
[7] [1979] 2 Lloyd's Rep. at 503.

The court disposed of an objection by the plaintiff that the exchange control regulations were not maintained or imposed consistently with the Articles. The report does not include the plaintiff's argument in support of this objection, but the court's reference to "very sweeping allegations which could perhaps be said of most member countries"[8] suggests that the argument was the incompatibility in principle of exchange controls or exchange restrictions with the broad objectives of the Articles. The treaty, however, does not invalidate exchange controls or all exchange restrictions. The Fund concluded, in a communication to one of the parties, that the Peruvian exchange controls were not inconsistent with the Articles. The reasons were stated earlier.[9]

The court rejected the objection of inconsistency with the Articles by referring to the *dictum* in the *Terruzzi* case that courts should not assume without evidence that the authorities of a member country administer their exchange control regulations in a manner contrary to the Articles. This *dictum* amounts to a presumption in favor of the consistency of exchange control regulations with the Articles, which places the burden of proving inconsistency on the plaintiff. But a defendant who relies on Article VIII, Section 2(b) necessarily asserts that exchange controls are maintained or imposed consistently with the Articles, and he should have the burden of proving this fact.

This allocation of the burden of proof is not intended to suggest that a court is debarred from raising the question of the application of Article VIII, Section 2(b) when the parties have failed to refer to the provision.[10] The only safe way to settle the question of consistency or inconsistency is to request a certificate from the Fund. The request can be made by a party or by the court itself if its procedures authorize this step. The reason why the Fund should be approached is that the answer may depend on the exercise of the Fund's discretionary powers to approve exchange restrictions if approval is required by the Articles. In the *Glass Fibres* case, it is not clear whether the court thought it necessary to rest on the *dictum* in favor of consistency, even though the Secretary of the Fund, acting with the authority of the Executive Board, had provided one of the defendants with a statement affirming the consistency with the Articles of the exchange control regulations cited in the case.[11]

---

[8] *Ibid.*, at 504.
[9] Gold, "Fund Agreement in the Courts—XV," pp. 300–301 in this volume.
[10] Gold, "Fund Agreement in the Courts—XIV," p. 259 in this volume.
[11] Gold, "Fund Agreement in the Courts—XV," p. 301 in this volume.

Another objection rejected by the court was that the restriction in this case was on the import of capital goods and was contained in the law relating to industry and not exchange control. The court held that this contention was not in accord with the evidence.

The court then turned to the "perplexing and difficult"[12] question of the effect of its findings on the claim against Royal Bank as the confirming bank. In the first part of this litigation, the court had concluded that, except in the case of fraud, a bank that confirms a letter of credit must pay against documents appearing to comply with the terms of the credit, and that the bank is not concerned with the question whether the goods complied with the terms of the contract of sale.[13] The problem was whether this principle was affected in any way by the Bretton Woods Order in Council. By stating the problem in this way, the court was asking whether fraud in the underlying contract between the beneficiary and the bank's customer at whose instance the letter of credit is arranged, which is a recognized exception to the principle of the independence of the letter of credit, is the only justification for the confirming bank's refusal to honor the instrument, or whether the Order in Council is a second and independent justification. The issue arose because the court held that in the circumstances of the case the established exception of fraud was not available to Royal Bank as a justification for refusing payment.

In examining the question whether the Order in Council was an independent justification for refusing to honor a letter of credit, the court discussed the decisions of the Court of Appeal in *Sharif v. Azad*[14] and *Batra v. Ebrahim*.[15] In the former case, the Court of Appeal permitted the plaintiff to recover on a check in England, notwithstanding the fact that the check was delivered as part of a plan to evade the exchange control regulations of Pakistan. The court in the *Glass Fibres* case noted the emphasis that the Court of Appeal had placed on the language of the regulations in *Sharif v. Azad*. They applied to "any person in or resident in Pakistan," but the parties to the action in England were resident in England. The court noted also the absence of any argument that the check was affected with fraud as between the parties.

---

[12] [1979] 2 Lloyd's Rep. at 504.

[13] *Ibid.*

[14] [1966] 3 All E.R. 785, [1966] 3 W.L.R. 1285. See Gold, "Fund Agreement in the Courts—IX," pp. 107–16 in this volume.

[15] *The Times* (London), May 3, 1977, p. 11. See Gold, "Fund Agreement in the Courts—XIV," pp. 258–65 in this volume.

In *Batra v. Ebrahim*, the two parties were resident in England, but the plaintiff failed. The court in the *Glass Fibres* case pointed out that the exchange control regulations of India, which were in issue in *Batra v. Ebrahim*, "were not expressly tied to residency."[16] This attempt to reconcile the two cases is an unhappy one. The words "involve the currency of any member" in Article VIII, Section 2(*b*) mean, according to one interpretation, that an exchange contract contrary to the exchange control regulations of a member is unenforceable only if performance of the contract would affect the member's balance of payments. According to another interpretation, performance must affect a member's exchange resources. On the basis of these interpretations, the residence of a contracting party within a member's territory, or the transfer of assets across its borders, is relevant under Article VIII, Section 2(*b*) whether or not the exchange control regulations in issue are formulated in terms of residence within the territory or the transfer of assets out of the territory.

The court explained that *Sharif v. Azad* had been decided on the basis of Section 30 of the Bills of Exchange Act, 1882, for which reason that case could be distinguished from one in which the question was the effect of the Order in Council on a confirmed letter of credit. This explanation of *Sharif v. Azad* adds nothing to the understanding of Article VIII, Section 2(*b*) and its possible application to letters of credit. The explanation amounts to no more than the proposition that the provision did not apply in *Sharif v. Azad* because the Bretton Woods Agreements Act and the Order in Council had not made it applicable in the circumstances of the case. The decision did not hold that the Bills of Exchange Act would have prevented a more extensive application of the provision. Earlier statute law would have been no more an obstruction than the traditional principles of private international law that the Court of Appeal in *Sharif v. Azad* recognized as inapplicable as a result of Article VIII, Section 2(*b*) and the Order in Council.

It is obvious that the Queen's Bench Division in the *Glass Fibres* case did not find guidance in the two earlier cases, although it may have thought that *Batra v. Ebrahim* gave it some support in denying recovery by the plaintiff. "After considerable hesitation,"[17] the court decided that the Order in Council should not be rendered ineffective by enforcing the letter of credit. Once any payment was made by the

---

[16] [1979] 2 Lloyd's Rep. at 504.
[17] *Ibid.*, at 505.

Royal Bank under the letter of credit, effect would be given to some extent to a monetary transaction in disguise, and therefore to an exchange contract that was contrary to the exchange control regulations of Peru.

The court rejected with some warmth the suggestion that the plaintiff should be allowed to recover half its claims under the letter of credit. That instrument could not be severed in this way. It was either enforceable in full or not at all. Judgment was given for the Royal Bank of Canada.

Some Comments on the Case in the Queen's Bench Division

1. The court of first instance noted the absence of authority on the effect that Article VIII, Section 2(*b*) had on letters of credit, but it seems that the decision of the New York Court of Appeals in *J. Zeevi and Sons, Ltd., et al. v. Grindlays Bank (Uganda) Limited*[18] was not cited, although decisions of courts in the United States on other aspects of the litigation were discussed, particularly on the issue of fraud in the underlying transaction. In the *Zeevi* case, the court held that a letter of credit issued as the result of an agreement between a Ugandan bank and an Israeli corporation was enforceable by the beneficiary of the letter of credit, notwithstanding the prohibition of Uganda's exchange control regulations. The court's primary motivation seems to have been the undesirability of a policy of refusing to enforce a letter of credit under which funds were to be made available in New York. The argument based on Article VIII, Section 2(*b*) was swept aside with the brief comment that a letter of credit was not an "exchange contract." This conclusion made it unnecessary for the court to examine other problems, such as the question whether the Ugandan exchange control regulations were consistent with the Articles.

Another case that the court might have wanted to consider, had it been cited, was the decision delivered by the Supreme Court of the Federal Republic of Germany on April 27, 1970, in which it was held that bills of exchange were within the reach of Article VIII, Section 2(*b*).[19]

---

[18] 37 N.Y. 2d 220, 333 N.E. 2d 168, 371 N.Y.S. 2d 892 (1975). See Gold, "Fund Agreement in the Courts—XII," pp. 219–21 in this volume.

[19] BGH Urt. v. 27.4.1970—II ZR 12/69 (Oldenburg), *Neue Juristische Wochenschrift*, Vol. 23 (August 20, 1970), pp. 1507–1508. See Gold, "Fund Agreement in the Courts—X," pp. 139–49 in this volume.

2. The *Glass Fibres* case was an action between two nonresidents of Peru, and discharge of the defendant's obligation to the plaintiff, taken in isolation, would not require any transfer of assets from Peru. On these facts alone, and on the basis of an economic interpretation of the currency "involved," there would have been no reason to hold that the letter of credit was unenforceable under Article VIII, Section 2(*b*) even if the underlying transaction was deemed to be a monetary one in disguise. But the court pointed out that enforcing the letter of credit would have made Banco Continental, a resident of Peru, liable to sell Peruvian soles to obtain U.S. dollars with which to repay Royal Bank, a nonresident of Peru, contrary to Peru's exchange control regulations.

It was possible that Royal Bank would not have had recourse against Banco Continental except by suit in Peru. It may be assumed that in these circumstances Peruvian courts would deny recovery as being in contravention of Peru's exchange control regulations. It is doubtful, however, that a plaintiff should be allowed to rely on such a response to the contention that Peru's balance of payments or exchange resources were affected and its currency involved within the meaning of Article VIII, Section 2(*b*).

3. In the United States, a surge of litigation and debate is taking place on the circumstances in which courts may grant injunctions restraining a bank from making payment on a letter of credit. Cases decided in the United States have influenced this sector of English law. Some of the questions raised in recent litigation in the United States are whether fraud in the underlying contract between the beneficiary of the letter of credit and the customer of the issuing bank is a basis for refusing relief, and whether fraud for this purpose connotes deceit, some other form of subjective behavior, or some form of objective behavior. The courts have found it difficult to reconcile the principle that commerce must be unimpeded, which leads them to hold that banks confirming letters of credit deal in documents and not goods, with the need to insist on basic honesty in commercial transactions.[20]

---

[20] Edward L. Symons, Jr., "Letters of Credit: Fraud, Good Faith and the Basis for Injunctive Relief," *Tulane Law Review*, Vol. 54 (February 1980), pp. 338–81. See also Dirk T. Biermann, "Letters of Credit," *Denver Journal of International Law and Policy*, Vol. 9 (Winter 1980), pp. 164–68; Herbert A. Getz, "Enjoining the International Standby Letter of Credit: The Iranian Letter of Credit Cases," *Harvard International Law Journal*, Vol. 21 (Winter 1980), pp. 189–252; Richard J. Driscoll, "The Role of Standby Letters of Credit in International Commerce: Reflections After Iran," *Virginia Journal of International Law*, Vol. 20 (Winter 1980), pp. 459–504.

So far, in the United States only the *Zeevi* case has raised the question of the effect of Article VIII, Section 2(*b*) on a letter of credit, but fraud in the underlying transactions was not alleged. The decision in that case protected the beneficiary of the letter of credit and the beneficiary's assignee. The decision of the Queen's Bench Division in the *Glass Fibres* case was in favor of the bank confirming the letter of credit and indirectly in favor of the issuing bank.

In some cases, the courts are called on to protect the issuing bank's customer. In cases involving Article VIII, Section 2(*b*), the interests of yet another entity can be prejudiced: the member of the Fund whose balance of payments or exchange resources would be affected by enforcement of the letter of credit. The protection of the member should not be made to depend on a demonstration of fraud in any form on the part of contracting parties. Such a demonstration is not required by Article VIII, Section 2(*b*). Even a contract that is entered into innocently may be caught by the provision. In the *Glass Fibres* case, the court emphasized the element of "a monetary transaction in disguise," but this approach was followed because of the narrow definition of exchange contracts adopted in the *Terruzzi* case and because the parties to the underlying contract were buying and selling goods.

4. The court's rejection of the argument that the restrictions in the case were on the importation of goods and were not exchange control regulations deserves a comment. The exchange control regulations of Peru's Decree Law No. 18275 applied directly to transactions in foreign exchange, and Decree Law No. 18891 made it a criminal offense to overvalue imports and obligations in foreign exchange, as well as to undervalue exports, in violation of the regime of foreign exchange certificates. The regulations were intended to control payments and transfers for international capital transfers and were obviously exchange control regulations within any reasonable meaning of the expression.

Suppose, however, that regulations are contained in a law relating to industry and the importation of capital goods as contended by the defendant. Regulations would not cease to be exchange control regulations by reason of that fact alone. Legislation frequently imposes restrictions on trade and augments them with regulations that deal with the financial aspects of restricted trade transactions. An importer might be required by law to obtain authority to make an import, and the same law might provide that an exchange license would be granted automatically if the import was authorized. In these circumstances there would be no restriction on the making of payments, but there would be a control of exchange. Whether there is a restriction on the making of payments depends on whether a discretion is exercised to permit, prohibit, or unduly delay payment. Under some laws, discretion is exercised with respect to both the trade and the financial aspects of transactions. These laws establish restrictions of a joint character on trade and payments.

Article VIII, Section 2(*b*) refers to exchange control regulations and not to the narrower concept of restrictions on the making of payments and transfers. A reasonable test to determine whether a measure is an exchange control regulation is whether its subject matter is the availability or use of exchange as such, but the regulation need not impose "a direct governmental limitation on the availability or use of exchange as such." [21]

Court of Appeal

The Court of Appeal, consisting of Lords Justices Stephenson, Ackner, and Griffiths, each of whom delivered an opinion, dealt with the two defenses of Article VIII, Section 2(*b*) and fraud in the underlying transaction. The Court of Appeal affirmed the decision of the Queen's Bench Division in favor of the defendant, but did so on the basis of the second defense while the lower court had rested its decision on the first defense.

On the subject of the first defense, the court held that the letter of credit contract between Glass Fibres and the defendant, considered in isolation, was not an exchange contract because it was a contract to pay U.S. dollars against documents and was not a contract to exchange one currency against another. The court followed the decision in the *Terruzzi* case in holding that "exchange contracts" in Article VIII, Section 2(*b*) meant contracts for the exchange of currencies, so that contracts involving securities or merchandise were not exchange contracts unless they were "monetary transactions in disguise."

The facts were analyzed by Lord Justice Stephenson as involving four contractual relationships, as follows:

(1) between Glass Fibres and Vitro for the sale and purchase of goods;

---

[21] Executive Board Decision No. 1034-(60/27), June 1, 1960, *Selected Decisions*, Ninth Issue, p. 210.

(2) between Vitro and Banco Continental for the opening of an irrevocable and transferable letter of credit in favor of Glass Fibres for the account of Vitro;

(3) between Banco Continental and Royal Bank by which Royal Bank confirmed the letter of credit opened by Banco Continental; and

(4) between Royal Bank and Glass Fibres as beneficiary of the letter of credit, which was the contract sued on in this case.

The fourth contract, however, came into existence to ensure payment of the U.S. dollars payable under the first contract. The first contract, by doubling the purchase price and providing for transfer of the excess to the United States, was a monetary transaction in disguise because it would result in an ultimate exchange of U.S. dollars for Peruvian soles in contravention of Peru's exchange control regulations. It was admitted that the regulations were maintained or imposed consistently with the Articles. The fourth contract was a necessary step toward the ultimate exchange of soles for dollars. Both the first and the fourth contracts, therefore, were exchange contracts, although this character was clearer in the latter contract than in the former. The main submission for Glass Fibres, however, was that the fourth contract was legally independent of the first contract. Glass Fibres contended that the independence of the contract for an irrevocable letter of credit was well established and commercially important. The court recognized the principle that the irrevocable obligations of banks, such as obligations under irrevocable confirmed letters of credit, guarantees, and performance bonds, were the life-blood of international commerce because they were separate legally from the underlying rights and obligations between merchants. A bank's obligation is to pay promptly and without question if the documents presented by the beneficiary are in accordance with the terms of the letter of credit, whether or not the documents conform to the terms of the underlying contract between the beneficiary and the issuing bank's customer. The bank must not pay if the documents are not in conformity with the terms of the letter of credit, however minor the nonconformity may be.

Lord Justice Stephenson considered the principle that the independence of the letter of credit would be undermined if the court looked beyond the letter of credit to its object and ultimate outcome or to other contracts connected with it, including exchange contracts. The contention had been made that a court must consider only the specific contract before it, so that the existence of an exchange contract could not be inferred by taking a variety of different contracts as a whole, none or only some of which, if taken separately, would constitute an exchange contract. The approach that refused to consider a scheme or arrangement as a totality did not recommend itself to Lord Justice Stephenson, who commented that

> almost every contract constituting a step towards an exchange contract would be enforceable and the currencies would in fact be illegally exchanged unless the last contract necessary to carry out the unlawful exchange required the help of a court of law to enforce it. That consequence might be thought to undermine to a surprising extent this important provision of the Bretton Woods Agreement.[22]

Lord Justice Stephenson discussed two decided cases that were relied on by the plaintiff to refute the proposition that the court could examine a scheme as a whole. The first was *Southwestern Shipping Corporation v. National City Bank of New York*,[23] which was decided by the New York Court of Appeals and which has been discussed earlier in this series.[24] Lord Justice Stephenson agreed that the majority of the New York Court of Appeals had isolated the contract sued on from the connected contracts.[25] He understood the decision to be based on the common law exception, which was not affected by Article VIII, Section 2(b), that if a party to an exchange contract that would be unenforceable under Article VIII, Section 2(b), if unperformed, turns over money or property to a third person for the use by the other party to the contract, the third party cannot rely on Article VIII, Section 2(b) to resist the claim of the other party to the money or property. Lord Justice Stephenson found the *Southwestern* case unhelpful in deciding whether the contract sued on in the case before him should be isolated.

His understanding of the *Southwestern* case can be stated in other words: transfer of the money or property to a third person for use of the other party to the contract amounted to performance of the contract. Article VIII, Section 2(b) applies to executory (unperformed) contracts and not to executed (performed) contracts.

Sharif v. Azad was the second of the two cases that Lord Justice Stephenson discussed. He remarked that, although there were striking

---

[22] [1981] 3 W.L.R. 254.

[23] 173 N.Y.S. 2d 509 (1958); 178 N.Y.S. 2d 1019 (1958); 190 N.Y.S. 2d 352 (1959); 80 S. Ct. 198 (1959).

[24] Gold, *Fund Agreement in the Courts* (1962), pp. 97–100, 102–108.

[25] He refers to them as contracts that "infringed" the Articles ([1981] 3 W.L.R. at 255), but this is obviously loose language.

similarities between it and the *Glass Fibres* case, there were also important dissimilarities. The facts must be repeated briefly in order to explain how he distinguished between the two cases. The plaintiff, a Pakistani citizen resident in England, sued the defendant, also a Pakistani citizen resident in England, on a sterling check drawn on a bank in England. Behind the check was a transaction between the plaintiff and Latif, a Pakistani citizen resident in Pakistan, by which the plaintiff had given Latif the sterling equivalent of the check in cash and had received in return a check in Pakistani rupees drawn by Latif on his bank in Pakistan, but with the payee's name left blank. The plaintiff took the rupee check to the defendant, who filled in the name of his brother as payee and sent the check to the brother in order to collect the rupees from Latif's bank. The object of the transaction was to evade Pakistan's exchange control regulations. The defendant pleaded that he had delivered the sterling check, on which the plaintiff was suing, in return for the rupee check provided by the plaintiff. The rupees were paid into the account of the defendant's brother but, as the result of action by the Pakistani authorities, the brother could not draw on them without official permission. The Court of Appeal in *Sharif v. Azad* held that the contract between the plaintiff and Latif would have been unenforceable as a result of Article VIII, Section 2(*b*) and the Order in Council, but the contract between the plaintiff and the defendant represented by the sterling check was separable, and the plaintiff could succeed on it.

One of the dissimilarities noted by Lord Justice Stephenson was the fact that the defendant's brother did receive rupees, even if they were blocked. Another dissimilarity was the fact that the plaintiff was suing not on a contract but on the sterling check issued in performance of it. Checks as negotiable instruments, which letters of credit are not, are regarded as equivalent to cash. Moreover, all members of the Court of Appeal in *Sharif v. Azad* appeared to have held that each of the two contracts, resulting in the sterling and rupee checks, was an exchange contract in itself.[26] The first two of these dissimilarities imply that the contracts in *Sharif v. Azad* had been executed by the delivery of checks, so that Article VIII, Section 2(*b*) was not applicable. More particularly, the sterling check was performance of the contract between the plaintiff and the defendant. The explanation of the case understood in this way would be the same as the explanation suggested by Lord Justice Stephenson's discussion of the *Southwestern* case.

---

[26] He cited *dicta* in the *Terruzzi* case in support of this view of the characterization of the contracts ([1981] 3 W.L.R. at 256–57).

Notwithstanding his rationalization of *Sharif v. Azad*, Lord Justice Stephenson found the case difficult to understand. He concluded that it depended on its special facts and that the law applicable to checks should not be applied to every action to enforce a letter of credit. *Sharif v. Azad* did not decide that every contract made in England by parties resident there was beyond the reach of Article VIII, Section 2(*b*), as *Batra v. Ebrahim* had demonstrated.

> The court must examine the particular contract sued on and its connection with the alleged breach of foreign currency regulations. If it "involves" those regulations and their breach[27]—and "involves" is a wide word (see *Reggazoni v. K.C. Sethia (1944) Ltd.* [1958] A.C. 301, 330, *per* Lord Somervell of Harrow)—it may offend against the article and be unenforceable, whether or not it is an exchange contract when looked at in isolation.
>
> For these reasons I feel free to distinguish *Sharif's* case and to consider whether the court is required by the nature of a letter of credit to look at it in all cases and circumstances, including the circumstances of this case, in isolation from those circumstances and so lend its aid to the enforcement of a contract declared unenforceable by Article VIII, section 2(*b*). I do not think that the court is required or entitled to do so. International trade requires the enforcement of letters of credit but international comity requires the enforcement of the Bretton Woods Agreement.
>
> I do not see why a court should shut its eyes to the object of the contract and with its eyes shut fall over backwards to avoid complying with the demands of international comity. On the contrary, the courts of this country should incline the other way and do their best to prevent breaches of the Bretton Woods Agreement to which this country is a party. In my judgment the courts of a country which is a party to the Agreement should do its best to promote both international comity and international trade. I have come to the conclusion that this court could best carry out this double duty in this case by enforcing the part of the sale agreement which does not offend against the law of Peru, and refusing to enforce the part of it which is a disguised monetary transaction by which currencies are to be exchanged in breach of that law. If this were the only defense to the plaintiffs' claim I would therefore proceed to allow the plaintiffs part of their claim.[28]

The defendant had argued that the letter of credit was illegal, void, or unenforceable under English common law principles. For example,

---

[27] Under the language of Article VIII, Section 2(*b*), exchange contracts, and not a member's exchange control regulations, must "involve" the member's currency.

[28] [1981] 3 W.L.R. at 258.

according to these principles, English courts will not enforce claims under contracts made in England and on their face lawful under English law if they require the performance of acts in another country that are unlawful there. The reason for these principles is international comity. Lord Justice Stephenson held that, even if the common law principle mentioned above was applicable to the *Glass Fibres* case on the facts, it was not applicable under the law:

> ... the Bretton Woods Agreement lays down the standard—or requirements—of comity in the area of exchange control which it covers: whether it extends to states who are not members of the International Monetary Fund or parties to the Agreement we do not have to consider. Article VIII, section 2(*b*) displaces the common law principle, as was clearly the opinion of Diplock L.J. in *Sharif v. Azad,* . . . with which I respectfully agree.[29]

The substitution in the field of exchange control of Article VIII, Section 2(*b*) when applicable for common law principles made it possible for Lord Justice Stephenson to dismiss any objection against severing contracts that might be based on common law principles. He held that the illegality under Peruvian law did not infect the whole range of contracts with illegality, which would be the consequence of the common law principles and which would deprive the plaintiff of all contractual rights to payment. He conceded that there were long-standing objections to severing entire contracts as there were to enforcing any part of a contract tainted with illegality. The case law, however, was not easy to reconcile, and no single principle or even clear guidelines could be derived from it on "when a court can award a plaintiff half a loaf and when it is bound to refuse him any bread."[30]

For Lord Justice Stephenson, it was relevant to the question of severability that Article VIII, Section 2(*b*) rendered exchange contracts unenforceable and not illegal. He would have been willing, but for his reaction to the other defense, to give effect "to so much of the plaintiffs' contract . . . as would not involve breaches of Peruvian law."[31]

In Lord Justice Ackner's opinion, if Glass Fibres had sued Vitro on the merchandise contract, Glass Fibres could have succeeded because the contract was not illegal and was not tainted as a whole by the overvaluation that was contrary to Peru's exchange control regulations. But Glass Fibres would not have been able to recover to the

---

[29] *Ibid.*, at 259.
[30] *Ibid.*, at 260.
[31] *Ibid.*, at 261.

extent of the overvaluation because to that extent the merchandise contract was a monetary transaction in disguise. He agreed that in exchange control matters the situation is regulated not by the general rules of English conflict of laws but by the Bretton Woods Agreements Act and the Order made under it.

The situation as described in this way was not changed because the action was on the confirmed letter of credit and not on the merchandise contract. Once a payment was made under the letter of credit, effect would be given, to some extent, to an exchange contract contrary to Peru's exchange control regulations. This result would follow because the contract required half of any payment to be transferred to the United States, to be held there for the benefit of Vitro. The principle of the immunity of the letter of credit from disputes between the buyer and the seller of goods, which they must settle between themselves without involving the bank, does not apply to a situation in which, as is established by *Batra v. Ebrahim*, the court is obliged by an international agreement not to enforce certain contracts. In that case, it will be recalled, the Court of Appeal held that the court must give effect to Article VIII, Section 2(*b*) even when the parties have not cited the provision.

Lord Justice Ackner also distinguished *Sharif v. Azad* from the case before the court. He explained the earlier case on the ground that both parties to it were resident in England, so that Pakistan's exchange control regulations were not contravened by enforcement of the claim. The cases could not be distinguished on this ground, however, because both Glass Fibres and Royal Bank were nonresidents of Peru. The second explanation by Lord Justice Ackner is more convincing: in *Sharif v. Azad* the payment of the rupees had been made, although into a blocked account, prior to the action. This explanation would be consistent with the suggested understanding of Lord Justice Stephenson's analysis of *Sharif v. Azad*. Lord Justice Ackner drew the same distinction between checks and letters of credit that had been drawn by Lord Justice Stephenson.

Lord Justice Griffiths made the problem of severability easier by treating the contract between Vitro and Glass Fibres as two agreements: an agreement for the purchase and sale of machinery and a "collateral agreement"[32] for overvaluation of the purchase price. The latter agreement was within Article VIII, Section 2(*b*), but not the former.

---

[32] *Ibid.*, at 278.

The letter of credit in isolation was not an exchange contract, he held, but it should not be looked at in isolation, because Vitro and Glass Fibres conspired together to use the letter of credit as a means of giving effect to an exchange contract in breach of Peru's exchange control regulations. The decisions that recognize the independence of letters of credit from underlying contracts establish that a bank is not concerned with possible breaches of an underlying contract, and not that the court must ignore the reality of a situation in which the letter of credit was not designed solely for the payment of goods and in which no dispute has arisen between the buyer and the seller.

> If Mr. Hirst's argument [that a court cannot look beyond a letter of credit] is right then the Order in Council relating to the unenforceability of exchange contracts will scarcely be worth the paper it is written on. In this case it so happens that there was a genuine sale contract which disguised the exchange contract but it would not be difficult to envisage the use of a completely spurious sale contract to disguise the exchange contract.
>
> Unless constrained by authority to do otherwise the court, in my view, ought to look at the whole arrangement and if it sees that the sale contract disguises an exchange contract it should refuse to enforce it through the medium of the letter of credit.[33]

Lord Justice Griffiths distinguished *Sharif v. Azad* from the *Glass Fibres* case for much the same reasons as those advanced by other members of the Court of Appeal, but he added another reason. The relevant regulations in *Sharif v. Azad* applied only to residents of Pakistan, but the relevant regulations of Peru were not confined to residents. Lord Justice Griffiths seems to have made this point in order to arrive at the view that Glass Fibres by providing the false invoice was itself in breach of the regulations. *Sharif v. Azad* did not bind him to follow a course that would "do a grave disservice to the obligations that this country accepted as a party to the Bretton Woods Agreement."[34]

Notwithstanding his view that Glass Fibres had violated Peru's exchange control regulations, Lord Justice Griffiths held that considerations of comity and public policy did not require that Glass Fibres as sellers should be deprived of the price of the goods they had sold. The sellers had fallen in with the scheme through weakness.

All three members of the Court of Appeal concurred in the conclusion that the defense based on Article VIII, Section 2(*b*), if it stood

---

[33] *Ibid.*, at 280.
[34] *Ibid.*

alone, would succeed in part but would not prevent recovery of the purchase price. All agreed, however, that because of the second defense no payments could be enforced under the letter of credit. The reason for this finding was a defect in the bills of lading against which Royal Bank would have been committed to make payments under the letter of credit. The bills of lading had been prepared and issued by an employee of the loading brokers for the shipping carriers of the merchandise purchased by Vitro from Glass Fibres. The employee made out the bills on December 16, 1976 but fraudulently altered the date to December 15, 1976 and fraudulently represented in them that the goods were on board on that earlier date. The letter of credit, it will be recalled, required shipment on or before December 15, 1976. The employee knew of the importance of the date, and it was possible that he was covering up his employer's failure to arrange the shipping on time. Neither Glass Fibres (or its assignee) nor Royal Bank knew of the fraud; the brokers and their employees were not the agents of either of these parties.

The Court of Appeal agreed that Royal Bank was not required, and indeed was not entitled, to pay under the letter of credit when it learned that the documents were not in conformity with the letter of credit if they had been completed honestly. The fraud of the person who makes out the documents vitiates the documents even though there is no fraud on the part of the seller of the goods or the beneficiary of the letter of credit or the seller-beneficiary who tenders the documents to the bank that confirms the letter of credit. There had been no earlier direct decision in England or the United States on the effect of the fraud of a third party. The decision can be understood to mean that, on facts such as those in the *Glass Fibres* case, it is the bank's duty to pay only on the presentation of conforming documents and that the onus is on the party presenting the documents to present conforming documents.

Some Comments on the Case in the Court of Appeal

1. The Court of Appeal decided the case in favor of the defendant on the basis of the second defense. It was unnecessary, therefore, for the court to consider the effect of Article VIII, Section 2(b). The views of the Lords Justices on that aspect of the case, though *obiter*, are of considerable interest as the most recent of the statements by English courts on the subject of Article VIII, Section 2(b).

2. An outstanding feature of the views of the Court of Appeal is the concern voiced by all members of the court that Article VIII, Sec-

tion 2(*b*), as an expression of public policy and international comity, should not be undermined. The reaction of some commentators to the *Terruzzi* case, not without justification, was that Article VIII, Section 2(*b*) would play a minimal role in England. Even though the *Terruzzi* case, from which there was no dissent, certainly represents an indefensibly narrow interpretation of Article VIII, Section 2(*b*), the *Glass Fibres* case shows that the provision can still have a substantial impact on litigation in England.

3. The earlier reaction to Article VIII, Section 2(*b*) as a provision of little practical effect is perhaps illustrated by the absence of a report of *Batra v. Ebrahim* in any of the standard series of English law reports. The case as reported in *The Times* (London) had much influence on the thinking of members of the Court of Appeal in the *Glass Fibres* case, particularly on the duty of courts to respect the public policy and international comity implicit in Article VIII, Section 2(*b*) and on the concept of unenforceability as it appears in that provision.

4. In the *Terruzzi* case, the Court of Appeal gave overriding effect to the undesirability of impediments to international trade, and the court took this position even though the contract sued on was entered into for the purpose of speculation in futures in metals. In the *Glass Fibres* case, the attitude of the Court of Appeal was that it had to balance the policy of freedom for trade with the policy of respecting the interests of other members of the Fund as expressed in their exchange control regulations.

5. A striking feature of the decision is the court's willingness to take account of all the steps that resulted from a plan to circumvent the exchange control regulations of a member and not to concentrate on the final step. Too often courts have looked only at the last step and have completed the circumvention that is the purpose of the plan. The Court of Appeal would have completed the plan[35] of Vitro and Glass Fibres and achieved a result contrary to Peru's exchange control regulations had the court considered only the letter of credit confirmed by Royal Bank for the benefit of Glass Fibres.

6. A question not clearly answered by the members of the Court of Appeal is whether their willingness to take account of all the relationships to which the plan gave rise was influenced by the fact that the plaintiff stood in the shoes of Glass Fibres, which was a

---

[35] Gold, *Fund Agreement in the Courts* (1962), pp. 106–108; Gold, "Fund Agreement in the Courts—XIV," pp. 266–67 in this volume.

participant in the plan. By taking all the relationships into account, the court was able to arrive at an amount that it considered Glass Fibres was entitled to as the seller of merchandise. It is not clear whether the Court of Appeal would have been similarly disposed to base its decision on all the relationships if the action had been between Banco Continental and Royal Bank.

7. A consequence of the refusal to look solely at the contract sued on is that the contract treated as unenforceable need not be in itself a contract for the exchange of one currency for another in accordance with the interpretation of "exchange contracts" in the *Terruzzi* case. The letter of credit required only that Royal Bank pay U.S. dollars to the beneficiary. It can be assumed that behind the letter of credit was an obligation by Vitro to pay Banco Continental in Peruvian soles the equivalent of the payments by Royal Bank and an obligation of Banco Continental to use the soles to obtain dollars with which to reimburse Royal Bank. Alternatively, Vitro might have been bound to obtain the dollars with soles in order to pay the dollars to Banco Continental. In either event, an exchange of one currency for another would occur, and this exchange would take place as a result of payments by Royal Bank under the letter of credit. The payments themselves, however, would not take the form of, or necessarily require, an exchange of currencies.

8. The concept of a monetary transaction in disguise is not clear. The intent may be to refer to a single design consisting of various steps of which at least one requires an exchange of one currency for another. Alternatively, the concept may cover cases in which no single step involves such an exchange, but the result of all the steps is that an exchange can be deemed to have occurred. Under either view, the monetary transaction in disguise is not a true exception to the *Terruzzi* interpretation of "exchange contracts." The exceptional aspect of the concept would be only the court's consideration of all the steps in an arrangement to circumvent exchange control regulations.

The Court of Appeal and those authors who favor the narrow interpretation of "exchange contracts" as adopted in the *Terruzzi* case and followed in the *Glass Fibres* case do not appear to treat the monetary transaction in disguise as an exception to their interpretation. They describe the transaction as an exception to the exclusion of contracts involving merchandise or securities from their interpretation.

9. The Court of Appeal ran together all relationships in the case but severed the contract between Glass Fibres and Vitro into two

parts. Lord Justice Griffiths was willing to regard that contract as consisting of two agreements. This approach had seemed unjustifiable to the lower court. The Court of Appeal found justification for its approach in Peru's exchange control regulations. The court understood Articles 1 and 2 of Decree Law No. 18275 as prohibiting the maintenance or establishment of deposits in a foreign currency in Peru or abroad. Therefore, the regulations did not reach the part of a contract that did not involve the maintenance or establishment of such deposits. The court treated Article 7 of Decree Law No. 18891 as if the offense of overvaluing imports implicitly preserved the validity of a transaction involving overvaluation to the extent of the true purchase price. There appears to have been no expert advice on this aspect of Peruvian law. The text of Article 7 can be read, at least in translation, to provide that the act of overinvoicing, and not the amount of invoicing, is the offense. The invoice as a whole is illegal on this reading and not partly legal and partly illegal.

10. Two consequences of severing the merchandise contract should be noted. First, the contract in circumstances similar to those in the *Glass Fibres* case becomes riskless for the exporter. This consequence may have induced Lord Justice Griffiths to point out that Glass Fibres and Vitro were not *in pari delicto* and that Glass Fibres was less at fault.

The other consequence, which members of the Court of Appeal did not discuss, was that the recovery it would have allowed Glass Fibres to make for its merchandise would have had the effect of condoning that part of the planned deposit abroad that Vitro and Glass Fibres had succeeded in making in contravention of Peru's exchange control regulations. The calculation concurred in by Lord Justice Stephenson is not completely clear, but in substance it appears to have been arrived at as follows. The true purchase price was doubled. An initial payment of 20 per cent of the full (i.e., double) contract price was made under the letter of credit. In accordance with the contract, half of this 20 per cent was transferred to the United States for the ultimate benefit of Vitro. The amount that the Court of Appeal would have been willing to award to Glass Fibres was half the full contract price less half the payment that had been made under the letter of credit. No deduction was made for the other half that reached Vitro. If this part had not been paid already, the court would not have enforced payment of it.

If the calculation by Lord Justice Stephenson was indeed the one described above, it could be defended perhaps on the ground that

Article VIII, Section 2(b) does not provide remedies in respect of contracts that have been executed or to the extent that they have been executed. This analysis might be justified if the court thought that it was being requested to make Vitro refund what it had received. A different view could prevail if the remedy were considered payment to Glass Fibres of the purchase price less the amount already paid to it. On this view, the full 20 per cent that had been paid to Glass Fibres under the letter of credit could be credited against the purchase price payable to it, even though this procedure would not force a surrender by Vitro of what it had gained.

11. The judgment that the Court of Appeal would have been willing to make in favor of the plaintiff had Article VIII, Section 2(b) been the only defense raises a problem of logic, at least on the reasoning of Lord Justice Ackner. He agreed with the lower court that once "any payment"[36] was made under the letter of credit, effect would be given, to some extent, to an exchange contract that was unenforceable under the provision. It is not obvious why this consequence should justify a decision in favor of the payment of half the amount of the letter of credit, because on the reasoning of Lord Justice Ackner this amount was a payment that was subject to sharing according to the contract between Vitro and Glass Fibres.

12. The decision of the Court of Appeal adds further authority to the proposition that unenforceability under Article VIII, Section 2(b) is not equivalent to illegality. Moreover, as *Batra v. Ebrahim* demonstrated, the unenforceability that is imposed by the provision does not have attached to it all the traditional incidents of unenforceability in English law.[37] Had this proposition not been true, an English court would not be able to call Article VIII, Section 2(b) into play in the absence of reliance on the provision by a party.

13. The view that Article VIII, Section 2(b) is an expression of the standard of international comity in the field of exchange control, and that this standard has displaced common law principles of comity in this field, may lead to interesting legal questions in the future. Lord Justice Stephenson has suggested one such question already in referring to the applicability of the standard to nonmembers of the

---

[36] [1981] 3 W.L.R. at 273.

[37] Gold, *Fund Agreement in the Courts* (1962), pp. 61–62, 85, 148–51; "Fund Agreement in the Courts—X," p. 144 in this volume; "Fund Agreement in the Courts—XIV," p. 260 in this volume; and "Fund Agreement in the Courts—XV," p. 298 in this volume.

Fund. There has been some speculation about the extent to which the Articles can be taken to express general principles of law that apply even to nonmembers. There has been more speculation, and more legal authority, on the question whether new principles of public policy have been enacted by the Articles among members even though these principles are not made explicit in the Articles.

The proposition that Article VIII, Section 2(*b*) can be taken to be the standard of comity in the field of exchange control that applies to nonmembers as well as members is not wholly indefensible in view of the common law principles referred to earlier. They developed without the benefit of the Articles. The nonrecognition of the interests of other countries that is dictated by certain traditional legal doctrines is based on a parochialism that increasingly appears to be inconsistent with interdependence among countries in modern conditions. Nevertheless, if Article VIII, Section 2(*b*) is broader than common law principles in the field of exchange control, the use of the provision as a standard that applies to nonmembers will be difficult to reconcile with the obvious spirit of Article VIII, Section 2(*b*). That spirit is one of collaboration among members, all of which undertake the same standard of behavior not only under that provision but also under the other provisions of the Articles. It may also be difficult to reconcile the recognition of Article VIII, Section 2(*b*) as the general standard of comity with the right of members to impose restrictions on exchange transactions with nonmembers.[38]

14. Whatever doubts the *Glass Fibres* case may suggest because of the willingness of the Court of Appeal to enforce payment of part of the amount of the letter of credit, the major importance of the case in relation to Article VIII, Section 2(*b*) is the affirmation that a letter of credit is not an absolute bar to the application of the provision. Moreover, the provision may be applied even though the circumstances do not involve fraud in the underlying transaction of the kind that is a recognized exception to the independence of a letter of credit.

II. Territorial Scope of Article VIII, Section 2(*b*)

KHARAGJTSINGH V. SEWRAJSINGH (NETHERLANDS)

On January 12, 1979 the Supreme Court of the Netherlands delivered its judgment on appeal from the Court of Justice of the Nether-

---

[38] Article XI, Section 2.

lands Antilles in a case involving some exchange control regulations of Surinam.[39] A.S. and his wife lived in a house in the Netherlands Antilles, under the law of which community property prevails between spouses. In 1974, A.S. sold the house to O.S., his brother, who was the respondent on appeal. The conveyance was completed in accordance with the law of the Netherlands Antilles, which did not require the wife's concurrence in the sale. At the time of the conveyance, Surinam, the Netherlands Antilles, and the Netherlands formed the Kingdom of the Netherlands. O.S. was a national and resident of Surinam, which became independent (and is now called Suriname) after the date of the conveyance but before the suit was filed. O.S. petitioned the court of first instance in the Netherlands Antilles for an order evicting the wife. She counterclaimed for rescission of the contract between the brothers. One of the grounds for her counterclaim was that O.S. as purchaser had failed to obtain a license in accordance with Surinam's exchange control regulations of 1947.

Under the regulations, a transaction entered into without the necessary authorization is void. The court of first instance and the Court of Justice of the Netherlands Antilles rejected the wife's counterclaim on the ground that the law of the Netherlands Antilles as the *lex situs* governed the conveyance, and the interests of Suriname were not fundamental enough to justify overriding the *lex situs*.

The wife appealed to the Supreme Court, alleging that the exchange control regulations of Suriname should be applied. Article VIII, Section 2(b) seems to have been cited, although not in the original grounds. The Procurator General urged that the decision of the Court of Appeal should be confirmed. There was no reason to apply the law of Suriname. Under the interregional law that applied among the three regions that constituted the Kingdom of the Netherlands at the time of the conveyance, the law of the Netherlands Antilles governed the contract. Under Article 3 of the Statute of the Kingdom, any matter that was not within the list of "Common Affairs" was governed by regional law. According to the law of the Netherlands Antilles, the conveyance was valid, but the legal situation would have been the same even if an international contract had been involved. The Supreme Court held that the law of the Netherlands Antilles applied and that the conveyance could not be rescinded because of noncompliance with Suriname's exchange control regulations. The court did not refer to Article VIII, Section 2(b).

---

[39] René van Rooij, Note, *Revue critique de droit international privé*, Vol. 69 (January–March 1980), pp. 69–79.

A commentator on the case has discussed at length the question whether Article VIII, Section 2(*b*) should have been applied.[40] He seems to hold the view that, because the court must take cognizance of the provision even if it is not relied on as a basis for suit, the court in this case must be taken to have rejected application of the provision. He appears to approve the decision because of the support it gives to a restricted application of Article VIII, Section 2(*b*). The discussion and conclusion rest on a fallacy. Article VIII, Section 2(*b*) renders certain contracts unenforceable if they are still executory and the aid of the court is invoked for specific enforcement or for damages for nonperformance. The concept of unenforceability necessarily implies that performance is still incomplete and can be enforced either specifically or by awarding damages. If a contract has been executed, Article VIII, Section 2(*b*) has no role. In particular, rescission of a contract cannot be obtained by relying on the provision. The silence of the Supreme Court on Article VIII, Section 2(*b*) should be taken to imply not a restrictive interpretation of the provision but its irrelevance to a request for rescission of an executed contract.

Novel questions would have arisen if a contract sued on had been executory in such circumstances of constitutional change. The circumstances at the date when the enforcement of performance is sought are decisive. At that time, Suriname had become independent and a member of the Fund. A relevant question then would have been whether the regional courts in the Netherlands Antilles were required to apply Article VIII, Section 2(*b*). The Netherlands is bound to ensure that exchange contracts within the reach of the provision "shall be unenforceable in the territories of any member." The "territories" of a member include regions with the constitutional status of the Netherlands Antilles.

A region such as the Netherlands Antilles is a component part of a member's territories and must be distinguished from a member's dependent territories. A member accepts the Articles on its "own behalf" and "in respect of" its dependent territories:

> By their signature of this Agreement, all governments accept it both on their own behalf and in respect of all their colonies, overseas territories, all territories under their protection, suzerainty, or authority, and all territories in respect of which they exercise a mandate.[41]

---

[40] *Ibid.*
[41] Article XXXI, Section 2(*g*).

The Netherlands must ensure that the courts of the Netherlands Antilles apply Article VIII, Section 2(b) when the exchange control regulations of another member are involved, because of the words "own behalf," and not "in respect of," in this provision, as well as the word "territories" in Article VIII, Section 2(b). The Supreme Court of Hong Kong in *White v. Roberts* had no doubt about this legal principle in a case involving the exchange control regulations of China.[42] Hong Kong is a dependent territory of the United Kingdom.

If the exchange control regulations of a region, such as the Netherlands Antilles, or a dependent territory, such as Hong Kong, are involved in an action in the courts of a member with which the region or territory is not connected, the member must apply Article VIII, Section 2(b) when the conditions of the provision are satisfied. The exchange control regulations are to be understood in both instances as those of the member that has accepted the Articles on its own behalf or in respect of its dependencies. Similarly, if the region or dependency has its own currency, that currency is a currency of the member, and the currency can be "involved" within the meaning of Article VIII, Section 2(b).

The provision has no application, however, to the exchange control regulations of a region or dependency of a member in the courts of the member or another of its dependencies. The words "any member" are wide and sometimes mislead observers into thinking that they apply to the legislator of exchange control regulations, so that even that member must treat exchange contracts as unenforceable under the provision if they are contrary to the member's own exchange control regulations, whether they are the regulations of a metropolitan territory, a region, or a dependency. It may seem anomalous that the courts of a region or dependency must apply Article VIII, Section 2(b) in favor of "foreign" members but not in favor of the member of which it is a region or dependency. There is no anomaly in this difference, however, because Article VIII, Section 2(b) is a provision designed to ensure cooperation among states. The reaction of a member's courts, wherever they are located within its territories, to the exchange control regulations of any of its territories is an internal matter governed exclusively by domestic law. That law may apply more rigorous sanctions than unenforceability when exchange contracts are contrary to the exchange control regulations of any of the member's territories.

---

[42] Gold, *Fund Agreement in the Courts* (1962), pp. 87–90.

The distinction between "foreign" and "internal" exchange control regulations that is drawn above is consistent with the Fund's view of Article VIII, Section 2(*a*):

> . . . no member shall, without the approval of the Fund, impose restrictions on the making of payments and transfers for current international transactions.

The Fund's understanding of "international" in this context is that the word applies to the making of payments and transfers for transactions between members. This understanding is supported by Article I(iv), which sets forth the purpose of the Fund that Article VIII, Section 2(*a*) is intended to make effective:

> To assist in the establishment of a multilateral system of payments in respect of current transactions between members and in the elimination of foreign exchange restrictions which hamper the growth of world trade.

As a result of this interpretation, a member is not required to obtain the approval of the Fund if it imposes restrictions on the making of payments and transfers for transactions between its own territories.

The freedom of a member to impose these restrictions or exchange control regulations may seem to be the anomaly, especially if a region or dependency has a currency and balance of payments of its own. In these circumstances, however, it might be expected that the member's laws would provide some form of reciprocal respect of "internal" exchange control regulations. The absence of a requirement of reciprocal respect in the Netherlands Antilles case is surprising. The commentator on the case has argued that there is an even stronger case for this form of respect, although not required by Article VIII, Section 2(*b*), than for the respect that must be accorded to "foreign" exchange control regulations in accordance with that provision.

An explanation of the Supreme Court's rejection of an obligation of respect among the regions may be the peculiarly intense attachment to the *lex situs* as the law that governs the disposition of interests in real property under private international law. The Supreme Court of the Netherlands held that "the considerable interest attaching for the Netherlands Antilles to the free functioning of legal commerce involving premises located in the Netherlands Antilles does not allow admitting in that country the nullity of the contract of sale provided for by the law of Suriname." [43] Traditional principles of the governing law

---

[43] Translated from *Revue critique de droit international privé* (cited in fn. 39), p. 69.

under private international law, even though the governing law is the *lex situs*, are not immune from the change wrought by Article VIII, Section 2(*b*) within its sphere. The authoritative interpretation of Article VIII, Section 2(*b*) that the Fund adopted on June 10, 1949 contains this sentence

> It also follows that such contracts will be treated as unenforceable notwithstanding that, under the private international law of the forum, the law under which the foreign exchange control regulations are maintained or imposed is not the law which governs the exchange contract or its performance.[44]

III. A Further Questionnaire on Article VIII, Section 2(*b*)

The fourteenth installment in this series was concluded with a list of twelve questions and answers relating to Article VIII, Section 2(*b*). The list can be supplemented on the basis of the two cases discussed in this installment.

(1) Should the defendant relying on Article VIII, Section 2(*b*) have the burden of proving the consistency of exchange control regulations with the Articles or should the plaintiff have the burden of proving inconsistency?

The defendant should have to demonstrate that all conditions of the provision are satisfied, including the consistency of the regulations with the Articles.

(2) Should the court determine the consistency of exchange control regulations without seeking the advice of the Fund?

The determination may depend on the Fund's exercise of discretionary powers, so that it may not be possible to find the answer by interpretation of the Articles. The only safe course is to seek the advice of the Fund.

(3) Does the answer to question (1) preclude the court from seeking the advice of the Fund?

If the court has authority under its procedures to seek the advice of the Fund, it should do so even if a party has not relied on Article VIII, Section 2(*b*) or even if a party has relied on the provision but has not obtained the advice of the Fund. A court should not permit the public policy of the provision to be frustrated by private parties.

(4) Does Article VIII, Section 2(*b*) justify the refusal of a bank to make payments under a letter of credit that it has issued or confirmed?

---

[44] Executive Board Decision No. 446-4, June 10, 1949, *Selected Decisions*, Ninth Issue, p. 202.

There is authority now that justifies the refusal because of the comity or public policy of the provision.

(5) Does the application of Article VIII, Section 2(*b*), in the circumstances referred to in question (4), depend on a demonstration of fraud in the underlying transaction that gives rise to the letter of credit of the kind that is recognized as an exception to the independence of the letter of credit from the underlying transaction?

The justification based on Article VIII, Section 2(*b*) does not depend on this demonstration.

(6) Must the exchange control regulations referred to in Article VIII, Section 2(*b*) constitute exchange restrictions?

Exchange control regulations are a broader category and they may, but need not, impose exchange restrictions. Exchange control regulations are within the scope of Article VIII, Section 2(*b*) if, for example, they augment restrictions on trade and even if payments are authorized automatically when imports are authorized.

(7) Can Article VIII, Section 2(*b*) be the basis for judicial rescission of an executed contract?

The concept of unenforceability implies that the contracts affected by the provision are still executory.

(8) Must a member ensure that courts in the dependencies in respect of which it has accepted the Articles apply Article VIII, Section 2(*b*) when the exchange control regulations of another member are in issue?

Yes.

(9) Must a member ensure that its courts or those of its dependencies apply Article VIII, Section 2(*b*) when the exchange control regulations of a dependency of another member are in issue?

Yes.

(10) Must a member ensure that its courts or the courts of its dependencies apply Article VIII, Section 2(*b*) when the exchange control regulations of one of its own dependencies are in issue, and must the courts of a member's dependency apply Article VIII, Section 2(*b*) when the exchange control regulations of the member or its other dependencies are in issue?

No.

(11) Does Article VIII, Section 2(*b*) apply to a member's own exchange control regulations when they are in issue in that member's courts?

No.

12

The Articles of Agreement and the U.S. Freeze of Assets, November 1979

Views of Courts and Others on Legal Aspects Relating to Article VIII, Section 2(*b*) of Fund's Articles

This chapter discusses the views of courts, legal scholars, legal practitioners, and officials on the relationship of the Articles of Agreement to the freeze of certain assets imposed by the President of the United States in November 1979. The chapter does not deal with the numerous other legal issues that have been discussed in connection with this action, except insofar as they have a bearing on the relationship of the U.S. measures to the Articles.

I. U.S. Executive Orders and Regulations

On November 14, 1979, the Secretary of the U.S. Treasury announced that President Carter had made an Order on that day blocking all official Iranian assets in the United States, including deposits in U.S. banks, their foreign branches, and their subsidiaries, in response to reports that the Government of Iran was about to withdraw its funds. The announced purpose of the Order was to ensure that the satisfaction of claims of the United States and its citizens against Iran would be provided for in an orderly manner. The Order did not affect the accounts of persons other than the Government of Iran, its Central Bank, and its other controlled entities. The precise amounts involved could not be ascertained at that time, but there was said to be no reason for disturbance in the foreign exchange or other markets. The President had taken this action pursuant to the International Emergency Economic Powers Act (IEEPA) under which the President has authority to deal with any unusual and extraordinary threat to the national security, foreign policy, or economy of the United States that has its source in whole or in substantial part outside the United States.

Executive Order 12170, which was the subject of the Secretary's statement, recited the President's authority under the Constitution and laws of the United States, including the IEEPA, to make the Order, stated that he found that the situation in Iran constituted an unusual and extraordinary threat of the kind mentioned above, and declared a national emergency in order to deal with the threat.

The Order continued:

> I hereby order blocked all property and interests in property of the Government of Iran, its instrumentalities and controlled entities and the Central Bank of Iran which are or become subject to the jurisdiction of the United States or which are in or come within the possession or control of persons subject to the jurisdiction of the United States.

Finally, the Secretary of the Treasury was authorized to employ all powers granted to the President by the IEEPA that were necessary to carry out the provisions of the Order.

On the same day, the Executive Director appointed by the United States made a statement in the Executive Board of the Fund that reflected the Secretary's statement and the Executive Order. The statement by the Executive Director did not invoke Executive Board Decision No. 144-(52/51). On November 28, 1979, the Executive Director in a memorandum to the Managing Director, which was circulated to the Executive Board on November 29, 1979, invoked that decision. He advised the Fund, in accordance with the decision and on behalf of the U.S. Government, that, with effect on November 14, 1979, the United States had issued regulations imposing restrictions on the making of certain payments and transfers by persons subject to the jurisdiction of the United States that involved the Government of Iran and its instrumentalities or controlled agencies. The Executive Director attached copies of the Executive Order and the regulations issued in accordance with it.

The Iranian Assets Control Regulations,[1] issued by the Foreign Assets Control Office of the U.S. Treasury, provided that:

> No property subject to the jurisdiction of the United States or which is in the posession of or control of persons subject to the jurisdiction of the United States in which on or after the effective date Iran has any interest of any nature whatsoever may be transferred, paid, exported, withdrawn or otherwise dealt in except as authorized; . . . .[2]

All dealings in any security registered or inscribed in the name of any Iranian entity were prohibited unless authorized by license.[3] Any transfer in violation of these provisions was null and void.[4]

Two vital definitions were as follows:

> . . . [T]he terms "property" and "property interest" or "property interests" shall include, but not by way of limitation, money, checks, drafts, bullion, bank deposits, savings accounts, debts, indebtedness, obligations, notes. . . .

as well as numerous other specified rights, assets, or instruments.[5]

> The term "persons subject to the jurisdiction of the United States" includes:
>
> (a) Any person wheresoever located who is a citizen or resident of the United States;
>
> (b) Any person actually within the United States;
>
> (c) Any corporation organized under the laws of the United States or of any state, territory, possession, or district of the United States; and
>
> (d) Any partnership, association, corporation, or other organization wheresoever organized or doing business which is owned or controlled by persons specified in paragraphs (a), (b), or (c) of this section.[6]

U.S.-owned or U.S.-controlled foreign firms, such as overseas branches or subsidiaries of domestic banks, were licensed to set off their claims against blocked accounts held by them.[7]

An amendment of the original Regulations, which became effective on November 19, 1979, declared that

> Deposits held abroad in currencies other than U.S. dollars by branches and subsidiaries of persons subject to the jurisdiction of the United

---

[1] 31 Code of Federal Regulations (CFR), Part 535.

[2] *Ibid.*, Part 535.201(a).

[3] *Ibid.*, Part 535.202.

[4] *Ibid.*, Part 535.203.

[5] *Ibid.*, Part 535.311.

[6] *Ibid.*, Part 535.329.

[7] *Ibid.*, Part 535.902. For other general licenses, see 31 CFR, Part 535.904.

States are unblocked, provided however that conversions of blocked dollar deposits into foreign currencies are not authorized.[8]

On April 28, 1980, the Executive Director appointed by the United States, recalling that he had notified the Managing Director of the Regulations under Executive Board Decision No. 144-(52/51), gave him notification under that decision of amendments issued on April 7 and 17, 1980. These amendments, he declared, imposed restrictions on the making of certain payments and transfers by persons subject to the jurisdiction of the United States that involved the Government of Iran, its instrumentalities or controlled entities, enterprises controlled by Iran, or persons in Iran. This notification and the amendments of the Regulations were circulated to the Executive Board. The period of 30 days referred to in Decision No. 144-(52/51), which is quoted later in this chapter, expired on each occasion without any action by members or by the Fund except as is noted later.

The notification of April 28, 1980 related to amendments of the Regulations made as a result of Executive Order 12205 of April 7, 1980. The restrictions on transactions, payments, and transfers were extended, and persons in Iran were added to Iran, Iranian governmental entities, and enterprises controlled by Iran as the parties with whom transactions, payments, and transfers were restricted. Persons subject to the jurisdiction of the United States were forbidden, by the amendment of April 17, 1980, to:

Make any payment, transfer of credit, or other transfer of funds or other property or interests therein, except for purposes of family remittances.

The Regulations issued in connection with Executive Order 12205 provided, however, that the prohibitions on financial transactions

shall not apply to transactions by any person subject to the jurisdiction of the United States which is a non-banking association, corporation or other organization organized and doing business under the laws of any foreign country. The U.S. parent of any such person must report to the Office of Foreign Assets Control any prospective transaction with Iran contained in paragraph (a) of the section ten days before any subsidiary enters into such a transaction.[9]

In July 1980 the Regulations were amended to provide that interest was to be credited back to December 1, 1979 on accounts in the hands of holders of certain blocked financial assets. The interest was to be frozen together with the principal. The purpose was to avoid an

---

[8] *Ibid.*, Part 535.566.
[9] *Ibid.*, Part 535.206(b).

unconvenanted benefit for the holders of the assets, who, it was assumed, had been able to earn interest on them, and to contribute to the successful outcome of discussions on a financial settlement between the banks and Iranian authorities.[10] The rate of interest and other matters relating to it were prescribed, but

> the duty to credit interest on any property . . . which, as of the effective date of this section, was held by a foreign branch or subsidiary of a U.S. person shall be determined in accordance with the local law of the host country of the foreign branch or subsidiary. Property in the form of a debt is not held outside the United States if the funds intended to pay that debt are held inside the United States.[11]

MOTIVATIONS OF U.S. MEASURES

The motivation stated in Executive Order 12170 was that "the situation in Iran constitutes an unusual and extraordinary threat to the national security, foreign policy and economy of the United States. . . . " The President's message to Congress on November 14, 1979 with respect to the Executive Order stated that:

> These events and actions put at grave risk the personal safety of United States citizens and the lawful claims of United States citizens and entities against the Government of Iran and constitute an extraordinary threat to the national security and foreign policy of the United States.

The two Executive Orders of April 1980 amplified the motivation stated in Executive Order No. 12170. Executive Order 12205 of April 7, 1980 added "in furtherance of the objective of United Nations Security Council Resolution 461 (1979) adopted on December 31, 1979."[12] The Executive Order of April 17, 1980 amplified the original motivation, so that it read:

> . . . the threat to the national security, foreign policy and economy of the United States. . . , and the added unusual and extraordinary threat to the national security, foreign policy and economy of the United States created by subsequent events in Iran and neighboring countries,

---

[10] Karin Lissakers, "Money and Manipulation," *Foreign Policy*, No. 44 (1981), p. 119; "A retrospective review of the Iranian 'hostages' settlement," *International Currency Review*, Vol. 13 (1981), pp. 54–62.

[11] 31 CFR, Part 535.205. See "U.S. Treasury regulations governing blocked Iranian assets," *International Currency Review*, Vol. 12 (1980), pp. 26–36, 38.

[12] Paragraph 6 of the Resolution provided that the Security Council

> "DECIDES to meet on 7 January 1980 in order to review the situation and in the event of non-compliance with this Resolution, to adopt effective measures under Articles 39 and 41 of the Charter of the United Nations."

A proposed resolution dealing with economic sanctions was vetoed by the U.S.S.R. on January 13, 1980.

including the Soviet invasion of Afghanistan, with respect to which I hereby declare a national emergency, and to carry out the policy of the United States to deny the use of its resources to aid, encourage or give sanctuary to those persons involved in directing, supporting or participating in acts of international terrorism. . . .[13]

Executive Order 12282 of January 19, 1981 and amendments of the Regulations revoked the restrictions imposed on payments and transfers for current international transactions that were contained in the earlier Executive Orders and Regulations and were the subject of notifications under Executive Board Decision No. 144-(52/51).[14]

II. Executive Board Decision No. 144-(52/51)

Decision No. 144-(52/51) was adopted by the Executive Board on August 14, 1952. The origins of the decision can be traced back to

---

[13] Fear of the effect on the U.S. dollar and the U.S. banking system of a sudden withdrawal of assets and defaults in the repayment of indebtedness is alleged to have been the motivation for the measures by Karin Lissakers, Deputy Director of the U.S. State Department's Policy Planning Staff, 1979–80, "Money and Manipulation," *Foreign Policy*, No. 44 (1981), pp. 107–26. A staff report prepared for the Committee on Banking, Finance and Urban Affairs of the U.S. House of Representatives, 97th Congress, 1st Session (Committee Print 97-5, July 1981), entitled *Iran: The Financial Aspects of the Hostage Settlement Agreement* (hereinafter cited as *Iran: The Financial Aspects (Committee Print 97-5)*), raises some question about the motivation of an economic emergency insofar as it was based on the impact of the withdrawal of balances on the U.S banking system (pp. 3–4, 13–14, 43). The Chairman of the Committee (p. v) records his opinion that:

"In light of the expansive interpretations given to the economic emergency authority under IEEPA in some government quarters during the Iran crisis, it would now be appropriate for the Congress to provide future administrations with clearer guidance as to those circumstances which should constitute an economic emergency under IEEPA."

[14] With the exception of stand-by letters of credit, performance bonds, and similar obligations, entered into prior to January 20, 1981 (31 CFR, Parts 535.438 and 535.579, February 24, 1981). See "U.S. Treasury regulations governing blocked Iranian assets," *International Currency Review*, Vol. 12 (1980), pp. 26–36, 38; *Emergency Economic Powers: Iran*, Hearing Before the Subcommittee on International Economic Policy and Trade of the Committee on Foreign Affairs, U.S. House of Representatives, 97th Congress, 1st Session, March 5, 1981, p. 13; *Iranian Asset Settlement*, Hearing Before the Committee on Banking, Housing, and Urban Affairs, U.S. Senate, 97th Congress, 1st Session, February 19, 1981, pp. 82–85; *The Iran Agreements*, Hearings Before the Committee on Foreign Relations, U.S. Senate, 97th Congress, 1st Session, February 17, 18, and March 4, 1981, p. 159.

See also Robert Carswell, "Economic Sanctions and the Iran Experience," *Foreign Affairs*, Vol. 60 (Winter 1981/82), p. 258, hereinafter cited as Carswell, *Economic Sanctions*. (Mr. Carswell was Deputy Secretary of the U.S. Treasury from 1977 to 1981.)

the imposition of restrictions by the United States in 1950 against China and North Korea and their residents during the action of the United Nations in Korea. At that time, the Fund took note of the restrictions pending the study of the Fund's jurisdiction under Article VIII, Section 2(*a*).

Executive Board Decision No. 144-(52/51) has been invoked by more than 30 members of the Fund that were imposing restrictions in connection with a variety of international situations. The United States has invoked the decision on the occasions on which it imposed restrictions on payments and transfers involving four countries and their residents. The only occasion on which the Fund has adopted a specific decision has been the one when the Fund deemed the earlier actions by the United States in relation to China and North Korea to be actions taken under Decision No. 144-(52/51).[15]

Decision No. 144-(52/51), which remains in effect as originally formulated, reads as follows:

PAYMENTS RESTRICTIONS FOR SECURITY REASONS: FUND JURISDICTION

Art. VIII, Sec. 2(*a*), in conformity with its language, applies to all restrictions on current payments and transfers, irrespective of their motivation and the circumstances in which they are imposed. Sometimes members impose such restrictions solely for the preservation of national or international security. The Fund does not, however, provide a suitable forum for discussion of the political and military considerations leading to actions of this kind. In view of the fact that it is not possible to draw a precise line between cases involving only considerations of this nature and cases involving, in whole or in part, economic motivations and effects for which the Fund does provide the appropriate forum for discussion, and the further fact that the Fund must exercise the jurisdiction conferred by the Fund Agreement in order to perform its duties and protect the legitimate interests of its members, the following policy decision is taken:

1. A member intending to impose restrictions on payments and transfers for current international transactions that are not authorized by Art. VII, Sec. 3(*b*) or Art. XIV, Sec. 2 of the Fund Agreement and that, in the judgment of the member, are solely related to the preservation of national or international security, should, whenever possible, notify the Fund before imposing such restrictions. Any member may obtain a decision of the Fund prior to the imposition of such restrictions by so indicating in its notice, and

---

[15] *History, 1945–65,* Vol. I: Chronicle, pp. 275–76. See also Margaret G. de Vries and J. Keith Horsefield and others, Vol. II: Analysis, pp. 259–60, 588–91; and Gold, *Membership and Nonmembership,* pp. 354–56.

the Fund will act promptly on its request. If any member intending to impose such restrictions finds that circumstances preclude advance notice to the Fund, it should notify the Fund as promptly as circumstances permit, but ordinarily not later than 30 days after imposing such restrictions. Each notice received in accordance with this decision will be circulated immediately to the Executive Directors. Unless the Fund informs the member within 30 days after receiving notice from the member that it is not satisfied that such restrictions are proposed solely to preserve such security, the member may assume that the Fund has no objection to the imposition of the restrictions.

2. The Fund will review the operation of this decision periodically and reserves the right to modify or revoke, at any time, the decision or the effect of the decision on any restrictions that may have been imposed pursuant to it.

PROCEDURE UNDER RULES H-2 AND H-3 AND DECISION No. 144-(52/51)

In a letter dated December 7, 1979 to the Managing Director, which was circulated to the Executive Board, the Governor of the Central Bank of Iran objected to the measures taken by the United States. Among the reasons for his objection were legal considerations of a general character drawn from the Articles, supported by reference to Article IV, Section 1 and Article I(ii). He requested that the case be submitted to the Executive Board and that the official views of the Fund be conveyed to him. The communication was treated as a complaint under Rules H-2 and H-3 of the Rules and Regulations:

H-2. If a member complains to the Executive Board that another member is not complying with its obligations concerning exchange controls, discriminatory currency arrangements, or multiple currency practices, the complaint shall give all facts pertinent to an examination.

H-3. Upon receipt of a complaint from a member, the Executive Board shall make arrangements promptly for consultation with the members directly involved.

The period of 30 days referred to in Decision No. 144-(52/51) would expire on December 29, 1979. Consultations under Rule H-3 would have to be completed in time to allow for discussion by the Executive Board before expiration of the period if an Executive Director requested discussion in accordance with the decision.

The Executive Board decided that the Managing Director should consult the two members directly involved by such contacts and communications as proved necessary. In communications of December 14, 1979 he drew to their attention Decision No. 144-(52/51) and offered his assistance. On December 19, 1979 the Governor of the Central Bank of Iran responded by describing the adverse effects of the Executive Order and asserting that it violated Article VIII, Section 2(a). He did not refer to Decision No. 144-(52/51). In a letter of December 22, 1979, following a meeting with the Managing Director, he requested an extension of the 30-day period under the decision to January 11, 1980, and that a meeting of the Executive Board be held on December 29, 1979 if this request was refused. The request for a meeting if an extension was not granted was withdrawn on December 27, 1979.

On December 27, 1979, the Executive Board decided to maintain the normal procedure as stated in the decision and not to extend the 30-day period. By a letter of the same date, the Acting Secretary of the U.S. Treasury wrote that the action of the United States was fully in accord with international law and Decision No. 144-(52/51).

The Temporary Alternate Governor of the Fund for Iran delivered a speech at the Annual Meeting of the Board of Governors in 1980 expressing his legal and economic objections to the U.S. measures and to the procedure the Fund had followed under Decision No. 144-(52/51). As part of his case, he rejected the assertion that the U.S. measures had been imposed for reasons of national or international security.[16]

The expiration of the 30-day period meant that the United States was entitled, without any notice to it by the Fund, to assume that the Fund had no objection to whatever restrictions on payments and transfers for current international transactions were imposed by the U.S. measures. The language of no objection is a traditional formulation for the "approval" that is required by Article VIII, Section 2(a). The traditional formulation is designed to avoid any impression of approbation that use of the word "approve" in a decision might convey. There is, however, no middle legal ground between approval and nonapproval under Article VIII, Section 2(a). The Fund announced in Executive Board Decision No. 144-(52/51) that it reserved the right to modify or revoke the effect of the decision on any restrictions imposed pursuant to it, but the Fund took no action of this kind in relation to the U.S. measures. The expiration of the period did not mean that consultation could not be resumed at any time under Rule H-3.

---

[16] *Summary Proceedings*, September 30–October 3, 1980, pp. 180–82.

Professor François Gianviti, who is Dean of the School of Law and Political Science of the University of Paris XII and a former member of the staff of the Fund's Legal Department, has speculated that the absence of an overt response by the Fund to the United States might have meant no more than that the Fund found no restrictions in the U.S. measures that required approval under Article VIII, Section 2(a).[17] This suggestion ignores the fact that the communications of the Executive Director appointed by the United States declared that the U.S. measures involved restrictions on payments and transfers for current international transactions and that the United States was obliged to give notice of them to the Fund under Decision No. 144-(52/51) because the restrictions were imposed for security reasons. The decision does not provide for silence by the Fund when there are no restrictions, precisely because of the uncertainty that would then be created. If there were no restrictions, the Fund would be required to find that the decision did not apply, because the Fund's silence entitles the member to "assume that the Fund has no objection to the imposition of the restrictions." The Fund distinguishes between the presence and absence of restrictions, as is shown by the fact that some of the notifications received by the Fund from the United States were found to deal with the interpretation of earlier restrictive measures or with procedures relating to them and not with new restrictions. For this reason, these notifications were not submitted to the Executive Board under the decision.

Although the treatment of a notification under the decision must be taken to imply a determination by the Fund that a member has imposed restrictions on payments and transfers for current international transactions and that all such restrictions as will be found to have been imposed are approved, neither the member's notification nor the memorandum transmitting it to the Executive Board includes an analysis or list of the measures that are deemed to be restrictions and that require approval under Article VIII, Section 2(a). The effect of the decision is to approve whatever restrictions on payments and transfers for current international transactions are in fact imposed by the member's measures. The absence of a tabulation of the restrictions can be explained as resulting from reluctance by the Fund and its members to become involved in the discussion of a political situation, but the procedure does produce uncertainty about the measures that are approved and the measures that do not require approval.

---

[17] François Gianviti, "Le blocage des avoirs officiels iraniens par les Etats-Unis (executive order du 14 novembre 1979)," *Revue critique de droit international privé*, Vol. 69 (1980), p. 295. (Hereinafter cited as Gianviti, *Le blocage*.)

III. Litigation Outside United States

FRANCE

It was not immediately obvious to all commentators that the Articles of Agreement might affect the litigation instituted as a result of the U.S. measures.[18] The possible relevance of the Articles became apparent to all after the decision of the *tribunal de grande instance* of Paris in *Central Bank of the Iranian State, Bank Markazi Iran v. Citibank Paris* on December 21, 1979.[19]

The plaintiff requested the court to order the defendant, a banking establishment with a registered place of business in Paris, to return the amount of US$50 million that the plaintiff had deposited with the defendant, or its equivalent in French francs, together with accrued interest on the account. The deposit had been made on August 17, 1976 and renewed on several occasions. The last maturity date under the contract was December 19, 1979. The plaintiff requested the court to act immediately in accordance with a summary procedure, on the ground that the defendant's obligation was indisputable and, under the banking law of France, had to be discharged in accordance with the contract.

The court, although noting that the defendant had admitted it was under obligation to restore the balance to the plaintiff, held that the issues were beyond the scope of summary proceedings, and referred the parties to further proceedings before a tribunal (*juges du fond*) that would examine the merits. The decision was preceded by the following clauses:

> Whereas the financial operation contemplated by the parties to the initial agreement is represented by an exchange of book money (*un échange de monnaie scripturale inscrite en compte*), performance of the final operation in reverse would seem to be incumbent on banking institutions where the currency is legal tender, in this case the United States of America;

> Whereas the argument put forth by Citibank Paris that it is unable effectively to carry out the said operation because of an executive order issued by the head of a foreign state under whose authority it falls as a branch of an American bank cannot be thoroughly assessed until the matter has been heard by *juges du fond*, it being noted that, as severe

---

[18] For example, in a broad examination of legal problems in "Legal repercussions of the freezing of Iranian assets and loans," *International Currency Review*, Vol. 12 (1980), pp. 25–39, there is no mention of the possible effect of the Articles.

[19] *Revue critique de droit international privé*, Vol. 69 (1980), pp. 382–84.

penalties attend the executive order, the debtor's possibilities for acting and deciding are limited;

Whereas, finally, to the extent that the executive order may be considered equivalent to an "exchange restriction", the actual operation of restitution must be assessed in the light of an interpretation of the Articles of Agreement of the International Monetary Fund, of which both France and the United States are members, and accordingly the intervention of the French judicial authorities, as requested by the Bank Markazi Iran, cannot be considered within the limited and provisional scope of summary proceedings; . . . .[20] (*Translation*)

Bank Markazi, on January 15, 1980, attached accounts of Citibank Paris held with the Bank of France and the Banque Internationale pour L'Afrique Occidentale (BIAO) and sought payment of its claim from these funds. In *Citibank Paris v. Central Bank of the Iranian State, Bank Markazi Iran*, the bank resisted the claim with the argument that, on the basis of both the agreement between the parties and standard practice in the Eurocurrency market, the claim could be satisfied only by having its correspondent in the United States transfer the U.S. dollars to another bank in the United States. The transfer would be subject to the Executive Order and could be paid, therefore, only from one blocked account to another.

The bank argued further that, even if it was decided that discharge of its obligation was not governed by U.S. law as the *lex loci solutionis*, the Articles obliged the court to take account of the Executive Order and respect the exchange control regulations that had been adopted by the United States.

Bank Markazi contended that the deposit was made, and an account opened, in Paris, with the consequence that the obligation of Citibank Paris was subject to the provisions of French law. The public policy of French law prevented enforcement of the Executive Order in France. With respect to Article VIII, Section 2(b), Bank Markazi argued that its contract with Citibank Paris was not an "exchange contract." Acceptance of the argument that Article VIII, Section 2(b) applied would pervert the Articles for a clearly political end. If, however, the court should hold that the case came within Article VIII, Section 2(b), so that the contract was unenforceable, the court should rescind the contract and order return of the amount deposited with interest.

---

[20] In an earlier decision, delivered on December 11, 1979, as the result of proceedings instituted on December 5, 1979, the court held that the deposit had been renewed by agreement between the parties for a period ending December 19, 1979, so that there were no grounds for summary proceedings at that date.

The court noted these arguments but did not base its reaction on them. The court's determination rested on the following considerations: the evidence did not lead conclusively to the legal system that the parties intended to select as the law governing their relationship; the parties disagreed on whether the funds for return of the deposit would come from New York or from Paris and on whether the deposit was subject to French law; the apparent corroboration of the contention of Citibank Paris by the language of telex exchanges between the parties ("payable at First National City Bank, New York," "funds at our disposal at First National City Bank, New York"); and the assertion of Citibank Paris that both the practice between the parties and the more general banking practice supported its premise that New York was the only place for return of the funds.

On the basis of these and other considerations, the court, on April 23, 1980, appointed three experts to examine the facts relating to the deposit, to describe the terms agreed upon between the parties, including those governing the deposit and return of the funds, and to verify the specific or general banking practices alleged by Citibank Paris.[21]

ENGLAND

Bank Markazi Iran instituted proceedings in London against the London branches of six U.S. banks and requested enforcement of its instructions for withdrawal or transfer of its dollar-denominated deposits with the defendants or damages for breach of contract.[22] The defendants argued that the contracts relating to these deposits were governed by the law of their home offices in New York or California, and that under these contracts repayment was illegal because of the U.S. measures. Another defense was that the customary and sole mechanism in use in London for the settlement of dealings in U.S. dollars, including withdrawals, was by interbank transfers in the United States, principally through the New York Clearing House Interbank Payments System (CHIPS) or the Federal Reserve System, and that it was an implied term of the contracts that dealings would

---

[21] *Gazette du Palais,* March 12–13, 1980, p. 8; *Journal du Droit International,* Vol. 107 (1980), pp. 330–31.

[22] *Iranian Assets Litigation Reporter,* May 2, 1980, pp. 639–50; May 16, 1980, pp. 790–802; June 20, 1980, pp. 1028–65; July 3, 1980, pp. 1098–1104. See also John E. Hoffman, Jr., "The Iranian Assets Litigation," *Private Investors Abroad—Problems and Solutions in International Business in 1980,* reprinted from Proceedings of the Southwestern Legal Foundation, 1980, pp. 329–65. (Hereinafter cited as Hoffman, *Iranian Assets Litigation.*)

be conducted in this way. A further defense was that if a valid claim were made for repayment, the place of performance would be in the United States or would necessarily involve acts performed within the United States. The defendants could not be required to make payment in a manner prohibited by the laws of the United States. A defense based on public policy asserted that the Government of Iran had threatened to disrupt the international monetary system by adversely affecting the value and utility of the principal international reserve currency, the U.S dollar. The last of the defenses that it is useful to note here is that the United Kingdom, the United States, and Iran were all members of the Fund, and that the U.S. measures were within the meaning of Article VIII, Section 2(b) and the Bretton Woods Agreements Order, 1946 of the United Kingdom that gave the provision the force of law in that country.

The plaintiff admitted the defendants' version of the procedure for London interbank dealings in Eurodollars but denied that this procedure was the only one that had been or could be followed. The procedure of clearing through New York or San Francisco was for convenience only and was not an implied term of the contracts. "In-house" transfers were carried out solely on the books of the London branch. The plaintiff was entitled to receive in London payment in cash or other negotiable security in dollars or any other currency that it requested and to have transfers honored in accordance with its instructions. No acts of performance were necessary in New York for satisfaction of the plantiff's rights.

The plaintiff denied the defendants' assertion of the law governing the contracts. The plaintiff's rights and the defendants' corresponding obligations were governed solely by English law. The fact that the Euromarket was established in order to avoid restrictive aspects of U.S. law, including exchange control provisions, was evidence that English law governed the contracts.

The plaintiff stated that Iran had publicly declared its willingness to honor debts that were its lawful obligations and to support the payment of due indebtedness by entities owned by the State. The plaintiff denied that its contracts with the defendants were exchange contracts. It wished only to have the currency of deposit transferred to a bank that was not owned or controlled by a U.S. bank. The plaintiff denied also that the U.S. measures were imposed consistently with the Articles, or that the currency of the United States was involved within the meaning of Article VIII, Section 2(b) and the Bretton Woods Agreements Order.

The assertion that transfers of U.S. dollars in New York would be necessary to satisfy the plaintiff's claim was involved in defenses that relied on both Article VIII, Section 2(b) and traditional private international law. It is useful, therefore, to note the explanation by Mr. John E. Hoffman, Jr., of New York of clearing systems in his article on the U.S. measures.[23]

He has written that custom and usage in the operation of a Eurocurrency account expressed in dollars require all transfers to be made in the United States because the only dollar-clearing mechanism exists in that country. For operations on Eurocurrency accounts expressed in another currency, a similar clearing mechanism exists in the country of the issuer of that other currency. The reason for this procedure is that ultimately a currency represents the obligation of the government that issues it, and is legal tender only in the country of issue. Therefore, money in the form of bank deposits is meaningless except insofar as it is payable within the issuing country in the form of liabilities of the central bank, which are equivalent to bank-notes.

The central banking system in the United States is composed of the Federal Reserve Banks, the Board of Governors of the Federal Reserve System, and the Federal Open Market Committee. The Federal Reserve Banks are the authorized issuers of U.S. currency. Funds on deposit at the Federal Reserve Banks represent direct liabilities of the central bank.

Bank deposits represent the obligations of a bank to the depositor. Performance of the obligation without delay depends directly on the liquidity of the bank holding the deposit. Liquidity can be ensured only through an interbank clearing mechanism that allows participants to know that payments will be sound, final (that is, payable in the form of central bank liabilities), and simultaneous with payments to other participants in the system.

A clearing system provides the structure through which participating banks offset inpayments and outpayments among themselves. Each can rely on the fact that outpayments can be made because inpayments will be received in good funds and speedily. Any net amounts that are due from a particular bank are settled by transferring balances or reserves that the bank maintains at the central bank. New York banks make these settlements through the New York Clearing House by transferring reserves at the Federal Reserve Bank of New York. If a bank has insufficient reserves, it must get them from other

---

23 Hoffman, *Iranian Assets Litigation*, pp. 347–50.

banks or from the Federal Reserve Bank and ultimately the bank may have to liquidate assets. Therefore, the Federal Reserve Banks act as the lenders of last resort to back up money in the form of bank credit, and banks must own demand liabilities of the central bank for the settlement of their obligations.

Mr. Hoffman has noted that although in theory clearings in dollars could exist outside the United States, the only clearing mechanism for settling large dollar transactions is in the United States. A clearing mechanism does not exist outside the United States because there is no economic incentive for establishing it, and indeed there are economic disincentives. Even if a clearing system for dollars were established in London notwithstanding the disincentives, the net payments arrived at among London banks would be settled through clearing systems in the United States. Mr. Hoffman has concluded that payment out of London dollar accounts requires essential acts of performance in the United States, and that, as a matter of contract law, whether English or U.S. law is applied, a court would not order a bank to operate in a way contrary to the law of the place of performance.

Other authors have discussed the effect of the clearing mechanism on the defense that private international law prevented enforcement of the depositor's claim whether action was brought in courts in the United States or elsewhere,[24] but the effect of private international

---

[24] A detailed inquiry into the clearing arrangements as they relate to Eurodollars and private international law is to be found in F.A. Mann, "Zahlungsprobleme bei Fremdwährungsschulden" ("Payments Problems in Connection with Foreign Currency Debts"), *Annuaire suisse de droit international*, Vol. XXXVI (1980), pp. 93–108. (Hereinafter cited as Mann, *Annuaire suisse*.) Dr. Mann asks the question whether the law must treat Eurodollar balances in the same way as other balances, so that, for example, the contract must be performed at the location of the branch bank and in case of doubt be treated as subject to the law of the country of location. He puts forward the hypothesis that a monetary debt is not involved, and that the creditor's right is to demand that the debtor bank procure a credit balance for the creditor, or for the party designated by him, through the CHIPS. Therefore, an essential part of performance takes place in New York, and even if the law of the country in which the debtor bank operates governs the contract, courts there will not treat as irrelevant the law of the place where necessary acts of performance must take place. Dr. Mann also concludes that this analysis, if correct, leads to the conclusion that dollars never leave the United States, and that the situs in New York of the dollar balances that are the subject of the procurement obligation is relevant for certain legal purposes.

Professor Gianviti has examined the application of French private international law to the U.S. measures (*Le blocage*, pp. 299–300), but apparently did not consider the clearing mechanism to be relevant. In his view, French law governed both the deposit contracts and the performance of them, and the contracts could be performed in francs if necessary. In his view, there was no stipulation

law on the application of the U.S. measures is not the subject of this chapter. The question whether the clearing mechanism was relevant to the defense of Article VIII, Section 2(b) would depend on whether the mechanism helped to satisfy the requirement of the provision that the U.S. dollar must be "involved" within the meaning of the provision. It is also possible that the clearing mechanism was relevant to the question whether the United States had legislative jurisdiction for the purpose of Article VIII, Section 2(b), if this question is different from the question of the involvement of a currency. These issues would arise only in courts outside the United States because the provision does not relate to the exchange control regulations of the country of the forum.

IV. Legislative Jurisdiction

When a member gives the Fund notification of restrictions under Executive Board Decision No. 144-(52/51), the Fund does not inquire whether the member imposing the restrictions, Terra, has authority under its national law or under international law to impose the restrictions.

Article VIII, Section 2(b) requires the courts of a member, Patria, to treat contracts as unenforceable when they are contrary to the exchange control regulations of Terra, provided that the regulations are consistent with the Articles. It is a necessary implication of Article VIII, Section 2(b), however, that Terra had jurisdiction to adopt the regulations.

The jurisdiction referred to here, which for convenience can be called legislative jurisdiction,[25] is not the jurisdiction to legislate that Terra has by virtue of its own law, but the jurisdiction that Patria

---

that France was not the place of performance. He does discuss the clearing arrangements in relation to the involvement of the U.S. dollar for the purpose of Article VIII, Section 2(b). See also "Symposium on the Settlement with Iran," *Lawyer of the Americas (The University of Miami Journal of International Law)*, Vol. 13 (1981), pp. 17–18 (hereinafter cited as *Miami Symposium*), and Carswell, *Economic Sanctions*, p. 250.

[25] Often referred to as "jurisdiction to prescribe," i.e., a state's authority to enact laws whether by legislation, executive act or order, or administrative rule or regulation. It is distinguished from "jurisdiction to enforce," i.e., a state's authority to compel compliance or impose sanctions for noncompliance with its administrative or judicial orders, and from "jurisdiction to adjudicate," i.e., a state's authority to subject persons or things to the process of its courts or administrative tribunals. See *Federal Trade Commission v. Compagnie de Saint-Gobain-Pont-a-Mousson*, 636 F. 2d 1300 (1980).

and all other members must recognize under public international law that Terra possesses in accordance with public international law. Whatever jurisdiction to legislate Terra has under its law, and whatever measures the authorities of Terra adopt in the exercise of that jurisdiction, will be recognized by the courts of Terra because their function is to apply the law of Terra, but it does not follow necessarily that Patria will agree that Terra has the jurisdiction that it has exercised.[26]

There are three possible approaches to the legislative jurisdiction that is implied in Article VIII, Section 2(*b*) as a basis for Terra's promulgation of exchange control regulations that will entitle it to support under the provision if all other conditions are met. The first approach is that the existence of legislative jurisdiction is to be demonstrated according to general principles that are recognized by international law and do not originate in the Articles. The second approach is that the words "involve the currency" in Article VIII, Section 2(*b*) have established a new principle of legislative jurisdiction for the purpose of that provision, and that this principle is independent of and replaces the general principles of legislative jurisdiction in the field of exchange control. The third approach is that the words "involve the currency" are themselves the recognition, and no more than an expression, of the general principles of legislative jurisdiction. The third approach resembles the first approach in requiring a demonstration of legislative jurisdiction according to general principles of international law, but the first approach, unlike the third approach, leaves open the possibility that the words "involve the currency" have a meaning that differs from the general principles. Under the first approach, therefore, it may be necessary to prove that two tests are met: legislative jurisdiction and involvement of the

---

[26] See, for example, David Lloyd Jones, "Protection of Trading Interests Act 1980," *Cambridge Law Journal*, Vol. 40 (1981), pp. 44–46; Douglas E. Rosenthal and Benjamin H. Flowe, Jr., "A New Approach to U.S. Enforcement of Antitrust Laws Against Foreign Cartels," *North Carolina Journal of International Law and Commercial Regulation*, Vol. 6 (1980), pp. 81–99; A.V. Lowe, "Blocking Extraterritorial Jurisdiction: The British Protection of Trading Interests Act, 1980," *American Journal of International Law*, Vol. 75 (1981), pp. 257–82; Andreas F. Lowenfeld, "Sovereignty, Jurisdiction, and Reasonableness: A Reply to A.V. Lowe," *American Journal of International Law*, Vol. 75 (1981), pp. 629–38; Werner Meng, "Neuere Entwicklungen im Streit um die Jurisdiktionshoheit der Staaten im Bereich der Wettbewerbsbeschränkungen," *Zeitschrift für ausländisches öffentliches Recht und Völkerrecht*, Vol. 41/3 (1981), pp. 469–513; Kenneth R. Feinberg, "Economic Coercion and Economic Sanctions: The Expansion of Extraterritorial Jurisdiction," *American University Law Review*, Vol. 30 (1981), pp. 323–48.

currency of the legislator. The second approach, like the third approach, requires only one test to be met, involvement of the legislator's currency, but the second approach, unlike the third, does not assimilate the test to the general principles of legislative jurisdiction under international law.

Simplicity should be one criterion for the choice of a solution, although not at the expense of other criteria. The criterion of simplicity suggests that a single test would be desirable, and therefore that the choice should lie between the second and third approaches. The third approach would be ideal because it would imply that the Articles do not call for any departure from recognized principles of legislative jurisdiction, but this approach would not satisfy other criteria if it did not lead to results compatible with the economic character of the Articles, particularly as the constitutive treaty of an organization concerned with the balance of payments of its members. If the results of the third approach were not satisfactory, the choice should be the second approach.

The Fund, however, has not interpreted what is meant by legislative jurisdiction for the purpose of Article VIII, Section 2(b). Nor does it examine the existence of legislative jurisdiction when approving exchange restrictions that require approval in order to be consistent with the Articles. The effect is that if the existence of legislative jurisdiction is challenged in a legal proceeding, it will be the function of the court to decide the question of legislative jurisdiction as a question of interpretation of the Articles and to apply the interpretation to the exchange control regulations that are in issue.

It will be seen that most of the authors who have discussed the problem of legislative jurisdiction have done so in general terms. They have not examined the problem in relation to Article VIII, Section 2(b).

The authors who have discussed the issue of legislative jurisdiction do not question the effectiveness of the Executive Order and the Regulations in courts in the United States. The question of legislative jurisdiction has been discussed in relation to courts outside the United States. An element in the debate has been the application of the measures to entities of the fourth category of persons: entities wheresoever organized or doing business that are owned or controlled by persons in the other three categories (citizens or residents, persons present in the United States, corporations organized under the laws of the United States or one of its subdivisions or subordinate territories). A second element in the measures that has aroused discussion about the existence of legislative jurisdiction is the application of the measures to assets wherever situated of entities subject to the jurisdiction of the United States.

These two elements have been controversial because they refer to entities or assets that are subject to the territorial jurisdiction of another country in which the entities do business or in which the assets are located. If legislative jurisdiction is claimed by another country, the problem for the courts of the country in which the persons do business or in which the assets are situated will be whether, under public international law, there is a recognized or an excessive assertion of jurisdiction by the foreign legislator. If in some circumstances two countries have legislative jurisdiction, the problem for the courts of the country in which persons do business or in which assets are situated will be whether, under the private international law of the forum, foreign law or local law is to apply if these laws have adopted contradictory norms for deciding issues that are before the courts.[27] But this solution is subject to Article VIII, Section 2(b) if the conditions of that provision are satisfied.

If it is assumed that the courts of Patria recognize that Terra has legislative jurisdiction to adopt exchange control regulations that affect entities doing business in Patria or assets situated there, and if it is assumed that the case litigated in Patria's courts comes within Article VIII, Section 2(b), the courts must treat an exchange contract that is contrary to the regulations as unenforceable. The courts cannot refuse to treat the contract in this way because it would be enforceable under the norms of Patria's private international law if Article VIII, Section 2(b) were ignored. (It is not necessary for the present purpose to decide whether Article VIII, Section 2(b) must be considered part of private international law. Nothing of substance in this or in the preceding paragraph would be altered by concluding that the provision is or is not part of private international law.)

The Executive Orders and the Regulations demonstrate an awareness by the U.S. authorities of the problem of legislative jurisdiction. For example, certain prohibitions of financial transactions did not apply to the transactions of persons subject to the jurisdiction of the United States as defined by the Regulations if the persons were nonbanking entities organized and doing business under the laws of a foreign country. The duty to credit interest on property that was

---

[27] See F.A. Mann, "The Doctrine of Jurisdiction in International Law," Hague Academy of International Law, *Recueil des Cours,* Vol. 111 (1964), pp. 9–162. (Hereinafter cited as Mann, *Jurisdiction.*)

held by a foreign branch or a subsidiary of a person subject to U.S. jurisdiction was to be determined in accordance with the local law of the host country. Deposits held abroad in currencies other than U.S. dollars by branches and subsidiaries of persons subject to the jurisdiction of the United States were unblocked. It is likely that the blocking of deposits was confined to those held in U.S. dollars because of considerations of legislative jurisdiction rather than a desire to emphasize the involvement of the U.S. dollar for the purpose of Article VIII, Section 2(b).

Mr. John F. Pritchard of New York and others have provided further evidence of awareness on the part of U.S. officials that legislative jurisdiction might be a problem. He has written that although banks in the United States were prevented by the original measures from instituting litigation with respect to blocked assets or from resorting to set-off against these assets, no such prohibitions applied to litigation involving assets held abroad or to the set-off of claims by banks against blocked overseas deposits. He has suggested that this distinction was made "because of the feeling of the Treasury Department that assets located abroad were less likely ultimately to be effectively restrained by the freeze order because of questions which would arise as to the extraterritorial application of the freeze order." [28] It has also been suggested that the distinction was made in order to encourage U.S. banks to defend the U.S. measures in litigation outside the United States. [29]

U.S. AUTHORS

Mr. Stanley Sommerfield, who was Director of the U.S. Treasury Department's Office of Foreign Assets Control when that Office issued the Regulations, has stated that there was a substantial body of

---

[28] In *The Iran Crisis and International Law, Proceedings of the John Bassett Moore Society of International Law*, Robert D. Steele, ed., a symposium held at the University of Virginia Law School, October 31–November 1, 1980, p. 57; see also p. 60. (Hereinafter cited as Steele, *Iran Crisis and International Law.*) See also Karin Lissakers, "Money and Manipulation," *Foreign Policy*, No. 44 (1981), p. 117; *Iranian Asset Settlement*, Hearing Before the Committee on Banking, Housing, and Urban Affairs, U.S. Senate, 97th Congress, 1st Session, February 19, 1981, pp. 21–22. The original prohibition on litigation in the United States was eliminated soon after promulgation. (See Steele, *Iran Crisis and International Law*, p. 60.) For an account of litigation and set-off abroad and in the United States, see Steele, pp. 57–75, and also Richard Fearon, "Note: Asset Freeze," *Harvard International Law Journal*, Vol. 21 (1980), pp. 523–28.

[29] *Iran: The Financial Aspects (Committee Print 97-5)*, pp. 57–58.

opinion in the Executive Branch of the U.S. Government and elsewhere in favor of a freeze that would be wholly domestic.

> That position largely stems from the belief that extraterritorial controls cause serious friction with other countries because it interferes with their exercise of their own sovereignty. There is no question that there is some interference. However, those same countries have never hesitated to impose this type of extraterritorial control when it served their national interests . . .
>
> [M]any will argue, including of course the Iranians, that the United States has no legal power to freeze dollars held at banks abroad, whether they are held at U.S. bank branches abroad, or held at European banks. Remember, the blocking action did in fact freeze the Iranian dollar assets held in European banks, as well as in dollars held by U.S. bank branches in Europe. . . .[30]

In Mr. Sommerfield's opinion, the U.S. measures were consistent with international law:

> There is a strong argument—the basis for which most people are not familiar with—to the effect that the Treasury's action in freezing these Iranian dollars held at banks abroad is valid under international law. This line of reasoning is based on the customary practices of international banks with respect to foreign currency holdings, plus the numerous precedents which exist in prior actions of foreign governments. These precedents range from the foreign exchange control regulations of many countries, to opinions of legal advisers to international agencies, to World War II economic warfare controls, and to inter-allied agreements reached after World War II among a number of the countries involved here. These actions all dealt with the question of what happened to extra-territorially controlled foreign exchange holdings.[31]

Mr. Sommerfield has expressed the view also that in banking practice and in international currency control practices there is a substantial question whether blocked U.S. dollars in the foreign branches of U.S. banks are located abroad or in the United States. In the latter event, he has said, they would be outside the jurisdiction of foreign courts.[32]

Professor Richard W. Edwards, Jr., of the University of Toledo, Ohio, has noted that the concept of "person subject to the jurisdiction of the United States" as defined by the Regulations

---

[30] Steele, *Iran Crisis and International Law*, p. 78.
[31] *Ibid.*, p. 79.
[32] *Ibid.*

is much broader than the traditional concept of "residency," which is the jurisdictional concept used in the exchange control regulations of most countries. The effect of the broad definition was, *inter alia*, to exercise U.S. jurisdiction over branches and subsidiaries of U.S. commercial banks even when those branches or subsidiaries were sited in other countries and doing business under their laws.[33]

Later in his article, he has written that the legislative jurisdiction of the United States under international law to control acts to be performed in France or England was questionable, and that the courts in France and England were not bound to respect this purported exercise of extraterritorial jurisdiction unless required to do so by Article VIII, Section 2(*b*).[34] The problem stated in this way implies that the provision may have created a new principle of legislative jurisdiction in accordance with what has been called earlier the second approach. Alternatively, the later statement can be read to be a summary of the plaintiff's contention. Elsewhere, it appears that in Professor Edwards' view legislative jurisdiction would exist if satisfaction of the plaintiff's claim required interbank transfers in the United States.[35]

Professor Edward Gordon of the Albany Law School has concluded that Article VIII, Section 2(*b*) confers legislative jurisdiction if the conditions of the provision are met and disposes of any foreign objection to the reach of the U.S. measures beyond the United States.[36] This view also is consistent with the second approach to the problem of legislative jurisdiction.

Mr. John E. Hoffman [37] has noted a number of reasons why the reaction of English courts on the issue of legislative jurisdiction had to be regarded as doubtful. One reason was the doctrine, which had been developed over decades by courts in the United States and was firmly established, that U.S. attachments do not reach foreign deposit accounts of U.S. banks. Doubt about the reaction of English courts on the question of legislative jurisdiction, he has written, induced the

---

[33] Richard W. Edwards, Jr., "Extraterritorial Application of the U.S. Iranian Assets Control Regulations," *American Journal of International Law*, Vol. 75 (1981), pp. 870–902, at 872. (Hereinafter cited as Edwards, *Extraterritorial Application.*)

[34] *Ibid.*, p. 880.

[35] *Ibid.*, pp. 880, 889–90. Professor Edwards has informed the author, in personal correspondence, that the alternative reading is the one that he intended.

[36] Edward Gordon, "The Blocking of Iranian Assets," *The International Lawyer*, Vol. 14 (1980), pp. 659–88, at 674–75.

[37] For the role of Mr. Hoffman in litigation involving, and legal problems related to, the U.S. measures, see *Iran: The Financial Aspects (Committee Print 97-5)*, pp. 29–39.

defendants not to rely on the unembellished assertion that the U.S. measures applied of their own force to deposit accounts outside the United States.[38]

Professor Andreas F. Lowenfeld of New York University School of Law has recommended that the test for determining whether a state has legislative jurisdiction should be whether the legislator has "real state interests." For the application of this test he has proposed nine criteria, and has evaluated a number of situations in the light of them, including the two that follow:

> Third was the case of Citibank's London branch, holding dollar deposits for an Iranian bank. This case was somewhat harder, but the nationality of the branch bank would tend to make the regulation reasonable, even against the depositor's expectations that he maintained a London, not a New York, account. Professor LOWENFELD would not say any U.S. regulation (for instance, one prescribing the maximum interest rate) could be applied to Citibank London, but the very strong interest of the United States in the freezing order, including the relation to the efforts to secure release of the hostages, would seem to support application of the freezing orders to the overseas branch in this case.
>
> Fourth was the case of any sterling deposits held by Citibank, London. Many of the same arguments applied as in the third case, but the application to foreign currency held abroad was again somewhat harder to support.[39]

It will be seen that Professor Lowenfeld's recommended test for determining the existence of legislative jurisdiction resembles the proposal by Dr. Mann quoted below, although in his brief outline of a simpler Ruritanian case Dr. Mann comes to a conclusion that differs from Professor Lowenfeld's.

In a discussion of Professor Lowenfeld's views, Mr. Mark B. Feldman, Deputy Legal Adviser, U.S. Department of State, made the following statement:

---

[38] Hoffman, *Iranian Assets Litigation*, pp. 346–47. See also Carswell, *Economic Sanctions* (p. 252): "Since the final settlement embodied in the Declarations of Algiers rendered litigation over the overseas blocking moot, one can only speculate whether in the end the courts of the U.K., and of France, West Germany and Turkey where litigation was also initiated by Iran, would have supported the blocking. Some knowledgeable legal experts think Iran in the end might have prevailed. . . ."

[39] "Extraterritoriality: Conflict and Overlap in National and International Regulation," in *American Society of International Law, Proceedings of the 74th Annual Meeting*, Washington, April 17–19, 1980 (1981), pp. 30–42, at 33–34. (Hereinafter referred to as *Extraterritoriality: Conflict and Overlap.*)

... [I]n the context of the present Iranian crisis, the United States took the view that freezing of Iranian assets held abroad by persons subject to U.S. jurisdiction was an appropriate and moderate response by the United States to serious violations of international law by the Iranian Government; that this response was justified under international law, and was a valid exercise of jurisdiction, particularly as applied to foreign branches of U.S. banks under the principle of nationality. Foreign courts should therefore give effect to the U.S. blocking orders, particularly where international law was part of the domestic law of the foreign jurisdiction.[40]

Public explanations by U.S. officials of the basis for legislative jurisdiction have varied. Mr. Sommerfield has cited past practice, Mr. Feldman has relied on the nationality of the branches of the U.S. banks, and Mr. Lloyd N. Cutler, Counsel to President Carter, has referred to the situs of the dollar balances:

> That case alone raised the most fascinating questions, particularly because we elected to block Iranian deposits not only within the United States but also within the branches of U.S. banks abroad where a very substantial amount was deposited.
>
> It raised the most fascinating juridical questions as to where the assets were. Is a dollar deposit in the London Branch of City Bank in London, or is it in New York? Since it is a dollar deposit, and since it must be kept on the books of the bank in New York, and all of the clearing runs through the New York Clearinghouse and the Federal Reserve in New York, there are very good arguments that it is a U.S. deposit and not a London deposit, at least as between sophisticated central banks like the Bank Markazi in Iran and City Bank or any other major U.S. bank with a branch in London ...
>
> There is an overarching issue, if we could get past all of these earlier points, about the extraterritorial reach of the U.S. statutes that as a matter of U.S. statutory law and U.S. constitutional law explicitly permit us to govern the conduct of U.S. banks with respect to their deposits abroad. Is that law entitled to the respect of the British court?[41]

English Authors

Dr. F.A. Mann was reported by the *Financial Times* of London as expressing the opinion that under English law the U.S. measures

---

[40] *Ibid.*, p. 42.

[41] *Ibid.*, pp. 44–45. See also *Emergency Economic Powers: Iran*, Hearing Before the Subcommittee on International Economic Policy and Trade of the Committee on Foreign Affairs, House of Representatives, 97th Congress, 1st Session, March 5, 1981, pp. 3, 12–13, 17; and *Miami Symposium*, pp. 14–16.

would not be recognized insofar as they applied to the subsidiaries and branches of U.S. banks in London.[42] He had delivered a similar opinion in his lectures on jurisdiction in international law in 1964:

> Or suppose a Ruritanian corporation carries on a banking business not only in Ruritania itself, but also, through branches and wholly-owned subsidiaries, in numerous other countries. Suppose further that Ruritania introduces legislation requiring all Ruritanian banks to disclose the names and assets of all their customers to the Ruritanian government. The Huber-Storyan approach would probably lend support to the legality of such a measure. Yet it cannot, or at least should not, be open to doubt that in so far as branches and subsidiaries outside Ruritania are concerned the legislation will have to be ignored by them as lacking international validity.[43]

In his lectures, however, Dr. Mann was critical of the territorial concept of jurisdiction and was in favor of a new approach that would base jurisdiction on the just and reasonable interests of the legislator.

> The problem, properly defined, involves the search for the State or States whose contact with the facts is such as to make the allocation of legislative competence just and reasonable. It is, accordingly, not the character and scope inherent in national legislation or attributed to it by its authors, but it is the legally relevant contact between such legislation and the given set of international facts that decides upon the existence of jurisdiction . . .
>
> Perhaps public international lawyers should now discard the question whether the nature of territorial jurisdiction allows certain facts to be made subject to a State's legislation. Rather should they ask whether the legally relevant facts are such that they "belong" to this or that jurisdiction.[44]

---

[42] *Financial Times*, November 16, 1979. For a more precise account of his views, see Mann, *Annuaire suisse.*

[43] Mann, *Jurisdiction*, p. 38.

[44] *Ibid.*, pp. 44–51. Note the following summary of a conference of the International Chamber of Commerce on the extraterritorial application of competition laws:

"It was generally agreed that whatever the basis for claiming subject-matter jurisdiction over foreign nationals in situations where conflicts with other countries are likely to arise if it is exercised, considerations of comity, involving the balancing of national interests, constitute one of the main factors in deciding whether there is jurisdiction or whether it should be exercised. More specific criteria for such balancing and more acceptable procedures for doing it need, however, to be agreed. It should not, as at present in private damage suits, be left solely to the courts of one of the interested countries, since this is not a simple task for them and they tend to conclude that national interests are so vital that they must necessarily override conflicting foreign interests." (*Business Law Review*, Vol. 2 (1981), p. 202.)

The problem then, he wrote, would be to determine the relevant points of contact, or to localize the legal relationships, but this approach was not to be pursued to the point at which it would interfere with the reasonable interests of other states.

French Authors

Both Professor Gianviti[45] and M. Christian Gavalda, Professor of Business and Banking Law of the University of Paris I, have held that French courts would not recognize that the United States had legislative jurisdiction to adopt the measures, but neither discusses this problem in relation to Article VIII, Section 2(b). Both rely on a principle of territoriality with respect to assets. Professor Gavalda gives special emphasis to the application of this principle to matters of banking.[46]

German Authors

Dr. Klaus Westrick of Frankfurt am Main has examined the question whether the U.S. measures would be effective under German law. He starts with a principle of national sovereignty, according to which one state cannot exercise sovereign acts over persons, things, or rights based in the territory of another state. On the basis of this principle, the U.S. measures would have no direct legal effect under German law on U.S. banks' branches or subsidiaries located in the Federal Republic. He treats Article VIII, Section 2(b), however, as "transcending the territorial principle," which implies that it establishes a new principle of legislative jurisdiction for the purpose of that provision.[47]

Dr. Hannes Schneider, also of Frankfurt am Main, has concluded that the U.S. measures, in their purported application to assets located abroad and to persons subject to the exchange control jurisdiction of another country, went beyond the legislative jurisdiction of the United States. Article VIII, Section 2(b) did not affect this conclusion:

---

[45] Gianviti, *Le blocage*, pp. 296–303.

[46] Christian Gavalda, "L'efficacité juridique en France de l'executive order du président Carter 'gelant' les avoirs officiels iraniens?" *Gazette du Palais*, December 16–18, 1979, pp. 2–3, and Note, *Gazette du Palais*, March 12–13, 1980, pp. 8, 17. See Lord Denning M.R. in *Power Curber International Ltd. v. National Bank of Kuwait S.A.K.* [1981] 1 W.L.R. at 1241.

[47] Klaus Westrick, "The Legality of Freeze Orders and the Extra-Territorial Effect of Foreign Freeze Orders in Germany in the Light of the Iranian Events," *International Business Lawyer*, Vol. 9 (1981), pp. 105–108, at 107. (Hereinafter cited as Westrick, *Legality of Freeze Orders*.)

I do not think that Article VIII, Section 2 (b), in plain words, cures the usurpation of international exchange control jurisdiction. Otherwise, the Bretton Woods Agreement would require each of its members to surrender its own legislative powers in the field of exchange control to the legislative powers of other members. This is something which states are normally not inclined to do.[48]

If the implication of this reasoning is that two members cannot have legislative jurisdiction in relation to the same exchange contract for the purposes of Article VIII, Section 2(b), the reasoning must be considered doubtful. It should be apparent that an exchange contract between the residents of two member countries—to take a simple example—should be subject to the legislative jurisdiction of both members. Article VIII, Section 2(b) does not require any member to surrender its legislative powers to the other. If the contracting parties are resident in Terra and Patria, the contract is contrary to the exchange control regulations of Terra, and suit is brought there, the court will dispose of the case by applying Terra's exchange control regulations whether or not the contract is contrary to Patria's exchange control regulations. If the contract is contrary to Patria's exchange control regulations but not Terra's, the court in Terra will declare the contract unenforceable under Article VIII, Section 2(b) because of Patria's exchange control regulations. The collaboration required by that provision does not displace the legislative jurisdiction of Terra. The situation is one in which Terra has not exercised its jurisdiction.

New York Litigation

The question of legislative jurisdiction arose in *The Chase Manhattan Bank, N.A. v. The State of Iran, et al.,*[49] which was decided by the United States District Court for the Southern District of New York on February 15, 1980. As of November 1979, Bank Markazi had three kinds of dollar accounts with Chase: a demand deposit account in New York, and both a "call account," which is similar to a demand deposit account in a U.S. bank, and a time deposit account in London. The last of these accounts was governed by English law by express agreement. On November 14, 1979, approximately $315 million was held in London and approximately $39 million in New York. As of the same date, the National Iranian Oil Company (NIOC) had approximately $77 million on deposit with Chase in London. Chase

---

[48] Hannes Schneider, "Problems of Recognition of the Carter Freeze Order by the German Courts," *International Business Lawyer*, Vol. 9 (1981), pp. 103–104, at 104. (Hereinafter cited as Schneider, *Problems of Recognition*.)

[49] *Iranian Assets Litigation Reporter*, February 22, 1980, p. 194.

claimed that, as of that date, Iran and various official entities of Iran were indebted to Chase in a total amount of approximately $348 million. On November 15, 1979, Chase, relying on the U.S. measures, transferred to New York the dollar balances of Bank Markazi and NIOC held in London in order to set off the claims against these balances.

On November 29, 1979, Bank Markazi instituted legal proceedings in London alleging that Chase was indebted to it in the sum of approximately $321 million, the amount of the London deposits at that time. On December 6, 1979 Chase brought this action against the State of Iran, Bank Markazi, and other official entities to have the court in New York enjoin the prosecution of the London action by Bank Markazi, and to declare the offset valid, or, alternatively, award damages.

Chase contended that it was entitled to a preliminary injunction because it was threatened with conflicting judgments if the litigation went ahead in courts in both the United States and England and because it would be subject to criminal penalties under the U.S. measures if it made any payment under an English judgment. Bank Markazi contended that it was entitled to sue in London, and that it was most appropriate for it to seek a ruling there on the issue of the effectiveness of the measures in relation to an English branch of a U.S. bank.

The court ruled against Chase. As the London action dealt with substantial accounts in London, the choice of a London forum could not be regarded as vexatious or unreasonable:

> From a fair and objective legal standpoint, the crucial connection of this controversy with England must be recognized. Perhaps the ultimate legal question involved is whether the President's blocking order, and the regulations thereunder, are valid under English law with respect to an English branch of an American bank. It is reasonable, to say the least, for Bank Markazi to seek a determination of this question in an English court.[50]

Judge Griesa concluded his opinion with the following comment:

> . . . [I]t is worth observing that the dollar is the recognized reserve currency for international trade. Bank Markazi's large dollar accounts were undoubtedly held in view of this circumstance. It would seem particularly inappropriate for this court to attempt to prevent Bank Markazi from litigating in England with respect to the status of its accounts in the international reserve currency.[51]

---

[50] *Ibid.*, p. 198.
[51] *Ibid.*, p. 199.

LEGISLATIVE JURISDICTION AND EVIDENCE OF ARTICLES

No provisions of the Articles deal directly with the question of legislative jurisdiction to adopt exchange control regulations. There are evidences in the Articles, however, that the drafters assumed a principle of territoriality for the purposes of certain provisions, although Article VIII, Section 2(b) is not among them. For example, Article XI, Section 1(iii) now provides, and has provided in the earlier versions of the Articles, that

Each member undertakes:

-
-
-

(iii) to cooperate with the Fund with a view to the application in its territories of appropriate measures to prevent transactions with non-members or with persons in their territories which would be contrary to the provisions of this Agreement or the purposes of the Fund.

Before the Second Amendment abolished the par value system, Article IV, Section 3 prescribed

The maximum and the minimum rates for exchange transactions between the currencies of members taking place within their territories. . . .

Section 4 of the same Article provided that:

Each member undertakes, through appropriate measures consistent with this Agreement, to permit within its territories exchange transactions between its currency and the currencies of other members. . . .[52]

The provisions of the original Article IV deserve notice for two reasons. One reason is that, as Appendix A shows, Article VIII, Section 2(b) was conceived originally as a measure in support of the par value system. The second reason is that the Fund never decided where exchange transactions were deemed to take place for the purposes of Article IV, Sections 3 and 4. The Legal Department advanced the view in 1955 that exchange transactions take place where the balances of currencies involved in the transactions are transferred and not where the contract for the exchange transaction is deemed to have been entered into.[53] On this view, an exchange transaction could take place in the territories of two members. It will be seen that the question has arisen of the territory or territories in which Eurodollar transactions take place.

---

[52] For similar provisions of the Second Amendment, which would apply if a par value system were introduced in the future, see Schedule C, par. 5.

[53] *History, 1945–65*, Vol. I: Chronicle, p. 405.

Article XIX(c) of the original Articles is even more pertinent. The provision was a link in a chain of provisions that defined a concept of monetary reserves. The concept was applied in the calculation of certain obligations of members. The provisions disappeared from the Articles in the Second Amendment, but the former Article XIX(c) is recalled because it was based on the assumption that the territorial sovereign had control of all banks within its territories, so that, to the extent that the Fund considered the holdings of these banks to be substantially in excess of working balances, the Fund could deem this excess to be official holdings:

> The holdings of other official institutions or other banks within its territories may, in any particular case, be deemed by the Fund, after consultation with the member, to be official holdings to the extent that they are substantially in excess of working balances; provided that for the purpose of determining whether, in a particular case, holdings are in excess of working balances, there shall be deducted from such holdings amounts of currency due to official institutions and banks in the territories of members or non-members specified under (d) below.

The Fund interpreted a member's "other official institutions" to be those that represented the member anywhere. Their excess holdings could be deemed to be official holdings because it was assumed that the holders would enjoy immunity from interference by the territorial sovereign with the member's control of them. "Other banks," however, which meant other than a member's central bank, were understood to be all banks within the territories of the territorial sovereign.[54]

Since 1974 there has been a movement among some members to coordinate official responsibility for supervising the activities of the subsidiaries and branches of foreign banks. A purpose of this development is to allocate responsibility as between parent and host (i.e., territorial) supervisory authorities. The result has been that the host authorities accept the principle of a degree of control by the parent authorities. In February 1975, the Governors of the Central Banks of the Group of Ten and Switzerland established a Committee on Banking Regulations and Supervisory Practices, with Mr. Peter Cooke of the Bank of England as its Chairman at this time (1981). The Committee produced a "Concordat" in 1975 that set out guidelines for the division of responsibility for supervising the solvency and liquidity of the foreign establishments of banks with headquarters in countries represented on the Committee. Different shades of responsibility are recognized for subsidiaries, branches, and joint ventures.

---

[54] *Selected Decisions*, Eighth Issue, p. 168.

The Concordat is not drafted with the precision of a legal instrument. It has been the subject of different interpretations by participating authorities on fundamental questions.[55] The Concordat and subsequent understandings resulting from the work of the Cooke Committee have not themselves modified, or led to modifications of, legal principles relating to legislative jurisdiction. Indeed, domestic laws based on territorial sovereignty have posed problems for supervisory authorities in seeking the collaboration that is the objective of the Concordat. Nevertheless, the interdependence that is recognized by the Concordat may make it desirable in the future to consider whether traditional principles of legislative jurisdiction in relation to banking should be re-examined. It will be interesting to see whether the moral responsibility of the supervisory authorities of the country of the head office for the solvency of a bank's foreign branches or subsidiaries will give weight to an assertion of legal authority over them.

CURRENCY AS BASIS FOR LEGISLATIVE JURISDICTION

Much has been made of the *dictum* of the Permanent Court of International Justice in the *Serbian Loans* case that "it is indeed a generally accepted principle that a State is entitled to regulate its own currency."[56] The *dictum* may suggest that there is unquestionable legislative jurisdiction if measures are adopted for the regulation of the legislator's currency whatever the reach of the regulation may be.

The *dictum* was delivered in the days before the Articles and was deprived by the Articles of much of whatever validity it had. Limitations remain on the scope of the doctrine as formulated by the court, but since the Second Amendment the doctrine has been reinforced to a large degree by the greater permissiveness of the Second Amendment in matters relating to exchange arrangements. Each member is now free to choose its exchange arrangements, provided that it does not maintain the external value of its currency in terms of gold,[57] and provided that it does not impose restrictions on payments and transfers for current international transactions or engage in multiple currency practices or discriminatory currency arrangements without

---

[55] See Michael Lafferty, "Centrepiece for international banking supervision," *Financial Times*, May 11, 1981, Section III, p. viii; "Central banks and Third World debt," *International Currency Review*, Vol. 13 (1981), pp. 7–9; Patrick Heininger, "Liability of U.S. Banks for Deposits Placed in Their Foreign Branches," *Law and Policy in International Business*, Vol. 11 (1979), pp. 903–1034.

[56] [1929] P.C.I.J., Series A, Nos. 20/21, at 44.

[57] Article IV, Section 2(b).

the approval of the Fund.[58] Furthermore, each member is free to determine the external value of its currency, provided again that certain obligations are observed, such as the obligation to avoid manipulating exchange rates or the international monetary system in order to prevent effective balance of payments adjustment or to gain an unfair competitive advantage over other members.[59]

The original U.S. Regulations were amended promptly to free deposits in currencies other than U.S. dollars held abroad by branches and subsidiaries of persons subject to the jurisdiction of the United States, without permitting the conversion of blocked dollar deposits into other currencies. The United States may have taken this step in order to strengthen the case for legislative jurisdiction. Whatever the reason may have been, to bring a case within Article VIII, Section 2(b) legislative jurisdiction must exist to control payments and transfers for current international transactions or capital transfers. Legislative jurisdiction may exist whether the controls relate to payments and transfers in the legislator's currency or some other currency. There is no principle that because a country may regulate its currency, the country has legislative jurisdiction over all payments and transfers made in the currency. There is no more substance to such an alleged principle than there would be to the contention that under private international law the law of a country governs all obligations expressed in the currency of the country as the so-called *lex monetae*. The U.S. Regulations were not based on a claim to legislative jurisdiction of this kind. They did not apply, for example, to Eurodollar deposits with banks that fell outside the definition of "persons subject to the jurisdiction of the United States."

If the Mann-Lowenfeld proposed approach to legislative jurisdiction were to prevail, the currency in which assets were denominated or some other connection with a currency might be among the circumstances to be taken into account in order to decide whether the interests of the issuer of the currency were sufficient to justify legislative jurisdiction. Professor Lowenfeld has been explicit about this possibility.[60]

It has been seen that Judge Griesa in *The Chase Manhattan Bank, N.A. v. The State of Iran, et al.* seems to have suggested that an English court was entitled to examine the question of the existence of legislative jurisdiction on the part of the United States because of the

---

[58] Article VIII, Section 3.
[59] Article IV, Section 1(iii).
[60] *Extraterritoriality: Conflict and Overlap*, p. 34.

role of the U.S. dollar in the international system. The implication of this view would be that the character of a currency might narrow the legislative jurisdiction of the issuer to regulate it.

V. "Exchange Contracts"

Definitions of the term "exchange contracts" in Article VIII, Section 2(b) by courts and scholars have fallen into two classes. One class consists of definitions formulated in terms of the exchange of one means of payment for another. The most common example is the exchange of one currency for another under a contract of purchase and sale. The other class is open ended and sweeps up all contracts that provide for a payment, or even for barter according to some theories. The exchange of currencies under a contract of purchase and sale is only one type of contract within this class. The contract between a depositor and a bank under which a deposit is made is another type within this broader class but is not within the first class.

Professor Gianviti has rejected the analysis of a contract of deposit under which the depositor may be repaid in a currency other than the one deposited as a purchase by the bank of one currency in return for another. This arrangement, however, illustrates for him the artificiality of the narrow definition of exchange contracts, because repayment in a currency other than the one deposited does amount to an exchange of currencies.[61]

Professor Gianviti has favored a wide interpretation. An exchange contract, in his opinion, means any contract containing an international monetary element. The definition covers all international monetary operations, whether they take the form of foreign exchange operations, international payments, or international transfers of funds. He has pointed out that if the narrow definition is coupled with the concept of unenforceability as a legal consequence that applies only to contracts that have not been executed, all that would remain of exchange contracts under Article VIII, Section 2(b) would be contracts in which one party transmits or promises to transmit one currency in return for the future transfer of another currency.[62] Forward exchange contracts would seem to constitute the bulk of the contracts within this definition.

---

[61] Gianviti, Le blocage, pp. 282–83.

[62] François Gianviti, "Le contrôle des changes étranger devant le juge national," Revue critique de droit international privé, Vol. 69 (1980), pp. 667–74.

Professor Edwards has noted the argument of the Bank Markazi that its deposit contracts with the defendant banks were not exchange contracts within the meaning of Article VIII, Section 2(b) because the depositor was claiming no more than the transfer of the same currency, Eurodollars, from a bank owned or controlled by a U.S. bank to a bank with a different ownership or control. Professor Edwards has supported the broader view of exchange contracts, according to which contracts of deposit would be exchange contracts.[63]

Mr. C.H. de Pardieu of Paris also has favored the broadest possible definition of exchange contracts,[64] but he, like some other authors, has fallen into the trap of incorporating in the definition a reference to the currency or the exchange resources of the legislator. This approach results in the redundancy of either the word "exchange" in "exchange contracts" or the words "which involve the currency of any member."

Suppose that a court adopts the narrow view that exchange contracts are confined to those that provide for the exchange of one means of payment against another or of one currency against another. In some countries a debt expressed and repayable in a foreign currency, whether as the result of a deposit or some other operation, can be discharged—at least in some circumstances—in the domestic currency.[65] This principle raises the question whether the possibility

---

[63] Edwards, *Extraterritorial Application*, pp. 888–89, 891.

[64] C.H. de Pardieu, "The Carter Freeze Order: Specific Problems Relating to the International Monetary Fund," *International Business Lawyer*, Vol. 9 (1981), pp. 97–102, at 98–99. (Hereinafter cited as de Pardieu, *Carter Freeze Order.*)

[65] "Under Swiss law it is perfectly legal and possible to enter into an obligation for the payment of foreign currency and the distinction between 'money of account' of a debt and its 'money of payment' is an elementary differentiation of monetary law. The money of account is the money which is owed and the question arises whether the payment of foreign currency can effectively be claimed and enforced or whether payment can be claimed and enforced in national currency only, in other words whether the money of payment necessarily is the national currency.

"Swiss law specifically deals with the question and the relevant section of our code says

'Where the contract provides for payment in a currency which is not legal tender at the place of payment the debt may be paid in national currency according to the rate of exchange on the due date, unless the contract calls for specific performance by use of the word "effective" or some similar addition.'

"There are, in other words, two different kinds of debts in foreign currency.

"If the contract provides specifically that valid payment can be made only in foreign currency, then the debtor can validly perform only by transferring foreign currency, in other words foreign bank-notes of the relevant country or credit instruments or credits, if the payor is deemed to have agreed in advance to accept the transfer of credit as payment. The obligation of the debtor has

of discharge in the domestic currency has the effect, in itself, of rendering a contract an exchange contract in accordance with the narrow definition. This conclusion is doubtful because the contract itself does not provide for performance in the domestic currency. The willingness of the creditor to receive the domestic currency, if not expressed in the contract as an agreed mode of performance, would not change the character of the contract: it would not be an exchange contract. This conclusion would be compatible with Professor Gianviti's criticism of the narrow view as logically indefensible.

Extension of the narrow view to contracts that can be discharged in domestic currency would not offend the policy of Article VIII, Section 2(b) or any other provision of the Articles. Courts that adopt the narrow view, however, are not likely to be willing to give the provision a liberal interpretation, although the decision of the English Court of Appeal discussed below is evidence of some willingness.

VI. "Involve the Currency"

One of the most difficult problems of interpreting Article VIII, Section 2(b) is the meaning of the words "involve the currency of any member." If the other conditions that are explicit or implicit in the provision are satisfied, the exchange control regulations of a member

---

some similarity to the one of a debtor having to furnish a certain amount of a commodity.

"If a contract does not provide specifically that the debtor can perform only in foreign currency, then the debtor having to make payment under Swiss law has the possibility to pay in currency of the country of the place of payment, the exchange rate applicable being the one on due date. In other words, in this case the debtor has the option of paying either the foreign currency, the money of account, or in the national currency.

"It seems that German, Italian and Austrian law provide for similar specific provisions. In France the same principle is also recognized by the courts and I would assume that similar rules would apply in most continental laws.

"The same alternative option does not apply, though, to the creditor. In fact, the creditor can claim the payment in the foreign currency only. In a law-suit for payment he has to claim the foreign currency due and even the judgement will be rendered for foreign currency.

"Only for purposes of *enforcement* in Switzerland Swiss law requires in a mandatory way that the claim in foreign currency be converted into Swiss currency. This conversion does, however, not constitute a change of the original claim and debt and does, in other words, not constitute novation. The debtor can continue to validly discharge himself by paying the amount in foreign currency despite a pending enforcement procedure." Marco A. Jagmetti, "Money and Payment," *International Business Lawyer*, Vol. 9 (1981), pp. 93–95. (Hereinafter cited as Jagmetti, *Money and Payment*.) See also Gianviti, *Le blocage*, p. 284.

must be recognized under the provision if the currency of that member is "involved." Some of the authors who have discussed the U.S. measures have addressed themselves, therefore, to the question whether the U.S. dollar was "involved" within the meaning of the provision.

Professor Gianviti has written that, in theory, the involvement of a currency may be determined by one of three possible criteria: (i) the nationality of the currency of payment, (ii) the location of assets, and (iii) the residence of parties.[66] He has analyzed these three criteria as follows:

(i) The currency owed by the banks affected by the U.S. measures was the U.S. dollar. Authors who define exchange contracts as contracts for the exchange of one currency in return for another would find the U.S. dollar involved only if the deposited dollars were to be exchanged for another currency. Authors who take a broader view of exchange contracts would deem a member's currency to be involved only if an exchange contract had an economic effect on a member by affecting its monetary system or exchange resources. The question then is whether the choice of the currency of payment is sufficient to have such an economic effect on the issuer of the currency.

Normally, according to Professor Gianviti, the nationality of the currency of payment does not have decisive economic importance of this kind. A payment in deutsche mark by a resident of the United States to a nonresident affects the U.S. balance of payments and therefore involves the currency of the United States. By contrast, a payment in U.S. dollars by a nonresident of the United States to another nonresident does not affect the U.S. balance of payments. Moreover, the specified currency of payment may turn out not to be the actual currency of payment. French law, for example, permits the French branch of a U.S. bank to discharge a dollar-denominated debt in an equivalent amount of francs.[67] The plaintiffs in French

---

[66] Gianviti, *Le blocage,* pp. 283–91.

[67] See fn. 64 *supra.* Note also Jagmetti, *Money and Payment* (p. 95):

"To minimize the risk of the creditor that he be paid in national currency instead of the Guest Currency of account, the optional right of the debtor to pay in national currency existing by law is usually excluded by the contract. Although the creditor cannot enforce in the foreign currency, at least the creditor will then usually have a clear title to receive damages for possible devaluations of the national currency ultimately received when it comes to enforcement."

Note further the European Convention on Foreign Money Liabilities of December 11, 1967 proposed by the Council of Europe, but not yet effective. Article 2 of the Annex:

"If a sum of money is due in a currency other than that of the place of pay-

litigation resulting from the U.S. measures requested payment in that form if the defendants refused to pay in dollars. The U.S. measures, however, forbade payments in another currency with the use of dollar-denominated accounts.

The criterion of the nationality of the currency of payment, therefore, was not acceptable. Furthermore, Professor Gianviti has not accepted the argument that the contracts of deposit affected the currency of the United States because the depositor could withdraw the deposited dollars, exchange them for other currencies, and in this way weaken the dollar in the exchange markets. The risk of such exchanges was independent of the deposit contracts. The exchanges could be made only after the contracts of deposit had been executed.

Professor Gianviti's analysis, however, would seem not to apply to the argument that discharge of the bank's obligation was possible in French francs. Payment in this form would not be an act taking place after discharge. On this assumption, the question then would be whether payment in French francs would necessarily require the bank to sell Eurodollars for francs, or to have entered into such a transaction at some time, in order to discharge its obligation.

(ii) Exchange controls regulate the transmission of domestic currency or foreign exchange from the legislator's territory because its exchange resources or money supply, and therefore its currency, is affected by such operations. The question whether the contracts to which the U.S. measures applied were assets located in the United States was complicated by the difficulty of determining where claims in the form of book money are located, and this difficulty was compli-

---

ment, the creditor may, if the debtor is unable, or alleges his inability, to make settlement in that currency, require payment in the currency of the place of payment."

Article 5 of the Annex:

"In the event of any proceedings for the recovery of a sum of money expressed in a currency other than that of the forum, the creditor may, at his choice, demand payment in the currency to which he is entitled or the equivalent in the currency of the forum at the rate of exchange at the date of actual payment."

Article 4 of the Convention:

"This Convention shall not prevent any Contracting Party from maintaining or introducing into its legislation provisions concerning exchange control or prohibiting in certain cases the conclusion of contracts and the payment in foreign money."

Article 5 of the Convention:

"This Convention shall be without prejudice to the provisions of any treaties, conventions or bilateral or multilateral agreements concluded or to be concluded, governing in special fields matters covered by this Convention."

cated in turn by the fact that the claims were to Eurodollars. Exchange control regulations treat bank deposit accounts as located where they can be encashed, whatever law governs the contract of deposit under private international law.

Eurodollars, Professor Gianviti has written, are created by double-accounting entries. The Eurobank credits its customer's account on its books with a sum in dollars, receiving in return a dollar credit on the books of a bank in the United States.[68] The economic effect of this accounting is to transfer dollars from the United States to Europe.[69] The legal effect is that a claim on a U.S. bank is transferred to a nonresident, the European bank. This claim "involves" the currency of the United States because credit of the funds to which the holder, the European bank, becomes entitled results in an outflow of dollars from the United States. The dollar is involved in this step, and U.S. exchange control regulations could impede the outflow.

At the same time, the legal effect is also the creation of a claim by the depositor against the European bank denominated in and repayable in the "guest currency"[70] in the country of deposit. Even if the claim is denominated in dollars, it is located in Europe, where it is repayable, and is outside the U.S. economy, so that the U.S. dollar is not "involved." Repayment of the depositor's claim in dollars could produce an outflow of dollars from the U.S. bank to the European bank, but this consequence would follow from the relationship between the European bank and the U.S. bank and not from the relationship between the depositor and the European bank. An attempt by the United States to impose exchange control regulations on this latter relationship would be for the purpose of giving effect to its political will and not of protecting its monetary economy.

---

[68] But see Jagmetti, *Money and Payment* (p. 95):

"This [U.S. clearing arrangements] has led some experts to say that all off-shore dollars are ultimately held in New York. Personally, I don't think that this is necessarily true. Normally it is true that every dollar-liability of a bank has its counterpart in a dollar claim towards a US bank, which in its turn has a claim towards the Federal Reserve System. But theoretically a dollar debt could be entered into by a European bank also without having covered itself at all by a dollar claim, the bank thus going short and assuming the full risk of changes in exchange rates or of defaulting due to the impossibility of getting dollars when its obligation is due. Or a bank could cover itself with a claim against a non US bank and so on, with the result of a completely closed circle of dollar claims and debts outside the US." See also Carswell, *Economic Sanctions*, pp. 261–62.

[69] But see fn. 67 *supra*.

[70] The terminology is that of Dr. Jagmetti (see fn. 65 *supra*).

In this analysis nothing is changed if the "European" bank is the branch of a U.S. bank. When the customer deposits money in the branch, the account of the branch at the home office is credited, and the branch opens an account for the customer on its own books. The relations of the branch with its customer are those of an independent bank situated in the country in which it does business.

Professor Gianviti and others have pointed out that this analysis of the residence of branches is compatible with the view that the United States itself has taken in not extending certain regulations to the foreign branches of U.S. banks. Eurodollar banking, they have pointed out, has been made possible by this view. To these experts, however, the reply may be made that if the practice of the United States is evidence of the legal position, the argument based on past practice has now been modified by the practice of the freeze.

The conclusion that Professor Gianviti has drawn from his analysis was reached before the decision of the English Court of Appeal in *United City Merchants (Investments) Ltd. and Others v. Royal Bank of Canada and Others.*[71] In that case, the court held that various contractual relationships connected with each other in a single design had to be considered together in order to see whether the court was being called upon to enforce an exchange contract contrary to the exchange control regulations of Peru. The Court of Appeal adopted this approach because it held that the design amounted to a monetary transaction in disguise. If, however, various contractual relationships are connected with each other overtly, it is arguable that the same approach should be followed even though there is no monetary transaction in disguise. Application of the policy of Article VIII, Section 2(b) should depend on effects and not on the intent to evade exchange control regulations. If this hypothesis were accepted, Professor Gianviti's twofold relationships could be considered together, and it might be found the the effect was an exchange contract involving the dollar. The link between the two relationships that would justify the view that they were not severable from each other would depend on whether the contract between the European branch of a U.S. bank and the depositor required repayment in dollars. Repayment of the deposit might then be considered a transfer of dollars from a bank resident in New York to a nonresident depositor, procured by the European branch on the instructions of the depositor pursuant to the contract between them. A transfer by way of repay-

---

[71] [1981] 3 W.L.R. 242.

ment to any other transferee on the instructions of the depositor would be equivalent to a direct transfer to the depositor itself.

(iii) In considering the criterion of the residence of the parties, Professor Gianviti has written that the French branch lacks independent legal personality,[72] and that this circumstance raises the question whether the branch is a resident of the United States. Exchange control regulations usually apply the criterion of the residence of parties as well as the criterion of the location of assets. Frequently, exchange control regulations forbid payments of domestic or foreign currency by residents to nonresidents because these payments have an adverse effect on the balance of payments of the residents' country. The payments are equivalent to a transfer of assets between the two countries. If the French branch were deemed to be a resident of the United States, the withdrawal of Iranian assets would be a payment by a resident to a nonresident. The French branch, however, is a resident of France and not the United States, which indeed has treated the branch as a nonresident and made it possible for the branch to engage in Eurodollar banking. Professor Gianviti has concluded, therefore, that the criterion of the residence of the parties does not justify the view that the U.S. dollar was "involved" in the sense of Article VIII, Section 2(b) in the contracts between the Iranian depositors and the branches of U.S. banks in France.

Professor Gianviti's analysis of the currency "involved" under Article VIII, Section 2(b) deserves further comment. In other published work he has rejected the effect of a contract on the balance of payments as the sole criterion of involvement, although he agrees that most often that criterion will suffice. His reasoning rests largely on

---

[72] This independence is legal and does not preclude financial dependence. For example:

"[C]ommercial banks can turn to central banks in the event of liquidity difficulties resulting from any abrupt withdrawal of funds. The great bulk of the recycling involving U.S. banks has occurred through U.S. head offices or foreign branches; the role of foreign subsidiaries or consortia in which U.S. banks participate has been minor. For instance, the assets of the foreign branches of U.S. banks are more than ten times as large as those of subsidiaries and consortia banks. Almost all of these foreign branches belong to U.S. banks that are members of the Federal Reserve System. The Federal Reserve is prepared, as a lender of last resort, to advance sufficient funds, suitably collateralized, to assure the continued operation of any solvent and soundly managed member bank that may be experiencing temporary liquidity difficulties associated with the abrupt withdrawal of petro-dollar—or any other—deposits." (From "Statement to Congress," Henry C. Wallich, Member, Board of Governors of the Federal Reserve System, Before Permanent Subcommittee on Investigations, Committee on Government Operations, U.S. Senate, October 16, 1974, *Federal Reserve Bulletin*, Vol. 60 (1974), p. 760.)

the assumption that the criterion of the balance of payments is confined to transactions between residents and nonresidents, while there are transactions between a country's residents in its foreign assets or between nonresidents in its foreign liabilities that have economic consequences for the country and are frequently subjected to the country's exchange control regulations. The criterion he prefers is one that encompasses the making or receipt of international payments and transfers or the holding or transmitting of international means of payment without limiting contracts to those that are made between a resident and a nonresident.

Professor Gianviti's rejection of the criterion of the balance of payments in favor of what he considers to be a broader criterion does not raise serious practical problems or provoke the objection that his criterion would be in collision with the policy of Article VIII, Section 2(b). Nevertheless, a closer examination of his view is desirable. The first question it suggests is whether there is a difference between the two criteria. He distinguishes between them on the ground that his criterion, but not the criterion of the balance of payments, encompasses transfers [73] of a country's foreign assets between residents and transfers of its foreign liabilities between nonresidents. The hypothesis that the balance of payments is confined to transactions between residents and nonresidents is not wholly in accord with the Fund's *Balance of Payments Manual.*[74]

The assumption that the balance of payments includes no transactions between residents or between nonresidents rests perhaps on the view that they produce no change in the balance of payments as a whole, but if this reason were valid many transactions between residents and nonresidents would be excluded because these transactions take the form of exchanges of economic values. The true question is whether transactions, whatever the parties to them, produce changes in any component of the balance of payments. The Fund's *Manual* shows that transactions between residents or between nonresidents may bring about changes in components of the balance of payments. A change may result, for example, from a transaction in foreign assets between a country's central authorities and another resident or from a transaction in foreign liabilities between a nonresident direct investor and a nonresident that is not a direct investor.

---

[73] In this discussion, "transfers" should be understood to embrace both "transfers" and "payments."

[74] *Balance of Payments Manual*, Fourth Edition, paragraphs 19, 30, 191, 365–67, 375–78.

It is likely that not all transactions between residents in a country's foreign assets and between nonresidents in its foreign liabilities produce changes in some component in the balance of payments. The question, however, is whether there is a persuasive argument why exchange contracts by which parties bind themselves to enter into the transactions that produce no changes should be within the protection of Article VIII, Section 2(b). Professor Gianviti's justification for preferring a criterion other than the effect that the enforcement of an exchange contract would have on the balance of payments is that the balance of payments is a purely accounting presentation and that the exclusive use of it for the purpose of Article VIII, Section 2(b) is inconsistent with economic reality and with the normal scope of exchange control regulations.

The balance of payments is certainly a statement based on accounting conventions,[75] but the question is why it should be considered an inadequate criterion for the purpose of Article VIII, Section 2(b) when it is of cardinal importance for so many other provisions of the Articles and so many functions of the Fund. Furthermore, the presentation of the balance of payments as recommended by the Fund's *Manual* has been prepared in consultation with national authorities and is designed to reflect the changes in the manner in which international transactions are conducted as well as changes in the international monetary system. The components of the presentation have been selected in order to provide the information considered important for understanding the relationship of an economy to the rest of the world. Finally, the criterion preferred by Professor Gianviti is itself grounded in convention. The criterion implies that by controlling all contracts by which foreign assets or domestic liabilities are created or transferred a country can mobilize the total resources of the country or prevent the reduction of them. This criterion may be consistent with a concept of legislative jurisdiction but its economic practicability can be questioned.

The argument that the criterion of the balance of payments is not consistent with the normal scope of exchange control regulations is blunted by the obvious limitation on the scope of Article VIII, Section 2(b). Its reach is shorter than the full length of the exchange control regulations that a member can impose. The provision is limited, for example, to exchange contracts and does not apply to noncontractual transfers even though they can affect a member's international position in the same way as contractual transfers.

---

[75] See, for example, D. Sykes Wilford, "An Economic View of the Balance of Payments," *Chase International Finance*, Vol. XVI (August 31, 1981), p. 8.

The argument is blunted also by calling in aid normal exchange control regulations. It is doubtful that there is a sufficiently uniform practice to justify the conclusion that there is a model exchange control. The effect might be to define "exchange contracts" for the purpose of Article VIII, Section 2(b) as any contracts that a particular exchange control authority happens to regulate. The view that the word "exchange" in the phrase "exchange contracts" in the provision should have the same meaning as in the phrase "exchange control regulations" in the provision and elsewhere in the Articles does not lead logically to the conclusion that "exchange contracts" are the contracts that are controlled by exchange control regulations whatever they happen to be. The proposition relating to the understanding of the word "exchange" has been advanced only to demonstrate the more limited, although important, point that the phrase "exchange contracts" should not be interpreted to mean only contracts for the exchange of currencies.

Notwithstanding these reactions to Professor Gianviti's views, there is much force in his conclusion that the U.S. dollar was not "involved," whether his test or the test of the balance of payments is applied. The withdrawal of the deposits would be a transaction between nonresidents, and the transfer between banks in the United States would be a transaction between residents. Neither the resources nor the balance of payments of the United States would appear to be affected by the withdrawal. A different conclusion would follow, however, if the two transactions were linked on the analogy of the English case cited under (ii) above in the discussion of Professor Gianviti's views on the currency "involved."

Professor Edwards has favored an interpretation of the currency "involved" that Professor Gianviti might classify as one based on the nationality of the currency of payment.[76] If a currency is named in a contract as the currency of payment or if payment or transfer in a currency is in fact necessary for performance, the contract should be taken to "involve" that currency. Professor Edwards has called his solution textual in approach: the currency "involved" is usually the currency that is named in the contract. He has recognized that most scholars prefer a criterion based on the economic consideration that a country's exchange resources are affected by a contract. Professor Edwards has stated that if this test were adopted—which he does not recommend—a broad view of the balance of payments should be applied. This view of the balance of payments should take account

---

[76] Edwards, *Extraterritorial Application*, pp. 889–94.

of a change in the country of residence of the nonresident to whom a legislator's resident was obligated. He has rejected the thesis that a quantitative test of the assets and liabilities of a country should be decisive. A currency might be involved if there were no change in them. It would seem, therefore, that if his preferred view of the currency "involved" did not prevail, he would choose an interpretation based on the balance of payments.[77]

Professor Edwards has claimed that, although his formulation of exchange contracts is not confined to contracts for the exchange of one currency against another, the English and U.S. cases that have adopted the narrow interpretation of exchange contracts support his view of the currency "involved." He has claimed, furthermore, that most or all of the other cases in which Article VIII, Section 2(b) has been applied are consistent with his theory of the currency "involved" even though that interpretation was not part of the *ratio decidendi*.

Professor Edwards has concluded that if it is customary banking practice, or if there is an implied term, that payments and transfers of Eurodollars are made through transfers in accounts with banks located in the United States, usually through the New York CHIPS, the U.S. dollar is "involved." This conclusion is justified by his textual theory of involvement because transfers of dollars through accounts in the United States would be necessary for performance of the deposit contracts. He has also maintained that, on the same assumption about customary practice or contractual terms, the economic approach to the involvement of a currency under Article VIII, Section 2(b) would lead to the same result as under the textual approach, because the transfer of assets situated within the United States to nonresidents would be the subject matter of the contracts.

Professor Edwards has discussed Professor Gianviti's conclusion that, on the assumption postulated by Professor Edwards, performance of the deposit contracts would not affect the resources of the United States because the contracts would be performed by the transfer of a U.S. liability between nonresidents. Professor Edwards is not persuaded by the argument that there is no effect on a member's resources, because economic consequences for the member can follow from changes in the countries to whose residents the member's residents have liabilities.

Professor Edwards has also considered the legal effect of a finding that the contracts affected by the U.S. measures included no implied

---

[77] *Ibid.*, pp. 893–94.

term that transfers had to be made through accounts located in the United States and that the use of these accounts was not necessary for performance of the deposit contracts. He has concluded that on his textual solution, the U.S. dollar would not be involved. If, however, the contracts called for payments in dollars, it is difficult to see why Professor Edwards' textual solution should not apply because the contracts did not deal, explicitly or implicitly, with the procedure for payment. The explanation may be that he admits the possibility that Eurodollars are not dollars.[78]

Professor Edwards would find the answer to the question whether the dollar was involved less clear if the economic approach were applied to circumstances in which there was no implied term requiring transfers through accounts in the United States, and in which the use of these accounts was not necessary. The answer would then depend, he holds, on whether the foreign branches of U.S. banks are residents of the countries in which they are located or residents of the United States. The Fund's statistical practice of regarding the branches as residents of the country in which they are located is no more than a helpful convention for compiling balance of payments statistics. It has been seen, however, that the practice was confirmed by the definition of monetary reserves in the original Articles. Professor Edwards has transformed the question of residence into the question whether the resources of the foreign branches of U.S. banks should be treated as resources of the United States, and his answer to this question would depend on whether the United States could be effective in marshaling the resources. Only in that event would it be justifiable for the United States to apply its exchange control regulations to the resources represented by dollar-denominated deposits with the foreign branches of U.S. banks. This analysis makes no sharp distinction between the question of legislative jurisdiction and the question of the involvement of a currency.

Professor Edwards has recognized that this line of reasoning is circular: exchange controls can be applied to resources that can be marshaled, and resources can be marshaled if exchange controls can marshal them. To break out of this circle, Professor Edwards relies on jurisdiction to enforce: whose courts could be effective in ensuring the performance of a contract? [79] Under this test, according to Professor Edwards, courts in England or France could not ensure effective performance if operations on accounts would be necessary in the

---

[78] Professor Edwards has informed the author that he holds open the possibility that Eurodollars may be a subcategory of U.S. dollars if in fact they must be cleared through a U.S. mechanism.

[79] See fn. 25 *supra*.

United States, and he concludes that on this assumption the U.S. dollar would be "involved."

There may be various reasons why Professor Edwards, in applying his textual solution, has emphasized the necessity for transfers through accounts in banks located in the United States, even if, it would seem, the deposit contracts with the foreign branches of U.S. banks call for payment in dollars. One reason appears to be the need to dispose of the contention advanced in the London litigation that Eurodollars are not really U.S. dollars but are a species of currency created by banks outside the United States and not controlled by U.S. authorities. A deposit of Eurodollars, it was contended in the litigation, is valued by reference to the U.S. dollar but is not a deposit of dollars, does not necessarily call for repayment in dollars, and can be repaid in other currencies. Perhaps for this reason Professor Edwards has insisted on transfer through banks in the United States as the procedure for repayment in order to involve actual dollars.

Professor Edwards has defended his preferred solution by pointing out that it puts contracting parties on notice of the member whose exchange control regulations they should heed.[80] He has argued that if an economic interpretation is chosen in order to give more weight to the public interest than to the interests of private parties, the Fund should exercise rigorous supervision of the necessity for exchange controls on both capital transfers and payments and transfers for current international transactions, so that controls would be kept to a minimum. In addition, the Fund should exercise close supervision of restrictions when imposed for reasons of national or international security.

These are telling considerations, although the degree of supervision exercised by the Fund should not depend on the choice of a criterion by which to determine whether a currency is involved. Furthermore, in the interpretation of Article VIII, Section 2(b) it must be recalled that the authority of members to control capital transfers without supervision by the Fund[81] was considered axiomatic.

Professor Edwards' preference for an avowedly textual over an economic interpretation of a provision of the Articles is disquieting.

---

[80] The forcefulness of the argument is stronger in relation to a currency if it is named in the contract as the currency of payment than if the transfer or payment is necessary for performance under the second part of Professor Edwards' textual solution.

[81] Except to determine whether the controls are being exercised in a manner that restricts payments and transfers for current international transactions.

One consequence, for example, would be that if the currency of payment is the U.S. dollar under a contract entered into between a resident of the United States and a resident of Terra, only the interests of the United States would be taken into account in applying Article VIII, Section 2(*b*). What rationale can be drawn from the Articles to explain why only the interests of the United States would deserve protection in this example?

Professor Edwards' theory makes Article VIII, Section 2(*b*) an instrument predominantly for the protection of those relatively few currencies that are used in international economic and financial activities. They are likely to be the currencies of members less in need of the protection of exchange control regulations than other members. This objection remains even if the theory does promote Professor Edwards' aim of minimum interference with the contracts of private parties.

There is one answer that might be made to the objection. One part of the test applied by Professor Edwards to determine whether a currency is involved is that the payment or transfer of a currency is necessary in fact to enable a party to perform according to his contract. This test might enable a payor required to pay in a currency foreign to him to argue in most cases that he must sell his own currency to obtain the foreign currency. This argument, if accepted, would give great breadth to the concept of the currency "involved." Professor Edwards does not intend to confine his test to cases in which the contracting parties agree, explicitly or implicitly, that a payment or transfer will be necessary in order to put one party in a position to perform or in which such an operation is called for by custom or usage. The facts will determine the outcome and not the intent of the parties. Professor Edwards treats the *Terruzzi* case as compatible with his theory because the contract called for payment in sterling and the defendant had sufficient sterling assets in England. (The defendant did not, because the plaintiff brought proceedings in Italy to enforce the English judgment.) If the defendant had insufficient sterling assets and had to sell lire to obtain sterling, Professor Edwards concludes that the lira would be "involved." (This view gives no independent meaning to sterling as the specified currency of payment.) The distinction, however, between the current need to sell lire to obtain sterling and a past sale by which sterling was obtained is not realistic. Nor is it realistic to distinguish between these sales of lire and a direct acquisition of sterling that the holder has retained and has not disposed of for lire.

Professor Edwards does not clarify what he means by "payments or transfers in currencies that are in fact necessary to performance of the contract." If an economic meaning is given to these words of the kind suggested in the preceding paragraph, contracting parties will not be on notice without further inquiry of the exchange control regulations with which they should concern themselves. But, if Professor Edwards' approach is followed, an obligee may not know whether the obligor has assets in the currency of payment within the jurisdiction of the forum (i.e., sterling balances in the *Terruzzi* case). Moreover, Professor Edwards does not deal with the case in which the obligor has such assets when undertaking his obligation but ceases to have them by the time of suit. The latter date is decisive for other purposes under the provision, but how can the obligee keep himself informed of the obligor's financial position?

Economic considerations of the kind that Professor Edwards does not take into account in interpreting the phrase "involve the currency" do not necessarily become irrelevant even if his views are accepted. If the involvement of a currency is not a new principle of legislative jurisdiction, some of these considerations, and perhaps all of them, although not recognized as economic, could come into play when the question to be decided is whether the member adopting exchange control regulations had legislative jurisdiction to adopt them.

VII. "Exchange Control Regulations"

Commentators have devoted much attention to the meaning of "exchange control regulations" as those words appear in Article VIII, Section 2(*b*). As a preface to the survey of the opinions of these commentators, it should be noted that the IEEPA authorizes the President of the United States to block assets under that statute but not to seize and use them as if the United States obtained ownership. The IEEPA differs from the Trading with the Enemy Act of the United States,[82] under which title to enemy property can be taken, but which is available only in time of war.[83]

Nevertheless, Professor Gianviti has characterized the U.S. measures as sequestration comparable to the sequestration of enemy property in time of war, which most authors, he declares, do not regard as exchange control because its purpose is punitive and not defensive.

---

[82] 50 U.S.C. §1701(b).
[83] Steele, *Iran Crisis and International Law*, p. 53.

Professor Gianviti has distinguished between restrictions under Article VIII, Section 2(a) and exchange control regulations under Article VIII, Section 2(b). The Fund's function, he has held, was to determine the character of the U.S. measures for the purpose of Article VIII, Section 2(a), but it was the responsibility of the courts to determine whether the measures were exchange control regulations for the purpose of Article VIII, Section 2(b). While the Fund has not adopted an interpretation of the concept of exchange control regulations in Article VIII, Section 2(b), Professor Gianviti's division of authority cannot be understood to mean that the Fund would be debarred from interpreting the concept. Nor should it be deduced that exchange restrictions can be imposed without exchange control regulations. Professor Gianviti implicitly recognizes that restrictions cannot exist without exchange control regulations by citing the Fund's guiding principle for the determination of restrictions [84] as support for his view that, in the practice of states, exchange controls deal directly with the making or receipt of international payments and transfers or with the holding or transmitting of international means of payment.[85]

Professor Gianviti has noted that the Fund does not limit restrictions to protective measures and that it accepts the view that measures of economic reprisal can constitute restrictions under the Articles. He has explained that certain authors would not concur in these conclusions, and that, if they are right, the motives of the United States for its measures would prevent them from being considered exchange control measures.[86]

---

[84] "The guiding principle in ascertaining whether a measure is a restriction on payments and transfers for current transactions under Article VIII, Section 2, is whether it involves a direct governmental limitation on the availability or use of exchange as such." (*Selected Decisions*, Ninth Issue, pp. 209–10.)

[85] For another discussion of the meaning of the concept of exchange control, see François Gianviti, "Le contrôle des changes étranger devant le juge national," *Revue critique de droit international privé*, Vol. 69 (1980), pp. 665–67.

[86] Gianviti, *Le blocage*, pp. 291–94. One of the authors he cites, although not with full concurrence, is Arthur Nussbaum (*Money in the Law, National and International*, Second Edition, 1950, pp. 455–57), who argued that the freeze of German property in March 1940 was not regarded by the Fund as a restriction under Article VIII, Section 2(b), because, if the Fund had taken this view, the United States would not have been able to accept the obligations of Article VIII, Sections 2, 3, and 4 in 1946. Professor Gianviti is not totally persuaded because the freeze may have been sufficiently relaxed by the time that the United States accepted the obligations. The Fund would have been able, however, to approve remaining restrictions, if there were any, under Article VIII, Section 2(a). Moreover, any remaining restrictions may have been on the transfer of capital and did not require approval.

Professor Gianviti would hesitate to classify the U.S. measures as exchange control regulations if the purpose—perhaps if the sole purpose—were to sequester assets for the benefit of creditors of the Iranian authorities. He has noted, further, that the measures extend beyond monetary assets and monetary operations. This fact would not deprive exchange control regulations of their character as such but would mean only that any measures that were not exchange control regulations would not fall within the scope of Article VIII, Section 2(*b*).

If the hypothesis that the test for determining whether a measure is an exchange control regulation is the legislator's motive of protecting itself, it must be noted that the United States asserted that it had this motive among others. Executive Order 12170 declared that there was an unusual and extraordinary threat to the economy of the United States as well as to its national security and foreign policy. Although the motivations were amplified, the mention of the threat to the economy was never abandoned. Suppose that the question of the meaning of exchange control regulations was before a court that treated motive as the test. Would the court hold that the legislator's statement of its motives was conclusive or would the court consider itself free to arrive at its own conclusions about motive?

An argument against reliance on motive in determining whether measures are exchange control regulations is that motives may be difficult to discover or they may be mixed. Motive is rejected by the Fund as the test of restrictions, with the result that the situation could arise in which measures could be considered restrictions by the Fund but not exchange control regulations by the courts. But, as noted already, restrictions cannot exist without exchange control regulations as the instruments for imposing the restrictions.

Professor Gianviti treats the relevance of motive as a hypothesis and does not give it his support. After noting certain features of the U.S. measures, he concludes that:

> Though it does not follow the classic model of exchange controls, either in its purpose or in its technique, the freeze may therefore be classified as a "rude" form of exchange control. The evolution of the American regulations tends to confirm this analysis.[87] (*Translation*)

According to Professor Edwards, the term "exchange control regulations" should apply to all regulations that in form directly control international payments and transfers, whether associated with current

---

[87] The word "rude" appears in the original as "rustique." (Gianviti, *Le blocage*, p. 294.)

transactions or with capital movements. Form is decisive and motive irrelevant. He has noted that some authors have held that the test of form for the purpose of determining what are restrictions under Article VIII, Section 2(*a*) is not necessarily applicable for the purpose of determining what are exchange control regulations under Article VIII, Section 2(*b*), and that in their view restrictions applied for reasons of security are not exchange control regulations. Some of these authors appear to him to have overlooked Executive Board Decision No. 144-(52/51). Professor Edwards has concluded that the U.S. measures were exchange control regulations.[88]

Mr. C.H. de Pardieu of Paris has noted the difference of opinion among authors on the question whether motive must be taken into account in determining whether measures are exchange control regulations. He has pointed out that protection of the economy of the United States was one of the motives for the adoption of the U.S. measures. The withdrawal and conversion of the deposits would have been a serious threat to the banking system of the United States and other countries. He has concluded, therefore, that one of the essential purposes of the United States was the protection of the U.S. currency by means of protecting U.S. financial resources. Another motive, he has written, was to provide for satisfaction of the claims of the United States and its citizens in an orderly manner. He has explained that although it might be questioned whether protecting the claims of U.S. creditors was equivalent to protecting U.S. financial resources, in his opinion the nonpayment of claims would have had a serious impact on the U.S. balance of payments that would have led to a decline in the external value of the dollar. He has concluded that even according to the strictest definition of exchange control regulations as measures intended to protect the financial resources of the legislator the U.S. measures were exchange control regulations.[89]

Dr. Klaus Westrick has come to the same conclusion. He seems to regard the conservation of assets for the benefit of creditors as an objective that justifies classification of the U.S. measures as exchange control regulations.[90]

---

[88] Edwards, *Extraterritorial Application*, p. 885.

[89] De Pardieu, *Carter Freeze Order*, pp. 98–99. See also Steele, *Iran Crisis and International Law*, p. 77, and U.S. oral argument in Case Concerning United States Diplomatic and Consular Staff in Tehran, *Department of State Bulletin*, Vol. 80 (May 1980), p. 56.

[90] "The Carter Freeze Order serves as a restriction of the flow of capital, as well as the securing of claims of the United States and its citizens against Iran, and as such seeks objectives in the currency law area. For this reason the Carter Order is to be considered a currency control measure within the meaning of Art. VIII. 2 b of the IMF treaty." (Westrick, *Legality of Freeze Orders*, p. 108.)

Miss Natalie A. Simon, a U.S. author who has focused on the question whether the U.S. measures were exchange control regulations within the meaning of Article VIII, Section 2(b), has favored a definition that includes some element of protection for the legislator.[91] The imprecision of this approach is illustrated by the author's various formulations of it: "protecting a nation's financial resources," "*imposed for purposes of protecting the nation's currency* [92] in periods of balance of payments disequilibrium," "their purpose is . . . to conserve the supply of the nation's currency," [93] "preserving the national currency," "the husbanding of foreign exchange." She has concluded that the U.S. measures were not exchange control regulations because the United States was not motivated exclusively by considerations of this character and because the measures prohibited transactions and not the acquisition or use of foreign exchange or domestic currency. The Regulations, however, provided in part that "no person . . . shall . . . in any transaction . . . make any payments, transfer of credit, or other transfer of funds. . . ." This prohibition was addressed directly to payments and not to the transactions that give rise to payments.

The attempts by authors to define exchange control regulations in terms of motivation fall into two classes. One approach is to specify the necessity for a particular motive, which is defined in terms of some economic objective, while the other approach is to exclude certain specified motives. Both approaches fail to recognize the multiplicity of possible motives, both economic and noneconomic, for exchange control regulations and the frequent admixture of motives when a member applies controls. Mr. Jozef Swidrowski, an expert formerly on the staff of the Fund, has listed no fewer than eight general categories and 28 specific examples of motives for controls on external transactions, but he has written that even this list was not complete.[94]

The U.S. measures illustrate another weakness of the attempt to define exchange control regulations in terms of motive. The measures were notified to the Fund under its decision on exchange restrictions imposed solely for the preservation of national or international

---

[91] Natalie A. Simon, "The Iranian Assets Control Regulations and the International Monetary Fund: Are the Regulations 'Exchange Control Regulations?' ", *Boston College International and Comparative Law Review*, Vol. IV (1981), pp. 203–23. (Hereinafter cited as Simon, *Regulations.*)

[92] Miss Simon's italics (*ibid.*, p. 209).

[93] "Currency" in this phrase is intended, perhaps, to mean monetary reserves.

[94] Jozef Swidrowski, "Controls on External Economic Transactions," *The University of Toledo Law Review*, Vol. 12 (1981), pp. 190–91.

security. The decision was intended to relieve the Fund, if possible, of the duty to examine political or military considerations. One of the announced motives for the measures was the protection of the economy of the United States. It follows, therefore, that political considerations can lead a member to take measures to achieve an economic objective.

In support of her conclusion that the U.S. measures were not exchange control regulations, Miss Simon has advanced the further argument that the measures were not confined to exchange but extended to other aspects of economic activity as well. It is common practice for members to adopt a set of measures that go beyond exchange restrictions or exchange controls. In these cases, neither logic nor legal prescription prevents a member's measures from being exchange restrictions or exchange control regulations to the extent that they meet whatever are the criteria for these concepts. The Fund is able to distinguish between measures that are within the area of its regulatory jurisdiction or other interests and those that are beyond the boundary. There is no legal or practical justification for the Fund to abandon its responsibilities because a member's measures are only partly within those responsibilities.

VIII. "Maintained or Imposed Consistently with This Agreement"

Article VIII, Section 2(b) provides that exchange contracts shall be unenforceable if the exchange control regulations that have not been observed are "maintained or imposed consistently with this Agreement." Professor Edwards has stated that restrictions approved by the Fund cannot be challenged by the courts as inconsistent with the Articles.[95] The implication of this view is that the exchange control regulations that impose the restrictions are consistent with the Articles and cannot be challenged. The restrictions involved in the U.S. measures were approved by the Fund under the special procedure of Executive Board Decision No. 144-(52/51).

Professor Edwards has written that consistency with the Articles should not be assumed simply because restrictions are approved under Article VIII, Section 2(a) or authorized by Article VI, Section 3 and do not need the approval of the Fund.[96] These restrictions should

---

[95] Edwards, *Extraterritorial Application*, p. 896.

[96] Some restrictions are authorized by Article VII, Section 2 or approved under Article VIII, Section 3.

be consistent with other provisions of the Articles, including Articles I and IV. He has recommended that in all cases it would be unwise for courts to refrain from seeking the guidance of the Fund on a question of consistency with the Articles.[97]

The view that the authorization of a restriction by or under a provision of the Articles is not conclusive on the question of consistency could put the Fund in the anomalous position of declaring, in response to an inquiry, that the Articles authorized or the Fund approved restrictions that were inconsistent with the Articles. The anomaly would be avoided, however, if the Fund were to take some action to express its objection to authorized restrictions under an express power in the Articles. For example, the Fund might find that a member, by applying restrictions on capital transfers, was not performing its obligations regarding exchange arrangements under Article IV. It is doubtful, however, that in practice the Fund would find that restrictions on capital transfers, even though authorized by Article VI, Section 3, were in violation of some other provision. The Fund has considered freedom to control capital transfers as something like a fundamental privilege of members. An illustration of this attitude is to be found in the Fund's decision that the freedom assured to members by Article VI, Section 3 is not impaired by the general language of Article VIII, Section 3 proscribing discriminatory currency arrangements.[98]

The Fund might be posed with less of a problem if requested to determine the consistency with the Articles of restrictions on payments and transfers for current international transactions that are authorized because they are imposed under the transitional arrangements of Article XIV, Section 2. Under Article XIV, Section 3, the Fund, if it deems such action necessary in exceptional circumstances, may make representations to a member that conditions are favorable for the withdrawal of any particular restriction or for the general abandonment of restrictions. If the Fund finds that the member persists in maintaining restrictions, the Fund may declare the member ineligible to use the Fund's general resources. If the Fund has made representations, and certainly if it has gone on to declare a member ineligible, the Fund might hold that the restrictions were now inconsistent with the Articles. It has never taken either action.

There remain for consideration nonrestrictive exchange control regulations. They are not authorized by any express provision, and

---

[97] See fn. 95 supra.
[98] Selected Decisions, Ninth Issue, p. 104.

there is no express provision under which the Fund can express its dissatisfaction with them.

Article VIII, Section 2(b) refers to exchange control regulations without distinguishing between those that are restrictive and those that are not. Why was the distinction not made, and why was the benefit of the provision made applicable to both categories of regulations? The answer to this question may be that even though exchange controls are not restrictive, they can still promote the policies of members. For example, exchange controls may be imposed in order to enable a member to collect information about capital transfers and decide whether it should prohibit capital transfers. If private parties ignore the controls, the effect might be capital outflow contrary to the policy that the member would wish to follow. Moreover, a member might wish to apply capital controls in order to curb inflow from members that were trying to control capital outflow.[99]

Miss Simon has concluded that although the U.S. measures were approved under Executive Board Decision No. 144-(52/51), approval for the purposes of Article VIII, Section 2(a) does not make restrictions consistent with the letter and spirit of the Articles for the purposes of Article VIII, Section 2(b).[100] This conclusion is supported with the argument that the common law principle that courts do not enforce foreign "revenue" laws is displaced by Article VIII, Section 2(b) only if exchange control regulations are imposed for balance of payments reasons. The argument rests on the questionable hypothesis that exchange control regulations are "revenue" laws, and fails to distinguish between the enforceability of revenue laws and the recognition of them for other purposes (such as the unenforceability of contracts).

Furthermore, the author has not reconciled her views on consistency with the Articles. On the one hand, she states that

> The only restrictions on current payments that could be justified under the Fund Agreement in light of its purposes and, thus, properly receive Fund approval, would be those that are necessary, temporary and imposed on balance of payments grounds.[101]

On the other hand, she recognizes that restrictions can be approved for reasons of security under Executive Board Decision No. 144-(52/

---

[99] See *History, 1945–65,* Vol. III: Documents, p. 179. These controls to curb capital inflow would be covered by the first, and not the second, sentence of Article VIII, Section 2(b). They illustrate the fallacy of interpreting the provision as if it were confined to the protection of the legislator's balance of payments or exchange resources.

[100] Simon, *Regulations,* p. 219.

[101] *Ibid.,* p. 218.

51). The first of these views should lead logically to the conclusion that the Fund's approval of restrictions for security reasons is *ultra vires*. Only then would the anomaly be avoided of the Fund's approval of restrictions that are not consistent with the spirit and letter of the Articles. The Fund has concluded, in the first sentence of Decision No. 144-(52/51), that all restrictions on the making of payments and transfers for current international transactions are subject to Article VIII, Section 2(a) and can be approved:

> Article VIII, Section 2(a), in conformity with its language, applies to all restrictions on current payments and transfers, irrespective of their motivation and the circumstances in which they are imposed.

The motivations are not confined to the balance of payments or the preservation of national or international security.

In confronting the problem of restrictions on payments and transfers for current international transactions that are imposed for reasons of security, the Fund had to choose among three theoretically possible solutions: the restrictions are not within the reach of Article VIII, Section 2(a) or other provisions of the Articles; they are subject to Article VIII, Section 2(a) but are not consistent with the Articles, so that they are always invalid; they are subject to Article VIII, Section 2(a), so that the Fund has a discretion to approve or not to approve them.

The problem of choice was brought to the attention of the Fund in a statement in the Executive Board on December 16, 1950 by the Executive Director appointed by the United States. The emergency in Korea was the occasion for his statement. He informed the Fund that on the following day the United States proposed to impose restrictions on payments and transfers within the jurisdiction of the United States that involved China and Korea and their nationals, with the exception of those portions that were under the control of China and Korea as recognized by the U.S. Government. The restrictions were being imposed not for economic or financial reasons but to assist the United Nations forces. The U.S. Government had given some consideration to the question of the applicability of the Articles to actions taken for the preservation of national and international security in time of war or an emergency in international relations. The Articles were not explicit on this point, but in view of the precedent of certain provisions of the GATT [102] and the proposed International

---

[102] The reference was to Article XXI of the GATT:
"Nothing in this Agreement shall be construed
(a) to require any contracting party to furnish any information the disclosure

Trade Organization (ITO) and the difficulties the Fund would have in endeavoring to evaluate actions to which the economic and financial criteria of the Articles did not apply, the tentative attitude of the U.S. Government was that the Fund should not be expected to act on such restrictions. The United States thought that the Fund should simply take note of an action that was proposed for security reasons. The Executive Board took a decision in accordance with this formulation in the case before it pending study of the general question of the Fund's jurisdiction.[103]

That study resulted in Executive Board Decision No. 144-(52/51), which represents the third of the three possible solutions noted above. The Fund's reluctance to create an exception to its jurisdiction that might be a precedent for other exceptions outweighed the disadvantages of the Fund's possible involvement in political disputes. Exceptions to the Fund's jurisdiction over restrictions might spread to its jurisdiction over exchange rates as well. Furthermore, if the Fund disclaimed jurisdiction over restrictions imposed for reasons of security, it would lack authority to compel the withdrawal of these restrictions. Finally, although restrictions imposed for reasons of security are not imposed for economic or financial reasons, the restrictions are economic or financial measures. Throughout the prolonged studies and discussions from which the decision emerged, there was no mention of the effect it would have under Article VIII, Section 2(b). Restrictions imposed for security reasons and approved under the decision have the same effect under Article VIII, Section 2(b) as restrictions approved under Article VIII, Section 2(a) by other procedures.

Professor Edwards has thought it absurd or unreasonable to expect courts in the member country against which restrictions are imposed

---

of which it considers contrary to its essential security interests; or

(b) to prevent any contracting party from taking any action which it considers necessary for the protection of its essential security interests

(i) relating to fissionable materials or the materials from which they are derived;

(ii) relating to the traffic in arms, ammunition and implements of war and to such traffic in other goods and materials as is carried on directly or indirectly for the purpose of supplying a military establishment;

(iii) taken in time of war or other emergency in international relations; or

(c) to prevent any contracting party from taking any action in pursuance of its obligations under the United Nations Charter for the maintenance of international peace and security." See John H. Jackson, *World Trade and the Law of GATT* (Indianapolis, Bobbs-Merrill, 1969), pp. 748–52.

[103] *History, 1945–65,* Vol. I: Chronicle, p. 275. See also *Summary Proceedings,* September 1951, pp. 45–46.

for security reasons to respect the restrictions under Article VIII, Section 2(*b*). This practical problem is not confined to restrictions imposed for reasons of security. Restrictions imposed for any reason may be detrimental to the interests of some members. Even closer parallels would exist if the Fund were to approve under Article VIII, Section 3 discriminatory currency arrangements involving restrictions for balance of payments reasons or if members were to impose restrictions on the use of a currency that the Fund had declared scarce under Article VII, Section 3.

Professor Edwards has made the further point that courts in third member countries may be reluctant to apply a provision when it compels them to take sides in a political dispute between two members. In view of these difficulties, he has recommended that Executive Board Decision No. 144-(52/51) should be revised so that the restrictions notified to the Fund under it would not be approved unless in particular cases the Fund were to adopt affirmative decisions to approve restrictions. A possible criterion for approval, he notes, could be that the restrictions were defensive and not imposed as a sanction that applied pressure against another member, but he has dismissed this criterion because it might be difficult to determine whether restrictions were defensive or offensive. He has cited the U.S. measures as an illustration of this difficulty because of the change he finds in the announced motivation for them. His preference would be approval by the Fund only when restrictions were called for by the Security Council of the United Nations.[104] The proposal is unrealistic if only because not all members of the Security Council are members of the Fund. Whatever can be said for or against this proposal, there is little reason to suppose that courts of the member against which the restrictions had been imposed would become less reluctant to apply Article VIII, Section 2(*b*) to them.

IX. Article VIII, Section 2(*b*) and Article VI, Section 3

Professor Gavalda has criticized the U.S. measures on the ground that they violated Article VI, Section 3. He has written:

> This type of measure seems glaringly to contradict the letter and the spirit of the Articles of Agreement. Article VI, Section 3 states that "no member may exercise these controls in a manner which will restrict payments for current transactions or which will unduly delay

---

104 Edwards, *Extraterritorial Application*, pp. 896–99.

transfers of funds in settlement of commitments, except as provided in Article VII, Section 3(*b*) and in Article XIV, Section 2."[105] (*Translation*)

The language of Article VI, Section 3 quoted by Professor Gavalda qualifies earlier language in the provision: "Members may exercise such controls as are necessary to regulate capital movements, . . ." His criticism is not clear, but it may mean that, even if balances are blocked as capital under the authority of Article VI, Section 3, the procedures for blocking must not restrict payments for current international transactions, and balances must be freed from blocking if the holder intends to make payments for current international transactions with them. Alternatively, he may be attributing to the words "unduly delay transfers of funds in settlement of commitments" in Article VI, Section 3 the meaning that balances must be unblocked whatever may be the purpose for which they are to be used if the commitments in discharge of which they are to be used were entered into before the blocking.

Neither of these interpretations of the words "unduly delay transfers of funds in settlement of commitments" is correct. Either interpretation would make the effective control of capital transfers impossible. The authority of members to control capital transfers was a fundamental objective of the negotiators of the Articles of Agreement. The Fund has been guided by this objective in interpreting the Agreement. Article VI, Section 3 has been understood to mean that if a member imposes controls on balances as capital, the member must administer the controls in such a way that the use of other balances in payments for current international transactions is not restricted. In addition, the member must not subject transfers of the proceeds of recent current transactions to undue delay.

The language of the clause in the provision that refers to undue delay gives some difficulty. It is not apparent why it was necessary to include the clause in Article VI, Section 3 because the restriction of payments and transfers is forbidden by Article VIII, Section 2(*a*), and undue delay in permitting transfers is a restriction. Moreover, it is not helpful to describe "transfers" as made in "settlement of commitments." Commitments are settled by the payments of payors to payees before payees make transfers of these receipts.

Notwithstanding these obscurities, the purpose of the words in Article VI, Section 3 must be taken to clarify the principle that undue delay in permitting the transfer of the proceeds of recent current

---

[105] Gavalda, *Gazette du Palais*, March 12–13, 1980, p. 17.

transactions is a restriction under Article VIII, Section 2(*a*) and that members must avoid this restriction in applying capital controls. Therefore, a member may not delay the transfer by a payee to his own country of the proceeds of a current international transaction and then take the position that the proceeds have become capital subject to control. This interpretation is supported by an unpublished draft of Article VI, Section 3 that was advanced at the Atlantic City Conference, which was held in preparation for the Bretton Woods Conference:

> No member country may control international capital movements in a manner which will restrict payments for current transactions or which will unduly delay transfers of funds in settlement of commitments arising from such transactions, except as provided in Article VI, Section 2 and Article X, Section 1.

No explanation of the deletion of the words "arising from such transactions" is available. It may be that they were thought to be unnecessary in a context that refers to "transfers" in conjunction with "payments for current transactions" because of the expression "payments and transfers for current international transactions" in Article VIII, Section 2(*a*).

Another possible explanation of the clause that refers to transfers in settlement of commitments in Article VI, Section 3 is that it is a surviving remnant of the time that preceded the drafting of the definition of payments for current transactions in Article XIX(*i*) of the original Articles.[106] Some of the payments listed in the definition were to be treated as payments for current transactions for reasons of policy even though economists would consider them to be capital transfers. To give effect to the policy reasons, the payments were included in earlier drafts of Article VI, Section 3 and Article VIII, Section 2(*a*), as follows:

> Subject to VI and X, 2, below, a member country may not use its control of capital movements to restrict payments arising out of current transactions in goods and services or to delay unduly transfer of earnings, interest and amortization.

> Not to impose restrictions on payments arising out of current transactions in goods and services or to delay unduly transfers of earnings, interest, and amortization, except as provided in X, 2, or to engage in discriminatory currency arrangements or multiple currency practices without the approval of the Fund.

---

[106] Article XXX(*d*) of the present Articles.

Probably, once the definition of payments for current transactions was settled or approaching finality, it became unnecessary to refer to earnings, interest, and amortization in either Article VI, Section 3 or Article VIII, Section 2(*a*). The draft of Article VI, Section 3 that emerged from Atlantic City, as quoted earlier, succeeded the draft of the first of the provisions quoted above in this paragraph.

If, as should be concluded, "transfers of funds in settlement of commitments" are transfers of the proceeds of recent current transactions, the provision does not deal with the unblocking of balances blocked as capital. It follows, first, that Article VI, Section 3 does not limit the authority of a member to control capital transfers, provided that payments and transfers for current international transactions are not impeded by undue delay or by a restriction of any other kind. It follows, second, that nothing in Article VI, Section 3 limits the authority of the Fund to approve restrictions on payments and transfers for current international transactions under Article VIII, Section 2(*a*). For these reasons, Professor Gavalda's objection based on Article VI, Section 3 cannot be accepted.

There is little disposition in these days to argue that Article VIII, Section 2(*b*) refers to exchange control regulations that affect payments and transfers for current international transactions but not to exchange control regulations that apply to capital transfers. Dr. Schneider, however, has written that the Supreme Court of the Federal Republic of Germany has expressed some doubt that the provision applies to capital controls, and in his opinion the question is entirely open in the Federal Republic.[107] It is useful, therefore, to note an argument in support of the broader impact of Article VIII, Section 2(*b*) that has not been noted hitherto.

Article VIII, Section 4(*a*) spells out the obligation of a member to convert holdings of its currency presented to it by other members. The obligation is subject to a number of exceptions in Article VIII, Section 4(*b*), one of which is that:

> (iii) the balances have been acquired contrary to the exchange regulations of the member which is asked to buy them.

The exception applies whether the balances were acquired contrary to exchange controls regulating either payments and transfers for current international transactions or transfers of capital. Article VIII, Section 2(*b*) and Article VIII, Section 4(*b*)(iii) can be regarded as

---

[107] Schneider, *Problems of Recognition*, p. 103.

related to each other in the sense that the first of these provisions deals with contracts that have not yet been performed by payment while the second of the two provisions deals with contracts that have been performed. If both kinds of regulation are covered by Article VIII, Section 4(b)(iii), both should be covered by Article VIII, Section 2(b).[108]

X. Reciprocity

Dr. Schneider has set forth four reasons why he doubts that courts in the Federal Republic of Germany would treat the U.S. measures as coming within the purview of Article VIII, Section 2(b).[109] One of these reasons is the expectation that a court would take the principle of reciprocity into consideration. He has written that this principle is deeply entrenched when the issue before a court of the Federal Republic is recognition of the acts of foreign jurisdictions. He notes the restrictive interpretation of "exchange contracts" by the English Court of Appeal in *Wilson, Smithett & Cope Ltd. v. Terruzzi*,[110] and by the New York Court of Appeals in *Banco do Brasil, S.A. v. A.C. Israel Commodity Co., Inc., et al.*,[111] and *J. Zeevi and Sons, Ltd., et al. v. Grindlays Bank (Uganda) Limited.*[112] Although he explains that the legal position in the United States is not finally settled and is less clear than in the United Kingdom, he nevertheless maintains that the *Zeevi* case has eliminated any doubt. He concludes that courts in the United States endorse as narrow a construction of Article VIII, Section 2(b) as do English courts. "It is conceivable, therefore, that a German court might resort to the principle of reciprocity and, in applying this principle, not give effect to the Presidential Order." [113]

The case decided by the Supreme Court of the Federal Republic of Germany on March 8, 1979 [114] does not support Dr. Schneider's expectation. The *Zeevi* case was decided on June 16, 1975. Although courts might be influenced by considerations of reciprocity, there is no valid doctrine of reciprocity in the application of Article VIII,

---

[108] It is not suggested, however, that the exchange control regulations covered by Article VIII, Section 2(b) are always those of the issuer of the currency to be converted under Article VIII, Section 4(b)(iii).

[109] Schneider, *Problems of Recognition*, pp. 103–104.

[110] [1976] 1 Q.B. 683; [1976] 1 Q.B. 703 (C.A.).

[111] 12 N.Y. 2d 371, 190 N.E. 2d 235, 239 N.Y.S. 2d 872 (1963).

[112] 37 N.Y. 2d 220, 333 N.E. 2d 168, 371 N.Y.S. 2d 892 (1975).

[113] Schneider, *Problems of Recognition*, p. 104.

[114] Gold, "Fund Agreement in the Courts—XV," pp. 294–99 in this volume.

Section 2(*b*). It is the function of the Fund to ensure that provisions of the Articles are observed properly. A court might legitimately take account of the decisions of foreign courts in order to arrive at a uniform interpretation of the provision, but uniformity is not the same as reciprocity. Uniformity justifies Dr. Schneider in citing the English and U.S. decisions, but reciprocity does not.

A condition of reciprocity could lead to a patchwork of bilateral applications of Article VIII, Section 2(*b*) with much diversity among decisions. Reciprocity would create a further problem when the courts of a member had not had an opportunity to interpret Article VIII, Section 2(*b*). The courts of other members would have no guidance in deciding how to apply Article VIII, Section 2(*b*) when the exchange control regulations in issue were those of the member whose courts had not spoken.

XI. Some Points of Principle

Some of the points of principle made in this survey can be summarized as follows:

1. If a member gives the Fund notice of the imposition of restrictions under Executive Board Decision No. 144-(52/51) and the Fund refrains from informing the member within 30 days after receiving the notice that the Fund is not satisfied that the restrictions are proposed solely for the preservation of national or international security, approval is given to whatever restrictions require approval under Article VIII, Section 2(*a*).

2. If a member receives no reaction from the Fund within 30 days, the absence of a reaction cannot be understood to mean that the Fund has concluded that there are no restrictions that require approval under Article VIII, Section 2(*a*).

3. A member adopting exchange control regulations is entitled to the support of Article VIII, Section 2(*b*) if the member had legislative jurisdiction in accordance with public international law to adopt the regulations. The Fund does not determine whether a member has legislative jurisdiction to adopt restrictions that are the subject of the procedure of Decision No. 144-(52/51).

4. Three approaches are possible in determining what is meant by legislative jurisdiction for the purpose of Article VIII, Section 2(*b*). The interpretation can be made in accordance with:

(i) general principles of legislative jurisdiction recognized by public international law, without reference to the Articles; or

(ii) the conclusion that a new principle of legislative jurisdiction is implicit in the concept of the involvement of a currency under Article VIII, Section 2(b) and that this principle replaces general principles of public international law on legislative jurisdiction for the purpose of Article VIII, Section 2(b); or

(iii) the concept of the involvement of a currency under Article VIII, Section 2(b), which concept is to be defined in accordance with general principles of international law on legislative jurisdiction. The Fund has not decided which is the correct approach.

5. Approaches (ii) and (iii) in 4 above would require only one test in order to decide both the existence of legislative jurisdiction and the involvement of a currency. Approach (iii), in contrast to (ii), would avoid the conclusion that Article VIII, Section 2(b) has created a new principle of legislative jurisdiction, but the choice between approaches (ii) and (iii) should depend on which would produce economic effects that are more compatible with the Articles.

6. Inasmuch as the Fund has not resolved what is meant by legislative jurisdiction for the purpose of Article VIII, Section 2(b), and inasmuch as the Fund does not inquire whether a member has legislative jurisdiction to impose particular exchange control regulations, these issues, if raised in legal proceedings, have to be decided by the courts.

7. If a member has legislative jurisdiction, the courts of another member must apply Article VIII, Section 2(b) if the conditions of the provision are satisfied. The court cannot refuse to do so on the ground that under its private international law the exchange contract sued upon would be enforceable if Article VIII, Section 2(b) were ignored.

8. Most commentators have discussed legislative jurisdiction in general terms and not in relation to Article VIII, Section 2(b). Therefore, they have not addressed themselves to the problem as set forth in 4 above.

9. The traditional view of legislative jurisdiction is strongly influenced by ideas of territoriality. There is evidence in the original Articles that the drafters accepted the concept of territoriality for certain purposes, although there is no evidence that Article VIII, Section 2(b) was among these purposes. Another view of legislative jurisdiction is that it is determined, after a consideration of all circum-

stances, by the conclusion that a particular legislator has sufficient national interest to justify legislative jurisdiction.

10. A country has broad but not unlimited powers to regulate its currency. These powers have been increased by the Second Amendment when compared with the original Articles. A member's power to regulate its currency does not mean that it has legislative jurisdiction over all payments and transfers in the currency. Under the second view of legislative jurisdiction in 9 above, however, the currency of payment or transfer might be one of the circumstances to be taken into account in evaluating a country's interest.

11. The narrow view of "exchange contracts" in Article VIII, Section 2(b) is that they are contracts for the exchange of one currency against another or one means of payment against another. The broad view is that they are contracts involving monetary elements. Under the latter view, contracts of deposit with banks are exchange contracts.

12. On the narrow view, the question arises whether a contract calling for payment in a foreign currency becomes an exchange contract solely by virtue of the fact that the law applied by the forum permits or requires the contract to be discharged by payment in the domestic currency.

13. An economic view of the currency "involved" under Article VIII, Section 2(b) is that it is the currency of the member whose balance of payments would be affected by performance of the exchange contract. A variant of this view is that the currency is that of the member whose exchange resources would be affected by performance. Exchange resources in this context have the broad meaning of potential national resources or, perhaps, resources that affect the international economic or financial position of the member. If there is any difference between the formulations in terms of the balance of payments and exchange resources, it would be principally in relation to some contracts between the residents of a country with respect to its foreign assets and between nonresidents with respect to its foreign liabilities.

14. A commentator who accepts the broader view of exchange contracts has concluded nevertheless that the withdrawal of a Eurodollar deposit does not "involve" the U.S. dollar under Article VIII, Section 2(b). The reason is that the contract between a depositor and a Eurobank (including branches and subsidiaries of a U.S. bank) can be performed at the situs of the bank and need not go through clear-

ing arrangements in the United States, from which the deduction is drawn that performance of the contract of deposit does not affect the U.S. balance of payments or the exchange resources of the United States. According to this theory, the contract of deposit is severable from the transfer of dollars from a U.S. bank to a Eurobank that occurs in the United States and enables the Eurobank to credit its customer, the depositor, with a sum in dollars on its books. This interbank transfer does "involve" the U.S. dollar within the meaning of Article VIII, Section 2(b), but an action to enforce the deposit contract is not an action to enforce an interbank transfer in the United States.

15. A question that has not been considered is whether, in view of a recent decision of the English Court of Appeal, the operations in the United States and elsewhere that are conducted in connection with Eurodollar deposits and withdrawals must be treated as locked together—in short, as not severable—for the purpose of determining whether the U.S. dollar is "involved."

16. Another commentator has supported a textual view of the currency "involved." The currency would be the one named in the contract as the currency of payment or transfer or a currency that must be paid or transferred so that the contract can be performed. The latter element in this formulation is intended to take account of clearing arrangements in the country of the issue of a currency that is a "guest currency" under the contract. On this view, Eurodollar deposit contracts "involve" the U.S. dollar. An avowedly noneconomic solution, however, is open to the objection that it may not be in harmony with the Articles. In addition, the interpretation would confine the benefits of Article VIII, Section 2(b) mainly to the few issuers of the currencies that are in widespread use in international payments.

17. Two approaches have been taken to the meaning of "exchange control regulations" in Article VIII, Section 2(b). One approach is based on form, the other on motive. Some commentators who favor the second approach require a motive of economic self-protection on the part of the legislator. Other commentators approach a definition by excluding particular motives, such as political retaliation. Motives can be hard to determine, and sometimes they are mixed. Executive Board Decision No. 144-(52/51) establishes that the motive for exchange control restrictions subject to Article VIII, Section 2(a) may be political.

18. If exchange control restrictions are approved under Article VIII, Section 2(a) or are authorized under other provisions of the Articles,

the regulations by which the restrictions are imposed fall within the scope of Article VIII, Section 2(*b*) as regulations "maintained or imposed consistently with this Agreement." A wedge cannot be driven between Article VIII, Section 2(*b*) and the provisions under which restrictions are approved, or the provisions by which they are authorized, by introducing motive as a further condition for the application of Article VIII, Section 2(*b*). The anomaly cannot be accepted that approved or authorized regulations may be inconsistent with the Articles. The Fund has certain powers, however, to disapprove or to express dissatisfaction with the maintenance of restrictions.

19. Article VI, Section 3 does not require a member to unblock capital balances because the holder of them wishes to make payments for current international transactions with the balances. Capital controls are among the regulations referred to in Article VIII, Section 2(*b*).

20. A member's courts should apply Article VIII, Section 2(*b*) without inquiring whether the courts of the member whose exchange control regulations are in issue grant reciprocal treatment. It is the function of the Fund to ensure that provisions of the Articles are observed properly. The jurisprudence of other courts is relevant not for the purpose of ensuring bilateral reciprocity but for the purpose of trying to achieve uniformity of interpretation by all courts in the territories of members.

APPENDIX A

A Note on the History of the Drafting of Article VIII, Section 2(*b*)

The publication of Volume XXVI of the *Collected Writings of John Maynard Keynes*[1] provides additional information on the origin of Article VIII, Section 2(*b*). This information confirms the knowledge derived from the Proceedings and Documents of the Bretton Woods Conference:[2] the provision was intended originally to support par values established under the Articles of the Fund by declaring contracts unenforceable if they dealt with the purchase and sale of currencies at exchange rates that were inconsistent with the Articles. The new material clarifies the motivation of the drafters of the first version of Article VIII, Section 2(*b*), but does not deal with the changes in the provision that occurred during the course of the Bretton Woods Conference. It does nothing, therefore, to confirm or to contradict that the changes were the result of a different motivation.

To explain the new material, it is necessary to say something about the provisions of the original Articles that dealt with exchange rates. Each member was expected to establish a par value for its currency directly or indirectly in terms of gold as a common denominator.[3] The initial par value was established in agreement with the Fund[4] and subsequent changes with its concurrence.[5] Article IV, Section 3 provided that exchange rates in exchange transactions in a member's territories involving the member's currency and another member's currency were not to differ from the parity between the two currencies by more than the limits referred to in the provision. Parity was the ratio between the par values of the two currencies. Article IV, Section 4(*a*) contained an obligation of members in general terms requiring them to collaborate with the Fund to promote exchange stability, to maintain orderly exchange arrangements with other members, and to avoid competitive exchange alterations.

---

[1] *Keynes, Vol. XXVI.*
[2] *Proceedings and Documents.*
[3] Article IV, Section 1(*a*).
[4] Article XX, Section 4.
[5] Article IV, Section 5.

Article IV, Section 4(*b*), which is most pertinent to this discussion, contained two sentences. The first sentence obliged each member to adopt appropriate measures consistent with the Articles to confine exchange transactions in its territories between its own currency and another member's currency within the limits defined in Article IV, Section 3. The second sentence, however, declared in effect that if a member's monetary authorities freely bought and sold gold for their own currency in transactions with the monetary authorities of other members, for the settlement of international transactions, at prices determined by the par value of the currency, plus or minus the margin prescribed by the Fund, the member engaging in this practice was deemed to be fulfilling its obligation with respect to exchange rates for its currency. The theory of the provision was that as par values were established in terms of gold, a member that was maintaining the value of its currency in relation to gold by means of official transactions with other members on the basis of the par value of its currency was maintaining the exchange stability of its currency. Nothing more should be expected of such a member. If exchange transactions involving its currency occurred in its territories outside the permitted limits around parity, these exchange rates had to be attributed to the behavior of the monetary authorities of the other member whose currency was involved in the exchange transactions.

The United States negotiated the inclusion in the Articles of the second sentence of Article IV, Section 4(*b*). The United States did not intend to centralize exchange transactions, intervene in the exchange markets to keep exchange transactions within the permitted limits, adopt legislation to declare that exchange transactions at exchange rates beyond these limits were illegal, or adopt exchange controls in any form.

The second sentence became the fundamental norm of the par value system because of the undertaking by the United States to engage in gold transactions in accordance with the second sentence of Article IV, Section 4(*b*). It is remarkable, therefore, that Keynes bitterly regretted his concurrence in the provision:

> The history of the matter is as follows. The clause originally ran as follows:
>
> "A member shall undertake not to allow exchange transactions in its market in currencies of other members at rates outside a prescribed range based on the agreed parities."
>
> We, then, weakly and illogically and mistakenly, allowed the Americans to contract out by the addition of what is now the second sentence, because they wanted to avoid having to bring before Congress a special law such as would be required to make black markets illegal. But they and we failed (inexcusably) to notice that this addition only prevented dealings in the dollar outside the permitted range and would allow black markets in other currencies. But we all assumed that the other members would forbid black

markets by law. Finally the lawyers altered the language, as being more tidy and in better form, to what it now is.[6]

The new illumination appears in a letter dated January 25, 1945 to Keynes from Sir Wilfrid Eady, Second Secretary of the U.K. Treasury and a member of the British delegation at Bretton Woods. The following passage is the relevant one.

> . . . at that time I was terribly preoccupied with the issues in IV (4)(b). I had always assumed that every signatory country would make it an offence against domestic law for its residents to deal in exchanges outside the approved parities. When the Americans said that they would not do that I was very shocked, because it seemed to me that under our ordinary procedure for supporting the exchanges by leaving an open order with the Bank's agents in New York, if there was any evidence that our exchange was moving to a discount on an individual transaction of importance, or possibly as a temporary trend, the agent would use the reserves to support the exchange. *I was fighting against the soothing suggestion of the Americans that if they made black market transactions unenforceable they would in fact have done the trick,* and that combined with their own *de facto* practice of buying and selling gold freely, was enough. In the end, after delivering a horrified lecture to the Americans about New York being the Black Market centre of the world, you thought I was making too much bother about the point, and that as the Americans would not in any case do anything to meet us we had better do the best we could. Out of that wreckage I saved IV (4)(a) which of course means nothing.
>
> I am not reviving this *infandum dolorem* merely in self-defence. I think the material point is that if the Gods are propitious, and we get a chance of making any amendments, we must attack IV (4)(b) as well as VIII (2)(a).[7]

The language (other than the Latin) that is emphasized in this passage probably refers to the original version of Article VIII, Section 2(*b*) and explains that it was intended by the U.S. delegation to compensate the British delegation for its disappointment that the U.S. monetary authorities would do nothing else to support exchange rates for sterling in the United States. Nobody deluded himself or others into thinking that an obligation to refuse the enforcement of unperformed contracts calling for exchange rates beyond the limits defined by the Articles was equivalent to positive action to prevent the entry into or to deny the performance of such contracts.

In a letter dated October 6, 1944 to White, Keynes expressed the hope that notwithstanding Article IV, Section 4(*b*) the United States would legislate.[8] It never did.

---

[6] *Keynes, Vol. XXVI,* p. 138. See also Dennis Robertson (*ibid.,* p. 127) on the original clause referred to by Keynes: "The intention of this clause was that the Americans should undertake to lighten the task of supporting the pound, the franc etc. against depreciation in terms of the dollar by forbidding anybody to deal in those currencies at a discount in the New York market: but the clause as amended specifically exempts them from giving any such undertaking."

[7] *Ibid.,* pp. 170–71 (emphasis added).

[8] "I take this opportunity to point out that the second sentence of IV 4(b)

By what process did Article VIII, Section 2(b) emerge in final form at Bretton Woods? The record begins with a joint proposal by the U.S. and British delegations offered at the opening of the Conference, which suggests that an understanding had been reached at the preparatory conference attended by a limited group of countries at Atlantic City in June 1944. The proposed text appeared in a provision entitled "Foreign Exchange Dealings Based on Par Values" that was the forerunner of Article IV, Sections 3 and 4. The draft contained a provision on the free purchase and sale of gold and also the following sentence:

> (c) Exchange transactions in the territory of one member involving the currency of any other member, which evade or avoid the exchange regulations prescribed by that other member and authorized by this Agreement, shall not be enforceable in the territory of any member.[9]

On July 7, 1944, the delegation of Poland proposed an addition to the provision on foreign exchange dealings. It can be regarded as the ancestor of the second sentence of Article VIII, Section 2(b), but it is also the first record of a provision in this field that refers to controls and restrictions:

> SECTION 8. To cooperate with other member countries in order to enable them to render really effective such controls and restrictions as these countries might adopt or continue, with the approval of the Fund, for the purpose of regulating international movements of capital.[10]

On July 9, 1944, the British delegation submitted a revised version of the original proposal:

> (c) Exchange transactions in the territory of one member involving the currency of any other member, which evade or avoid the exchange regulations prescribed by that other member and authorized by this Agreement, shall be an offense in the territories of all members.[11]

This revision substituted the concept of an offense for the remedy of unenforceability. Keynes remained under the impression even after the Bretton Woods Conference that the purpose of Article IV, Section 4 was to require members, other than the United States, to declare "black markets in weak

---

by which, in effect, the U.S. contracts out of this clause, is in fact illogical. For, whilst gold convertibility prevents the dollar from depreciating, it does not prevent *other* currencies from depreciating in the New York market. Thus unless you legislate to the contrary, New York will become, as Einzig has been eager to point out, the chartered black market where all dubious transactions and weak currency deals will be concentrated. Let us hope that in spite of the Statue of Liberty pointing to New York as, under the Constitution, the proud home of black markets as the symbol of Freedom, you will in fact legislate!" (*Ibid.*, p. 143.)

[9] *Proceedings and Documents*, pp. 54–55. The draft was discussed by Committee 1 of Commission I on July 6, 1944, and discussion of it "disclosed various difficulties of a legal nature." The draft was referred to the Drafting Committee (p. 217).

[10] *Ibid.*, p. 230. (See also p. 288.)

[11] *Ibid.*, p. 334. This proposal also was referred to the Drafting Committee of Commission I (pp. 287–88). See also p. 341, in which the language is "be an offense in the territory of any member."

currencies" illegal. He seems to have regarded this action as the primary "appropriate measure."[12]

On July 11, 1944, the Drafting Committee of Commission I submitted the following language as a possible variant but not as a definite recommendation. This proposed text would still have been included in the provision on foreign exchange dealings:

> (c) Exchange transactions in the territory of one member involving the currency of any other member which are outside the prescribed variation from parity set forth in (a) above shall not be enforceable in the territory of any member country.
>
> Each member agrees to cooperate with other members in their efforts to effectuate exchange regulations prescribed by such members in accordance with this Agreement.[13]

Committee 1 of Commission I discussed three versions on July 12, 1944: the original joint proposal, the British revision, and the Drafting Committee's variant. The British delegation was willing to resile from its revision if the joint proposal was accepted. The U.S. delegation preferred the Drafting Committee's text but asked for more time to consider the matter. Committee 1 referred all three texts to Commission I.[14]

The reporting delegate of Committee 1 emphasized that the Drafting Committee's text would render not enforceable "only transactions outside the prescribed variation from parity." He explained also that this text would accomplish the purpose of the proposal made by the Polish delegation. This proposal was then withdrawn.[15]

Commission I did not make a choice. The Chairman referred the problem to a new Special Committee on July 13, 1944.[16] The Special Committee recommended, on July 14, 1944, that the Drafting Committee be asked to reconcile the differences between its language and the original joint proposal in order to clarify that there was no intent to impose criminal rather than civil penalties.[17] On the same day, clarification of the problem was still being sought in a meeting of Commission I, and the Drafting Committee was called into action again.[18]

On July 16, 1944, a Working Draft of the Articles was circulated for the Drafting Committee. For the first time, the provision appears as Article VIII, Section 2(*b*), and in a form close to the final text:

> (b) Exchange contracts, which involve the currency of any member and are contrary to the exchange control regulations of that member maintained or imposed consistently with this Agreement, shall be unenforceable in the territories of any other member.

---

12 See, for example, *Keynes, Vol. XXVI*, p. 138.
13 *Proceedings and Documents*, p. 502.
14 *Ibid.*, p. 543.
15 *Ibid.*, p. 576.
16 *Ibid.*, p. 599.
17 *Ibid.*, p. 605.
18 *Ibid.*, p. 628.

> In addition, members may, by mutual accord, co-operate in measures for the purpose of making the respective exchange control regulations of either member more effective, provided that such measures and regulations are consistent with this Agreement.[19]

Nothing further appears in the record until July 18, 1944 when a text of the Articles of Agreement was circulated in which the final version of Article VIII, Section 2(b) appeared for the first time. The accompanying second report of the Drafting Committee declares that:

> All the material contained in this report has been approved in principle by the Commission at previous sessions. The present report contains, however, a new formulation of certain provisions to which I should specifically draw the attention of the Commission.
> These are: . . .
> 2. Paragraph (b) of Section 2 of Article VIII on pages 17 and 18 dealing with the enforceability of exchange contracts contrary to the exchange control regulations of members and measures of cooperation to enforce exchange control regulations. . . .[20]

This recorded history of the drafting of Article VIII, Section 2(b) is obviously unsatisfying. The record is silent at the very point at which an explanation of the transfer of the provision from a context dealing with exchange rates to one dealing with the general obligations of members would be invaluable. There has been much speculation about the implications of this transfer. The extrusion of the provision from the context in which it was included for so much of the Conference suggests that the provision was no longer confined to exchange transactions at exchange rates inconsistent with the Articles. This deduction might imply that exchange contracts were not confined to contracts for exchange transactions, but this reading would not be the only one that was possible. The provision could be read to mean that no such radical departure from the earlier drafts was intended, and that the purpose of the new language and the new context was to render unenforceable contracts for exchange transactions that were contrary to exchange control regulations whether they dealt with exchange rates or other aspects of a member's exchange arrangements.

There are alternative arguments to support the thesis that Article VIII, Section 2(b) went beyond anything that had been agreed already by the Commission. One argument rests on the assumption that the Drafting Committee's phrase "all the material" was meant to apply to Article VIII, Section 2(b) and the Articles as a whole. On this assumption, the former agreement by the Commission can be taken to have been that only unenforceability was intended and not criminal sanctions. The only evidence of agreement on principle in the record is on this aspect of the provision. The weakness of this explanation is the implication that the Drafting Committee held the view that other aspects of the provision raised no issues of principle that needed to be drawn to the attention of Commission I.

---

[19] *Ibid.*, p. 671.
[20] *Ibid.*, p. 808.

The alternative and better explanation is that the Drafting Committee was conscious of a departure from or extension of what had been approved in principle earlier. This explanation can be supported by comparing the Working Draft of July 16, 1944 prepared for the Drafting Committee with the text of the Articles circulated with the second report of the Drafting Committee dated July 18, 1944. This comparison has force if Commission I took no action to approve changes in principle in the period between circulation of the two documents. There is no record of such action, and some evidence that the Commission did not meet after July 16, 1944 until it met to consider the second report of the Drafting Committee.[21]

The comparison referred to above involves the six provisions, including Article VIII, Section 2(*b*), that are listed as new formulations. The comparison shows important differences of principle between the two texts in the content of the six provisions. These differences negate any conclusion that the Drafting Committee was referring to matters of drafting and not substance.

Article V, Section 7 in the Working Draft would have permitted a member to purchase with gold any part of the Fund's holdings of its currency;[22] the later version narrowed this form of repurchase to holdings in excess of a member's quota.[23] This change prevented a member from making its currency scarce in the Fund and transformed the rationale of the provision into a privilege for members to avoid the necessity to pay periodic charges to the Fund on holdings of the member's currency. The same provision created an additional repurchase obligation for a member because of the receipt of a third member's currency in transactions with other members. In the earlier version of the provision, this obligation accrued only with the consent of the third member, the issuer of the currency;[24] in the later version, there was no necessity for this consent.[25] There are other differences in the repurchase provisions of the two versions.

Article XII, Section 5 on voting in the earlier version contains no modification of computations to take account of a uniform change in par values accompanied by a decision to waive adjustment of the Fund's holdings of currencies;[26] this modification is included in the later version.[27]

The earlier version of Article XVI on liquidation of the Fund[28] does not contain the provisions of the later version that authorize the Fund to suspend the operation of certain provisions in the event of an emergency

---

[21] *Ibid.*, p. 698.
[22] *Ibid.*, p. 665.
[23] *Ibid.*, p. 775.
[24] *Ibid.*, p. 667.
[25] *Ibid.*, p. 776.
[26] *Ibid.*, p. 680.
[27] *Ibid.*, pp. 789–90.
[28] *Ibid.*, p. 684.

or the development of unforeseen circumstances threatening the operations of the Fund.[29]

Differences exist between the two versions of Article XIX on the explanation of terms. The definition of current transactions is an outstanding example.[30] The definition is crucial in the activities of the Fund.

The last of the listed provisions, Article XX, which sets forth the final provisions, contains variations of substance between the two texts. For example, the later but not the earlier version provides that changes in a par value communicated but not yet established by a member whose metropolitan territory had been occupied by the enemy could be made only by agreement with the Fund.[31] Again, only the later version provides that changes in par value agreed under the final provisions were not to be taken into account in calculating the extent to which subsequent changes depart from the initial par value.[32]

The differences in the two texts of Article VIII, Section 2(b) are minor, but the implication that the Commission had not approved, in whole or in part, the principle of the listed provisions before July 18, 1944 can be drawn for Article VIII, Section 2(b) also. The explanation can still be that the text of the provision presented on July 18, 1944 departed from the last version approved in principle by the Commission or filled a gap that had never been filled by the Commission.

One author [33] has concluded that on July 14, 1944, Commission I had approved the text of Article VIII, Section 2(b) as it appeared in the Working Draft for the Drafting Committee dated July 16, 1944. His conclusion is based on the following passage in the published minutes of a meeting of Commission I on July 14, 1944:

> Article VIII, General Obligations of Members, was adopted as presented by the Drafting Committee, with the inclusion of section 2, Exchange Controls on Current Payments, and section 3, Multilateral Clearing, as reworded (see wording in Document 329 and recommendation in Document 374).[34]

Reference to Documents 329 (July 13, 1944) [35] and 374 (July 14, 1944) [36] shows clearly that Article VIII, Section 2(b) had not been "reworded" in the form that appeared in the Working Draft when Commission I met on July 14, 1944. At that meeting, the forerunner of Article VIII, Section 2(b) was still part of the exchange rate provisions. Document 374 refers to

---

[29] *Ibid.*, pp. 793–94.
[30] *Ibid.*, pp. 687, 797.
[31] *Ibid.*, pp. 690, 800.
[32] *Ibid.*, p. 800.
[33] John S. Williams, "Extraterritorial Enforcement of Exchange Control Regulations Under International Monetary Fund Agreement," *Virginia Journal of International Law*, Vol. 15 (1975), pp. 318–96, at 326–28.
[34] *Proceedings and Documents*, p. 628.
[35] *Ibid.*, pp. 544–46.
[36] *Ibid.*, pp. 604–608.

Document 343, in which the reporting delegate set forth the joint proposal, the British revision, and the Drafting Committee's preferred text. All three versions dealt with exchange transactions or exchange rates. Moreover, the published minutes on which the author bases his conclusion show that the draft forerunner of Article VIII, Section 2(*b*) that was before the Commission was included not in Article VIII, but in Article IV on exchange rates:

> In the discussion of article IV a question was raised concerning the application of section 3(c) (Document 343, p. 3), which was referred to the Drafting Committee for clarification.[37]

Some unpublished informal minutes of Commission I confirm that what the Commission was approving in principle at its meeting of July 14, 1944 was an approach involving a reconciliation of the three versions based on exchange transactions and exchange rates as part of the provisions on exchange rates and in a form that would not call for criminal penalties. The Commission had only these versions before it. The minutes also suggest that there was no further consideration of the provision by the Commission before July 16, 1944:

> Delegate from U.S.: I believe that it was the view of the Special Committee last night that that language needed certain further definition to make it perfectly clear that cooperation did not include the necessity for imposing criminal penalties in any country which enforced the regulations of another country. On the other hand, there would be some effort made to express the feeling that we should work out some way of cooperating but not so as to involve any use of criminal penalty.
>
> Delegate from U.S.: I should add that it was the agreement of the Committee in substance. It was also the opinion of this Committee that the appropriate language for this purpose should be prepared by the Drafting Committee.
>
> Chairman: The statement has been made that the recommendation of the Committee was one of substance; that there are, I gather, some changes to be made in form and possibly in language, but in no way is there to be any alteration in form of [*sic*] substance so that a vote on this at this stage would be either approval or disapproval, and if it be approved, that any change we make in the Drafting Committee would not come before this Commission for another vote unless any member felt redrafting further would involve a change of substance. Am I correct in the recommendation?

The Commission accepted the recommendation.

The deductions drawn by the author mentioned above from his treatment of the *travaux préparatoires* in support of his interpretation of the provision cannot be accepted. The argument of another author on the basis of the conclusion that the text of July 18, 1944 represented no change in the substance of Article VIII, Section 2(*b*) is similarly unacceptable.[38]

---

[37] *Ibid.*, p. 628.

[38] F. A. Mann, *The Legal Aspect of Money*, Third Edition (Oxford, 1971), p. 435, fn. 1. The history and analysis of Article VIII, Section 2(*b*) as presented in this Appendix support the conclusions drawn in Gold, *Fund Agreement in the Courts* (1962), pp. 62–66.

The new information in Volume XXVI of Keynes' papers suggests an explanation of the reason why Article VIII, Section 2(*b*) was moved from the provisions on exchange transactions and exchange rates and why its substance was changed late in the Conference. The explanation may be that some members of the British delegation became aware during the Conference that the original version of Article VIII, Section 2(*b*) did nothing to diminish Keynes' concern about exchange rates for sterling in transactions in the United States. With that realization, it would have become logical to retain the idea of collaboration that was the basis for the provision but to detach it from provisions on exchange transactions and exchange rates and to give it as ample a scope as possible. It was then desirable to draw this change of substance to the attention of Commission I on July 18, 1944. This analysis would be a further reason to doubt the correctness of the English Court of Appeal's decision in *Wilson, Smithett & Cope Ltd. v. Terruzzi.*

Finally, what can be said of Article VIII, Section 2(*b*) in relation to the Second Amendment of the Fund's Articles? In the fourteenth installment of the *Fund Agreement in the Courts* [39] it is said that nothing bearing on the interpretation of the provision should be read into the fact that the provision was not modified. It was not examined during the drafting of the Second Amendment and no proposal was made to amend it. Nevertheless, there is one inference that can be drawn from this fact. It has been seen that the provision had its origin in the par value system and was designed to encourage respect for exchange rates consistent with that system in exchange transactions. If the Fund had held the view that there was an indissoluble tie between the exchange rates of a par value system and Article VIII, Section 2(*b*), it would have been necessary to modify the provision because of the abrogation of the par value system.

Even those who advocate a narrow interpretation of "exchange contracts," however, do not assert that the provision applies only if contracts for exchange transactions are contrary to those exchange control regulations that prescribe limits on exchange rates for exchange transactions. The retention of Article VIII, Section 2(*b*) without modification supports this interpretation, but retention is neutral on the question whether the provision is or is not confined to contracts for exchange transactions.

---

[39] Pp. 257–58 in this volume.

APPENDIX B

Judicial Application of Gold Units of Account

The breakdown of the par value system after the announcement by the President of the United States on August 15, 1971 of the official inconvertibility of the dollar followed by the failure in March 1973 of the system of central rates and wider margins for exchange transactions under the Fund's decision of December 18, 1971 [1] left organizations and courts with no obvious solution of the problem of applying units of account defined in terms of gold. Many of these units of account are to be found in domestic legislation that gives effect to conventions in which the unit of account is the Poincaré franc or the Germinal franc, both of which are defined in terms of a quantity of gold.[2]

Gold units of account are usually to be found in treaties that limit the liability of an entrepreneur in a particular activity for damage or loss sustained by others as a result of the entrepreneur's pursuit of that activity. Courts in many countries have been called on to apply these provisions. Gold units of account, however, are not confined to treaties that limit liability.

A mass movement has taken place, and is still continuing, to substitute the SDR for gold as the unit of account in treaties. The amendment of many treaties has been proposed for this purpose, but the problem remains until sufficient acceptances are received to make the amendment effective. Some commentators have expressed doubt that certain of the proposed amendments limiting liability will take effect because inflation has already made the limits on recoveries in the proposals unfairly low. It is probable, however, that, sooner or later, a new unit of account will have to be substituted for gold in all treaties in which the unit of account is defined in terms of gold.

---

[1] *Selected Decisions*, Eighth Issue, pp. 14–17. For the revised decision, see pp. 18–21.

[2] Poincaré franc = 65.5 milligrams, nine-tenths fine. Germinal franc = $\frac{10}{31}$ gram, nine-tenths fine.

Three developments have been occurring in order to solve the problem of applying a gold unit of account in the period before an amendment does become effective.[3] First, when there are administrators of a treaty, they have sometimes taken action, by interpretation or regulation, to require the SDR to be applied as the unit of account. Second, in some countries, the legislature has solved the problem for courts by means of a statute substituting the SDR for a gold franc and prescribing the formula for substitution. In some countries, a department of government has issued orders, binding on the courts, on how a gold franc is to be translated into the domestic currency. The translation is made via the SDR.

When none of these developments has occurred, the courts themselves are faced with the necessity of finding a solution if they have to apply a gold unit of account. The Second Amendment of the Fund's Articles provides no explicit solution. On the contrary, it has made the problem more acute not only by abrogating the former official price of gold but also by outlawing it for the future as a denominator or common denominator in terms of which the external value of a currency or currencies may be maintained.[4]

Decisions Before April 1, 1978

As the Second Amendment took effect on April 1, 1978, it is convenient to divide decisions on gold units of account by reference to that date. The division is not clean cut, however, because, as will be seen, it is possible that decisions after April 1, 1978 may have to be made on the basis of events that occurred before that date.

Before the Second Amendment, a few courts based their decisions on the market price of gold,[5] and earned the approval of some commenta-

---

[3] These various developments are discussed in detail in the following pamphlets by Joseph Gold: Pamphlet No. 19; Pamphlet No. 22; *SDRs, Gold, and Currencies: Third Survey of New Legal Developments*, IMF Pamphlet Series, No. 26 (Washington, 1979); *SDRs, Currencies, and Gold: Fourth Survey of New Legal Developments*, IMF Pamphlet Series, No. 33 (Washington, 1980); *SDRs, Currencies, and Gold: Fifth Survey of New Legal Developments*, IMF Pamphlet Series, No. 36 (Washington, 1981). (Hereinafter cited as Gold, Pamphlet No. 26, No. 33, and No. 36, respectively.)

[4] Article IV, Section 2(b); Schedule C, par. 1.

[5] For example, *Zakoupolos v. Olympic Airways Corp.*, Judgment No. 256/1974 of the Court of Appeals, Athens, Greece, February 15, 1974 (in which the price of gold on the Athens Stock Exchange was applied under an interpretation of statutes of 1937 and 1946, and not because of international monetary developments); *Re Motor Ship "Saga,"* Lower Court, Göteborg, Sweden, October 2, 1973 (Gold, Pamphlet No. 19, pp. 30–31, fns. 54–56); *Balkan Bulgarian Airlines v. Tammaro*, T. Treves, "Sulla Conversione in Moneta Nazionale Dei Limiti Di Responsabilità In Franchi Oro Della Convenzione Di Varsàvia," *Il Diritto Marittimo* (1978), pp. 83–91, decided October 25, 1976 by a Milan court (Gold, Pamphlet No. 33, pp. 90–92); *Reed v. Wiser*, 555 F. 2d 1079 (2d Cir.), certiorari

tors.[6] Some of the courts have taken intellectual shortcuts to decision. They have said, for example, that the issue was whether the "true price" of gold or the price set by the United States should prevail,[7] or that an ambiguous reference to gold should be interpreted liberally in favor of the citizen because a limitation of liability toward him was an encroachment on his rights.[8] Often, approval by commentators was based on the thesis that there was no alternative to the market price as the solution that met the test of universal applicability. Some commentators have had additional reasons for endorsing this solution. For example, the market price of gold is regarded as compensation for the inadequacy of limits on liability that results from inflation. Again, the market price is approved because it reduces the great disparity that has developed in some jurisdictions between the damages that can be recovered in domestic death and injury cases and the limits under conventions regulating international activities that result in death and injury.

Other courts faced with the problem before April 1, 1978 rejected the solution of the market price.[9] The Supreme Court of the Netherlands took this position in *Hornlinie v. Société Nationale des Pétroles Aquitaine (The Hornland)* as early as April 14, 1972.[10] The issue in the case was the amount of Netherlands guilders to be deposited, at the rate prevailing on May 2, 1969, as the equivalent of an amount of Poincaré francs established by the provisions of the Commercial Code of the Netherlands that gave effect to the Treaty Concerning the Limitation of Liability of Owners of Seagoing Vessels signed at Brussels on October 10, 1957. Under the provi-

---

denied 434 U.S. 922 (1977); *Florencia Cia Argentina de Seguros S.A. v. Varig S.A.,* decided by the National Court of Appeals, Buenos Aires, August 27, 1976 ([1977] *Uniform Law Review* 198) (in which the court was influenced by earlier decisions applying what it considered to be the most realistic rate of exchange when there were multiple rates of exchange for the domestic currency); *Télé-Montage Inc. v. Air Canada* (1976) C.S. (*Recueils de Jurisprudence du Québec*) 228 (without discussion of the issue); *Miller v. American Airlines, Inc.,* County Court of Judicial District of York, Toronto, Ontario, October 4, 1977.

[6] See authors cited in Gold, Pamphlet No. 19, p. 30, fn. 53; Marc S. Moller, "Gold Up—Warsaw Damage Limitations Down," *New York Law Journal,* October 17, 1980, pp. 1–2; Aleksander Tobolewski, "The Special Drawing Right in liability conventions: An acceptable solution?" *Lloyd's Maritime and Commercial Law Quarterly,* May 1979, pp. 169–80; Paul P. Heller, "Converting the Goldfranc—a reply from an unconverted," *Air Law,* Vol. 5 (1980), pp. 33–34. For some early cases rejecting the market price, see Gold, *Fund Agreement in the Courts* (1962), pp. 6–8.

[7] *Florencia Cia Argentina de Segusos S.A. v. Varig S.A.* [1977] *Uniform Law Review* 198.

[8] *Miller v. American Airlines, Inc.* (See fn. 5 *supra.*)

[9] See, for example, *Companhia de Seguros Maritimos v. Varig,* decided by the Federal Court of Appeals, Brazil, June 3, 1975 (Civil Appeal No. 35, 737–Guanabara).

[10] *Nederlandse Jurisprudentie,* 1972, No. 269, pp. 728–38. (Gold, "Fund Agreement in the Courts—XI," pp. 177–82 in this volume.)

sions of the Commercial Code, the amounts to which liability can be limited are expressed as specified numbers of Poincaré francs per ton of the ship's net tonnage. Translation into guilders is to be made at the rate of the day on which the shipowner-defendant complies with the order of the court to make a deposit or provide security in a proceeding brought to limit liability.

In *The Hornland*, the shipowner argued that the calculation should be made on the basis of the par value of the guilder as defined in terms of gold on the relevant date. The claimant contended that since the institution of the "two-tier system" of gold markets in 1968, the official price of gold was relevant only for central banks and that for all other purposes the price ruling in the nonofficial market was the only appropriate one. This argument was based on the two-tier system and not on the ineffectiveness of par values after August 15, 1971.

The Supreme Court held that the calculation must be made by reference to the most recent par value of the guilder, which had been established under the Fund's Articles in 1961. The drafters of the Brussels Convention must have had the monetary character of gold in mind and not its commercial value. Most of the negotiating countries were members of the Fund. They chose an artificial currency rather than a given weight of gold as such. Constancy of purchasing power was not a criterion for choosing between the two contending views of par value and nonofficial market price. Neither of them would achieve this stability of purchasing power. Computations based on the market price would result in higher currency limits on liability, but the amounts yielded in this way would be determined by such influences as speculation and not by changes in the purchasing power of the currency to be deposited. Furthermore, the objective of uniformity that was sought by the Brussels Convention would be better served by the common valuation of gold that most parties to the treaty had accepted by becoming members of the Fund. What survived in this reasoning and affected the later decisions of the Supreme Court that were not based on par values was the rejection of the market price of gold.

German courts also refused to apply the market price of gold in cases decided before the Second Amendment became effective. *Transarctic Shipping Corporation, Inc. Monrovia, Liberia v. Krögerwerft (Kröger Shipyard) Company* [11] involved provisions of the Commercial Code of the Federal Republic that gave effect to the same provisions of the Brussels Convention as were in issue in *The Hornland*. A provision of the Code declared that the equivalent of amounts of Poincaré francs in deutsche mark were to be calculated by reference to the "parity" of the currency. The most recent par value of the deutsche mark was established under the Articles on October 27, 1969, and in accordance with the law of the Fund was still in effect.[12]

---

[11] *European Transport Law*, Vol. 9 (1974), pp. 701–10. (Gold, Pamphlet No. 19, pp. 17–22.)

[12] Gold, "Fund Agreement in the Courts—XIII," pp. 232–33 in this volume.

On June 29, 1973, however, a central rate for the deutsche mark became effective under the Fund's decision on central rates and wider margins. The central rate for the deutsche mark was expressed in terms of the SDR, which at that time was still defined by reference to gold. The Fund's decision on the "basket" method of valuing the SDR did not come into operation until July 1, 1974.

The Fund's decision on central rates and wider margins was an attempt by the Fund to minimize disorder in circumstances in which members were not observing the obligations respecting exchange rates that were imposed on members by the Articles. Central rates and wider margins, however, were not practices that could be validated under the Articles,[13] although some observers thought that they had been validated by the decision.

The Hanseatic Higher Regional Court at Hamburg decided on July 2, 1974 that one purpose of requiring calculations to be made on the basis of par values was to avoid the use of market prices for gold, because market prices were subject to severe and often speculative pressures. After the collapse of the system of central rates in March 1973 and the entry into force of the European common margins arrangement ("the snake"), par values had lost most of their practical meaning. The legal provisions requiring the application of par values rested on the assumption that all members of the Fund would respect the provisions. Members were observing central rates and not par values. The application of central rates would promote the underlying objectives of the legal provisions more effectively than would a literal application of the par values to which they referred.

The pragmatism of this decision was carried further by the decision of the Hamburg District Court (Division 64), delivered on December 29, 1976, in the *Matter of the Khendrik Kuivas*.[14] The issue in this case involved the same legal provisions as in the earlier German case, but the Fund's first decision on the basket method of valuing the SDR was now in effect. The court held that it had to take account of this development in the international monetary system. The court decided that the calculation must be made according to the definition of the SDR in terms of gold in the Fund's Articles and the definition of the Poincaré franc in terms of gold. According to this formula, the rounded amount of 15 Poincaré francs was equal to one SDR. (This solution will be referred to from time to time as "the SDR solution.") The value of the deutsche mark in terms of the SDR would be determined by the most recent announcement of it by the Fund.

DECISIONS AFTER APRIL 1, 1978

The Rotterdam District Court applied the market price of gold in a case decided on May 12, 1978 under provisions of domestic law that gave effect

---

[13] *Ibid.*, pp. 235–36.
[14] Gold, Pamphlet No. 22, pp. 56–59.

to the Convention on the Contract for the International Carriage of Goods by Road (CMR), which took effect on July 2, 1961. Under the provisions, the compensation payable by a carrier liable for the loss of goods is calculated by reference to the value of the goods at the time and place at which they were accepted for carriage, but compensation is not to exceed 25 Germinal francs per kilogram. The claim in this case was for the nondelivery of goods accepted for delivery in Rotterdam in 1969. The full value of these goods exceeded the maximum amount under the convention when calculated on the basis of the last central rate for the guilder in terms of gold, but was less than the maximum when calculated on the basis of the market price of gold. The court awarded the full value of the goods on the latter basis.[15]

In the case of *The Breda*,[16] the Amsterdam District Court, on January 10, 1979, came to the same conclusion as had been reached in *The Hornländ*, even though in the meantime the Second Amendment had become effective and the Netherlands, by adopting the Act Relating to the Exchange Rate of the Guilder, had repealed, with effect on August 1, 1978, the Act on the Par Value of the Guilder.[17] The vessel had collided on August 20, 1978 with an installation owned by the State. The relevant legal provisions were the same as in *The Hornland*. The shipowner petitioned to limit its liability according to the formula that 15 Poincaré francs were equal to one SDR. The State, as claimant, argued that in the absence of any official price for gold under the law of the Netherlands or under international law, the limit on liability should be determined by reference to the market price of gold on the day on which the shipowner complied with the order of the court to make a deposit or provide security.

The court recognized that the Second Amendment had made it necessary to repeal the Act on the Par Value of the Guilder. A statute governing the application of gold units of account was in preparation but had not yet become effective. Nor was any rule of international law in force. If the market price were applied because of repeal of the Act on the Par Value of the Guilder, the consequence would be that on August 1, 1978 the limits

---

[15] *Avandero N.V. v. Westeuropese Transportmaatschappij Wetram N.V.*, *Schip en Schade*, 1979, Vol. 23, No. 5, p. 162. The market price was applied by the Court of the Principal Civil Judge, Bangalore, India, on August 11, 1978 (*Kuwait Airways Corporation v. Sanghi*, Regular Appeal No. 54/77). The par value of the rupee established under the Articles was rejected on the ground that neither the Warsaw Convention nor Indian legislation giving effect to it stated that the par value was to apply. Although the case was decided after April 1, 1978, the issue was taken to be the price of gold on April 22, 1977 when the lower court delivered its judgment. At that date, the rupee still had a par value in terms of gold under the Articles.

[16] *Koninklijke Nederlandse Stoomboot Maatschappij B.V. v. State of the Netherlands*, *Schip en Schade*, 1979, No. 29, pp. 76–79.

[17] See Gold, Pamphlet No. 33, p. 82.

on liability were increased by 250 per cent compared with the limits on July 31, 1978, but there was no reason to believe that the legislature had intended the repeal to have this effect. It was implausible that the new statute when enacted would prefer the market price to the SDR solution in view of the widespread movement to substitute the SDR for gold as a unit of account.

The market price solution would frustrate the intent of the convention, which had assumed that gold would have a monetary function. For the brief period before a new measure was in operation, a solution was required that would not lead to results radically different from those that had prevailed before August 1, 1978 or were likely to prevail in the future. Arguments could be found to support the SDR solution, but that solution would give no role at all to a price for gold.

The Supreme Court decided, after this examination, that the gap in the law had to be filled by applying the central rate for the guilder expressed in terms of gold that was most recently in effect as the result of official action. This solution would apply until the gap was filled in some other way by steps at the national or international level, or until it was demonstrated that special circumstances had occurred that called for some modification of the solution. The court held that its solution was compatible with the language and intent of relevant legal provisions, avoided unreasonable results, did not anticipate a future and still uncertain legislative measure, and was in accordance with the price used in monetary transactions between the central banks of members of the Fund. The court also held that the State's application of the par value until August 1, 1978 and the absence of direct statutory recognition of the central rate did not weaken the justification for the solution chosen by the court.

The Supreme Court's reference to the monetary price in gold transactions between the central banks of members of the Fund did not give adequate weight to the impact of the Second Amendment. Until March 31, 1978 the monetary authorities of members continued to be bound, if they dealt in gold between themselves, to respect the par value of the currency for which the currency was bought and sold. The substitution of the central rate for the par value in these gold transactions would not have been in accordance with the Articles.[18] Once the Second Amendment became effective, the official price of gold disappeared and members were freed from the obligation to observe any specific price in their transactions.

---

[18] See Gold, Pamphlet No. 32, p. 37. See the Invitation to Bid in the Fund's gold auctions that began in May 1976. Until the Second Amendment became effective, one term provided that "No bid may be submitted by the governmental or monetary authorities of a member of the Fund or by an agent acting on behalf of these authorities at a price inconsistent with the Articles of Agreement of the Fund, but the Bank for International Settlements may submit bids." (See, for example, *IMF Survey*, Vol. 5 (May 17, 1976), p. 150.)

Three decisions of French courts must be noted. On August 24, 1978, the Le Havre Commercial Court decided a case in which the owner of a Moroccan freighter sought to limit its liability under the Brussels Convention and related provisions of French law after colliding with a Soviet trawler in French waters. The owner of the freighter sought to limit its liability on the basis of the relationship between the Poincaré franc and the most recent par value of the French franc under the Articles. The court held that the correct basis for the calculation was that par value adjusted in accordance with the retail price index for June 1978 as determined by the National Institute for Statistics and Economic Research. This basis for calculation resulted in an amount of French francs that was slightly more than double the amount the owner had proposed to deposit.[19] The solution implied the view that the negotiators of the Brussels Convention intended to adopt a unit of account that would reflect stable purchasing power, which was not the view of the Netherlands Supreme Court in *The Hornland.*

The other two decisions were affected by the fortuitous circumstance that the Convention for the Unification of Certain Rules Relating to International Carriage by Air (the Warsaw Convention) was signed on October 12, 1929 soon after the Poincaré franc had been defined, by the law of June 25, 1928, as the currency of France. The decisions were influenced by the further fortuitous circumstance that the proceedings in the two cases were conducted in French tribunals. Under the Warsaw Convention, as subsequently amended by the Protocol done at The Hague on September 28, 1955, and made effective in France, an air carrier's liability for loss of checked baggage is limited to a specified number of units per kilogram, and the translation of units into national currencies is to be made according to their gold value at the date of judgment. The unit is equivalent to the Poincaré franc as defined by France's law of June 25, 1928.

In *Société Egyptair v. Chamie*,[20] the Court of Appeal of Paris, on January 31, 1980, decided an appeal from a decision that the *tribunal de grande instance* of Paris had delivered on October 6, 1978. The passenger's claim was for baggage lost in the course of a flight on July 26, 1976. The lower court had accepted the passenger's argument that the Poincaré franc had to be applied by reference to the market price of gold in Paris. The carrier argued that the Warsaw Convention itself rejected the market price and that the Second Amendment could not affect the application of the convention. Therefore, the most recent par value of the French franc, established under the Fund's Articles on August 10, 1969, was the proper basis for calculating the limits on liability under the convention. The *Avocat Général*, in his

---

[19] P.Y. Nicolas, "La conversion du 'franc' des conventions internationales de droit privé maritime," *Droit maritime français 1980*, Vol. 32, pp. 579–88, at 581–82.

[20] *Droit maritime français 1980*, Vol. 32, pp. 285–94.

observations, referred to the extravagant consequences of applying the market price.

The Court of Appeal noted that conventions drafted more recently than the Warsaw Convention and the Hague Protocol continued to use the Poincaré franc without adopting the market price of gold by which to value it. (The court did not refer to the even more recent practice in favor of the SDR solution.) The court also noted that France had never established a central rate for the franc. The par value had been abrogated as a result of the Second Amendment. The application of a price index to adapt the last par value was unacceptable to the court because the choice of an index would depend on the court's subjective preferences. The term in the carrier's tickets defining its liability by reference to the U.S. dollar could not be applied because that currency was not convertible into gold. For this reason, the term was inconsistent with the Warsaw Convention.[21]

The Court of Appeal rejected the solution of the market price because the contracting parties to the Warsaw Convention had agreed that the translation of the Poincaré franc into national currencies would be made according to the value of currencies in terms of gold as established by the states issuing the currencies. The market price had no official national or international monetary character and was the result of private transactions motivated by speculation. The court concluded that as the market price was inappropriate and as the abrogation of the par value for the French franc on April 1, 1978 made it impossible to translate the Warsaw unit into the national currency of France, the only solution was to recognize that the current French franc was the successor to the Poincaré franc. One Poincaré franc was to be deemed equal to one current French franc, without relating them to gold. This solution ignores the fact that in the negotiation of the Warsaw Convention the Poincaré franc defined in terms of gold was substituted for the "French franc" because of objections to a national currency.

The court noted that the French franc was recognized as a currency of payment for international obligations. The court, in discussing the term referring to U.S. dollars in the tickets, did not mention that the U.S. dollar had this same quality. Nor did the court regard the inconvertibility of the French franc into gold as an impediment to its decision.

---

[21] Article 23 of the Warsaw Convention prohibits terms that tend to relieve the carrier of liability or to reduce the limits laid down in the convention, but not terms that increase the carrier's liability (Peter Martin, "The Price of Gold and the Warsaw Convention," *Air Law*, Vol. 4 (1979), p. 74; Praveen M. Singh, "International Air Charter Transportation in Australia," *Air Law*, Vol. 5 (1980), pp. 221, 227). Moreover, increased limits expressed in SDRs have been approved, or not objected to, by civil aviation authorities (see, e.g., U.S. Civil Aeronautics Board's Order 81-3-143, March 24, 1981). Whether or not there is an increase, or the amount of the increase, depends on a determination of how the Poincaré franc must be valued.

The effect of the decision was that a limit of 250 French francs per kilogram was substituted for an amount somewhat less than the 100 French francs that would have been payable on the carrier's thesis. The court may have been influenced by the economic inadequacy of the limits in the convention as a result of inflation. It will be recalled, however, that the Supreme Court of the Netherlands refused to assume that the legislature intended the abrogation of the par value of the guilder to bring about an increase of 250 per cent in the limits under the Brussels Convention when translated into guilders.

Since the end of June 1975, the monetary authorities of France have valued their gold at the end of each semester according to the average over the preceding three months of the daily U.S. dollar price of gold in London translated into French francs at the franc-U.S. dollar rate in Paris during the same period. The Court of Appeal refused to follow this technique, but in rejecting it the court gave as its reason the official inconvertibility of the French franc. In *Linee Aeree Italiane v. Riccioli*,[22] an Italian court refused to follow the central bank's practice of relating the valuation of the bank's gold holdings to the market price, because this technique was no more than an accounting convention. In *Florencia Cia Argentina de Seguros S.A. v. Varig S.A.*,[23] an Argentine court referred to the practice of the central bank in support of the court's application of the market price.

The Court of Appeal in *Société Egyptair v. Chamie* did not make the point that the practices of monetary authorities in valuing their gold holdings are so diverse [24] that to follow the method of valuation of the domestic monetary authorities would defeat the objective of a universal and uniform standard of value that inspires the drafters of conventions. The same objection can be made to the solution that assumes the current French franc to be the legal successor to the Poincaré franc as the unit of account chosen by all contracting parties. The objection could be met if all contracting parties were willing to make the same assumption, but there is no evidence of this willingness.

The decision of the Court of Appeal is not compatible with the view expressed in *The Hornland* that the negotiators of the Brussels Convention had chosen the Poincaré franc because it had become a fictitious currency. They had not wished to link the unit of account to an actual currency, because a link of that character would have made the unit of account subject to the devaluations and revaluations of the currency.

In *Linee Aeree Italiane v. Riccioli*,[25] however, the court declared that the drafters of the Warsaw Convention had chosen a currency as the unit of

---

[22] Judgment 609/197, November 14, 1978.
[23] See fn. 5 *supra*.
[24] Gold, Pamphlet No. 22, pp. 52–55; No. 26, pp. 32–35; No. 33, pp. 87–90.
[25] See fn. 22 *supra*.

account, even though the currency was fictitious, in preference to an amount of gold as such. The court drew the conclusion that the drafters had intended a unit of account that was to be applied through the exchange system and not through the gold market. The court could have gone on to recall that the Fund has not regarded the price of gold in any currency as an exchange rate for that currency, and therefore it has not been able, even if it had wished, to approve a market price for gold as a multiple currency practice under Article VIII, Section 3. The Fund defines an exchange rate as the rate at which one currency is exchanged for another currency.

The legal provisions involved in *Société Egyptair v. Chamie* were the subject of proceedings in the later case of *Pakistan International Airlines v. Compagnie Air Inter S.A. et al.*, decided by the Court of Appeal of Aix-en-Provence on October 31, 1980.[26] The claim was for the loss of some packages in the course of transportation by air by a number of carriers in April 1974. One issue was how 13,500 Warsaw units were to be translated into current French francs. The insurance company subrogated to the rights of the consignee argued that it was entitled to 13,500 current French francs. The court referred to an implicit reference by the insurance company to the Jamaica Accord.[27] The court held that the Accord had not been submitted to the legislature and did not constitute an international treaty binding on France.

The court was right in its view of the "Accord." That document was no more than a communiqué that the Interim Committee of the Board of Governors of the Fund on the International Monetary System had issued in Jamaica on June 12, 1975.[28] The communiqué included a statement of the principles that the Committee wanted the Executive Board to observe in drafting the provisions of the Second Amendment on gold. One of the principles was that the official price of gold should be abolished. The Court of Appeal decided, correctly, that the Second Amendment was the only legal instrument of the Fund that had to be considered.

The court then made two points, neither of which appears in the judgment delivered in *Société Egyptair v. Chamie*. First, the Second Amendment "prohibits the fixing of a gold par value as a denominator of the national

---

[26] *La Compagnie d'Aviation "Pakistan International Airlines" v. La Compagnie Air Inter S.A., La Société Transport et Groupages de France, La Société Helvetia Saint Gall, La Société KLM Royal Dutch Airlines, et autres*, No. 79/2278.

[27] The Court of Appeal of Paris in *Société Egyptair v. Chamie* referred to the Jamaica Accord ("accords de la Jamaïque") as follows:

"Considering that the Jamaica accords, which France signed, eliminated from April 1, 1978 all reference to gold for the determination of the official value of national currencies and, therefore, that of the present French franc; . . . ." (*Translation*)

There was no signature of the Jamaica Accord by anyone.

[28] IMF Press Release No. 75/22; reproduced in *Annual Report*, 1975, pp. 99–101.

449

currency, but . . . does not intend to prohibit all national regulations that institute, save for exchange regulations, a relation between gold and national currency." [29] This view is correct: the Second Amendment prohibits maintenance by a member of the external value of its currency in terms of gold,[30] but does not prohibit the valuation of the currency in terms of gold for other purposes.[31] The court deduced from this principle that it was free to decide how to translate a gold unit of account into French francs. The fallacy in this deduction is that it conflicts with the intent of the contracting parties to conventions of the kind in issue to establish a common standard of valuation because such a standard would achieve an equivalence among currencies based on their external value. It should not be assumed that because the Second Amendment does not prohibit a member's attribution of a gold value to its currency for some purposes, the member is free to choose any value in applying conventions. Unless the chosen value is based on the external value of the currency and is related to some standard that can ensure an equivalence of external value among currencies, the universality and uniformity that are objectives of the conventions will not be achieved.

The Court of Appeal concluded that it was free to attribute to the Poincaré franc a value equivalent to the current French franc [32] and that this solution was not inconsistent with the Second Amendment. There was no inconsistency because the solution did not have the effect of maintaining the external value of the French franc in terms of gold.

The court's reasoning would lead to strange results if the Germinal franc was the unit of account that was being applied under a treaty and this franc also was treated as equivalent to the current French franc. The Germinal and Poincaré francs were defined in terms of different amounts of gold. The only way to avoid the anomaly referred to would be to regard the Poincaré franc as equivalent to the current French franc and, for the purpose of applying the Germinal franc, to adapt that relationship according to the ratio between the Poincaré and Germinal francs in terms of gold. The justification for considering the Poincaré rather than the Germinal franc as equivalent to the French franc would be that the Poincaré franc was created later than the Germinal franc.

---

[29] *Translation* of: ". . . interdit la fixation d'une parité or prise comme dénominateur de la monnaie nationale, mais que cette disposition n'a pas pour effet de prohiber tous les règlements nationaux instituant, en dehors des dispositions de change, une relation entre l'or et la monnaie nationale; . . . ."

[30] Article IV, Section 2(*b*).

[31] Gold, Pamphlet No. 22, pp. 3–5; No. 26, pp. 51–57; No. 33, pp. 81–83.

[32] According to the defendant's memorandum of law (p. 42) referred to in fn. 34 *infra*, the solution according to which the Poincaré franc is deemed to be equivalent to the current French franc was approved by *dictum* in *Kinney Shoe Corporation v. Alitalia Airlines* (United States District Court, Southern District of New York, 1980) and adopted by a decision of the same court in *Wood v. British West Indian Airways* (July 7, 1980). Both cases are unreported.

The second point made by the Court of Appeal was that the Second Amendment could have no effect on a contract of carriage entered into in April 1974. In *Société Egyptair v. Chamie* also, the contract preceded the Second Amendment, but in that case the court did not dwell on dates. On the view taken by the court in the later case, it is difficult to understand why the court complicated its consideration of the case by dealing at all with the Second Amendment.

Finally, the court was not embarrassed in arriving at its decision by any statute that established a par value for the French franc. If there had been a statute, the par value would have been defined in terms of an amount of gold that differed from the definition of the Poincaré franc. France is a country in which the Executive is empowered to determine the external value of the currency.

The decision of the Netherlands Supreme Court in *Giants Shipping Corporation v. State of the Netherlands (The Blue Hawk)*,[33] on May 1, 1981, is likely to become a leading case in the Netherlands [34] and to be cited in litigation in the courts of other countries as well. The relevant legal provisions were the same as in *The Hornland* and *The Breda*. The proceedings arose out of a collision on December 29, 1978 in which the Blue Hawk collided with some installations owned by the State. The issue was whether the market price of gold or the SDR solution should be adopted. As in *The Breda*, the State of the Netherlands, the aggrieved party, based its claim on the market price, arguing that no other method of calculation was

---

[33] *Rechtspraak van de Week*, May 30, 1981, pp. 321–30. In their briefs, both parties and the Attorney General of the Supreme Court made extensive use of the pamphlets cited in fn. 3 *supra*.

[34] The confusing state of jurisprudence in the Netherlands before the decision is illustrated further by two decisions in early 1979 not discussed in this article. On January 18, 1979, the Roermond Court adopted the market price solution (*Schip en Schade*, 1979, 45), and on March 9, 1979, the Groningen Court adopted the SDR solution (*Schip en Schade*, 1979, 90).

The SDR solution was adopted by the Civil Court of Rome for the purposes of the Warsaw Convention in *Linee Aeree Italiane v. Riccioli* (November 14, 1978; Judgment 609/1979), on the grounds that there was no way in which the equivalence between the Italian lira and the Poincaré franc could be calculated, and that the SDR solution approximated an official value. An earlier decision of the same court (*Fida Cinematografica v. Pan American World Airways*, October 13, 1976) adopted the market price, but both parties appear to have accepted it. (Defendant's memorandum of law in *Franklin Mint Corporation et al. v. Trans World Airlines, Inc.*, United States District Court, Southern District of New York, July 31, 1981, pp. 32–34.)

No mention was made of the *Riccioli* case in *Cosida S.p.A. v. British Airways European Division* (Court of Appeals of Milan, June 9, 1981), in which the court refused to reverse a decision of October 3, 1977 based on the average market price of gold in the London and Zurich markets (because there was no free market in Italy). For another case in which the court was willing to apply the market price, see *Salvati e Santori v. Alitalia* (Court of Appeals of Rome, June 29, 1981).

possible under Netherlands law. The State contended that as a consequence of the statute by which the Netherlands had approved the Second Amendment, application of the last par value of the guilder was prohibited. Similarly, the last central rate could not be applied, because it too was defined, although indirectly, in terms of gold.

In the proceedings in the lower courts, the Rotterdam District Court ruled in favor of the market price of a quantity of gold corresponding to the specified number of Poincaré francs, translated into Netherlands currency at the rate of the day on which the shipowner complied with the court's ruling. The Court of Appeal reversed the ruling to the extent that it referred to the market price, but the court refrained from deciding what was the correct method of calculation. The reason for the reversal was that it was not known whether or when the shipowner would comply with the District Court's ruling. The determination in favor of the market price, therefore, was premature. The Court of Appeal probably took into account the possibility that by the time the shipowner complied new legal provisions might be in effect and that they might be retroactive.

The Supreme Court held that the decision on the method of valuation could not be deferred, and it decided in favor of the SDR solution. The court noted that since the date of the decision in *The Hornland* the Second Amendment and the statute abrogating the par value of the guilder had become effective. For the Netherlands, gold had lost all monetary significance, and therefore gold as a unit of account no longer served the objectives of the Brussels Convention. In these circumstances, a gap existed in the relevant provisions. National or international steps would have to be taken to fill the gap. Agreement on a Protocol to the Brussels Convention had been reached on December 21, 1979 as an international measure, but it was not yet in operation. In the Netherlands, the Lower House of Parliament had adopted the draft of an Act Governing the Conversion of Units of Account Expressed in Gold into Netherlands Currency,[35] which would give legislative force to the SDR solution, but the bill had not yet passed into law.

The gap remained, but the courts were not entitled to refrain from deciding the problem of the method of valuation. A standard accepted in international monetary transactions had to be found for determining international uniform limits of liability in accordance with the objectives of the Brussels Convention. The market price of gold did not meet this test, but the SDR did. The SDR had been adopted by members of the Fund. It had been defined formerly in terms of gold. A link had been created between the SDR and gold, because, when the basket method of valuing the SDR had been introduced, the Fund ensured that the value of the SDR in terms of

---

[35] Session II, 1978/1979, Bill No. 15459.

452

currencies would be the same immediately before and immediately after the transition to the new method of valuation. The SDR solution would be compatible with the changes that had been made or were being made in international conventions and national laws, including the draft law that was being proposed in the Netherlands.

The State advanced an argument in favor of applying the practice that the Netherlands Bank followed in valuing its gold holdings. The central bank values its gold at 70 per cent of the lowest average annual price in the preceding three years. In principle, this method of valuation is applied at the end of every three years. The State argued that the central bank's formula would overcome the objections based on the extreme escalation of the market price and the fluctuations in it. Moreover, recognition of the formula would be consistent with the spirit of the decision in *The Breda* by recognizing "the official gold price."

The central bank's formula, it should be noted, was a national measure that has not been endorsed by the Fund or by other international action. When the Supreme Court of the Netherlands applied the central rate for the guilder in *The Breda*, the court attached importance to the Fund's recognition of the central rate. Moreover, the Fund's decision on central rates rested on the assumption of a common method of valuing gold.[36] In *The Blue Hawk*, the Supreme Court made no reference to the central bank's formula. It is fair to infer that the court found the State's argument in favor of it unpersuasive.

The Supreme Court took note of the State's objection that valuation of the Poincaré franc at $\frac{1}{15}$ of the SDR meant lower effective limits on liability because of the decline in the purchasing power of the SDR compared with the purchasing power of the amount of gold in the definition of the Poincaré franc. The court held that the inadequacy of limits on liability because of the decline in purchasing power was a problem for the negotiators of conventions and amendments of them and for national legislators, but not for the courts. International action had been taken already in the form of the proposed Convention on Liability for Maritime Claims that had been adopted in London on November 19, 1976. The convention, when effective, would establish much higher limits of liability, expressed in SDRs, for the purposes of the Brussels Convention. This dismissal of the argument based on purchasing power made it unnecessary for the court to point out that there is no systematic connection between the market price of gold and the loss of purchasing power of currencies or the SDR.

Although the Supreme Court held, as it had in *The Breda*, that there was a gap in the law, the court was not content to find a solution that might

---

[36] The second of the Fund's decisions on central rates (see fn. 1 *supra*) did not rest on this assumption.

have no more than temporary efficacy.[37] The forcefulness of the decision is even greater than it would have been in any event because the process for finding a legislative solution was already in train. The State had contended that the SDR solution would be objectionable as an "anticipatory interpretation."

The court did not deal with the argument that the market price of gold might defeat one of the objectives of conventions that limit liability. This objective is to reduce litigation and encourage speedier recoveries by aggrieved parties, while at the same time protecting entrepreneurs against unpredictable and possibly ruinous losses. The prospects for achieving this objective depend on the ability of an entrepreneur that must pay damages to compare, with reasonable certainty, the loss that has been suffered and the amount that must be deposited as a condition of limiting the entrepreneur's liability. The fluctuating price of gold might increase the difficulty of making this comparison. The inducement to limit liability might be lessened, and entrepreneurs might prefer to litigate issues of liability and the extent of loss. The SDR solution also produces fluctuations in the amounts of recoveries, but the fluctuations tend to be more moderate than those resulting from the market price of gold.

A General View of the Cases

The courts have adopted a variety of solutions for the problem of translating a gold unit of account into a currency of recovery: the last par value of the currency, the last central rate of the currency, the last par value adapted according to an index, the market price of gold, the present French franc, and the SDR. The central bank's method of valuing its gold holdings has been referred to in order to support the solution of the market price. All solutions other than the market price specifically reject the market price.

The Second Amendment has provided a more obvious legal basis for applying the SDR solution, although that solution could be followed even in a case that has to be decided by reference to the state of affairs after July 1, 1974 and before April 1, 1978. During that period, the Fund applied a basket valuation of the SDR for the purpose of operations and transactions in SDRs and also as the Fund's unit of account for general purposes. The Fund's action necessarily implied the legal fiction of a gold value for the SDR basket during this period. The justification for this fiction was that the efficacy of the Articles demanded a solution in circumstances in which no currency could be said to have a gold value.

The main opponent of the SDR solution, although a weakening one, remains the market price solution. There is no need to rehearse in detail the

---

[37] The State had argued that *The Breda* was wrongly decided because the foundation on which it rested—the international currency arrangements under the Fund's decision on central rates—had ceased to exist in 1978. Furthermore, *The Breda* could be distinguished because it was based on the supposition, which had proved to be unfounded, that the gap in the law would be temporary.

legal arguments for, and the practical advantages of, the SDR solution. An objection to the market price, however, that does not seem to be sustainable is that the market price could not provide an approach toward the uniformity that is an objective of the conventions in which gold is still the unit of account. An approach to uniformity would be achieved if there were to be agreement among the contracting parties to a convention on the solution of the market price and on the method of selecting and applying a market price.[38] Gold, however, is no longer recognized by the monetary authorities of most countries in the world as an acceptable unit of account. The unilateral or multilateral actions of countries in favor of the SDR solution show how unlikely it is that general agreement could be reached on a gold unit of account.

Uniformity has been one objective in choosing gold as a unit of account; stability has been another. An argument made in some proceedings in opposition to the SDR is that it fluctuates in value and therefore has no claim to acceptance that is superior to the market price of gold. The fluctuation of the SDR, however, is determined by exchange rates for currencies and in accordance with systematic principles. Moreover, a degree of stability is achieved because the basket method of valuing the SDR mitigates the variability of exchange rates for individual currencies. The market price of gold has neither of these characteristics.

The case for the SDR differs in at least one respect from the former case for gold as a unit of account. A reason for the choice of gold in the past was that many countries defined the value of their currencies in terms of gold either by usage or under the compulsion of the Articles of Agreement once the Articles had become effective. Countries are free under the Second Amendment to define the value of their currencies in terms of the SDR, and some members do so, but the practice is not widespread.

The case for the SDR as the unit of account does not depend on the argument that gold has lost all monetary significance. Gold has lost much of its former legal status in the international monetary system, but it would go too far to hold that it has no monetary significance whatsoever. The Executive Board's Report to the Board of Governors on the Proposed Second Amendment referred to "the objective of the gradual reduction of the role of gold in the system"[39] and not to the immediate or total elimina-

---

[38] Even so, no more than an approach to uniformity would be achieved because of the spread of "special contracts" increasing the limits on liability under the Warsaw Convention (see fn. 21 *supra*). Some countries require their national airlines to enter into special contracts, but the amounts are not uniform. These differences, however, do not support the case for either the market price or the SDR solution.

[39] *Proposed Second Amendment*, Part II, Chapter I, Section 1, p. 43. See also Joseph Gold, "Gold in International Monetary Law: Change, Uncertainty, and Ambiguity," *Journal of International Law and Economics*, Vol. 15 (1981), pp. 323–70.

tion of its role. Gold continues to be held in the monetary reserves of members. It may be accepted by the Fund from members instead of SDRs or currency in operations or transactions authorized by the Articles, although at a price agreed, on the basis of market prices, for each operation or transaction,[40] and provided that the decision to accept gold is supported by a majority of 85 per cent of the total voting power.[41] Gold continues to have practical importance as a reserve asset, but its practical role and its residual legal position in international monetary law have not preserved the function of gold as a standard of value accepted by monetary authorities for international purposes.

A fundamental change has occurred in the circumstances existing at the time of the conclusion of the conventions in which gold is the unit of account. It is not suggested that parties have invoked, or should invoke, the change as a ground for terminating or withdrawing from a convention. These actions could be taken only by contracting parties. The criteria, according to Article 62 of the Vienna Convention on the Law of Treaties, that would justify action by contracting parties are that the circumstances in which change has occurred were an essential basis of the consent of parties to be bound by the treaty and that the effect of the change is radically to transform the extent of obligations under the treaty. Changes of this character do not authorize courts to hold that treaties are no longer binding, but the changes have influenced courts to find solutions that are not dictated by a defunct monetary system. *The Blue Hawk, Miliangos v. George Frank (Textiles) Ltd.,*[42] *Matter of the Khendrik Kuivas,* and *Lively Ltd. and Another v. City of Munich*[43] are examples of this judicial realism.

The problem of applying the gold unit of account in the Warsaw Convention is before a number of courts in the United States.[44] Plaintiffs are advancing claims on the basis of the market price of gold and are arguing that any other solution requires amendment of the convention. Defendants are relying on the SDR solution, but in default of its adoption by the court are averring that an appropriate solution would be the last official price of gold or the current French franc. The defendant's case in favor of the SDR is strengthened by the fact that the Fund itself moved to the SDR, defined in relation to a basket of currencies, as its unit of account before the Second Amendment and at a time, therefore, when the Articles still referred to gold as the unit of account and defined the SDR in terms of gold.

On November 6, 1981 the United States District Court for the Southern District of New York decided in favor of the last official price of gold in the United States, although the court declared that if it had been writing on a

---

[40] Article V, Section 12(*d*).
[41] Article V, Section 12(*b*).
[42] [1975] 3 All E.R. 801.
[43] [1976] 3 All E.R. 851.
[44] See fn. 32 *supra* for some earlier cases.

clean slate it would have found the arguments in favor of the SDR solution most persuasive. The court relied on two considerations in arriving at its decision. First, internal memoranda of the Civil Aeronautics Board, obtained by attorneys under the Freedom of Information Act, appeared to favor the solution adopted by the court. The Civil Aeronautics Board was the government agency most intimately concerned with the issue, and its view, therefore, came as close as anything to a governmental interpretation. Second, the printed tariffs of all domestic carriers, including the defendant in this case, based the dollar value of the limitation amounts in the Warsaw Convention on the last official price of gold. The court seemed to imply that, for this reason, the interpretation was a contractual one between the parties.[45]

Some parties in these cases have stressed the inequity of applying solutions other than the market price of gold, because of the decline in the purchasing power of currencies and of the SDR. These solutions are said to ignore the stability that the drafters of conventions sought by defining a unit of account in terms of gold. The argument assumes that the drafters were intent upon ensuring stability in the purchasing power of the limits imposed on recoveries. The likelihood, however, is that the drafters were seeking stability in exchange value among currencies rather than stability in the purchasing power of individual currencies. The former kind of stability could be achieved, but the latter kind would have required a further technique. It would have been necessary, for example, to adopt not only a unit of account but also an index to achieve the objective of stable purchasing power. The negotiators of conventions drafted during the life of the par value system under the Articles might have assumed that changes would be made in par values to reflect persistent changes in the purchasing power of currencies.

---

[45] *Franklin Mint Corporation et al. v. Trans World Airlines, Inc.*, 81 Civ. 1700 (WK); 525 F. Supp. 1288; 16 Av. Cas. 18,024.

APPENDIX C

Unenforceability of Exchange Contracts, the GATT, and Nonmembers of the Fund

Because the benefits of Article VIII, Section 2(b) are available only to members, an effort has been made to impose a similar obligation on non-members of the Fund that become contracting parties to the GATT.

Article XV, paragraph 4 of the GATT inspired this effort. The provision declares that contracting parties to the GATT "shall not, by exchange action, frustrate the intent of the provisions of the Articles" of the Fund. Under paragraph 6 of the provision, a nonmember of the Fund must enter into "a special exchange agreement" with the CONTRACTING PARTIES to the GATT to give effect to the obligation to avoid exchange action that frustrates the intent of the Fund's Articles. Obligations under a special exchange agreement become part of the obligations imposed by the GATT. The Fund and the CONTRACTING PARTIES collaborated on the preparation of a model special exchange agreement.[1] The model contains the following provision (Article VII, paragraph 3), which obviously is based on Article VIII, Section 2(b) of the Fund's Articles:

> Exchange contracts which involve the currency of any contracting party and which are contrary to the exchange control regulations of that contracting party maintained or imposed consistently with the Articles of Agreement of the Fund or with the provisions of a special exchange agreement entered into pursuant to paragraph 6 of Article XV of the General Agreement, shall be unenforceable in the territories of ———. In addition, the Government of ——— may, by mutual accord with other contracting parties, co-operate in measures for the purpose of making the exchange control regulations of either contracting party more effective, provided that such measures and regulations are consistent with this agreement or with another special exchange agreement entered into pursuant to paragraph 6 of Article XV of the General Agreement or with the Articles of Agreement of the Fund, whichever may be applicable to the contracting party whose measures or regulations are involved.

The beneficiaries of this provision are members of the Fund and non-members that enter into a special exchange agreement. The provision

---

[1] For the text, see GATT, *Basic Instruments and Selected Instruments* (Geneva, May 1952), Vol. II, pp. 115 *et seq.*, and Gold, *Membership and Nonmembership*, pp. 536–45.

applies to the exchange control regulations of a member of the Fund that are consistent with the Fund's Articles or the exchange control regulations of a nonmember that are consistent with its special exchange agreement as a contracting party to the GATT. The obligation under the provision quoted above is undertaken by the signatory of a special exchange agreement. Nothing in the Articles or the GATT or the special exchange agreement binds a member of the Fund to treat exchange contracts as unenforceable because they are contrary to the exchange control regulations of the signatory of a special exchange agreement. The signatory does benefit, however, from the obligations undertaken by the signatories of other special exchange agreements.

Only a few special exchange agreements have been entered into, and none has been in operation since April 1954. It proved to be impractical to expect countries that had decided not to become members of the Fund or that had withdrawn from it to enter into detailed agreements that imposed obligations comparable to those imposed by the Articles. Furthermore, the signatories of special exchange agreements did not receive the rights of membership. For many years, therefore, the CONTRACTING PARTIES have exercised their authority to grant waivers of obligations under the GATT by exempting nonmembers of the Fund from the obligation to sign a special exchange agreement. Instead, a nonmember that becomes a contracting party signs a Protocol for Accession that deals with its position under the GATT and its relations with the CONTRACTING PARTIES. A Protocol contains language along the following lines:

> . . . so long as ———— is not a member of the International Monetary Fund, it will act in exchange matters in accordance with the intent of the General Agreement and in a manner fully consistent with the principles laid down in the text of the [model] special exchange agreement. . . .

If, on the complaint of a contracting party, the CONTRACTING PARTIES find that a nonmember has taken exchange action contrary to the intent of the GATT, they may decide that the nonmember shall sign a special exchange agreement.[2]

It is not known whether courts in nonmember countries have refused to enforce contracts that were contrary to the exchange control regulations of members of the Fund as the result of a special exchange agreement or a Protocol for Accession.[3]

---

[2] For a more detailed account of special exchange agreements, see Gold, *Membership and Nonmembership*, pp. 426–45.

[3] No such decisions were referred to by Iván Meznerics in his discussion in 1963 of the application of foreign exchange laws of other countries by the courts of socialist states ("Application of Foreign Exchange Laws by Foreign Courts," *Acta Juridica Academiae Scientiarum Hungaricae*, Vol. V, Fasc. 1–2 (1963), pp. 74–77). For a sympathetic attitude to the exchange control regulations of other countries, with certain qualifications, under the law apart from Article VIII, Section 2(b), see F.A. Mann, "The Private International Law of Exchange Control in General," Ch. XII in *The Legal Aspect of Money*, Third Edition (Oxford, 1971), pp. 399–430.

Although the signatory of a special exchange agreement would not get the benefit of Article VIII, Section 2(*b*) for its exchange control regulations in the courts of a member, it would receive a different benefit. A member that applied exchange restrictions against the contracting party might be acting in violation of its obligations under the Articles. Article XI declares that nothing in the Articles affects the right of a member to impose restrictions on exchange transactions with nonmembers or with persons in their territories unless the Fund finds that such restrictions prejudice the interests of members and are contrary to the purposes of the Fund. Under the Fund's Rules and Regulations, if the Fund finds that restrictions imposed by a member on exchange transactions with a nonmember or with persons in its territories are prejudicial to the interests of members and contrary to the purposes of the Fund, the Fund must present a report to the member. The report must set forth the Fund's views and may request the member to abolish or modify the restrictions.[4] Under another Rule,[5] the Fund has decided that there would be prejudice to members and inconsistency with the purposes of the Fund if a member were to impose restrictions on exchange transactions with a nonmember that had entered into a special exchange agreement or against persons in its territories. This finding would not apply if the member would be authorized by the Articles, in similar circumstances, to apply restrictions against members and persons in their territories. The Rule also declares that a member may request the Fund to approve in advance restrictions on exchange transactions with a nonmember or persons in its territories.[6]

These Rules might have an effect on the attitudes of courts to the exchange control regulations of a member that affect a nonmember. Suppose that Patria, a member of the Fund, imposes exchange restrictions against Regio, a nonmember, and that these restrictions are deemed by the Fund to be prejudicial to the interests of members and contrary to the purposes of the Fund. Suppose further that suit is brought in the courts of Terra, a member, to enforce an exchange contract that is contrary to the exchange control regulations of Patria that are directed against Regio. Article VIII, Section 2(*b*) would not be applied by the courts of Terra because the exchange control regulations would not be maintained or imposed consistently with the Articles.

The foregoing discussion of restrictions against a member and persons in its territories under Article XI and the Fund's Rules and Regulations applies only to restrictions on exchange transactions. Other exchange restrictions or exchange control regulations would not be affected by the legal provisions that have been discussed.

---

[4] Rule M-5, *By-Laws, Rules and Regulations,* Thirty-Seventh Issue (Washington, January 1, 1981), p. 47.

[5] Rule M-6, *ibid.,* pp. 47–48.

[6] Gold, *Membership and Nonmembership,* pp. 446–51.

A nonmember is free to take action to support the exchange controls of other countries for whatever reason it sees fit, which may be the protection of its reputation as a financial center. The Swiss National Bank, for example, has entered into an Agreement on the Prudence Required in Accepting Funds and on the Handling of Bank Confidentiality with almost all domestic banks and quasi-bank finance companies. Among the objectives of the Agreement, which entered into force on July 1, 1977, is the prevention of prohibited acts made possible by an improper use of the confidentiality of banking, the acceptance of funds that banks can recognize as having stemmed from punishable activities, and the aiding and abetting of capital flight or deception practiced on domestic or foreign authorities. An Arbitration Commission is empowered to investigate and punish violators of the Agreement. It has imposed fines for violations, and has turned the proceeds over to the Red Cross. The tribunal's decisions are subject to appeal to the Zurich Superior Court. The Agreement is in force until June 30, 1982 and can be extended for one further year.[7]

Abetting capital flight is a violation of the Agreement when three conditions are satisfied:

(a) the bank gives active support to a transaction, especially by organizing meetings with clients abroad for the purpose of accepting funds;

(b) the law of the country in which the client is domiciled restricts the investment of funds abroad; and

(c) a capital transfer out of that country has occurred.

In contrast to Article VIII, Section 2(b), which deals with exchange contracts that are executory (not yet performed or not yet performed in full), the Agreement deals with contracts involving capital flight that have been executed (performed).[8]

---

[7] *Neue Zürcher Zeitung*, November 28, 1980, p. 19. It has been reported that the agreement is to be extended (*Journal of Commerce*, December 23, 1981, p. 6A). The banks in Liechtenstein have entered into a similar agreement with their Government.

[8] "Kapitalflucht, Identitätsprufung, Täuschungsmanöver, Herkunft von Geldern ("Capital Flight, Identity Check, Deceptive Practices, Origin of Funds"), *Der Schweizer Treuhänder*, Vol. 55 (March 1981), pp. 26–28. This article discusses some of the Commission's cases. See also *New York Times*, November 28, 1980, pp. D1, 4.

APPENDIX D

Article VIII, Section 2(*b*), Governments, Private Parties, and Arbitration

An arbitrator has adopted an interpretation of Article VIII, Section 2(*b*) that is uniquely in error.[1] The award has not been published but has been made available to the author of a book on commercial arbitration who has discussed the effect of the Articles on the award.[2] This Appendix is based solely on his discussion of the award.

A dispute arose from a contractual relationship concluded in 1964, under which a Pakistani cement manufacturer, PPCI, undertook to repay a debt owed to the plaintiff, an Indian corporation, by delivering, over a period of years, defined quantities of cement. A separate but related contract was entered into between the plaintiff and the defendant, a Pakistani bank, under which the defendant agreed to pay to the plaintiff 94 Pakistani rupees in respect of each ton of cement not delivered by PPCI under its contract with the plaintiff. Hostilities broke out between the two countries in 1965, and both adopted legislative measures impeding commercial intercourse.

PPCI failed to make the deliveries required for the first three years (1965–67), and the plaintiff invoked the arbitration clause in the guarantee contract. The plaintiff claimed damages in respect of PPCI's failure to deliver. The defendant relied on various defenses, among which only the one relating to the Articles need be mentioned.

The author of the book referred to above discusses this defense as follows:

> The defendant contended that to enforce the guarantee contract would require him to make payment out of Pakistan contrary to Pakistani currency legislation. This would not only violate the public policy of Pakistan, but would also be contrary to Article VIII of the *Agreement on the International Monetary Fund* which provided that sovereign States would respect the

---

[1] International Chamber of Commerce (ICC) Award, No. 1664, Doc. No. 410/2104, March 15, 1972.

[2] Julian D.M. Lew, *Applicable Law in International Commercial Arbitration, A Study in Commercial Arbitration Awards* (New York and the Netherlands. 1978), pp. 405–409. See also pp. 545–46. Professor David Flint of the Faculty of Law, The New South Wales Institute of Technology, has drawn the author's attention to the arbitration and Mr. Lew's book.

exchange controls of other States. This last contention the arbitrator rejected because only a State could invoke the provisions of an international agreement. The arbitrator stated:

"The Agreement on the International Monetary Fund is an international treaty which is only binding on States. Private persons or legal entities are not admitted to invoke the provisions of a treaty between States. The Defendant cannot rely in the present proceedings on an alleged or intended violation by the State of India of Pakistani Exchange Control Regulations because:

(i) . . .

(ii) any such intended violation would be directed against the provisions of a treaty between States, provisions which are not directly applicable in regard to either the Defendant or the Claimant."[3]

There is no principle that private parties cannot invoke the provisions of a treaty. The question whether rights or obligations have been affected by the provisions of a treaty must not be confused with the question whether one of the contracting parties to the treaty has violated it. If a treaty purports to affect the rights or obligations of private parties and if these effects are automatically, or have been made, binding on the courts, the parties may rely on the provisions of the treaty and the courts must apply them. If a contracting party to the treaty has violated it, the remedy for the violation will have to be sought at the international level. The remedy cannot be pursued by private parties. Nevertheless, they may be able to invoke a violation in proceedings between them. For example, Article VIII, Section 2(*b*) is intended to affect the rights and obligations of private parties, and members must ensure that the provision is effective. If members fail to take any necessary step for this purpose, other members can complain to the Fund, and the Fund may react to the violation. A plaintiff in judicial proceedings, however, may reply to the defendant's reliance on Article VIII, Section 2(*b*) that the member in whose courts the proceedings are brought has failed to give the provision the necessary force of law.

Both India[4] and Pakistan[5] have adopted measures to give the force of law to Article VIII, Section 2(*b*). They have done so because the provision is intended to affect the rights and obligations of private parties, and the measures they have taken are necessary under their laws to make the provision effective. The contract that was the subject of the arbitration discussed above seems to have been governed by the law of India.[6]

A question of interpretation can arise about the intent of a provision. Is it intended to affect the rights and obligations of private parties? Keynes

---

[3] Lew, *op. cit.*, p. 409.

[4] Ordinance No. XLVII of 1945 to implement the International Monetary Fund and Bank Agreements, Section 5 and Schedule, Part I, *Gazette of India*, December 24, 1945.

[5] Act No. XLIII of 1950 to implement the International Monetary Fund and Bank Agreements, Section 5 and Schedule, Part I, *Gazette of Pakistan*, July 8, 1950.

[6] Lew, *op. cit.*, p. 337.

was concerned about a question of interpretation of Article VIII, Section 2(*a*) that raised this issue.[7] His attitude was influenced by the consideration that virtually all rights and obligations under the Articles are between members. There has never been any doubt, however, that Article VIII, Section 2(*b*) affects the rights and obligations of private parties.

The parties to an arbitration may choose the law that is to govern the arbitrator. If they choose a particular law, does the reference to the chosen law include the international obligations of the chosen legislator? There is authority that the obligations are included in the absence of an express exclusion of them.[8] On this proposition, a reference to the law of India as the governing law of a contract that an arbitrator is to apply would require the arbitrator to respect Article VIII, Section 2(*b*). But the authority referred to would also permit the parties to exclude the provision. The Fund's interpretation of Article VIII, Section 2(*b*) declares that members must ensure that their judicial and administrative authorities will apply Article VIII, Section 2(*b*),[9] but the interpretation is not necessarily comprehensive in this respect.

The answer to the question whether an arbitrator can heed an agreement by the parties that Article VIII, Section 2(*b*) or other international obligations shall not be applied by him as part of the governing law would depend on whether the autonomy of the will of the parties is the exclusive principle for the choice of law by an arbitrator. Among the theories on the legal basis of arbitration is the jurisdictional theory, according to which the power of the state is recognized to control and regulate all arbitrations that take place within its jurisdiction.[10]

It is possible, moreover, that an arbitrator would refuse to respect the parties' exclusion of Article VIII, Section 2(*b*) on the ground that it violated international public policy.[11] It is possible also that a court called upon to enforce an arbitral award that had ignored Article VIII, Section 2(*b*) would refuse enforcement on the ground that its public policy had been flouted.[12]

---

[7] Gold, *Occasional Paper No. 6.*
[8] Lew, *op. cit.,* pp. 89–90.
[9] *Selected Decisions,* Ninth Issue, p. 201.
[10] Lew, *op. cit.,* pp. 52 *et seq.* See also pp. 111 *et seq.*
[11] *Ibid.,* p. 104.
[12] *Ibid.,* pp. 561–65.

SELECTED BIBLIOGRAPHY

Selected Bibliography

Certain publications cited in this volume are listed here by author or title. Most of them, including a number of works by the author, were issued by the International Monetary Fund. The bibliography is also a guide to the short titles that have been used for many of the works cited.

Annual Report, 19—
International Monetary Fund, *Annual Report of the Executive Directors for the Fiscal Year Ending June 30, 1947* (Washington, 1947), and *Annual Report of the Executive Directors for the Fiscal Year Ended April 30, 1958, 1972, 1974,* and *1975* (Washington, 1958, 1972, 1974, and 1975).

Balance of Payments Manual
International Monetary Fund, *Balance of Payments Manual,* Third Edition (Washington, 1961) and Fourth Edition (Washington, 1977).

Gold, *Fund Agreement in the Courts* (1962)
Gold, Joseph, *The Fund Agreement in the Courts* (Washington, 1962).

Gold, Joseph, *The Fund's Concepts of Convertibility,* IMF Pamphlet Series, No. 14 (Washington, 1971).

Gold, *Membership and Nonmembership*
Gold, Joseph, *Membership and Nonmembership in the International Monetary Fund: A Study in International Law and Organization* (Washington, 1974).

Gold, Occasional Paper No. 6
Gold, Joseph, *The Multilateral System of Payments: Keynes, Convertibility, and the International Monetary Fund's Articles of Agreement,* IMF Occasional Paper No. 6 (Washington, 1981).

Gold, Pamphlet No. 3
Gold, Joseph, *The International Monetary Fund and Private Business Transactions,* IMF Pamphlet Series, No. 3 (Washington, 1965).

Gold, Pamphlet No. 6
Gold, Joseph, *Maintenance of the Gold Value of the Fund's Assets,* IMF Pamphlet Series, No. 6 (Washington, 1965; Second Edition, 1971).

Gold, Pamphlet No. 11
Gold, Joseph, *Interpretation by the Fund,* IMF Pamphlet Series, No. 11 (Washington, 1968).

Gold, Pamphlet No. 19
Gold, Joseph, *Floating Currencies, Gold, and SDRs: Some Recent Legal Developments,* IMF Pamphlet Series, No. 19 (Washington, 1976).

Gold, Pamphlet No. 22
> Gold, Joseph, *Floating Currencies, SDRs, and Gold: Further Legal Developments*, IMF Pamphlet Series, No. 22 (Washington, 1977).

Gold, Pamphlet No. 26
> Gold, Joseph, *SDRs, Gold, and Currencies: Third Survey of New Legal Developments*, IMF Pamphlet Series, No. 26 (Washington, 1979).

Gold, Pamphlet No. 32
> Gold, Joseph, *The Rule of Law in the International Monetary Fund*, IMF Pamphlet Series, No. 32 (Washington, 1980).

Gold, Pamphlet No. 33
> Gold, Joseph, *SDRs, Currencies, and Gold: Fourth Survey of New Legal Developments*, IMF Pamphlet Series, No. 33 (Washington, 1980).

Gold, Pamphlet No. 36
> Gold, Joseph, *SDRs, Currencies, and Gold: Fifth Survey of New Legal Developments*, IMF Pamphlet Series, No. 36 (Washington, 1981).

Gold, *Selected Essays*
> Gold, Joseph, *Legal and Institutional Aspects of the International Monetary System: Selected Essays* (Washington, 1979).

Gold, Joseph, *Voting Majorities in the Fund: Effects of the Second Amendment of the Articles*, IMF Pamphlet Series, No. 20 (Washington, 1977).

History, 1945–65
> Horsefield, J. Keith, *The International Monetary Fund, 1945–1965: Twenty Years of International Monetary Cooperation* (Washington, 1969).

IFNS
> International Monetary Fund, *International Financial News Survey*, Vol. 23 (1971).

International Monetary Fund, *Balance of Payments Concepts and Definitions*, IMF Pamphlet Series, No. 10 (Washington, 1968; Second Edition, 1969).

International Monetary Fund, *By-Laws, Rules and Regulations*, Thirty-Second Issue (Washington, July 10, 1974) and Thirty-Seventh Issue (Washington, January 1, 1981).

International Monetary Fund, *Eighth Annual Report on Exchange Restrictions* (Washington, 1957), *Eleventh Annual Report on Exchange Restrictions* (Washington, 1960), *Twelfth Annual Report on Exchange Restrictions* (Washington, 1961), *Thirteenth Annual Report on Exchange Restrictions* (Washington, 1962), and *Fifteenth Annual Report on Exchange Restrictions* (Washington, 1964).

International Monetary Fund, *IMF Survey* (various issues).

International Monetary Fund, *Selected Decisions of the Executive Directors and Selected Documents,* Fifth Issue (Washington, July 10, 1971).

International Monetary Fund, Trade and Payments Division (Bahram Nowzad, Chief), *The Rise in Protectionism,* IMF Pamphlet Series, No. 24 (Washington, 1978).

Keynes, Vol. XXVI
Moggridge, Donald, ed., *The Collected Writings of John Maynard Keynes, Vol. XXVI: Activities 1941–1946, Shaping the Post-War World, Bretton Woods, and Reparations* (Macmillan and Cambridge University Press, for the Royal Economic Society, 1980).

Proceedings and Documents
Proceedings and Documents of the United Nations Monetary and Financial Conference, Bretton Woods, New Hampshire, July 1–22, 1944, Department of State Publication 2866, International Organization and Conference Series I, 3 (Washington, 1948).

Proposed Second Amendment
International Monetary Fund, *Proposed Second Amendment to the Articles of Agreement of the International Monetary Fund: A Report by the Executive Directors to the Board of Governors* (Washington, March 1976).

Selected Decisions, Second Issue
International Monetary Fund, *Selected Decisions of the Executive Directors,* Second Issue (Washington, September 1963).

Selected Decisions, Third Issue
International Monetary Fund, *Selected Decisions of the Executive Directors and Selected Documents,* Third Issue (Washington, January 1965).

Selected Decisions, Sixth Issue
International Monetary Fund, *Selected Decisions of the International Monetary Fund and Selected Documents,* Sixth Issue (Washington, September 30, 1972).

Selected Decisions, Seventh Issue
International Monetary Fund, *Selected Decisions of the International Monetary Fund and Selected Documents,* Seventh Issue (Washington, January 1, 1975).

Selected Decisions, Eighth Issue
International Monetary Fund, *Selected Decisions of the International Monetary Fund and Selected Documents,* Eighth Issue (Washington, May 10, 1976).

Selected Decisions, Ninth Issue
International Monetary Fund, *Selected Decisions of the International Monetary Fund and Selected Documents,* Ninth Issue (Washington, June 15, 1981).

Summary Proceedings

International Monetary Fund, *Summary Proceedings of the Sixth Annual Meeting of the Board of Governors*, September 1951 (Washington, 1951), *Summary Proceedings of the Twenty-Sixth Annual Meeting of the Board of Governors*, September 27–October 1, 1971 (Washington, 1971), and *Summary Proceedings of the Thirty-Fifth Annual Meeting of the Board of Governors*, September 30–October 3, 1980 (Washington, 1980).

INDEXES

Index A. Provisions of Articles of Agreement Cited

Original Articles

473

First Amendment

Second Amendment

Index B. Rules and Regulations Cited

Index C. Decisions of Executive Board Cited

Index D. Table of Cases Cited

FRANCE

Index E. Authors

References to the author's works have not been included in this Index.
A number of his works that have been referred to have been listed
in the Selected Bibliography.

491

Index F. Subjects

References in this index are to the first page only of a
discussion that extends through several pages.

A

ACT OF STATE, 3, 43, 53, 121, 123, 126, 131, 229
ACTS ABROAD, ILLEGAL, 226, 229, 272, 375
APPRECIATION, 165, 304, 312, 322
ARBITRATION, 236, 306, 462
ARGENTINA, 441, 448
ARTICLES OF AGREEMENT OF FUND
  Amendment of: domestic steps for acceptance of, 285, 292; national sovereignty and, 287, 293; unanimity in, 293
  And bilateral treaties, 122, 156, 267
  And private international law, 3
  And private parties, 3, 462–64
  Article VIII, Section 2(b): and private international law, 346; legislative history, 429
  As constituting international monetary system, 316, 325, 328
  As declaratory of public international law, 136
  Authoritative interpretation by Fund, 4, 5, 110, 143; request for, 7; rescission or modification of, 8
  Binding force of amendment of, 286
  Exchange rates under, 33, 36
  Informal interpretation by Fund, 8
  Interpretation: competence of national courts on, 291; economic approach to, 3, 12, 145, 263, 406
  Second Amendment, 2; and Sixth General Review of Quotas, French constitutional problem relating to, 285
  Transitional arrangements, 130, 414
ATLANTIC CITY CONFERENCE, 86, 419

B

Balance of Payments Manual, 83, 145, 274, 401
BANK FOR INTERNATIONAL SETTLEMENTS, 307, 310, 329

BELGIUM, 5, 218, 226, 272
Bonnes mœurs, 227
BRAZIL, 35
BRETTON WOODS CONFERENCE, 14, 154, 216, 225, 253, 429
BRUSSELS CONVENTION, 1957, 177, 441, 448, 452

C

CANADA, 441
CAPITAL AND CURRENT ACCOUNT PAYMENTS, 79, 126, 137, 196
  Insurance and, 81
CAPITAL CONTROLS, 13, 80, 86, 125, 135, 208, 224, 418, 421, 427
CAPITAL TRANSFERS, 14, 80, 84, 93, 125, 135, 208, 224, 268, 275, 301, 414, 419, 421
CARRIAGE OF GOODS BY ROAD CONVENTION, 444
CENTRAL RATES, 167, 184
  And wider margins, 164, 185, 235, 250, 303, 443
CERTIFICATE BY FUND, 414
COMITY, 200, 345, 464
  Articles the standard in relation to exchange control, 345
  Exchange control and nonmembers, 352
  Promotion of, 344
COMMITTEE OF BOARD OF GOVERNORS ON INTERPRETATION, 8
COMMON AGRICULTURAL POLICY, 171, 243
CONDEMNATION OF PROPERTY FOR BENEFIT OF FUND, 40
CONFISCATION, 126, 128, 133, 220, 225
CONFISCATORY LAWS, 227
CONTRACTS, ILLEGAL, 156
CONVERSION FACTORS, 102
CONVERTIBILITY OF CURRENCIES, 14
  External, 174
COUNTERVAILING DUTIES, 104
Cours forcé, 78, 119

492

495

Index G. Summary of Conclusions or Principles